Augustus R. Cazauran

The Democratic Speaker's Hand-Book

Augustus R. Cazauran

The Democratic Speaker's Hand-Book

ISBN/EAN: 9783337403980

Printed in Europe, USA, Canada, Australia, Japan

Cover: Foto ©Suzi / pixelio.de

More available books at **www.hansebooks.com**

THE DEMOCRATIC SPEAKER'S HAND-BOOK:

CONTAINING EVERY THING NECESSARY FOR THE DEFENSE OF THE NATIONAL DEMOCRACY IN THE COMING PRESIDENTIAL CAMPAIGN, AND FOR THE ASSAULT OF THE RADICAL ENEMIES OF THE COUNTRY AND ITS CONSTITUTION.

COMPILED BY
MATTHEW CAREY, Jr.

"Can such things be,
And overcome us like a summer's cloud,
Without our special wonder?"

PREFACE.

The editor and compiler of this work, from his previous professional occupation, was enabled to accumulate a vast amount of material, which, properly condensed and arranged, would be of service to Democratic speakers and editors, in the great National duty they are called upon to discharge to their country in the existing Presidential campaign. Wishing to contribute to the cause, which he believes to be the cause of good government, and the only hope for the restoration of a Constitutional Union, as much of personal service as he may be capable of rendering, he has prepared the book which follows with a view of facilitating the Democratic champions of the Constitution in the great work of defense and assault which is to distinguish them during this campaign, and which is to rescue the nation from the anarchy of Radicalism, or consign it permanently to the disintegrating and destructive influences of that revolutionary school. His great difficulty has been to condense a great deal into as little space as possible; and while his book omits very much that he would like to embrace in it, in order to bring it within the space to which he is restricted, he believes it will serve, to a great extent, to relieve the use of the ponderous scrap-books and authorities which are so burdensome to the prosecution of an active political campaign.

The nomination of Horatio Seymour and Francis P. Blair, jr., by the National Democratic Convention, and the distinct and patriotic platform upon which they were placed, gives assurance to the nation that the ancient Guard of the Constitution is still intact, and that, like the famous Guard of Napoleon, it "never surrenders." Should it triumph in this, the most critical hour of the nation's peril, a return of the Government to its natural and Constitutional motion will give repose to domestic strife, security to the individual rights of the citizens, restored Constitutional governments to oppressed and proscribed States, and protection to each of the co-ordinate branches of the Government against the assaults of either or both of the others. It will reinvigorate and put in exercise the discarded checks and balances of the Constitution; and, by making its administration in all of its departments to conform to the organic law, it will re-elevate the nation to its former position of commanding respect, and place it on the highway to still greater achievement than the most hopeful votaries of the system ever anticipated, or the most sanguine prophet stretched his vision to foresee. Should this result be the crowning compensation of the present Democratic effort, the contribution toward it, though small, of this endeavor to aid the champions of the public liberty in the fierce struggle for the right, will afford a sufficient satisfaction to the editor for the labor this work has cost.

The arrangement of matter is not as perfect as was intended, owing to the delay in procuring and preparing portions of it after other parts referring to the same subject had necessarily been furnished to the printer—a difficulty inseparable from a work prepared, as this has been, in a great hurry, and under circumstances of great embarrassment.

The political classification of Congressmen on certain votes is according to their party associations at the time when they were called upon to act on the various questions.

To the Democratic speakers and editors of the country the compiler and editor dedicates his labors, because upon them depends the good work which is to produce the fruit of a restored Constitution, on the first Tuesday after the first Monday in November next.

THE DEMOCRATIC SPEAKER'S HAND-BOOK.

CONSTITUTION OF THE UNITED STATES.
ITS ABNEGATION BY RADICALISM.

WE the People of the United States, in order to form a more perfect Union, establish Justice, insure domestic Tranquillity, provide for the common defense, promote the general welfare, and secure the blessings of Liberty to ourselves and our Posterity, do ordain and establish this CONSTITUTION for the United States of America.[1]

ARTICLE I.

SECTION 1. All legislative powers herein granted shall be vested in a Congress of the United States, which shall consist of a Senate and House of Representatives.

SEC. 2. The House of Representatives shall be composed of members chosen every second year by the people of the several States, and the electors in each State shall have the qualifications requisite for electors of the most numerous branch of the State Legislature.[2]

No person shall be a Representative who shall not have attained to the age of twenty-five years, and been seven years a citizen of the United States, and who shall not, when elected, be an inhabitant of that State in which he shall be chosen.

Representatives and direct taxes shall be apportioned among the several States which may be included within this Union, according to their respective numbers, which shall be determined by adding to the whole number of free persons, including those bound to service for a term of years, and excluding Indians not taxed, three-fifths of all other persons. The actual enumeration shall be made within three years after the first meeting of the Congress of the United States, and within every subsequent term of ten years, in such manner as they shall by law direct. The number of Representatives shall not exceed one for every thirty thousand, but each State shall have at least one Representative; and until such enumeration shall be made, the State of New Hampshire shall be entitled to choose three, Massachusetts eight, Rhode Island and Providence Plantations one, Connecticut five, New York six, New Jersey four, Pennsylvania eight, Delaware one, Maryland six, Virginia

---

[1] The Preamble violated by the Radical party, in this: that the blessings of liberty are denied to the people of ten States, who, by act of Congress, are subjected to the government of Military despotisms, and to the people of Tennessee, who, by an usurping Radical State Government, erected upon the ruins of the legitimate Constitution of the State, and acting under the cover of an irregular bogus Constitution, have deprived a majority of the White people of their dearest franchises, and are imposing upon them the most cruel and oppressive measures, pretending to be laws, and sustained by the United States Army, a partisan Militia, armed with Federal bayonets, and a ruling horde of illiterate and brutal negro suffragans.

[2] This section violated inasmuch as the duly elected Representatives of ten States of the Union are arbitrarily excluded from their rightful seats by the Radical majority in the House of Representatives.

ten, North Carolina five, South Carolina five, and Georgia three.[1]

When vacancies happen in the representation from any State, the Executive authority thereof shall issue writs of election to fill such vacancies.[2]

The House of Representatives shall choose their Speaker and other officers; and shall have the sole power of impeachment.

SEC. 3. The Senate of the United States shall be composed of two Senators from each State, chosen by the Legislature thereof, for six years; and each Senator shall have one vote.[3]

Immediately after they shall be assembled in consequence of the first election, they shall be divided as equally as may be into three classes. The seats of the Senators of the first-class shall be vacated at the expiration of the second year, of the second class at the expiration of the fourth year, and of the third class at the expiration of the sixth year; so that one-third may be chosen every second year; and if vacancies happen by resignation, or otherwise, during the recess of the Legislature of any State, the Executive thereof may make temporary appointments until the next meeting of the Legislature, which shall then fill such vacancies.[4]

No person shall be a Senator who shall not have attained to the age of thirty years, and been nine years a citizen of the United States, and who shall not, when elected, be an inhabitant of that State for which he shall be chosen.

The Vice-President of the United States shall be President of the Senate, but shall have no vote, unless they be equally divided.

The Senate shall choose their other officers, and also a President *pro tempore*, in the absence of the Vice-President, or when he shall exercise the office of President of the United States.

The Senate shall have the sole power to try all impeachments. When sitting for that purpose, they shall be on oath or affirmation. When the President of the United States is tried, the Chief Justice shall preside: And no person shall be convicted without the concurrence of two-thirds of the members present.

Judgement in cases of impeachment shall not extend further than to removal from office, and disqualification to hold and enjoy any office of honor, trust, or profit, under the United States; but the party convicted shall nevertheless be liable and subject to indictment, trial, judgment and punishment according to law.

SEC. 4. The times, places and manner of holding elections for Senators and Representatives, shall be prescribed in each State by the Legisla-

---

[1] This section violated in this: that the direct tax on cotton was levied without reference to any such apportionment, and while ten States, whose product of cotton in 1866 and 1867 was taxed, were denied their Constitutional representation in Congress, by the Radical majority in each branch of the same. In this: that no enumeration was had in the cotton-producing States in 1860, the end of the term of ten years, nor since; and yet a direct tax on cotton was levied in the absence of the same. In this: that this clause especially provides for a representation in the United States House of Representatives from Virginia, North Carolina, South Carolina and Georgia, and yet a representation from those States in said house is arbitrarily excluded by the Radical majority in said House.

[2] This section violated in this: that vacancies existed in the representation of ten States; the elections to fill which were held under writs issued by the Executives thereof, but the Representatives chosen were denied admission by the Radical majority in Congress.

[3] This section violated in this: that Senators from ten States are denied their rightful seats in the Senate by the Radical majority in that body, and laws are passed in the absence of those Senators violently excluded therefrom.

[4] This section violated in this: that its rule of classification is defeated by the exclusion entirely from the Senate, by the Radical majority therein, of the Senators from ten States, preventing the choice of one-third of the Senators every two years.

ture thereof; but the Congress may at any time, by law, make or alter such regulations, except as to the places of choosing Senators.

The Congress shall assemble at least once in every year, and such meeting shall be on the first Monday in December, unless they shall by law appoint a different day.

Sec. 5. Each House shall be the judge of the elections, returns and qualifications of its own members; and a majority of each shall constitute a quorum to do business; but a smaller number may adjourn from day to day, and may be authorized to compel the attendance of absent members, in such manner and under such penalties as each House may provide.[1]

Each House may determine the rule of its proceedings, punish its members for disorderly behavior, and, with the concurrence of two-thirds, expel a member.[2]

Each House shall keep a journal of its proceedings, and from time to time publish the same, excepting such parts as may in their judgment require secrecy; and the yeas and nays of the members of either House, on any question, shall, at the desire of one-fifth of those present, be entered on the journal.

Neither House during the session of Congress shall, without the consent of the other, adjourn for more than three days, nor to any other place than that in which the two Houses shall be sitting.

Sec. 6. The Senators and Representatives shall receive a compensation for their services, to be ascertained by law, and paid out of the Treasury of the United States. They shall in all cases except treason, felony, and breach of the peace, be privileged from arrest during their attendance at the session of their respective Houses, and in going to and returning from the same; and for any speech or debate in either House, they shall not be questioned in any other place.

No Senator or Representative shall, during the time for which he was elected, be appointed to any civil office under the authority of the United States, which shall have been created, or the emoluments whereof shall have been increased, during such time; and no person holding any office under the United States shall be a member of either House during his continuance in office.

Sec. 7. All bills for raising revenue shall originate in the House of Representatives; but the Senate may propose or concur with amendments, as on other bills.

Every bill which shall have passed the House of Representatives and the Senate, shall, before it become a law, be presented to the President of the United States; if he approve, he shall sign it; but if not, he shall return it, with his objections, to that House in which it shall have originated, who shall enter the objections at large on their journal, and proceed to reconsider it. If, after such reconsideration, two-thirds of that House shall agree to pass the bill, it shall be sent, together with the objections, to the

---

[1] This section violated in this: that the Senators and Representatives from ten States are excluded from each House by the Radical majority therein, and a majority of the number chosen without counting them, assume to act as a quorum instead of a majority of the entire number of the Senators and Representatives from all the States.

[2] This section violated in this: that members of both Houses are driven from or excluded from admission into the same, upon the fraudulent pretenses of contest or illegality of election, by a mere majority vote of said Houses; these pretenses being manufactured to avoid the necessity of a two-third vote under this section, not always so certain of attainment. See case of Mr. Stockton, Senator from New Jersey; Gen. Morgan, Representative from Ohio; and Messrs. Brown and Young, Representatives from Kentucky. The two latter gentlemen were never admitted. Their exclusion was a negative violation of this clause however.

other House, by which it shall likewise be reconsidered, and if approved by two-thirds of that House, it shall become a law. But in all such cases the votes of both Houses shall be determined by yeas and nays, and the names of the persons voting for and against the bill shall be entered on the journal of each House respectively. If any bill shall not be returned by the President within ten day (Sundays excepted) after it shall have been presented to him, the same shall be a law in like manner as if he had signed it, unless the Congress by their adjournment prevent its return, in which case it shall not be a law.

Every order, resolution, or vote to which the concurrence of the Senate and House of Representatives may be necessary (except on a question of adjournment), shall be presented to the President of the United States; and before the same shall take effect, shall be approved by him, or being disapproved by him, shall be re-passed by two-thirds of the Senate and House of Representatives, according to the rules and limitations prescribed in the case of a bill.

Sec. 8. The Congress shall have power

To lay and collect taxes, duties, imposts, and excises, to pay the debts and provide for the common defense and general welfare of the United States; but all duties, imposts, and excises, shall be uniform throughout the United States;[1]

To borrow money on the credit of the United States;

To regulate commerce with foreign nations, and among the several States, and with the Indian tribes;

To establish an uniform rule of naturalization, and uniform laws on the subject of bankruptcies, throughout the United States;

To coin money, regulate the value thereof, and of foreign coin, and fix the standard of weights and measures;

To provide for the punishment of counterfeiting the securities and current coin of the United States;

To establish post-offices and post roads;

To promote the progress of science and useful arts, by securing for limited times to authors and inventors the exclusive right to their respective writings and discoveries;

To constitute tribunals inferior to the Supreme Court;

To define and punish piracies and felonies committed on the high seas, and offenses against the law of nations;

To declare war, grant letters of marque and reprisal, and make rules concerning captures on land and water;

To raise and support armies; but no appropriation of money to that use shall be for a longer term than two years;

To provide and maintain a navy:

To make rules for the government and regulation of the land and naval forces;

To provide for calling forth the militia to execute the laws of the Union, suppress insurrections and repel invasions;

To provide for organizing, arming, and disciplining the militia, and for governing such part of them as may be employed in the service of the United States, reserving to the states respectively the appointment of the officers and the authority of training the militia according to the discipline prescribed by Congress;

To exercise exclusive legislation, in all cases whatsoever, over such district (not exceeding ten miles square), as may, by cession of particular States and the acceptance of Congress, become the seat of the Government of the United States, and to exercise like authority over all places

---

[1] This section violated inasmuch as cotton, a product of but a section of the United States, was taxed in 1866 and 1867, which consequently could not have been uniform throughout the United States.

purchased, by the consent of the legislature of the State in which the same shall be, for the erection of forts, magazines, arsenals, dock-yards, and other needful buildings; and

To make all laws which shall be necessary and proper for carrying into execution the foregoing powers, and all other powers vested by this Constitution in the government of the United States, or in any Department or officer thereof.

SEC. 9. The migration or importation of such persons as any of the States now existing shall think proper to admit, shall not be prohibited by the Congress prior to the year one thousand eight hundred and eight, but a tax or duty may be imposed on such importation, not exceeding ten dollars for each person.

The privilege of the writ of *habeas corpus* shall not be suspended, unless when in cases of rebellion or invasion the public safety may require it.[1]

No bill of attainder or *ex post facto* law shall be passed.[2]

No capitation, or other direct, tax shall be laid, unless in proportion to the census or enumeration hereinbefore directed to be taken.[3]

No tax or duty shall be laid on articles exported from any state.[4]

No preference shall be given by any regulation of commerce or revenue to the ports of one State over those of another: nor shall vessels bound to, or from, one State, be obliged to enter, clear, or pay duties in another.

No money shall be drawn from the Treasury, but in consequence of appropriations made by law; and a regular statement and account of the receipts and expenditures of all public money shall be published from time to time.

No title of nobility shall be granted by the United States: and no person holding any office of profit or trust under them, shall, without the consent of the Congress, accept of any present, emolument, office, or title, of any kind whatever, from any king, prince, or foreign State.[5]

SEC. 10. No State shall enter into any treaty, alliance, or confederation; grant letters of marque and reprisal; coin money, emit bills of credit, make anything but gold and silver coin a tender in the payment of debts, pass any bill of attainder, *ex post facto* law, or law impairing the obligation of contracts, or grant any title of nobility.

No State shall, without the consent of the Congress, lay any imposts, or duties on imports or exports, except what may be absolutely necessary for executing its inspection laws: and the net produce of all duties and imposts, laid by any State on imports or exports, shall be for the use of the Treasury of the United States; and all such laws shall be subject to the revision and control of Congress.

---

[1] This section violated inasmuch as the writ of *habeas corpus* is arbitrarily suspended by the Military Commanders of ten States in this Union, acting under the authority of the Radical Congress, and by Gen. G. H. Thomas, Military Commander of Tennessee and Kentucky, who asserts the right to seize a citizen of Tennessee at his home, drag him to Kentucky, and by a mere order confine him in a military dungeon. *Vide* case of Mr. Milliken, of Tennessee; T. W. Roberts, and other citizens of Eutaw, Greene county, Alabama; confined for a while in Tortugas; Col. W. H. McCardle, of the Vicksburg Times, and other cases too numerous to mention.

[2] This section most flagrantly violated by the act wresting jurisdiction from the Supreme Court, in the McArdle case, when a decision, it was believed, was about to be made declaring the reconstruction acts unconstitutional.

[3] This clause also violated by Cotton Tax.

[4] This clause also violated by Cotton Tax.

[5] This clause violated by Mr. Anson Burlingame, a High-priest of Radicalism, in this: that he accepted, without the consent of Congress, while holding the position of U. S. Minister to China, the place of Chief of the Chinese Embassy to the reigning powers of the world, and was received by the Radical Congress, whose consent he contemned, with the highest honors.

No state shall, without the consent of Congress, lay any duty of tonnage, keep troops or ships of war in time of peace, enter into any agreement or compact with another State, or with a foreign power, or engage in war, unless actually invaded, or in such imminent danger as will not admit of delay.

ARTICLE II.

SEC. 1. The Executive power shall be vested in a President of the United States of America. He shall hold his office during the term of four years, and, together with the Vice-President, chosen for the same term, be elected as follows:

Each State shall appoint, in such manner as the legislature thereof may direct, a number of electors, equal to the whole number of Senators and Representatives to which the State may be entitled in the Congress; but no Senator or Representative, or person holding an office of trust or profit under the United States, shall be appointed an elector.

[The electors shall meet in their respective States, and vote by ballot for two persons, of whom one, at least, shall not be an inhabitant of the same State with themselves. And they shall make a list of all the persons voted for, and of the numbers of votes for each; which list they shall sign and certify, and transmit sealed to the seat of the Government of the United States, directed to the President of the Senate. The President of the Senate shall, in the presence of the Senate and House of Representatives, open all the certificates, and the votes shall then be counted. The person having the greatest number of votes shall be the President, if such number be a majority of the whole number of electors appointed; and if there be more than one who have such majority, and have an equal number of votes, then the House of Representatives shall immediately choose by ballot one of them for President; and if no person have a majority, then from the five highest on the list the said House shall in like manner choose the President. But in choosing the President, the votes shall be taken by States, the Represrentation from each State having one vote; a quorum for this purpose shall consist of a member or members from two-thirds of the States, and a majority of all the States shall be necessary to a choice. In every case, after the choice of the President, the person having the greatest number of votes of the electors shall be the Vice-President. But if there should remain two or more who have equal votes, the Senate shall choose from them by ballot the Vice-President.[1]]

The Congress may determine the time of choosing the electors, and the day on which they shall give their votes; which day shall be the same throughout the United States.

No person except a natural born citizen, or a citizen of the United States at the time of the adoption of this Constitution, shall be eligible to the office of President; neither shall any person be eligible to that office who shall not have attained to the age of thirty-five years, and been fourteen years a resident within the United States.

In case of the removal of the President from office, or of his death, resignation, or inability to discharge the powers and duties of the said office, the same shall devolve on the Vice-President, and the Congress may by law provide for the case of removal, death, resignation, or inability, both of the President and Vice-President, declaring what officer shall then act as President, and such officer shall act accordingly, until the disability be removed, or a President shall be elected.

The President shall, at stated times, receive for his services a compensa-

---

[1] This clause of the Constitution has been annulled. See 12th Article of the amendment.

tion, which shall neither be increased nor diminished during the period for which he shall have been elected, and he shall not receive within that period any other emolument from the United States, or any of them.

Before he enter on the execution of his office, he shall take the following oath or affirmation:

"I do solemnly swear (or affirm) that I will faithfully execute the office of President of the United States, and will, to the best of my ability, preserve, protect, and defend the Constitution of the United States."

SEC. 2. The President shall be commander-in-chief of the army and navy of the United States and of the militia of the several States, when called into the actual service of the United States; he may require the opinion in writing of the principal officer in each of the executive departments upon any subject relating to the duties of their respective offices; and he shall have power to grant reprieves and pardons for offenses against the United States, except in cases of impeachment.[1]

He shall have power, by and with the advice and consent of the Senate, to make treaties, provided two-thirds of the Senators present concur; and he shall nominate, and by and with the advice and consent of the Senate, shall appoint ambassadors, other public ministers and consuls, judges of the Supreme Court, and all other officers of the United States, whose appointments are not herein otherwise provided for, and which shall be established by law. But the Congress may by law vest the appointment of such inferior officers as they think proper in the President alone, in the courts of law, or in the heads of departments.

The President shall have power to fill up all vacancies that may happen during the recess of the Senate, by granting commissions, which shall expire at the end of their next session.[2]

SEC. 3. He shall, from time to time, give to the Congress information of the state of the Union, and recommend to their consideration such measures as he shall judge necessary and expedient; he may, on extraordinary occasions, convene both Houses, or either of them; and in case of disagreement between them, with respect to the time of adjournment, he may adjourn them to such time as he shall think proper; he shall receive ambassadors and other public ministers; he shall take care that the laws be faithfully executed; and shall commission all the officers of the United States.

SEC. 4. The President, Vice-President, and all civil officers of the United States, shall be removed from office on impeachment for and conviction of treason, bribery, or other high crimes and misdemeanors.

ARTICLE III.

SEC. 1. The judicial power of the United States shall be vested in one Supreme Court, and in such inferior courts as the Congress may from time to time ordain and establish. The judges, both of the Supreme and inferior courts, shall hold their offices during good behavior, and shall, at stated times, receive for their services a compensation, which shall not be diminished during their continuance in office.

SEC. 2. The judicial power shall

---

[1] This clause held in contempt by the Radical majority in the House of Representatives, in passing a Supplementary Reconstruction Bill during the present session, seizing the right of assignment from the President in order to enable Gen. Grant to appoint supple Radical tools in command of the departments embracing the ten unrepresented States. Bill not acted on in Senate. Violated by section 2 of the Act of March 2, 1867, requiring the President to send all orders to the army through Gen. Grant, and forbidding army officers from obeying his orders otherwise sent; also, fixing army headquarters at Washington.

[2] This clause violated by the Tenure of Office Bill, and the President impeached by the Radical House of Representatives for exercising his authority under the same; thirty-seven Radical Senators voting to convict him therefor and remove him from office.

extend to all cases in law and equity arising under this Constitution, the laws of the United States, and treaties made, or which shall be made, under their authority; to all cases affecting ambassadors, other public ministers, and consuls; to all cases of admiralty and maritime jurisdiction; to controversies to which the United States shall be a party; to controversies between two or more States; between a State and citizens of another State; between citizens of different States; between citizens of the same State claiming lands under grants of different States; and between a State, or the citizens thereof, and foreign States, citizens, or subjects.[1]

In all cases affecting ambassadors, other public ministers, and consuls, and those in which a State shall be party, the Supreme Court shall have original jurisdiction. In all the other cases before mentioned, the Supreme Court shall have appellate jurisdiction, both as to law and fact, with such exceptions, and under such regulations as the Congress shall make.

The trial of all crimes, except in cases of impeachment, shall be by jury, and such trial shall be held in the State where the said crimes shall have been committed; but when not committed within any State, the trial shall be at such place or places as Congress may by law have directed.[2]

SEC. 3. Treason against the United States shall consist only in levying war against them, or in adhering to their enemies, giving them aid and comfort. No person shall be convicted of treason, unless on the testimony of two witnesses to the same overt act, or on confession in open court.

The Congress shall have power to declare the punishment of treason; but no attainder of treason shall work corruption of blood or forfeiture, except during the life of the person attainted.

ARTICLE IV.

SEC. 1. Full faith and credit shall be given in each State to the public acts, records, and judicial proceedings of every other State. The Congress may, by general laws, prescribe the manner in which such acts, records, and proceedings shall be proved, and the effect thereof.[3]

SEC. 2. The citizens of each State shall be entitled to all privileges and immunities of citizens in the several States.[4]

A person charged in any State with treason, felony, or other crime, who shall flee from justice, and be found in another State, shall, on demand of the executive authority of the State from which he fled, be delivered up, to be removed to the State having jurisdiction of the crime.[5]

No person held to service or labor in one State, under the laws thereof,

---

[1] This clause attempted to be violated by the Radical majority in the House of Representatives, in passing a bill forbidding the Supreme Court to take cognizance of cases arising under the reconstruction legislation of Congress. Since violated by Congress snatching jurisdiction from the Supreme Court in the McArdle case.

[2] This clause violated by the manifold Military Commissions, which have sat on the liberties of citizens, and executed them without law or jury, and by the several Military commanders in the unrepresented States.

[3] This section violated by the arbitrary abnegation of the legitimate State authorities of the South by the reconstruction legislation of Congress, which sets over them military rulers who set aside at their own caprice the public acts, records, and judicial proceedings of the same, and interrupts the cognizance upon the part of the States of the public acts, records and judicial proceedings of each other.

[4] This clause violated by the recent act of Congress admitting Arkansas to representation, and the recent Omnibus act, admitting certain other States to representation which ratify the constitutions of the bogus organization of said States, which require certain oaths to be taken as a necessary prerequisite to the enjoyment of certain privileges and immunities in those States; and in other modes to be seen by an examination of the same: an incapacity to take the oath working this unconstitutional proscription.

[5] This clause violated by the Radical State authorities of New York, who went into Louisi-

escaping into another, shall, in consequence of any law or regulation therein, be discharged from such service or labor, but shall be delivered up on claim of the party to whom such service or labor may be due.

SEC. 3. New States may be admitted by the Congress into this Union; but no new State shall be formed or erected within the jurisdiction of any other State; nor any State be formed by the junction of two or more States, or parts of States, without the consent of the Legislatures of the States concerned as well as of the Congress.[1]

The Congress shall have power to dispose of and make all needful rules and regulations respecting the territory or other property belonging to the United States, and nothing in this Constitution shall be so construed as to prejudice any claims of the United States, or of any particular State.

SEC. 4. The United States shall guarantee to every State in this Union a republican form of government, and shall protect each of them against invasion; and on application of the Legislature, or of the Executive (when the Legislature can not be convened), against domestic violence.[2]

ARTICLE V.

The Congress, whenever two-thirds of both Houses shall deem it necessary, shall propose amendments to this Constitution; or, on the application of the Legislatures of two-thirds of the several States, shall call a convention for proposing amendments, which, in either case, shall be valid to all intents and purposes, as part of this Constitution, when ratified by the Legislatures of three-fourths of the several States, or by conventions in three-fourths thereof, as the one or the other mode of ratification may be proposed by the Congress; provided that no amendment which may be made prior to the year one thousand eight hundred and eight shall in any manner affect the first and fourth clauses in the ninth section of the first Article; and that no State, without its consent, shall be deprived of its equal suffrage in the Senate.

ARTICLE VI.

All debts contracted and engagements entered into, before the adoption of this Constitution, shall be as valid against the United States under this Constitution, as under the Confederation.

This Constitution, and the laws of the United States which shall be made in pursuance thereof; and all treaties made, or which shall be made, under the authority of the United States, shall be the supreme law of the land; and the Judges in every State shall be bound thereby, anything in the Constitution or laws of any State to the contrary notwithstanding.[3]

The Senators and Representatives before mentioned, and the members of the several State Legislatures, and all executive and judicial officers, both

---

ana and seized a prisoner without a demand upon the Governor thereof, and spirited him away to New York in contempt of a writ of *habeas corpus* and in defiance of the military interposition of Gen. Hancock. Violated also by the Radical Governor of Tennessee, who declines to respect any demand upon him from the Governor of any other State, when the criminal is what he calls a loyal citizen.

[1] This section violated by the division of the Commonwealth of Virginia, by the Radical party in Congress, with the approval of President Lincoln, cutting off from the same the State of West Virginia, without the consent of Virginia

[2] This clause is violated in this, that the Radical Congress does not guarantee to Tennessee a Republican form of government, but permits it to be dominated over by a licentious and tyrannical oligarchy, and that it imposed upon ten States of the South a military despotism.

[3] This clause is violated by the Radical Congress, which openly and unblushingly legislates without reference to the existence of the Constitution, and in violation of its letter and spirit. It is no longer mentioned by them in argument or regarded in action. It is not named either in the platform at Chicago or in the letter of acceptance either of Grant or Colfax.

of the United States and of the several States, shall be bound by oath or affirmation, to support this Constitution; but no religious test shall ever be required as a qualification to any office or public trust under the United States.[1]

ARTICLE VII.

The ratification of the conventions of nine States, shall be sufficient for the establishment of this Constitution between the States so ratifying the same.

Amendments.

ART. 1. Congress shall make no law respecting an establishment of religion, or prohibiting the free exercise thereof; or abridging the freedom of speech or of the press, or the right of the people peaceably to assemble, and to petition the government for a redress of grievances.[2]

ART. 2. A well regulated militia being necessary to the security of a free State, the right of the people to keep and bear arms shall not be infringed.[3]

ART. 3. No soldier shall in time of peace be quartered in any house without the consent of the owner; nor in time of war, but in a manner to be prescribed by law.[4]

ART. 4. The right of the people to be secure in their persons, houses, papers, and effects, against unreasonable searches and seizures, shall not be violated; and no warrants shall issue but upon probable cause, supported by oath or affirmation, and particularly describing the place to be searched, and the persons or things to be seized.[5]

ART. 5. No person shall be held to answer for a capital or otherwise infamous crime, unless on a presentment or indictment of a grand jury, except in cases arising in the land or naval forces, or in the militia when in actual service in time of war, or public danger; nor shall any person be subject for the same offense, to be put twice in jeopardy of life or limb; nor shall be compelled, in any criminal case, to be witness against himself; nor be deprived of life, liberty, or property, without due process of law; nor shall private property be taken for public use without just compensation.[6]

ART. 6. In all criminal prosecutions, the accused shall enjoy the right to a speedy and public trial, by an impartial jury of the State and district wherein the crime shall have

---

[1] This clause violated in this: that Congress adds to the oath prescribed in it, certain tests, embraced in what is called the iron-clad oath, and requires parties eligible to the offices named, and who are able to take the oath prescribed in the Constitution, to subscribe to the extra constitutional oath, thus excluding them from those offices by such indirect means, when incompetent or indisposed to take it.

[2] This article is violated with impunity in ten States of the South. Witness the destruction in August, 1867, of the Constitutional Eagle, a Democratic paper, published at Camden, Ark., by a band of U. S. soldiers in command of an officer of the armies of the U. S., for strictures on the indecent exposure of their persons in the town by the soldiers aforesaid; the suppression by Gen. Grant, in 1866, of the Richmond Enquirer; the threat of Brig.-Gen. Shepherd, commanding at Mobile, to the Editors of the Mobile Register and Advertiser; the arrest and imprisonment of Col. W. H. McArdle, Editor of the Vicksburg Times; the arrest and imprisonment of the Editors of the Memphis Avalanche by a Radical Judge; the arrest of the Editors of the Ledger, by the same; and other cases too numerous to mention.

[3] This article not regarded in the ten States of the South, the militia in the same being disbanded, and the right to bear arms being taken away or given at the discretion of their military rulers.

[4] This article, the violation of which no officer of the army of the U. S. will deny, because the houses of citizens, for quarters of officers of all grades from General down, and for troops, were occupied to a great extent in the South, for a long time since the war, against the consent of, and in many instances without compensation to, the owners, and are to a much less extent so occupied now.

[5] This article, now the subject of violation daily in all of the Military Districts of the South, more particularly in the command of Gen. Meade and that of the sub-commander of the State of Arkansas.

[6] The next note applies as well to this article.

been committed, which district shall have been previously ascertained by law, and to be informed of the nature and cause of the accusation; to be confronted with the witnesses against him; to have compulsory process for obtaining witnesses in his favor; and to have the assistance of counsel for his defense.[1]

ART. 7. In suits at common law, where the value in controversy shall exceed twenty dollars, the right of trial by jury shall be preserved; and no fact tried by jury shall be otherwise re-examined in any court of the United States than according to the rules of the common law.[2]

ART. 8. Excessive bail shall not be required, nor excessive fines imposed, nor cruel and unusual punishments inflicted.[3]

ART. 9. The enumeration in the Constitution of certain rights, shall not be construed to deny or disparage others retained by the people.[4]

ART. 10. The powers not delegated to the United States by the Constitution, nor prohibited by it to the States, are reserved to the States respectively, or to the people.[5]

ART. 11. The judicial power of the United States shall not be construed to extend to any suit in law or equity commenced or prosecuted against one of the United States by citizens of another State, or by citizens or subjects of another State, or by citizens or subjects of any foreign State.

ART. 12. The electors shall meet in their respective States, and vote by ballot for President and Vice-President, one of whom, at least, shall not be an inhabitant of the same State with themselves; they shall name in their ballots the person voted for as President, and in distinct ballots the person voted for as Vice-President; and they shall make distinct lists of all persons voted for as President, and of all persons voted for as Vice-President, and of the number of votes for each, which lists they shall sign and certify, and transmit sealed to the seat of government of the United States, directed to the President of the Senate: the President of the Senate shall, in the presence of the Senate and House of Representatives, open all the certificates, and the votes shall then be counted; the person having the greatest number of votes for President shall be the President, if such number be a majority of the whole number of electors appointed; and if no person have such a majority, then from the persons having the highest numbers, not exceeding three, on the list of those voted for as President, the House of Representatives shall choose immediately by ballot the President. But in choosing the President, the votes shall be taken by States, the representation from each State having one vote; a quorum for this purpose shall consist of a member or members from two-thirds of the States, and a majority of all the States shall be necessary to a choice. And if the House of Representatives shall not choose a President whenever the

---

[1] This article, not regarded in the District of North and South Carolina, commanded by Gen. Canby; nor in that of Georgia, Florida and Alabama, commanded by Gen. Meade; nor in that of Mississippi and Arkansas, lately put in command of Gen. McDowell.

[2] This article, in the ten States of the South, and in Kentucky and Tennessee, in any case where a negro or a white loyalist (as a carpet-bagger is officially designated), is the plaintiff, and a white man is defendant, is set aside, and the authority of an officer of the Freedman's Bureau is supreme. The same where their positions are reversed.

[3] This article utterly obsolete in the Southern States. Look into the horrible prisons at Dry Tortugas, and reflect that drum-head Court Martials are in session all over the ten Southern States, and continue to send citizens to it and other kindred prisons.

[4] Congress exercises no respect for any enumeration of rights, but claims unlimited powers, as is shown in previous notes and hereafter in this book, and utterly denies to the ten States of the South and the people thereof the rights reserved to them.

[5] This article is violated in the same manner as Article 9, and the same note applies to it

right of choice shall devolve upon them, before the fourth day of March next following, then the Vice-President shall act as President, as in the case of the death or other constitutional disability of the President.

The person having the greatest number of votes as Vice-President, shall be the Vice-President, if such number be a majority of the whole number of electors appointed; and if no person have a majority, then from the two highest numbers on the list, the Senate shall choose the Vice-President: a quorum for this purpose shall consist of two-thirds of the whole number of Senators, and a majority of the whole number shall be necessary to a choice.

But no person constitutionally ineligible to the office of President shall be eligible to that of Vice-President of the United States.[1]

DECLARATION OF INDEPENDENCE.
Its Vital Principles Violated by the Radicals.

WHEN, in the course of human events, it becomes necessary for one people to dissolve the political bands which have connected them with another, and to assume, among the powers of the earth, the separate and equal station to which the laws of nature and of nature's God entitle them, a decent respect to the opinions of mankind requires that they should declare the causes which impel them to a separation.

We hold these truths to be self-evident: that all men are created equal; that they are endowed by their Creator with certain inalienable rights; that among these are life, liberty, and the pursuit of happiness. That to secure these rights, governments are instituted among men, deriving their just powers from the consent of the governed; and that, whenever any form of government becomes destructive of these ends, it is the right of the people to alter or to abolish it, and to institute a new government, laying its foundations on such principles, and organizing its powers in such form, as to them shall seem most likely to effect their safety and happiness. Prudence, indeed, will dictate that governments, long established, should not be changed for light and transient causes; and, accordingly, all experience hath shown, that mankind are more disposed to suffer, while evils are sufferable, than to right themselves by abolishing the forms to which they are accustomed. But, when a long train of abuses and usurpations, pursuing invariably the same object, evinces a design to reduce them under absolute despotism, it is their right, it is their duty, to throw off such government, and to provide new guards for their future security. Such has been the patient sufferance of the colonies, and such is now the necessity which constrains them to alter their former systems of government. The history of the present king of Great Britain is a history of repeated injuries and usurpations, all having, in direct object, the establishment of an absolute tyranny over these States. To prove this, let facts be submitted to a candid world:

He has refused his assent to laws the most wholesome and necessary for the public good.

---

[1] The notes to the Constitution, in so far as they refer to the existence of Military government in ten States of the South, were prepared preparatory to the admission to representation in Congress of some of those States under bogus constitutions, and with bogus Senators and Representatives. This does not change the force of the notes, for the Military power itself exercises a supervisory control, which amounts to as absolute a despotism as its exclusive sway. It is the more offensive since it becomes the means of giving violent support if necessary to the rotten boroughs which substitute the real States, and which are in the possession and under the government of a gang of vagrant Radicals. Gen. Grant's order to Gen. McDowell, directs him not to turn over the Government of Arkansas absolutely; but "as rapidly as he deems it prudent." In other words, not to be in a hurry until after the Presidential election.

He has forbidden his governors to pass laws of immediate and pressing importance, unless suspended in their operations till his assent should be obtained; and, when so suspended, he has utterly neglected to attend to them.

He has refused to pass other laws for the accommodation of large districts of people, unless those people would relinquish the right of representation in the legislature—a right inestimable to them, and formidable to tyrants only.

He has called together legislative bodies at places unusual, uncomfortable, and distant from the depository of their public records, for the sole purpose of fatiguing them into compliance with his measures.

He has dissolved representative houses repeatedly, for opposing with manly firmness his invasions on the rights of the people.

He has refused, for a long time after such dissolutions, to cause others to be elected; whereby the legislative powers, incapable of annihilation, have returned to the people at large for their exercise; the State remaining, in the mean time, exposed to all the danger of invasion from without, and convulsions within.

He has endeavored to prevent the population of these States; for that purpose, obstructing the laws for naturalization of foreigners, refusing to pass others to encourage their migration hither, and raising the conditions of new appropriations of lands.

He has obstructed the administration of justice, by refusing his assent to laws for establishing judiciary powers.

He has made judges dependent on his will alone for the tenure of their offices and the amount and payment of their salaries.

He has erected a multitude of new offices, and sent hither swarms of officers to harass our people, and eat out their substance.

He has kept among us, in time of peace, standing armies, without the consent of our legislature.

He has affected to render the military independent of, and superior to the civil power.

He has combined, with others, to subject us to a jurisdiction foreign to our Constitution, and unacknowledged by our laws; giving his assent to their acts of pretended legislation:

For quartering large bodies of armed troops among us:

For protecting them, by a mock trial, from punishment for any murders which they should commit on the inhabitants of these States:

For cutting off our trade with all parts of the world:

For imposing taxes on us without our consent:

For depriving us, in many cases, of the benefits of trial by jury:

For transporting us beyond seas to be tried for pretended offenses:

For abolishing the free system of English laws in a neighboring province, establishing therein an arbitrary government, and enlarging its boundaries so as to render it at once an example and fit instrument for introducing the same absolute rule into these colonies:

For taking away our charters, abolishing our most valuable laws, and altering, fundamentally, the powers of our governments:

For suspending our own legislatures, and declaring themselves invested with power to legislate for us in all cases whatsoever.

He has abdicated government here, by declaring us out of his protection, and waging war against us.

He has plundered our seas, ravaged our coasts, burnt our towns, and destroyed the lives our people.

He is, at this time, transporting large armies of foreign mercenaries to complete the works of death, desolation, and tyranny, already begun, with circumstances of cruelty and perfidy scarcely paralleled in the most barbarous ages, and totally unworthy the head of a civilized nation.

He has constrained our fellow-citizens, taken captive on the high seas, to bear arms against their country, to become the executioners of their friends and brethren, or to fall themselves by their hands.

He has excited domestic insurrections among us, and has endeavored to bring on the inhabitants of our frontiers the merciless Indian savages, whose known rule of warfare is an undistinguished destruction of all ages, sexes, and conditions.

In every stage of these oppressions, we have petitioned for redress in the most humble terms. Our repeated petitions have only been answered by repeated injuries. A prince, whose character is thus marked by every act which may define a tyrant, is unfit to be the ruler of a free people.

Nor have we been wanting in attention to our British brethren. We have warned them, from time to time, of attempts by their legislature, to extend an unwarrantable jurisdiction over us. We have reminded them of the circumstances of our emigration and settlement here. We have appealed to their native justice and magnanimity, and we have conjured them, by the ties of our common kindred, to disavow these usurpations, which would inevitably interrupt our connexions and correspondence. They, too, have been deaf to the voice of justice and consanguinity. We must, therefore, acquiesce in the necessity which denounces our separation, and hold them, as we hold the rest of mankind—enemies in war; in peace, friends.

We, therefore, the Representatives of the United States of America, in General Congress assembled, appealing to the Supreme Judge of the world for the rectitude of our intentions, do, in the name and by the authority of the good people of these colonies, solemnly publish and declare that these United Colonies are, and of right ought to be, free and independent States; that they are absolved from all allegiance to the British crown, and that all political connexion between them and the State of Great Britain is, and ought to be, totally dissolved; and that, as free and independent States, they have full power to levy war, conclude peace, contract alliances, establish commerce, and do all other acts and things which independent States may of right do. And, for the support of this declaration, with a firm reliance on the protection of Divine Providence, we mutually pledge to each other our lives, our fortunes, and our sacred honor.

Indorsement of the foregoing by the Radical National Convention.

Resolved, That we recognize the great principle laid down in the Declaration of Independence as the true platform of democratic Government, and we hail with gladness every effort toward making these principles a living reality on every inch of American soil.—*Chicago Platform.*

The Indorsement a Swindle.

This Declaration of Independence it will be seen by reference to the Chicago Platform, was affirmed by the Radical Convention, while all allusion to the Constitution was pretermitted. The Albany Argus shows up the Radical violation also of the Declaration of Independence. Says the Argus:

Who can deny that this indictment against George the Third does not apply to Congress? It sounds as though it was especially written to meet the usurpation of the men at Washington.

A miscalled Republican Congress has been guilty of acts of tyranny which render them unfit to rule a free people.

They have dissolved representative governments of States in times of peace.

They have annulled State Governments, and refused to receive representatives elected to that body.

They have overthrown tribunals established by the people, and erected military tribunals in their stead.

They keep large standing armies to eat

out the substance of the people, and to resist and defeat the popular will.

They have annulled the right of trial by jury in ten States, and substituted martial-law in its place.

They have declared the military to be superior to the civil power, and stigmatize all as "disloyal" who resist such a usurpation of power.

They have suspended Legislatures in ten States, and assume to legislate for the people.

They have removed Governors of States by military edicts, because they would not violate the oaths they had taken to support the Constitution.

And worse than all, they made a military dictator superior to the President, usurped the powers of the Supreme Court, and declare themselves the government independent of the State, and "outside of the Constitution." A Congress "whose character is thus marked by every act which may define a tyrant, is unfit to rule a free people."

Senator Saulsbury graphically portrays the violation by the Radicals of both the Constitution and Declaration of Independence.

The Republican party waged three wars at one and the same time. A war against the Southern States, a war against their political opponents, and a war against the Constitution of the United States. In the prosecution of these wars they were guilty of almost every offense for the commission of which our fathers declared their independence of the British Crown and made war to secure that independence. I will say nothing of their action in respect to the people of the South. Against those who adhered to the Union, and who were much more devoted to the Constitution and Government of the United States than they were themselves, they were guilty of the following offenses charged in the Declaration of Independence:

1st. They dissolved Legislatures for opposing with manly firmness their invasions on the rights of the people. 2d. They obstructed the administration of justice by imprisoning Judges and officers of the law. 3d. They attempted to make Judges dependent on their will alone for the tenure of their offices and the payment of their salaries. 4th. They erected a multitude of new offices and sent among them swarms of officers to harass the people and eat out their substance. 5th. They kept among the people, who were at peace among themselves, standing armies, without the consent of their Legislature. 6th. They rendered the military independent of and superior to the civil power. 7th. They subjected the people to a jurisdiction foreign to their Constitution and unacknowledged by their law. 8th. They quartered large bodies of armed troops among them. 9th. They protected officers and troops from punishment for murder and other crimes committed by them. 10th. They cut off the trade of the people among themselves and with other parts of the world. 11th. They deprived the people in many cases of the benefits of the trial by jury. 12th. Without authority of law their President exercised the following powers which belong exclusively to Congress, and was thereby guilty of usurpation, which usurpation was approved by the Republican party, and thus it became their act: 1, he increased the army; 2, he increased the navy; 3, he appropriated the public money; 4, he regulated commerce with foreign nations; 5, he regulated commerce between the States; 6, he contracted debt on behalf of the nation; 7, he suspended the writ of *habeas corpus*. 13th. The following powers, denied both to Congress and the President, their President exercised, which exercise of unauthorized power they approved, and thereby are guilty as a party of the usurpation themselves: 1, he proclaimed martial-law; 2, he arrested without legal warrant; 3, imprisoned and punished without conviction and legal trial; 4, punished under *ex post facto* or non-existing law; 5, introduced *lettres de cachet*, bastiles, and the midnight secret proceedings of the Inquisition; 6, interdicted reports; 7, favored some ports to the prejudice of others; 8, regulated the commerce of a State within its own bounds; 9, impaired the freedom of speech and of the press; 10, infringed the people's right to keep and bear arms; 11, made unreasonable searches and seizures; 12, prohibited emigration and required passports; 13, dismissed the police of cities in States not proclaimed in insurrection, and appointed others in their place; 14, interfered by the military force with the freedom of elections in the States; 15, took private property for public use without just compensation. 14th. This party has conferred the elective franchise upon the negro in the District of Columbia against the will of the people. 15th. They have placed Governors over the people against their will and in violation of their laws, by military force. 16th. They have caused pretended Legislatures to be elected in the States against the will of the people in the same manner and by the same employment of the same means. 17th. They have by the same means appointed pretended conventions to form and revise the Constitutions of the States. 18th. They have forced illegal State Constitutions upon the people against their wills. 19th. They have appropriated money out of the public Treasury; for the support of negroes living in idleness, and have levied taxes upon the white citizens for that purpose. 20th. They have attempted to deprive the people of the States of the power to determine evidence and regulate the judicial proceedings of their own courts, in violation of their laws and Constitutions. 21st. They have deprived the State courts of the jurisdiction to hear and determine questions relating to the rights of persons, liberty, and property within the State, and to pass and determine upon the guilt or innocence of those accused of crimes committed within the State. 22d. They have authorized the arrest and punishment of Judges for deciding questions of law against their enactment. 23d. They have annulled the Constitutional authority and prerogatives of the Executive of the United States. 24th. They have banished the citizens from family and home without trial. 25th. They have violated every one of the twelve amendments to the Constitution designed to protect the people in the enjoyment of their rights of persons, liberty, and property. 26th. They have sacrificed the lives of half a million men in a war which they might easily have averted, and have burdened the industry of the people by the creation of a debt amounting to billions of dollars.

"And now there was no foe in arms
T' unite their factions with alarms,
But all reduced and overcome,
Except their worst, themselves, at home,
Who'd compass'd all they pray'd and swore
And fought and preach'd and plunder'd for;
Subdued the nation, church, and state,
And all things but their laws and hate.
But when they came to treat and transact,
And share the spoil of all they'd ransack'd
To botch up all they'd torn and rent,
Religion and the Government,
They met no sooner, but prepared
To pull down all the war had spared.
Agreed in nothing but t' abolish,
Subvert, extirpate, and demolish.
And all conjoined to do their best
To damn the public interest."

And yet, Mr. President, this Republican party, with this record, instead of calling upon the rocks and mountains to hide them from the face of an outraged and indignant people, coolly charge the members of the Democratic party with being disloyal and with being unfaithful to the Constitution and laws of their country. O shame, where is thy blush!

Radical Platform.
NOT A WORD IN IT ABOUT THE CONSTITUTION.

The following is the Platform adopted by the Republican National Convention recently in session in Chicago:

The National Union Republican party of the United States, assembled in National Convention in the city of Chicago, on the 20th day of May, 1868, make the following declaration of principles:

1. We congratulate the country on the assured success of the reconstruction policy of Congress as evidenced by the adoption, in a majority of the States lately in rebellion, of Constitutions securing equal civil and political rights to all, and regard it as the duty of the Government to sustain those Constitutions and prevent the people of such States from being remitted to a state of anarchy or military rule.

2. The guarantee by Congress of equal suffrage to all loyal men in the South was demanded by every consideration of public safety, of gratitude and of justice, and must be maintained while the question of suffrage in all the loyal States, properly belongs to the people of those States.

3. We denounce all forms of repudiation as a national crime, and national honor requires the payment of the public indebtedness in the utmost good faith to our creditors at home and abroad, not only according to the letter, but the spirit of the laws under which it was contracted.

4. It is due to the labor of the nation that taxation should be equalized and reduced as rapidly as national faith will permit.

5. The national debt, contracted as it has been, for the preservation of the Union for all time to come, should be extended over a fair period for redemption, and it is the duty of Congress to reduce the rate of interest thereon whenever it can honestly be done.

6. That the best policy to diminish our burden of debt is to improve our credit, that capitalists will seek to lend us money at lower rates of interest than we now pay, and must continue to pay so long as repudiation, partial or total, open or covert, is threatened or suspected.

7. The Government of the United States should be administered with the strictest economy. The corruptions which have been so shamefully nursed and fostered by Andrew Johnson, call loudly for radical reform.

8. We profoundly deplore the un-

timely and tragic death of Abraham Lincoln, and regret the accession of Andrew Johnson to the Presidency, who has acted treacherously to the people who elected him and the cause he was pledged to support; has usurped high legislative and judicial functions; has refused to execute the laws; has used his high office to induce other officers to violate the laws; has employed his executive power to render insecure the lives, property, peace, and liberty of the citizens; has abused the pardoning power; has denounced the National Legislature as unconstitutional; has persistently and habitually resisted, by every means in his power, every proper attempt at the reconstruction of the States lately in rebellion; has perverted the public patronage into an engine of wholesale corruption, and has been justly impeached for high crimes and misdemeanors, and properly pronounced guilty thereof by the votes of thirty-five Senators.

9. The doctrine of Great Britain, and other European powers, that because a man is once a subject he is always so, must be resisted at every hazard by the United States as a relic of the feudal times, not authorized by the law of nations, and at war with our national honor and independence. Naturalized citizens are entitled to be protected in all their rights of citizenship as though they were native-born. No citizen of the United States, native or naturalized, must be liable to arrest or imprisonment by any foreign power, for acts done or words spoken in this country; and, if so arrested and imprisoned, it is the duty of the Government to interfere in his behalf.

10. Of all who were faithful in the trials of the late war, there were none entitled to more especial honor than the brave soldiers and seamen who endured the hardships of the camp and cruise, and imperiled their lives in the service of the country. The bounties and pensions appropriated by law for these brave defenders of the Union are obligations never to be forgotten. The widows and orphans of the gallant dead are the wards of the people—a sacred legacy bequeathed to the United States' protecting care.

11. Foreign emigration, which in the past has added so much to the wealth and increased the resources of this nation—the asylum of all nations—should be fostered by a liberal and just policy.

12. This Convention declares its sympathy with all oppressed people who are struggling for their rights.

Resolved, That we recognize the great principles laid down in the Declaration of Independence as the true platform of democratic government, and we hail with gladness every effort toward making these principles a living reality on every inch of American soil.

Resolved, That we highly commend the spirit of magnanimity and forgiveness with which men who have served in the rebellion have now frankly and honestly co-operated with us in restoring the peace of the country, and are reconstructed. They are received back into the Union of the loyal people. We favor the removal of the restrictions imposed upon the late rebels as soon as the spirit of rebellion has died out.

General Grant's Letter of Acceptance.

The following is General Grant's reply to the nomination of the Chicago Convention:

WASHINGTON, May 29, 1868.

To General Joseph R. Hawley, President National Union Republican Convention:

In formally accepting the nomination of the National Union Republican Convention of the 21st of May instant, it seems proper that some statement of views beyond the mere acceptance of the nomination should be expressed. The proceedings of the Convention were marked with wisdom, moderation, and patriotism, and, I believe, express the feelings of the great mass of those who sustained the country through its recent trials. I indorse the resolutions. If elected to the office of President of the United States, it will be my endeavor to administer all the laws in good faith, with economy, and with the view of giving peace, quiet, and protection everywhere. In times like the present it is impossible, or at least eminently improper, to lay down a policy to be adhered to, right or wrong, through an administration of four years. New political issues, not foreseen, are constantly arising; the views of the public on old ones are constantly changing, and a purely administrative officer should always be left free to execute the will of the people. I always have respected that will, and always shall. Peace, and universal prosperity, its sequence, with economy of administration, will lighten the burden of taxation, while it constantly reduces the national debt. Let us have peace.

With great respect, your obedient servant,

U. S. GRANT.

He does not mention the Constitution once.

Speaker Colfax's Letter of Acceptance.

The following is the reply of Speaker Colfax to the Committee announcing his nomination by the Chicago Convention:

WASHINGTON, May 30, 1868.

Hon. J. R. Hawley, President of the National Union Republican Convention:

DEAR SIR: The platform adopted by that patriotic convention over which you presided, and the resolutions which so happily supplement it, so naturally agree with my views as to a just national policy, that my thanks are due to the delegates as much for this clear and auspicious declaration of principles, as for the nomination with which I have been honored and which I gratefully accept. When a great rebellion, which imperiled the national existence was at last overthrown, the duty, of all others, devolving on those intrusted with the responsibilities of legislation, evidently was to require that the revolted States should be readmitted to participation in the Government against which they had erred, only on such a basis as to increase and fortify, not to weaken or endanger, the strength and power of the nation. Certainly no one ought to have claimed that they should be readmitted under such rule that their organization as States could ever again be used, as at the opening of the war, to defy the national authority or to destroy the national unity. This principle has been the pole-star of those who have inflexibly insisted on the Congressional policy your convention so cordially indorsed. Baffled by executive opposition, and by persistent refusals to accept any plan of reconstruction proffered by Congress, justice and public safety at last combined to teach us that only by an enlargement of suffrage in those States could the desired end be attained, and that it was even more safe to give the ballot to those who loved the Union than to those who had sought ineffectually to destroy it. The assured success of this legislation is being written on the adamant of history, and will be our triumphant vindication. More clearly, too, than ever before, does the nation now recognize that the greatest glory of a republic is, that it throws the shield of its protection over the humblest and weakest of its people, and vindicates the rights of the poor and the powerless as faithfully as those of the rich and the powerful. I rejoice, too, in this connection, to find in your platform the frank and fearless avowal that naturalized citizens must be protected abroad, at every hazard, as though they were native-born. Our whole people are foreigners, or descendants of foreigners; our fathers established by arms their right to be called a nation. It remains for us to establish the right to welcome to our shores all who are willing, by oaths of allegiance, to become American citizens. Perpetual allegiance, as claimed abroad, is only another name for perpetual bondage, and would make all slaves to the soil where first they saw the light. Our national cemeteries prove how faithfully these oaths of fidelity to their adopted land have been sealed in the life-blood of thousands upon thousands. Should we not then be faithless to the dead if we did not protect their living brethren in the full enjoyment of that nationality for which, side by side with the native-born, our soldiers of foreign birth laid down their lives? It was fitting, too, that the representatives of a party which had proved so true to national duty in time of war, should speak so clearly in time of peace for the maintenance, untarnished, of the national honor, national credit, and good faith as regards its debt, the cost of our national existence. I do not need to extend this reply by further comment on a platform which has elicited such hearty approval throughout the land. The debt of gratitude it acknowledges to the brave men who saved the Union from destruction, the frank approval of amnesty based on repentance and loyalty, the demand for the most thorough economy and honesty in the Government, the sympathy of the party of liberty with all throughout the world who long for the liberty we here enjoy, and the recognition of the sublime principles of the Declaration of Independence, are worthy of the organization on whose banners they are to be written in the coming contest. Its past record can not be blotted out or forgotten. If there had been no Republican party, slavery would to-day cast its baneful shadow over the republic. If there had been no Republican party, a free press and free speech would be as unknown, from the Potomac to the Rio Grande, as ten years ago. If the Republican party could have been stricken from existence when the banner of rebellion was unfurled, and when the response of "No coercion!" was heard at the North, we would have had no nation to-day. But for the Republican party daring to risk the odium of tax and draft laws, our flag could not have been kept flying in the field until the long hoped for victory came. Without a Republican party the Civil Rights bill—the guarantee of equality under the law to the humble and the defenseless, as well as to the strong—would not be to-day upon our national statute-book. With such inspiration from the past, and following the example of the founders of the republic, who called the victorious General of the Revolution to preside over the land his triumphs had saved from its enemies, I can not doubt that our labors will be a success that shall bring restored hope, confidence, prosperity, and progress, South as well as North, West as well as East, and, above all, the blessings under Providence of national concord and peace.

Very truly yours,
SCHUYLER COLFAX.

The Constitution has become of so little concern in Radical eyes that even the Sophomore Colfax fails to reverence it with a mention.

General Grant's Record.

REGULATONS IN RELATION TO NEGROES.

HEADQUARTERS DEPARTMENT OF THE TENNESSEE, }
CORINTH, MISS., August 11, 1862.   }

* * Officers and soldiers are positively prohibited *from enticing slaves to leave their masters.* * * It is enjoined on all commanders to see that this order is executed strictly under their own direction. By command of

U. S. GRANT, Major-General.

[From the World, July 28, 1863.]

GRANT'S POLITICS—HE VOTED FOR DOUGLAS.

The Galena (Ill.) *Advertiser* settles the vexed question as to Gen. Grant's political status. While in the army he never voted, but after he settled in Galena he declared himself a Democrat, and voted in 1860 for Stephen A. Douglas for President. It should be understood that it requires a good deal of moral courage for a business man in Northern Illinois to acknowledge himself a Democrat. That section of the country is more intensely and bigotedly Abolition than even Massachusetts or the Western Reserve.

ON IOWA SOLDIERS VOTING.

HEADQUARTERS DEPARTMENT OF THE TENNESSEE, }
VICKSBURG, MISS., August 4, 1863.   }

L. G. BYINGTON, Esq.:

Sir—Your letter of the 6th of July, asking if citizens of the State of Iowa will be allowed to visit this army and distribute tickets when the election is held for soldiers to vote, etc., is just received. In reply I will state that loyal citizens of Northern States will be allowed to visit the troops from their States at any time. *Electioneering, or any other course calculated to arouse discordant feelings, will be prohibited.* The volunteer soldiers of the army will be allowed to hold an election, if the law gives them the right to vote, and no power shall prevent them from voting the ticket of their choice.

I have the honor to be, very respectfully, your obedient servant.

U. S. GRANT, Major-General.

HE WAS "NEVER AN ANTI-SLAVERY MAN."

Senator Wilson, in a speech before the American Anti-Slavery Society, in December, 1863, quoted the following extract from a letter written by Gen. Grant to Hon. E. B. Washburne:

I have never been an anti-slavery man, but I try to judge justly of what I see. I made up my mind when this war commenced that the North and South could only live together in peace as one nation, and they could only be one nation by being a free nation. Slavery, the corner-stone of the so-called Confederacy, is knocked out, and it will take more men to keep black men slaves than to put down the rebellion. Much as I desire peace, I am opposed to any peace until the question of slavery is forever settled.

TERMS OF GEN. LEE'S SURRENDER.

APPOMATTOX COURT HOUSE, April 9, 1865.

Gen. R. E. LEE, Commanding C. S. A.

* * * The officers to give their individual paroles not to take arms against the Government of the United States until properly exchanged, and each company or regimental commander sign a like parole for the men of their commands. * * * This done, each officer and man will be allowed to return to their homes, *not to be disturbed by the United States authority so long as they observe their parole and the laws in force where they reside.*

Very respectfully,
U. S. GRANT, Lieut.-Gen.

[The Southern armies subsequently surrendered in substantially the same terms.]

HE IMPLORES PARDON FOR GEN. LEE AND GEN. PICKETT.

RICHMOND, VA., June 13, 1865.

LEE, GEN. R. E.—For benefit and full restoration to all rights and privileges extended to those included in amnesty proclamation of the President of 20th May, 1865.

HEADQUARTERS ARMY OF THE U. S. }
June 16, 1865.   }

Respectfully forwarded through the Secretary of War to the President, *with earnest recommendation* that the application of Gen. Robert E. Lee *for amnesty and pardon may be granted him.*

The oath of allegiance required by the

recent order of the President to accompany application, does not accompany this, for the reason, as I am informed by General Ord, the order requiring it had not reached Richmond when this was forwarded.

U. S. GRANT, Lieut.-General.

Headquarters Armies of the United States, July 18, 1867.

Official copy: GEO. K. LEET, Ass't Adj. Gen.

RICHMOND, VA., June 13, 1865.

LEE, GENERAL ROBERT E.—Understanding that he and other officers are to be indicted by grand jury at Norfolk, Virginia, states his readiness to be brought to trial, but had supposed the terms of his surrender protected him; therefore prays, etc.

HEADQUARTERS ARMY U. S., June 16, 1865.

In my opinion, the officers and men paroled at the Appomattox Court House, and since, upon the same terms given to Lee, can not be tried for treason so long as they observe the terms of their parole. This is my understanding. Good faith, as well as true policy, dictates that we should observe the conditions of that convention. Bad faith on the part of the Government, or a construction of that convention subjecting officers to trial for treason, would produce a feeling of insecurity in the minds of all the paroled officers and men. If so disposed they might even regard such an infraction of terms by the Government as an entire release from all obligations on their part. I will state, further, that the terms granted by me met with the hearty approval of the President at the time, and of the people generally. The action of Judge Underwood, in Norfolk, has had an injurious effect, and I would ask that he be ordered to quash all indictments found against prisoners of war, and to desist from further prosecution of them.

U. S. GRANT, Lieut.-General.

Headquarters Armies of the United States, July 18, 1867.

Official copy: GEO. K. LEET, Ass't Adj. Gen.

[Cipher.]
HEADQUARTERS ARMY UNITED STATES, WASHINGTON, May 6, 1865.

Maj. Gen. HALLECK, Richmond, Virginia.

Since receipt of your dispatch of 3d, I think it will be advisable to leave Hunter alone for the present. Although it would meet with opposition in the North to allow Lee the benefit of amnesty, *I think it would have the best possible effect toward restoring good feeling and peace in the South to have him come in.* All the people, except a few political leaders in the South, will accept whatever he does as right, and will be guided to a great extent by his example.

Headquarters Armies United States, July 18, 1867.

Official copy: GEO. K. LEET, Ass't Adj. Gen.

WASHINGTON, D. C., March 12, 1865.

PICKETT, GEN. GEO. E.—Presents history of his case, refers to surrender and agreement of April 9, 1865, and asks for protection from prosecution for treason.

HEADQUARTERS ARMY UNITED STATES, March 16, 1866.

Respectfully forwarded to his Excellency, the President of the United States, *with the recommendation that clemency be extended in this case,* or assurance given that no trial will take place for the offense charged against George E. Pickett.

HIS OPINION ON NEGRO SUFFRAGE.

[Extract from Senator Doolittle's speech at Milwaukee, October 2, 1865.]

The other day, when Gen. Grant was here, spending several hours with him in free conversation upon this subject, among others, he expressed to me the same opinion. Said I, "General Grant, I never quote private conversation without express permission. Am I permitted to state what you now state to me?" Said he, "Certainly, there is no concealment on my part." And he stated to me in the conversation that a considerable portion of the troubles between the whites and the blacks that had already occurred, was in consequence of the unwise attempt to force negro suffrage in those States. He said further, that if the Federal Government were to attempt to do it and enforce it, it would undoubtedly produce war between the two races there.

GEN. GRANT ON ARBITRARY ARRESTS.

[Cincinnati Telegram (Oct. 3, 1867,) to the Chicago Times.]

There was much excitement in Newport, yesterday, at the arrest of Rev. L. D. Huston. * * * Gen. Grant immediately telegraphed Gen. Palmer, at Louisville, directing the unconditional release of the distinguished divine. Subsequent to this action by Gen. Grant, Rev. Geo. Maley, an old acquaintance of the General and his family, called upon Gen. Grant, and after a brief interview in a social character, Father Maley inquired: "General, what can you do for Dr. Huston?" "I have already ordered his unconditional release. *It is time that military arrests and military commissions were at an end* We are now at peace, and if any citizen commits any political offense he should be *taken before the civil courts and there tried for his crime.*"

REPORT ON THE CONDITION OF THE SOUTHERN STATES.

HEADQUARTERS ARMIES OF UNITED STATES,
WASHINGTON, D. C., December 18, 1865.

* * * With your approval, and also that of the Honorable Secretary of War, I left Washington City on the 27th of last month for the purpose of making a tour of inspection through some of the Southern States, or States lately in rebellion, and to see what changes were necessary to be made in the disposition of the military forces of the country; *how these forces could be reduced and expenses curtailed, etc.*; and to learn, as far as possible, the feelings and intentions of the citizens of those States toward the General Government. * * Both in traveling and while stopping, I saw much and conversed freely with the citizens of those States, as well as with officers of the army who have been stationed among them. The following are the conclusions come to by me: I am satisfied that the mass of thinking men of the South accept the present situation of affairs in good faith. The questions which have heretofore divided the sentiments of the people of the two sections —slavery and States' rights, or the right of a State to secede from the Union—*they regard as having been settled forever by the highest tribunal—arms—that man can resort to.* I was pleased to learn from the leading men whom I met, that they not only accepted the decision arrived at *as final*, but, now that the smoke of battle has cleared away and time has been given for reflection, that *this decision has been a fortunate one for the whole country,* they receiving like benefits from it with those who opposed them in the field and in council. * * *There is such universal acquiescence in the authority of the General Government throughout the portions of the country visited by me, that the mere presence of a military force, without regard to numbers, is sufficient to maintain order.* The good of the country and economy require that the force kept in the interior, where there are many freedmen (*elsewhere in the Southern States than at ports upon the sea-coast no force is necessary*), should all be white troops. The reasons for this are obvious, without mentioning many of them. The presence of black troops, lately slaves, demoralizes labor, both by their advice and by furnishing in their camps a resort for the freedmen for long distances around. White troops generally excite no opposition, and therefore a small number of these can maintain order in a given district. * * My observations lead me to the conclusion that the citizens of the Southern States *are anxious to return to self-government within the Union as soon as possible;* that while reconstructing they want and require protection from the Government; that they are earnest in wishing to do what they think is required by the Government, *not humiliating to them as citizens*, and that if such a course was pointed out *they would pursue it in good faith.* It is to be regretted that there can not be a greater commingling at this time between the citizens of the two sections, and particularly of those intrusted with the law-making power.

I did not give the operations of the Freedmen's Bureau that attention I would have done if more time had been at my disposal. Conversations on the subject, however, with officers connected with the Bureau, lead me to think that in some of the States its affairs have not been conducted with good judgment or economy, and that the belief, widely spread among the freedmen of the Southern States, that the lands of their former owners will, at least in part, be divided among them, *has come from the agents of this Bureau.* This belief is seriously interfering with the willingness of the freedmen to make contracts for the coming year.

* * In some instances, I am sorry to say, the freedman's mind does not seem to be disabused of the idea that a freedman has a right to live without care or provision for the future. The effect of the belief in division of lands *is idleness and accumulation in camps, towns and cities*. In such cases I think it will be found that vice and disease *will tend to the extermination, or great reduction of the colored race.*

I have the honor to be, very respectfully, your obedient servant,

U. S. GRANT, Lieut.-General.

His Excellency A. Johnson, President of the United States.

SUPPRESSION OF NEWSPAPERS.

HEADQUARTERS ARMIES OF THE U. S.,
WASHINGTON, Feb. 17, 1866.

You will please send to these headquarters as soon as practicable, and from time to time thereafter, such copies of newspapers published in your department as contain sentiments of disloyalty and hostility to the Government in any of its branches, and state whether such paper is habitual in its utterance of such sentiments. *The persistent publication of articles calculated to keep up a hostility of feeling between the people of different sections of the country can not be tolerated.* This information is called for with a view to their suppression, which will be done from these headquarters only.

By order of Lieut.-Gen. Grant.

T. S. BOWERS, Asst. Adj.-Gen.

GRANT'S SPEECH AT CINCINNATI, IN SEPTEMBER, 1866.

A foolish person named Baker protests in the Cincinnati *Gazette* against the outrageous distortion of Gen. Grant's remarks in the theater the other night, by the *Enquirer;* which reports them thus:

"SIR: I am no politician. The President of the United States is my Commander-in-Chief. *I consider this demonstration in opposition to the President of the United States. Andrew Johnson.* If you have any regard for me you will take your men away. I am greatly annoyed at this demonstration. I came here to witness this theatrical performance. I will be glad to see you all to-morrow when the President arrives."

Baker's own version is:

"I am no politician. The President of the United States is my superior officer, and I am under his command. I beg, if you have any regard for me, to march your company away, as I do not wish to be thus annoyed. *I consider this merely a political demonstration for a selfish and political object, and all such I disapprove of.* I came here to enjoy the performance, but I shall be glad to see you all to-morrow at the Burnet House."

"Strange such a difference there should be 'Twixt tweedle-dum and tweedle-dee."

[From the Missouri Republican, Sept. 20, 1866.]
GRANT AND THE PRESIDENT—LETTER FROM HIS FATHER.

COVINGTON, KY., July 20, 1866.

E. C. COLLINS, Esq: * * You know enough about Ulysses to know that to accept the Presidency would be to him a sacrifice of feeling and personal interest. *He could not well stand the trial of being a candidate for public favor;* and his present position is in every way a much better one than that of President. But if there should seem to be the same necessity for it two years hence as now, I *expect he will yield.*

Yours, etc., J. R. GRANT.

ON THE SUBJECT OF SENDING TROOPS TO BALTIMORE, IN THE OCTOBER ELECTION OF 1866.

WASHINGTON, Oct. 24, 1866.

The conviction is forced on my mind that *no reason now exists for giving or promising the military aid of the Government to support the laws of Maryland.* The tendency of giving such aid or promise would be to produce the very result intended to be averted. So far, there seems to be merely a very bitter contest for political ascendancy in the State. Military interference *would be interpreted as giving aid to one of the factions,* no matter how pure the intentions or how guarded and just the instructions. It is a contingency I hope never to see arise in this country, while I occupy the position of General in-Chief of the Army, to have to send troops into a State, in full relations with the General Government, on the eve of an election, to preserve the peace. If insurrection does come, the law provides the method of calling out forces to suppress it. No such condition seems to exist now.

Very respectfully, your obedient servant,
(Signed.) U. S. GRANT, General.
His Excellency Andrew Johnson, President of the United States.

Yet he now openly defends the holding of elections, in ten of the States of the South, under military auspices.

MARTIAL-LAW IN THE SOUTH TO BE DEPLORED.

In the month of January, 1867, Gen. Sheridan addressed a letter to Gen. Grant, which the latter referred to the Secretary of War, recommending the application of martial-law to the State of Texas. The following extract is from Gen. Grant's indorsement of Sheridan's letter:

"The necessity for governing any portion of our territory by martial-law *is to be deplored;* if resorted to, it should be *limited in its authority, and should leave all local authorities and civil tribunals free and unobstructed* until they prove their inefficiency or unwillingness to perform their duties.

"U. S. GRANT, General."

He is now the willing instrument of the Radical power in making the martial-law supreme in the States of the South.

[From the Official Report.]
THE IMPEACHMENT INVESTIGATION—GENERAL GRANT'S TESTIMONY.

WASHINGTON, July 18, 1867.

Gen. Ulysses S. Grant sworn and examined by Mr. Eldridge—Q. Did you after that time [his appointment as General, July, 1866,] have any interviews with the President in reference to the condition of the rebel States? A. I have seen the President frequently on the subject.

Q. Did you have any interviews with him on the subject of granting amnesty or pardon to the officers of the Confederate army, or to the people of those States? A. Not that I am aware of. *I have occasionally recommended a person for amnesty.* I do not recollect any special interview that I have had on the subject. I recollect speaking to him once or twice about the time that he issued his proclamation. I thought myself at that time that there was *no reason why, because a person had risen to the rank of General, he should be excluded from amnesty* any more than one who had failed to reach that rank. I thought his proclamation all right so far as it excluded graduates from West Point or from the Naval Academy, or persons connected with the Government, who had gone into the rebellion; but I did not see any reason *why a volunteer who happened to rise to the rank of General should be excluded any more than a Colonel.* I recollect speaking on that point. *Neither did I see much reason for the twenty thousand dollar clause.* These are the only two points that I remember to have spoken of at the time. I afterward, however, told him that I thought he was much nearer right on the twenty thousand dollar clause than I was.

* * * * * *

Q. Did you give your opinion to the President that his proclamation interfered with the stipulations between yourself and Gen. Lee? A. No, sir. I frequently *had to intercede for Gen. Lee and other paroled officers, on the ground that their parole,* so long as they obeyed the laws of the United States, *protected them from arrest and trial.* The President at that time occupied *exactly the reverse grounds, viz:* that they should be tried and punished. He wanted to know when the time would come that they should be punished. I told him not so long as they obeyed the laws and complied with the stipulation. That was the ground that I took.

Q. Did you not also insist that that applied as well to the common soldier? A. Of course, it applied to every one who took the parole; but that matter was not canvassed, except in case of some of the leaders. I claimed that, in surrendering their armies and arms, they had done what they could not all of them have been compelled to do, as a portion of them could have escaped. But they surrendered in consideration of the fact that they were to be exempt from trial so long as they conformed to the obligations which they had taken; and they were entitled to that.

Q. You looked on that in the nature of a parole, and held that they could only be tried when they violated that parole? A. Yes; that was the view I took of the question.

Q. That is your view still? A. Yes, yes; unquestionably.

Q. Did you understand that to apply to General Lee? A. Certainly.

Q. That was your understanding of the arrangement which you made with Gen. Lee? A. That was my understanding of an arrangement which I gave voluntarily. Gen. Lee's army was the first to surrender, and I believed that with such terms all the rebel armies would surrender, and that we would thus avoid bushwhacking and a continuation of the war in a way that we could make very little progress with, having no organized armies to meet.

Q. You considered that the like terms were given by Gen. Sherman to the armies which surrendered to him? A. Yes, sir; *to all the armies that surrendered* after that.

* * * * * *

Q. Did you give those views to the President? A. I have stated these views to the President frequently, and, as I have said, he disagreed with me in those views. He insisted on it that the leaders must be punished, and wanted to know when the time would come that those persons could be tried. I told him when they violated their parole.

Q. Did you consider that that applied to Jefferson Davis. A. No, sir; he did not take any parole.

Q. He did not surrender? A. No, sir. It applied to no person who was captured— only to those who were paroled.

Q. Did the President insist that Gen. Lee should be tried for treason? A. He contended for it.

Q. And you claimed to him that the parole which Gen. Lee had given would be violated in such trial? A. I did. *I insisted on it that Gen. Lee would not have surrendered his army,* and given up all their arms, if he had supposed that after surrender he was going to be tried for treason and hanged. I thought we got a very good equivalent for the lives of a few leaders in getting all their arms and getting themselves under control, bound by their oaths to obey the laws. That was the consideration which I insisted upon we had received.

Q. Do you recollect at any time urging the President to go further in granting amnesty than he had gone in his proclamation? A. Just as I said before, I could not see any reason why the fact of a volunteer rising to the rank of General should exclude him any more than any other grade. And with reference to the twenty thousand dollar clause, I thought *that a man's success in this world was no reason for his being excluded from amnesty;* but I recollect afterward saying to the President that I thought he was right in that particular, and I was wrong. In reference to the other, I NEVER CHANGED MY VIEWS.

Q. Did you not give your opinion at all that amnesty ought to be granted to those people *to any extent?* A. I know that *I was in favor of some proclamation of the sort,* and perhaps I may have said so. It was necessary to do something to establish civil governments and civil law there. *I wanted to see that done,* but I do not think I ever pretended to dictate what ought to be done.

Q. Did you not advise? A. I do not think I ever did. I have given my opinions, perhaps, as to what has been done, but I do not think I advised any course myself any more than *I was very anxious to see* something done to restore civil governments in those States. * * * There were no governments there when the war was over, and *I wanted to see some governments established, and wanted to see it done quickly.* I did not pretend to say how it should be done or in what form.

Q. By Mr. Williams—Did you ever advise the pardon of Gen. Lee? *Yes, sir.*

Q. Were you ever consulted on that question by the President? A. Gen. Lee forwarded his application for amnesty by me, and *I forwarded it to the President, approved.*

Q. Did you have any conversation about it with the President? A. I do not recollect having any conversation with him on the subject. I think it probable that *I recommended verbally the pardon of General Johnston,* immediately after the surrender of his army, on account of the address he delivered to his army. I thought it in such good tone and spirit that we should distinguish between him and others who did not appear so well. I recollect speaking of that, and saying that *I should be glad if General Johnston received his pardon,* on account of the manly manner in which he addressed his troops.

Q. By the Chairman—You supposed his pardon would have a good effect? A. Yes; I thought it would *have a good effect.*

Q. By Mr. Marshall—I understand you to say that you were very anxious, at the close of the war, that *civil governments should be established in some form as speedily as possible,* and that you so advised the President. A. *I so stated frequently in his presence.*

Q. I wish to know whether, at or about the time of the war being ended, you advised the President that it was, in your judgment, best *to extend all liberal policy toward the people of the South,* and to restore as speedily as possible the fraternal relations which existed prior to the war between the two sections? A. I know that immediately after the close of the rebellion *there was a very fine feeling manifested in the South, and I thought we ought to take advantage of it as soon as possible;* but since that there has been an evident change. I may have expressed my views to the President.

Old Man Grant sounds his boy "Ulyss" on the Subject of Negro Suffrage.

The General's father came to town the other day, and stopped with "Ulyss," as he calls his boy, whom he found seated at his fireside, smoking, of course, and surrounded by members of his private and military family. About the first thing the old gentleman did, after shedding his overcoat, was to come at his unpumpable offspring with "Ulyss, are you in favor of nigger suffrage?" [No response, only vigorous puffs]. "I say, Ulyss, are you in favor of nigger suffrage?" "What do you think of it?" inquired the General, with Yankee shrewdness. The old one states his position: he's for an intelligence qualification, and so on. "Well, now, Ulyss, I've answered your question, I want you to answer mine: Are you in favor of nigger suffrage? If you are, you'll get beat all hollow, with all your popularity, for Ohio went fifty thousand against it, and if she was to vote again on it to-morrow, she'd go a hundred thousand the same way." "I haven't talked politics much for the last five or six years," was the reply of Ulysses, "the Silent." At last accounts the old gentleman was in doubt as to the position of "Ulyss" on negro suffrage.

General Grant and Congress.

COVINGTON, KY., January 11, 1868.

To the Editor of the Pittsburg Commercial:

When in Washington in September last, I wrote to my brother, Dr. A. B. Nixon, of Sacramento, California, a private family letter, some extracts from which found their way into the newspaper. * * * The concluding sentences as they appear in your weekly edition of the 1st instant, are as follows:

"He (General Grant) has told me since I have been here this time, that he approves of everything that Congress has done; but that they did not go far enough in taking the work of reconstruction into their own hands. I do hope this may be owing to local and merely temporary causes. After having stood up so well in more trying times, he should surely stand firm now."

In some of the papers it is printed "they should stand firm now."

* * * * The extract, down to the words "their own hand," is correct. Then, in a separate paragraph, the letter proceeded to speak of the defeat of the Republican party in the recent State election in California, in relation to which defeat were employed the concluding sentences, viz: "I do hope that this may be owing to local and merely temporary causes," etc.

* * * * * *

Very respectfully,

JOHN S. NIXON.

General Grant on our Hebrew Fellow-Citizens

HEADQUARTERS 13TH ARMY CORPS, DEP'T OF THE TENNESSEE, OXFORD, MISS., Dec. 17, 1862.

General Order No. 11].

The Jews, as a class, violating every regulation of trade established by the Treasury

Department, also department orders, are hereby expelled from the department within twenty-four hours from the receipt of this order by post commanders.

They will see that all this class of people are furnished with passes and required to leave; and any one returning after such notification, will be arrested and held in confinement until an opportunity occurs of sending them out as prisoners, unless furnished with permits from these headquarters.

No passes will be given this people to visit headquarters for the purpose of making personal application for trade permits.

By order of Major-General Grant.

J. A. RAWLING, A. A. G.

Official: J. LOVELL, Capt. and A. A. G.

This infamous order was ruthlessly and savagely carried into effect, without discrimination and without delay, in that inclement season of the year. The Evansville *Courier* remarks, truly:

Our Jewish fellow-citizens are proverbially industrious, honest, and loyally attached to our Government and institutions. Far from having been in any way identified with armed resistance to the then existing Government, they were found by thousands in the ranks of the Union soldiers, doing good service in the ranks to restore the Union.

The above inhuman order was for some time wholly unknown to President Lincoln, who finally rescinded it; but we are impressed with the belief that he was ignorant of the order and its effect, until the following preamble and resolution was offered in Congress by Mr. Pendleton (Dem.), of Ohio:

"WHEREAS, On the 17th day of December, 1862, Major-General Grant, commanding the department of the Tennessee, did publish the following order, to-wit: (here followed the above order, *verbatim.*) And in pursuance thereof did cause many peaceable citizens of the United States, residents in the said department, to be expelled therefrom within twenty-four hours, without allegation of special misconduct on their part, and on no other proof than that they were members of a certain religious denomination; and,

"WHEREAS, The said order, in its sweeping condemnation of a whole class of citizens, without discriminating between the guilty and the innocent, is illegal and unjust, and in its execution is tyrannical and cruel; therefore,

"*Resolved,* That the said order deserves the earnest condemnation of this House, and of the President and Commander-in-Chief."

In introducing this resolution, Mr. Pendleton demanded the previous question, which was seconded. The rest of the story is thus told by the *Globe:*

On ordering the main question there were—ayes 28, noes 30 (no quorum voting). Mr. Pendleton demanded tellers.

Tellers were ordered; and Messrs. Pendleton and Buffington were appointed.

The main question was not ordered; the tellers having reported—ayes 41, noes 60.

Mr. WASHBURNE (Rad.) This resolution censures one of our best Generals without a hearing, and I move that it be laid upon the table.

Mr. HOLMAN demanded the yeas and nays.

The yeas and nays were ordered.

The question was taken; and it was decided in the affirmative—yeas 56, nays 53.

This vote, though not so strictly party as the vote on the same proposition in the Senate, was still a party vote. Several Republicans, it is true, voted in the negative; but no Democrats voted in the affirmative. Not one.

In the sequel, we are informed that Mr. Pendleton's resolution was lost in the House.

In the Senate of the United States Mr. Powell, of Kentucky (Democrat), on the 19th of January, 1862, introduced the following resolution:

Resolved, by the Senate of the United States, That the said order of Major-General Grant, expelling the Jews, as a class, from the Department of which he is in command, is condemned as illegal, tyrannical, cruel and unjust, and the President is requested to countermand the same.

Mr. HALE. I hope the Senator will not insist on the reading of the resolution. I see by the papers that that order has been rescinded.

Mr. POWELL. I have a motion to make in regard to it, and I wish it to be read.

Mr. HALE. It was read when it was originally offered, and it is not worth while to read it again.

Mr. POWELL. I insist on the reading.

The Secretary, accordingly, completed the reading of the resolution, whereupon Mr. Powell said:

Mr. President—Gentlemen may say, the order having been revoked, it is unnecessary that this body should take any action upon it. That seems to be the intimation of the gentleman from New Hampshire. I look upon the matter otherwise. I have in my possession documents that go to establish the fact beyond the possibility of a doubt that the Jews, residents of the city of Paducah, Kentucky, some thirty gentlemen in number, were driven from their homes and their business by virtue of this order of Gen. Grant, only having the short notice of four and twenty hours; *that the Jewish women and children of that city were expelled under that order; that there was not a Jew left, man, woman, or child, except two women who were prostrate on beds of sickness.* I have the evidence before me, set forth in a petition, and attested by some twelve or fourteen of the most respectable Union citizens of the city of Paducah, among others the surveyor of the port, that those Jews of Paducah had at no time been engaged in trade within the active lines of Gen. Grant; that they had all the while been engaged in legitimate business at their homes, and that there was but one Jew, a resident of Paducah, who had gone out of the State into the cotton region; and that one was not at home, and consequently was not expelled from his residence by this ruthless order.

Mr. President, if we tamely submit to allow the military power thus to encroach on the rights of the citizen, we shall be setting a bad and most pernicious example to those in command of our army. We should administer to those in command of our armies the sternest rebuke for such flagrant outrages upon the rights of the citizen. These people are represented by the most respectable citizens of Paducah to be loyal men. Many of them are men who were not engaged in commerce. They were mechanics, attending to their daily avocations at their homes. In my judgment, it is incumbent on this Senate, as the matter is before them, to pass the resolution, and let General Grant and all the other military commanders know that they are not to encroach upon the rights and privileges of the peaceful loyal citizens of this country. Pass the resolution, and the example will be of the greatest importance, particularly at this time, when the constitutional rights of the citizens are being stricken down and trodden under foot throughout the entire country by the executive and military power. We have submitted already too long and tamely to the encroachments of the military upon the civil rights of the citizen. Many of these Jews who were expelled from Paducah were known to me for many years as highly honorable and loyal citizens. This order expels them as a class from the entire department, and prevents them having a pass to approach his person to ask a redress of grievances. General Grant might just as well expel the Baptists, or the Methodists, or the Episcopalians, or the Catholics, as a class, as to expel the Jews. All are alike protected in the enjoyment of their religion by the Constitution of our country. They are inoffensive citizens; and it is set forth in papers that I have before me that two of the Jews who were expelled had served three months in the army of the United States in defense of the Union cause.

There is no excuse for General Grant for issuing the order. It may be said that some Jews in his department had been guilty of illegal traffic. If so, expel them. I do not wish to shield a Jew or a Gentile from just punishment for the infraction of the law. He should have directed his order to the offenders, and should have punished them; but, sir, so far from doing that, he punishes a whole people as a class; without specific charge, hearing, or trial, he drives out inoffensive, loyal people, men, women and children, from a city far distant from his headquarters, without giving them the least opportunity to meet and repel charges that might be brought against them. Such conduct is utterly indefensible. I regret that General Grant issued such an order. General Grant's conduct heretofore as a soldier has been that of a brave and gallant officer; he has fought well on many fields; for that I commend him. But while I commend him for his gallant conduct I must censure him for this most atrocious and illegal order. It is inhuman and monstrous. It would be unworthy the most despotic government in the most despotic period of the world's history. Sir, we should rebuke such conduct. I regret that some other less meritorious officer of the army had not issued this order. I regret that General Grant has issued it; but, sir, we owe it to ourselves, we owe it to the civil and religious liberty of the citizen, to put our condemnation upon it.

I think I have couched the resolution in the mildest terms possible. It is my duty, in vindication of the rights of my constituents—these Jews who have been so grossly and cruelly wronged—to urge this resolution to its passage. It will be a landmark in the future to teach these military gentlemen that they are not thus to encroach on the civil and religious rights of the citizen, whether he be Jew or Gentile. I should be the last man here who would wish to visit with censure any commander of any department of the army for justly punishing those who had been violators of the law in his department; and I trust I shall be the last to palliate or excuse any commander, however meritorious his conduct in other matters may have been, who thus strikes cruelly and inhumanly at a class of people, driving them from their homes—men, women, and children—upon the shortest notice. Their houses are closed up, and many of their stores, they inform me, are left without an occupant, containing thousands of dollars' worth of goods.

The Senate, in my judgment, owes it to itself to vindicate the laws and the rights of these persecuted Jews. I do for them what I would do for any other citizens of this nation, or for any other constituents that I have. I hope that the amendment I propose may be adopted, and that part of the resolution asking the President to countermand the order (for the Commander-in-Chief, to his honor be it spoken, has most promptly revoked it) be stricken out, and let the preamble and resolution, censuring this order and denouncing it as illegal, cruel, and inhuman, be passed by the Senate.

Mr. Clark (Rad.), of New Hampshire, though affecting to disapprove the order, moved the indefinite postponement of the resolution, the suppression, that is to say, of the whole question, on the pretended ground that Gen. Grant had not been heard! On this motion, Mr. Powell asked for the yeas and nays, which were ordered. Mr. Anthony (Rad.), of Rhode Island, then artfully suggested to Mr. Clark that a better disposition would be to refer the resolution to the Committee on Military Affairs. The suggestion Mr. Clark refused to accept, his refusal being seconded by Mr. Wilson (Radical), of Mass., who, though like Mr. Clark himself, affecting to disapprove the order, expressed the hope that the resolution would be either quashed entirely or laid on the table. Upon this hint, Mr. Hale (Radical), of New Hampshire, spoke, moving to lay the resolution on the table, which was carried as follows:

Ayes—Anthony, Arnold, Browning, Collamer, Clark, Cowen, Dixon, Doolittle, Foote, Foster, Grimes, Hale, Harlan, Harris, Henderson, Howe, King, Lane (of Indiana), Morrill, Pomeroy, Rice, Sherman, Sumner, Ten Eyck, Trumbull, Wade, Wiley, Wilson (of Massachusetts), and *Wright*—30.

Nays—*Davis, Harding, Latham, Nesmith,* Powell, Saulsbury, Wilson (of Missouri)—7.

The only Democrat who voted in the affirmative was Mr. Wright, of New Jersey. No Republican voted in the negative. Not one. Such was the fate of this resolution in the Senate.

This savage tyrant, says the Louisville (Ky.) *Journal,* is the same General Grant, whose name adorns the Radical ticket as candidate for the office of President of the United States. Some men have honors thrust upon them, and although a man's birth or occupation is nothing when weighed against his noble nature, talents and rectitude as a man and an American citizen, yet we think all these should be brought to bear on the minds of the people when one becomes a candidate for public honors and emoluments. The *animus* of Order No. 11 may at any time of popular commotion be aimed at any other class of men as well as at the Jews. Violating trade, indeed! Why, that order was violated everywhere.—Here, in our most loyal city, it was notoriously so. No; the Jews were persecuted because they were Jews, and nothing else.

General Grant and the Bondholders.
THEIR SECRET CIRCULAR.

NEW YORK, January 1, 1868.

This Circular was very freely mailed to the customers of Mr. A. T. Stewart, throughout the United States, and was indignantly regarded by many of them, to mean that this merchant prince intended to govern his future accommodations by the character of their replies:

SIR: At a public meeting at the Cooper Institute, in this city, held on the evening of December 4, 1867, attended by a vast number of our recognized thinking people, and visited by a throng unable to gain admittance, sufficiently numerous to fill five times the space of the large hall in that building, General Ulysses S. Grant was placed in nomination as the candidate of the people, irrespective of party, for the office of President of the United States.

The multitude who participated in this movement, were assisted by officers, vice-presidents and secretaries, citizens drawn from every business, profession and pursuit; *belonging to a class not usually found at political gatherings,*[1] and representing the indus-

---

[1] Meaning the aristocratic bondholders and millionaires. They would not have been found at this meeting, but for their concern for their bonds.

try, property and intelligence of this great city, to a degree unknown in any previous instance of a public meeting convened for a like purpose. Indeed, it appeared as if the people, sickened with politics and politicians, and anxious alone for the prosperity of the country, and perpetuity of our Union, had met in their might and taken into their own hands the business of declaring, in advance of political conventions, who should be their next Chief Magistrate and ruler. It may also be remarked, that while ignoring politicians, they likewise ignored "party platforms," the expedient of politicians, and determined to present the name of that man for President whose past services to our country give assurance that he is equally entitled to confidence, whether occupying a civil office or leading our armies to victory.

To effectuate this purpose, and to further, in all proper ways, the nomination of Gen. Grant, the undersigned committee, emanating from that meeting, were appointed, in the belief that by communicating the views and actions of that vast assemblage to their fellow-countrymen in all parts of the Union, it would stimulate others, controlled by like desires, to break from the lead of the mere political traders who have too long held the people in bondage, and, as business men, and lovers of our country, meet together in their various villages, towns and cities, and with one voice announce as their common choice for President, the name of General Ulysses S. Grant.

It is for this object we address you, entertaining the hope that you will at once take measures toward bringing about a public meeting in your locality, called by men of business and all true citizens, who, regardless of party, and seeking alone the prosperity of our country, are willing to forget political strife, and join hands in one united effort to place in the Presidential office the man who, of all others named for that high position, is emphatically the choice of the people.

Knowing that you will, in a matter so vitally affecting the future prosperity of our country, be governed by like motives as controlled us in entering upon this movement, and that your position in the community where you reside, will enable you to shape, if not lead, public opinion in your locality, we trust, that on receipt of this, after conference with your neighbors, you will at once issue a call for a public meeting, irrespective of party, for the nomination of General Grant as the choice of the people for President of the United States.

We will be much pleased to hear your views, and be informed of the state of the public mind in your district, respecting this movement.

All communications may be addressed to Henry Hilton, Chairman of the Executive Committee, No. 262 Broadway, N. Y.

Very respectfully yours.

ALEX. T. STEWART,* Chairman.

COMMITTEE.

W. B. Astor,* HAMILTON FISH,*
JAMES BROWN,* PETER COOPER,*
MOSES TAYLOR,* JONATHAN STURGES,*
F. B. CUTTING,[1] ROBERT D. STUART,*
W. T. BLODGETT,* B. B. SHERMAN,*
S. B. CRITTENDEN,* C. K. GARRISON,*
JAMES HARPER,* W. E. DODGE,*
M. H. GRINNELL,* JOHN COCHRANE,[3]
JOHN Q. JONES,* JOHN E. WILLIAMS,*
S. WETMORE, WILLIAM H. WEBB,*
F. S. WINSTON,* JAMES H. BANKER,*
HENRY HILTON,[2] C. VANDERBILT,*
ALEXANDER T. STEWART.*

EXECUTIVE COMMITTEE.

M. H. GRINNELL,* WILLIAM E. DODGE,*
C. K. GARRISON, JOHN COCHRAN,[3]
HENRY HILTON.[2]

Grant Charged with Drunkenness by Wendell Phillips.

[From the Anti-Slavery Standard.]

Rumors reach us from Washington, coming from different and trustworthy sources, that Gen. Grant has been seen unmistakably drunk in the streets of that city within a few weeks. We know nothing ourselves of the truth of these rumors. We make no charge against Gen. Grant in this respect. But even the possibility of the truth of these reports is of too much momentous importance to be lightly dealt with. The nation is bound to inquire as to the habits of candidates for high office. After the experience of the last three years it has no right to run the slightest risk in this respect. No public man, whose friends are asking for him high office, ought to complain of the strictest scrutiny by the public as to his habits in this particular. We call, therefore, on the National and State temperance societies to investigate these reports. They have this subject in their special charge. They are bound to give us the facts, and save us from even the possibility of such another infliction as the nation now suffers. Especially we call on Hon. Henry Wilson, a pledged teetotaler, to see that the whole truth in this matter is

---

* Bondholders—The cream of the rich aristocratic "ton" of New York.

[1] A rich New York lawyer. The legal adviser of many of these bondholders.

[2] An Ex-Judge. Also, lawyer for many of his bondholder associates.

[3] A political weathercock, and military fizzle.

given to the country. He has devoted himself to the advocacy of Grant's claims. As a temperance man, he is bound to see that we run no risks of this kind. Living in Washington, he must know, or have ample means of knowing the truth as to this matter. If we are unnecessarily anxious, let him relieve us by trustworthy assurances that Grant is now a temperate man, fully able, on all occasions, to withstand this temptation. If the fact is not so, let him explain to his temperance associates how he dares to ask their votes for Grant. It is perilous enough to give the Presidency to a man who was, confessedly, an inveterate drunkard two or three years ago. But it will be the gravest crime to give it to him if that vice still holds him in its iron grasp.

WENDELL PHILLIPS.

Doubt about Grant's Name.

[From "Early Life of General Grant," written by his Father; New York Ledger, March 14, 1867.]

"I believe he went by the name of 'Uncle Sam' [at West Point], on account of his initials, 'U. S.' A superstitious person might almost think there was something providential about these significant initials being stuck on to him, for they were not given to him at his christening. When the question arose after his birth what he should be called, his mother and one of his aunts proposed Albert, for Albert Gallatin; another aunt proposed Theodore; his grandfather proposed Hiram, because he thought that was a handsome name. His grandmother—grandmother by courtesy—that is his mother's step-mother—was a great student of history, and had an enthusiastic admiration for the ancient commander Ulysses, and she urged that the babe should be named Ulysses. I seconded that, and he was christened Hiram Ulysses; but he was always called by the latter name, which he himself preferred when he got old enough to know about it. But Mr. Hamer [who nominated him as a cadet] knowing Mrs. Grant's name was Simpson, and that we had a son named Simpson, somehow got the matter a little mixed in making the nomination, and sent the name in Ulysses S. Grant instead of Hiram Ulysses Grant. My son tried in vain afterward to get it set right by the authorities, and I suppose he is now content with his name as it stands."

Grant as a Talker.

HE THREATENED TO RESIGN AND CAST HIS LOT WITH THE SOUTH.

The editor of the Randolph Citizen recalls some interesting reminiscenses of the great Reticent. He had a tongue at one time, it would seem:

In the summer of 1861 General Grant, then Colonel of the Twenty-first Illinois Regiment of Infantry, was stationed at Mexico, on the North Missouri Railroad, and had command of the post. He remained several months, mingling freely with the people, regardless of the peculiar shade of any one's political opinions; and as the distinguished Colonel had then no thought of aspiring to the Presidency or a dictatorship, no occasion existed for the reticence to which latterly he owes the greater part of his popularity. Ulysses the Silent was then Ulysses the Garrulous, and embraced every fair opportunity which came in his way to express his sentiments and opinions in regard to political affairs. One of these declarations we distinctly remember. In a public conversation in Ringo's banking-house, a sterling Union man put this question to him: "What do you honestly think was the real object of this war on the part of the Federal Government?"

"Sir," said Grant, "I have no doubt in the world that the sole object is the restoration of the Union. I will say further, though, that I am a Democrat—every man in my regiment is a Democrat—and whenever I shall be convinced that this war has for its object anything else than what I have mentioned, or that the Government designs using its soldiers to execute the purposes of the abolitionists, I pledge you my honor as a man and a soldier that I will not only resign my commission, but will carry my sword to the other side, and cast my lot with that people."

The Story of Washington v. the Story of Grant— The Ethics of 1776 v. the Ethics of 1868.

All remember the story of Washington and the cherry tree. The friends of Grant seek to match it thus:

When Ulysses S. Grant was a little boy, his father bought him a hatchet. Ulysses was so delighted that he went about hatcheting everything he could find. One fatal day, after things had been going on thus and so, for more than a week, Ulysses cut down one of his fathers favorite pear trees. When the old gentleman saw the ruin of his favorite pear tree, he went to U. S. and said:

"U. S., who cut down my favorite pear tree?"

"I can not tell a lie," said Ulysses; "Ben. Johnson cut it down with his hatchet."

"My dear son," said the old gentleman, spanking him, "I would rather have you tell a thousand lies than lose so fine a tree."

Grant Cowhides Senator Chandler, of Michigan, in 1851.
[From the Augusta Sentinel.]

In the winter of 1850-1, Gen. Grant was stationed with his regiment in Detroit, the home of Hon. Zach. Chandler, Senator from Michigan, the man who, in 1861, thought the country needed a little blood-letting. At that time Grant was a lieutenant in the service, and was decidedly a very fast young man. He had a little Indian pony he used to ride up and down the street on a clean jump. It so happened that, on one occasion, he slipped and fell on the icy sidewalk in front of Zach. Chandler's house. Therefore he brought suit against Chandler for neglect to clean his sidewalk.

The next day the following complaint was lodged in the Mayor's Court of the city of Detroit:

"*State of Michigan, City of Detroit, ss :—* Ulysses S. Grant being duly sworn deposeth and saith, that on or about the 10th day of January, A. D. 1851, and for twenty-five days previous thereto, Zachary Chandler did neglect to keep his sidewalk free and clear from snow, in and on Jackson avenue, in front of the house occupied by him, and did then and there commit many other acts contrary to the ordinances of said city. Further deponent saith not.
"U. S. GRANT.

"Sworn, and subscribed before me, this 10th day of January, A. D. 1851.
"J. VAN RENSSELER, City Clerk."

The reader will perceive by this complaint that Zachary, even at that remote day, practiced the doctrines of contempt for law which have since made him a Radical great man. Under this complaint, his sacred person was seized by a vile tip-staff, and he was carried into the dread presence of justice; but he was unabashed, and scorned any aid save his own. He appeared as his own counsel, and Ulysses and he appeared face to face. Imagine the meeting! It was like the sun and moon hob-nobbing. Zachary denied that he had a house; and asserted that if he had one there was no walk in front of it; and that, if there was a walk, Ulysses was never on it; and that if he was on it, he fell down because he was drunk.

Such was Zachary's defense, and it filled Grant's martial soul with such ire that he forthwith proceeded to a sadler's and purchased a rawhide—a strong, tough, supple, stinging implement—with which he went forth to meet Zachary. They met—"'twas in a crowd"—in Jefferson avenue. Ulysses approached on Zachary's center and gave him a cut, which Zachary evaded by a flank movement, in executing which he exposed his rear, which his wary enemy immediately attacked with such vigor that Zach. summoned his legs to his aid, and displayed for the first time those masterly powers of retreat which afterward immortalized him at Bull Run. Ulysses, being short-legged, attempted in vain to follow him, and was soon distanced. Thus ended the fight.

Grant a General at the Discretion of the President.
A SUBORDINATE NOT A SUPERIOR.

By the express language of the Constitution of the United States the President is made "Commander-in chief of the army and navy, and of the militia of the several States when called into the actual service of the United States." And the old act of Congress restoring the grade of General fully conforms to the constitutional prerogative of the President, as in the following explicit language:

Be it enacted, etc., That the grade of General be revived; that the President is authorized to appoint, with the advice and consent of the Senate, a General of the army, to be selected from among those officers most distinguished for courage, skill and ability; *who being commissioned as General, may be authorized, under the direction and during the pleasure of the President, to command the armies of the United States.*

It will be seen that by this law the President is authorized to appoint a General of the army, to command the forces of the United States under the direction and during the pleasure of the President, and not in defiance of his will and in contempt of his supreme authority.

The Israelites of St. Louis on Grant.

A St. Louis paper publishes a long card, signed by about two hundred Israelites of that city, in which the order referred to is reproduced and denounced. The signers, disclaiming anything of a partisan spirit, protest that while some are Radicals, some Conservatives, and some Democrats, all agree in the determination to oppose Grant's election. The card thus concludes:

Shall we as Israelites vote for such a man? Will the 2,300 votes from Israelites in this city help make a President with the name of U. S. Grant, who, attaining power by accident, issued an order expelling all Israelites, whether guilty or not, from his department, merely because they were Israelites? Hardly can we believe that, in view of this insult, and unrevoked as the outrage stands, there will be one low enough found in our midst to think of it. Without being prophets, we hazard the prediction that there will be as few Israelitic votes cast for General Grant next November as he had occasion to make arrests under his infamous order.

The feeling expressed in the above is the feeling that must animate the whole Hebrew population of the United States.

Indecent Ferocity of the Radical Press toward the Jews.

Thus we quote from the McMinnville *Enterprise*, one of the papers selected by Gov. Brownlow to do the legal advertising in the Third Congressional District of Tennessee, which says:

The *Union and Dispatch* says 2,000 Jews in St. Louis will vote against Gen. Grant because, while in command at Vicksburg, he issued an order expelling Jews from his camps. That paper might as well have said that 2,000 rebels in St. Louis will vote against Gen. Grant. The Jews as a class of men have no politics outside of money. Gold is the idol of their hearts, and in the general they are all things to all men for the sake of money. During the war, here in the South they were on the side of the rebellion fully nine-tenths, if not ninety-nine one hundredths of them. And so treacherous were they that Gen. Grant was under the necessity of expelling them from his lines.

The Harrisburg *Telegraph*, the Radical central organ in Pennsylvania, says:

The Jews of the Southwest, or such of them as were suttlers and bummers in the armies under Grant, it will be remembered, behaved shamefully, robbing, debauching and demoralizing the troops to such a degree that he was compelled to eject them from his lines."

Senator James Harlan, of Iowa, on Grant as a General.

Yes, the rebels thought his capture of Fort Donelson in the winter was very unseasonable.—[*Evansville Journal.*

But *did* Grant capture Fort Donelson? Hear what Rev. Jas. Harlan, Radical Senator from Iowa, says on that point. We quote from the Congressional Globe, of May 9, 1862:

"At Fort Donelson, the right wing of our army, which was under his immediate command, was *defeated and driven back several miles from* the enemy's works. The battle was restored by Gen. Smith, the enemy's works stormed, and thus a victory was finally won."

Grant's capture of Fort Donelson, eh? Not much.—[*Vincennes Sun.*

Grant's Letter of Acceptance.

"SLUMKEY FOREVER!"

Gen. Grant's declaration that he will have no policy "but the will of the people" to guide him in the administration of the Government, reminds the New York World of a similar declaration of the great Mr. Pickwick, of his policy at the great election at Eatonswill, between the Buffs and the Blues, in which the Hon. Samuel Slumkey was the candidate of the Blues, and the Hon. Horatio Fizkin of the Buffs.

"Slumkey forever!" roared the honest and independent.

"Slumkey forever!" echoed Mr. Pickwick, taking off his hat.

"No Fizkin!" roared the crowd.

"Certainly not!" shouted Mr. Pickwick.

"Who is Slumkey?" whispered Mr. Tupman.

"I don't know," replied Mr. Pickwick. "Hush, don't ask any questions; it's always best to do what the mob does on these occasions."

"But suppose there are two mobs," suggested Mr. Snodgrass.

"Shout with the largest," replied Mr. Pickwick.

Volumes could not have said more.

"The Tail Wags the Dog!"

There is a conundrum of the Lord Dundreary style of wit: "Why does a dog wag his tail?" The answer is: "Because the dog is bigger than the tail, for, if it were not so, the tail would wag the dog."

This was, until lately, a mere supposition, although it was generally accredited as a fact, because no such combination of dog and tail, as the reverse implies, had been found to furnish proof to the contrary. We have now a living example which justifies the wisdom of the conundrum. It is to be found in the Grant and Colfax nomination; and the wagging business is faithfully illustrated in Grant's and Colfax's letters of acceptance. Supposing Grant to represent the body and brain of the animal, and Colfax the animal's tail, we have a tail bigger than the dog; and, by reading the documents, it will be discovered that the tail palpably wags the dog. The truth of the theory has been vindicated by practice, but the celebrated conundrum is henceforth valueless, as it presupposes a fixed and unalterable relation between dog and tail.—[*Mo. Republican.*

Grant a Tyrant.

Grant is essentially a tyrant. As late as 1866, three years after the war closed, he suppressed the Richmond (Va.) *Enquirer*, because he did not like its political course. Its editor (Mr. Pollard) had an interview with him, which he thus reported:

"It was evident that I had nothing to hope from him, for he said to me expressly that if he had the authority he would that day suppress the New York *News*, the Cincinnati *Enquirer*, and the Chicago *Times*, adding that the 'Copperhead papers of the North,' as he designated them, were doing quite as much harm as the papers in the South."

The only reason, therefore, that prevents him from establishing a general censorship over the press North as well as South, is the want of authority. He admits that he has the disposition. Appeals to reason and conscience, which he can not answer, he would silence with the brute force of a despot. Such is Gen. Grant.—[*Cincinnati Enquirer.*

Grant's Reticence.

HE SWINGS AROUND THE CIRCLE WITH ANDREW JOHNSON— HE INDORSES THE PRESIDENT'S SPEECHES.

[From the Chicago Times, Jan. 26, 1868.]

Grant's uniform silence and meaningless expression of countenance have rendered his appearance much the same, whether under the deepening and intensifying influence of liquor, or merely reflecting the natural stolidity of his composition. The same absence of sensibility always characterizes his thoughts and movements. Appeal to the mental and moral man with all the acuteness of suffering, or cut away at him with broadswords of argument, and Grant would no more feel them than would a rhinoceros the pricking of a pin.

Grant possesses only one pronounced characteristic, which is an imperviousness that resists everything except the desire for drinking and smoking.

* * * * *

The country has not yet forgotten the Presidential excursion, popularly known as "Swingin' round the circle." The country also remembers that Gen. Grant was one of the most prominent men in the Presidential party. It was at a time when the name of Grant was synonymous with loyalty, patriotism and success. The Radicals held up their hands in holy horror that this idol of the people should accompany a governmental party that was in favor of thirty-six States in the Union, instead of twenty-five; that advocated the extension of federal rights to the whole country; that preferred civil authority over military despotism.

The explanations of Gen. Grant's presence with this party were as unsatisfactory as they were various. Many said that he accompanied the President as an officer on the staff of the Commander-in-Chief. Subsequent events have proved that Grant does not regard the President as Commander-in-Chief. Others said that he was ordered to go, and obeyed as a military subordinate should always obey a superior. But there have been instances since that prove Grant not so willing and ready in subordination. At first, none were willing to admit that Grant had committed himself to the Presidential policy; but, before the excursion had come to an end, the Radicals regarded Grant as tainted with sentiments of Unionism, and treacherously favoring a speedy return to peace and prosperity.

* * * * *

Whatever his motive for joining the party may have been, he looked upon it as an excellent occasion for a prolonged and uninterrupted "drunk." He did not draw a sober breath from the time the party reached Niagara until after it had landed in Chicago.

At Niagara Falls he made only one appearance in the open air, and that in a carriage, supported by a couple of friends. On the way to Buffalo, at Tonawanda, Admiral Farragut excused General Grant from making an appearance, because he was "played out." At Buffalo and other places, Secretary Seward excused Grant's non-appearance on account of "illness." The truth is, and it is well known to every man who accompanied the excursion, that Grant was sent to Cleveland by another train in order to give him the time and opportunity to sober off. This, however, was not the General's pleasure. He preferred to remain drunk; and, on the way from Cleveland to Detroit, he was in a staggering condition of drunkenness, and only made his way through the cars with support on each side, and his appearance on the platform at stations with the same assistance. The reporters of the New York *Tribune* and of the Chicago *Republican*, who were in attendance, telegraphed to their respective journals that Grant was in the condition described.

It is equally true that Grant, on several occasions during this trip, committed himself fully to the conservatism represented by Mr. Johnson at the time, and denounced by the Radical party. At Detroit, Seward, speaking to the people from the balcony of the hotel, said: "Let me tell those who are trying to make a distinction between General Grant and the President, that nothing in this world could divide him from the President, or me from him and the President;" and General Grant acquiesced in his customary silence. Mr. Seward has kept faith and General Grant has broken it.

At Battle Creek, Michigan, there was a great crowd and loud calls for General Grant, while Secretary Seward was expounding the President's policy for restoring the Union. "Gentlemen," the Secretary continued, with Grant by his side, "if you expect to hear anything different from General Grant from what the President would tell you, you are very much mistaken. The General allows me to do his speaking, and I allow him to do my fighting, and we have neither of us as yet fought or spoken against the other." The Secretary then turned to General Grant, who bowed in acquiescence amid the cheers of the crowd, and concluded, "That is General Grant's speech."

There is but one alternative for Grant in regard to his position at that time. Either he shared the convictions and approved the policy of the President, which were fundamentally the same then as they are now, or he was too stupidly drunk to deny the sentiments attributed to him before such vast crowds of his countrymen. Both conclusions are equally discreditable in the turn that affairs have recently taken.

"**Cursed be the Soul of Benjamin Franklin**"—Also that of Ulysses Grant.

[From the Anti-Slavery Standard.]

All readers of Swift know what sort of ideas *nice* men usually have. They swallow a camel of bad actions, but strain at a gnat of plain words. "I could easily have escaped," said the wretch who picked the old pensioner's pocket, "but conscientious scruples prevented my traveling on the Sabbath."

Here is a man with a princely revenue, and a more than princely title, conferred on him—for what? That he may make the flag protect loyalty wherever it floats. No thanks to him that it floats in honor at New York or Boston. His soldiership is shown when loyal men are safe under it in Galveston and New Orleans. If we have indeed conquered Tennessee and Louisiana, then Memphis and New Orleans are ours. Grant's soldiership is proved when loyal men may walk those streets in safety. While in half the Southern cities loyal men hide themselves, and rebels, fully armed, stalk defiantly abroad, the head of our army is either no soldier or he is the willing tool of traitors. Imagine Wellington smoking at Tattersall's, or any other horse market, while Ireland was in such condition as the South is to-day! He never earned his "Iron Duke" by any such effeminacy. While Durant quits New Orleans because its streets are not safe for Union men—while riot rules Memphis and blood flows at New Orleans—while Union men, all over the South, hide themselves from rebels, Grant flaunts his undeserved title in the face of a disgraced nation, and filches his unearned salary from an impoverished people.

"But Johnson won't let him do his duty." Then do not let him take title and pay for a duty he is not allowed to discharge. But the excuse is sheer falsehood. If Grant had done, at the time of the New Orleans riot, what Fremont or Butler would have done—gone to New Orleans and begun to do his duty—Johnson would not have dared to cripple him with restrictions. Had he done so, and Grant had returned to say to Congress and the country, "Union men were shot down in New Orleans because the White House would not let me do my duty," Johnson would have ceased to be President in thirty days. The same is true of Memphis and Texas. When through Grant's hands passed the report that Texas could be ruled only by martial-law, and it was not instantly after put under martial-law, Grant wrote "no soldier" or "traitor's tool" on his own record. We speak in earnest, for there is not a more disgraceful blot on our record—and that is a daring statement—than the nation's cruel desertion of Union men at the South. For this Grant is the front sinner. He, more than any other man, could have prevented it. Of him it is more emphatically true than of any other loyal man, that he is responsible for it. The blood at Memphis and New Orleans will blight in history half of his Virginia laurels. If we were Grant we should feel more remorse for the Union murders of 1867, than pride in the Virginia victories of 1865. We should know ourself more truly the cause of the first than of the last. General Thomas reporting several hundred Union murders in his district, all unpunished and most of them uninvestigated, and yet—Grant a soldier! Grant knows that ten of these promptly and thoroughly punished in each State would put an end to this state of things. The bullies would creep back into their dens. He knows that he has ample strength to punish these crimes. Why he does not punish them, every man must decide for himself. If the reason be Mr. Johnson's opposition, Grant knows that, any time during the last two years, ten decisive words from himself would have obliged Johnson instantly to desist from his opposition and set the whole nation indignantly against him. Grant is ten times as strong as Mr. Johnson. Leaving those ten words unspoken, is Grant's guilt. And it is this party, so greedy for office, and so faithless to principle, that it leaves the Barbara Freitchies and Robert Smalls to be victims of those it pretends to have conquered; these Jew leeches, intriguing to filch from the people all they covet, no matter whether it is in the bond or not—with their dawdling candidate, bartering blood for coin—it is this party who affect such horror at what they consider an irreverent phrase? Here is a party waiving justice and honor, and content to stand behind a dumb candidate, neutral on all questions, provided greedy bondholders will help elect him; a party which has sold out to the National Banks and Belmont, and like Pecksniff about to join swindlers, they cry "fie! oh, fie!" when things are called by their right names!

WENDELL PHILIPS.

Grant did not want to be President.

There is another "short speech" by Gen. Grant. It is dated "Nashville, Tenn., January 20, 1864," and addressed to Hon. Isaac N. Morris, of Quincy, Ills. In this short speech Gen. Grant says:

* * * * * *

Allow me to say, however, that I am not a politician, never was, and hope never to be, and could not write a political letter.

In your letter, you say that I have it in my power to be the next President. This is the last thing in the world I desire. I would regard such a consummation as being highly unfortunate for myself, if not for the country. Through Providence, I have attained to more than I ever hoped, and with the position I now hold in the regular army, if allowed to retain it, will be more than satisfied. I certainly shall never shape a sentiment, or the expression of a thought, with a view of being a candidate for office. I scarcely know the inducement that could be held out to me to accept office, and unhesitatingly say that I infinitely prefer my present position to that of any civil office within the gift of the people.

Grant's Murderous Tactics.

[From the N. Y. World.]

We have already shown the respective forces and losses of Generals Grant and Lee, between the Rapidan and the James, and, as prefatory to some further historical light on General Grant's soldiership, reproduce them:

Grant, on assuming command, May 4, 1864, had of effective men, besides the reserve, when he crossed the Rapidan, 125,000.

Lee, at the same date, had an effective force of 52,000.

Grant's reinforcements up to the battle of Cold Harbor, June 3, were 97,000.

Lee's reinforcements, up to the same date, were 18,000.

Grant's total force, including reinforcements, was 222,000.

Lee's total force, including reinforcements, was 70,000.

Returns to their respective governments showed that, when both armies had reached the James, June 10, the number of Grant's army that had been put *hors du combat* was 117,000.

Up to the same date, the number of Lee's men who had been put *hors du combat* was 19,000.

The two armies then met in front of Petersburg.

It will be seen that Grant's total force, including reinforcements, was 152,000, and his loss 98,000 in excess of Lee's, or that, with a force outnumbering his opponent's three to one, this bungler lost every other man in his army, while Lee lost but two out of every nine—or, to put it still differently, that Grant lost just six thousand men more than one and a-half times Lee's entire army. That Grant succeeded is true, but a General would have accomplished the same result with less means and less loss. Gen. Lee was not conquered by fighting him, but by exhausting his resources.

He stood on the defensive for nearly a year after Grant assumed command in the East, although the Confederacy was even then, when Grant crossed the Rapidan, tottering and well nigh spent by three years' exertion in a strenuous and unequal struggle. It is certainly just to credit Grant with the capture of Lee; but there is a debit as well as a credit side to the account. What General Scott called "the economy of life by means of head work," will be sought for in vain in the campaigns of Gen. Grant. His successes have been won by a prodigal expenditure of his soldiers. In his last and greatest campaign, he pitted an enormous army against a small one, and sacrificed twice as many men as Gen. Lee had under his command. It is not justice, but adulation, to praise him as if he had conquered an army as large as his own. It is not justice, but an affront to humanity, to give him as much credit as if he had achieved the same result without such wholesale sacrifices of men. Gen. Jackson won his brilliant victory at New Orleans, with 7,000 men against a British army of 12,000. Gen. Taylor had but 6,000 men at Buena Vista, and the Mexicans twice that number. Gen. Scott had 8,000 men at Cerro Gordo, the Mexicans 12,000. The splendid victory of Contreras was achieved by Scott with 4,500, against 12,000 Mexicans. Gen. Scott, in his report to the Secretary of War, speaking of the battles in front of Mexico, said: "And I assert, upon accumulated and unquestionable evidence, that in not one of these conflicts was this army opposed by less than three and a-half times its numbers—in several of them by a yet greater excess." If it be said that Grant had disadvantages of ground and position to encounter in advancing through an enemy's country, the same is equally true of Scott, who nevertheless, with greatly inferior numbers, advanced rapidly from triumph to triumph, while Grant, operating with superior numbers, against a nearly exhausted foe, required a whole year to capture Richmond, which finally succumbed to exhaustion, rather than to military genius.

Grant's Cruelty to Prisoners.

Let the sufferers at Belle Isle, Libby, Andersonville, and other Southern prisons—sufferers because of the very necessities of the country—read this.

In December, 1863, Butler was appointed Commissioner of Exchange, and by March, 1864, effected a basis of exchange with the Confederate Commissioner, man for man. He then details the further proceedings in the matter thus:

Mr. Ould left on the 31st of March, with the understanding that I would get authority and information from my Government, by which all disputed points possible could be adjusted, and would then confer with him further, either meeting him at City Point or elsewhere for that purpose. In the mean time the exchanges of sick and wounded and special exchanges should go on.

Lieutenant-General Grant visited Fortress Monroe on the 1st of April, being the first time I ever met him.

To him the state of the negotiations as to exchange were verbally communicated, *and most emphatic verbal directions were received from the Lieutenant-General not to take any step by which another able-bodied man should be exchanged until further orders from him.*

On the 14th of April, Butler received a telegram from General Grant, at Washington, stating that the whole subject of exchange of prisoners had been referred to him, as follows:

WASHINGTON, April 14, 1864.

MAJOR-GENERAL BUTLER: Your report respecting negotiations with Commissioner Ould for the exchange of prisoners of war *has been referred to me for my orders.*

Until examined by me, and my orders thereon are received by you, *decline all further negotiations.*

U. S. GRANT, Lieut.-Gen.

Six days later, after General Grant had "examined," he sent a long telegram to Butler, stating that he had been empowered "to give such instructions as I may deem proper," and he gave instructions of which Butler says:

"Of course these instructions, in the then state of negotiations, rendered any further exchange impossible and retaliation useless."

Butler says he then made an effort to have the sick and wounded excepted, so that they might be exchanged, and he received the following telegram in reply:

WASHINGTON, April 30, 1864.

MAJOR-GENERAL B. F. BUTLER: Receive all the sick and wounded the Confederate authorities send you, *but send no more in exchange.*

U. S. GRANT, Lieut.-Gen.

Upon this extraordinary "instruction" Butler remarks as follows:

"To obtain delivery of even sick and wounded prisoners without any return would be a somewhat difficult operation, save that the enemy, by giving us our wounded and sick in their hands, we retaining all the rebel sick and wounded in ours, burdened us with the care and cost of *all* the sick and wounded on both sides—an operation of which it is difficult to see the strategetic value, and only to be defended because of its humanity in rescuing our wounded from the destitution and suffering permitted to them by the Confederates."

In August, the Confederate Commissioner renewed his offer of March, man for man, and again Butler was, as it appears, disposed to accede, but again General Grant interposed, and in a telegram sent to Butler, August 18, 1864, said:

On the subject of exchange, I differ from General Hitchcock. It is hard on our men, held in Southern prisons, not to exchange them, but it is humanity to those left in the ranks to fight our battles. Every man released on parole or otherwise becomes an active soldier against us at once, either directly or indirectly. If we commence a system of exchange which liberates all prisoners taken, we will have to fight on until the whole South is exterminated. If we hold those caught, they amount to no more than dead men. At this particular time, to release all rebel prisoners North, would insure Sherman's defeat, and would compromise our safety here.

U. S. GRANT, Lieut.-Gen.

It is proper to state that these extracts appear in the report of the Committee on the Conduct of the War, a public document wherein the reader may find some other matters explanatory of that murderous system of warfare, whereby Grant has wrought himself to greatness on dead men's bones.

Grant Instructs his Military Commanders to be Radical Congressional Tools.

WASHINGTON, August 3, 1867.

To Major-Gen. John Pope:

I think your views sound—sound both in the construction which you give to the laws of Congress and the duties of the supporters of a good Government to see that when reconstruction is effected no loop-hole is left open to give trouble and embarrassment thereafter. It is certainly the duty of district commanders to study what the framers of the reconstruction laws wanted to express as much as what they do express, and to execute the laws according to that interpretation. This I believe they have generally done, and, so far, have the approval of all who approve the Congressional plan of reconstruction.

(Signed.) U. S. GRANT, Gen'l.

Grant's Indorsement of the Action of the Military Commanders of the South.

"In their civil capacity they are entirely independent of both the General and Secretary, except in the matters of removals, appointments and details, where the General of the army has the same powers as have district commanders. It is but fair to the district commanders, however, to state that, while they have been thus independent in their civil duties, there has not been one of them who would not yield to a positively expressed wish, in regard to any matter of civil administration, from either of the officers placed over them by the Constitution, or acts of Congress, so long as that wish was in the direction of a proper execution of law, for the execution of which they alone are responsible. I am pleased to say that the commanders of the five military districts have executed their difficult trust faithfully and without bias from any judgment of their own as to the merit or the law they were executing."

Grant, Senior, Makes a Speech.

If Hiram is reticent, the venerable author of his existence lets off his mouth occasionally, as witness the following extract from a letter to the Cincinnati *Enquirer*, dated at Mineral Point, Wis., May 27, 1868:

Gentlemen, there never was such a nomination made as the one the Radicals have made in nominating my son as President, and Colfax is a very good man for the position of Vice-President. He said he was glad that Ben Wade was not put in as Vice, for he had not a bit of sense, and talked too much, and would have been the means of the Radical ticket losing at least a hundred thousand votes in Ohio—do n't believe in letting negroes vote; says it is too much like trying to make them equal to the whites, and said the only reason he thought they ought to have been freed for, was financially and politically, not because they were not in their place, for he thought the only place they were fit for was as slaves, for they are not able to take care of themselves, and he told a story to illustrate the fact. Said the only way they would work and only way to treat them was by using the whip freely. He thinks the people will be ashamed of giving the negro his freedom. He says Gen. Palmer made a fool of himself at the Convention in his speech. He do n't think much of Palmer or the platform. He said he advised them to leave nigger out of the platform, for he told them if they did not they would be beat; and said one of the most disgusting things he ever witnessed was the nigger delegates at the convention at Chicago. If he had his way he would have kicked them out. He said never—no, never—would he be willing for niggers to vote; he thinks the more they are educated the worse it is for them, and says he do n't believe in educating them. He do n't believe in them voting in the South or any place else. They have no civil rights at all; this country was made to be ruled by white men and not niggers; thinks the Freedmen's Bureau the greatest swindle the world ever saw. He said he had seen the time when he had nothing to eat, and the United States did not feed him, but he had to work or starve. And as long as they indulged the nigger in idleness the longer they would have to; and said if he had ten cents and it would educate a nigger, he would throw it in the fire before they should have it. Says he thinks it will beat the General, and will be glad if he is defeated.

Before he was done talking every one of the Rads had left, and the old gentleman was talking to Democrats. I heard all the above conversation.

Gen. Grant when He was Sam. Grant, at Galena.

[From the Galena (Ill.) Democrat.]

U. S. Grant, or S. U. Grant, came to this city about nine years ago. His father was a resident of Covington, Ky., had a leather store here, and was engaged, through his two sons, Orville and Simpson Grant, in the purchase of hides, which were shipped to Covington. Hither came Ulysses, after he wandered out of the United States army, and was employed as a kind of porter about the establishment. He was equally unknown to fame or to society here, and so remained until his good luck came into play with that of the Black Republican dynasty of A. Lincoln.

It has been repeatedly stated that Grant voted for Douglas at the Presidential election of 1860, which resulted in the triumph of

"Black Old Abe and the eternal nigger!"

Again, it has been said that both he and his brother voted for A. Lincoln. His brother did vote the Republican ticket, but Sam. did not vote at all. He told one gentleman that, if he did vote, he would prefer to do so for Bell and Everett, the Know-Nothing candidates. To another gentleman he expressed his preference for Judge Douglas, adding, however, that he did not like to oppose the wishes of his father and brother, who were Republicans; thus exhibiting the same vacillating course in politics that he does at present. Know-Nothingism appears at all times to be his predominating political characteristic.

But few of our citizens knew U. S. or S. U. Grant during his residence here; and it was not until the title of General was attached to his name that they began to inquire: "Who and what is this General Grant who is announced as a distinguished citizen of Galena?"

"We never knew him!" "What is he—what did he do here?" Everybody seemed astonished that we "had a Bourbon among us," and had ignorantly been nursing a military genius in our midst, who was destined (politically at least) to overslaugh all competitors.

It is generally understood that there is, and has been for some time past, in fact, ever since General Grant loomed up in the political horizon, quite a contest or rivalry as to the particular individual who first lent Grant a helping hand—both E. B. Washburne and Dick Yates claiming the merit of being his benefactor.

It appears that on the breaking out of the rebellion, U. S. or S. U. Grant (we had better call him Sam., for short) wandered to Springfield, and obtained temporary employment as a clerk or peace adjutant in the office of that moral, sober and exemplary chief magistrate, Governor Richard Yates, then busily attempting to organize the militia of Illinois. It was here the first stroke of good luck occurred to him. A regiment was being organized, and Dick was about to appoint a certain A. B. Colonel thereof, against whom the officers of the embryo corps rebelled stoutly. "Who, then, shall I appoint?" said his Excellency. "Anybody but a politician," responded the Captains and Lieutenants present. "There's Captain Grant; how will he do—he's a West Pointer?" says Dick (Sam. was writing at a table in the room). "Content," answered the officers, and Grant was immediately commissioned by the Governor Colonel of the Twenty-first Illinois Regiment, and who, probably, in that capacity, was the best appointment that Dick had made.

Ulysses Sam., or Sam. Ulysses, after his singularly accidental fortune in getting the regiment, had next to raise the funds to equip himself. His present admirers were not the men to assist him; they stood aloof, although many of them at the time were making money out of army contracts. He was poor; they were rich. His own family refused to aid him; and, had it not been for the kindness of a gentleman who was a Democrat, and had been at one time connected with his father in business, he would not have been able to purchase his outfit.

Up to this time it is said that Sam. Grant had never known E. B. Washburne, or Washburne known Sam., although some members of his family had politically stood by Washburne The Congressman had often passed and repassed the unknown hero in blessed ignorance of who and what he was.

When and where they found out their respective merits is unknown to us. So also others of our citizens, who now adulate, fawn upon, and worship Grant, hailing him as the "Agamemnon" of the army, never recognized him, patronized him, or extended to him the right hand of fellowship until Washburne led the way, after he had been manufactured into a General, and then it was that he was first deemed worthy of their distinguished consideration.

Such is a brief sketch of the Galena career of "Uncle Sam." Grant, as he was want to be called by his old comrades in the regular army. We have "naught extenuated or set down in malice." His good luck in things personal had adhered to him thus far. As we have before remarked, the very men who knew him not, who never extended to him their hands in friendship, or their hospitality to him, or his family, or even visited them—who, in fact, while he was in the humble employ of his father, under the direction of his younger brother, gave him the cold shoulder—are now his most obsequious servants, and, in conjunction with, and at the nod of E. B. Washburne, purchased and furnished for him a house, at the enormous expense of some sixty thousand dollars, making the whole country ring with their generosity. On the other hand, the few who, out of pity for his poverty and forlorn condition, showed him kindness, appear to have been totally forgotten by this distinguished "citizen of Galena."

What Grant Thinks of Himself as a Statesman.

[From the New York World.]

If Hiram Ulysses Grant is now running as a statesman, and not as a soldier, he will speedily go to the wall. The fact is, that General Grant's connection with public affairs, outside of the army, has been so slight that he has had very little opportunity to display the "statesmanship" the *Times* exhibits for him, and so far from assuming such qualities to himself, Grant has respectfully disclaimed them. Two years ago he wrote a letter to Mr. Morris, in which he said: "I am not a politician, never was, and hope never to be, and could not write a political letter"—as his recent letter of acceptance shows, and even in that letter he declares that he has no policy of his own, which is a singular position for a "statesman." Sumner thought so little of Grant's views of the situation of civil affairs in the South as to characterize his report as a "whitewashing" one. But Hiram Ulysses Grant has put upon record his opinion of his own abilities as a statesman. When Lewis D. Campbell was appointed United States Minister to Mexico, the President, October 20, 1866, instructed General Grant, through the Secretary of War, to accompany Campbell to Mexico, if he thought fit, or to proceed to some point on the frontier most suitable and convenient for communication with that Minister, "to give him the aid of his advice in carrying out the instructions of the Secretary of State." General Grant asked to be excused, and suggested Sherman, Hancock, or Sheridan, for the duty. To the Secretary of War he said: "I would not dare to counsel the Minister in any matter beyond stationing troops on United States soil. * * * I sincerely hope I may be excused from undertaking a duty so foreign to my office and tastes as that contemplated." To the President, asking to be excused, he wrote: "It is a diplomatic duty for which I am not fitted either by education or taste. It has necessarily to be conducted with the State Department, with which my duties do not connect me. Again, then, I most respectfully but urgently repeat my request to be excused from the performance of a duty entirely out of my sphere, and one, too, which can be so much better performed by others." The President excused him, and the *Times* will be good enough to excuse us if we do not believe that Grant possesses qualities which he so utterly disclaims himself.

A Case of Cotton Speculation—Grant the Father, and Grant the Son—An Ugly Affair.

We reproduce, says the Cincinnati *Enquirer*, the proceedings of a very important Court case, as published at the time in the Cincinnati papers, and which created much talk. It was the case of Jesse R. Grant (the father of General Hiram Ulysses Grant), who sued the Mack Brothers on a contract entered into between the parties, December, 1862.

Was it in view of this arrangement between Jesse R. Grant and the Mack Brothers, and in order that it might be as profitable to the parties as possible, that General Grant issued his inhuman order of December 17, 1862, requiring all Jews to be expelled from his department (that of Tennessee) within twenty-four hours from the receipt of that order by post commanders? And did Jesse R. Grant comply with the regulations of trade established by the Treasury Department, before his son issued to him a trade permit? And was he furnished at the public expense with transportation and other facilities to get cotton into the loyal States?

These questions might have found a solution had the case not been compromised. The plaintiff took a few dollars and dismissed the case. Its developments promised to be an ugly affair, and not very creditable to the Commander of the Department of the Tennessee. It was, therefore, prudently taken out of Court. The following is the case as reported and published in the Cincinnati papers, May 17, 1864:

SUPERIOR COURT.

General Term—Jesse R. Grant *v.* Mack Brothers. Judge Hoadly delivered the opinion. The case was reserved from special term on demurrer to the petition. The action was instituted for the settlement of a partnership account.

The plaintiff avers that in December, 1862, he entered into a partnership with defendants for the purchase of cotton in the military department of U. S. Grant; the condition of said agreement that defendants were to furnish the capital and the men to purchase and ship the cotton, and the plaintiff to procure at the headquarters of Gen. Grant a permit to purchase it, secure transportation, and such other facilities as might be consistent with the usages and interests of the army. The plaintiff was to receive one-fourth share of the net profits of sales, after deducting from gross proceeds the necessary expenses. The petition further states that there was a realized profit in the defendants' favor of not less than $40,000, and that they refuse to render any account, or pay the plaintiff his proportion.

The defendants claim that the plaintiff contributed, by his own showing, neither capital nor lawful service to the copartnership, and that their agreement to pay him a share of the profits is, therefore, without sufficient consideration.

The Court can not presume that the plaintiff intended to allege that he undertook that which was prohibited by law. His acts and promises may have been illegal, and the partnership one for a forbidden enterprise; but in the absence of an answer so averring, the Court can not assume it, unless the averments are inconsistent with any other theory.

The purchase of cotton in the military department commanded by General Grant was illegal, unless carried on by permission of the President, obtained through the Treasury Department.

The plaintiff avers that he was to go to the headquarters of General Grant and procure a permit to purchase cotton. Whether this was expected to be obtained from the General himself, from some member of his staff, or a Treasury agent at headquarters, is not stated. Whether the plaintiff was to procure it as a personal favor, or by the use of personal influence, or in the ordinary mode of business, is not shown. The Court could not presume he was to get his permit from an officer not authorized by law to give it, or that he was to procure it as the reward of personal, political or other illegitimate influence. They must rather infer that he proposed to solicit and procure a permit in the ordinary and proper way, from a Treasury agent having authority to issue it.

Again: It is averred that plaintiff was to and did secure transportation. This may have been done by procuring from some Quartermaster, or other officer controlling it, the improper and illegal use of Government horses and wagons, or steamboats; or he may have hired horses and wagons from the people of the country, and secured steamboat transportation in the usual way. The mere fact that he was to secure transportation at the headquarters of General Grant, is not decisive.

The other item of service, the "procuring of such other facilities as might be consistent with the usages and interests of the army," is open to the same double reading. These facilities, whatever they were, may have been procured by honest or dishonest influences.

For these reasons, the defense suggested must be presented by answer. The theory that the employment of the plaintiff was to procure the illegal co-operation of the military in a private enterprise, must be alleged by sworn answer. If true, it was equally disgraceful to the defendants and the plaintiff, and, if proven, would insure the dismissal of the petition with reprobation to the two parties, upon the principle, among others, *in pari delicto, potior est conditio defendentis*. Demurrer overruled, and leave to answer.

Judge Storer agreed with the other members of the Court on the question of the pleadings, and felt constrained to say that the whole of the trade, as disclosed in this proceeding, was not only disgraceful, but tends directly to disgrace the country. It is the price of blood.

Grant's Military Discipline.

How He Punishes Private Soldiers.

A clerical *claqueur* of Gen. Grant, the Rev. J. L. Crane, ex-chaplain of his regiment, ventilates his recollections of the great oyster. Among other things he says:

He is always cheerful. No toil, cold, heat, hunger, fatigue or want of money depresses him. He does his work at the time, and he requires all under his command to be equally prompt. I was walking over the camp with him one morning after breakfast. It was usual for each company to call the roll at a given hour. It was now probably a half hour after the time for that duty. The Colonel was quietly smoking his old meerschaum, and talking and walking along, when he noticed a company drawn up in line and the roll being called. He instantly drew his pipe from his mouth and exclaimed: "Captain, this is no time for calling the roll. Order your men to their quarters immediately." The command was instantly obeyed, and the Colonel resumed his smoking and walked on, conversing as quietly as if nothing had happened. For this violation of dicipline, those men went without rations that day, except what they gathered up privately from among their friends of other companies. Such a breach of order was never witnessed in the regiment afterward while he was its Colonel. This promptness is one of Grant's characteristics, and it is one of the secrets of his success.

Now, this ex-chaplain is either a Reverend prevaricator, or Grant practiced a cruel discipline upon his private soldiers. For an irregularity in roll-call he punished the private soldiers by taking from them their rations that day, and compelled them to impose upon their friends for something to eat. The men were not to blame for any irregularity in roll-call. They have nothing to do but to obey it. The company commander should alone have been punished. To order the men to suffer on that account was a small display of the military despot.

What Grant and Colfax think of the Soldiers.

General Grant has written to the Military Committee of the House of Representatives, asking for an increase of one-third in the pay of army officers, but he has not a word to say for the private soldier.

An Indiana soldier addresses a note to the Indianapolis *Sentinel*, in which he details the treatment he received at the hands of Mr. Colfax, as follows:

In the winter of 1862, I was in the Patent Office Hospital, in Washington City, during convalescence, after a very hard spell of fever. A friend called upon me. Through him I succeeded in getting a standing pass. This friend requested me to visit him. He was clerking in the Treasury Department; was also attending lectures as a medical student, and had to be absent from his duties every day. He requested me to write for him two hours every day to keep up his books, at the same time requesting me to try and secure the situation, as he was going to give it up. I thought I would then call upon Mr. Colfax, and perhaps, through his instrumentality, I might facilitate my discharge and secure the situation as clerk in the department. I therefore called on him, at his residence. I was clothed as well as a clean, decent suit of soldier's clothes would allow. A finely dressed gentleman came in immediately behind me; a colored boy met us in the reception room. He asked for our cards; the citizen laid his upon the waiter. I informed him I had none. He then left the room. In a few minutes Mr. Colfax made his appearance. He spoke in a very affable way to the citizen gentleman, not deigning to notice me. In a short time the gentleman left me, and Mr. Colfax, turning shortly around, in no very amiable way, said: "Well, what will you have?" I then, in as few words as possible, explained the object of my visit. In reply, he said that he had no time to fool away with soldiers. I then immediately left, thinking to myself that perhaps I might do him a favor some day, on the same principle. Perhaps the time is coming when I might vote for him; but I could not, nor would not, even for Supervisor. To the above I am willing to be qualified.   N. M. MOORE.

Colfax and Foreigners.

In 1854–5, when Know-Nothingism sought the disfranchisement and proscription of every foreigner and Roman Catholic in the country on account of his birthplace and religion, Mr. Schuyler Colfax was a bright and shining light in the organization. The Indianapolis *Sentinel* states that there was no fiercer or more proscriptive Know-Nothing in the land. Could he have had his way, not a foreigner or Roman Catholic would to-day be allowed to hold office or even vote. In order to show our foreign born citizens what manner of man he is, we give the oaths which he took when initiated into the Know-Nothing Lodge, as follows:

First Degree.—In the presence of Almighty God and these witnesses you do solemnly promise and swear that * * * you will not vote, nor give your influence, for any man, for any office in the gift of the people, unless he be an American born citizen, in favor of Americans ruling America, nor if he be a Roman Catholic.

Second Degree.—In the presence of Almighty God and these witnesses you do solemnly and sincerely swear * * * if it may be legally done, you will, when elected or appointed to any official station conferring on you power to do so, remove all foreigners, aliens or Roman Catholics from office or place, and that you will in no case appoint such to any office or place in your gift.

Now, when, against his utmost efforts, the Know-Nothing organization has been utterly defeated and swept from existence, the Radicals expect these same foreigners and their descendants to vote to make Mr. Schuyler Colfax Vice-President. Can they forget and forgive the vindictive proscription with which he pursued them?

Opinion of Colfax in the West.

The Cleveland *Plaindealer* says of Colfax, that he is a "politician by trade, and is notorious in Indiana as a chronic office-beggar;" that "he was elected to Congress in 1854 by the Know-Nothing party, and he was one of the most bitter, loud-mouthed defamers of our foreign-born fellow-citizens in that memorable campaign;" and that "he is best known as a mere partisan intriguer, as full of Radical bitterness as old Thad. himself, and possessed of neither strength or comprehensiveness of mind nor generosity of disposition." *

Views of the Framers of the Constitution as to the Danger of Legislative Usurpations.
[From the National Intelligencer, January 30, 1868.]

In the Federal Convention of 1787, when Edmund Randolph, in opening the main business, commented on the difficulty of the crisis, and the necessity of preventing the fulfillment of the prophesies of the American downfall, the resolutions which he proposed contemplated not only that a national judiciary be established, but that the Executive and a convenient number of the national judiciary ought to compose a council of revision, with authority to examine every act of the national legislature before it shall operate. (Madison Papers, vol. 2, p. 733.) On the same day Mr. Charles Pinckney laid before the House his draft, which, as to the courts, provided that "one of these courts shall be termed the Supreme Court," whose jurisdiction shall extend to all cases arising under the laws of the United States (Ib. 743-4), and shall be appellate, except in certain specified cases.

On the 30th of May, 1787, when the Convention proceeded to consider the proposition to establish a National Government consisting of a *supreme* legislative, executive and judiciary, Mr. Butler said that "he had opposed the grant of powers to Congress (Ib. 748) heretofore, because the whole power was vested in one body. The proposed distribution of the powers with the different bodies changed the case, and would induce him to go great lengths." In the subsequent debates, Mr. Gerry expressed doubts whether the judiciary ought to form a part of the council of revision, "as they will have a sufficient check against encroachments on their own department by their exposition of the laws, which involved a power of deciding on their constitutionality. In some States the judges had already set aside laws as being against the Constitution. This was done, too, with general approbation." (Ib. 783.) On his motion, the clause was postponed, and the Convention considered a proposition to give the national executive a right to negative any legislative act which shall not be afterward passed by certain parts of each branch.

Mr. Wilson thought "neither the original proposition nor the amendment went far enough. If the legislative, executive, and judiciary ought to be distinct and independent, the executive ought to have an absolute negative. Without such a self-defense, the legislature can at any moment sink it into non-existence." (Ib. 784.) Mr. Hamilton was also for giving the executive an absolute negative. (Ibid.) Mr. Madison supposed that if a proper proportion of each branch should be required to overrule the objections of the executive, it would answer the same purpose as an absolute negative. (Ib. 786.) Mr. Wilson thought "the requiring a large proportion of each house to overrule the executive's check, might do in peaceable times; but there might be tempestuous moments in which animosities may run high between the executive and legislative branches, and in which the former ought to be able to defend itself." (Ib. 786-7.) The Convention decided against giving the executive absolute negative—against giving the executive absolute power to suspend a legislative act; but to give the executive alone, without the judiciary, the revisionary control of the laws, unless overruled by two-thirds of each branch. (Ib. 790.)

Then the Convention agreed to establish a national judiciary, to consist of one supreme tribunal, and of inferior tribunals (Ib. 791); and empowered the national legislature to institute the latter. (Ib. 799.) Mr. Madison said, "an effective judiciary establishment, commensurate to the legislative authority, was essential. A government without a proper executive and judiciary would be the mere trunk of a body without arms or legs to act or move." (Ib. 799.)

A portion of the Convention still desired that the judiciary should aid the executive in the revision of the laws. Mr. Madison observed that "the great difficulty in rendering the executive competent to its own defense arose from the nature of republican government"—"an association of the judges in his revisionary function would both

---

* For more of Grant's and Colfax's record, see other parts of this book.

double the advantage and diminish the danger. It would also enable the judiciary department the better to defend itself against legislative encroachments—whether the object of the revisionary power was to restrain the legislature from encroaching on the other co ordinate departments. or on the rights of the people at large; or from passing laws unwise in their principle or incorrect in their form—the utility of annexing the wisdom and weight of the judiciary to the executive seemed incontestible." (Ib. 810–11.) Colonel Mason was "for giving all possible weight to the revisionary institution. The executive power ought to be well secured against legislative usurpations on it. The purse and the sword, ought never to get into the same hands, whether legislative or executive." (Ib. 811.) The decision of the Convention was, however, against joining the judges to the executive in the way proposed.

After this decision, when the Convention proceeded to consider the jurisdiction of the judiciary, Mr. Madison proposed "that the jurisdiction shall extend to all cases arising under the national laws; and to such other questions as may involve the national peace and harmony;" which was agreed to *nem con.* (Ib. 1,137–8.)

Mr. Wilson made another effort to have the judiciary associated with the executive in the revisionary power. He thought "the judiciary ought to have an opportunity of remonstrating against projected encroachments on the people as well as on themselves." Adverting to its having been said that the judges, as expositors of the laws, would have an opportunity of defending their constitutional rights, he admitted there was weight in this observation; but he thought "this power of the judges did not go far enough." He said: "Laws may be unjust, may be unwise, may be dangerous, may be destructive; and yet may not be so unconstitutional as to justify the judges in refusing to give them effect. Let them have a share in the revisionary power, and they will have an opportunity of taking notice of those characters of the law, and of counteracting by the weight of their opinions the improper views of the legislature." (Ib. 1,161–2.)

Mr. Madison seconded the motion, considering that it would be "useful to the community at large, as an additional check against a pursuit of those unwise and unjust measures which constituted so great a portion of our calamities." He said: "If any solid objection could be urged against the motion, it must be on the supposition that it tended to give too much strength, either to the executive or judiciary. He did not think there was the least ground for this apprehension. It was much more to be apprehended, that, notwithstanding this co-operation of the two departments, the legislature would still be an overmatch for them. Experience in all the States had evinced a powerful tendency in the legislature to absorb all power into its vortex. This was the real source of danger to the American constitutions, and suggested the necessity of giving every defensive authority to the other departments that was consistent with republican principles" (Ib. 1,163.)

Mr. Strong thought, with Mr. Gerry, the power of making ought to be kept distinct from that of expounding the laws. Mr. Governor Morris said: "The interest of our executive is so inconsiderable and so transitory, and his means of defending it so feeble, that there is the justest ground to fear his want of firmness in resisting encroachments. He was extremely apprehensive that the auxiliary firmness and weight of the judiciary would not supply the deficiency. He concurred in thinking the public liberty in greater danger from legislative usurpations than from any other source. It had been said that the legislature ought to be relied on as the proper guardians of liberty. The answer was short and conclusive. Either bad laws will be pushed or not. On the latter supposition, no check will be wanted. On the former, a strong check will be necessary—and this is the proper supposition." (Ib. 1,165–6.) Mr. L. Martin objected to the association of the judges with the executive. He said: "As to the constitutionality of laws, that point will come before the judges in their official character. In this character they have a negative on the laws. Join them with the executive in the revision, and they will have a double negative." (Ib. 1,166.)

Madison said: "If a constitutional discrimination of the departments on paper were a sufficient security to each against encroachments upon the others, all farther provisions would be superfluous. But experience has taught us a distrust of that security, and that it is necessary to introduce such a balance of powers and interests as will guarantee the provisions on paper." (Ib. 1,167.) Colonel Mason, adverting to the danger that the Legislature would pass unjust and pernicious laws, said this restraining power "would have the effect not only of hindering the final passage of such laws, but would discourage demagogues from attempting to get them passed." To Mr. Martin's argument, he replied that the judges, in their expository capacity, could impede, in one case only, the operation of laws. They could declare an unconstitutional law void. But with regard to every law, however unjust, oppressive or pernicious, that did not come plainly under this description, they would be under the necessity, as judges, to give it a free course. He wished the further use to be made of the judges of giving aid in preventing every improper law." (Ib. 1,168.) Mr. Wilson's motion for joining the judiciary in the revision of laws, was, however, decided in the negative, there being—ayes 3, noes 4.

The resolutions of the Convention having been referred to a committee, that committee accordingly reported a constitution providing that "the jurisdiction of the Supreme Court shall extend to all cases arising under laws passed by the Legislature of the United States," and that in certain cases the jurisdiction should be original, and in other cases it should be appellate.

There was still a desire for greater impediments to improper laws. Mr. Governor Morris said: "The most virtuous citizens will often, as members of a legislative body, concur in measures which afterward, in their private capacity, they will be ashamed of. Encroachments of the popular branch of the Government ought to be guarded against." "If the Executive be overturned by the popular branch, as happened in England, the tyranny of one man will ensue." (Ib., vol. 3, p. 1,335.) Mr. Wilson was most apprehensive of a dissolution of the Government from the Legislature swallowing up all the other powers. (Ib. 1,336.) A motion to require *three-fourths* instead of *two-thirds* of each House to overrule the dissent of the President was now adopted, there being ayes 6 and noes 4. (Ib. 1,337.) Subsequently a committee reported a constitution requiring only *two-thirds* of each House to approve a bill (Ib. 1,548), and the Constitution with this provision was adopted.

In lieu of the words, "the jurisdiction of the Supreme Court," was inserted the words "the judicial power;" and the words, "this Constitution and the" were inserted before the word "laws." (Ib. 1,439.) There was a motion to insert, "in all other cases before mentioned the judicial power shall be exercised in such manner as the Legislature shall direct;" but the motion did not prevail. Having disagreed to this motion by a vote of six against, to two for it (Ib. 1,439), the Convention adopted the Constitution with the provisions as to the judicial power now found in article 3; secs. 1, 2, 3.

The Constitution providing in so many words that "the judicial power *shall extend to all* cases in law and equity arising under this Constitution, the laws of the United States, and treaties made, or which shall be made under their authority, it is not for a Congress elected under that Constitution to enact that the judicial power shall not extend to all cases arising under that Constitution or under those laws. In all such cases, other than cases affecting ambassadors, other public ministers, and consuls, and those in which a State shall be a party, the Supreme Court has, under the Constitution, appellate jurisdiction, both as to law and fact, with such exceptions and under such regulations as the Congress shall make.* The power of Congress to make such exceptions and regulations should, of course, be exercised consistently with, and in subordination to the Constitution. It should be exercised consistently with, and in subordination to the plain provision that "the judicial power shall extend to all cases, in law and equity, arising under this Constitution," or "the laws of the United States."

It is plain, beyond all doubt, that the Convention recognized the judiciary as having, and intended they should have, the power of deciding on the constitutionality of acts of Congress, and holding the same void so far as inconsistent with the Constitution. And until it shall be done, we should be slow to believe that Congress will pass any act to prevent the judiciary from so deciding. We should be slow to believe that the desire to prevent such decision is so strong as to induce members, bound by oath to support the Constitution, to violate that oath and commit willful perjury. But if so wicked a deed shall be done, we may hope and trust that a reverence for principles of *Magna Charta*, existing long before the American Constitution, is still felt by some American, no less than by some English judges. For centuries before that Constitution, it was a principle of English law, that no matter whence commandments should come to the contrary, the judges should not omit or delay to do right in any point; that no judge should be excused by pleading even the danger of his life from the menaces of the sovereign. (Cotton, p. 364; 2 Hume's Eng., ch. 18, p. 339.)

The distinction is plain between the power to create a new court and appoint new judges in it, and the power of judges of a court which has been created and established to determine matters in it. (Jentlemen's case, 6 Rep., 11b.) In the fifth year of the reign of *James the First*, Coke, C. J., with the consent of all the judges, informed that sovereign that no King after the Conquest, assumed to himself to give any judgment in any cause whatsoever which concerned the administration of justice, but these were solely determined in the courts of justice. The King claiming to determine

---

* Those words became necessary or proper, on account of the power given to Congress to establish *inferior* courts.

a controversy, and urging that he and others had reason as well as the judges, Coke answered, "That true it was that God had endowed his Majesty with excellent sense and great endowments of nature; but his Majesty was not learned in the laws of his realm of England, and causes which concern the life, or inheritance, or goods, or fortunes of his subjects are not to be decided by natural reason, but by the artificial reason and judgment of law, which law is an act which requires long study and experience before that a man can attain to the cognizance of it; and that the law was the golden metwand and measure to try the causes of the subject, and which protected his Majesty in safety and peace"—with which the King was greatly offended, and said "that then he should be under the law, which was treason to affirm," which Coke answered by citing *Bracton's* words: "*Quod rex non debet esse sub homine, sed sub deo et lege.*" (12 Rep , 63, 4, 5.) If, on the one hand, some members of the present Congress may seem in some respects to resemble James the First, it is to be hoped, on the other hand, that American judges holding their offices during good behavior, will, if there should be occasion for it, show not less of the moral firmness and independence that should characterize the discharge of judicial duty, than was manifested by English judges in the reign of that sovereign, though without the benefit of such tenure. It is a pleasant thing to remember that in the twelfth year of that reign, when the King commanded his Attorney-General to signify by letters his pleasure to the judges that the argument of a certain case should be deferred, that nevertheless the argument proceeded, the judges answering that they held those letters to be contrary to law, and such as they could not obey by oath. (Francklin's Annals, 17, 18; Woolwich's Life of Coke, pp. 108–111.)

C. R.

A Radical Light v. the Early Fathers.

The conceit of the wise men of the Radical power in Congress is well illustrated by the following extract from a speech of Mr. Bingham, the judicial syringe of Radicalism, who, in the face of these opinions, daily imposes upon the country such trash as this:

In the debate on the Judiciary bill, he laid down the right of the people, through Congress, to control the decisions of the Supreme Court, by reducing or increasing the number of judges:

"The rights of the people of this country are to be respected, and those whom they send to this Congress are clothed by the Constitution with power to compel even the Supreme Court to respect those rights; and to that end, if need be, to reduce that Court to a single person, if you please, and thereby compel unanimity, at least in a decision which may deny the people's rights and violate the people's laws. It will not do for any man who ever read the Constitution of the United States, and understands the plainest words of our mother tongue, to rise in his place here and say that the Congress of the United States can not reduce that tribunal to a single judge, or, if you please, to but two or three judges."

A Radical Mob in the Senate of the United States.

[Special to the Cincinnati Commercial.]

WASHINGTON, May 6.

When Mr. Bingham took his seat, Senator Wilson rose to submit a motion that the Senate retire for consultation. He had scarcely time to address the Chair, when, to the right of the Chair, in the gentlemen's gallery, a few spectators commenced to stamp their feet and clap their hands in approval of Mr. Bingham's speech. It was promptly suppressed by the Chief-Justice, but very quickly spread through the entire galleries, increasing in violence as it went around, until it amounted to a disorderly uproar. Even the ladies were quick to catch the contagion, and gave vent to their enthusiasm as earnestly as those of the other sex.

The Chief-Justice rapped when it was too late. He might as well have tried to extinguish a prairie fire with a syringe; when he rose from his seat and cried "Order," with all the voice he could put into the word, he was only laughed at; and for very spite hundreds who had remained silent till then joined in the demonstration, and made the Senate Chamber a bedlam. Some stood up while they clapped their hands, and others kept their seats that they might be enabled to use both hands and feet in the uproar.

While the noise was at its loudest, the Chief-Justice, in an angry tone, ordered the Sergeant-at-arms to clear the galleries, but it was manifest that without the consent of the offenders, the order could not be executed. A few cried out, "He can't do it, he hasn't men enough; we won't go out;" and there were indications for a time that they meant what they said, and were determined not to be put out. The door-keepers attempted to enforce the order by announcing it, but they found the crowd very slow to move. The Senators began to get alarmed, for really the scene began to smack of the French Revolution, when the crowd used to overawe the National Assembly.

Mr. Grimes angrily asked, after surveying the scene, why the order was not enforced forthwith, to which the Chief-Justice, who seemed to be getting quite nervous, replied that it certainly would be enforced. A volley of hisses for Grimes came next, and that, too, from the most respectable part of the galleries. Many a finely-dressed lady contributed to them. An attempt was made to get up a more violent insult in the way of a loud "bah," and some hootings were heard such as the rabble sometimes deal out to stump-speakers they don't like.

Mr. Trumbull quickly came to the relief of Grimes, with a motion that the offenders be arrested, as well as the galleries cleared. "I would like to see you do it!" shouted several of the retiring offenders in reply.

The galleries were by this time about half cleared, but not because of the order of the Chief-Justice. It got out that the court was about to retire, or adjourn, and those who had left had done so under this impression. Suddenly a few men cried out: "Hold on! They ain't going to adjourn. Let us see this thing out!" Then came a halt, and hundreds took their seats again, with the utmost unconcern, and totally indifferent to the order for their ejection.

Mr. Cameron, amid the din and confusion, rose to hope that the galleries would not be cleared. He did not believe it fair to punish all for the offense of some, and hoped none but those who had made the demonstration would be put out.

Messrs. Fessenden and Johnson sharply called Mr. Cameron to order, and insisted that the clearance be proceeded with; at which there was another volley of hisses and a few more hootings, and the scene looked more revolutionary than ever.

Meantime, in the corridors, a few hundreds of the ejected had formed into a crowd, and commenced singing "Old Grimes is dead, that poor old man!"

They were joined by the ladies with great glee. Between the verses the Iowa Senator was liberally and maliciously cursed and damned as a traitor and Copperhead. One man attempted to make a speech against Grimes and the other renegades, but the tumult was too great for him, and all around him were too much interested in the song, which was thought to be peculiarly appropriate and piquant. "Will the ladies help us to sing?" "Certainly they will," said another, and so they did.

While this extraordinary scene was taking place in the corridors, and within the hearing of the high court of impeachment, Senators were wondering what still kept the galleries at least half full. Mr. Sherman attempted to solve the mystery by suggesting to the Chief-Justice that perhaps those who remained in the galleries did not understand the nature of the order. The Chief-Justice repeated the order for their benefit, and again instructed the Sergeant-at-arms to enforce it, which he, with the aid of the Capitol employés he could find, proceeded at once to do.

Finally all were cleared but the reporters' and the diplomatic gallery. The occupants of these thought themselves exempt from the rule. The Sergeant-at-arms quickly dispersed these by sending the *posse* to eject them. The British Minister at first remonstrated, then went out to find the Sergeant-at-arms, and then again tried to secure the interposition of Mr. Sumner, but all to no purpose. He and all his choice company of distinguished foreigners had to leave.

The reporters were the last and most reluctant to obey. They insisted that they had committed no offense, and ought not to be interfered with. A few of them shouted to Senatorial friends to know if they, too, must go. They received, in reply, a laugh, which they construed affirmatively, and which they responded to with a loud groan, and a muttering comment that this was a "— o' a way." The *Tribune* correspondent protested that the loyal press ought to pitch into Grimes. The *Times* man swore like a trooper, while about twenty, who had smuggled themselves into the gallery with the *Herald* reporters, joined in a most unearthly and fiendish moan, supplemented with the remark from one of them that he "wished some fellow would put a box of nitro-glycerine under the court and explode it." One of the fourth estate insisted on three groans for Grimes and Trumbull, and was about to start them in the presence of the court, but just then a deputy sergeant-at-arms caught him by the coat-collar and lifted him into an adjoining room. An indignation meeting of the Republican reporters was extemporized in the corridors, but before they had come to any resolution, one of them, imitating the example of Donnelly in the House of Representatives, proposed that they should all go out and take a drink, which was agreed to with great unanimity.

It took nearly half an hour to clear the galleries. The scenes attendant upon the process have been only faintly described above. The picture could scarcely be overdrawn, for nothing like it for indecency has ever been witnessed before. Some seven years ago, when Senator Andrew Johnson made a Union speech in reply to Mr. Lane, of Oregon, and the galleries deliberately rose and gave nine cheers for the Union and the flag, Vice-President Breckenridge caused them to be cleared. There was no disorder attending the execution of that order, and since then, until to-day, no such order has been executed.

Rev. Henry Ward Beecher on Reconstruction.

HIS LETTER TO THE SOLDIERS' AND SAILORS' CONVENTION.

PEEKSKILL, August 30.

Charles G. Halpine, Brevet Brigadier-General; Henry W. Slocum, Major-General; Gordon Granger, Major-General; Committee:

Gentlemen: I am obliged to you for the invitation which you have made to me, to act as Chaplain to the Convention of Sailors and Soldiers about to convene at Cleveland. I can not attend it, but I heartily wish it, and all other conventions, of what party soever, success, whose object is the restoration of all the States late in rebellion to their Federal relations.

Our theory of Government has no place for a State except in the Union. It is justly taken for granted, that the duties and responsibilities of a State in Federal relations, tend to its political health, and to that of the whole nation. Even Territories are hastily brought in, often before the prescribed conditions are fulfilled, as if it were dangerous to leave a community outside of the great body politic.

Had the loyal Senators and Representatives of Tennessee been admitted at once on the assembling of Congress, and, in moderate succession, Arkansas, Georgia, Alabama, North Carolina and Virginia, the public mind of the South would have been far more healthy than it is, and those States which lingered on probation to the last, would have been under a more salutary influence to good conduct than if a dozen armies watched over them.

Every month that we delay this healthful step complicates the case. The excluded population, enough unsettled before, grow more irritable; the army becomes indispensable to local government, and supersedes it; the Government at Washington is called to interfere in one and another difficulty, and this will be done inaptly, and sometimes with great injustice; for our Government wisely adapted to its own proper functions, is utterly devoid of those habits, and unequipped with the instruments, which fit a centralized government to exercise authority in remote States over local affairs. Every attempt to perform such duties has resulted in mistakes which have excited the nation. But whatever imprudence there may be in the method, the real criticism should be against the requisitions of such duties of the General Government.

The Federal Government is unfit to exercise minor police and local government, and will inevitably blunder when it attempts it. To keep half a score of States under Federal authority, but without national ties and responsibilities; to oblige the central authority to govern half the territory of the Union by Federal civil officers, and by the army, is a policy not only uncongenial to our ideas and principles, but pre-eminently dangerous to the spirit of our Government. However humane the ends sought and the motives, it is in fact, a course of instruction, preparing our Government to be despotic, and familiarizing the people to a stretch of authority which can never be other than dangerous to liberty.

I am aware that good men are withheld from advocating the prompt and successive admission of the exiled States by the fear, chiefly, of its effects upon parties, and upon the freedmen.

It is said that, if admitted to Congress, the Southern Senators and Representatives will coalesce with Northern Democrats, and rule the country. Is this Nation, then, to remain dismembered to serve the ends of parties? Have we learned no wisdom by the history of the last ten years, in which just this course of sacrificing the Nation to the exigencies of parties plunged us into in to rebellion and war?

Even admit that the power would pass into the hands of a party made up of Southern men, and the hitherto dishonored and misled Democracy of the North, that power could not be used just as they pleased. The war has changed, not alone institutions, but ideas. The whole country has advanced. Public sentiment is exalted far beyond what it has been at any former period. A new party would, like a river, be obliged to seek out its channels, in the already existing slopes and forms of the continent.

We have entered a new era of liberty. The style of thought is freer and more noble. The young men of our times are regenerated. The great army has been a school, and hundreds of thousands of men are gone home to preach a truer and nobler view of human rights. All the industrial interests of society are moving with increasing wisdom toward intelligence and liberty. Everywhere, in churches, in literature, in natural science, in physical industries, in social questions, as well as in politics, the Nation feels that the winter is over, and a new spring hangs n the horizon, and works through all the elements. In this happily changed and advanced condition of things, no party of the retrograde can maintain itself. Everything marches, and parties must march.

I hear, with wonder and shame and scorn, the fear of a few, that the South once more, in adjustment with the Federal Government, will rule this nation! The North is rich, never so rich; the South is poor, never so poor. The population of the North is nearly double that of the South. The industry of the North, in diversity, in forwardness and productiveness, in all the machinery and education required for manufacturing, is half a century in advance of the South. Churches in the North crown every hill, and schools swarm in every neighborhood; while the South has but scattered lights, at long distances, like lighthouses twinkling along the edge of a continent of darkness. In the presence of such a contrast, how mean and craven is the fear that the South will rule the policy of the land! That it will have an influence, that it will contribute, in time, most important influences or restraints, we are glad to believe. But, if it rises at once to the control of the Government, it will be because the North, demoralized by prosperity, and besotted by groveling interests, refuses to discharge its share of political duty. In such a case, the South not only will control the Government, but it ought to do it!

2. It is feared with more reason that the restoration of the South to her full independence, will be detrimental to the freedmen. The sooner we dismiss from our minds the idea that the freedmen can be classified and separated from the white population, and nursed and defended by themselves, the better it will be for them and us. The negro is part and parcel of Southern society. He can not be prosperous while it is unprospered. Its evils will rebound upon him. Its happiness and reinvigoration can not be kept from his participation. The restoration of the South to amicable relations with the North, the reorganization of its industry, the reinspiration of its enterprise and thrift will all redound to the freedmen's benefit. Nothing is so dangerous to the freedmen as an unsettled state of society in the South. On him comes all the spite, and anger, and caprice, and revenge. He will be made the scapegoat of lawless and heartless men. Unless we turn the Government into a vast military machine, there can not be armies enough to protect the freedmen while Southern society remains insurrectionary. If Southern society is calmed, settled, and occupied and soothed with new hopes and prosperous industries, no armies will be needed. Riots will subside, lawless hangers on will be driven off or better governed, and a way will be gradually opened up to the freedmen, through education and industry, to full citizenship, with all its honors and duties.

Civilization is a growth. None can escape that forty years in the wilderness who travel from the Egypt of ignorance to the promised land of civilization. The freedmen must take their march. I have full faith in the results. If they have the stamina to undergo the hardships which every uncivilized people has undergone in their upward progress, they will in due time take their place among us. That place can not be bought, nor bequeathed, nor gained by sleight of hand. It will come to sobriety, virtue, industry and frugality. As the nation can not be sound until the South is prosperous, so, on the other extreme, a healthy condition of civil society in the South is indispensable to the welfare of the freedmen!

Refusing to admit loyal Senators and Representatives from the South to Congress will not help the Freedmen. It will not secure for them the vote. It will not protect them. It will not secure any amendment of our Constitution, however just and wise. It will only increase the dangers and complicate the difficulties. Whether we regard the whole nation, or any section of it, or class in it, the first demand of our time is, entire reunion.

Once united, we can, by schools, churches, a free press and increasing free speech, attack each evil and secure every good.

Meanwhile the great chasm which rebellion made is not filled up. It grows deeper and stretches wider? Out of it rise dread specters and threatening sounds. Let that gulf be closed, and bury in it slavery, sectional animosity, and all strifes and hatreds.

It is fit that the brave men, who, on sea and land, faced death to save the nation, should now, by their voice and vote, consummate what their swords rendered possible.

For the sake of the freedmen, for the sake of the South and its millions of our fellow-countrymen, for our own sake, and for the great cause of freedom and civilization, I urge the immediate reunion of all the parts which rebellion and war have shattered. I am, truly, yours,

HENRY WARD BEECHER.

The Democratic Platform of 1864.

The Democratic National Convention which assembled in Chicago on the 30th of August, 1864, nominated George B. McClellan and George H. Pendleton for the Presidency and Vice-Presidency, and adopted the following platform, as reported by Mr. Guthrie, Chairman of the Committee:

Resolved, That in the future, as in the past, we will adhere with unswerving fidelity to the Union under the Constitution as the only solid foundation of our strength, security, and happiness as a people, and as a frame-work of government equally conducive to the welfare and prosperity of all the States, both Northern and Southern.

Resolved, That this Convention does explicitly declare, as the sense of the American people, that after four years of failure to restore the Union by the experiment of war, during which, under the pretense of a military necessity, or war power higher than the Constitution, the Constitution itself has been disregarded in every part, and public liberty and private right alike trodden down and the material prosperity of the country essentially imperiled — justice, humanity, liberty, and the public welfare demand that immediate efforts be made for a cessation of hostilities, with a view to an ultimate convention of the States, or other peaceable means, to the end that at the earliest practicable moment peace may be restored on the basis of the Federal Union of the States.

Resolved, That the direct interference of the military authorities of the United States in the recent elections held in Kentucky, Maryland, Missouri, and Delaware, was a shameful violation of the Constitution; and a repetition of such acts in the approaching election will be held as revolutionary, and resisted with all the means and power under our control.

Resolved, That the aim and object of the Democratic party is to preserve the Federal Union and the rights of the States unimpaired; and they hereby declare that they consider that the administrative usurpation of extraordinary and dangerous powers not granted by the Constitution; the subversion of the civil by military law in States not in insurrection; the arbitrary military arrest, imprisonment, trial, and sentence of American citizens in States where civil law exists in full force; the suppression of freedom of speech and of the press; the denial of the right of asylum; the open and avowed disregard of State rights; the employment of unusual test-oaths, and the interference with and denial of the right of the people to bear arms in their defense, is calculated to prevent a restoration of the Union and the perpetuation of a government deriving its just powers from the consent of the governed.

Resolved, That the shameful disregard of the Administration to its duty in respect to our fellow-citizens who now are, and long have been prisoners of war in a suffering condition, deserves the severest reprobation, on the score alike of public policy and common humanity.

Resolved, That the sympathy of the Democratic party is heartily and earnestly extended to the soldiery of our army and sailors of our navy, who are, and have been in the field and on the sea, under the flag of their country; and in the event of its attaining power, they will receive all the care, protection, and regard that the brave soldiers and sailors of the Republic have so nobly earned.

Negro Privileges in Railroad Cars.

On the 27th of February, 1863, pending a supplement to the charter of the Washington and Alexandria Railroad Company, Mr. Sumner offered this proviso to the first section:

That no person shall be excluded from the cars on account of color.

Which was agreed to—yeas 19, nays 18, as follows:

YEAS—Messrs. Arnold, Chandler, Clark, Fessenden, Foot, Grimes, Harris, Howard, King, Lane (of Kansas), Morrill, Pomeroy, Sumner, Ten Eyck, Trumbull, Wade, Wilkinson, Wilmot, Wilson (of Massachusetts)—19.

NAYS — Messrs. Anthony, *Bayard, Carlile, Cowan, Davis,* Henderson, Hicks, Howe, *Kennedy,* Lane (of Indiana), *Latham, McDougal, Powell, Richardson, Saulsbury, Turpie,* Willey, *Wilson* (of Missouri)—18.

March 2.—The House concurred in the amendment without debate, under the previous question.

Radicals in Roman, Democrats in *Italic.*

President Lincoln's Letter on Politics, to Horace Greeley.

EXECUTIVE MANSION,
WASHINGTON, Friday, August 22, 1862.

Hon. HORACE GREELEY:

Dear Sir: I have just read yours of the 19th instant, addressed to myself through the New York *Tribune.*

If there be in it any statements or assumptions of fact which I may know to be erroneous, I do not now and here controvert them.

If there be any inferences which I may believe to be falsely drawn, I do not now and here argue against them.

If there be perceptible in it an impatient and dictatorial tone, I waive it in deference to an old friend whose heart I have always supposed to be right.

As to the policy I "seem to be pursuing," as you say, I have not meant to leave any one in doubt. I would save the Union. I would save it in the shortest way under the Constitution.

The sooner the national authority can be restored, the nearer the Union will be— the Union as it was.

If there be those who would not save the

NEGRO SUFFRAGE.

Union unless they could at the same time save slavery, I do not agree with them.

If there be those who would not save the Union unless they could at the same time destroy slavery, I do not agree with them.

My paramount object is to save the Union and not either to save or destroy slavery.

If I could save the Union without freeing any slave, I would do it—and if I could save it by freeing all the slaves, I would do it—and if I could save it by freeing some and leaving others alone, I would also do that.

What I do about slavery and the colored race, I do because I believe it helps to save the Union, and what I forbear, I forbear because I do not believe it would help to save the Union.

I shall do less whenever I shall believe what I am doing hurts the cause, and shall do more whenever I believe doing more will help the cause.

I shall try to correct errors when shown to be errors, and I shall adopt new views so fast as they appear to be true views.

I have here stated my purpose according to my view of official duty, and I intend no modification of my oft-expressed personal wish that all men everywhere could be free.

Yours,   A. LINCOLN.

Negro Suffrage.

THE WHITE MAN'S PLATFORM.

I hold that this Government was made on the white basis, by white men, for the benefit of white men and their posterity forever, and should be administered by white men, and none others. I do not believe that the Almighty made the negro capable of self-government.—*Stephen A. Douglas.*

Hear President Lincoln in reply:

I AM NOT, NOR EVER HAVE BEEN, IN FAVOR OF MAKING VOTERS OR JURORS OF NEGROES, nor of qualifying them to hold office, nor intermarrying them with white people, and I will say, in addition to this, that there is a PHYSICAL DIFFERENCE between the white and black race, which, I believe, *will forever forbid the two races living together on terms of social and political equality*—and, inasmuch as they can not so live, while they do remain together, there must be a position of superior and inferior, and I, as much as any other man, am in favor of having the SUPERIOR POSITION ASSIGNED TO THE WHITE RACE.

Two years before the death of Daniel Webster he said:

IF THESE IMPERTINENT *Fanatics and Abolitionists* ever get the power in their own hands, they will *override the Constitution, set the Supreme Court at defiance,* change and make laws to suit themselves, lay violent hands on those who differ with them in opinion or dare question their fidelity; and finally, bankrupt the country and deluge it in blood.

On September 2, 1843, twenty-five years ago, Henry Clay said:

The agitation of the question in the free States will first *destroy all harmony, and finally lead to disunion*—*perpetuate the war*—*the extinction of the African race*—*ultimate military despotism.*

But the great aim and object of your tract should be to arouse the laboring classes of the free States against abolition. Depict the consequences to them of immediate emancipation. The slaves being free, would be dispersed throughout the Union; they would enter into competition with free labor; with the American, the Irish, the German; reduce his wages, be confounded with him, and affect his moral and social standing. And as the ultras go both for abolition and amalgamation, show that their object is to unite in marriage the laboring white man and the laboring black woman, to reduce the white laboring man to the despised and degraded condition of the black man.

I would show their opposition to Colonization. Show its humane, religious and patriotic aim. That they are to separate those whom God had separated. Why do the Abolitionists oppose Colonization? To keep and amalgamate together the two races, in violation of God's will, and to keep the blacks here, that they may interfere with, degrade and debase the laboring whites. Show that the British Government is co-operating with the Abolitionists, for the purpose of dissolving the Union, etc. You can make a powerful article that will be felt in every extremity of the Union. I am perfectly satisfied it will do great good. Let me hear from you on this subject.

Mr. Jefferson, the very man who is the author of the Declaration of Independence, when speaking upon the subject of races, said:

Nothing is more certainly written in the book of fate than that these people (the negroes) are to be free. Nor is it less certain that the two races—equally free—can not live in the same Government. Nature, habit, opinion, have drawn indelible lines of distinction between them.

Radical Views on Negro Suffrage.

Governor Morton, of Indiana, now U. S. Senator, in his annual message to the Legislature, Nov. 14th, 1865, speaking of Southern reconstruction, said:

The subject of suffrage is, by the national Constitution, expressly referred to the determination of the several States, and it can not be taken from them without a violation of the letter and spirit of that instrument.

But without stopping to discuss theories or questions of Constitutional law, and leaving them out of view, it would, in my opinion, be unwise to make the work of reconstruction depend upon a condition of such doubtful utility as negro suffrage.

It is a fact so manifest, that it should not be called in question by any, that a people who are just emerging from the barbarism of slavery, are not qualified to become a part of our political system, and take part, not only in the government of themselves and their neighbors, but of the whole United States. So far from believing that negro suffrage is a remedy for all of our national ills, I doubt whether it is a remedy for any, and rather believe that its enforcement by Congress would be more likely to subject the negro to a merciless persecution, than to confer upon him any substantial benefit. By some it is thought that suffrage is already cheap enough in this country; and the immediate transfer of more than a half million of men from the bonds of slavery, with all the ignorance and degradation upon them which the slavery of generations upon Southern fields has produced, would be a declaration to the world that the exercise of American suffrage involves no intellectual or moral qualifications, and that there is no difference between an American freeman and an American slave, which may not be removed by a mere act of Congress.

Mr. Spalding, a Radical Representative from Ohio, in the course of a debate in the House, on the 18th of March, 1868, on a bill making universal suffrage obligatory on the States said:

I wish to remark that only last October I was called upon, as a citizen of Ohio, to vote on the proposition to amend the Constitution of that State by inserting a right for the free black to vote, equally with the white. I not only voted cheerfully for that provision as amendatory of my State Constitution, but I used all my influence with the citizens in my section of the State to induce them to engraft that provision on our State Constitution. It was unsuccessful. We were in advance of the sentiment of our people, and they voted it down by forty thousand majority. Now, I would like to see the member of Congress from the State of Ohio who would come here and have the boldness to vote for the passage of this bill, which cuts directly, in my judgment, across the Constitution of the United States, and really decides the action of the people of my State, who have refused to insert in their own Constitution of State government this general right of suffrage for the blacks as well as the whites.

Sir, I believe the day may come when our Constitution, the great bulwark of our liberties, shall be so amended as that all free people may vote at the polls. God hasten the day when that right shall be extended! But so long as the Constitution remains as it is, I will suffer my right arm to drop from its socket sooner than vote for any such bill as that now before the House. In saying this, I am bold to affirm that I speak the sentiment of a large majority of my colleagues on this floor, irrespective of party. I should regard the passage of this bill at this hour as the death-knell of our hopes as a political party in the Presidential canvass.

In the course of the debate it came out that the Supreme Court of Pennsylvania had decided, under the *old* Constitution of that State, framed in the year 1790, that the word "freeman" meant *white freeman*, and that, in the present Constitution (framed about thirty years ago), the word "white" had been expressly introduced. Moreover, it appears that, only a few days ago, in the lower House of the Pennsylvania Legislature—a body in which the Republicans have a large majority—out of *ninety* members, *only thirteen* voted in favor of negro suffrage. It appeared, moreover, that, by a recent decision of Judge Agnew—a man placed on the bench of the Supreme Court of Pennsylvania by the Republican party—it had been determined that a negro had no right to a seat in a railway car provided for the accommodation of white people. In short, it appeared that the Pennsylvania Radicals, in advocating the doctrine of universal suffrage and universal social equality, did so with reference to the Southern States, and not with reference to Pennsylvania, as does the Radical Platform adopted at Chicago.

James Hughes, of Indiana, says the Cincinnati *Enquirer*, is one of the ablest and most prominent of the Radical leaders in that State. He is a bold and positive man, of very decided views upon public questions. He is the intimate friend of Morton, and of other Republican leaders, and is thoroughly acquainted with their secret views and with the objects at which they ultimately aim. As a member of the Indiana Legislature from Monroe county he lately gave an account of his stewardship, at Bloomington. The Indianapolis *Herald* had a special reporter there, who thus reports the leading portion of his speech:

"I am opposed to negro suffrage, not because they are negroes, or are black, for those are matters of taste and prejudice, but because the right of suffrage has already been too much extended and cheapened in this country. While I am opposed to extending the right of suffrage to the negroes, I am in favor of disfranchising one-half the white people in this country. Our fathers committed a great and fatal mistake in extending as they did the right of suffrage. All history proves that there is but one interest that is conservative, and that can be safely intrusted with the governing power, and that is the property interest. When a man is possessed of property he has a stake in the country and desires a strong and stable government, and will not endanger his property by unwise legislation or by involving the country in war. The great defect in our form of government has been the want of strength and power in the Federal Government. It will be impossible to govern this vast and rapidly increasing country under the operation of universal suffrage. Our system of government has been materially and radically changed during the war, and it can never be restored to what it was prior to the war. The Constitution is not worth the paper upon which it is written. The first effect of universal suffrage will be to make the Government more nearly approach a pure democracy, but this can not last long. We will follow the example of other governments. The strife of factions will go on until, ultimately, either the Senate or the President will assume the control, when we will have a strong and stable government. The British Government is the best government that has ever existed on the face of God's earth, and the sooner ours assimilates itself to that of the British Government, the better it will be for the country. I do not hesitate to declare, no matter how unpopular it may be, that if the negro race, and one-half of the white race, had good masters and mistresses, they would be much better off and the Government would be safer and stronger."

Reservations of the States.

DANGERS OF CONSOLIDATION—INSTRUCTIONS TO DELEGATES IN THE CONTINENTAL CONGRESS.

The Pennsylvania instructions contain the following reservation:

"Reserving to the people of this colony the sole and exclusive right of regulating the internal government and police of the same."

And, in a subsequent instruction, in reference to suppressing the British authority in the colonies, Pennsylvania uses this language:

"Unanimously declare our willingness to concur in a vote of the Congress declaring the United Colonies free and independent States, provided the forming the government and the regulation of the internal police of this colony be alway reserved to the people of the said colony."

Connecticut, in authorizing her delegates to vote for the Declaration of Independence, attached to it the following condition:

"Saving that the administration of government, and the power of forming governments for, and the regulation of the internal concerns and police of each colony, ought to be left and remain to the respective colonial legislatures."

New Hampshire annexed this proviso to her instructions to her delegates to vote for independence:

"Provided the regulation of our internal police be under the direction of our own Assembly:

New Jersey imposed the following condition:

"Always observing that, whatever plan of confederacy you enter into, the regulating the internal police of this province is to be reserved to the colonial legislature"

Maryland gave her consent to the Declaration of Independence upon the condition contained in this proviso:

"And that said colony will hold itself bound by the resolutions of a majority of the United Colonies in the premises, provided the sole and exclusive right of regulating the internal government and police of that colony be reserved to the people thereof."

Virginia annexed the following condition to her instructions to vote for the Declaration of Independence:

"Provided that the power of forming government for, and the regulations of the internal concerns of the colony, be left to respective colonial legislatures."

Debate in the Convention which Framed the Constitution.

John Dickinson, adverted in the Convention, with prophetic and far-seeing sagacity, to the division of the country into distinct States as "the chief source of *stability*" to our political system. "It is this," he said, "which is the ground of my consolation for the future fate of my country. Without this, and in case of the consolidation of the States into one great republic, we might read its fate in the history of those which have gone before it."

Mr. Rives, in his second volume of the Life of Madison, shows with how much jealousy and alarm the Eastern States in the Convention contemplated the future growth and power of the new States of the West. Mr. Governor Morris, though at that time a delegate of the State of Pennsylvania, was made the spokesman and interpreter of this jealous feeling of the Eastern States. He said:

"He looked forward to that range of new States which would soon be formed in the West. These States will know less of the public interest than the old; will have an interest, in many respects, different; in particular, will be little scrupulous of involving the country in wars, the burdens and operations of which would fall chiefly on the maritime States. Among other objections," he added, "it must be apparent they would not be able to furnish men, equally enlighted, to share in the administration of the common interests. If the Western people get the power into their hands, they will ruin the Atlantic interests." Finally, he said, "seeing the dangers from this quarter, he should be obliged to vote for the vicious principle of equality in the second branch, in order to provide some defense to the Northern States against it;" and he also declared that "he thought the rule of representation in the first branch ought to be so fixed as to secure to the Atlantic States the prevalence in the national councils."

This hint was immediately taken by Mr. King and Mr. Gerry, of Massachusetts; and the latter, repeating the alarm sounded by Mr. Morris, and declaring that "if the Western States acquire power they will abuse it, will oppress commerce, and draw our wealth into the Western country," actually submitted to the Convention a proposition that, whatever might be the future population of the new States of the West, "the total number of their representatives shall *never* exceed the total number of the representatives of the old States." This invidious attempt on the part of some of the old States to bind the infant Hercules of the West in perpetual swaddling bands met with an indignant protest from others, and especially from the oldest of them all, Virginia. Col. Mason said:

"The new States of the West must be treated as *equals*, and subjected to no degrading discriminations. They will have the same pride and other passions which we have, and will either not unite with or speedily revolt from the Union, if they are not, in all respects, placed on an *equal footing* with their brethren."

Mr. Madison said: "With regard to the Western States, I am clear and firm in the opinion that no unfavorable distinctions are admissible, either in point of justice or policy."

The proposition of Mr. Gerry and Mr. King was rejected—Massachusetts, Connecticut, Maryland and Delaware voting for it; New Jersey, Virginia, North Carolina, South Carolina and Georgia against it, and Pennsylvania divided.

The great principle of the equal right of all the States, says Mr. Rives, to representation in the national councils by one and the same rule, was thus victoriously and permanently established in the Constitution against all the efforts and devices of sectional jealousy or ambition to thwart and defeat it.

In September, 1796, we find in Washington's Farewell Address, this language:

"The alternate domination of one faction over another, sharpened by the spirit of revenge, natural to party dissension, which in different ages and countries has perpetrated the most horrid enormities, is itself a frightful despotism. But this leads at length to a more formal and permanent despotism. The disorders and miseries, which result, gradually incline the minds of men to seek security and repose in the absolute power of an individual; and sooner or later the chief of some prevailing faction, more able or more fortunate than his competitors, turns this disposition to the purposes of his own elevation on the ruins of the public liberty."

"An extremity of this kind," he adds, "ought not to be entirely out of sight."

Is not this prophetic of the existing condition of things in the nation, and will not the whole prophesy be fulfilled if Grant is elected?

Mr. Calhoun, in his speech on the National Bank, September 26, 1837, speaking of the States' Rights party, said:

We are the sworn enemies both of executive and legislative usurpations; and of the two, more opposed, if possible, to the latter than the former; because in the nature of things, they must take precedence in the order of time. Without legislative, there could be no executive usurpations. Congress must first encroach on the powers of the States before the executive can become strong enough to encroach on its powers;

These views were not altogether original with Mr. Calhoun; for in his speech on the joint resolution in reference to the Madison Papers, February 20, 1837, he said that

> He had been much struck with the sagacity and foresight of Mr. Jefferson, in a remark of that great statesman, that legislative usurpation would always precede executive, but that executive would always succeed legislative usurpation.

Warnings.

Washington left this solemn warning to his countrymen:

> The spirit of encroachment tends to consolidate the departments all in one, and thus to create, whatever the form of government, a *real despotism*. The necessity of reciprocal checks in the exercise of the political power, by dividing and distributing it into different depositories, and constituting each the guardian of public weal against invasions by the others, has been evinced by experiments ancient and modern, some of them in our country, and under our own eyes.—[*Farewell Address.*

James Madison said:

> The accumulation of all powers, legislative, executive and judiciary, in the same hands, whether of one or few, or many, may be called the definition of tyranny.—[*Federalist.*

John Adams said:

> A total separation of the Executive from the Legislative power, and of the Judicial from both, and a balance in the Legislature by three independent equal branches, and perhaps the three only discoveries in a constitution of a free government since the institutions of Lycurgus. * * If not invented by the English nation, they have never been imitated by any other except by their own descendants in America. If there is one certain truth to be collected from the history of all ages, it is this: that the people's rights and liberties, and the democratical mixture in a constitution can never be preserved without a strong Executive, or, in other words, without separating the executive power from the legislative."—[*History of Republics.*

The present condition of our national affairs was thus painted lately by a Pennsylvania statesman. Mr. Woodward said:

> He looked upon any interference whatever with the course of judicial action as not only a great indelicacy, but as a most dangerous precedent. The Tenure of Office Bill had virtually destroyed the independence of the Executive Department of the Government, and now this bill was aimed at the Judicial Department. What were the people to understand? Just this—that the Legislative Department of the country was determined to consolidate all the powers of the Government in its own hands into a grand legislative oligarchy; the country to be governed by the legislature, and the legislature to be governed by—the Lord knew who.

The Corruption of the Radical Party.

WHERE THE PEOPLE'S MONEY GOES—RADICAL CORRUPTION THE BASIS OF OUR FINANCIAL TROUBLES.

In a speech in the House of Representatives, January 9, 1868, Mr. Marshall, of Illinois, truly said that a majority of the Federal officials seemed to have adopted the maxim:

> A little thieving is a dangerous art,
> But thieving largely is a noble part;
> As vile to rob a hen-roost of a hen,
> But stealing largely makes us gentlemen.

Is it to be wondered that the National Debt is increasing; that high tariffs and onerous tax bills are fashionable, when the party which holds the legislative power of the Government is represented by men who bask in fortunes accumulated in forays on the public treasury, and who uphold every dishonest official against the power of removal vested by the Constitution in the President, if he belongs to the dominant party and contributes to its political successes from his ill-gotten gains, and augments the personal fortunes of their party leaders?

Behold, fellow-citizens, the unblushing effrontery with which a high man of the Radical party boasts upon the floor of Congress that he had made the experiment of buying high public officials. Mr. John Covode, of Pennsylvania, said in the House of Representatives, in a debate on the Pacific Raiload Bill (we quote from the N. Y. *Tribune's* report of the proceedings of May 12, 1868):

Mr. Covode (Rep.), Penn., spoke as one having experience in organizing transportation, and declared that railroads in Pennsylvania could afford to carry freight for one-third of what it could be carried for on the Pacific Railroad; one reason being the supply of fuel in Pennsylvania, and the absence of it along the lines of the Pacific Railroad. The time had not come to fix the tariff of prices on the Pacific Railroad. If he owned the Pacific Railroad he would not hesitate a moment if he wanted to charge exhorbitant prices. He could buy three men cheaper than he could buy two hundred, he had made the experiment [laughter], and knew what could be done with the head of a department. He had acquired some knowledge on the subject at this session. The heads of departments were purchasable if members of Congress were, and should know better than the representatives of the people what the wants of the people were.

Mr. Elliot asked Mr. Covode the average price of members of the Cabinet, but the gentleman made no reply.

A fit accompaniment to this shameless boast of Mr. Covode, was the declaration of Mr. Thaddeus Stevens, a few days afterward. Certainly, if a man could not be hurt by perjury, stealing would not destroy him:

Mr. Ross—I ask the gentleman from Pennsylvania whether, in his opinion, Senators would be justified in perjuring themselves for the purpose of procuring a conviction of the President.

Mr. STEVENS—Well, sir, I do not think it would hurt them.

FIVE RADICAL SENATORS FOR SALE.

Colonel Edmund Cooper, Assistant Secretary of the Treasury, in his examination before the House Managers, was asked whether he had been approached on the subject of using money for acquittal of the President. He answered he had; that a person professing to act on authority of Hon. S. C. Pomeroy, Senator from Kansas, proposed that for $40,000, cash in hand, he (Pomeroy) would control four Radical votes in the Senate and his own, so as to insure the acquittal of the President. The witness professed to doubt his authority, and then the person brought a letter from Senator Pomeroy, dated Senate Chamber, day blank, substantially as follows:

Sirs: I will, in good faith, carry out any arrangement made with my brother-in-law, Willis Gaylord, to which I am a party.
S. C. POMEROY,
United States Senate.

Gen. Butler objected to the witness testifying as to the substance of the letter, saying that he (Butler) would produce it then.

Willis Gaylord was then introduced by the person who first called on witness, and read the letter to witness and Gaylord. The person who first came then retired.

Thereupon Mr. Gaylord renewed the proposition contained in the letter, namely: $40,000 to secure five votes, and the patronage of the Administration to be thrown in for Pomeroy in the State of Kansas.

The witness believed that this proposition from the Senator was intended to entrap him, and, acting under that belief, determined that he would lead them on until he could expose them. The witness assigned as reasons for this belief, that the Senator was a strong partisan; that he felt bitterly toward the President, and that if money was his object, the party to which he belonged was much better able to pay than the Administration.

In addition to which, the person, in enumerating the names of Senators which Mr. Pomeroy proposed to control, included the name of Mr. Morton, of Indiana, and witness did not believe such an assertion to be possible. The name of Senator Nye was also included.

The interviews with witness were sought by the party professing to act for Senator Pomeroy. He brought letters showing his authority to so act.

On this point, the Louisville *Journal*, which enjoys the reputation of being cautious in its statements, avers that General Steedman offered the Impeachment Managers a dinner if they would examine him, and that he agreed to prove that Senator Pomeroy's vote was offered him for ten thousand dollars.

SENATOR POMEROY'S PREVIOUS CHARACTER.

The Leavenworth (Kansas) *Conservative* thus enlightens us in regard to Pomeroy's antecedents. It says:

"Pomeroy and his brother-in-law have been in this business of buying and selling before. The first adventure of this kind in Kansas, was in the Legislature of 1861, when he purchased forty-nine Republican members to support him for Senator, over Marcus J. Parrott, and paid them out of the money deposited with him by the generous people of the East, to purchase food and raiment for the starving poor of Kansas. Men are now living in Kansas who know about the amount paid to each member, and who saw a portion of the money paid to be purchased. It appears he is not now in the purchasing line; he is occupying the *role* of salesman! Kansas! are you not proud of your Senator?"

Thurlow Weed on the Same Subject.

In the New York *Commercial Advertiser*, of the 27th, appears the following from Thurlow Weed, its editor:

"What is given of my testimony, with one or two not important errors, is given accurately. It contains nothing to explain or regret. I have neither done an act, nor said a word, in relation to the impeachment and trial of the President, that I would not do and say again.

"If the result of my information and observations teaches me anything, it is that Senators Grimes, Fessenden, Fowler, Henderson, Trumbull, Ross and Van Winkle, voted upon their convictions of duty.

"In explanation of the propositions made to myself, I have just this to say:

"Senator Pomeroy either intended to dispose of three votes (including his own) or he was willing that his friends should use his name to make money; or, as some believe, there was a conspiracy between Butler and Pomeroy to implicate the President, thus obtaining new material for impeachment.

"My reasons for this belief are, that several months since Mr. Leggett, an intimate friend of Senator Pomeroy, wanted the appointment of Postmaster at Leavenworth, Kansas. He was supported by Pomeroy, who wrote a letter which was shown to the Postmaster-General, promising his (Pomeroy's) vote for Presidential confirmation, and his influence against impeachment. The Postmaster-General was furnished with a copy of Senator Pomeroy's letter (copied from the original in his possession), and Leggett received a postal agency. Some three weeks ago Leggett appears before Colonel Cooper with a letter from Senator Pomeroy, saying that he would carry out in good faith any 'arrangements' made with Mr. Gaylord, who is Pomeroy's brother-in-law; whereupon Leggett and Gaylord undertake, for money, to obtain the votes of Senators Pomeroy, Nye and Tipton. I did not believe that Senators Nye and Tipton had authorized this 'arrangement,' nor did I believe that either of them would vote against the conviction of the President. But I did and do believe that Senator Pomeroy baited the hooks with which his friend Leggett, and his brother-in-law, Gaylord, fished. Whether they caught anything or not I am unable to say. Nothing, certainly, from me, or with my consent.

"THURLOW WEED."

Beast Butler Bluffed by a Witness.

Mr. Cornelius Wendell being before the Radical Managers for examination— Butler presented a telegram to the witness, signed "C. W.," and asked him if it was his. Wendell declined answering, and Butler threatened to consign him to prison to keep Woolley company. "No you won't," said Wendell. "You have one white elephant on hand now, and don't know what to do with it; besides, if I tell anything, I shall tell all I know. Do you wish me to do so, General?"

Here the witness gave General Butler a significant look, when the latter promptly replied:

"No further questions. If the Managers wanted the witness again, they would send for him."

What Is It?

Manager Logan, who was present, remarked, aside: "What could witness have known which Butler did not wish told?" That's the question.

A Radical Organ on this Subject.

The New York *Evening Post*, a Radical paper, says that the offer to Mr. Cooper, supposed to come from Mr. Pomeroy, was to sell his own vote and those of Senators Nye and Tipton, for thirty thousand dollars. This offer, if it really deserves so much noise as has been made over it, would certainly indicate that votes were a drug in the market, and that the wealthy Kansas Senator and his friends, in entering on the business, had determined at once to fix their rates so low as to defy competition. For the present, it is safe to decline believing that the proposition was other than a trap set to catch Mr. Johnson, but sprung very curiously on its authors.

What Senator Trumbull Hints About it.

Mr. Trumbull, a gentleman who weighs his words well, and never commits himself to important statements without strong evidence for them, has written to his friend, Mr. Kœrner, as follows:

"The stories about corruption or improper motives influencing any Republican to vote against conviction are, of course, false. *All the pressure, and it was very great—more than you know of—was on the other side, as an investigation. if one is ever had, will show.* But for outside pressure, I think no such vote as thirty-five could have been obtained for conviction on the eleventh article."

A Grave Suspicion of Butler.

A Washington special to the Indianapolis *Journal* gives the following account of a tilt between the Beast and a witness, supposed to be Mr. Valkenburgh:

Butler was awfully indignant at a charge that he attempted to appropriate a one thousand dollar bill of Woolley's money. The following is the statement received from the witness:

Butler—"What became of the money Woolley left in your hands?"

Witness—"I have it in my pocket."

Butler—"Produce it, and the papers contained in the envelope."

Witness—"Here is the money; the papers you can't have."

Butler received the package of money, and directed the witness to leave the room, which he declined to do, saying he was responsible for the money, and was not willing to leave it in Butler's hands.

Butler threatened to arrest him.

Witness denied his power.

Butler proceeded to count the money, and said, "I find here $16,100."

Witness—"I'll swear I handed you $17,100."

Butler—"Then you had better count it yourself."

Witness—"If you will raise that newspaper, I think you will find a thousand dollar bill under it."

Manager Logan now, for the first time, interfered and remarked: "Yes, General, I see the corner sticking out."

Butler—"Oh, yes! I did not see it."

The statement has been made public on authority of the witness, who is a gentleman of known integrity, and the matter is the topic of general conversation.

How they Accuse each Other.

The debate between Donnelly and Washburne, two leading Radical members of Congress, will be remembered for its indecency. They charged each other with every known crime except murder. An investigating committee of Radical members whitewashed the affair thus:

They found, in regard to what took place in the House, that Mr. Donnelly withdrew the offensive portions of his speech, and disclaimed any imputation upon the honesty, integrity or private character of Mr. Washburne, whereupon the latter gentleman withdrew what he said about Donnelly. This disposed of the matter so far as what occurred in the debate was concerned, but left remaining the letter written by Mr. Washburne, which the committee next considered. They found in it no charge of bribery or corruption against Mr. Donnelly, as a member of Congress, but only charges touching his action and character years before he came to Congress, and thereupon determined that such matters were not a proper subject for investigation by the House. Mr. Donnelly asked their investigation, and Mr. Washburne held himself ready to show the grounds of his allegations with the fullest inquiry by calling witnesses to sustain all his charges. The committee refused, however, to enter upon the investigation, and directed its chairman to ask the House to discharge them from further consideration of the subject.

This is cool, considering the manner they spoke of each other, which is well illustrated by the following extract from the speech of Donnelly. He says of Washburne:

"If there be in our midst one low, sordid, vulgar soul, of barely mediocre intelligence, one heart callous to every kindly sentiment and every generous impulse, one tongue leprous with slander, one mouth which is like unto a den of foul beasts giving forth deadly odors; if there be here one character which, while blotched and spotted all over, yet raves and rants and blackguards like a prostitute, it is the gentleman from Illinois."

This is the man who "carries Ulysses S. Grant in his breeches pocket."

How a Poor Senator Becomes Mysteriously Rich.

Senator Harlan, says the Des Moines *Statesman*, was not worth one thousand dollars, and was teaching school and preaching a little for his daily bread, when he was elected to the United States Senate twelve years ago. He has lived for four years in a house in Washington City, for which he paid thirty thousand dollars, and the furniture of the house cost twenty thousand dollars; the yearly expenses of his family average from seven to ten thousand dollars a year; he also has a private residence in Mount Pleasant, worth twelve thousand dollars; and all this money—*where did it come from?* His salary as Senator has never more than half paid his expenses of living—where did the *balance* of the money come from? O Senator Harlan, Senator Harlan, you are a gay deceiver! Under the pretense of laboring to free the nigger, you have burdened your pockets with the "root of all evil." Under the guise of a minister of the Gospel, you have imposed taxes upon the people grievous to be borne. You are now laboring to subvert the liberties of the American people; take care, lest the oak you are bending rebound not to your destruction.

The Transactions of a Massachusetts Member of Congress at New Orleans.

The many charges of corruption which attached to Beast Butler's administration as Major-General commanding at New Orleans, induced the Government to cause a little inquiry, and accordingly the keen and witty James T. Brady, of New York, and Gen. Baldy Smith, were commissioned to make the necessary investigations, which they did, making a voluminous report to the Secretary of War, containing statements the most damaging to the reputation of General Butler. Congress, with its characteristic curiosity, after some time had elapsed, also determined to know something about the secrets unfolded by Messrs. Brady and Smith, and adopted a resolution calling for their report. The resolution was adopted, but the indomitable Secretary of War declined to gratify Congress, on the ground that "the good of the public service demanded that the desired documents should not be made public." This accounts for the milk in the Cocoa-nut. Beast Butler's zeal in behalf of Stanton's continuance in the War Department arose from a prudent concern for his own interests. Stanton is alleged to have destroyed this report before leaving. A correspondent got a peep at it, before its decease, and gives the following extracts from the evidence. It was published in the New York *Herald* and Brooklyn *Eagle*:

Mr. Jacob Barker, examined February 9, 1865—States that when General Butler arrived in New Orleans he told witness that he had no money, or very little, in the military chest—about $100; witness at his request loaned him $5,000, afterward paid; "about this time he told me (Barker) that he wanted more money, $100,000, on his own account, for his bill in Boston; I agreed to let him have it; he took the greater portion, for which he gave me his exchange on Boston, which was honorably paid;" "of this money he drew most of it on me for gold in favor of his brother; subsequently he told me that his object in this negotiation was to get funds to loan his brother."

Mr. B. F. Smith, examined 27th February, 1865.—A resident of New Orleans for twenty-two years; was there when General Butler arrived; that he was interested with Col. A. J. Butler, brother of General Butler, in carrying goods across the lake, consisting of salt, quinine, shoes, corn, groceries and liquors, which went mostly into the hands of the rebels, as Col. Butler well knew; he (witness) received one-third of the profits realized upon them. The witness was asked, "Do you believe that General Butler knew about this trade?" "Yes, sir; I told him; he asked me the question; and thirteen thousand dollars' worth went after that;' Gen. Butler had informed him that no more goods should go out unless cotton returned; went to the rebel authorities—General Lovell; returned and told him (Butler) what General Lovell had said; had no difficulty in getting in or out; had five or six schooners chartered; Colonel Butler got everything fixed up; French, Provost-Marshal-General under Butler, signed the passes; that after his interview with the rebel General he reported progress to General Butler and Colonel Butler, and that the cotton came in and the goods went out; value of the goods between $12,000 and $13,000; 196 bales of cotton at 45 cents a pound; Colonel Butler did not give him $2,500; the rebel party offered witness $10,000 for his interest in the thing. States further—Does not know what his claim was against Butler, but that he was to have one-third of the net proceeds; paid ten cents a pound for the cotton, and got forty-five cents, amounting to about $30,000; made about two hundred per cent. on the goods; salt sold at thirty dollars per sack; made about seventy-five per cent. upon the cotton. Witness further says that he was a rebel at the time, and did not take the oath until after these transactions.

W. W. Watson, examined March 1, 1865.—states that the witness Smith did a great deal of business during General Butler's administration; at the time he saw Smith the business was not carried on very well, and Smith told Gen. Butler that he would retire; says he has no doubt he filled out the General's passes in a written form; saw his book and his passes that were not signed by the General, but that General Butler filled the passes up; witness proceeds: "He (Smith) cleared three vessels from here (New Orleans) to Matamoras, among which was the Mary Davis; when Admiral Farragut was informed of it he sent a gun-boat and took the supercargo (Reed), General Butler's brother-in-law; Farragut took his pass and went up to the General with it, and asked him if that was his handwriting, to which the General replied, "That is A. J.'s handwriting." A. J. Butler was then arrested and paroled, and afterward taken up by a picket and brought back to New Orleans, and having given security in $30,000 bond, finally ran away. The permits Colonel Butler made out contained a great variety of articles, and instanced one, to a man named Long, to take a vessel of about eighty tons to Mobile, laden with provisions, etc. He was to bring back the money belonging to the Merchant's Bank. Colonel Butler and Mr. French made out the list of medicines, and assisted in getting the medicines to send by this vessel; says that he has reason to suppose that General Butler was interested in these operations, but did not know the fact, but gives as a reason that they had no money until General Butler got $320,000 out of the city treasury, and that he saw the first thousand dollars counted out on the table in Colonel Butler's office. General Butler, General Shepley and Duer gave an order to deliver this money to A. J. Butler, and it passed into his hands; did not see the money used, but A. J. Butler asked him to pass $20,000 to a planter on the coast, which he refused to do; states further that A. J. Butler was engaged in removing crops from plantations to the city; boat used was guarded by from twenty five to fifty soldiers; the boat would return to the city with 700 or 800 hogsheads of sugar, and he understood that this sugar was seized and sent to New York through the hands of A. J. Butler & Co., or their agents; the boats employed were the Iberville, Laura Hill, the Empire Parish and the Lieutenant Morris, which were in the employ of the United States Government; the Iberville was chartered by Col. Schaffer and Mr. Bloomer, who did the outside business for Butler, at five thousand dollars per month; these boats paid no freight to the Quartermaster's Department; witness paid the wagoners and teamsters employed in the work; the boats all passed out of the port of New Orleans free of any charge or tax; says he suggested to General Butler that the Government transports might be ballasted with sugar; the General replied that it would not be proper, for the port was not open, but finally said he might do so, provided it was "sand" instead of "sugar;" did not pay Butler any freight upon this ballast; but commenced going around to persons who wanted to ship sugar to New York, and told them that it would be taken for ten dollars a hogshead, and to say that it was sand if any inquiries were made about it; the port was not opened until the middle of June; this sugar was shipped in May; General Butler said it would break the blockade in the eyes of foreign governments if we were found shipping from here (New Orleans) before the port was opened; when Colonel Butler came here (New Orleans), he sent Capt. Turner and desired an introduction to me (Watson); I went down, and he (the Colonel) stated that he had been informed I was the only person capable or willing to do business, and as there was a great deal of shipping to be done, that if I would do it he would furnish offices, stationery and clerks, and would divide with me; I declined doing so, when he sent for me again and insisted on my doing so; I heard him say to the captains of vessels, "When you arrive in New York, lay off in the harbor, go to the Quartermaster and get your charter cancelled, then haul alongside the pier and discharge your cargo to the consignees, who will pay you two dollars a hogshead; keep your mouths shut." States that he engaged the freight for ten dollars a hogshead; does not know what became of the other eight dollars, but supposed the Government consigned to the Quartermaster and collected the freight in New York; supposed everything was proper; Colonel Schaffer cancelled his bonds by paying $60,000, as they would not bear investigation. (Pages 149 to 156.)

George Honnewell, examined May 5, 1865, states that on the 17th of September, 1862, Gen. Butler compelled him to sell to him the steamer Nassau for $31,360 in current funds; he called it $28,000 in greenbacks; he gave me his check on the Citizens' Bank for $31,360, equal to $28,000 in United States Treasury notes; I had offered to charter her to the Government for $50 a day, and if that was too much they might have had her for $40; he (Butler) said he was going to send her on a perilous errand and could not charter her; Gen. Butler sold the steamer a few days afterward for $40,000 in greenbacks; he afterward chartered her to the Government for $350 a day—$10,500 a month; I saw the check for the first month's charter.

The public interest which demands the suppression of these facts required Stanton's retention in office, to screen other delinquents, and accounts for the onslaught on the Executive.

A Disinterested Legislator.

A Washington correspondent, speaking of things at the Capital, writes:

Apropos of the great deal that is being said about the motives of the seven Republican Senators in voting against impeachment, it is not unworthy of remark that a great deal of the legislation of Congress is engineered and pushed forward by members and Senators who are personally and pecuniarily interested in its success. This is notably the case in regard to that vast amount of legislation which takes place every year in the interest of the Pacific Railroad. A great work this railroad is, no doubt, but its importance would not be materially lessened if Congressmen were not stockholders to the extent that they are. Mr. Oakes Ames, of Massachusetts, is a member of the House Committee on the Pacific Railroad. He owns a million dollars' worth of stock in the enterprise. So of other members of the committee, in the

Senate as well as in the House. Under this state of the case it is not much wonder that every day or two there comes from the committee a bill for a big subsidy in money or land for an enterprise in which the Government has already sunk millions of dollars, which it may reasonably expect never to see again in this world or the next. I shall not be guilty of impugning the motives of so patriotic a gentleman as Mr. Ames. In all he does as a member of the committee, he is, of course, influenced by no considerations but those of the public good. He never, for a moment, thinks of the million dollars in stock which he has at home, nor how it may be affected in value by any action of his committee. But, after all, wouldn't it be creditable to his disinterestedness either to sell his stock or withdraw from the committee?

The New Radical Secretary of the Senate.

The New York correspondent of the Charleston *Courier*, in his letter of the 6th, says:

The choice of Gorham as Secretary of the Senate to succeed Forney, tells the story. This man has always been known in California as the most notorious lobbyist, who bought his Republican nomination for the Governorship last year, and so disgusted the honest voters that every Republican paper in San Francisco opposed his election. Defeated by the most honest men in his State, by his own party friends in his own home, the revolutionary faction of the Senate takes him to its own bosom, to make use of him while the dirty work of tampering with the electoral votes is going on.

The St. Louis *Democrat*, a leading Radical organ, last September, when the news came of the overthrow of the Radicals by the Democracy of California, accounted for the defeat of its friends on the ground that the Radical candidates and leaders were such a set of rascals that the Radical voters of California would not support them. Alluding to the charges made against Gorham by the Radical papers of California, the *Democrat* said: "It is claimed that he obtained the nomination (for Governor) by foul means, and that he has been a legislative corruptionist." And then it adds: "His election would have been regarded as the triumph of rascality and fraud." It administered the lash to its corrupt party, a portion of whom nominated Gorham, and said: "It is high time that the Republican party should learn it can not nominate *corruptionists* with impunity." And then it said that it rejoiced over Gorham's defeat, "because the defeat of unworthy men, by whatsoever party they may be nominated, is to be earnestly desired by every patriot and honest citizen."

These are but a few of the countless evidences which might be produced to exhibit the rotten corruption of the Radical party in Congress. It will not do for the Chicago Platform to lay at the door of the President the immense expense of administering the Government. He is powerless to spend a cent without a previous appropriation by Congress. All of the profligate sources of expenditure, such as the occupation of the Southern States by a standing army; their government at the expense of the National Treasury by extravagant military satraps, instead of by governments of their own, at their own cost; the Freedmen's Bureau; the heavy contingent extravagances of Congress, and all the other wasteful dissipations of the national finances, are emanations from Congressional recklessness and corruption, and are the objects of his vehement protests.

By the passage of the Tenure-of-Office Bill, they have stolen from him the power of dismissing dishonest officials, and by the action of their Senate, which fails to confirm his new appointments, the preying vultures of Radicalism are left to fatten upon the robbery and waste of the public Treasury, wrung from an impoverished and suffering people. This is no fancy picture. In the House of Representatives a short time since—

"Mr. Brooks called attention to the case of the Collector of the Eighth District of New York. That office had been badly filled, so that no revenue could be obtained, and he (Brooks) had, for over a year, made an effort to effect a change. Some five or six Democrats had been nominated by the President, and all of them rejected, until finally he had to recommend a Republican, whose appointment was confirmed. Thus, for over a year, under the Tenure-of-Office act, millions of, or certainly thousands on thousands of dollars had been lost to the revenue by the maladministration of that office.

"Mr. Woodward instanced a similar case in his district, where seven responsible men had been rejected one after another."

In the debate on the Tax Bill, in the discussion of the amendment offered by Mr. Jenckes to the 57th section, proposing to give to the District Attorney the power to discontinue suits in *qui tam* actions on a *nolle prosequi* in criminal cases—

"Mr. Schenck (Radical) argued against the amendment, and stated that 'the whisky ring' had its aiders and abettors as often in the District Attorneys as in all other officers in the law. He had in his mind one proof furnished to the Committee of Ways and Means—the case of a Judge in one of the Federal courts, and of a District Attorney, who had divided the black-mail between them, which was the consideration of them letting off some sixty culprits arraigned before the Court. He trusted that would result yet in an impeachment of that Judge. The committee ought not to throw everything into the power of the District Attorney so that he should hold a veto over all the cases. He was perfectly willing that in a proper case a District Attorney should have his remedy against any possibility of the ends of justice by continuing his case, if if witnesses are spirited out of the way."

The New Albany (Ind.) *Ledger* says: "We know a soldier who is minus an arm, and who was left on the battle-field for dead, who was nominated by the President for the position of Assessor of Internal Revenue for this district, but was nevertheless rejected by the Senate, simply and only because he was a Democrat, for his qualifications were undoubted. Such is a specimen of Radical love for armless soldiers. Such is the 'pride they take in bestowing civil offices upon men who honorably and efficiently served their country in the army.'"

The Whisky Ring at Richmond, Va.

The facts developed on the 11th of June, 1868, in the Federal Court at Richmond, the Chief-Justice presiding, show an astonishing degree of corruption among the "whisky ring" of that city. We give some of the particulars from the *Whig*:

"The parties on trial are J. H. Anderson, Collector of Internal Revenue; J. H. Patterson, Assessor; and Goldman Shepherd, Richard Anderson, Horatio Anderson, McCreary, Manson and Elsom, subordinates.

"Colonel Clarkson, one of the largest distillers in this section, testified that an agreement had been entered into by the distillers on the south side of the James, and John H. Anderson and John H. Patterson, internal revenue officers of the Fourth District, by which more than ten thousand dollars had been paid them for granting said distillers the privilege of shipping large quantities of spirits distilled by them, without the payment of the revenue tax. The aggregate loss to the Government by this arrangement was over $250,000. It was further agreed that these revenue officers should realize $50,000 annually for these privileges. Many of their subordinate officers were parties to the agreement and profited by their connection with it.

"Dr. Clendenin, the next witness, before testifying, desired to know whether an indictment could be found against him upon any testimony he might give in the case?

"Mr. Chandler, United States District Attorney, replied, that not upon any evidence he himself might give.

"In June or July, Mr. Goldman came to witness and said he thought he would not be doing justice to himself in the office he held unless he made some money above his salary. He then offered witness' firm certain privileges in evading the United States tax on whisky if it would give him $500. Witness referred him to his partner (Mr. Parrish), with whom the arrangement proposed was consummated. Under it a good deal of whisky was shipped, and the money promised the Government officers paid. A second contract was made, Mr. Parrish representing the Howlett distillery, in which witness also had an interest; Mr. Richard F. Walker, the Roxdale distillery, and Mr. Denmead, the Denmead distillery. The four distilleries were to pay $30,000 per annum, to be divided between them, for the privilege of shipping five-sixths of all the whisky they might distill free of Government tax——the revenue officers to make the arrangements by which this could be effected?"

The parties have since been convicted, and are in the New York penitentiary.

Who is Responsible?

Mr. McCulloch, Secretary of the Treasury, in his indorsement on Mr. Commissioner Rollins' resignation, fixes it:

"This communication is partial because it attributes the present deranged condition of the internal revenue service to the removals and appointments made by the President, while it must be clear to the mind of the Commissioner that this demoralization is attributable in part to the antagonism between the executive and legislative branches of the Government, which has prevented harmony of action between them in regard to appointments and to the Tenure-of-Office act, but mainly to the high duties upon distilled liquors, tobacco, etc., which have created an irresistible temptation to fraud on the part of revenue officers, as well as on the part of manufacturers, dealers, and others.

"It is incorrect in that it alleges that the numerous recommendations of the Commissioner for removal of assessors and collectors, even for the grossest misconduct, have been almost always disregarded, while the truth is that in all cases in which recommendations for removals were accompanied by evidence of incompetency or misconduct on the part of the officers, the recommendations were promptly responded to by the President.

"It is unjust and disrespectful to the President, because the records of the bureau show that the falling off of the revenue in the districts in which removals were made by the President, in 1866, was not comparatively greater than in the districts in which no changes took place.

"That, in fact, the revenues of the fiscal year, ending June 20, 1867, during which the removals were made, were entirely satisfactory, coming up very closely to the liberal estimates of the department. The demoralization of the service and the decline of the revenues have chiefly occurred during the present fiscal year, long after the officers removed by the President had been reinstated, or others whose nominations had been approved by the Senate had taken the places of appointees of the President. It was for these reasons, and for no others, that the communication could not be received, and was returned to the Commissioner. The return of it is also justified by the fact that copies of it were sent to the press before it was handed to the Secretary. It must, therefore, have been intended for the public rather than for the files of the department.

HUGH McCULLOCH,
Secretary of the Treasury.
JUNE 13, 1868.

The Whisky Tax Stealing Business.

WHAT A RADICAL JOURNAL THINKS OF IT.

[From the New York Times.]

Of the seven collection districts in New York City, for instance, the distilling business is confined mainly to two; while in the third district (Brooklyn) the number of distilleries increased from about twenty in May, 1866, to upward of ninety by the 1st of the following September. It has been repeatedly proven that the whisky manufactured in this district for six months in that year, did not pay four cents on the gallon. Yet the officers of every district in this locality must suffer for the frauds committed in these two or three districts. It is a fact well known to all familiar with internal revenue matters, that the frauds which have so disgraced the country are mainly confined to some fifteen or sixteen districts, and to correct them it is only necessary to remove the present incumbents in these districts and put honest men in their places.

This done, and the service cleaned of a score or more of leeches in the shape of Inspectors, Special Agents, and Revenue Agents, it would be purged of corruption, and the revenue largely collected, even under the present law.

But they are not removed. On the contrary, men whose misconduct in office is well known and understood, are retained in office. This is distinctly stated by the Commissioner, and is assigned as his reason for resigning his office. The Secretary admits the fact, but insists that it is not the President who is responsible for this failure, but that it is to be attributed to the unfortunate conflict going on between the President and Congress. This, doubtless, is true; but the question still recurs, which party is it that, notwithstanding this controversy, is responsible for the failure to remove corrupt men from office?

* * The frauds in New York and elsewhere, in the winter and spring of 1867, were simply frightful, and they were largely, but not entirely, to be found in the districts where Mr. Johnson had made removals. In one of these districts, false and fraudulent bonds to the amount of about $750,000 were accepted, and whisky representing taxes to this amount was released from bond on them. In another district, on Saturday night, as the Collector was to surrender his office to his successor on the following Monday morning, he accepted a bond for one hundred thousand dollars, and released the whisky represented in it. But neither the principal nor either of the sureties who signed this bond could ever be found. But these frauds were by no means confined to the appointees of Mr. Johnson. Some of the worst men ever in the revenue service were the appointees of Mr. Lincoln. These frauds so reduced the market value of whisky that no man could afford to pay the tax, and fraud thus became a necessity of doing business under the law.

To prevent future changes for political reasons Congress passed the Tenure-of-Office Bill. By the provisions of this act, the President can not remove an officer even for cause.

If the officer is guilty of misconduct in office during a recess of the Senate, he may suspend him from office, but if the misconduct occurs during a session of Congress, the most he can do is to send a name to the Senate, the incumbent retaining the office until his successor is confirmed.

Notwithstanding the notorious corruption of the service, we believe it is a fact that *no person has ever been removed from office under this law.* Its only effect thus far has been to give practical immunity to thieves, and they have not been slow to avail themselves of its benefits.

To get a man out of office under this law you must first convince the Commissioner that the officer complained of has been guilty of misconduct in office. He must then convince the Secretary of the Treasury, who must convince the President, who must in turn convince the Senate.

In five or six cases we believe the Commissioner has succeeded in convincing the President that officers have been guilty of corruption in office. In these cases the President has suspended the delinquents and reported the cases to the Senate. It is a curious fact, one worth noting as we are passing along, that all of these delinquents were, we believe, Republicans. We do not intimate that this fact rendered it easy for the Commissioner to convince the President that these men had been guilty of misconduct in office, nor that it was this fact which made it difficult, and, in fact, impossible, for the President to convince the Senate of their guilt. In no instance, so far as we are informed, has the President found a Democrat guilty of such misconduct in office as to warrant his suspension from office; nor has the Senate, in any case, approved the suspension of a Republican. This fact tells the whole story of our difficulties.

Some Radical Officials Come to Grief.

AN EX-SPEAKER OF THE N. Y. ASSEMBLY IN THE PENITENTIARY.

[From the Rochester (N. Y.) Union.]

Dispatches from New York to-day announce the sentence of Theophilus C. Callicott, Collector of Internal Revenue, Richard C. Enright and John S. Allen, to the Albany penitentiary, for defrauding the Government of taxes to a large amount by means of bogus whisky bonds. The New York *Express* of last evening gives a sketch of the scene in court. Judge Nelson directed the prisoners to stand up, and after a few remarks on the enormity of their offenses, sentenced Callicott to imprisonment in the Albany Penitentiary for two years and to pay a fine of $10,000. Judge Benedict sentenced the other two—Enright to the Albany Penitentiary for eighteen months, and to pay a fine of $2,500, and Allen to be imprisoned in the same place for one year and to pay a fine of $2,000.

The return of Callicott to Albany as a convict in its penitentiary is suggestive. On attaining his majority he was a Democrat from principle, and soon after, when he entered active life as a lawyer, with fair natural and acquired talent, he showed such signs of promise that the Democracy of his district in Brooklyn elected him to the Assembly. This was in 1850. In 1863 he was re-elected. The Assembly of that year was politically a tie, and there was a long struggle for the Speakership. This struggle also involved the succession to Preston King in the United States Senate, Governor Morgan, who had just gone out of the Executive chair, being an ambitious candidate.

The Republican leaders were on the ground, prominent among them Horace Greeley, and they canvassed the entire Democratic side for a time in vain to find a Judas who would sell himself. Finally they debauched Callicott—bribed him with money, one of the checks for which, from the Republican State Committee, was unearthed at the time and exposed. Callicott was elected Speaker, Morgan was elected United States Senator, and all the villainous participants in the work for a time prospered. Callicott sought a re-election at the hands of his new-made friends. He ran as the "Union"—the "loyal" candidate, and had the active personal support of Horace Greeley and the open advocacy of the New York *Tribune*. The "loyal" men of the district, although they liked the treason, detested the traitor to his party, and out of a vote of 5,837 Callicott received just 272. Spurned on all sides by honest men, Greeley and Morgan still stood by their protege. They did not violate the well-known principle of honor among, etc. They induced the late lamented Lincoln to give Callicott a cotton agency on the Mississippi, and when that ran out they procured for him the Internal Revenue Collectorship, Morgan securing his confirmation against all the facts that were brought to bear as to his character, and showing his unfitness for the trust. From the Collectorship he goes back to Albany—not to resume the Speakership of the Assembly, but to occupy a felon's cell.

Hon. S. S. Marshall, of Illinois, in a Speech in the House of Representatives, January 9, 1868.

The men holding the public offices of the country under the Presidential appointment are men appointed either by Mr. Lincoln or Mr. Johnson with the approbation of the Senate of the United States. It is a notorious fact that no member of the Democratic party proper can pass the ordeal of the Senate for any appointment. The appointments throughout the country have been made from men within the Republican party. So far as my colleague's speech was intended to have a partisan bearing, let me say that he must know that the Democratic party proper has had no part or lot in the collection of the revenues of the Government. Secretary McCulloch stated on oath before the Judiciary Committee that nineteen out of twenty of the officials in his Department were not only not Democrats but Radicals, supporters of the policy of Congress; and Mr. Rollins, the Commissioner of Internal Revenue, admitted to be a strong Radical, was present when the testimony was given and assented to the statement. So it is all over the country.

The effort of my colleague to give this matter a partisan turn must be met, and may be rightfully met, in this way: in all Governments, frauds occasionally occur. Now and then, under every Administration, a scoundrel gets into office. Even under good old Democratic Administrations there occasionally got into office some man who perpetrated frauds upon the Government; but they were promptly turned out when the fact was discovered. It was not till the advent of the Republican party to power that robbery of the people became a fine art (laughter) and was indulged in all over the country. A distinguished Republican Senator from New Hampshire (Mr. Hale) has testified in the Senate, and a distinguished Republican Representative from Massachusetts (Mr. Dawes) has testified in this House, that more of the money of the people was stolen during the first year of Mr. Lincoln's Administration than the entire expenses of conducting the Government during the four years of Mr. Buchanan's Administration. And, sir, that inundation of thievery which commenced then has been growing and rolling and swelling from that day to this, until the people are brought to poverty in one section of the country and to starvation in another. If the party that brought about this thing has any remedy to offer, it is time the remedy should be presented. When the people are crying for relief from the enormous burdens which are weighing them down, it is high time that this party, now upon its last legs, and about to retire from power forever, should inaugurate some system by which the people may be hereafter protected from such robbery as that by which they have suffered. There are many ways of introducing reform and protecting the interests of the people. I know of one method which I think would be infallible, and I hope my colleagues, or if that be hopeless, at least that the honest masses who have been deceived by the false pretensions of the party in power, will join me in bringing about the desired reform.

I do not, I must confess, have very strong hopes that my colleague will unite in the proposed effort, but the remedy is a palpable one, and that is to go back to the old principles and practice of Democratic Administration, bring in a Democratic President and a Democratic Congress, and introduce the principles of economy and justice which were always carried out when that party was in power. Then this robbery of the people will cease. I will guarantee it, sir. The history of our Government, from its foundation to the present time, furnishes irrefragable evidence that this is the remedy, and now the only remedy.

My colleague proposes one plan by which to increase the revenue from the whisky tax. I propose another plan, and that is to get rid right now of this party which has thus wronged and oppressed the people, and brought desolation, ruin, mourning and woe to our fair land. Let the slick, unctuous gentlemen around me bow themselves out of these Halls, and let the old-fashioned Democratic Administration come into power, and I will guarantee that we will have an Administration which will relieve the people of the enormous burdens which are now crushing out their very lives, and that we will drive the thieves and money-changers in disgrace and ignominy from this great temple of liberty which they have been polluting and desecrating.

Mr. MAYNARD. Let me ask the gentleman a question. Mr. Floyd, one of the old fashioned economists, has unfortunately departed, but can he inform us whether Jacob Thompson is accessible, and what means we shall resort to in order to get him back? (Laughter.)

Mr. MARSHALL. I have heard charges against these men, and they may be true, but Mr. Buchanan's Administration was not a favorite of mine. I have, however, the testimony of leading Republicans for saying that the stealing during the first year of Mr. Lincoln's Administration amounted to a larger sum than it cost to run Mr. Buchanan's Administration for four years, stealing and all. (Great Laughter.)

This thing of stealing, sir, has become a wholesale business, and has grown to most appalling proportions since the advent of the Republican party to power, and it will cease, in my judgment, the very day that it goes out of power, and not one moment sooner. The present condition of the country, sir, ought not to be considered cause for surprise or wonder to any one who has brains enough to comprehend the natural and inevitable connection and sequence between cause and effect. Similar causes would produce similar results in any age or in any country. The Abolition, now called the Republican or Radical, party was founded on the maxim, which they spread out on their banners and boldly proclaimed to the world, that "the United States Constitution is a covenant with death and an agreement with hell," and that there was a higher law than the Constitution, and no man was bound by its provisions or obligations. And this party, since it came into power, has been true to this theory upon which it was founded. Every feature and principle of that sacred instrument, and every safeguard put there for the protection of the rights and liberties of the citizen, have been openly and defiantly trampled under foot by this party. And now its great leaders and Representatives upon this floor openly proclaim that they are administering the Government "outside of" and in open defiance of the Constitution. No wonder, Mr. Speaker, that all sense of moral obligation has been destroyed among their followers. No wonder that the floodgates have been broken down, and a deluge of crime, debauchery, and prostitution, political, moral, and social, has swept over the land. When the chosen and select prophets of the sect openly and defiantly disregard the sanctions and guarantees of that great charter which they have just sworn to support, why should we wonder that the lesser lights and disciples should feel resting lightly upon them the obligations of the commandment which says, "Thou shalt not steal," or be surprised when we see them engaged in wholesale plunder and debauchery?

It was the most natural thing in the world that, when the leaders were engaged in violating their duties to the country and its Constitution, the lesser lights should practice upon the rules of venality which has been laid down for them and go to filling their pockets. And they have done it with a vengeance.

These robbers are now rioting in luxury all over the land, while the honest, industrious laboring people are borne down with poverty and taxation. The very bread which they make by the sweat of their brow is wrested from them before it reaches the mouths of their children, and one-half of the revenue wrung from them is taken to feed and clothe lazy, vagabond negroes, or put into the hands and pockets of these plunderers.

This system must cease, and there is a remedy for it; and the only remedy is to go back to the original principles of the Government; to reinstate that party in power which for sixty years safely and economically carried on the Government, and successfully prosecuted two great foreign wars without any oppression of the citizen, any violation of the safeguards of the Constitution, and without sending one single Federal tax-gatherer among the people to eat out their substance.

And how dare my colleague or any gentleman, in the presence of public and well-known facts, charge any of these frauds upon the President or upon any one outside of the party now in power? By an act of Congress the President is stripped of his rightful power for the correction of these evils. He can not remove a single man from office, not even one of his own Cabinet ministers, or appoint a single man to office without the consent of your Radical Senate. The consequence is that, while the offices are now filled by Radicals, all new appointments must be made from that party. It is sufficient for the Senate to know that a man is a friend of the President or an opposer of the Radical measures of Congress to secure his rejection; and, therefore, rather than have these offices vacant that are necessary to be filled for the public service, he time and again sends in men of the Radical party, the very elect of the party, and they are the only ones who can be confirmed for positions of any importance. He has not the power to select men of his own choice. Why, even for the very highest offices in the land, although opposing Congress in its miscalled "reconstruction" policy, the President takes the elect of the Radical party. Look at our foreign missions where vacancies have occurred. Mr. Bancroft was appointed to one, and Mr. Raymond to another. Then Mr. Greeley, the very head and front of the party, was nominated for one of the first positions under the Government. It is not true that the President, even where he has had the power of appointment, has confined himself to his own friends in making the selection. He had been compelled, in all these revenue cases, so far as my knowledge extends, either to take men of the dominant party or those with whom they were satisfied, or leave the offices unfilled. And if, in selecting among them, he finds one thief out of a dozen, I do not think it is at all remarkable, and I am only surprised that he has not been more unlucky than he has in this particular.

The Object of the War, the Restoration of the Union.

In the House of Representatives, on the 22d of July, 1861, the day after the battle of Manassas, Mr. Crittenden offered the following resolution:

"*Resolved, That the present deplorable civil war has been forced upon the country by the disunionists of the Southern States now in revolt against the constitutional Government and in arms around the Capital;* that in this national emergency Congress, banishing all feeling of mere passion or resentment, will recollect only its duty to the whole country; that this war is not waged upon our part in any spirit of oppression, nor for any purpose of conquest or subjugation, nor purpose of overthrowing or interfering with the rights or established institutions of those States; but to defend and maintain the supremacy of the Constitution and to preserve the Union with all the dignity, equality, and rights of the several States unimpaired; that as soon as these objects are accomplished the war ought to cease."

The question being divided, the House adopted the first clause of the resolution, being the part in italics, by a vote of 122 to 2.

The second clause of the resolution, beginning with the words "that in this national," etc., and ending "the war ought to cease," was adopted—yeas 119, nays 2, as follows:

YEAS—Messrs. Aldrich, Allen, Alley, Babbitt, Goldsmith F. Bailey, Joseph Baily, Baxter, Beaman, Francis P. Blair, Samuel S. Blair, Blake, George H. Browne, Buffinton Calvert, Campbell, Chamberlain, Clark, Cobb, Colfax, F. A. Conkling, Roscoe Conkling, Cooper, Corning, Cox, Crittenden, Curtis, Cutler, Dawes, Delano, Diven, Duell, Dunlap, Dunn, Edwards, English, Fenton, Fessenden, Fouke, Franchot, Frank, Gooch, Granger, Grider, Gurley, Haight, Hale, Harding, Harrison, Holman, Horton, Jackson, Johnson, Kelley, William Kellogg, Killinger, Law, Lazear, Leary, Lehman, Logan, Loomis, McClernand, Mallory, Menzies, Mitchell, Moorhead, Anson P. Morrill, Justin S. Morrill, Morris, Nixon, Noble, Nugen, Odell, Olin, Patton, Pendleton, Perry, Pike, Pomeroy, Porter, Reid, Alexander H. Rice, John H. Rice, Richardson, Robinson, Edward H. Rollins, James S. Rollins, Sheffield, Shellabarger, Sherman, Smith, Spaulding, John B. Steele, William G. Steele, Stratton, Francis Thomas, Train, Trowbridge, Upton, Vallandigham, Van Horn, Van Valkenburgh, Van Wyck, Verree, Vibbard, Wadsworth, Charles W. Walton, E. P. Walton, Ward, Webster, Wheeler, Whaley, Albert S. White, Chilton A. White, Wickliffe, Windom, Woodruff, Worcester, Wright—119.

NAYS—Messrs. Potter, Riddle—2.

Every Radical, except two, voting for it.

July 24, 1861.—Mr. Johnson, of Tennessee, offered substantially the same resolution in the Senate, which was passed July 25—yeas 30, nays 5, as follows:

YEAS—Messrs. Anthony, Browning, Chandler, Clark, Cowan, Dixon, Doolittle, Fessenden, Foot, Foster, Grimes, Harlan, Harris, Howe, Johnson of Tennessee, Kennedy, King, Lane (of Indiana), Lane (of Kansas), Latham, Morrill, Nesmith, Pomeroy, Saulsbury, Sherman, Ten Eyck, Wade, Wilkinson, Willey, Wilson—30.

NAYS—Messrs. Breckenridge, Johnson (of Missouri), Polk, Powell, Trumbull—5.

Every Radical, except one, voting for it.

THE POSITION OF THE STATE DEPARTMENT.

In a letter to Mr. Dayton, United States Minister to France, as late as February 6, 1863, with reference to a proposed mediation suggested by M. Drouyn de l'Huys, French Premier, through M. Mercier, Mr. Seward says:

It is true, indeed, that peace must come at some time, and that conferences must attend, if they are not allowed to precede the pacification. There is, however, a better form for such conferences than the one which M. Drouyn de l'Huys suggests. The latter would be palpably in derogation of the Constitution of the United States, and would carry no weight, because destitute of the sanction necessary to bind either the disloyal or the loyal portions of the people. On the other hand, the Congress of the United States furnishes a constitutional forum for debates between the alienated parties. Senators and Representatives from the loyal portion of the people are there already, freely empowered to confer; and seats also are vacant, and inviting Senators and Representatives of the discontented party who may be constitutionally sent there from the States involved in the insurrection. Moreover, the conferences which can thus be held in Congress have this great advantage over any that could be organized upon the plan of M. Drouyn de l'Huys namely: that the Congress, if it were thought wise, could call a national convention to adopt its recommendations, and give them all the solemnity and binding force of organic law. Such conferences between the alienated parties may be said to have already begun. Maryland, Virginia, Kentucky, Tennessee and Missouri—States which are claimed by the insurgents—are already represented in Congress, and submitting with perfect freedom, and in a proper spirit, their advice upon the course best calculated to bring about, in the shortest time, a firm, lasting, and honorable peace. Representatives have been sent, also, from Louisiana, and others are understood to be coming from Arkansas.

There is a preponderating argument in favor of the congressional form of conference over that which is suggested by M. Drouyn de l'Huys, namely: that while an accession to the latter would bring this Government into a concurrence with the insurgents in disregarding and setting aside an important part of the Constitution of the United States, and so would be of pernicious example, the congressional conference, on the contrary, preserves and gives new strength to that sacred writing which must continue through future ages the sheet anchor of the Republic.

You will be at liberty to read this dispatch to M. Drouyn de l'Huys, and to give him a copy, if he shall desire it.

To the end that you may be informed of the whole case, I transmit a copy of M. Drouyn de l'Huys' dispatch.

I am, sir, your obedient servant,
WILLIAM H. SEWARD.

PRESIDENT LINCOLN TO HON. FERNANDO WOOD.

EXECUTIVE MANSION,
WASHINGTON, December 12, 1862.

HON. FERNANDO WOOD:

My Dear Sir: Your letter of the 8th, with the accompanying note of same date, was received yesterday.

The most important paragraph in the letter, as I consider, is in these words: "On the 26th of November last, I was advised by an authority which I deemed likely to be well informed, as well as reliable and truthful, that the Southern States would send representatives to the next Congress, provided that a full and general amnesty should permit them to do so. No guarantee or terms were asked for other than the amnesty referred to."

I strongly suspect your information will prove to be groundless; nevertheless, I thank you for communicating it to me. Understanding the phrase in the paragraph above quoted—"the Southern States would send representatives to the next Congress"—to be substantially the same as that "the people of the Southern States would cease resistance, and would reinaugurate, submit to, and maintain the national authority within the limits of such States, under the Constitution of the United States," I say that in such case the war would cease on the part of the United States; and that if within a reasonable time "a full and general amnesty" were necessary to such end, it would not be withheld.

I do not think it would be proper now to communicate this, formally or informally, to the people of the Southern States. My belief is that they already know it; and when they choose, if ever, they can communicate with me unequivocally. Nor do I think it proper now to suspend military operations to try an experiment of negotiation.

I should, nevertheless, receive with great pleasure, the exact information you now have, and also such other as you may in any way obtain. Such information might be more valuable before the 1st of January than afterward.

While there is nothing in this letter which I shall dread to see in history, it is, perhaps, better for the present that its existence should not become public. I therefore have to request that you will regard it as confidential. Your obedient servant,

ABRAHAM LINCOLN.

From the foregoing it will be seen that President Lincoln promised the security of a full and general amnesty to protect Senators and Representatives from the Seceded States, who would attend and take their seats in Congress, and thus preserve their persons from arrest, and any condition other than full freedom.

The Disunionists of the Radical Party.

WHAT ITS PROMINENT LEADERS THOUGHT OF DISUNION—WHAT THEY DID TO PROVOKE A DISRUPTURE.

It is not necessary to encumber this work with a history of the causes which ended in an attempted dissolution of the Union. That the Democratic party is in nowise responsible for it, no honest man will gainsay. That it used every effort to prevent the dire culmination, and its bloody consequences, is equally true. That the Radical party, which is now vociferous in its hypocritical canting about the terrible crime of disunion, is under the party leadership of men who were diligent in devising and exercising the means, with the criminal purpose of provoking a disruption of the Union, is susceptible of the clearest proof. That it is now in its daily history, in and out of Congress, acting upon the hypothesis that the Union was dissolved, will not be denied even by its own oracles. That disunion, which they now affect to regard with so much horror, was their favorite agency for years before the war, by which they hoped to accomplish their unholy designs—their own words shall attest. Let us look into history a little and reproduce what it records. Let us recall the incendiary work of Hinton Rowan Helper, which was indorsed, published and circulated by them to inflame the Northern mind to an irreconcilable discontent with any further fellowship with their Southern brethren. That it was the text book of the Radical, or, as it was then called, the "Republican" party, is apparent from the indorsement of its views and revolutionary objects, by the leading representative men of that party in Congress. So shocked was the conservative temper of the country by the character of this book that, when it came to be exposed, Mr. John Sherman, at present a Radical Senator from the State of Ohio, who indorsed it, was coerced by public sentiment to withdraw from the position of Republican nominee for the Speakership of the House of Representatives and give way to another Republican who had not indorsed it.

The following passages we *extract from this amiable work:*

"Our own banner is inscribed: No co-operation with slaveholders in politics; no fellowship with them in religion; no affiliation with them in society; no recognition of pro-slavery men, except as ruffians, outlaws and criminals.

" Immediate death to slavery; or, if not

immediate, unqualified proscription of its advocates during the periods of its existence.

"It is our honest conviction, that all the pro-slavery slaveholders deserve at once to be reduced to a parallel with the basest criminals that lie fettered within the cells of our public prisons.

"We are determined to abolish slavery at all hazards—in defiance of all the opposition, of whatever nature it is possible for the slaveocrats to bring against us. Of this they may take due notice, and govern themselves accordingly.

"We believe it is, as it ought to be, the desire, the determination, and the destiny of the Republican party to give the death-blow to slavery."

Among other things, it proposed "to land military forces in the Southern States, who shall raise the standard of freedom, and call the slaves to it, and such free persons as may be willing to join it." The purpose was thus more fully developed:

"Our plan is to make war, openly or secretly as circumstances may dictate, upon the property of slaveholders and their abettors, not for its destruction, if that can be easily avoided, but to convert it to the use of the slaves. If it can not be thus converted, we advise its destruction. Teach the slaves to burn their masters' buildings, to kill their cattle and hogs, to conceal and destroy farming utensils, to abandon labor in seed-time and harvest, and let the crops perish."

This is but a small sample of the blood-thirsty theories and advices of this work which was circulated by the hundreds of thousands throughout the North, and among the slaves of the South, as a campaign document of the Republican party. It was the device of its genius to invoke disunion and bloodshed. We have quoted enough of it to give its true character.

Let us recur a little further to history. About that time a well-known politician, N. P. Banks, Jr., was Governor of Massachusetts, a position to which he had been repeatedly chosen, notwithstanding his avowal that in a certain contingency, not specified, he would be willing to "let the Union slide." It was during the occupation of the executive chair by the same chief magistrate, that the banner of the Commonwealth, at a period of high political excitement, was substituted for the flag of the United States upon the staff of the State House, and continued to be there displayed for days, at least, and until public notice, called to a fact the significance of which could not be mistaken, caused the restoration of the national ensign to its accustomed place. Another chief magistrate of the same Commonwealth, Ex-Governor Andrew, while peace was yet unbroken, had accepted, on the part of the State, the present of a Revolutionary musket from a conspicuous Abolition clergyman, who had himself declared "a drum-head Constitution" the only one worthy of regard—and with due ceremonies, in the presence of the members of the legislative assembly, in session, had welcomed the giver with a formal and enthusiastic address, at the capital of the State; and, rather as a symbol of what guns might be expected to do afterward, it may be thought, than for the past achievements of an ordinary relic of the old Revolutionary War, "with dewy eye and trembling lips," had actually imprinted a kiss of affection upon the body of the weapon. A very aged citizen of the same Commonwealth, Josiah Quincy, Jr., of high social and literary position, while the amalgamation process was going forward between the Whigs and Republicans, had published a pamphlet, during Mr. Buchanan's administration, in which he urged it as the duty of the North to "take possession of the Government."*

"There were a very few pulpits at the North, at this period," says a distinguished Massachusetts lawyer, "to which a pastor would venture to invite a brother clergyman from a slave State, should such a one happen to be in the neighborhood, to preach a Gospel addressed to all nations, in any one of which, at the time of its promulgation, slavery was the common practice, and in regard to which practice it contains no reproof. The American Tract Society had already been formally divided; the main office remaining at New York, while the New England seceding branch had its head-quarters at Boston, and became an active organ of abolition."

At a mass meeting, held at South Farmingham, Massachusetts, in October, 1860, a leading Republican Senator of the North (Mr. John P. Hale), who had been the candidate of the Free-soil party for President a few years previously, said: "The South talked about dissolving the Union if Lincoln was elected. The Republicans would elect him, just to see if they would do it. *The Union was more likely to be dissolved if he was not elected.*"—*Report of Boston Courier, October 12.*

In the Chicago Convention, at which Lincoln and Hamlin were nominated, after the resolutions had been read, Judge Jessup, of Pennsylvania, by whom they had been

---

* This paragraph is from "Lunt's Origin of the War."

reported, said that he "desired to amend a verbal mistake in the name of the party. It was printed in the resolutions 'the National Republican party.'" He wished to strike out the word *National*, as that was not the name by which the party was properly known." The correction was made.—*Report in New York Tribune of May* 18.

It thus openly professed itself "sectional."

A few brief extracts from the speeches, delivered before the war, by the high priests of Radicalism, will form a proper conclusion to this short reference to the disunionism of that organization anterior to the war:

"Although I am not one of that class of men who cry for the perpetuation of the Union, though I am willing in a certain state to let it slide. I have no fear for its perpetuation."—*General N. P. Banks, of Massachusetts, at Portland, Maine, in* 1856.

"I would have Judges who believe in a higher law and an anti-slavery Constitution, an anti-slavery Bible, and an anti-slavery God."—*Hon. Anson Burlingame, at Faneuil Hall, in* 1855.

On the 16th of January, 1855, the Rev. Mr. Beecher said, in a lecture in New York, on the subject of cutting the North from the South:

"Two great powers that will not live together are in our midst, and tugging at each other's throats. They will search each other out, though you separate them a hundred times. And if by an insane blindness you shall contrive to put off the issue, and send this unsettled dispute down to your children, it will go down, gathering volume and strength at every step, to waste and desolate their heritage. Let it be settled now. Clear the place. Bring in the champions. Let them put their lances in rest for the charge. Sound the trumpet, and God save the right!"

At a public meeting held in his church, to promote emigration to Kansas, the Rev. Henry Ward Beecher made the following remarks, as we find them in the report of the New York *Evening Post*:

"He believed that the Sharp rifle was truly a moral agency, and there was more moral power in one of those instruments, so far as the slaveholders of Kansas were concerned, than in a hundred Bibles."

"The object to be accomplished is this: That the free States shall take possession of the Government by their united votes. Minor interests and old party affiliations and prejudices must be forgotten. We have the power in number; our strength is in union."—*Simon Brown, Massachusetts Free-soil candidate for Lieut.-Governor in* 1855.

"There never was an hour when this blasphemous and infamous government should be made, and now the hour was to be prayed for when that disgrace to humanity should be dashed to pieces forever."—*Rev. Andrew T. Foss, of New Hampshire, at the American Anti-Slavery Society meeting at New York, May* 13, 1857.

"My most fervent prayer is that England, France, and Spain, may take this slavery-accursed nation into their special consideration; and when the time arrives for the streets of the cities of this 'land of the free and home of the brave' to run with blood to the horses' bridles, if the writer of this be living, there will be one heart to rejoice at the retributive justice of Heaven."—*Mr. W. O. Duval.*

"So long as this blood-stained Union existed, there was but little hope for the slave."—*W. Lloyd Garrison, at New York, May* 13, 1857.

"I will continue to experiment no longer—it is all madness. Let the slaveholding Union go, and slavery will go with the Union down into the dust. If the Church is against disunion, and not on the side of the slave, then I pronounce it as of the devil."—*W. Lloyd Garrison, at New York, August* 1, 1855.

"I would not be understood as desiring a servile insurrection; but I say to Southern gentlemen, that there are hundreds of thousands of honest and patriotic men who will 'laugh at your calamity, and will mock when your fear cometh.'"—*Hon. J. R. Giddings.* (See his Book of Speeches, pages 159-60.)

"Massachusetts has already made it a penal offense to help to execute a law of the Union. I want to see the officers of the State brought into collision with those of the Union.

"No union with slaveholders. Up with the flag of disunion, that we may have a free and glorious union of our own."—*W. Lloyd Garrison.*

This Union, it is a lie, an imposture, and our first business is to seek its overthrow. *Boston Liberator.*

We confess that we intend to trample under foot the Constitution of this country. Daniel Webster says: "You are a law-abiding people;" that the glory of New England is, "that it is a law-abiding community." Shame on it, if this be true; if even the religion of New England sinks as low as its statute book. But I say *we are not a law-abiding community.* God be thanked for it!— *Wendell Phillips, of Massachusetts, at a Free Soil meeting in Boston, May,* 1849.

Wendell Phillips issued a pamphlet in 1850, reviewing Mr. Webster's speech "on the constitutional rights of the States," in which is the following:

"We are disunionists, not from any love of separate confederacies, or as ignorant of the thousand evils that spring from neighboring and quarrelsome States; but we would get rid of this Union."

He wished for the dissolution of the Union, because he wanted Massachusetts to be left free to right her own wrongs. If so, she would have no trouble in sending her ships to Charleston and laying it in ashes. *Edward Quincy, of Mass., at New York, May* 13, 1857.

On the 1st of February, 1850, the same petitions praying a dissolution of the Union were presented in the Senate by Mr. Hale, of New Hampshire.

Mr. Webster, of Mass., suggested that there should have been a preamble to the petition in these words:

"Gentlemen, members of Congress, whereas, at the commencement of the session, you and each of you took your solemn oaths in the presence of God and the Holy Evangelists, that you would support the Constitution of the United States, now, therefore, we pray you to take immediate steps to break up the Union and overthrow the Constitution of the United States as soon as you can. And as in duty bound we will ever pray."

But three Senators voted for the reception of the petition, viz:

Messrs. Chase, Hale, and Seward.

They (the South) tell you that they are willing to abide by the ballot-box, and willing to make that the last appeal. If we fail there, what then? We will drive it back, sword in hand, and, so help me God! believing that to be right, I am with them. [Loud cheers, and cries of "Good."]—*James Watson Webb, at the Philadelphia Convention that nominated Fremont in* 1856.

There was no Union with the South. Let us have a Union, said he, or let us sweep away this remnant which we call a Union. I go for a Union where all men are equal, or for no Union at all, and I go for right. *Senator Wade, of Ohio, in a speech to a mass-meeting of the Republicans, held in the State of Maine, in* 1855, *according to the Boston Atlas.*

Patriotic Efforts to Avert Disunion.

LEADING RADICALS OPPOSE ADJUSTMENT—FRIGID SATISFACTON WITH WHICH THEY WELCOMED DISUNION.

On the 4th of February, 1861, representatives from twenty States, met in what was known as the "Peace Conference," to devise some means of averting disunion, which was then imminent. The Radical Governors mostly sent partisans of their own school, to represent their States in this body. Against all the propositions adopted by the Conference, the votes, in the same, of Maine, Vermont and Iowa, represented by entire Republican delegations, were cast. Massachusetts, which was represented by a full delegation of Republicans, voted against all except one, and did not vote on that. New Hampshire, with a like delegation, voted against all but two. The States whose delegations were composed of men of both parties, voted generally for the propositions.

They were substantially as follows:

I. Slavery was prohibited in Territory north of the parallel of 36° 30', and permitted south of that line. No law was to be passed by Congress or the local legislatures, to prevent the taking of slaves into the latter territory; and on either side of the line, territory with inhabitants sufficient, and with Republican form of government, was to be admitted either with or without involuntary servitude, as its constitution might provide.

II. No future acquisition of territory was to be made, except by discovery, and for certain national purposes, without the concurrence of a majority of the Senators from the free States and the slave States respectively.

III. Congress was to have no power, by construction of the Constitution, or by any amendment of it, to interfere with slavery in any State, or in the District of Columbia, or in places within the exclusive jurisdiction of the United States; nor to prohibit the transportation of slaves from one slave State or Territory to another; but they were not to be taken through States or Territories in which the laws forbade such transit. Slaves were not to be brought into the District of Columbia for sale, or to be kept there on the way to sale.

IV. No such construction was to be placed on the article of the Constitution which provides for the delivery of fugitives from service or labor, as to prevent States from passing laws for the enforcement of that provision.

V. The foreign slave-trade was to be forever prohibited.

VI. The provisions of the Constitution for the delivery of fugitives from service or labor, and in relation to the apportionment of Representatives and direct taxes, were not to be amended or abolished without the consent of all the States.

VII. Congress was to provide by law for the payment, by the United States, to the owner, of the full value of any slave rescued by violence or intimidation, or whose recovery might be prevented by the same means.

On the 2nd of March, 1861, they were offered to the Senate by Mr. Crittenden of Kentucky, after the adoption of the House Constitutional Amendment, and pending the Crittenden propositions, and they were rejected—yeas 7, nays 28—as follows:

YEAS—Messrs. Crittenden, Douglas, Harlan, Johnson (of Tennessee), Kennedy, Morrill, and Thompson—7.

NAYS—Messrs. Bayard, Bigler, Bingham, Bright, Chandler, Clark, Dixon, Fessenden, Foot, Foster, Grimes, Gwin, Hunter, Lane, Latham, Mason, Nicholson, Polk, Pugh, Rice, Sebastian, Sumner, Ten Eyck, Trumbull, Wade, Wigfall, Wilkinson, and Wilson—28.

March 1, 1861, Mr. McClernand moved to suspend the rules for the purpose of receiving the recommendation of the Peace Congress, which was rejected—yeas 93, nays 67, as follows:

YEAS—Messrs. Chas. F. Adams, Green Adams, Adrain, Aldrich, Wm. C. Anderson, Avery, Barr, Barrett, Bocock, Boteler, Brabson, Branch, Briggs, Bristow, Brown, Burch, Burnett, Campbell, Horace F. Clark, John B. Clark, John Cochrane, Corwin, James Craig, John G. Davis, De Jarnette, Dunn, Etheridge, Florence, Foster, Fouke, Garnett, Gilmer, Hale, Hall, Hamilton, J. Morrison Harris, John T. Harris, Haskin, Hatton, Hoard, Holman, William Howard, Hughes, Jenkins, Junkin, W. Kellogg, Killinger, Kunkel, Larrabee, J. M. Leach, Leake, Logan, Maclay, Mallory, Chas. D. Martin, Maynard, McClernand, McKenty, McKnight, McPherson, Milson, Milward, Laban T. Moore, Moorhead, Edward Joy Morris, Nelson, Niblack, Nixon, Olin, Pendleton, Peyton, Phelps, Porter, Pryor, Quarles, John H. Reynolds, Rice, Riggs, James C. Robinson, Sickles, Simms. Wm. N. H. Smith, Spaulding, Stevenson, William Stewart, Stokes, Thomas, Vance, Webster, Whiteley, Winslow, Woodson, and Wright—93.

NAYS—Messrs. Alley, Ashley, Bingham, Blair, Brayton, Duffinton, Burlingame, Burnham, Cary, Case, Coburn, Colfax, Conway, Burton Craige, Dawes, Delano, Duell, Edgerton, Eliot, Ely, Fenton, Ferry, Franck, Gooch, Graham, Grow, Gurley, Helmick, Hickman, Hindman, William A. Howard, Hutchins, Irvine, Francis W. Kellogg, Kenyon, Loomis, Lovejoy, McKean, Morrill, Morse, Palmer, Perry, Potter, Pottle, Christopher Robinson, Royce, Ruffin, Sedgwick, Sherman, Somes, Spinner, Stanton, Stevens, Tappan, Tompkins, Train, Vandever, Van Wyck, Wade, Waldron, Walton, Cadwalader C. Washburn, Elihu B. Washburne, Wells, Wilson, Windom, and Woodruff—67.

It will be seen that but one Radical voted for them in the Senate, and that but three Southern Representatives voted against the motion to suspend the rules to receive them in the House.

The Crittenden Resolutions.

On the 2nd of March, 1861, the Senate came to a vote on the peace propositions of Mr. Crittenden of Ky., recommending several Constitutional amendments, of substance as follows:

1st. A division of territory into free and slave on the line of 36° 30′, prohibiting Congress or the Territorial Legislature from abolishing or interfering with slavery south of that line, and providing for the admission of new States with population sufficient for one representative in Congress.

2nd. Amending the Constitution so as to prohibit interference by Congress with slavery in the States by abolishing it in any places within its exclusive jurisdiction.

3d. Prohibiting the abolition of slavery in the District of Columbia, as long as it existed in Maryland and Virginia, and permitting officers of the Government and members of Congress to bring their slaves with them into the District during their official service, and taking them out from the District.

4th. Congress to have no power to interfere with the inter-State slave trade.

5th. Paying the owner for his fugitive slave where the U. S. Marshall is prohibited from recovering him by local violence; the Government to sue and recover, from the county in which the rescue occurred, the value of the slave, and it, in turn, to sue and recover from the wrong-doers or rescuers.

6th. No future amendment to the Constitution to affect these amendments, nor the third paragraph of the second section of the 4th article of the Constitution, nor to give Congress the power to interfere with or abolish slavery in the States.

The proposition also recommended the passage by Congress of joint resolutions against the repeal of the Fugitive Slave Law, and in favor of laws punishing the rescuers of fugitive slaves; the repeal, by the several States who had passed such enactments, of what was known as the personal liberty laws; the amendment of the Fugitive Slave Law, so as to give the Commissioner the same fee, whether he decided for or against the claimant, and to restrict the power to summons a *posse comitatus* to cases of actual resistance, and the passage of the most stringent and effectual laws for the suppression of the African slave trade.

The entire proposition was rejected.

YEAS—Messrs. Bayard, Bigler, Bright, CRITTENDEN, Douglas, Gwin, Hunter, Johnson (of Tennessee), Kennedy, Lane, Latham, Mason, Nicholson, Polk, Pugh, Rice, Sebastian, Thomson and Wigfall—19.

NAYS—Messrs. Anthony, Bingham, Chandler, Clark, Dixon, Doolittle, Durkee, Fessenden, Foot, Foster, Grimes, Harlan, King, Morrill, Sumner, Ten Eyck, Trumbull, Wade, Wilkinson and Wilson—20.

Every Radical present voted against it. The same proposition had been introduced in the House of Representatives on the 27th of February, and had been rejected, as follows:

YEAS—Messrs. Adrain, WILLIAM C. ANDERSON, Avery, Barr, Barrett, Bocock, Boteler, Bouligny, Brabson, Branch, BRIGGS, BRISTOW, Brown, Burch, Burnett, Horace F. Clark, John B. Clark, John Cochrane, Cox, James Craig, Burton Craig, John G. Davis, De Jarnette, Dimmick, Edmundson, English, Florence, Fouke, Garnett, GILMER, Hamilton, J. MORRISON HARRIS, John T. Harris, Hatton, Holman, William Howard, Hughes, Jenkins, Kunkel, Larrabee, JAMES M. LEACH, Leake, Logan, Maclay, MALLORY, Charles D. Martin, Elbert S. Martin, MAYNARD, McClernand, McKenty, Millson, Montgomery, LABAN T. MOORE, Isaac N. Morris, Nelson, Niblack, Noell, Peyton, Phelps, Pryor, QUARLES, Riggs, Jas. C. Robinson, Rust, Sickles, Simms, William Smith, WILLIAM N. H. SMITH, Stevenson, James A. Stewart, Stokes, Stout, Thomas, Vallandigham, VANCE, WEBSTER, Whitely, Winslow, Woodson and Wright—80.

NAYS—Messrs. Charles F. Adams, Aldrich, Alley, Ashley, Babbitt, Beale, Bingham, Blair, Blake, Brayton, Buffinton, Burlingame, Burnham, Butterfield, Campbell, Carey, Carter, Case, Coburn, Clark B. Cochrane, Colfax, Conkling, Conway, Corwin, Covode, H. Winter Davis, Dawes, Delano, Duell, Dunn, Edgerton, Edwards, Eliot, Ely, Etheridge, Farnsworth, Fenton, Ferry, Foster, Frank, French, Gooch, Graham, Grow, Hale, Hall, Helmick, Hickman, Hindman, Hoard, William A. Howard, Humphrey, Hutchins, Irvine, Junkin, Francis W. Kellogg, William Kellogg, Kenyon, Kilgore, Killinger, DeWitt C. Leach, Lee, Longnecker, Loomis, Lovejoy, Marston, McKean, McKnight, McPherson, Moorhead, Morrill, Morse, Nixon, Olin, Palmer, Perry, Pettit, Porter, Potter, Pottle, E. R. Reynolds, Rice, Christ. Robinson, Royce, Scranton, Sedgwick, Sherman, Somes, Spaulding, Spinner, Stanton, Stevens, William Stewart, Stratton, Tappan, Thayer, Theaker, Tompkins, Train, Trimble, Vandever, Van Wyck, Verree, Wade, Waldron, Walton, Cadwalader C. Washburn, Elihu B. Washburne, Wells, Wilson, Windom, Wood and Woodruff—113.

But one Southern Representative, it will be seen, voted against it. Every Radical voted against it. Every Democrat for it.

In the Senate of the United States, on the 3d of January, Mr. Douglas said:

"I believe this to be a fair basis of amicable adjustment. If you, of the Republican side, are not willing to accept this, nor the proposition of the Senator from Kentucky, Mr. Crittenden, pray tell us what you are willing to do. I address the inquiry to the Republicans alone, for the reason that, in the Committee of Thirteen, a few days ago, every member from the South, including those from the cotton States (Messrs. Davis and Toombs), expressed their readiness to accept the proposition of my venerable friend from Kentucky, as a final settlement of the controversy, if tendered and sustained by the Republican members. Hence, the sole responsibility of our disagreement, and the only difficulty in the way of an amicable adjustment, is with the Republican party."

Indeed, Mr. Toombs himself, in a speech to the Senate, January 7th, speaking, of course, for those with whom he was acting as well as for himself, after suggesting the conditions which he would prefer, and would accept "for the sake of peace—permanent peace"—proceeded:

"I am willing, however, to take the proposition of the Senator from Kentucky, as it was understood in committee, putting the North and the South on the same ground, prohibiting slavery on one side, acknowledging slavery and protecting it on the other; and applying that to all future acquisitions, so that the whole continent, to the north pole, shall be settled upon the one rule, and to the south pole, under the other."

This was in exact conformity with the propositions of the Peace Conference, and, moreover, the principle of the Missouri Compromise. Mr. Crittenden, also, in a published letter to Mr. Anderson, of Cincinnati, dated March 27, 1861, remarks, in reference to the resolutions which bear his name:

"I believe if those measures, thus offered, had been, at a suitable time, promptly adopted by the Congress of the United States, it would have checked the progress of the rebellion and revolution, and saved the Union."

On the day of the final disposition of the question, March 3, 1861, Mr. Pugh, of Ohio, declared, in a speech to the Senate: "Before the Senators from the State of Mississippi left this chamber, I heard one of them, who now assumes, at least, to be President of the Southern Confederacy, propose *to accept it* (that is, the Crittenden proposition), *and to maintain the Union, if that proposition could receive the vote it ought to receive from the other side of this chamber.*

"Therefore, of all your propositions, of all your amendments, knowing as I do, and knowing that the historian will so write it down, *at any time before the first of January* a two-thirds vote for the Crittenden Resolutions, in this chamber, would have saved every State in the Union, but South Carolina."

Mr. Douglas followed Mr. Pugh on this occasion, and remarked:

"The Senator has said that if the Crittenden proposition could have passed, early in the session, it would have saved all the States, except South Carolina. *I firmly believe it would.*

"I can confirm the Senator's declaration that Senator Davis himself, when on the Committee of Thirteen, *was ready at all times to compromise on the Crittenden proposition.* I will go further, and say that Mr. Toombs was also."

It was stated in the public prints, early in November, 1861, when actual war had been on foot but a few months, that Mr. Lincoln made known his "regrets that he did not urge the adoption of the Crittenden Compromise."

The following passage is an extract from a letter addressed by him, from Washington, to Mr. Hays, of Chicago, dated December 29, 1860:

"*Many of the Republican leaders desire a dissolution of the Union, and urge war as a means of accomplishing disunion;* while others are Union men in good faith. We have now reached a point where a compromise on the basis of mutual concession or disunion and war is inevitable."

In another letter of Mr. Douglas, addressed to Mr. Taylor, of New York, and dated on the same day, he wrote:

"We are now drifting rapidly into civil war, which must end in disunion. This can only be prevented by amendments to the Constitution, which will take the slavery question out of Congress. Whether this can be done, depends upon the Republicans. *Many of their leaders desire disunion on party grounds*, and here is the difficulty. God grant us safe deliverance, is my prayer."

A Senator from Ohio (Mr. Pugh) declared in his place, on the day preceding the final adjournment of Congress (March 3, 1861), that the resolutions had "been petitioned for by a larger number of electors of the United States, than any proposition that was ever before Congress."

Mr. Douglas, in a letter dated at Washington, February 2, 1861, and addressed to a paper in Tennessee, says, with the purpose of dissuading the people of that State from taking part with secession:

"You must remember that there are disunionists *among the party leaders* at the North as well as at the South; men whose hostility to slavery is stronger than their fidelity to the Constitution, and who believe that the disruption of the Union would draw after it, as an inevitable consequence, civil war, servile insurrection, and finally, the utter extermination of slavery in all the Southern States. * * * The Northern disunionists, like the disunionists of the South, are violently opposed to all compromises and Constitutional amendments, or efforts at conciliation, whereby peace should be restored and the Union preserved. *They are striving to break up the Union, under the pretense of unbounded devotion to it.* They are struggling to overthrow the Constitution, while professing undying attachment to it, and a willingness to make any sacrifice to maintain it.

"They are trying to plunge the country into civil war, as the surest means of destroying the Union, upon the plea of enforcing the laws and protecting the public property. If they can defeat any adjustment or compromise, by which the points at issue may be satisfactorily settled, and keep up the irritation, so as to induce the border States to follow the cotton States, they will feel certain of the accomplishment of their ultimate designs. *Nothing will gratify them so much,* or contribute so effectually to their success, as the secession of Tennessee and the Border States. Every State that withdraws from the Union increases the relative power of the Northern abolitionists to defeat a satisfactory adjustment."

In a debate in the Senate on the state of the Union, on the 10th December, 1860, when affairs had so nearly ripened into open secession, Mr. Dixon, of Connecticut, declared that the true way to restore harmony was "by cheerfully and honestly assuring to every section its constitutional rights. *No section professes to ask more. No section ought to offer less.*" He added, that three-quarters of his constituents would uphold him in this position. Whereupon, Mr. Davis' colleague, Mr. Brown, of Mississippi, said: "If the same spirit could prevail which actuates the Senator who has just now taken his seat, *a different state of things might be produced in twenty days.*"—*Congressional Globe*, December 11, 1860.

Mr. Douglas declared, February 29, 1860, in reply to a speech of Mr. Seward:

"I repeat that their resistance (that of the Republican or Radical party) to carrying out in good faith the settlement of 1820, their defeat of the bill for extending it to the Pacific Ocean, was the sole cause of the agitation of 1850, and gave rise to the necessity of establishing the principle of non-intervention by Congress with slavery in the Territories. Hence, I am not willing to sit here and allow the Senator from New York, with all the weight of authority he has with the powerful party of which he is the head, to arraign me and the party to which I belong with the responsibility for that agitation which rests solely upon him and his associates."

The following passage is an extract of a speech, delivered by a very eminent citizen of New York, the late Judge Wm. Duer, at Oswego, in that State, August 6, 1860:

"The Republican party is a conspiracy, under the forms, but in violation of the spirit of the Constitution of the United States, to exclude the citizens of 'slaveholding States from all share in the government of the country, and to compel them to adopt their institutions to the opinions of the citizens of the free States.'"

How the Leading Radicals treated the Crisis.

Governor Andrew, of Massachusetts, in his message, January 5, 1861, remarked:

"And the single question now presented to the nation is this: shall a reactionary spirit, *unfriendly to liberty,* be permitted to subvert democratic-republican government, organized under constitutional forms?"

In other words, the Governor of Massachusetts was afraid to do any thing to abate the disunion spirit, for fear that a patriotic reaction might overwhelm him and his co-conspirators of the Radical party. In evidence, beyond what has already appeared, to support this statement, among a mass of similar testimony, the following may suffice. Mr. Wade, a Senator from Ohio, made the following declarations in a published speech: (These extracts are made from Carpenter's "Logic of History," a book published at Madison, Wisconsin, in 1864.)

"And, after all this, to talk of a Union! Sir, I have said you have no Union. I say you have no Union to-day worthy of the name. I am here *a conservative man,* knowing, as I do, that the only salvation to your Union (that is, according to the resolve of Mr. Wade and others) is that you divest it entirely from all the taints of slavery. If we can't have that, then *I go for no Union at all, but I go for a fight.*"

"WASHINGTON, February 11, 1861.

"MY DEAR GOVERNOR: Governor Bingham and myself telegraphed to you on Saturday, *at the request of Massachusetts and New York,* to send delegates to the Peace Compromise Congress. They admit that we were right and they were wrong; that *no Republican State* should have sent delegates; but they are here, and can't get away. Ohio, Indiana, and Rhode Island are coming in, and there is some danger of Illinois; and now they beg us, for God's sake, to come to their rescue, and *save the Republican party* from rupture. I hope you will send *stiff-backed men* or none. The whole thing was gotten up against my judgment and advice, and will end in thin smoke. Still, I hope, as a matter of courtesy to some of our erring brethren, that you will send the delegates.

"Truly your friend,
"Z. CHANDLER.

"His Excellency, Austin Blair.

"P. S. Some of the manufacturing States think that *a fight* would be awful. Without a little blood-letting, this Union will not, in my estimation, be worth a curse."

Mr. Seward was unwilling to do any thing then. He might, however, in one, two, or an indefinite number of years. In the Senate, on the 12th of January, 1861, he said:

"After the angry excitements of the hour have subsided, and calmness once more shall have resumed its accustomed sway over the public mind—then, and not till then—one, two, or years hence—I should cheerfully advise a convention of the people, to be assembled in pursuance of the Constitution, to consider and decide whether any and what amendments of the organic national law ought to be made."

The Boston *Courier,* of January 25, 1861, published a Washington dispatch, saying:

"Senator Wilson has just returned from Massachusetts; says the Republicans there are stronger than ever in their faith. He states that *the Democrats and Bell and Everett men* told him that *now was the time to settle the question of slavery.* The secession movement in South Carolina" (and similar causes referred to) "confirmed his constituents in their determination *to dispose of the question now and forever.* When asked how they would dispose of it, the Senator intimated *that remained to be seen.*

Mr. Thurlow Weed, than whom no one could be more conversant with the whole subject, declared in the Albany *Journal,* edited by him:

"The chief architects of the rebellion, before it broke out, avowed that they were aided in their designs by the ultra Abolitionists of the North. This *was too true, for without such aid the South could never have been united against the Union.*"

Mr. Andrew Johnson, now President of the United States, declared, in a speech, just before the rebellion broke into open violence:

"There are two parties in existence who want dissolution. Slavery and a Southern Confederacy is the hobby. *Sumner wants to break up the Government,* and so do the Abolitionists generally. They hold that, if it survives, the Union can not endure. Secessionists argue that, if the Union continues, slavery is lost. Abolitionists want no compromise; but they *regard peaceable secession as a humbug.*

"The two occupy the same ground. Why,

abolition is dissolution; dissolution is secession; one is the other. Both are striving to accomplish the same object."

The South Encouraged to Dissolution.
Secession a Peaceful Right.

Mr. Ben. Wade announced in a speech in the Senate, as it is reported in the *Congressional Globe*, third session, Thirty-fourth Congress, page 25, bolder disunion doctrine than was ever avowed by Messrs. Davis or Yancey:

"But Southern gentlemen stand here and in almost all their speeches, speak of the dissolution of the Union, as an element of every argument, as though it were a peculiar condescension on their part that they permitted the Union to stand at all. If they do not feel interested in upholding the Union—if it really trenches on their rights—if it endangers their institutions to such an extent that they can not feel secure under it—if their interests are violently assailed by means of the Union, I am not one of those who expect that they will long continue under it. I am not one of those who would ask them to continue in such a Union. It would be doing violence to the *platform of the party to which I belong*. We have adopted the old Declaration of Independence as the basis of our political movements, which declares that any people when their government ceases to protect their rights—when it is so subverted from the true purposes of government as to oppose them—have the right to recur to fundamental principles, and, if need be, to *destroy the government under which they live*, and to erect on its *ruins* another more conducive to their welfare. I hold that they have *this right. I will not blame any people for exercising it*, whenever they think the contingency has come. * * * *You can not forcibly hold men in this Union, for the attempt to do so, it seems to me, would subvert the first principles of the Government under which we live.*"

January 12, 1848, the late President Lincoln in App., *Congressional Globe*, first session, Thirtieth Congress, page 94, proclaimed in Congress that,

"Any people, any where, being inclined and having the power, have the right to rise up and shake off the existing government and form a new one that suits them better. Nor is this right confined to cases in which the people of an existing government may choose to exercise it."

December 17, 1860, Horace Greeley, in the New York *Tribune*, says:

"If the Declaration of Independence justified the secession from the British Empire of 3,000,000 colonists in 1776, we do not see why it should not justify the secession of 5,000,000 of Southerners from the Union in 1861."

November 9, 1860, the same journal says:

"Whenever a considerable section of our Union is all deliberately resolved to go out, we shall resist all coercive measures designed to keep them in. We hope never to live in a Republic whereof one section is pinned to another by bayonets."

November 26, 1860, the same journal again says:

"If the cotton States unitedly and earnestly wish to withdraw peaceably from the Union, we think they should and would be allowed to do so. Any attempt to compel them by force to remain would be contrary to the principles enunciated in the immortal Declaration of Independence—contrary to the fundamental ideas on which human liberty is based."

March 2, 1861, nearly six weeks before the assault upon Fort Sumter, the same journal again said:

"We have repeatedly said, and we once more insist, that the great principle embodied by Jefferson in the Declaration of Independence, that governments derive their just powers from the consent of the governed, is sound and just; and that, if the slave States, the cotton States, or the Gulf States only, choose to form an independent nation, *they have a moral right to do so*."

Of course Southern members of Congress must have had the opportunity of knowing the private opinions of Northern members of the two branches, and, probably, of those members of the administration, whose views of the situation more or less coincided with those of the Secretary of the Treasury.

Even General Scott, at the head of the military force of the Union, on the 3d of March, 1861, the day after Mr. Greeley's announcement of his views, in his published letter to Mr. Seward, proposed as his final and apparently favorite alternative, in "the highly disordered condition of our (so late) happy and glorious Union, say to the seceded States—*wayward sisters, depart in peace!*"

Negro Suffrage.

Votes on, in Congress, on the 18th of March, 1864.

The House passed, without a division, a bill in the usual form, to provide a temporary government for the Territory of Montana.

March 31—The Senate considered it, when Mr. Wilkinson moved to strike from the second line of the fifth section (defining the qualifications of voters), the words "white male inhabitant" and insert the words: "male citizen of the United States, and those who have declared their intention to become such;" which was agreed to—yeas 22, nays 17, as follows:

YEAS—Messrs. Brown, Chandler, Clark, Collamer, Conness, Dixon, Fessenden, Foot, Foster, Grimes, Hale, Harlan, Harris, Howard, Howe, Morgan, Morrill, Pomeroy, Sumner, Wade, Wilkinson, Wilson—22.

NAYS—Messrs. Buckalew, Carlile, Cowan, Davis, Harding, Henderson, Johnson, Lane (of Indiana), Nesmith, Powell, Riddle, Saulsbury, Sherman, Ten Eyck, Trumbull, Van Winkle, Willey—17.

The House disagreed to the amendments of the Senate, and a Committee of Conference recommended that it recede from its disagreement to the above, among other amendments of the Senate. The recommendation was rejected by the House on the 15th of April, when, on a motion to adhere to its amendments, and ask another Committee of Conference, Mr. Webster moved instructions:

"And that said committee be instructed to agree to no report that authorizes any other than free white male citizens, and those who have declared their intention to become such, to vote."

Which was agreed to—yeas 75, nays 67, as follows:

YEAS—Messrs. James C. Allen, Wm. J. Allen, Baily, Augustus C. Baldwin, Francis P. Blair, Bliss, Brooks, James S. Brown, Wm. G. Brown, Chanler, Clay, Coffroth, Cox, Cravens, Creswell, Henry Winter Davis, Dawson, Denison, Eden, Eldridge, Finck, Ganson, Grider, Hall, Harding, Benjamin G. Harris, Herrick, Holman, Hutchins, William Johnson, Kalbfleisch, Kernan, Knapp, Law, Lazear, Long, Mallory, Marcy, McBride, McDowell, McKinney, Wm. H. Miller, James R. Morris, Morrison, Nelson, Noble, Odell, Pendleton, Radford, Saml. J. Randall, W. H. Randall, Robinson, Rogers, James S. Rollins, Ross, Scott, Smith, Smithers, Stebbins, John B. Steele, Wm. G. Steele, Strouse, Stuart, Sweat, Thomas, Tracy, Voorhees, Webster, Whaley, Wheeler, Chilton A. White, Joseph W. White, Winfield, Fernando Wood, Yeaman—75.

NAYS—Messrs. Alley, Allison, Ames, Anderson, Ashley, John D. Baldwin, Baxter, Beaman, Blaine, Boutwell, Boyd, Broomall, Ambrose W. Clark, Cobb, Cole, Dawes, Deming, Driggs, Dumont, Farnsworth, Frank, Gooch, Grinnell, Higby, Hooper, Hotchkiss, Asahel W. Hubbard, John H. Hubbard, Jenckes, Julian, Kelley, Francis W. Kellogg, Orlando Kellogg, Loan, Longyear, Marvin, McClurg, McIndoe, Samuel, F. Miller, Morrill, Daniel Morris, Leonard Myers, Norton, Charles O'Neill, Orth, Patterson, Perham, Pike, Pomeroy, Price, Alexander H. Rice, John H. Rice, Edward H. Rollins, Schenck, Shannon, Sloan, Stevens, Thayer, Upson, Van Valkenburgh, Elihu B. Washburne, William B. Washburn, Williams, Wilder, Wilson, Windom, Woodbridge—67.

The Senate declined a further conference on these terms, when a free conference was had, which resulted in the passage of a suffrage clause, similar to that in the act organizing Idaho, which confined suffrage to white males at first election; the qualifications of voters, afterward, to be determined by the Territorial Legislature.

In the Senate, May 26, 1864, the bill for the registration of voters in the city of Washington being under consideration. Mr. Sumner moved to amend the bill by adding this proviso:

"*Provided*, That there shall be no exclusion of any person from the registry on account of color."

May 27—Mr. Harlan moved to amend the amendment by making the word "person" read "persons," and adding the words—

"Who have borne arms in the military service of the United States, and have been honorably discharged therefrom."

Which was agreed to—yeas 26, nays 12, as follows:

YEAS—Messrs. Anthony, Chandler, Clark, Collamer, Conness, Dixon, Fessenden, Foot, Foster, Grimes, Hale, Harlan, Harris, Johnson, Lane (of Indiana), Lane (of Kansas), Morgan, Morrill, Pomeroy, Ramsey, Sherman, Ten Eyck, Trumbull, Wade, Willey, Wilson—26.

NAYS—Messrs. Buckalew, Carlile, Cowan, Davis, Hendricks, McDougall, Powell, Richardson, Saulsbury, Sumner, Van Winkle, Wilkinson—12.

May 28—Mr. Sumner moved to add these words to the last proviso:

"*And provided further*, That all persons, without distinction of color, who shall, within the year next preceding the election, have paid a tax on any estate, or been assessed with a part of the revenue of said District, or been exempt from taxation, having taxable estate, and who can read and write with facility, shall enjoy the privilege of an elector. But no person now entitled to vote in the said District, continuing to reside therein, shall be disfranchised hereby."

Which was rejected—yeas 8, nays 27, as follows:

YEAS—Messrs. Anthony, Clark, Lane (of Kansas), Morgan, Pomeroy, Ramsey, Sumner, Wilkinson—8.

NAYS—Messrs. Buckalew, Carlile, Collamer, Cowan, Davis, Dixon, Fessenden, Foot, Foster, Grimes, Hale, Harlan, Harris, Hendricks, Hicks, Johnson, Lane (of Indiana), McDougall, Morrill, Powell, Saulsbury, Sherman, Ten Eyck, Trumbull, Van Winkle, Willey, Wilson—27.

The other proposition of Mr. Sumner, amended on motion of Mr. Harlan, was then rejected—yeas 18, nays 20, as follows:

YEAS—Messrs. Anthony, Chandler, Clark, Dixon, Foot, Foster, Hale, Harlan, Howard, Howe, Lane (of Kansas), Morgan, Pomeroy, Ramsey, Sherman, Sumner, Wilkinson, Wilson—18.

NAYS—Messrs. Buckalew, Carlile, Cowan, Davis, Grimes, Harris, Hendricks, Hicks, Johnson, Lane (of Indiana), McDougall, Morrill,

Nesmith, Powell, Richardson, Saulsbury, Ten Eyck, Trumbull, Van Winkle, Willey—20.

The bill then passed the Senate, and afterward the House, without amendment.

An act to regulate the elective franchise in the District of Columbia, was vetoed by the President. This act provided that each and every male person, excepting paupers and persons under guardianship, of the age of twenty-one years and upward, who has not been convicted of any infamous crime or offense, and excepting persons who may have voluntarily given aid and comfort to the rebels in the late rebellion, and who shall have been born or naturalized in the United States, and who shall have resided in the said District for the period of one year, and three months in the ward or election precinct in which he shall offer to vote, next preceding any election therein, shall be entitled to the elective franchise, and shall be deemed an elector and entitled to vote at any election in said District, without any distinction on account of color or race.

On the 7th of January, 1866, the President vetoed it.

Same day, the Senate passed it, notwithstanding the President's objections, by a two-thirds vote—yeas 29, nays 10, as follows:

YEAS—Messrs. Anthony, Cattell, Chandler, Conness, Cragin, Creswell, Edmunds, Fessenden, Fogg, Fowler, Frelinghuysen, Grimes, Henderson, Howard, Howe, Kirkwood, Lane, Morgan, Morrill, Poland, Ramsey, Ross, Sherman, Stewart, Sumner, Trumbull, Wade, Willey, Williams—29.

NAYS—Messrs. Cowan, Dixon, Doolittle, Foster, Hendricks, Johnson, Nesmith, Norton, Patterson, Van Winkle—10.

January 8—The House passed it — yeas 113, nays 38, as follows:

YEAS—Messrs. Alley, Allison, Ames, Arnell, Delos R. Ashley, James M. Ashley, Baker, Baldwin, Banks, Barker, Baxter, Beaman, Benjamin, Bidwell, Bingham, Blaine, Boutwell, Brandegee, Bromwell, Broomall, Buckland, Bundy, Reader, W. Clarke, Sidney Clarke, Cobb, Cook, Cullom, Culver, Darling, Dawes, Defrees, Delano, Deming, Dixon, Dodge, Donnelly, Driggs, Eckley, Eggleston, Farnsworth, Farquhar, Ferry, Garfield, Grinnell, Abner C. Harding, Hart, Hawkins, Hayes, Henderson, Higby, Hill, Holmes, Hooper, John H. Hubbard, James R. Hubbell, Ingersoll, Jenckes, Julian, Kasson, Kelley, Kelso, Ketcham, Koontz, George V. Lawrence, William Lawrence, Loan, Longyear, Lynch, Marston, Marvin, Maynard, McClurg, McRuer, Mercur, Miller, Morrill, Moulton, Myers, Newell O'Neill, Orth, Paine, Patterson, Perham, Pike, Plants, Price, Raymond, Alexander H. Rice, John H. Rice, Sawyer, Schenck, Scofield, Spalding, Starr, Stokes, Thayer, Francis Thomas, John L. Thomas, jr., Trowbridge, Upson, Van Aernam, Burt Van Horn, Hamilton Ward, Warner, Elihu B. Washburne, Welker, Wentworth, Williams, James F. Wilson, Stephen F. Wilson, Windom, and Speaker Colfax—113.

NAYS—Messrs. Ancona, Bergen, Campbell, Chanler, Cooper, Dawson, Eldridge, Finck, Glossbrenner, Aaron Harding, Hise, Hogan, Chester D. Hubbard, Humphrey, Hunter, Kerr, Kuykendall, Latham, Leftwich, McCullough, Niblack, Nicholson, Noell, Phelps, Radford, S. J. Randall, W. H. Randall, Ritter, Rogers, Ross, Shanklin, Strouse, Taber, Nathaniel G. Taylor, Nelson Taylor, Trimble, Andrew H. Ward, Winfield—38.

Whereupon the Speaker of the House declared the bill a law.

In the Senate, Messrs. Brown, Harris, Pomeroy, Sprague and Wilson, who voted for the bill originally, did not vote on this vote.

Messrs. Buckalew, Davis, Riddle and Saulsbury, who voted against the bill originally, did not vote on this vote.

Mr. Johnson, who did not vote on the original bill, voted against it now.

In the House, Messrs. Anderson, Blow, Conkling, Eliot, Griswold, Hale, Hotchkiss, Demas Hubbard, jr., Hubbard, Laflin, McIndoe, Moorhead, Morris, Pomeroy, Rollins, Shellabarger, Sloan, Stevens, R. T. Van Horn, W. B. Washburn and Woodbridge, who voted for the bill originally, did not vote on this vote.

Messrs. Benjamin, Cullom, Darling, Farquhar, Plants and J. L. Thomas, jr., who did not vote on the bill originally, voted for it now.

Messrs. Boyer, Denison, Goodyear, Harris, E. N. Hubbell, LeBlond, Marshall, McKee, Rousseau, Sitgreaves, Stillwell, Thornton and Whaley, who voted against the bill originally, did not vote now.

Messrs. Humphrey, McCullough, Trimble and Winfield, who did not vote originally, voted against the bill now.

In the Senate, January 10, 1861, pending the bill to amend the organic acts of the Territories,

This substitute was adopted:

"That from and after the passage of this act there shall be no denial of the elective franchise in any of the Territories of the United States, now or hereafter to be organized, to any citizen thereof, on account of race, color, or previous condition of servitude, and all acts or parts of acts, either of Congress or the legislative assemblies of said Territories inconsistent with the provisions of this act, are hereby declared null and void."

The vote was—yeas 24, nays 8, as follows:

YEAS — Messrs. Anthony, Conness, Cragin, Creswell, Edmunds, Fessenden, Fogg, Foster, Fowler, Grimes, Henderson, Howard, Howe, Kirkwood, Lane, Morgan, Morrill, Poland, Sherman, Stewart, Sumner, Wade, Willey, Williams—24.

NAYS—Messrs. Buckalew, Hendricks, Johnson, Norton, Patterson, Riddle, Saulsbury, Van Winkle—8.

Same day—The House concurred—yeas 104, nays 38, as follows:

YEAS—Messrs. Alley, Allison, Ames, Arnell, James M. Ashley, Baker, Baldwin, Banks, Barker, Baxter, Beamen, Benjamin, Bidwell, Bingham, Blaine, Boutwell, Bromwell, Broomall, Buckland, Bundy, Reader W. Clarke, Sidney Clarke, Cobb, Cook, Cullom, Culver, Davis, Defrees, Delano, Deming, Dixon, Dodge, Donnelly, Driggs, Eckley, Eggleston, Farnsworth, Farquhar, Ferry, Garfield, Grinnell, Abner C. Harding, Hart, Hawkins, Higby, Hill, Holmes, Hooper, Demas Hubbard, jr., John H. Hubbard, James R. Hubbell, Ingersoll, Jenckes, Julian, Kasson, Kelso, Ketcham, Koontz, George V. Lawrence, W. Lawrence, Loan, Longyear, Lynch, Marston, Maynard, Marvin, McClurg, McRuer, Mercur, Miller, Morrill, Moulton, Myers, Orth, O'Neill, Paine, Perham, Plants, Price, Raymond, John H. Rice, Rollins, Sawyer, Schenck, Scofield, Spalding, Stokes, Thayer, John L. Thomas, jr., Trowbridge, Upson, Van Aernam, Burt Van Horn, Hamilton Ward, Warner, Elihu B. Washburne, Henry D. Washburn, William B. Washburn, Welker, Wentworth, Williams, James F. Wilson, Stephen F. Wilson, Windom—104.

NAYS—Messrs. Ancona, Bergen, Boyer, Campbell, Chanler, Cooper, Dawson, Denison, Eldridge, Finck, Glossbrenner, Aaron Harding, Hise, Hogan, Chester D. Hubbard, Edwin N. Hubbell, Humphrey, Johnson, Latham, Le Blond, Leftwich, Niblack, Nicholson, Noell, Samuel J. Randall, William H. Randall, Ritter, Rogers, Ross, Shanklin, Sitgreaves, Taber, Nathaniel G. Taylor, Thornton, Trimble, Andrew H. Ward, Whaley, Winfield—38.

The failure of the President to sign, or return this bill with his objections, within ten days after presentation to him, made it a law.

In the Senate, January 9, 1861, the bill for the admission of Nebraska, passed—yeas 24, nays 15, with the third section in these words:

"That this act shall take effect with the fundamental and perpetual condition that within said State of Nebraska there shall be no abridgment or denial of the exercise of the elective franchise, or of any other right, to any person by reason of race or color, excepting Indians not taxed."

YEAS—Messrs. Anthony, Cattell, Chandler, Conness, Cragin, Creswell, Edmunds, Fogg, Fowler, Henderson, Howard, Kirkwood, Lane, Morrill, Poland, Ramsey, Ross, Sherman, Stewart, Sumner, Van Winkle, Wade, Willey, Williams—24.

NAYS—Messrs. Buckalew, Cowan, Dixon, Doolittle, Foster, Grimes, Hendricks, Howe, Johnson, Morgan, Nesmith, Norton, Patterson, Riddle, Saulsbury—15.

In the House, January 15, 1867, the third section of the bill, as it became a law, was substituted for the above. It is as follows:

"That this act shall not take effect except upon the fundamental condition that within the State of Nebraska there shall be no denial of the elective franchise, or of any other right to any person by reason of race or color except Indians not taxed, and upon the further fundamental condition that the Legislature of said State, by a solemn public act, shall declare the assent of said State to the said fundamental condition, and shall transmit to the President of the United States an authentic copy of said act. Upon receipt whereof the President, by proclamation, shall forthwith announce the fact; whereupon said fundamental condition shall be held as a part of the organic law of the State; and thereupon, and without any further proceeding on the part of Congress, the admission of said State into the Union shall be considered as complete. Said State Legislature shall be convened by the Territorial Governor within thirty days after the passage of this act, to act upon the condition submitted herein."

The vote on this substitute was as follows:

January 15—The third section as it stands, was substituted for that adopted above by the Senate—yeas 88, nays 70, as follow:

YEAS—Messrs. Alley, Allison, Ames, Anderson, James M. Ashley, Baldwin, Banks, Baxter, Blaine, Boutwell, Brandegee, Broomall, Cobb, Cook, Cullom, Culver, Dawes, Deming, Dixon, Dodge, Donnelly, Driggs, Eckley, Eliot, Ferry, Garfield, Grinnell, Griswold, Hart, Higby, Holmes, Hooper, Demas Hubbard, jr., John H. Hubbard, Ingersoll, Jenckes, Julian, Kelley, Kelso, Ketcham, Koontz, Kuykendall, Loan, Longyear, Lynch, Marston, Marvin, Maynard, McClurg, McIndoe, McRuer, Mercur, Moorhead, Morrill, Morris, Moulton, Newell, O'Neill, Orth, Paine, Patterson, Perham, Pike, Price, Raymond, Alexander H. Rice, John H. Rice, Rollins, Sawyer, Schenck, Schofield, Spalding, Stevens, Thayer, Trowbridge, Upson, Van Aernam, Burt Van Horn, Hamilton Ward, Warner, Elihu B. Washburne, William B. Washburn, Welker, Wentworth, Williams, James F. Wilson, Stephen F. Wilson, Windom—88.

NAYS—Messrs. Ancona, Delos R. Ashley, Baker, Benjamin, Bergen, Bingham, Boyer, Bromwell, Buckland, Bundy, Campbell, Chanler, Reader W. Clarke, Cooper, Davis, Dawson, Defrees, Delano, Denison, Eldridge, Farnsworth, Farquhar, Finck, Glossbrenner, Goodyear, Hale, Aaron Harding, Abner C. Harding, Hawkins, Henderson, Hill, Hise, Hogan, Chester D. Hubbard, Edwin N. Hubbell, J. R. Hubbell, Humphrey, Hunter, Johnson, Kerr, Latham, George V. Lawrence, LeBlond, Leftwich, Marshall, McKee, Miller, Niblack, Nicholson, Plants, Radford, Samuel J. Randall, William H. Randall, Ritter, Rogers, Shanklin, Shellabarger, Sitgreaves, Stillwell, Stokes, Strouse, Taber, Nathaniel G. Taylor, Nelson Taylor, Francis Thomas, John L. Thomas, jr., Thornton, Andrew H. Ward, Henry D. Washburn, Whaley—70.

Same day the bill passed—yeas 103, nays 55.

On the 16th of January the Senate agreed to the above amendment of the House:

YEAS—Messrs. Anthony, Cattell, Chandler, Conness, Cragin, Fessenden, Fogg, Fowler, Frelinghuysen, Grimes, Henderson, Howard, Kirkwood, Lane, Morgan, Morrill, Poland, Ramsey, Sherman, Sprague, Stewart, Sumner, Van Winkle, Wade, Willey, Williams, Wilson, Yates—28.

NAYS—Messrs. Buckalew, Cowan, Dixon, Doolittle, Edmunds, Foster, Harris, Hendricks, Johnson, Nesmith, Norton, Patterson, Riddle, Saulsbury—14.

The President vetoed the bill, and it was passed over his veto and became a law, Feb. 9, 1867.

The bill for the admission of Colorado passed the House January 15, with a third section exactly the same as that contained in the Nebraska bill published above, except that it provides that the Governor elect of said State shall convene the Legislature instead of the Territorial Governor, and that he shall do so in sixty days instead of thirty, as provided in the Nebraska bill.

1867, January 15—the bill passed—yeas 90, nays 60, as follows:

YEAS—Messrs. Alley, Allison, Ames, Anderson, Delos R. Ashley, James M. Ashley, Baldwin, Banks, Baxter, Benjamin, Boutwell, Brandegee, Bromwell, Broomall, Bundy, Reader W. Clarke, Cobb, Cook, Cullom, Culver, Dawes, Delano, Deming, Dixon, Dodge, Donnelly, Driggs, Eckley, Eliot, Farquhar, Ferry, Garfield, Grinnell, Griswold, Henderson, Higby, Hill, Holmes, Hooper, Demas Hubbard, jr., John H. Hubbard, J. R. Hubbell, Ingersoll, Jenckes, Julian, Kelley, Koontz, George V. Lawrence, Longyear, Marston, Marvin, McClurg, McIndoe, McRuer, Mercur, Miller, Moorhead, Morris, Moulton, Newell, O'Neill, Orth, Paine, Perham, Plants, Price, Alexander H. Rice, John H. Rice, Rollins, Sawyer, Schenck, Shellabarger, Spalding, Stokes, Thayer, Francis Thomas, John L. Thomas, jr., Trowbridge, Upson, Van Aernam, Burt Van Horn, Warner, Henry D. Washburn, William B. Washburn, Welker, Wentworth, Williams, James F. Wilson, Stephen F. Wilson, Windom—90.

NAYS—Messrs. Ancona, Baker, Bergen, Bingham, Blaine, Boyer, Buckland, Campbell, Cooper, Davis, Defrees, Denison, Eldridge, Finck, Glossbrenner, Goodyear, Hale, Aaron Harding, Abner C. Harding, Hart, Hawkins, Hise, Hogan, Chester D. Hubbard, Edwin N. Hubbell, Humphrey, Hunter, Johnson, Kelso, Kerr, Kuykendall, Latham, LeBlond, Lefwich, Lynch, Marshall, Maynard, McKee, Morrill, Niblack, Nicholson, Pike, Radford, Samuel J. Randall, Raymond, Ritter, Rogers, Ross, Shanklin, Sitgreaves, Stillwell, Strouse, Taber, Nathaniel G. Taylor, Nelson Taylor, Thornton, Andrew H. Ward, Hamilton Ward, Elihu B. Washburne, Whaley—60.

January 16—the Senate agreed to the bill with the third section as it stands—yeas 27, nays 12, as follows:

YEAS—Messrs, Anthony, Cattell, Chandler, Conness, Cragin, Fessenden, Fowler, Frelinghuysen, Grimes, Harris, Henderson, Howard, Kirkwood, Lane, Morrill, Poland, Ramsey, Sherman, Sprague, Stewart, Sumner, Van Winkle, Wade, Willey, Williams, Wilson, Yates—27.

NAYS—Messrs. Buckalew, Dixon, Doolittle, Edmunds, Foster, Hendricks, Johnson, Nesmith, Norton, Patterson, Riddle, Saulsbury—12.

Personal Liberty of the American Citizen.

RADICAL CONTEMPT OF CONSTITUTIONAL FREEDOM.

The cool indifference with which the Radical members of the United States Senate and House of Representatives viewed the outrages committed upon the rights of citizens during the war, and the cruel antagonism with which they confronted any inquiry into or condemnation of the illegal imprisonment of citizens who had been dragged from their homes and confined in dungeons by the mere *ipse dixit* of President Lincoln, Stanton, or any of the rulers of that day, can be well illustrated by the reproduction of a few votes in Congress.

In the Senate, December 16, 1862, Mr. Saulsbury offered the following resolution:

"*Resolved*, That the Secretary of War be and is hereby directed to inform the Senate whether Dr. John Law and Whitely Meredith, or either of them, citizens of the State of Deleware, have been arrested and imprisoned in Fort Delaware; when they were arrested and so imprisoned; the charges against them; by whom made; by what order they were arrested and imprisoned; and that he communicate to the Senate all papers relating to their arrest and imprisonment."

Which was laid upon the table.

YEAS—Messrs. Anthony, Arnold, Browning, Chandler, Clark, Collamer, Dixon, Doolittle, Fessenden, Field, Foote, Foster, Grimes, Hale, Harlan, Harris, Howard, Howe, King, Lane (of Kansas), Morrill, Sumner, Ten Eyck, Trumbull, Wade, Wilkinson, Wilmot, Wilson (of Mass.), and *Wright*—29.

NAYS—Messrs. *Bayard, Carlile*, Cowan, *Davis, Harding*, Henderson, *Kennedy, Nesmith, Powell*, Rice, *Saulsbury*, Willey, *Wilson* (of Mo.)—13.

In the House of Representatives, December 1, 1862, Mr. Cox offered the following preamble and resolution:

"WHEREAS, Many citizens of the United States have been seized by persons acting or pretending to be acting, under the authority of the United States, and have been carried out of the jurisdiction of the States of their residence, and imprisoned in the military prisons and camps of the United States, without any public charge being preferred against them, and without any opportunity being allowed to learn or disprove the charges made, or alleged to be made, against them; and whereas, such arrests have been made in States where there was no insurrection or rebellion, or pretense thereof, or any other obstruction against the authority of the Government: and whereas, it is the sacred right of every citizen of the United States, that he shall not be deprived of liberty without due process of law, and when arrested, that he shall have a speedy and public trial by an impartial jury of his countrymen: Therefore,

"*Resolved*, That the House of Representatives do hereby condemn all such arrests as unwarranted by the Constitution and laws of the United States, and as a usurpation of power never given up by the people to their rulers, and do hereby demand that all such arrests shall hereafter cease, and that all persons so arrested and yet held should have a prompt and public trial, according to the provisions of the Constitution."

Which was laid on the table—yeas, 80; nays, 40. The nays were:

Messrs. Ancona, Baily, Biddle, Jacob B. Blair, Calvert, Corning, Cox, Crittenden, English, Fouke, Granger, Grider, Haight, Hall, Harding, Holman, Knapp, Law, Lazear, Menzies, Morris, Noble, Norton, Nugen, Odell, Price, Richardson, Sheffield, Shiel, John B. Steele, William G. Steele, Stiles, Benjamin F. Thomas, Francis Thomas, Vallandigham, Ward, Chilton A. White, Wickliffe, Wright and Yeaman—40.

December 1—Mr. Richardson offered the following resolution:

"*Resolved*, That the President of the United States be requested to inform this House what citizens of Illinois are now confined in the Forts Warren, Lafayette and Deleware, or the Old Capitol Prison, and any other forts or places of confinement; what the charges are against said persons; also, the places where they were arrested. That the President be further requested to inform this House of the names of persons that have been arrested in Illinois and taken to and confined in prisons outside of the limits of said State, and who have been released; what were the charges against each of them; by whom the charges were made; also, by whose order said arrests were made, and the authority of law for such arrests."

Which was laid on the table—yeas, 74; nays, 40. The nays were:

Messrs. Ancona, Baily, Biddle, Calvert, Roscoe Conkling, Conway, Corning, Cox, Crittenden, Dunn, English, Fouke, Granger, Grider, Hall, Harding, Holman, Wm. Kellogg, Knapp, Law, Lazear, Leary, Menzies, Morris, Noble, Norton, Nugen, Odell, Porter, Price, Richardson, Shiel, John B. Steele, William G. Steele, Stiles, Benjamin F. Thomas, Vallandigham, Ward, Chilton A. White and Wright—40.

December 22.—Mr. May offered the following resolution:

"*Resolved*, That the Secretary of State be requested to communicate to this House a copy of an order which, on or about the 28th of November, 1861, he caused to be read to State prisoners confined in Fort Warren, whereby they were forbidden to employ counsel in their behalf, and informed that such employment of counsel would be regarded by the Government and by the State Department as a reason for prolonging the term of their imprisonment."

Which was laid upon the table—yeas, 63; nays, 48. The nays were:

Messrs. William Allen, William J. Allen, Ancona, Biddle, Burnham, Calvert, Clements, Cobb, Cox, Cravens, Crittenden, Dunn, English, Granger, Grider, Hale, Harding, Johnson, William Kellogg, Kerrigan, Knapp, Law, Lazear, Leary, May, Morris, Noble, Norton, Nugen, Pendleton, Price, Robinson, James S. Rollins, Shiel, Smith, Benj. F. Thomas, Francis Thomas, Vallandigham, Vibbard, Voorhees, Wadsworth, Ward, Chilton A. White, Wickliffe, Woodruff, Worchester, Wright and Yeaman—48.

On the 17th of December, 1863, Mr. Harrington offered a preamble followed by these resolutions:

"*Resolved, by the House of Representatives of the United States*, That no power is delegated by the Constitution of the United States, either to the legislative or executive power, to suspend the privilege of the writ of *habeas corpus* in any State loyal to the Constitution and Government, not invaded, and in which the civil and judicial powers are in full operation.

"*Resolved*, That Congress has no power, under the Constitution, to delegate to the President of the United States the authority to suspend the privilege of the writ of *habeas corpus*, and imprison at his pleasure, without process of law or trial, the citizens of the loyal States.

"*Resolved*, That the assumption of the right by the Executive of the United States, to deprive the citizens of such loyal States of the benefits of the writ of *habeas corpus*, and to imprison them at his pleasure, without process of law, is unworthy the progress of the age, is consistent only with a despotic power unlimited by constitutional obligations, and is wholly subversive of the elementary principles of freedom upon which the government of the United States, and that of the several States, is based.

"*Resolved*, That the Judiciary Committee be instructed to prepare and report a bill to this House protecting the rights of the citizens in the loyal States, in strict accordance with the foregoing provisions of the Constitution of the United States."

Which was negatived—yeas 67, nays 90, as follows:

YEAS—Messrs. James C. Allen, Wm. J. Allen, Ancona, Augustus C. Baldwin, Bliss, Brooks, Brown, Chanler, Coffroth, Cox, Cravens, Dawson, Denison, Eden, Edgerton, Eldridge, English, Finck, Ganson, Grider, Hall, Harding, Harrington, Benjamin G. Harris, Herrick, Holman, William Johnson, Kernan, King, Knapp, Law, Le Blond, Long, Mallory, Marcy, McAllister, McDowell, McKinney, Middleton, Wm. H. Miller, James R. Morris, Morrison, Nelson, Noble, Odell, John O'Neill, Pendleton, Perry, Radford, Samuel J. Randall, Robinson, Rogers, Ross, Scott, John B. Steele, Wm. G. Steele, Stiles, Strouse, Stewart, Voorhees, Wadsworth, Ward, Wheeler, Chilton A. White, Joseph W. White, Winfield, Wood—67.

NAYS—Alley, Allison, Ames, Arnold, Ashley, John D. Baldwin, Beaman, Blaine, Blow, Boutwell, Brandegee, Broomall, William G. Brown, Ambrose W. Clark, Freeman Clarke, Clay, Cobb, Cole, Cresswell, Henry Winter Davis, Thomas T. Davis, Dawes, Dixon, Donnelly, Driggs, Dumont, Eckley, Eliot, Farnsworth, Fenton, Frank, Garfield, Gooch, Grinnell, Hale, Higby, Hooper, Hotchkiss, Asahel W. Hubbard, John H. Hubbard, Hulburd, Jenckes, Julian, Kasson, Kelley, Francis W. Kellogg, Orlando Kellogg, Loan, Longyear, Lovejoy, Marvin, McBride, McClurg, McIndoe, Samuel F. Miller, Moorhead, Morrill, Dan'l Morris, Amos Myers, Leonard Myers, Norton, Charles O'Neill, Orth, Perham, Pike, Pomeroy, Price, Wm. H. Randall, Alexander H. Rice, John H. Rice, Edward H. Rollins, Schenck, Scofield, Shannon, Sloan, Smithers, Spalding, Stevens, Thayer, Tracy, Van Valkenburgh, Elihu B. Washburne, William B. Washburn, Whaley, Williams, Wilder, Wilson, Windom, Woodbridge—90.

Among the parties seized and imprisoned was Brigadier-General Charles P. Stone, who was in command of the Federal forces in the defeat at Ball's Bluff. His imprisonment was understood to have been instigated by Senator Sumner, of Massachusetts. The Senate addressed the President for information as to his arrest, who replied as follows:

"EXECUTIVE MANSION, WASHINGTON, May 1, 1862.

"*To the Senate of the United States:*

"In answer to the resolution of the Senate, in relation to Brigadier-General Stone, I have the honor to state that he was arrested and imprisoned under my general authority, and upon evidence which, whether he be guilty or innocent, required, as appears to me, such proceedings to be had against him for the public safety. I deem it incompatible with the public interest, as also, perhaps, unjust to General Stone, to make a more particular statement of the evidence.

"He has not been tried, because, in the state of military operations at the time of his arrest and since, the officers to constitute a court-martial, and for witnesses, could not be withdrawn from duty without serious injury to the service. He will be allowed a trial without any unnecessary delay; the charges and specifications will be furnished him in due season, and every facility for his defense will be afforded him by the War Department.

"ABRAHAM LINCOLN."

Under the head of Military Arrests, this subject is again referred to; also in history of Reconstruction, in a subsequent part of this book.

Indemnity Act.

The third session of the Thirty-seventh Congress passed an act of indemnity, which not only approved of all these illegal arrests, but protecting the President against all suits for damages arising therefrom, and giving him the power, during the war, to suspend the writ of *habeas corpus* anywhere he might see fit. This bill passed the House of Representatives, March 2, 1863, by yeas and nays as follows:

YEAS—Messrs. Aldrich, Arnold, Ashley, Babbitt, Baker, Baxter, Beaman, Bingham, Jacob B. Blair, Samuel S. Blair, Blake, William G. Brown, Buffinton, Campbell, Casey, Chamberlain, Clark, Colfax, Frederick A. Conkling, Roscoe Conkling, Conway, Cutler, Davis, Dawes, Delano, Dunn, Edgerton, Eliot, Ely, Fenton, S. C. Fessenden, Tho's A. D. Fessenden, Fisher, Flanders, Franchot, Frank, Goodwin, Gurley, Hahn, Hale, Harrison, Hooper, Horton, Hutchins, Julian, Kelley, Francis W. Kellogg, Wm. Kellogg, Killinger, Lansing, Leary, Lehman, Loomis, Low, McIndoe, McKean, McKnight, McPherson, Marston, Maynard, Mitchell, Moorhead, Anson P. Morrill, Nixon, Olin, Patton, Timothy G. Phelps, Pike, Pomeroy, Porter, John H. Rice, Riddle, Edward H. Rollins, Sargent, Sedgwick, Segar, Shanks, Shellabarger, Sherman, Sloan, Spaulding, Stevens, Stratton, Francis Thomas, Trimble, Trowbridge, Van Horn, Van Valkenburgh, Van Wyck, Verree, Walker, Wall, Wallace, Washburne, Wheeler, Albert S. White, Wilson, Windom, Worcester—99.

NAYS—Messrs. *William Allen, William J. Allen, Ancona, Biddle, Calvert, Cravens, Crisfield, Delaplaine, Dunlap, English, Granger, Grider, Hall, Harding, Holman, Johnson, Knapp, Kerrigan, Law, Mallory, May, Menzies, Morris, Noble, Norton, Nugen, Pendleton, Perry, Price, Robinson, Shiel, Smith, John B. Steele, William G. Steele, Stiles, Benjamin F. Thomas, Vallandigham, Voorhees, Wadsworth, Ward, Chilton A. White, Wickliffe, Wood, Woodruff, Yeaman*—45.

Same day, the bill passed the Senate, without a record of the yeas and nays, owing to a misunderstanding respecting the putting of the vote.

The history of the passage of this act, and the attending circumstances, are as follows:

During the session a bill was passed in the House of Representatives, introduced by Mr. Stevens, entitled "An act to indemnify the President, and other persons, for suspending the privilege of the writ of *habeas corpus*, and acts done in pursuance thereof."

This bill was the subject of the following protest in the House of Representatives, on 22d of December, 1862, against its passage:

We protest against the passage of the bill:

"1. Because it purports to deprive the citizen of all existing, peaceful, legal modes of redress for admitted wrongs, and thus constrains him tamely to submit to the injury inflicted, or to seek illegal and forcible remedies.

"2. Because it purports to indemnify the President and all acting under his authority for acts admitted to be wrongful, at the expense of the citizen upon whom the wrongful acts have been perpetrated, in violation of the plainest principles of justice, and the most familiar precepts of constitutional law.

"3. Because it purports to confirm and make valid, by act of Congress, arrests and imprisonments which were not only not warranted by the Constitution of the United States, but were in palpable violation of its express prohibitions.

"4. Because it purports to authorize the President, during this rebellion, at any time, as to any person, and everywhere throughout the limits of the United States, to suspend the privilege of the writ of *habeas corpus*, whereas by the Constitution the power to suspend the privilege of that writ is confided to the discretion of Congress alone, and is limited to the places threatened by the dangers of invasion or insurrection.

"5. Because, for these and other reasons, it is unjust and unwise, an invasion of private rights, an encouragement to lawless violence, and a precedent full of hope to all who would usurp despotic power and perpetuate it by the arbitrary arrest and imprisonment of those who oppose them.

"6. And finally, because in both its sections it is 'a deliberate, palpable, and dangerous' violation of the Constitution, according to the plain sense and intention of that instrument,' and is therefore utterly null and void.

Geo. H Pendleton, C. A. Wickliffe,
W. A. Richardson, Charles J. Biddle,
J. C. Robinson, J. A. Cravens,
P. B. Fouke, Elijah Ward,
James R. Morris, Philip Johnson,
A. L. Knapp, John D. Stiles,
C. L. Vallandigham, D. W. Voorhees,
C. A. White, G. W. Dunlap,
Warren P. Noble, Hendrick B. Wright,
W. Allen, H. Grider,
William J. Allen, W. H. Wadsworth,
S. S. Cox, A. Harding,
E. H Norton, Charles B. Calvert,
George K. Shiel, James E. Kerrigan,
S. E. Ancona, Henry May,
J. Lazear, R. H. Nugen,
Nehemiah Perry, George H. Yeaman,
C. Vibbard, B. F. Granger,
John Law.

The motion to enter this protest was tabled—yeas 75, nays 41.

The above bill of Mr. Stevens was amended in the Senate, and finally passed that body, January 28—yeas 33, nays 7, as follows:

YEAS—Messrs. Anthony, Arnold, Browning, Chandler, Clark, Collamer, Cowan, Dixon, Doolittle, Fessenden, Foot, Foster, Grimes, Hale, Harlan, Harris, Henderson, Hicks, Howard, King, Lane (of Indiana), Lane (of Kansas), Morrill, Pomeroy, Sherman, Sumner, Ten Eyck, Trumbull, Wade, Wilkinson, Willey, Wilmot, Wilson (of Massachusetts)—33.

NAYS—Messrs. *Bayard, Carlile, McDougal, Powell, Turpie, Wall, Wilson* (of Missouri)—7.

The House non-concurred in the amendments, and a Committee of Conference having met, agreed upon a report, which was agreed to in both Houses, and which resulted in the Act of March 3, 1863, known as the Indemnity Act, the vote upon which is given in the first part of this chapter.

VOTE ON THE SUSPENSION OF HABEAS CORPUS.

Pending the consideration of the original House bill in the Senate,

1863, February 19—Mr. Powell moved to strike out the third section authorizing the President to suspend, by proclamation, the writ of *habeas corpus* in certain contingencies; which was rejected—yeas 13, nays 27, as follows:

YEAS—Messrs. *Bayard, Carlile,* Cowan, *Kennedy, Latham, Nesmith, Powell, Rice, Richardson, Saulsbury, Turpie,* Willey, *Wilson* (of Missouri)—13.

NAYS—Messrs. Anthony, Arnold, Chandler, Clark, *Davis,* Dixon, Doolittle, Fessenden, Foot, Grimes, Harris, Henderson, Hicks, Howard, Howe, King, Lane (of Indiana), Lane (of Kansas), Morrill, Pomeroy, Sherman, Sumner, Ten Eyck, Trumbull, Wilkinson, Wilmot, Wilson (of Massachusetts)—27.

The Sherman and Johnston Armistice.

HOW TWO SOLDIERS AGREED TO FIX AN ENDURING PEACE—GENERAL SHERMAN'S VIEW OF THE WAR—ITS PURPOSES, AND THE LOGICAL EFFECT OF ITS CLOSE.

First, The contending armies now in the field to maintain their *statu quo* until notice is given by the commanding General of either one to its opponent, and reasonable time—say 48 hours—allowed.

Second, The Confederate armies, now in existence, to be disbanded, and conducted to their several State capitals, there to deposit their arms and public property in the State arsenals; and each officer and man to execute and file an agreement to cease from acts of war, and abide action of both State and Federal authority. The number of arms and munitions of war to be reported to the Chief of Ordnance at Washington city, subject to future action of the Congress of the United States, in the mean time to be used solely to maintain peace and order within the borders of the States respectively.

The recognition by the Executive of the United States of the several State governments in their officers and legislatures, taking oath prescribed by the Constitution of the United States, and where conflicting State governments have resulted from the war, the legitimacy of all shall be submitted to the Supreme Court of the United States.

Fourth, The re-establishment of all Federal Courts in the several States, with powers as defined by the Constitution of the United States, and of the States respectively.

Sixth, The Executive authority of the Government of the United States, not to disturb any of the people by reason of the late war, so long as they live in peace and quiet, and abstain from acts of armed hostility, and obey laws in existence at any place of their residence.

In general terms, war to cease; a general amnesty, so far as the Executive power of the United States can command, or on condition of disbandment of the Confederate armies, and the distribution of arms, and resumption of peaceful pursuits by officers and men, as hitherto composing the said armies. Not being fully empowered by our respective principals to fulfill these terms, we individually and officially pledge ourselves to promptly obtain necessary authority, and to carry out the above programme.

W. T. SHERMAN,
Maj.-Gen. Command'g the Army of the U. S. in N. C.

J. E. JOHNSTON,
Gen. Command'g Confederate States Army in N. C.

Signed April 18, 1865.

This memorandum was rejected by the President and Cabinet, and Sherman was directed to resume hostilities at once. General Johnston, when informed of the decision of the Government, surrendered his command on the same terms as those granted to General Lee.

General Sherman, in his report of the operations of his command in North Carolina, dated May 9, 1865, addressed to General Rawlins, Chief of Staff, says:

"The points on which he (General Johnston) expressed especial solicitude were, lest their States were to be dismembered and denied representation in Congress, or any separate political existence whatever, and that the absolute disarming of his men would leave the South powerless and exposed to depredations by wicked bands of assassins and robbers.

"President Lincoln's message of 1864; his Amnesty proclamation; General Grant's terms to General Lee, substantially extending the benefits of that proclamation to all officers above the rank of colonel; the invitation to the Virginia Legislature to reassemble in Richmond by General Weitzel, with the approval of Mr. Lincoln and General Grant, then on the spot; a firm belief that I had been fighting to re establish the Constitution of the United States; and last, not least, the general and universal desire to close a war, any longer without organized resistance, were the leading facts that induced me to pen the 'memorandum of April 18th, signed by myself and General Johnston.'

"* * * My letter to the Mayor of Atlanta has been published to the world, and I was not rebuked by the War Department for it.

"My letter to Mr. N. W., at Savannah, was shown by me to Mr. Stanton before its publication, and all that my memory retains of his answer is that he said, like my letters generally, it was sufficiently 'emphatic, and could not be misunderstood.'

"But these letters asserted my belief that, according to Mr. Lincoln's proclamations and messages, when the people of the South had laid down their arms and submitted to the lawful power of the United States, *ipso facto*, the war was over as to them; and, furthermore, that if any State in rebellion would conform to the Constitution of the United States, 'cease war,' ELECT SENATORS AND REPRESENTATIVES TO CONGRESS, if admitted (of which each House of Congress alone is the judge), that State became *instanter* as much in the Union as New York or Ohio. Nor was I rebuked for this expression, though it was universally known and commented on at the time."

How Beaten Impeachers make War on Women.

THE MEANEST OF THE MEAN RADICAL PLOTS EXPOSED — CONGRESS VS. MISS VINNIE REAM.

By reference to the preceedings in another chapter, in the case of Mr. C. W. Woolley, it will be seen, that the House, on the 28th of May, made the following location of the Legislative Bastile for the confinement of that gentleman:

"*Resolved*, That the rooms A and B, opposite the room of the Solicitor of the Court of Claims, in the capitol, be and are hereby assigned as guard-room and office of the capitol police, and are for that purpose placed under charge of the Sergeant-at-arms of the House, with power to fit the same up for the purpose specified."

The Washington correspondent of the New York *World* (J. B. S), in his dispatch of May 29, exposes the low motive for the selection of those two rooms:

"Rooms A and B, designated in Mr. Bingham's resolution, were never designated as such until yesterday morning, when, in accordance with instructions from one or more of the managers, the letters A and B were pasted on the doors of those rooms. The apartment to which the letter B was affixed was the one intended for the prisoner Woolley. The apartment to which the letter A was affixed is the one hitherto occupied by Miss Vinnie Ream, an artist employed by Congress to model and complete a marble statue of Abraham Lincoln for the Capitol. This room was originally offered Miss Ream by a Congressional committee, without her solicitation, and has been used by her as a studio with the tacit and cordial consent of both Houses of Congress. It is an out-of-the-way delightful little place in the basement of the Capitol, hallowed by the modest presence of a lady and the tokens of her art. The best, the most venerable, and the most distinguished men of the Senate and the House, and the highest dignitaries of the Government have been proud and glad to repair once in a while to this remote nook in the great building where the legislative business of the nation is carried on, and to encourage with their presence and their words the efforts of one, almost a child in years, to vindicate the confidence reposed in her genius and her skill. But this girl, than whom a braver or a more aspiring enthusiast never lived, this young devotee to an art her endeavors to perfect herself in which have, I am assured by her friends, been from the first so arduous and uninterrupted as to endanger her health and cause her to forswear in a great measure the social enjoyments appropriate to her age, is at last singled out by the dishonored and beaten scoundrels who were at the head of the impeachment, as a victim. Why? Because, as it is ridiculously alleged, Miss Ream 'influenced' the vote of a Senator for the acquittal of the President. In order that this falsehood may be the more completely exposed, I proceed to state, in their order, some facts which were, and some which were not, mentioned in this afternoon's debate. Mr. Ross, of Kansas, whose vote assisted to kill the impeachment, is the Republican Senator alluded to as having been persuaded by Miss Ream. Mr. Ross is a gentleman, whose family, consisting of a wife and several children, reside at his Kansas home. Sent here to represent that State in the Senate, Mr. Ross applied for and has since occupied rooms at the house of his old acquaintance and neighbor in Kansas, Mr. Robert L. Ream. This circumstance, associated with the facts that Miss Vinnie Ream is the daughter of Mr. Ream aforesaid, and that she resides with her parents, and with the assertion that whatever patriotic sympathies she had were far from being associated with the Radical cause, led some persons who assemble in the Radical caucuses at the Capitol to organize a base scheme for the success of the impeachment. Mr. George W. Julian, of Indiana, a Radical member who was once publicly cowhided by General Meredith, and who deserves another hundred lashes on his bare back for the despicable errand that he went upon, proceeded, doubtless at the instance of his confederates, to Miss Ream's studio. To that apartment, in common with all who choose to enter it during the hours set apart for the reception of visitors, he had been accustomed occasionally to repair. Miss Ream might have presumed, for aught I know, that this Indiana demagogue was kindly disposed to her. Nevertheless her instincts were too acute not to induce her to repel with maidenly indignation the charge that he covertly insinuated that she had expressed her desire to Senator Ross as to his vote on the impeachment. Satisfied as he must have been that she had not done so, the wily Julian forthwith expressed himself nearly as follows:

"'But you ought to use your influence for the sake of the great Republican party. If Mr. Ross don't vote for conviction, you will be ruined.'

"The sweet temper of the lady thus addressed was not quite proof against this shameful appeal. The gray-haired diplomat retired, previously, however, receiving an intimation from Miss Ream that, although she was not informed of Senator Ross' intention, and had no right to know of or inquire into it, she supposed that he, being a Republican, would vote for the conviction of the President. This dastardly threat of Julian against a trembling girl is the very threat that Butler and his gang are now carrying into effect. The apartment in the Capitol which she has occupied is taken from her, not because the prisoner (Woolley) has to be incarcerated in it, for he is to be put into the adjoining room, but because Woolley's imprisonment is a sort of excuse for making the studio an office for Woolley's keepers.

"The statue of Mr. Lincoln, now being molded by Miss Ream, in clay, can not be removed, and the Radicals of the House are rejoiced. They are delighted for this reason: this clay model, upon which Miss Ream has been engaged for months, is the inception of that work upon which she is not only to base her reputation as a sculptor, but upon which she most depends for pecuniary reward. If it is neglected, it will shrink, crack to pieces, and be destroyed. All the artist's labor will have been in vain. There will be nothing left save a shattered, shapeless mass, to be moistened, after it is too late, by a young girl's tears.

"Butler, particularly, gloats over the prospect of such a consummation. He crossed to the Democratic side of the House yesterday, and declared that, so long as he had anything to do with the Committee on Appropriations, Miss Vinnie Ream should not receive a dollar on account of her labor. He said to-day, in effect, that the country desired no statue of Mr. Lincoln from her hands. This creature, too flatteringly called 'the Beast,' has a daughter; yet in neither his nature, nor in Bingham's, nor in the natures of any of the men in Congress—run mad with partisanship and the thirst for vengeance—does there seem to be an instinct sensitive enough to shrink from the immolation of a helpless girl upon the altar of a lost and shameful cause."

The New York *Gazette*, says: "Butler shows himself a coward—for the first time, in our opinion. His recent reference to her brings a blush to an American face. A member of the United States Congress, upon the floor of the House, announces that a matter of great political moment to the country shall be carried to a successful result 'in spite of all the women in the basement of the Capitol'"—that is, in spite of Miss Vinnie Ream, a little sculptress, and the only woman "in the basement of the Capitol." No remark so belittling to the importance of American politics was ever made by a public man, even in the halls of Congress."

A Bastile in the National Capitol.
IMPRISONMENT OF A CITIZEN BY THE ORDER OF BEAST BUTLER.

The *National Intelligencer*, published at Washington, contains the following:

"A bastile is established, and the day is not distant, as things go, when the instruments and means of torture of which history has a horrible record—the rack, the wheel, and the thumb screw—will be applied to innocent victims until their agonized shrieks shall resound through the vaulted arches of the Capitol."

This statement of the *Intelligencer* is too true. Its apprehensions for the future are too well founded. It will be recollected that Butler, acting for the impeachment managers, who were carrying on an investigation as to the alleged purchase of certain Radical Senators to vote for the acquittal of the President, seized upon the manuscript of all the telegraphic messages which had been sent off from Washington about that time. This illegal and unjustifiable outrage is coolly defended by him and his party in the House as the mere use of "a *subpena duces tecum*," which he says was the exercise of an ordinary power. Among other dispatches, he seized upon and pried into the private telegrams of Mr. C. W. Woolley, a citizen of Cincinnati, then in Washington on business.

Summoning Mr. Woolley before the managers, Butler, being the only one present, subjected him to all manner of rude, abusive, and insulting indignities, such as placing him in the custody of the Sergeant-at-arms, and ordering that no one be permitted to speak to him. Some of the other managers being brought in, the witness was again introduced, Butler continuing the same course toward him, and at one time telling him that he lied. On the morning of the 27th of May, as described by a Washington correspondent, witness desired a consultation with his counsel for fifteen minutes, as to the propriety of certain questions which were asked him. This was refused, and the managers asked him with reference to this dispatch:

"*To Sheridan Shook, New York:*

"My business is adjusted. Place ten to my credit to-day, with Gillis, Harney & Co., No 24 Broad street. Answer
"(Signed) HOOPER."

To this witness replied:

"This is a private and confidential communication, passing between counsel and client. It has reference to business in that relation, and to nothing else, and had no reference whatever to the trial of the President or to the articles of impeachment proffered against him, nor to the conduct or result of the trial, nor to the votes of any person, nor any allusions thereto whatever."

They inquired if that was all the witness had to reply to the question, and he answered that it was, and requested, if his answer was not sufficiently explicit and full, that he might be taken to the bar of the House to receive its orders in the premises. The following question was then proposed to witness:

"Did you send a telegram to Sheridan Shook, dated the 12th of May, as follows: 'The five should be had. May be absolutely necessary.'"

To which witness gave the same reply which is set forth in full to the question above quoted; repeating the request thus made to be subjected to the instructions of the House. Gen. Butler thereupon remarked that he would offer a resolution to place the witness in solitary confinement until the 4th of March, 1869; and witness was thereupon recommitted to the custody of the Sergeant-at-arms. Witness considers that he can not divulge matters that come to him under the protection and sanction of the relation of client and counsel, and if he should make such disclosures under any circumstances, they can be made only when demanded by competent authority, which possesses the power to punish for a refusal to disclose. When the authority which can punish for a refusal to disclose requires it to be done at the peril of incurring a penalty, the disclosure is not voluntary, but coerced, and the witness is protected. The committee can not punish, and it is their duty on an issue between them and a witness to submit the matter to the House, and let it take action in relation thereto.

Mr. Woolley, in his protest filed with the committee on the 21st inst., explicitly states as follows:

"But in thus presenting this constitutional shield against vague and general and unsupported inquiries, your petitioner intends no disrespect to the House of Representatives or its managers, and tenders himself ready and willing to comply with any resolution or order that may be passed by the House of Representatives in the premises; and in the meantime he humbly prays that this, his protest and refusal, may be presented to the House."

"The managers were in possession of the private bank account of Mr. Woolley, and it was in regard to the use that he made of a certain $25,000 about which Butler inquired. Woolley refusing to tell that, the first difference between them then occurred. Mr. Woolley on this point, however, complied so far with the demands of the inquisition as to state into whose hands he had placed checks for the amount of money in question—a gentleman in New York, and, as I understand, one or more gentlemen in Cincinnati. The witness distinctly avowed, at the same time, as he had avowed during the whole course of his examination, that he had never offered or used money to influence Senators or other parties to secure the acquittal of the President."

His refusal to respond, on the 27th of May, to the question relating to the dispatch sent to Sheridan Shook, caused him to be brought before the bar of the House, where, after a long squabble over his answer, the following resolution was offered by Mr. Boutwell:

"*Resolved,* That the said Charles W. Woolley be committed to and detained in close custody by the Sergeant-at-arms in the Capitol during the remainder of the session, or until discharged by the further order of the House, to be taken when he shall have purged the contempt upon which he was arrested, by testifying before the committee authorized to continue the investigation which the managers were conducting when the contempt was committed by said Woolley."

After a debate, Mr. Woolley (at the bar of the House), then said:

Mr. Speaker, I ask leave to make a statement to the House.

The Speaker—The witness at the bar asks, through the Speaker, permission to make a statement.

Mr. Boutwell—I have no objection.

The Speaker—It requires unanimous consent.

No objection was made.

Mr. Woolley—I desire to say, Mr. Speaker, that I expect to answer such questions as the House may judge to be proper.

Mr. Boutwell—It is only necessary to say that that is substantially—

Mr. Woolley—In other words, Mr. Speaker, if the committee and myself differ as to the propriety of a question, I will ask them, as I did on my first examination, to bring me to the bar of the House, and ask the order of the House upon it, and I will abide by the order of the House.

Mr. Boutwell—This House must see that its power, through its committees, will be at an end if a person summoned as a witness may demand and receive from the House an arrangement which will destroy the just authority of the committee, and render every effort at investigation utterly useless; for whatever may be demanded and received by this witness, may be demanded and received by any other witness that any other committee of this House may call before it. I insist upon the previous question.

The question was taken and the resolution of Mr. Boutwell was passed—yeas 81, nays 28.

NAYS—Messrs. Allison, Ames, Arnell, James M. Ashley, Baldwin, Beaman, Benton, Bingham, Blaine, Boutwell, Bromwell, Broomall, Butler, Cake, Churchill, Reader W. Clark, Sidney Clark, Cobb, Coburn, Covode, Dodge, Donnelly, Driggs, Ela, Eliot, Ferriss, Ferry, Fields, Garfield, Halsey, Harding, Higby, Hooper, Hopkins, Chester D. Hubbard, Hunter, Judd, Julian, Kelsey, Ketcham, Koontz, Laflin, Geo. V. Lawrence, Wm. Lawrence, Loan, Logan, Mallory, Maynard, McCarthy, McClurg, Mercur, Moore, Moorhead, Morrill, Myers, Newcomb, O'Neill, Orth, Paine, Perham, Pike, Plants, Polsley, Raum, Sawyer, Schofield, Starkweather, Aaron F. Stevens, Stokes, Taylor, Trowbridge, Upson, Burt Van Horn, Robt. T. Van Horn, Ward, Elihu B. Washburne, William B. Washburn, Welker, Thos. Williams, John T. Wilson and Windom—81.

NAYS—Messrs. *Adams, Boyer, Brooks, Burr,* CARY, *Eldridge, Getz, Glossbrenner, Golladay, Grover, Haight, Hotchkiss, Johnson, Jones, Kerr, Knott, Marshall, McCormick, Morgan, Nicholson,*

Phelps, Pruyn, Randall, Ross, Sitgreaves, Taber, Lawrence S. Trimble and Van Trump—28.

Yeas all Radicals; nays all Democrats except Gen. Cary. So the Radicals indorsed the proposition for the imprisonment of an American citizen in a legislative bastile.

BASTILE AT THE CAPITOL.

"Mr. Bingham—I am instructed by the select committee charged with the investigation of alleged corruption in the matter of the impeachment of the President, to report the following resolution and put it on its passage:

"'*Resolved*, That rooms Nos. A and B, opposite the room of the Solicitor of the Court of Claims, in the Capitol be, and are hereby, assigned as guard-room and office of the Capitol police, and are for that purpose placed under the charge of the Sergeant-at-arms of the House, with power to fit the same up for the purpose specified.'

"I desire to say that there are no rooms at present assigned by order of the House in which to detain persons ordered into the custody of the Sergeant-at-arms. There is such an order now in process of execution. The person Woolley is at present detained in the room of the Committee on Foreign Affairs, and the resolution was that he be detained in custody in the Capitol. The committee are satisfied that a room ought to be assigned to the use of the Sergeant-at-arms, so that this witness may be detained beyond the power of possibility, by trick or circumvention on the part of any person, to defeat the administration of justice."

This resolution was passed, and Mr. Woolley was put in confinement in those rooms. According to the *Tribune*, one of those rooms "forcibly reminds one of a dungeon," and the other "has arched ceilings of brick; the walls, as well as the ceilings, are much soiled, evidently by the dampness which generates in the heavy masses of masonry of which they are composed." Yet this is deemed a fit place for an American citizen who is accused of no crime, and is charged with nothing but refusing to answer Butler's insolent questions concerning his private affairs.

A Candidate for Vice-President.

THE TURNKEY AT THE CAPITOL BASTILE.

It is said that Mr. Colfax, the candidate of the Radicals for the Vice-Presidency, is practically the turnkey at the Capitol bastile. Mr. Ordway, being a kind-hearted man, is not considered sufficiently trustworthy *Viva* the new jailor or turnkey. Persons wishing to see prisoners must apply to Speaker Colfax.—[*National Intelligencer.*

A TEN-STRIKE AT THE AMERICAN BASTILE, JUNE 1.

Mr. Van Trump introduced the following:

"*Whereas*, As by a former order of this House certain rooms in the basement of the Capitol are now being fitted up as a prison-house or bastile for the incarceration of free-born but deluded American citizens, who yet have the uparalelled audacity to dare to claim the absolute privilege of constitutional guarantees and laws; and,

"*Whereas*, Also, it is essentially important that said legislation of the House should be strong and well secured in order to prevent the escape of such contumacious and dangerous State prisoners; and,

"*Whereas*, Also, it is the duty of the public law-givers also to preserve the consistency and symmetry of history, and to adopt kindred means to sustain the public order and insure the safety of the public weal, in accordance with the precedents and practices of former and coincident periods in the history the popular liberty;

"*Therefore, be it hereby resolved, etc.*, That the Committee on Military Affairs be instructed to enter into negotiations with the ladies of the Mount Vernon Association for the purchase of a well-known historical key, now in the possession of the said Association of Mount Vernon, and formerly used in turning the bolts of the French bastile in Paris during the mild and humanitarian administration of French affairs in 1793, and that the same, if so purchased, shall be used in the said new Capitol prison, now being up as aforesaid."

Mr. Stevens (Rad.) Penn., objected to its reception, and it was not received.

A Palpable Violation of the Constitution.
[From the Boston Post.]

"Here is the case: A citizen goes to Washington on private business during the impeachment trial. He deposits a considerable amount of money in a bank there. Some of his papers and telegraphic dispatches are seized, unlawfully and without warrant, and he simply *suspected* of having used some of his money to influence votes in the impeachment case. This, on oath, he denies *in toto*; but on being questioned as to how he did dispose of a part of his money, he declines to answer, as he says it was only used in his private business and not for the purpose of influencing any vote on impeachment. Because he declines to tell for what he used his own money, he is charged with contempt of the House of Representatives, and a prison is prepared for him in the Capitol of the Union, by order of a majority of the House of Representatives. Where in the Constitution is the power given the House of Representatives thus to seize private citizens, and imprison them by its order for constructive contempt? Section 5, article I, provides that 'the House may punish its members for disorderly behavior,' but we find in article III, section 2, that 'the trial of all crimes, except in cases of impeachment, shall be by jury;' and article V of the amendments to the Constitution provides that 'no person shall be held to answer for a capital or otherwise infamous crime, unless on a presentment, or indictment of a grand jury, except in cases arising in the land or naval forces, or in the militia when in actual service in time of war or public danger; nor shall any person be subject for the same offense to be twice put in jeopardy of life or limb; nor shall he be compelled, in any criminal case, to be a witness against himself, nor be deprived of life, liberty, or property, without due process of law; nor shall private property be taken for public uses, without just compensation.' Again—article VI of the amendments, says: 'In all criminal prosecutions, the accused shall enjoy the right to a speedy and public trial, by an impartial jury of the State or District wherein the crime shall have been committed, which District shall have been previously ascertained by law, and to be informed of the nature and cause of the accusation; to be confronted with the witnesses against him; to have compulsory process for obtaining witnesses in his favor; and to have the assistance of counsel for his defense.' So article IV of the amendments provides that 'the right of the people to be secure in their persons, houses, papers, and effects, and against unwarrantable searches and seizures, shall not be violated; and no warrants shall issue, but upon probable cause, supported by oath or affirmation, and particularly describing the place to be searched and the person or things to be seized.' And once again—article IX declares that 'the enumeration in the Constitution of certain rights shall not be construed to deny or disparage others retained by the people.' In defiance of all these provisions of the Constitution, the majority of the House of Representative have resolved that a citizen shall by their simple order, be imprisoned in close confinement in the guard-room of the Capitol Police until he shall fully answer their questions; and that, meanwhile, no person shall communicate with him in writing or verbally except by order of the House. Shame! that such an act can be done in this country, at this age of the world! Have we no law? Has anarchy already asserted her sway, and are we ruled by a Star Chamber partisan committer, a Directory of frantic fanatics, men who seize persons and papers without warrant or process, who deny the victim of their malice even the society of his wife, family, or counsel? Can American citizens suffer such dishonor at the hands of this majority?

* * * * *

In this confinement, Mr. Woolley remained until after Mr. Sheridan Shook, his client, had been examined, and he having disclosed the information which the managers had endeavored to elicit from Mr. Woolley, the latter, relieved from the necessity, of any further assertion of his rights, agreed to appear and answer; whereupon he was released, first being subjected to the outrage of an additional day's confinement to await the pleasure of the managers to examine him. It turned out that the bulk of the money which had given the managers so much concern, had been handed by him to his friend Mr. Van Valkenberg, who had deposited it in the safe at the Metropolitan Hotel, Washington, for him. Thus ended this anomalous and outrageous proceeding. Should the Radicals get control of all the Departments of the Government, what citizen will be free from the vindictive and cruel use of such despotic torture. Then, as the *National Intelligencer* truly says, "the rack, the wheel and the thumb screw, will be applied to innocent victims until their agonized shrieks shall resound through the vaulted arches of the Capitol."

How Senators are Ostracised by the Senate.

HOW REPRESENTATIVES ARE IMMOLATED BY THE HOUSE—RADICAL BLOWS AT THE RIGHT OF REPRESENTATION, STATES' RIGHTS, AND POPULAR SOVEREIGNTY.

On the 4th of December, 1865, Mr. John P. Stockton (Dem.) was sworn in as United States Senator from the State of New Jersey, for the six years beginning the 4th of March, 1865. A protest was presented, signed by several Radical members of the Legislature of New Jersey, against the legality of his election, on the ground that he only received a plurality of the votes of the members present in the joint convention of the two Houses. This was true, but the joint convention had prescribed as its rule that such plurality should elect. The whole subject was referred to the Committee on the Judiciary, and that committee, through Mr. Trumbull, its chairman, reported that the joint convention had a right to prescribe that rule of election, and that Mr. Stockton was duly elected and entitled to the seat. About this time the difference between the Congress and the President, on the subject of reconstruction, became very wide and irreconcilable. It was necessary for the Radicals to have a clear majority of two thirds in the Senate and House, to combat successfully the *veto* power of the President. In the Senate this proportion was so nicely balanced as not to make it a working certainty on all questions. To bring this about, was the end; as to the means, the Radical Senators were not all of them particularly particular. The way to help the matter was to get Mr. Stockton out of his seat and a Radical Senator in it—the Executive and Legislature of New Jersey having passed into the hands of the Radical power. Accordingly, on the 22d of March, the resolution of the Committee on the Judiciary declaring Mr. Stockton entitled to his seat, was brought to a vote, with the following result:

YEAS—Messrs. Anthony, Buckalew, Cowan, Davis, Foster, Guthrie, Harris, Henderson, Hendricks, Johnson, Lane (of Kansas), McDougall, Morgan, Nesmith, Norton, Poland, Riddle, Saulsbury, Stewart, Trumbull, Willey—21.

NAYES—Messrs. Brown, Chandler, Clark, Conness, Cragin, Cresswell, Fessenden, Grimes, Howe, Kirkwood, Lane (of Indiana), Nye, Pomeroy, Ramsey, Sherman, Sprague, Sumner, Wade, Wilson, Yates—20.

Before the vote was announced, Mr. Morrill (Rad.), of Maine, said to the Secretary, "Call my name."

The Secretary—"Mr. Morrill."

Mr. Morrill—I vote nay.

This, it will be seen, increased the negative vote to 21, which made it a tie vote, which would have negatived the resolution and expelled Mr. Stockton. Mr. Morrill had voted in violation of his pair with Mr. Wright (Dem.), who was sick at his home in New Jersey, and who would not have gone home had it not been for this pair He had been telegraphed to, and had declined to relieve Mr. Morrill of the obligation of the arrangement. This disreputable conduct of Mr. Morrill left Mr. Stockton but one remedy. With an exhibition of manhood in the highest degree creditable, he freed himself from the inferior or personal aspect of the question, and as the Senator for his State—the rightful Senator as he conscientiously believed, he voted aye, which passed the resolution.

On the next day, Mr. Sumner (Radical) moved to amend the journal by striking out the vote of Mr. Stockton. After a long debate, Mr. Sumner withdrew his motion, and Mr. Poland moved to reconsider the vote confirming Mr. Stockton's right to his seat, which was agreed to. Mr. Sumner then offered the following:

Resolved, That the vote of Mr. Stockton be not received in determining the question of his seat in the Senate, which was agreed to.

Mr. Clark, on March 27th, moved to amend the original resolution, to the effect that Mr. Stockton was not entitled to the seat, which was agreed to. The resolution as amended was then passed by the following vote:

Yeas the same as the negative vote on the first original resolution, with the addition of Messrs. Howard, Riddle and Williams, and the exception of Messrs. Morrill, Foster and Stewart. Nays the same as the affirmative vote on the original resolution, with the exception of Mr. Stockton, prohibited from voting. Mr. Riddle (Dem.) voted aye with a view of moving a reconsideration, which was not done, because it would have proven fruitless. Mr. Stockton was thus, without justice, and against every idea of right, expelled from the Senate, and the sovereignty of New Jersey was ruthlessly insulted. A Radical Senator was chosen to Mr. Stockton's rightful place, and a working majority of two-thirds secured to the revolutionary conspirators in the Senate.

The House was discovered to be in the same fix as the Senate. A working majority of two-thirds in that body was not certain to be always attainable for the revolutionary measures of the Congress, when the test of a Presidential veto might make such a majority necessary. Accordingly, the seats of four Democrats were found to have contestants, with shallow pretences of claims that, in the better days of the Republic, would have disgraced the parties that made them. These were the seats of Messrs. James Brooks of New York, D. W. Voorhees of Indiana, Alexander H. Coffroth of Pennsylvania, and Augustus C. Baldwin of Michigan—all staunch defenders of the Constitution. The seats were given by a party majority, without reference to the right, to Messrs. William E. Dodge, Henry D. Washburn, W. H. Koontz, and Rowland E. Trowbridge—all Radicals, favoring every scheme of the Congressional conspirators against the national peace and public welfare. It were a useless consumption of space to enter into the details of these several contests, and of the frivolous pretexts upon which the Democratic incumbents were ejected, and the bogus contestants installed in these Representative places. The general course of the Radical party in Congress, in making their decisions on such questions with an eye alone to the politics of the parties, without regard to the right, renders such a reference to it unnecessary. Suffice it to say, that by this change in the House, a *facile* majority of two-thirds was erected, to give color of law to the legislative pretences of the Congress, whenever they failed to meet the approval of the President.

Nor was the Congress which succeeded it, and which now burlesques the national Legislature at Washington, less scrupulous about the question of right, whenever a seat in either of the bodies composing it became a subject of contest. If anything, it was more ambitious of a disreputable infamy in this respect than its predecessor. Mr. Philip Frank. Thomas had been elected a United States Senator, from Maryland, for the term beginning March 4, 1867. He was a Democrat, and had been what is denominated a loyal citizen during the war. He had a son who served in the Confederate army, and whom he had endeavored by appeals to dissuade from such service. Finding him inexorable, with true parental solicitude he gave him a hundred dollars, to serve him in the event of his becoming a victim to any of the casualties of war, which might throw him into the hands of the Union army, and require the use of Union money to alleviate his misfortunes. This natural action of the father was regarded as a crime in Radical morals. His failure to inform on his son, and have him imprisoned before his departure as a traitor to the United States, was claimed to be an aggravation of the other offense. In addition to this, Mr. Thomas had, upon his election to the Senate, addressed the Legislature of Maryland against the policy of the Radical majority in Congress, and denounced it in becoming and patriotic terms. Upon the presentation of his credentials, the doors of the Senate were closed upon him, and after a delay of nearly one year before final action was had, he was declared incompetent for these reasons to act as a Senator, and his seat was decided to be vacant. Thus, for near a year, Maryland was permitted to have but one-half of her proper representation in the Senate, and then her commission was insultingly flaunted back in her face, and she was virtually coerced by the Radical majority in the Senate into repudiating an honored citizen, who was her deserving choice, and made to send another gentleman in his place. It is pertinent to state that Mr Thomas was competent to take the iron-clad oath, which shows that, when that unconstitutional barrier can be overcome by a patriot and statesman, the Radical majority are not particular about getting up new means to override the prerogatives of a State which is obnoxious to them in politics.

In the House, the practice of this species of illegal and unconstitutional proscription was carried to the greatest excess. Criminal is no adjective for the license with which it was indulged by that body. To this writing, George W. Anderson—a Radical pretending to be a Representative from the Eighth Congressional District of Missouri—is shamelessly tolerated to occupy a seat belonging to Mr. Switzler, his Democratic opponent. Anderson knows and feels this to be the case; the House knows and feels it; and the Radical Committee on Elections of the House has so reported; but there he is, kept to vote for the infamous measures which the Radical *genii* invent to disturb the longed-for peace of the country.

At the very opening of the Congress—On the 3d day of July, 1867, the credentials of the following members elect from Kentucky, were presented: L. S. Trimble, John Young Brown, J. Proctor Knott, A. P. Grover, Thomas L. Jones, Jas. B. Beck, Geo. M. Adams and John D. Young.

Mr. Logan, of Illinois, offered the following preamble:

"WHEREAS, There is good reason to believe that, in the election recently held in the State of Kentucky for Representatives to the Fortieth Congress, the legal and loyal voters in the several districts in said State have been overawed, and prevented from a true expression of their will and choice at the polls, by those who have sympathized with, or actually participated in, the late rebellion, and that such elections were carried by the votes of such disloyal and returned rebels; and, whereas, it is alleged that several of the Representatives elect from that State are disloyal"—with a resolution that the credentials of all, except those of Mr. Adams, be referred to the Committee on Elections, which was adopted.

Mr. Adams, who was excepted, was a Democrat, and had an unexceptionable record as a gallant officer of the Union army. This latter qualification was the pretence for the exception in his case. The real motive was to avoid, by the admission of this single member from Kentucky, the appearance of the true purpose of the Radicals, which was to strike a blow at the representation of Kentucky in the House of Representatives, because of the uncompromising position of that Commonwealth as a Democratic State. After a tedious delay, during which time Kentucky, though entitled to eight Representatives, had but one on the floor, all these gentlemen were admitted except Messrs. John Young Brown and John D. Young. Mr. Brown was perfectly competent to take the iron-clad oath. He had been a loyal citizen during the war, but that was not sufficient to commend him to Radical favor. A rising young statesman of extraordinary powers, Radicalism had felt his blows, and in his person they had an opportunity to indulge a dual resentment—that of political hostility to him, and of malignant hatred for his people and State. At the beginning of the war Mr. Brown favored the position of neutrality which Kentucky had assumed, and had written a letter warmly in opposition to the contribution of men or arms to the subjugation of the South. This was the position of the Legislature of Kentucky, which assembled in May, 1861, which, by an almost unanimous vote in the lower House, passed the following resolutions:

"*Resolved*, by the House of Representatives, That this State and the citizens thereof should take no part in the civil war now being waged except as mediators and friends to the belligerent parties; and that Kentucky should, during the contest, occupy the position of strict neutrality; and your committee unanimously recommend the adoption of the following resolution:

"*Resolved*, That the act of the Governor in refusing to furnish troops or military force upon the call of the Executive authority of the United States, under existing circumstances, is approved."

Among the names of the members voting for those resolutions are Oscar H. Burbridge, brother of the General; Curtis F. Burnam, afterward the Republican candidate for United States Senator; Milton J. Cook, now Radical Senator in Kentucky; W. L. Neale, Republican candidate for State Treasurer in 1865; and many others whose loyalty would, from the Republican stand-point, compare favorably with the majority of the members on the Radical side of the House.*

It was the position of the Louisville *Journal*, the potential organ of the Union party of Kentucky, which, in May, 1861, said:

"In our judgment, the people of Kentucky have answered this question in advance; and the answer, expressed in every conceivable form of popular expression, and finally clinched by the glorious vote of Saturday, is, arm Kentucky, efficiently, but rightfully and fairly, with the clear declaration that the arming is not for offense against either the Government or the seceding States, but purely for defense against whatever power sets hostile foot upon the actual soil of the Commonwealth. In other words, the Legislature, according to the manifest will of the people, should declare the neutrality of Kentucky in this unnatural and accursed war of brothers, and equip the State for the successful maintenance of her position at all hazards."

In fact, it was the position at that time of that party and its leaders, in Kentucky, which afterward lent to the cause of the Federal Government so much of that influence which prevented that State from carrying out what appeared at one time probable—a complete union with the Confederacy in its struggle.

Mr. Brown was shown, in the evidence taken in the trial, to have been a Union man. Indeed, at the time when his speeches were delivered, which were the pretext for his rejection, he was the Union candidate for Congress, and was engaged in a canvass for the Union. But he was also a Democrat, and an unyielding foe to the Radical enemies of the Constitution, and was, in his late canvass, one of the most effective orators against their machinations; and these being his offenses, the rights of his constituents were violated to visit punishment upon him, and to spite them for the six thousand one hundred and six majority by which they sent him to Congress. His seat, notwithstanding this immense majority, was declared vacant—but three Radicals voting to receive him—and is still vacant, for the people will have no one else as their Representative, and the House insists upon regulating their choice for them.

In the case of Mr. John D. Young (Democrat), from the same State, he defeated that notorious wretch, Sam. McKee, by fourteen hundred and seventy-nine majority. He was also a loyal man during the war. But his sympathies were alleged to have been with the South. McKee claimed the seat upon such barefaced and mean bases of contest that but one of the Radical members of the Committee on Elections could stomach them. All of them were willing to proscribe Mr. Young from taking his rightful seat, and reported in favor of declaring it vacant.

One Charles Upson, from Michigan, however, reported not only in favor of declaring Young not entitled, but also in favor of giving the seat to McKee. The face of the Congress lit up with a smile at the coolness of this proposition; but this did not deter McKee and his champion, Upson; for they knew full well, from their long association with it, the unscrupulous character of the Radical majority in Congress. Before the question had yet been acted on in the House, influences were set at work to induce a majority of the Election Committee to assimilate their views with those of the illustrious Upson. It succeeded, and withdrawing their original report, they coincided with that of the unscrupulous Michigander. They reported that Young was not entitled, and that McKee was entitled. The figures by which they overcame Young's majority of 1479, are a mathematical wonder, and deserve something more than a mere reference. They admit that Young received 9042 votes, McKee 7563 votes, and Thomas Green 862 votes. Young's official majority, 1479. They find that of the votes received

---

*From speech of the Hon. J. B. Beck, of Kentucky, in the House of Representatives, February 1, 1868.

by Mr. Young, 625 were given by men proven to have been in the rebel army, and, by the rule laid down, not entitled to vote; for, say the committee, "persons who had been in the rebel army had no right to vote or to act as officers of election." They were paroled prisoners of war, and especially exempted from the amnesty proclaimed by the President, May 29, 1865, and, adds the committee, "there appears to have been no other act of amnesty up to the time of this election (in the Ninth Kentucky District) which could include them." The committee throw out these votes, thus reducing Young's majority, at one stroke, to 854, and still further diminish it by eight votes proven to have been cast for him by deserters—leaving but 846 to overcome. This they accomplish in the manner following, to-wit: Ex-rebels, they contend, can not legally act as judges of elections, and where there were such, the elections, in such precincts, are not valid. All of these precincts gave Young majorities ranging from fifty-one to one hundred and thirty-two. Thereupon the committee throw out the vote of these polls, and arrive at the following conclusion: That 1516 votes were illegally cast. Deduct Young's official majority, 1479, and McKee's legal majority is 41.

The House agreed to the report, and McKee was admitted to the seat for which he had been defeated by fourteen hundred and seventy-nine majority. Great criminals have at times been known to exhibit some blush of shame when they had descended to some low and groveling meanness which they regarded as depreciative of the refined rascality for which they had been distinguished, and the skillful exercise of which they looked upon as an accomplished and creditable motion. It is upon some such hypothesis that we alone can credit the appearance of McKee with which the newspaper correspondents compliment him when he appeared before the House to take the oath and qualify for the office into which he had so basely stolen. He was unable to look up, and seemed to confess by his appearance a sensibility to his turpitude, and a consciousness that his lips were sealing an oath to support a Constitution which by that very sacred testimony he was lowly, and with the most degrading baseness, meanly violating. This is the creature whose elevation to office is made the means of outraging the rights of an upright, honorable gentleman who is justly entitled to it, and of striking a blow at the sacred right of representation as unjust as it is offensive to the people of his district. That such a fellow is spoken to by men representing the country in Congress, or is permitted to speak to them, is a melancholy evidence of the moral decay of the times. That he is tolerated as a Representative, and made the subject of a straining violation of the Constitution, to put him into place, is the best evidence that intolerant Radicalism intends, if its power is prolonged, to leave us no vestige of constitutional government.*

This does not complete the list of Radical outrages in this matter of contested elections. General George W. Morgan, a gallant officer of the Federal army, well known as "Cumberland Gap Morgan," was elected to Congress from the Columbus District in Ohio, as an uncompromising Democrat and thorough opponent of Radicalism. One Delano, a Radical, wanted his place, and forged a contest for that purpose, asserting technical and lying objections to the legal qualifications of certain judges, and objections to certain voters that they were "deserters," when it was proved that they were not. It was not pretended that the majority of votes were not cast for Morgan. He was got rid of by throwing out the votes cast for him by *bona fide* voters sufficient to give the majority to Delano. The Thirteenth Ohio District is known to be Democratic. In 1867, Thurman, Democratic candidate for Governor, carried the district by a majority of 2,178 in an aggregate of 27,906. The Radical Congress outraged that Democratic community by putting in a Radical as its Representative who was rejected by the people. Mr. Morgan, in closing his speech upon the report of the committee ejecting him from his seat, made a prediction which we believe will be fulfilled. He said: "I will be sent back by the majestic voice of an outraged people—not by three hundred—but by ten times three hundred majority." Mr. Delano will enjoy his stolen honors until the 4th of March next.

This closes the cases of outrages upon the constitutional right of representation to which we have deemed it proper to call the attention of the people of the country. They are the bold and undeniable advertisement by the Radicals that they regard nothing in their administration of the Government but the one paramount idea of unfaltering allegiance to their party—an end which justifies all means. Before it the Constitution, Law, Right, Justice, and everything that attests political virtue, and personal integrity, must give way, and the Government be administered according to the unbounded licentiousness of whatever may be their caprice, and with the sole view of their personal and party aggrandizement—

---

*In the chapter on the "Condition of Tennessee," it will be seen that the House practiced the reverse action in the matter of the Tennessee members. Why? Because they were Radicals.

at all sacrifice, whether of its dearest forms or the expenditure of blood, to maintain their political ascendancy. It is of this party that Grant and Colfax are the boasted standard-bearers. The former a confessed ally of the two Houses of Congress in all of their atrocious villanies, and the latter one of the most experienced of the conspirators themselves, who has smiled again and again at the fortune of his party, obtained at the expense of his country. Is there not enough public virtue left to rebuke these Catalines? We believe the election in November will prove that there is.

The Tenure-of-Office Bill.

AN ACT REGULATING THE TENURE OF CERTAIN CIVIL OFFICES.

Be it enacted by the Senate and House of Representatives of the United States of America in Congress assembled, That every person holding any civil office to which he has been appointed by and with the advice and consent of the Senate, and every person who shall hereafter be appointed to any such office, and shall become duly qualified to act therein, is, and shall be, entitled to hold such office until a successor shall have been, in like manner, appointed and duly qualified, except as herein otherwise provided: *Provided,* That the Secretaries of State, of the Treasury, of War, of the Navy, and of the Interior, the Postmaster-General, and the Attorney-General shall hold their offices respectively for and during the term of the President by whom they may have been appointed, and for one month thereafter, subject to removal by and with the advice and consent of the Senate.

SEC. 2. That when any officer appointed as aforesaid, excepting Judges of the United States Courts, shall, during the recess of the Senate, be shown, by evidence satisfactory to the President, to be guilty of misconduct in office, or crime, or for any reason shall become incapable or legally disqualified to perform its duties, in such case, and in no other, the President may suspend such officer, and designate some suitable person to perform, temporarily, the duties of such office until the next meeting of the Senate, and until the case shall be acted upon by the Senate; and such person, so designated, shall take the oaths and give the bonds required by law to be taken and given by the person duly appointed to fill such office; and in such case it shall be the duty of the President, within twenty days after the first day of such next meeting of the Senate, to report to the Senate such suspension, with the evidence and reasons for his action in the case, and the name of the person so designated to perform the duties of such office. If the Senate concurs, the President may remove the officer and appoint a successor. If the Senate does not concur, the suspended officer resumes his office, and receives again the official salary and emoluments. The President, in case he shall become satisfied that the suspension by him of a civil officer was made on insufficient grounds, shall be authorized, at any time before reporting the suspension to the Senate, to revoke the suspension and reinstate the officer in the performance of the duties of his office.

SEC. 3. The President shall have power to fill all vacancies which may happen during the recess of the Senate, by reason of death or resignation, by granting commissions which shall expire at the end of their next session. And if no appointment, by and with the advice and consent of the Senate, shall be made to such office so vacant or temporarily filled during the next session of the Senate, the office shall remain in abeyance, without any salary, fees or emoluments attached thereto, until it shall be filled by appointment thereto, by and with the advice and consent of the Senate; and during such time all the powers and duties belonging to the office shall be exercised by such other officer as may by law exercise such powers and duties in case of a vacancy in such office.

SEC. 4. No term of office, the duration of which is limited by law, shall be extended by this act.

SEC. 5. Persons accepting or exercising office contrary to this act, are declared to be guilty of a high misdemeanor, and, upon trial and conviction thereof, shall be punished by a fine not exceeding $10,000, or by imprisonment not exceeding five years, or both.

SEC. 6. Every removal, appointment, or employment made, had or exercised contrary to the provisions of this act, and the making, signing, sealing, countersigning or issuing of any commission or letter of authority for or in respect to any such appointment or employment, are declared to be high misdemeanors, and, upon trial and conviction thereof, persons guilty thereof shall be punished by a fine not exceeding $10,000, or by imprisonment not exceeding five years, or both: *Provided,* That the President shall have power to make out and deliver, after the adjournment of the Senate, commissions for all officers whose appointment shall have been advised and consented to by the Senate.

SEC. 7. It shall be the duty of the Secretary of the Senate, at the close of each session, to deliver to the Secretary of the Treasury, and to each of his assistants, and to each of the Auditors, and to each of the Comptrollers in the Treasury, and to the

Treasurer, and to the Registrar of the Treasury, a full and complete list, duly certified, of all the persons who shall have been nominated to and rejected by the Senate during such session, and a like list of all the offices to which nominations shall have been made and not confirmed and filled at such session.

SEC. 8. The President shall notify the Secretary of the Treasury when he has made an appointment to office without the consent of the Senate; and it shall be the duty of the Secretary of the Treasury thereupon to communicate such notice to all the proper accounting and disbursing officers of his department.

SEC. 9. No money shall be paid or received from the Treasury, or paid or received from or retained out of any public moneys or funds of the United States, to or by or for the benefit of any person appointed to or authorized to act in or holding or exercising the duties or functions of any office contrary to the provisions of this act; nor shall any claim, account, or other instrument providing for or relating to such payment, receipt or retention, be presented, passed, allowed, approved, certified or paid by any officer of the United States, or by any person exercising the functions or performing the duties of any office or place of trust under the United States, for or in respect to such office, or the exercising or performing the functions or duties thereof; and persons who shall violate any of the provisions of this section shall be deemed guilty of a high misdemeanor, and, upon trial and conviction thereof, shall be punished therefor by a fine not exceeding $10,000, or by imprisonment not exceeding ten years, or both.

The bill was passed over the President's veto on March 2, 1867.

The Senate repassed it—yeas 35, nays 11, as follows:

YEAS—Messrs. Anthony, Cattell, Chandler, Conness, Cragin, Edmunds, Fessenden, Fogg, Foster, Fowler, Frelinghuysen, Grimes, Harris, Henderson, Howard, Kirkwood, Lane, Morgan, Morrill, Nye, Poland, Pomeroy, Ramsey, Ross, Sherman, Sprague, Stewart, Sumner, Trumbull, Van Winkle, Wade, Willey, Williams, Wilson, Yates—35.

NAYS—Messrs. *Buckalew, Cowan, Davis, Dixon, Doolittle, Hendricks, Johnson, Nesmith, Norton, Patterson, Saulsbury*—11.

Same day—The House repassed it—yeas 138, nays 40, as follows:

YEAS—Messrs. Alley, Allison, Ames, Anderson, Arnell, Delos R. Ashley, James M. Ashley, Baker, Baldwin, Banks, Barker, Baxter, Beaman, Benjamin, Bidwell, Bingham, Blaine, Blow, Boutwell, Brandegee, Bromwell, Broomall, Buckland, Bundy, R. W. Clarke, S. Clarke, Cobb, Conkling, Cook, Cullom, Darling, Davis, Dawes, Defrees, Delano, Deming, Dixon, Dodge, Donnelly, Driggs, Dumont, Eckley, Eggleston, Eliot, Farnsworth, Farquhar, Ferry, Garfield, Grinnell, Griswold, Hale, Abner C. Harding, Hart, Hawkins, Hayes, Henderson, Higby, Hill, Holmes, Hooper, Hotchkiss, A. W. Hubbard, Chester D. Hubbard, John H. Hubbard, James R. Hubbell, Hulburd, Ingersoll, Jenckes, Julian, Kasson, Kelley, Kelso, Ketcham, Koontz, Laflin, George V. Lawrence, William Lawrence, Loan, Longyear, Lynch, Marquette, Marston, Marvin, Maynard, McClurg, McIndoe, McKee, McRuer, Mercur, Miller, Moorhead, Morrill, Morris, Moulton, Myers, Newell, O'Neill, Orth, Paine, Patterson, Perham, Pike, Plants, Pomeroy, Price, William H. Randall, Raymond, Alexander H. Rice, John H. Rice, Rollins, Sawyer, Schenck, Scofield, Shellabarger, Sloan, Spalding, Starr, Stokes, Thayer, Francis Thomas, Trowbridge, Upson, Van Aernam, Burt Van Horn, Robert T. Van Horn, Hamilton Ward, Warner, Henry D. Washburn, William B. Washburn, Welker, Wentworth, Whaley, Williams, James F. Wilson, Stephen F. Wilson, Windom, Woodbridge, and Speaker Colfax—138.

NAYS—Messrs. *Ancona, Bergen, Boyer, Campbell, Chanler, Cooper, Dawson, Eldridge, Finck, Glossbrenner, Goodyear, Aaron Harding, Hise, Hogan, Edwin N. Hubbell, Humphrey, Hunter, Jones, Latham, LeBlond, Leftwich, Marshall, McCullough, Niblack, Nicholson, Radford, Sam. J. Randall, Ritter, Rogers, Ross, Shanklin, Sitgreaves, Strouse, Taber, Nelson Taylor, Thornton, Trimble, Andrew H. Ward, Winfield, Wright*—40.

Whereupon the Speaker of the House declared the bill to be a law.

Impeachment of President Johnson.

This movement was first initiated on the 17th of December, 1866, by one James M. Ashley, an infamously notorious Representative from Ohio, who charged the President with certain high crimes and misdemeanors, and proposed an investigation by the Committee on the Judiciary, into the same. His resolution to that effect was adopted by a vote of—yeas 108, nays 39. Messrs. Davis, Dodge, Hawkins, Hubbell, Latham, Raymond, Spalding and Whaley, Radicals, voting with the Democrats, in the negative. The committee, at the close of the Congress, reported an incompleteness of their labors, and placed upon file the evidence they had accumulated, with a recommendation that the investigation be continued by their successors.

Mr. Rogers (of New Jersey), in a minority report of the Committee, reported that not one word of evidence had been adduced to sustain the charges.

On the 7th of March, 1867, Mr. Ashley renewed his proposition, when, on motion of Mr. Sydney Clarke, of Kansas, the Committee on the Judiciary were instructed to report on the charges preferred against the President on the first day of the meeting of the House, after the recess hereafter to be determined.

On the 25th of November, they submitted therewith their report, or rather three reports. Messrs. Boutwell, Williams, Thomas, Lawrence and Churchill agreed in favor of impeachment, and submitted this resolution:

"*Resolved*, That Andrew Johnson, President of the United States, be impeached of high crimes and misdemeanors."

Messrs. Wilson and Woodbridge were not in favor of impeachment, and reported thus:

"*Resolved*, That the Committee on the Judiciary be discharged from the further consideration of the proposed impeachment of the President of the United States, and that the subject be laid upon the table."

Messrs. Marshall and Eldridge (Democrats) were opposed to the whole proceeding.

On the 6th of December the House took up the report. The next day the report came up, and the House reached the main business, and the resolution "that Andrew Johnson, President of the United States, be impeached of high crimes and misdemeanors," was lost—yeas 57, nays 108; absent or not voting 22. Thus closed the impeachment movement.

We give the following analysis of the vote, from the *Tribune* Almanac:

THOSE WHO VOTED FOR IMPEACHMENT.

MAINE—1.
1. John Lynch.

NEW HAMPSHIRE—2.
1. Jacob H. Ela,   2. Aaron F. Stevens.

MASSACHUSETTS—2.
7. George S. Boutwell,   5. Benjamin F. Butler.

NEW YORK—3.
22. John C. Churchill,   27. Hamilton Ward.
25. William H. Kelsey,

PENNSYLVANIA—9.
7. John M. Broomall,   2. Charles O'Neill,
21. John Covode,   9. Thaddeus Stevens,
4. William D. Kelley,   23. Thomas Williams,
13. Ulysses Mercer,   18. Stephen F. Wilson.
3. Leonard Myers,

MARYLAND—1.
4. Francis Thomas.

OHIO—5.
10. James M. Ashley,   4. William Lawrence,
6. Reader W. Clarke,   3. Robert C. Schenck.
17. Ephraim R. Eckley,

INDIANA—6.
6. John Coburn,   8. Godlove S. Orth,
3. Morton C. Hunter,   11. John P. C. Shanks,
5. George W. Julian,   10. William Williams.

MICHIGAN—1.
5. Rowland E. Trowbridge.

ILLINOIS—6.
7. H'y. P. H. Bromwell,   4. Abner C. Harding,
8. Shelby M. Cullom,   1. Norman B. Judd,
2. Jno. F. Farnsworth   At large. Jno. A. Logan.

WISCONSIN—3.
3. Amasa Cobb,   1. Halbert E. Paine.
2. Benj. F. Hopkins,

MINNESOTA—1.
2. Ignatius Donnelly.

IOWA—2.
4. William Loughridge,   2. Hiram Price.

MISSOURI—7.
9. George W. Anderson,   2. Car'n. A. Newcomb,
4. Joseph J. Gravely,   1. William A. Pile,
7. Benjamin F. Loan,   6. Robert T. Van Horn.
5. Joseph W. McClurg,

TENNESSEE—6.
6. Samuel M. Arnell,   8. David A. Nunn,
2. Horace Maynard,   3. William B. Stokes,
4. James Mullins,   5. John Trimble.

CALIFORNIA—1.
2. William Higby.

KANSAS—1.
1. Sidney Clarke.

Total voting in the affirmative 57—all Republicans.

THOSE VOTING AGAINST IMPEACHMENT.

MAINE—4.
2. Sidney Perham,   4. John A. Peters,
3. James G. Blaine,   5. Frederick A. Pike.

NEW HAMPSHIRE—1.
3. Jacob Benton.

VERMONT—3.
2. Luke P. Poland,   1. Fred. E. Woodbridge.
3. Worthington C. Smith,

MASSACHUSETTS—7.
2. Oakes Ames,   1. Thomas D. Eliot,
8. John D. Baldwin,   4. Samuel Hooper,
6. Nathaniel P. Banks,   9. Wm. B. Washburn.
10. Henry L. Dawes,

RHODE ISLAND—1.
2. Nathan F. Dixon.

CONNECTICUT—4.
4. *Wm. H. Barnum*,   1. *Richard D. Hubbard*,
2. *Julius Hotchkiss*,   3. H'y. H. Starkweather

NEW YORK—20.
21. Alexander H. Bailey,   26. Wm. S. Lincoln,
8. *James Brooks*,   18. James M. Marvin,
7. *John W. Chanler*,   23. Dennis McCarthy,
16. Orange Ferris,   14. *John V. L. Pruyn*,
19. Wm. C. Fields,   10. Wm. H. Robertson,
15. John A. Griswold,   3. *Wm. E. Robinson*,
17. Calvin T. Hulburd,   6. *Thomas E. Stewart*,
30. *J. M. Humphrey*,   1. *Stephen Taber*,
12. John H. Ketcham,   31. Henry Van Aernam,
20. Addison H. Laflin,   11. Chas. H. Van Wyck.

NEW JERSEY—4.
2. *Charles Haight*,   4. John Hill,
5. George A. Halsey,   3. *Charles Sitgreaves*.

PENNSYLVANIA—11.
6. *Benjamin M. Boyer*,   22. James K. Moorhead,
8. *J. Lawrence Getz*,   1. *Samuel J. Randall*,
15. *A. J. Glossbrenner*,   5. Caleb N. Taylor,
16. William H. Koontz,   11. *D. M. Van Auken*,
24. Geo. V. Lawrence,   12. *G. W. Woodward*.
14. George F. Miller,

DELAWARE—1.
1. *John A. Nicholson*.

MARYLAND—4.
2. *Stevenson Archer*,   3. *Charles E. Phelps*,
1. *Hiram McCullough*,   5. *Frederick Stone*.

WEST VIRGINIA—2.
1. Chester D. Hubbard,   3. Daniel Polsley.

OHIO—13.
16. John A. Bingham,   5. *William Mungen*,
9. Ralph P. Buckland,   15. Tobias H. Plants,
2. Samuel F. Cary,   18. Rufus P. Spalding,
1. Benjamin Eggleston,   12. *Philip Van Trump*,
19. James A. Garfield,   14. Martin Welker,
8. Corn. W. Hamilton,   11. John T. Wilson.
13. George W. Morgan,

INDIANA—4.
4. *Wm. S. Holman*,   1. *Wm. E. Niblack*,
2. *Michael C. Kerr*,   7. H'y D. Washburn.

MICHIGAN—4.
1. Fernan. C. Beaman,   4. Thomas W. Ferry,
6. John F. Driggs,   2. Charles Upson.

KENTUCKY—6.

8. George M. Adams, 5. Asa P. Grover,
7. James R. Beck, 6. Thomas L. Jones,
3. Jacob S. Golladay, 4. J. Proctor Knott.

ILLINOIS—7.

12. Jehu Baker, 11. Samuel S. Marshall,
10. Albert G. Burr, 9. Lewis W. Ross,
6. Burton C. Cook, 3. Elihu B. Washburne.
5. Ebon C. Ingersoll,

WISCONSIN—3.

4. Chas. A. Eldridge, 6. Cad. C. Washburne.
5. Philetus Sawyer,

IOWA—4.

3. William B. Allison, 6. Asahel W. Hubbard,
5. Grenville M. Dodge, 1. James F. Wilson.

MISSOURI—1.

8. John F. Benjamin.

TENNESSEE—1.

7. Isaac R. Hawkins.

CALIFORNIA—2.

1. Samuel B. Axtell, 3. James A. Johnson.

NEVADA—1.

1. Delos R. Ashley.

Total voting in the negative, 108, of whom 67 were Republicans, and 41 were Democrats.

ABSENT OR NOT VOTING.

ILLINOIS—13. Green B. Raum.
INDIANA—9. Schuyler Colfax.
KENTUCKY—2. John Y. Brown; 1. Lawrence S. Trimble; 9. John D. Young. These three are not yet in the House.
MASSACHUSETTS—3. Ginery Twitchell.
MICHIGAN—3. Austin Blair.
MINNESOTA—1. William Windom.
MISSOURI—3. James R. McCormick.
NEBRASKA—1. John Taffe.
NEW JERSEY—1. William Moore.
NEW YORK—2. Demas Barnes; 13. Thomas Cornell; 4. John Fox; 5. John Morrissey; 24. Theodore M. Pomeroy; 28. Lewis Selye; 29. Burt Van Horn; 9. Fernando Wood.
OHIO—7. Samuel Shellabarger.
OREGON—1. Rufus Mallory.
PENNSYLVANIA—10. Henry L. Cake; 20. Darwin A. Finney; 17. Daniel J. Morrill; 19. Glenni W. Scofield.
RHODE ISLAND—1. Thomas A. Jenckes.
TENNESSEE—1. Robert B. Butler.
WEST VIRGINIA—2. Bethuel M. Kitchen.

Total absent or not voting, 22; of whom 18 are Republicans and 4 are Democrats.

Messrs. Wilson and Woodbridge, the two Radicals who disagreed with their Radical colleagues, said, in their report, what becomes interesting in view of their subsequent efforts in favor of impeachment. Its conclusion is as follows:

"A great deal of the matter contained in the volume of testimony reported to the House is of no value whatever. Much of it is mere hearsay, opinions of witnesses, and no little amount of it is utterly irrelevant to the case. Comparatively a small amount of it could be used on a trial of this case before the Senate. All of the testimony relating to the failure to try and admission to bail of Jefferson Davis, the assassination of President Lincoln, the diary of J. Wilkes Booth, his place of burial, the practice of pardon brokerage, the alleged correspondence of the President with Jefferson Davis, may be interesting to a reader, but is not of the slightest importance so far as a determination of this case is concerned. Still much of this irrelevant matter has been interwoven into the majority report, and has served to highten its color and to deepen its tone. Strike out the stage effect of this irrelevant matter and the prominence given to the Tudors, the Stuarts and Michael Burns, and much of the play will disappear, and settle down upon the real evidence in the case—that which will establish, in view of the attending circumstances, a substantial crime, by making plain the elements which constitute it, and the case in many respects dwarfs into a political contest. In approaching a conclusion, we do not fail to recognize the stand-points from which this case can be reviewed, the legal and the political. Viewing it from the latter, the case is a success. The President has disappointed the hopes and expectations of those who placed him in power; he has betrayed their confidence and joined hands with their enemies; he has proved false to the express and implied conditions which underlie his elevation to power, and in our view of the case deserves the censure and condemnation of every well-disposed citizen of the republic. While we acquit him of impeachable crimes, we pronounce him guilty of many wrongs. This contest with Congress has delayed reconstruction, and inflicted vast injury upon the people of the rebel States. He has been blind to the necessities of the times and to the demands of a progressive civilization, enveloped in the darkness of the past, and seems not to have detected the dawning brightness of the future. Incapable of appreciating the grand changes which the past six years have wrought, he seeks to measure the great events which surround him by the narrow rules which adjusted public affairs before the rebellion, and its legitimate consequences destroyed them and established others. Judge him politically, condemn him, but the day of political impeachment would be a sad one for the country. Political unfitness and incapacity must be tried at the ballot-box, not in the high court of impeachment. A contrary rule might leave to Congress but little time for other business than the trial of impeachments. But we are not now dealing with political offenses. Crimes and misdemeanors are now demanding our attention. Do these, within the meaning of the Constitution, appear? Rest the case upon political offenses, and we are prepared to pronounce against the President, for such offenses are numerous and grave. If Mexican experience is desired, we need have no difficulty, for there almost every election is productive of a revolution. If the people of this republic desire such a result, we have not yet been able to discover it; nor would we favor it if its presence were manifest. While we condemn and censure the political conduct of the President, and judge him unwise in the use of his discretionary powers, and appeal to the people of the republic to sustain us, we still affirm that the conclusion at which we have arrived is correct. We, therefore, declare that the case before us, presented by the testimony and measured by the law, does not declare such high crimes and misdemeanors within the meaning of the Constitution as require 'the interposition of the constitutional power of this House,' and recommend the adoption of the following resolution:

"*Resolved*, That the Committee on the Judiciary be discharged from the further consideration of the proposed impeachment of the President of the United States, and that the subject be laid upon the table.

"JAMES F. WILSON,
"F. E. WOODBRIDGE."

On the 21st of February, 1868, when the news reached Congress of the attempted removal of Mr. Stanton, the Secretary of War, by the President, Mr. John Covode offered, in the House of Representatives, the following resolution as a question of privilege:

"*Resolved*, That Andrew Johnson, President of the United States, be impeached for high crimes and misdemeanors."

This resolution was referred to the Committee on Reconstruction.

After a secret deliberation of seven hours' duration, the following resolution was adopted:

"WHEREAS, The Senate has received and considered the communication of the President, stating that he had removed Edwin M. Stanton, Secretary of War, and had designated the Adjutant-General of the army to act as Secretary of War *ad interim*; therefore,

"*Resolved*, By the Senate of the United States, that, under the Constitution and laws of the United States, the President has no power to remove the Secretary of War, and to designate any other officer to perform the duty of that office *ad interim*."

On the 22d of February, Mr. Stevens, from the Committee on Reconstruction, made a report, signed by himself, Messrs. Boutwell, Bingham, Hulburd, Farnsworth, Beaman and Paine, which concluded with the following resolution:

"*Resolved*, That Andrew Johnson, President of the United States, be impeached of high crimes and misdemeanors."

On the 24th of February the House came to a vote.

During the vote excuses were made for the absence of Messrs. Robinson, Benjamin, Washburn (Ind.), Williams (Ind.), Van Horn (Mo.), Trimble (Tenn.), Pomeroy, Donnelly, Koontz, Maynard, and Shellabarger.

The Speaker stated that he could not consent that his constituents should be silent on so grave an occasion, and therefore, as a member of the House, he voted yea.

The vote resulted — yeas 126, nays 47, as follows:

YEAS—Messrs. Allison, Ames, Anderson, Arnell, Ashley (Nev.), Ashley (Ohio), Bailey, Baker, Baldwin, Banks, Beaman, Beatty, Benton, Bingham, Blaine, Blair, Boutwell, Bromwell, Broomall, Buckland, Butler, Cake, Churchill, Clarke (Ohio), Clarke (Kan.), Cobb, Coburn, Cook, Cornell, Covode, Cullom, Dawes, Dodge, Driggs, Eckley, Eggleston, Eliot, Farnsworth, Ferris, Ferry, Fields, Gravely, Griswold, Halsey, Harding, Higby, Hill, Hooper, Hopkins, Hubbard (Ia.), Hubbard (W. Va.), Hulburd, Hunter, Ingersoll, Jenckes, Judd, Julian, Kelley, Kelsey, Ketcham, Kitchen, Laflin, Lawrence (Pa.), Lawrence (Ohio), Lincoln, Loan, Logan, Loughridge, Lynch, Mallory, Marvin, McCarthy, McClurg, Mercur, Miller, Moore, Moorhead, Morrill, Mullins, Myers, Newcomb, Nunn, O'Neill, Orth, Paine, Perham, Peters, Pike, Pile, Plants, Poland, Polsley, Price, Raum, Robertson, Sawyer, Schenck, Scofield, Seyle, Shanks, Smith, Spalding, Starkweather, Stevens (N. H.), Stevens (Pa.), Stokes, Taffee, Taylor, Trowbridge, Twitchell, Upson, Van Aernam, Van Horn (N. Y.), Van Wyck, Ward, Washburn (Wis.), Washburne (Ill.), Washburn (Mass.), Welker, Williams (Pa.), Wilson (Iowa), Wilson (Ohio), Williams (Pa.), Windom, Woodbridge, and Speaker—126.

NAYS—Messrs. *Adams, Archer, Axtell, Barnes, Barnum, Beck, Boyer, Brooks, Burr,* CARY, *Chanler, Eldridge, Fox, Getz, Glossbrenner, Golladay, Grover, Haight, Holman, Hotchkiss, Hubbard* (Conn.), *Humphrey, Johnson, Jones, Kerr, Knott, Marshall, McCormick, McCullough, Morgan, Morrissey, Mungen, Niblack, Nicolson, Phelps, Pruyn, Randall, Ross, Sitgreaves, Stewart, Stone, Taber, Trimble* (Ky.), *Van Auken, Van Trump, Wood, Woodward*—47.

Messrs. Boutwell, Stevens, Bingham, Wilson, Logan, Julian and Wade, were appointed to prepare articles of impeachment, and they reported the following:

"ARTICLE 1. Recited the fact of the President suspending Stanton, and that of the Senate refusing to concur in such suspension; and charged the order of the President removing Stanton and appointing Gen. Thomas Secretary of War *ad interim*, after the refusal of the Senate to concur in his suspension, to be a high misdemeanor in office.

"ART. 2. That, on the 21st day of February, in the year of our Lord 1868, at Washington, in the District of Columbia, said Andrew Johnson, President of the United States, unmindful of the high duties of his oath of office, and in violation of the Constitution of the United States, and contrary to the provisions of an act entitled 'An act regulating the tenure of certain civil offices,' passed March 2, 1867, without the advice and consent of the Senate, then and there being in session, and without authority of law, did appoint one L. Thomas to be Secretary of War *ad interim*, by issuing to said Lorenzo Thomas a letter of authority, in substance as follows, that is to say:

"EXECUTIVE MANSION,
"WASHINGTON, D. C., February 21, 1868.

"*Sir:* The Hon. Edwin M. Stanton having been this day removed from office as Secretary of the Department of War, you are hereby authorized and empowered to act as Secretary of War *ad interim*, and will immediately enter upon the discharge of the duties pertaining to that office. Mr. Stanton has been instructed to transfer to you all the records, books, papers and other public property now in his custody and charge. Respectfully yours,
"ANDREW JOHNSON.
"To Brevet Major-Gen. L. Thomas, Adjutant Gen. U. S Army, Washington, D. C.

"Whereby said Andrew Johnson, President of the United States, did then and there commit, and was guilty of a high misdemeanor in office.

"ART. 3. That said Andrew Johnson, President of the United States, on the 21st day of February, in the year of our Lord one thousand eight hundred and sixty-eight, at Washington, in the District of Columbia, did commit, and was guilty of a high misdemeanor in office, in this: That without authority of law, while the Senate of the United States was then and there in session, he did appoint one Lorenzo Thomas to be Secretary for the Department of War *ad interim*, without the advice and consent of the Senate, and in violation of the Constitution of the United States, no vacancy having happened in said office of Secretary for the Department of War during the recess of the Senate, and no vacancy existing in said office at the time, and which said appointment so made by Andrew Johnson of said Lorenzo Thomas is in substance as follows, that is to say:

"EXECUTIVE MANSION,
"WASHINGTON, D. C., February 21, 1868.

"*Sir:* The Hon. E. M. Stanton having been this day removed from office as Secretary for the Department of War, you are hereby authorized and empowered to act as Secretary of War *ad interim*, and will immediately enter upon the discharge of the duties pertaining to that office. Mr. Stanton has been instructed to transfer to you all the records, books, papers, and other public property now in his custody and charge. Respectfully yours,
"ANDREW JOHNSON.
"To Brevet Major-Gen. L. Thomas, Adjutant-Gen. U. S. A., Washington, D. C."

Article 4 charged the President with an unlawful conspiracy with Lorenzo Thomas, and other persons unknown, on the 21st of February, 1868, by intimidation and threats, to prevent Edwin M. Stanton from discharging his lawful duties as Secretary of War, in violation of the act of July 31, 1861, to define and punish certain conspiracies, thereby committing a high crime in office.

Article 5 the same as article 4, except that it charged a conspiracy by force to violate Tenure-of-Office act, thereby committing a high misdemeanor in office.

Article 6 charged a conspiracy with Thomas to take by force possession of the property of the United States in the War Department, in violation of the act of July 31, 1861, and the Tenure-of-Office act, thereby committing a high crime in office.

Article 7 charged a conspiracy with Thomas to prevent the execution of the Tenure-of-Office act, thereby committing a high misdemeanor in office.

Article 8 charged a conspiracy with Thomas to take by force possession of the property of the United States in the War Department, in violation of the Tenure-of-Office act, thereby committing a high misdemeanor in office.

Article 9 charged that the President, by bringing before him Major-Gen. Wm. H. Emory, U. S. A., and instructing him that part of a law, passed March 2, 1867, which requires that all orders and instructions from the President or Secretary of War relative to the army, should issue through the General of the army, was unconstitutional and not binding on him, was guilty of a high misdemeanor in office.

An animated debate sprang up on the question of the adoption of the above articles, which was continued until March 2, when they were adopted, and Speaker Colfax announced as managers of the impeachment trial, on the part of the House, Messrs. Thaddeus Stevens, B. F. Butler, John A. Bingham, George S. Boutwell, J. F. Wilson, T. Williams and John A. Logan.

It was then ordered that the articles agreed to by the House, to be exhibited in its name and in the name of the people of the United States, against Andrew Johnson, President of the United States, in maintenance of the impeachment against him for high crimes and misdemeanors in office, be carried to the Senate by the managers appointed to conduct such impeachment.

On the 3d of March, Gen. Butler proposed an additional article, remarking that, with but a single exception, the managers favored the adoption of the article. He strongly urged the reception of the charges he had prepared, saying:

"The articles already adopted presented only the bone and sinew of the offenses of Andrew Johnson. He wanted to clothe that bone and sinew with flesh and blood, and to show him before the country as the quivering sinner that he is, so that hereafter, when posterity came to examine these proceedings, it might not have cause to wonder that the only offense charged against Andrew Johnson was a merely technical one. He would have him go down to posterity as the representative man of this age, with a label upon him that would stick to him through all time."

The article was adopted—yeas 87, nays 41; the only Republicans voting in the negative being Messrs. Ashley (Nev.), Coburn, Griswold, Laflin, Mallory, Marvin, Pomeroy, Smith, Wilson (Ind.), Wilson (Ohio), Windom and Woodbridge.

This article was made the tenth on the list, and is as follows:

"ARTICLE 10. That said Andrew Johnson, President of the United States, unmindful of the high duties of his high office and the dignity and proprieties thereof, and of the harmony and courtesies which ought to exist and be maintained between the executive and leisglative branches of the Government of the United States, designing and intending to set aside the rightful authorities and powers of Congress, did attempt to bring into disgrace, ridicule, hatred, contempt and reproach, the Congress of the United States, and the several branches thereof, to impair and destroy the regard and respect of all the good people of the United States for the Congress and the legislative power thereof, which all officers of the Government ought inviolably to preserve and maintain, and to excite the odium and resentment of all good people of the United States against Congress and the laws by it duly and constitutionally enacted; and in pursuance of his said design and intent, openly and publicly, and before divers assemblages of citizens of the United States, convened in divers parts thereof, to meet and receive said Andrew Johnson as the Chief-Magistrate of the United States, did, on the eighteenth day of August, in the year of our Lord one thousand eight hundred and sixty-six, and on divers other days and times, as well before as afterward, make and declare, with a loud voice, certain intemperate, inflammatory and scandalous harangues, and therein utter loud threats and bitter menaces, as well against Congress as the laws of the United States duly enacted thereby, amid the cries, jeers and laughter of the multitudes then assembled in hearing, which are set forth in the several specifications hereinafter written, in substance and effect, that is to say:"

[The specifications to this article embraced extracts from his speeches made at the Executive Mansion, on the 18th of August, 1866, and on what is commonly known as the "swinging around the circle" trip, at Cleveland and St. Louis.

On the same day Mr. Bingham offered still another article. It was adopted by the same vote as the previous articles:

"ARTICLE 11. That the said Andrew Johnson, President of the United States, unmindful of the high duties of his office and his oath of office, and in disregard of the Constitution and laws of the United States, did, heretofore, to-wit: On the 18th day of August, 1866, at the City of Washington, and in the District of Columbia, by public speech, declare and affirm in substance, that the Thirty-ninth Congress of the United States was not a Congress of the United States authorized by the Constitution to exercise legislative power under the same, but, on the contrary, was a Congress of only part of the States, thereby denying and intending to deny, that the legislation of said Congress was valid or obligatory upon him, the said Andrew Johnson, except in so far as he saw fit to approve the same, and also thereby denying the power of the said Thirty-ninth Congress to propose amendments to the Constitution of the United States. And in pursuance of said declaration, the said Andrew Johnson, President of the United States, afterward, to wit: On the 21st day of February, 1868, at the City of Washington, D. C., did unlawfully and in disregard of the requirements of the Constitution that he should take care that the laws be faithfully executed, attempt to prevent the execution of an act entitled 'An act regulating the tenure of certain civil offices,' passed March 2, 1867, by unlawfully devising and contriving and attempting to devise and contrive means by which he should prevent Edwin M. Stanton from forthwith resuming the functions of the office of Secretary for the Department of War, notwithstanding the refusal of the Senate to concur in the suspension theretofore made by the said Andrew Johnson of said Edwin M. Stanton from said office of Secretary for the Department of War; and also by further unlawfully devising and contriving, and attempting to devise and contrive means then and there to prevent the execution of an act entitled 'An act making appropriations for the support of the army for the fiscal year ending June 30, 1868, and for other purposes,' approved March 20, 1867. And also to prevent the execution of an act entitled 'An act to provide for the more efficient government of the rebel States,' passed March 2, 1867. Whereby the said Andrew Johnson, President of the United States, did then, to wit, on the 21st day of February, 1868, at the City of Washington, commit and was guilty of a high misdemeanor in office."

Want of space precludes the intermediate details, including those of the trial. The public are sufficiently acquainted with them.

On the 19th of May, 1868, the Senate came to a vote, beginning with the eleventh article. The following named Senators, nineteen in number, voted not guilty:

Messrs. Bayard, Buckalew, Davis, Dixon, Doolittle, *Fessenden, Fowler, Grimes, Henderson*, Hendricks, Johnson, McCreery, Norton, Patterson (Tennessee), *Ross*, Saulsbury, *Trumbull, Van Winkle*, Vickers.

And the following, caring nothing for country, but everything for party, voted for conviction:

Messrs. Anthony, Cameron, Cattell, Chandler, Cole, Conklin, Conness, Corbett, Cragin, Drake, Edmunds, Ferry, Frelinghuysen, Harlan, Howard, Howe, Morgan, Morrill (Me.), Morrill (Vt.), Morton, Nye, Patterson (N. H.), Pomeroy, Ramsey, Sherman, Sprague, Stewart, Sumner, Thayer, Tipton, Wade, Willey, Williams, Wilson, Yates.

The Senate, sitting as a high court of impeachment, without voting on the other articles, adjourned to the 26th of May. On that day the high court resumed its session, and disposed of the second and third articles, and declared, by precisely the same vote which was cast on May 16, on the eleventh article, that the President was not guilty of the high crimes and misdemeanors charged in those articles. As the President could not be convicted on the remaining first, fourth, fifth, sixth, seventh, eighth, ninth and tenth articles, by unanimous consent, a judgment of acquittal on the second, third and eleventh articles was entered in the journal of the court, and in pursuance of a motion made by Senator Williams, of Oregon, Chief-Justice Chase declared that the Senate, sitting as a court of impeachment stood adjourned without day.

INDECENT OUTSIDE PRESSURE PENDING THE VOTE.

WASHINGTON, May 13, 1868.

The following telegram was received to-day from St. Louis:

To Hon. J. B. Henderson:

There is intense excitement here. Meeting called for to-morrow night. Can your friends hope that you will vote for the eleventh article? If so, all will be well.
[Signed] E. W. FOX.

To which Senator Henderson replied:

WASHINGTON, May 13, 1868.

E. W. Fox, St. Louis:

Say to my friends that I am sworn to do impartial justice according to the law and the evidence, and I will try to do it like an honest man.
[Signed] J. B. HENDERSON.

LETTER FROM MISSOURI DELEGATION TO MR. HENDERSON.

Before the Senate met the delegation had agreed upon the request contained in the following letter, and presented the same to Mr. Henderson:

WASHINGTON, D. C. May 12, 1868.

Hon. J. B. Henderson, U. S. Senator:

SIR—On a consultation of the Radical members of the House of Representatives from Missouri, in view of your position on impeachment articles, we ask you to withhold your vote on any article upon which you can not vote affirmatively. The request is made because we believe the safety of the loyal people of the United States demands the immediate removal of Andrew Johnson from the office of President of the United States.

Respectfully, &c.

Signed by Messrs. Anderson, Pile, Newcomb, Gravelly, McClurg, Loan and Benjamin. Mr. Van Horn is absent from the city.

Senator Henderson addressed the following letter to the Missouri Congressional delegation.

WASHINGTON CITY, May 14, 1868.

GENTLEMEN: In an interview with you on the day before yesterday. You suggested that my position on the impeachment question was against the almost unanimous wish of the Union party of our State, and that you feared violence and bloodshed might follow the President's acquittal. Inasmuch as I owed my position here to that party, and expected to support its men and measures in the coming canvass, equally as I deprecated the consequences you thought might follow, though I did not anticipate nor fear any such result; yet, in order to place myself beyond the possible censure of those whom I know to be my best friends, I at once proposed to tender to the Governor my resignation as Senator. To this you did not consent, and I then requested you as my friends to consult together and determine what you thought was proper for me to do under the circumstances. You did so, and the result was, that, believing the safety of the country and interests of the loyal people of the United States demanded the immediate removal of Andrew Johnson, you asked me to withhold my vote on any article upon which I can not vote affirmatively.

So soon as I had time to read and consider the paper, I found that I could not comply with the request without that degree of humiliation and shame to which I was satisfied you, as honorable gentlemen, would not wish to subject me. I had already spoken in the Senate, and I thought conclusively, at least to my mind, against eight of the articles, and had informed you I was no less decided in my judgment against the efficiency of others, leaving me in doubt only as to one. If, with the clear conviction expressed in the full Senate, I should now sit silent, I would forfeit my self-respect and stand defenseless before the world.

You agreed to reconsider your opinion, and although you at first resolved to adhere to it, I am gratified that on further reflection you agreed with me that it was quite unreasonable, but you still insisted on your opinion that my duty required my vote to be so cast or withheld, as might seem necessary on some of the articles, so as to secure conviction.

I at once mentioned the difficulty attending the suggestion. Senators had been and were so reticent on the subject, that I could not ascertain their position. I knew them to be greatly divided, and were liable to change their minds at any moment before the final vote should be taken. But as you expressed a desire that I should not resign unless it became absolutely necessary to have a successor in my place favorable to conviction, I promised to give you the result of my conclusion, as soon as I could ascertain the probable result in one or two articles.

Since that time I have seriously reflected over the whole matter, and have come to the conclusion that, having been sworn to try this case on the principles of impartial justice, and to render a verdict according to the law and the evidence, I can not shirk or divide that responsibility with others. It is for the House to find articles of impeachment. It is for the Senate to try them. If I resign before the vote, it strikes me I have come short of my oath; and as you are pleased to place this matter on purely political grounds, you will permit me to say, my resignation can be of no possible service to you. A proper sense of delicacy would prevent my successor from voting, he not having heard the case, and you are aware that voting in the negative and declining to vote, will be practically the same. Should he forego delicacy, and secure the conviction by his vote, the manner of obtaining it will defeat every conceivable advantage to be derived.

I have, therefore, resolved to stand by the obligations of my oath, honestly discharge my duty as it is given me to know it, and appealing to heaven for the rectitude of my intentions, I am determined to follow the dictates of conscience, and trust to a generous and upright people for the vindication of my conduct.

Your friend,
JOHN B. HENDERSON.

[Correspondence of the Cincinnati Commercial.]
WASHINGTON, May 14.

It was stated in these dispatches, on Tuesday night, that telegrams had been sent from here to get up popular demonstrations in favor of impeachment. Senator Anthony's paper, the Providence *Journal*, of yesterday, comes to hand here with the statement that the following telegram was sent to several gentlemen in that city who are more or less conspicuous in local politics:

"WASHINGTON, May 12, 1868.

"Great damage to the peace of the country and the Republican cause if impeachment fails. Send to your Senators before Saturday public opinion, by resolutions, letters and delegations.

"ROBERT C. SCHENCK, Chm'n."

That paper, in commenting upon it, says that such a telegram coming from such a source awakened in many minds a profound feeling of surprise and mortification. General Schenck, it adds, has mistaken his own duty, and he has mistaken the Senators from Rhode Island and the people they represent. *Per contra*, however, the following from General Burnside to General Schenck was received last night.

"PROVIDENCE, R. I., May 13.

"Rhode Island is a law and order State. She is in favor of impeachment, because she believes the President has violated the law of the land. A. E. BURNSIDE."

The following resolutions were adopted by the Fourth Ward Republican Club of Washington:

"*Resolved*, That any Representative or Senator of the United States, who, at this hour of peril, deserts the party that placed him in power, by voting for the acquittal of Andrew Johnson, will be forever infamous, and deserve the execrations of every lover of his country.

"*Resolved*, That we impeach Senators Fessenden, Trumbull and Grimes, at the bar of justice and humanity, as traitors, before whose guilt the infamy of Benedict Arnold becomes respectability and decency."

The following telegraphic dispatch, signed

by a number of men, including delegates to the Chicago Convention, has been received by General Schenck:

LEAVENWORTH, KAN., May 13.

"We hope and pray there will be no division among our Senators in the conviction of Andrew Johnson, as there is none whatever among the Republicans of Kansas."

The Iowa members had an informal caucus, and concluded that "Mr. Grimes was beyond any appeals to his honor, or to his conscience, or to his party," and they would turn him over to the tender mercies of his outraged and betrayed constituency.

"The Illinois delegation, we are told, had a caucus, lasting nearly two hours, attended by all the Republican members. Mr. Trumbull *was denounced by each one, and most severely by Messrs. Judd and Cook*, who have heretofore been his devoted friends. His motives were impugned and the unanimous verdict was that he was engaged in a deep and damnable conspiracy, and that any argument or appeal to him would be lost."

The *Tribune* went still further in its brutal attacks, and says, of Trumbull, Fessenden, and Grimes:

"The infamous notoriety which they had obtained made every stranger ask to have them pointed out to him. Nobody who had the least regard for his reputation ventured near them. *Can one touch pitch and not be defiled?* seemed to be the unanimous sentiment. Grimes curled himself up on his seat, *as mean, repulsive, and noxious as a hedge hog in the cage of a traveling menagerie;* and so they sat, the target of scoffs, while five hundred lorgnettes were scanning their faces for some indication in their facial lines of the *deep, dark treachery of their hearts.* Fessenden busied himself with his correspondence. Indignant New Englanders asked, what has New England done that she should have such a representative? * * The journal of yesterday gave little evidence of the *treachery* of Trumbull, the *falsehood* of Fessenden, or the *party treason* of Grimes."

The following telegraphic dispatches were sent to the conscientious Senator from Kansas. Mr. Ross, who refused to commit perjury by finding the President guilty in obedience to outside clamor and dictation. Thereupon, the Jacobins at home sent him dispatches, of which the following are specimens:

"LEAVENWORTH, May 16, 1868.

"Hon. E. G. Ross, U. S. Senator, Washington, D. C.:

"Your telegram received. Your vote is dictated by Tom Ewing, not by your oath. Your motives are Indian contracts and greenbacks. Kansas repudiates you as she does all perjurers and skunks.

"D. R. ANTHONY, and others."

"To E. G. Ross:

TOPEKA, May 16, 1868.

"Probably the rope with which Judas hung himself is lost, but the pistol with which Jim Lane committed suicide is at your service. L. D. BAILEY."

Wendell Phillips Denounces Mr. Chase and the Senate.

In a letter from Washington, Wendell Phillips says: "The Chief Justice of the Supreme Court is his ally. Salmon P. Chase, mad with the Presidential fever, and desperate in the consciousness of baffled plans, meanly jealous of Wade, and perhaps cherishing the forlorn hope of a Democratic nomination, joins forces with the enemy, and stands as the Presidential ally. It has been known for a long time that the relations between the Chief-Justice and the President were more cordial than was made necessary by the mere official relations of the parties; and last Wednesday night the rooms of the Chief-Justice, filled with the gay and fashionable winter society of Washington, were startled as by electric shock, when the doors were flung open, and the usher, in a loud voice, announced, "the President of the United States and daughter." Very few of those who were present with me will soon forget the significant looks which passed from face to face through these brilliant and crowded rooms as the unusual event of the President of the United States attending an evening reception of the Chief-Justice was fully realized. His carping letter to the Senate—his refusal, at first, to obey the mandates to appear as its presiding officer—and his decisions of the following day, are but the unfolding of a plot to obstruct and defeat as far possible the conviction of the President. How far he may be able to work harm, depends, of course, on the firmness of the Senate; but in any event, he is a serious obstacle, with evil intentions only limited by his courage; which latter, fortunately, is not great. He seems determined to maintain the consistency of a public career which may be summed up in these words: He never had an opportunity to serve his party that he did not betray it.

"The Senate itself is the next great danger. There is reason to believe that a serious defection exists among the Republicans on this question. Ross, of Kansas, and Sprague, of Rhode Island (Chase's son-in-law), are already counted secure as two of the seven Republicans it is necessary to win over to prevent a conviction. The more than probable defection of Fessenden would carry at least four more gentlemen who hang on his skirts. The folly of Congress in not providing for the suspension of the President during trial, will soon be evident. The boundless opportunity this gives the culprit to corrupt his judges, will not remain unimproved.'

Senator Fessenden on the Pressure.

Senator Fessenden, in a letter dated June 25, 1868, to Governor Bullock and others, of Boston, writes:

"The excitement elsewhere, however, was trifling when compared with that which prevailed at the Capital. Here a change of administration had long been contemplated, and was now counted on as a certainty. That looked-for change had its usual attendants. The coming in of a new President could hardly have warmed into life a more numerous brood of expectants, or stimulated more extensive hopes of honors and profits. The city was filled with men ready to jump into places to be made vacant, as they hoped and believed, for their benefit. Gamblers thronged the saloons, staking more than they were able to pay upon conviction or acquittal. As these hopes rose or fell with the rumors of the hour, as impeachment stock went up or down upon the political exchange among the crowd of hungry expectants, so for the time rose and fell the character and reputation of those Senators upon whose votes the result was supposed to depend; while the telegraph was at hand to carry over its wires to the homes and friends of those Senators every calumny which disappointed ambition could imagine, or cupidity and malignity could invent, and while a portion of the press, claiming for itself a character for decency, and even for Christian virtue, stood ready to indorse and circulate the lie.

"What effect such a condition of things might have had upon the conclusions of Senators, it is not easy to determine. The result has shown that in the estimation of that portion of the public which I have attempted to delineate, it was of little consequence what the opinion of Senators might be upon particular questions, so that conviction and removal were secured. The immediate cause of impeachment, and the main article upon which it was founded, was the removal of the Secretary of War. Two honorable and learned Senators, not included in "the seven," announced their opinions that the President was not guilty upon this article, and it was not considered in them an error of judgment, much less a betrayal of party, so long as they were able to vote for conviction upon the eleventh. Other Senators in their opinions declared themselves unable to sustain the fourth, fifth, sixth, seventh, ninth and tenth. No articles could be found which would secure the vote of thirty-five Senators except the second, third and eleventh. And yet the political orthodoxy of Senators was saved by a vote for conviction upon something. To all such the full right of independent judgment was fully conceded, while such as claimed and exercised the same right upon all the articles were unsparingly denounced as traitors, and proclaimed infamous in advance by a Manager who had substantially declared in the House, that without the eleventh article the whole were good for nothing."

Shameless Inconsistency of Senators.

During the debate on the Tenure-of-Office Bill, Mr. Edmonds, of Vt., a member of the Committee of Conference which settled the final shape of the bill, said, on behalf of the committee, that they thought, "after a great deal of consultation and reflection:"

"That it was right and just that the Chief Executive of the nation, in selecting these named Secretaries, who, by law and by the practice of the country, and officers analogous to whom by the practice of all other countries, are the confidential advisers of the Executive respecting the administration of all his departments, *should be persons who were personally agreeable to him, in whom he could place entire confidence and reliance*, and that, whenever it should seem to him that the state of relations between him and any of them had become so as to render that relation of confidence and trust and personal esteem inharmonious, he should in such case be allowed to dispense with the services of that officer in vacation, and have some other person act in his stead."

Mr. Williams, of Oregon, who prepared the original bill, said that there were good reasons why the power of the President over his Secretaries should be excepted out of the limitations. He said:

"The chief reason that influenced me to make the exception was, that I thought something was due to the President of the United States—to that office. This bill undertakes to reverse what has heretofore been the admitted practice of the Government; and it seemed to me that it was due to the exalted office of the President of the United States, the Chief Magistrate of the nation, that he should exercise this power; that he should be left to choose his own Cabinet, and that he should be held responsible, as he will be, to the country for whatever acts that Cabinet may preform."

Mr Fessenden, of Maine, maintained the same view of the intent of the law, and enforced it on the high grounds of public expediency. The head of a department should possess the power over the subordinates, and the President over the Secretaries. He said:

"In my judgment, in order to the good and proper management of a department, it is necessary that that power should exist in the head of it, and quite as necessary that the power should exist in the President with reference to the few men who are placed about him to share his councils, be his friends and his agents."

Mr. Sherman, of Ohio, spoke even more decidedly, even to indignation, that any Secretary should attempt to defeat the desire of the President to get rid of him.

The following are some of the emphatic passages of his speech, which now apply to Mr. Stanton:

"Now, I say that if a Cabinet officer should attempt to hold his office for a moment beyond the time when he retains the entire confidence of the President, I would not vote to retain him, nor would I compel a President to have about him, in these high positions, a man in whom he did not entirely trust, both personally and politically.

"Any gentleman fit to be a Cabinet Minister, who receives an intimation from his chief that his longer continuance in that office is unpleasant to him, would necessarily resign. If he did not resign, it would show that he was unfit to be there. I can not imagine a case where a Cabinet officer would hold on to his place in defiance and against the wishes of his chief; and if such a case should occur, I certainly would not by any extraordinary or ordinary legislation protect him in the office in defiance of what would be regarded in every constitutional government as the proper one, namely, to retire when he separates or differs in opinion from his chief.

"I take it that no case can arise, or is likely to arise, where a Cabinet Minister will attempt to hold on to his office after his chief desires his removal. I can scarcely conceive of such a case. I think that no gentleman, no man with any sense of honor, would hold a position as a Cabinet officer after his chief desired his removal.

"And if I supposed that either of these gentlemen was so wanting in manhood, in honor, as to hold his place after the politest intimation by the President of the United States that his services were no longer needed, I certainly, as a Senator, would consent to his removal at any time, and so would we all."

Yet all these Senators, except one, were the active partisans of impeachment.

Thaddeus Stevens was the chief prosecutor of the President to impeachment, on the score of his having asserted the power to remove a refractory and offensive member from his Cabinet. Mr. Stevens was, a few years ago, member of the Pennsylvania State Convention for the framing of a State constitution; and therein he was the stoutest advocate for the necessity that an Executive should have the fullest power to appoint and to remove his own Cabinet.

He said:

"But, if you take the appointments from the Governor, it may, and probably often will, happen, that he will be of one party, and entertain one set of principles, and they be of another party, and hold entirely opposite principles; discord and opposition must then disturb their counsels, and injure the interests of the State."

Again:

"Why vest the power of appointment in the Legislature? Their legitimate duty is to enact laws, and not to appoint those who are to execute them. Sufficient inducements are now held out to them to make them swerve from the path of duty, without multiplying the temptations by placing the patronage of this great State at their disposal."

And still again, as if predicting the course he is now pursuing as an evil to be carefully provided against, he said:

"The Governor and the Senate would either be of the same political party or hostile parties; if of the same party, the Senate would be no check upon the Governor, as there would be perfect concert before the nomination, and, therefore, this supervising power would be useless. If they were of hostile parties, constant and bitter collisions would exist between them, which would greatly disturb the faithful discharge of their other duties."

And so they have done and are continuing to do now, and this same Mr. Stevens is the Moloch of discord.

A Radical Organ Denounces the Conspiracy.

[From the New York Evening Post.]

These proceedings are clearly unlawful and revolutionary. If, on an impartial trial, the impeached President should be convicted, the country would doubtless accept the result as one on the whole satisfactory. But what respect is a verdict entitled to which is got by threats against the judges, by the secret solicitations of the prosecutors, and by open demands that judges shall either vote for conviction or withhold their votes altogether.

Setting aside for the moment the unlawful, atrocious and revolutionary character of these proceedings, we ask, what will be the use, or the force or value of a verdict so gained? Suppose that when the high court re-assembles on Saturday, it gives a verdict against the accused—what character or moral force will, or can, such a verdict have? Will it not be plain to the least discerning that this end has been reached by the unlawful and unjust interference of the prosecutors; by secret solicitations and public threats of the judges; by means which, if they were employed by the public prosecutors in the trial of a pickpocket, would arouse a storm of just indignation?

A Two-Edged Quotation.

The Baltimore *Sun* says that Manager Logan, in the printed speech he has filed in the impeachment case, quotes from Shakspeare, saying we (the managers) thought "if it were done, when 'tis done, then 'twere well it were done quickly." This very appropriate quotation is from "Macbeth," when he is about to murder "Duncan." It was an apt quotation, and the parallel suggested would have been still more complete if Mr. Logan had proceeded with other extracts from the same soliloquy of "Macbeth:"

"We but teach
Bloody instructions, which being taught, return
To plague the inventor."
"Besides, this Duncan hath been
So clear in his great office, that his virtues
Will plead, like angels, trumpet-tongued against
The deep damnation of his taking off."

Now and Then.

In 1864, when the Republicans wanted Mr. Blair put out of the Cabinet, the following paper was presented to President Lincoln:

"The theory of our government, the early and uniform practical construction thereof, is that *the President should be aided by a Cabinet council agreeing with him in political principle and general policy*, and that all important measures and appointments should be the result of their combined wisdom and deliberation. The most obvious and necessary condition of things, *without which no administration can succeed*, we and the public believe does not exist, and, therefore, such selections and changes in its members should be made as will secure to the country unity of purpose and action in all material and essential respects, more especially in the present crisis of public affairs.

"The Cabinet should be *exclusively composed* of statesmen who are *the cordial, resolute, unwavering supporters of the principles and purposes above mentioned.*"

This paper was signed by the following Republican Senators, among whom will be found a large number who voted for conviction. They were agreed to punish, in Mr. Johnson, as a *crime*, what they urged upon Mr. Lincoln as a *duty*. These are the names of the signers:

Massachusetts—Charles Sumner, Henry Wilson.
Ohio—Benj. F. Wade, John Sherman.
New York—Preston King, Ira Harris.
Pennsylvania — David Wilmot, Edgar Cowan.
Maine—L. M. Morrill, W. P. Fessenden.
Connecticut—James Dixon, L. S. Foster.
Vermont—Solomon Foot, Jacob Collamer.
New Hampshire—D. Clark, John P. Hale.
Rhode Island—H. B. Anthony.
Michigan—Zachariah Chandler.
Illinois—O. H. Browning, Lyman Trumbull.
Iowa—James Harlan, James W. Grimes.
Kansas—S. C. Pomeroy.
Wisconsin—J. R. Doolittle, T. O. Howe.

Disreputable Conduct of an Interested Party.

Had President Johnson been convicted, B. F. Wade, Senator from Ohio, and President *pro tempore* of the Senate, would have succeeded to his high place. Yet, he had the brazen audacity to present himself to be sworn in as a trier, and voted for conviction. Mr. Hendricks, of Indiana, objected to his qualification, but withdrew it. During the debate, Mr. Bayard, of Delaware, administered him the following withering rebuke:

"He argued against the right of Senator Wade to take the oath, the object of the Constitution being to exclude the person who was to be benefited by the deposition of the President from taking part in the proceedings leading to such deposition. He proceeded to argue that the character of the body in trying impeachment was that of a court, not that of a Senate. He could not conceive on what ground the question as to the character of the body was introduced, except it was that Senators, cutting themselves loose from the restraints of their judicial character, might give full swing to their partisan passions. If he stood in the same position as the Senator from Ohio, the wealth of the world would not tempt him to sit in such a case."

Butler Loser on Impeachment.

A Washington correspondent writes as follows:

"There is a report, which a good many people credit, that Butler had a large amount of money staked on impeachment. It is said that George Wilkes, who was very busy in Washington during the impeachment *furore*, was betting Ben's money, with Ben's consent, of course; and that the patriot of Lowell and Dutch Gap, would have pocketed quite a comfortable sum if Wade had gone in with the apple blossoms. Perhaps his disappointment on this head was one cause of the rage he exhibited on the heels of the impeachment fiasco."

Effort to Impeach Washington.

ISSUES BETWEEN GEORGE WASHINGTON AND CONGRESS — IMPEACHMENT PREVENTED BY THE PEOPLE.

[From the New York Commercial Advertiser.]

The trial of President Johnson recalls the attempts made in 1795 to destroy the character of President Washington, with an intention, had it succeeded, to impeach him. The parties combined to accomplish these objects consisted of—

First. The opponents of the funding scheme of Alexander Hamilton.

Second. The partisans of the French Directory.

Third. The opponents of the excise law.

This combination assailed Washington with a bitterness and vigor never since surpassed in this country. The vials of party wrath were poured out against him through a malignant press. We are told by Chief-Justice Marshall: His military and political character was attacked with equal violence, and it was averred that he was totally destitute of merit, either as a soldier or statesman. The calumnies with which he was assailed were not confined to his public conduct; even his qualities as a man were the subjects of detraction. That he had violated the Constitution in negotiating a treaty without the previous consent of the Senate, and in embracing within that treaty subjects belonging exclusively to the Legislature, were openly maintained, for which an impeachment was publicly suggested; and that he had drawn from the Treasury, for his private use, more than the salary annexed to his office, was asserted without a blush. This last allegation was said to be supported by extracts from the Treasury accounts, which had been laid before the Legislature, and was maintained with the most persevering effrontery.

In addition to the insurrection in the western counties of Pennsylvania, which Washington believed to have been "fomented by the self-created societies who were laboring to effect some revolution in the Government," the President was embarrassed by divisions and dissensions in his Cabinet, and a want of fidelity on the part of some members of the Cabinet, and was also confronted by a serious dispute with the House of Representatives, arising out of his refusal to comply with a resolution of the House requesting the President to lay before it the instructions, correspondence, and other documents relative to the treaty with Great Britain negotiated by Mr. Jay. His biographer, Washington Irving, says:

"Washington, believing that these papers could not be constitutionally demanded, resolved from the first moment, and from the fullest conviction of his mind, to resist the principle which was evidently intended to be established by the call of the House; he only deliberated on the manner in which this could be done with the least bad consequences."

Washington, in his answer, after observing that to admit the demand would establish a dangerous precedent, concluded by declaring that, "as it was essential to the due administration of the Government that the boundaries fixed by the Constitution between the different departments should be observed, a just regard to the Constitution and to the duty of his office forbid a compliance with the request."

This decided answer subjected President Washington to numerous misrepresentations and fabrications, which, says Marshall, "were with unwearied industry pressed upon the public in order to withdraw the confidence of the nation from its chief." Amid all these difficulties, President Washington pursued the even tenor of his way; but that his magnanimous heart received a deep wound from these persecutions and misrepresentations, there is ample evidence in his letters.

To Jefferson, he writes: "Until within the last year or two I had no conception that parties would or ever could go the length I have been witness to; nor did I believe until lately that it was within the bounds of probability, hardly within those of possibility, that, while I was using my utmost exertions to establish a national character of our own, and wished, by steering a steady course, to preserve this country from the throes of a desolating war, I should be accused of being the enemy of one nation, and subject to the influence of another; and, to prove it, that every act of my administration would be tortured, and the grossest and most insidious misrepresentations of them be made, by giving one side of a subject, and that too in such exaggerated and indecent terms as could scarcely be applied to a Nero, a notorious defaulter, or even to a common pickpocket."

Again, we are informed that when the Minister of the French Republic set the acts of the United States Government at defiance and threatened the Executive with an appeal to the people, and the latter, notwithstanding the indignity thus offered to their Chief Magistrate, sided with their aggressors, and exulted in open defiance of his national policy, he became weary and impatient, and being handed one of those scandalous libels in circulation, called "The Funeral of George Washington," wherein the President was represented as placed upon a guillotine, a horrible parody on the late decapitation of the French King, "burst forth," writes Jefferson, "into one of those transports of passion beyond his control; inveighed against the personal abuse which had been bestowed upon him, and defied any man on earth to produce a single act of his since he had been in this Government which had not been done in the purest of motives. He had never repented but once having slipped the moment of having resigned his office, and that was every moment since. In the agony of his heart he declared that he had rather be in his grave than in his present situation; that he had rather be on his farm than to be made Emperor of the World; 'and yet,' said he, indignantly, 'they are charging me with wanting to be a king.' From Randolph, Secretary of State, he demanded an explanation of his statements to the French Minister (contained in an intercepted dispatch of the latter to his Government), which reflected on the purity of conduct as well as fidelity of the Secretary to his superior. The explanation was promised, and Mr. Randolph resigned on the spot."

The country finally took the alarm, and came to the defense of the President. The General Assembly of Maryland passed a unanimous resolution to the following effect: That, "observing with deep concern a series of efforts, by indirect insinuation or open invective, to detach from the First Magistrate of the Union the well-earned confidence of his fellow-citizens, they think it their duty to declare, and they do hereby declare, their unabated reliance on the integrity, judgment, and patriotism of the President of the United States."

Meetings were held in every part of the Union to express the public feeling in the matters referred to in this communication. The result was, that the character of the illustrious Washington came out of the ordeal without a stain upon it; and the people, although they did not all espouse his views, avowed their readiness to support him in the exercise of his constitutional functions.

Is the President Bound to Execute an Unconstitutional Law?—An Unpublished Letter of Jefferson's.

[From the New York World, May 15.]

By the civility and public spirit of the possessor, we are furnished with a transcript of the following letter of President Jefferson, written in the first year of his administration. It is superscribed
"Free.
"TH. JEFFERSON.
"EDWARD LIVINGSTON, ESQ.,
"Mayor of New York."

Mr. Livingston was, at that time, United States District Attorney at New York, as well as Mayor of the city. The pertinent bearing of the letter on the impeachment of President Johnson, will be manifest on perusal:

"WASHINGTON, November 1, 1801.

"DEAR SIR: I some days ago received a letter from Messrs. Denniston and Cheetham, of the most friendly kind, asking the general grounds on which the *nolle prosequi* in Duane's case ought to be presented to the public, which they propose to do. You are sensible I must avoid committing myself in that channel of justification, and that, were I to do it in this case, I might be called on by other printers in other cases where it might be inexpedient to say anything. Yet, to so civil an application. I can not reconcile myself to the incivility of giving no answer. I have thought, therefore, of laying your friendship under contribution, and asking you to take the trouble of seeing them and of saying to them, that the question being in the line of the law, I had desired you to give them the explanation necessary. My text of explanation would be this: The President is to have the laws executed. He may order an offense, then, to be prosecuted. If he sees a prosecution put into a train which is not lawful, he may order it to be discontinued and put into legal train. *I found a prosecution going on against Duane for an offense against the Senate, founded on the Sedition act.* I AFFIRM THAT ACT TO BE NO LAW BECAUSE IN OPPOSITION TO THE CONSTITUTION, AND I SHALL TREAT IT AS A NULLITY WHEREVER IT COMES IN THE WAY OF MY FUNCTIONS. *I therefore directed that prosecution to be discontinued and a new one to be commenced, founded on whatsoever other law might be in existence against the offense. This was done, and the Grand Jury, finding no other law against it, declined doing anything against the bill.* There appears to me to be no weak part in any of these positions or inferences. There is, however, in the application to you to trouble yourself with the question. For this I owe apology, and build it on your goodness and friendship. Health and happiness *cum cæteris votis.*
"TH. JEFFERSON."
"EDWARD LIVINGSTON, ESQ."

A Stanton Case during the elder Adams' Time.

On the 10th day of March, 1800, President Adams addressed to Colonel Pickering, then Secretary of State, a note, which I will read:

"May 10, 1800.

"*T. T. Pickering, Secretary of State, Philadelphia*—SIR: As I perceive a necessity of introducing a change in the administration of the Office of State, I think it proper to make this communication of it to the present Secretary of State, that he may have an opportunity of resigning if he chooses. I should wish the day on which his resignation is to take place to be named by himself. I wish for an answer to this letter on or before Monday morning, because the nomination of a successor must be sent to the Senate as soon as they sit.

"With esteem, I am, sir, your most obedient and humble servant,
"JOHN ADAMS."

Colonel Pickering replied in an extraordinary strain, declining to resign; whereupon Mr. Adams sent him this laconic notice, which bears date May 12, 1800:

"May 12, 1800.
"*To Timothy Pickering, Philadelphia—*
SIR: Divers causes and considerations, essential to the administration of the Government, in my judgment requiring a change in the Department of State, you are hereby discharged from any further service as Secretary of State.
"JOHN ADAMS,
"President of the United States."
[*Works of John Adams, Vol. IX, pp. 54, 55.*]

Observe in this, that Mr. Adams saw fit to peremptorily discharge Colonel Pickering. The same day, May 12, the President sent a brief announcement of the removal to the Senate, which reads as follows:

"MONDAY, May 12, 1800.
"*Gentlemen of the Senate:* I nominate the Honorable John Marshall, Esq., of Virginia, to be Secretary of State, in place of the Honorable Timothy Pickering, Esq., removed.
"JOHN ADAMS."

That was all the official notice the Senate had of the removal, before or since. Mr. Adams, in one of his Cunningham letters, calls this one of the most deliberate, virtuous and disinterested actions of his life.

A Radical Attorney-General on the Power of the President to Remove an Officer.

Congress, in 1865, passed a law vesting the power of appointing the Assistant Revenue Collectors by the District Collectors.

Mr. McCulloch, Secretary of the Treasury, submitted to the Attorney-General these three questions:

1. Whether the provisions of the act of March 3, 1865, vesting the appointment of Assistant Assessors in the Assessors of the respective assessment districts, is constitutional?

2. If it is unconstitutional, in whom is the power of appointing Assistant Assessors by law vested?

3. If the President is, by law, vested with that power, should he exercise it against the express provision of the act of Congress, before any judicial determination has been had of the two preceding questions?

These make exactly the Stanton case. A law is passed restricting the President's power of appointment. Is it constitutional? and if not constitutional, can the President lawfully exercise the power of appointing before the courts have pronounced on the constitutionality of the law?

Mr. Speed gave his opinion that the law was unconstitutional, and, further, that it is not only within the power to make the appointments constitutionally, but that "it is clearly his duty to do so."

"If he fully concurs in the view I have taken on this question, there is no escape from the conclusion that he alone can lawfully fill the offices. It is his duty to do all that he has lawful power to do, when the occasion requires an exercise of authority. To do otherwise, on whichever occasion, would be *pro tanto* an abdication of his high office."

The Attorney-General went on to state that the true arbiter in cases of conflict of appointment, is the Supreme Court, and that when two persons challenge the authority of exercising the powers of an office, "the question would then be peculiarly one for judicial determination."

"In the absence of authoritative exposition of the law by that [the Judicial] Department, it is equally the duty of the officer holding the Executive power of the Government to determine for the purposes of his own conduct and action, as well the operation of conflicting laws, as of the constitutionality of any one."

Here is the official opinion of Mr. Stanbery's immediate predecessor, the Attorney-General of Mr. Lincoln, a Radical of the most confirmed stamp, who has just been publicly addressing the Radicals of Kentucky to move them into action in support of Congress.

Conclusion of the Speech of Judge Woodward, of Pennsylvania, on the Resolution of Impeachment.

Mr. Speaker, I shall not feel that my whole duty to the House and the country is done unless I allude to another objection to this impeachment movement, which my friend from New York [Mr. Brooks] glanced at, and for which the gentleman from Ohio [Mr. Bingham] and the two gentlemen from Illinois [Mr. Farnsworth and Mr. Logan] poured out upon his head a flood of vituperative eloquence. At the risk of similar denunciations I take it upon me to deny your right to impeach anybody.

and the present Senate's right to try any impeachment.

Says the Constitution: "The House of Representatives shall have the sole power of impeachment," and "the House of Representatives shall be composed of members chosen every second year by the people of the several States." This House of Representatives is not so composed; but, on the contrary, the Representatives chosen from ten of the "several States" have been and are excluded from these Halls. I do not say if they were absent voluntarily they could prevent your exercise of the impeaching power; for then they would form, though personally absent, a part of the composition of the House; but so long as you prevent their entering into its composition, you are not the House of Representatives, to whom the Constitution commits the "sole power of impeachment." Our functions in this regard have been likened to those of a grand jury which consists of twenty-three men. And suppose, sir, a majority of a grand jury should get possession of the jury-room and bar the door against a minority of their fellows, as well entitled to be there as the majority, would the findings of such a jury be respected? By no court in Christendom. On the contrary, their acts would be set aside, and very likely themselves punished for their contempt of the law.

Then, as to the Senate, the Constitution says, "the Senate shall have the sole power to try all impeachments," and that the "Senate of the United States shall be composed of two Senators from each State." The ten excluded States are entitled to twenty Senators upon that floor, and until they are admitted and incorporated into the body, I deny that it is the Senate to whom the Constitution commits the power to try impeachments. What criminal was ever before arraigned before a court from which twenty of his legal triers had been excluded? Yet you propose to arraign the man who represents in his person thirty-five millions of freemen before just such a dismembered bench. You have no right to do it. Your might makes it not right. A giant's strength is good, but it is tyrannous to use it as a giant.

The flippant reply to this grave suggestion is that we pass laws, and therefore we are a House and Senate to impeach. But the answer is, your legislative powers have not been questioned—your impeaching powers are. I am not bound to take even a valid objection to the jurisdiction of a court who sits to adjudicate my civil rights, nor is my objection to its jurisdiction to try me for crimes and misdemeanors impaired by my failure to make timely objection in behalf of my civil rights. The question of jurisdiction is raised now, and now is the time to decide it. It could not be decided before it was raised, and hence I conclude all the legislation we have done does not constitute us the court to originate and try impeachments which the Constitution contemplates.

Mr. Speaker, so sure I am that the American people will respect this opinion, that I will say, if I were the President's counselor, which I am not, I would advise him, if you prefer articles of impeachment, to demur both to your jurisdiction and that of the Senate, and to issue a proclamation giving you and all the world notice that, while he held himself impeachable for misdemeanors in office before the constitutional tribunal, he never would subject the office he holds in trust for the people to the irregular, unconstitutional, fragmentary bodies who propose to strip him of it. Such a proclamation, with the army and navy in hand to sustain it, would meet a popular response that would make an end of impeachment and impeachers.

Chancellor Kent's Opinion.

Chancellor Kent's remarks on the subject are as follows:

"On the first organization of the Government it was made a question whether the power of removal in case of officers appointed to hold at pleasure, resided nowhere but in the body which appointed, and, of course, whether the consent of the Senate was not requisite to remove. This was the construction given to the Constitution while it was pending for ratification before the State conventions, by the author of the Federalist. But the construction which was given to the Constitution by Congress, after great consideration and discussion, was different. The words of the act (establishing the Treasury Department) are: 'And whenever the same shall be removed from office by the President of the United States, or in any other case of vacancy in the office, the assistant shall act.' This amounted to a legislative construction of the Constitution, and it has ever since been acquiesced in and acted upon as a decisive authority in the case. It applies equally to every other officer of the Government appointed by the President, whose term or duration is not specially declared. It is supported by the weighty reason that the subordinate officers in the executive department ought to hold at the pleasure of the head of the department, because he is invested generally with the executive authority, and the participation in that authority by the Senate was an exception to a general principle, and ought to be taken strictly. The President is the great responsible officer for the faithful execution of the law, and the power of removal was incidental to that duty, and might often be requisite to fulfill it."

The Finale—The Retreat of Stanton.

WAR DEPARTMENT,
WASHINGTON, May 26, 1868.

SIR: The resolution of the Senate of the United States, of the 21st of February last, declaring that the President has no power to remove the Secretary of War, and designate any other officer to perform the duties of that office *ad interim*, having this day failed to be supported by two-thirds of the Senators present and voting on the articles of impeachment preferred against you by the House of Representatives, I have relinquished the charge of the War Department and have left the same, and the books, archives, papers, and property in my custody as Secretary of War, in care of Brevet Major-General Townsend, the senior Adjutant-General, subject to your direction.

(Signed) E. M. STANTON,
Secretary of War.

To the President.

A History of Reconstruction.

POLICY OF PRESIDENTS LINCOLN AND JOHNSON, AND THAT OF CONGRESS—THE ABUSES UNDER THE CONGRESSIONAL POLICY—THE FRUITS OF ITS WORKINGS—SOVEREIGN STATES WIPED OUT AND ROTTEN BOROUGHS SUBSTITUTED.

By reference to the chapter in this work on the Purposes of the War, it will be seen that the paramount object was to restore the States to the Union, with all the rights and powers intact which they possessed at the time of their attempted secession. Congress so declared, on the 23d of December, 1861. Mr. Seward so stated in his dispatches to Foreign Governments. Mr. Lincoln's Executive action seemed to be possessed of that object as its primary idea. His first efforts, says the *World's* history of the matter, were in Louisiana:

"New Orleans was captured in April, 1862, and shortly after, as General Butler testified before the Committee on the Conduct of the War, it was intimated to him, from Washington, that the election of two members of Congress from Louisiana would be desirable; and he further testified that he sent General Weitzel to make an expedition into the Lafourche district for the express purpose of including territory enough within the Federal lines to warrant the election of a second Congressman. Eight months (Nov. 14, 1862) after the occupation of New Orleans, by command of General Butler, Military Governor, Brigadier-General G. F. Shepley issued an order in which he said: 'Whereas the State of Louisiana is now, and has been, without any Representatives in the Thirty-seventh Congress of the United States of America; and whereas, a very large majority of the citizens of the First and Second Congressional Districts in this State, by taking the oath of allegiance, have given evidence of their loyalty and obedience to the Constitution and laws of the United States,' etc. The election for two members of Congress was held, but the members chosen were refused seats.

"Still further, under the direction of the President, a reorganization of the State government was ordered; the State Constitution was revised by a Convention, submitted to the people, and ratified; a legislature was chosen; in March, 1864, Michael Hahn was elected Governor by the people; subsequently, the Legislature chose United States Senators, one of whom was Hahn, then Governor; and in the following popular election, J. Madison Wells was chosen Governor of the State. Although the United States Senators and Representatives elect were refused admission, the State Government, as reorganized under the Lincoln-Banks plan, was never interfered with by Congress till the final Reconstruction Acts were passed."

Then the Legislature, being discovered to be composed of a Democratic majority, was ordered by General Sheridan not to reassemble. Governor Wells, though a Radical, was personally obnoxious to General Sheridan, and was removed. A new Governor was, however, appointed by him, and the State Government thus formed was continued to a great extent in operation.

The following is the letter of the President on the subject:

EXECUTIVE MANSION,
WASHINGTON, June 19, 1863.

Gentlemen: Since receiving your letter, reliable information has reached me that a respectable portion of the Louisiana people desire to amend their State Constitution, and contemplate holding a convention for that object. This fact alone, it seems to me, is a sufficient reason why the General Government should not give the committee the authority you seek, to act under the existing State Constitution. I may add, that while I do not perceive how such a committee could facilitate our military operations in Louisiana, I really apprehend it might be so used as to embarrass them.

As to an election to be held in November, there is abundant time without any order or proclamation from me just now. The people of Louisiana shall not lack an opportunity for a fair election for both Fed eral and State officers by want of anything within my power to give them.

Your obedient servant,
A. LINCOLN.

President Lincoln, on July 8, 1864, issued this proclamation:

"WHEREAS, at the late session, Congress passed a bill 'to guarantee to certain States, whose governments have been usurped or overthrown, a republican form of government,' a copy of which is hereunto annexed;

"AND WHEREAS, the said bill was presented to the President of the United States for his approval, less than one hour before the *sine die* adjournment of said session, and was not signed by him;

"AND WHEREAS, the said bill contains, among other things, a plan for restoring the States in rebellion to their proper practical relation in the Union, which plan expresses the sense of Congress upon that subject, and which plan it is now thought fit to lay before the people for their consideration:

"Now, THEREFORE, I, Abraham Lincoln, President of the United States, do proclaim, declare, and make known, that, while I am (as I was in December last, when by proclamation I propounded a plan for restoration) unprepared, by a formal approval of this bill, to be inflexibly committed to any single plan of restoration; and, while I am also unprepared to declare that the free State constitutions and governments already adopted and installed in Arkansas and Louisiana shall be set aside and held for nought, thereby repelling and discouraging the loyal citizens who have set up the same as to further effort, or to declare a constitutional competency in Congress to abolish slavery in States, but am at the same time sincerely hoping and expecting that a constitutional amendment abolishing slavery throughout the nation may be adopted, nevertheless I am fully satisfied with the system for restoration contained in the bill as one very proper plan for the loyal people of any State choosing to adopt it, and that I am, and at all times shall be, prepared to give the Executive aid and assistance to any such people, so soon as the military resistance to the United States shall have been suppressed in any such State, and the people thereof shall have sufficiently returned to their obedience to the Constitution and laws of the United States, in which cases Military Governors will be appointed, with directions to proceed according to the bill."

The Arkansas government was erected under express instructions from the President to Major-General Steele, commanding United States forces. Here is President Lincoln's letter:

"EXECUTIVE MANSION, }
"WASHINGTON, January 20, 1864. }

"*Major-General Steele:* Sundry citizens of the State of Arkansas petition me that an election may be held in that State, at which to elect a Governor; that it be assumed at that election, and thenceforward, that the constitution and laws of the State, as before the rebellion, are in full force, except that the constitution is so modified as to declare that there shall be neither slavery nor involuntary servitude, except in the punishment of crimes, whereof the party shall have been duly convicted; that the General Assembly may make such provisions for the freed people as shall recognize and declare their permanent freedom, and provide for their education, and which may yet be construed as a temporary arrangement suitable to their present condition as a laboring, landless, and homeless class; that said election shall be held on the 28th March, 1864, at all the usual places of the State, for all such voters as may attend for that purpose; that the voters attending at each place at 8 o'clock in the morning of said day may choose judges and clerks of election for that purpose; that all persons qualified by said constitution and laws, and taking the oath presented in the President's proclamation of December 8, 1863, either before or at the election, and none others, may be voters; that each set of judges and clerks may make returns directly to you on or before the —— day of —— next; that in all other respects said election may be conducted according to said modified constitution and laws; that, on receipt of said returns, when 5,406 votes shall have been cast, you can receive said votes and ascertain all who shall thereby appear to have been elected; that, on the —— day of —— next, all persons so appearing to have been elected, who shall appear before you at Little Rock and take the oath, to be by you severally administered, to support the Constitution of the United States and the modified constitution of the State of Arkansas, shall be declared by you qualified and empowered to immediately enter upon the duties of the offices to which they shall have been respectively elected.

"You will please order an election to take place on the 28th of March, 1864, and returns to be made in fifteen days thereafter.

"A. LINCOLN."

Under President Lincoln's authority thus enunciated, a new State government was organized, with Isaac Murphy as Governor, who is reported to have received nearly 16,000 votes. Also, a Lieutenant Governor and other State officers, and members of both branches of the Legislature. This organization was preserved until the advent of Major General Ord, as commander of that District, when, the Democrats being discovered to have control of both branches of the Legislature, he ordered them not to reassemble, and removed all the officers elected by it. The Governor, who was a Radical, he permitted to continue in office, and he nominally administered it until the advent of the bogus rotten borough government.

"The Olustee expedition was undertaken mainly for the purpose of "opening up" a Congressional District in Florida; indeed, President Lincoln may be said to have been represented on the ground in the person of his Private Secretary, Mr. John Hay, who accompanied it.

"President Lincoln's efforts at restoration in Tennessee date from his appointment of Andrew Johnson as Military Governor of that State. Governor Johnson began the work of reorganization by calling a convention, which forever abolished slavery in the State, declared the ordinance of secession null and void, and repudiated the Confederate debt. Under the reorganization effected by Andrew Johnson, William G. Brownlow, March 4, 1865, was claimed to have been elected Governor by a popular vote. Congress never interfered with this reorganization or reconstruction of the State;* and Tennessee, Louisiana, Florida and Arkansas, were the only States in which Mr. Lincoln was able to accomplish anything in the way of "restoration."

Upon the accession of President Johnson, after the death of Mr. Lincoln, he proceeded, the war having been closed, to carry out the policy of his predecessor. He appointed Provisional Governors in each of the late separated States, except Virginia (in which the Pierpont government had, from an early period in the war, been recognized), Tennessee, Louisiana, and Arkansas, in which governments existed under the plan of Mr. Lincoln. Under these Provisional Governments, elections for conventions of the people of the several States, for the choice of State and local officers, and for the election of Representatives to Congress from all the States, were ordered. The main qualification for an elector for delegates to the convention was the exhibition of his duly-certified signature to the Amnesty Oath contained in the President's proclamation of May 29, 1865.

---

* On the contrary, Congress recognized and readmitted the State to representation under it.

Delegates to the conventions were accordingly elected in the several States. In North Carolina the convention met in October, 1865, declared the secession ordinance null and void, and passed ordinances prohibiting slavery forever in the State, repudiating the Confederate debt, and dividing the State into seven Congressional Districts. November 9, these ordinances were submitted to the people and approved; and on the same day State officers and members of Congress were elected. December 1, the Legislature ratified the anti-slavery amendment; and December 15, Jonathan Worth, elected in November, was qualified as Governor of the State. In Mississippi the convention met August 14, and passed the required ordinances respecting slavery in the State and the secession ordinance. On the first Monday in October, State officers and members of Congress were elected. The Legislature met October 16, and the next day Benjamin G. Humphreys was inaugurated Governor. November 27, the Legislature declined to ratify the anti-slavery amendment. The Georgia convention submitted the anti-slavery, anti-secession and Confederate debt repudiation ordinances to the people; November 15, State officers and members of Congress were elected; and December 5, the Legislature ratified the anti-slavery amendment. The Alabama convention passed the required ordinances. In November, State officers (R. M. Patton, Governor), and members of Congress were elected; December 2, the Legislature ratified the anti-slavery amendment, and December 5, Provisional Governor Parson received a telegram from Secretary Seward, conveying the congratulations of the President, that, by its vote ratifying the anti-slavery amendment, the State of Alabama "being the twenty-seventh, fills up the complement of two-thirds, and *gives the amendment finishing effect as a part of the organic law of the land.*" South Carolina, by order of Provisional Governor Perry, called a convention, which ordered a State election October 18, when James L. Orr was elected Governor. November 13, the Legislature ratified the anti-slavery amendment, and November 22, members of Congress were elected. Florida annulled the secession ordinance, abolished slavery, and repudiated the rebel debt. November 29, State officers and a Representative to Congress were elected; and December 28, the Legislature ratified the anti-slavery amendment. In Virginia the administration of Governor Francis H. Pierpoint, having been recognized by the President's order of May 9, 1865, the State government continued without interruption; and October 12, 1865, Representatives in Congress were elected.

From the date of Brownlow's election, March 4, 1865, as Governor of Tennessee, the government in that State has been unmolested by Congress. Texas annulled the secession ordinance, abolished slavery, and repudiated the rebel debt. The provisional government of Hamilton was followed by an elected State government, headed by Governor Throckmorton. In October, 1865, when Isaac Murphy was elected Governor of Arkansas, President Johnson telegraphed to him that there would be no interference with the "present organization of State government," and added, "I have learned * * * that all is working well, and you will proceed and resume the former relations with the Federal Government, and all aid in the power of the Government will be given in restoring the State to its former relations."

When the Senators and Representatives, elected under the auspices of these organizations, appeared, the doors of Congress were coldly shut upon them. This, too, in face of the fact that delegations from Tennessee* and Virginia, had, at times during the war, occupied seats and discharged all the functions appertaining to them. Congress then, after long incubation, tried its hand. Let us see what it brought forth.

"Reconstruction" Measures of Congress.

An Act to Provide for the More Efficient Government of the Insurrectionary States.

WHEREAS, No legal State governments or adequate protection for life or property now exist in the rebel States of Virginia, North Carolina, Georgia, Mississippi, Alabama, Louisiana, Florida, Texas and Arkansas; and whereas, it is necessary that peace and good order should be enforced in said States until loyal and republican State governments can be legally established: Therefore,

Be it enacted, etc., That said rebel States shall be divided into military districts and made subject to the military authority of the United States, as hereinafter prescribed, and for that purpose Virginia shall constitute the first district; North Carolina and South Carolina the second district; Georgia, Alabama and Florida, the third district; Mississippi and Arkansas the fourth district; and Louisiana and Texas the fifth district.

SEC. 2. That it shall be the duty of the President to assign to the command of each of said districts an officer of the army, not below the rank of Brigadier General, and to detail a sufficient military force to enable such officer to perform his duties and enforce his authority within the district to which he is assigned.

SEC. 3. That it shall be the duty of each officer, assigned as aforesaid, to protect all persons in their rights of person and property; to suppress insurrection, disorder and violence, and to punish, or cause to be punished, all disturbers of the public peace and criminals, and to this end he may allow local civil tribunals to take jurisdiction of and to try offenders; or when, in his judgment, it may be necessary for the trial of offenders, he shall have power to organize military commissions or tribunals for that purpose; and all interference under color of State authority with the exercise of military authority, under this act, shall be null and void.

SEC. 4. That all persons put under military arrest by virtue of this act shall be tried without unnecessary delay, and no cruel or unusual punishment shall be inflicted; and no sentence of any military commission or tribunal hereby authorized, affecting the life or liberty of any person, shall be executed until it is approved by the officer in command of the district, and the laws and regulations for the government of the army shall not be affected by this act, except in so far as they conflict with its provisions: *Provided*, That no sentence of death under the provisions of this act shall be carried into effect without the approval of the President.

SEC. 5. That when the people of any one of said rebel States shall have formed a constitution of government in conformity with the Constitution of the United States in all respects, framed by a convention of delegates elected by the male citizens of said State twenty-one years old and upward, of whatever race, color, or previous condition, who have been resident in said State for one year previous to the day of such election, except such as may be disfranchised for participation in the rebellion, or for felony at common law, and when such constitution shall provide that the elective franchise shall be enjoyed by all such persons as have the qualifications herein stated for electors of delegates, and when such constitution shall be ratified by a majority of the persons voting on the question of ratification who are qualified as electors for delegates, and when such constitution shall have been submitted to Congress for examination and approval, and Congress shall have approved the same, and when said State, by a vote of its Legislature elected under said Constitution, shall have adopted the amendment to the Constitution of the United States, proposed by the Thirty-ninth

---

*The delegation from Tennessee was afterward admitted upon the ratification, by the Legislature, of the anti-slavery amendment.

Congress, and known as Article XIV, and when said article shall have become a part of the Constitution of the United States. said State shall be declared entitled to representation in Congress, and Senators and Representatives shall be admitted therefrom on their taking the oaths prescribed by law, and then and thereafter the preceding sections of this act shall be inoperative in said State: *Provided*, That no person excluded from the privilege of holding office by said proposed amendment to the Constitution of the United States shall be eligible to election as a member of the convention to frame a constitution for any of said rebel States, nor shall any such person vote for members of such convention.

Sec. 6. That until the people of said rebel States shall be by law admitted to representation in the Congress of the United States, any civil governments which may exist therein shall be deemed provisional only, and in all respects subject to the paramount authority of the United States at any time to abolish, modify, control, or supercede the same; and in all elections, to any office under such provisional governments, all persons shall be entitled to vote, and none others, who are entitled to vote under the provisions of the fifth section of this act; and no person shall be eligible to any office under any such provisional governments who would be disqualified from holding office under the provisions of the third article of said constitutional amendment.

Passed March 2, 1867.

The bill passed the House on February 20, 1867, by the following vote: Yeas 128 (all Republicans), nays 46 (all Democrats, except Hawkins, of Tenn.; James R. Hubbell, of Ohio; and Kuykendall, of Illinois). The Senate passed the bill on the same day: Yeas 35 (all Republicans except Johnson, of Maryland), nays 7 (all Democrats). The bill was vetoed March 2. Both Houses of Congress repassed it on the same day, the House by a vote of 138 (all Republicans), nays 51 (all Democrats, except Hale, of N. Y.; Hawkins, of Tenn.; Kuykendall, of Ill.; Stillwell, of Ind., and Latham, of W. Va.); the Senate by a vote of—yeas 38 (all Republicans except Johnson, of Maryland), nays 10 (all Democrats).

The Constitutional Amendment.

The following is the proposed article of the Constitution which must be adopted by the Legislature before the State can be represented in Congress:

Resolved by the Senate and House of Representatives of the United States of America, in Congress assembled, two-thirds of both Houses concurring, That the following articles be proposed to the Legislatures of the several States as an amendment to the Constitution of the United States, which, when ratified by three fourths of said Legislatures, shall be valid as a part of the Constitution, namely:

Article —, Section 1. All persons born or naturalized in the United States, and subject to the jurisdiction thereof, are citizens of the United States and of the State wherein they reside. No State shall make or enforce any laws which shall abridge the privileges or immunities of citizens of the United States, nor shall any State deprive any person of life, liberty or property without due process of law, nor deny to any person within its jurisdiction the equal protection of the laws.

Sec. 2. Representatives shall be apportioned among the several States according to their respective numbers, counting the whole number of persons in each State, excluding Indians not taxed. But whenever the right to vote at any election for electors of President and Vice-President, or for United States Representatives in Congress, executive or judicial officers of a State, or members of the Legislature thereof, is denied to any of the male inhabitants of such States, being twenty-one years of age and citizens of the United States, or in any way abridged, except for participation in rebellion or other crime, the basis of representation therein shall be reduced in the proportion which the number of such male citizens shall bear to the whole number of male citizens twenty-one years of age in such State.

Sec. 3. No person shall be a Senator or Representative in Congress, or elector of President or Vice-President, or hold any office, civil or military, under the United States, or under any State, who, having previously taken an oath as a member of Congress, or as an officer of the United States, or as a member of any State Legislature, or as an executive or judicial officer of any State, to support the Constitution of the United States, shall have engaged in insurrection or rebellion against the same, or given aid or comfort to the enemies thereof; but Congress may, by a vote of two-thirds of each House, remove such disability.

Sec. 4. The validity of the public debt of the United States, authorized by law, including debt incurred for the payment of pensions and bounties for services in suppressing insurrection or rebellion, shall not be questioned; but neither the United States nor any State shall assume or pay any debt or obligation incurred in aid of insurrection or rebellion against the United States, or claim for the loss or emancipation of any slave; but all such debts, obligation and claim shall be held illegal and void.

SEC. 5. The Congress shall have power to enforce, by appropriate legislation, the provisions of this article.

Passed June 13, 1866.

Supplemental "Reconstruction" Act of Fortieth Congress.

An Act supplementary to an act entitled "An act to provide for the more efficient government of the rebel States," passed March second, eighteen hundred and sixty-seven, and to facilitate restoration.

Be it enacted, etc., That before the first day of September, eighteen hundred and sixty-seven, the commanding General in each district defined by an act entitled "An act to provide for the more efficient government of the rebel States," passed March second, eighteen hundred and sixty-seven, shall cause a registration to be made of the male citizens of the United States, twenty-one years of age and upward, resident in each county or parish in the State or States included in his district, which registration shall include only those persons who are qualified to vote for delegates by the act aforesaid, and who shall have taken and subscribed the following oath or affirmation: "I, ——, do solemnly swear (or affirm), in the presence of Almighty God, that I am a citizen of the State of ——; that I have resided in said State for —— months next preceding this day, and now reside in the county of ——, or the parish of ——, in said State (as the case may be); that I am twenty-one years old; that I have not been disfranchised for participation in any rebellion or civil war against the United States, nor for felony committed against the laws of any State or of the United States; that I have never been a member of any State legislature, nor held any executive or judicial office in any State and afterward engaged in insurrection or rebellion against the United States, or given aid or comfort to the enemies thereof; that I have never taken an oath as a member of Congress of the United States, or as an officer of the United States, or as a member of any State legislature, or as an executive or judicial officer of any State, to support the Constitution of the United States, and afterward engaged in insurrection or rebellion against the United States, or given aid or comfort to the enemies thereof; that I will faithfully support the Constitution and obey the laws of the United States, and will, to the best of my ability, encourage others so to do, so help me God;" which oath or affirmation may be administered by any registering officer.

SEC. 2. That after the completion of the registration hereby provided for in any State, at such time and places therein as the commanding General shall appoint and direct, of which at least thirty days' public notice shall be given, an election shall be held of delegates to a convention for the purpose of establishing a constitution and civil government for such State loyal to the Union, said convention in each State, except Virginia, to consist of the same number of members as the most numerous branch of the State legislature of each State in the year eighteen hundred and sixty, to be apportioned among the several districts, counties or parishes of such State by the commanding General, giving to each representation in the ratio of voters registered as aforesaid, as nearly as may be. The convention in Virginia shall consist of the same number of members as represented the territory now constituting Virginia in the most numerous branch of the legislature of said State in the year eighteen hundred and sixty, to be apportioned as aforesaid.

SEC. 3. That at said election the registered voters of each State shall vote for or against a convention therefor under this act. Those voting in favor of such a convention shall have written or printed on the ballots by which they vote for delegates, as aforesaid, the words "For a convention," and those voting against such a convention shall have written or printed on such ballots the words "Against a convention." The person appointed to superintend said election, and to make return of the votes given thereat, as herein provided, shall count and make return of the votes given for and against a convention; and the commanding General to whom the same shall have been returned shall ascertain and declare the total vote in each State for and against a convention. If a majority of the votes given on that question shall be for a convention, then such convention shall be held as hereinafter provided; but if a majority of said votes shall be against a convention, then no such convention shall be held under this act: *Provided*, That such convention shall not be held unless a majority of all such registered voters shall have voted on the question of holding such convention.

SEC. 4. That the commanding General of each district shall appoint as many boards of registration as may be necessary, consisting of three loyal officers or persons, to make and complete the registration, superintend the election, and make return to him of the votes, list of voters, and of the persons elected as delegates by a plurality of the votes cast at said election; and upon receiving said returns he shall open the same, ascertain the persons elected as delegates according to the returns of the officers who conducted said election, and make proclamation thereof; and if a majority of the votes given on that question be for a convention, the commanding General, within sixty days from the date of election, shall notify the delegates to assemble in convention, at a time and place to be mentioned in the notification, and said convention, when organized, shall proceed to frame a constitution and civil government according to the provisions of this act and the act to which it is supplementary; and when the same shall have been so framed, said constitution shall be submitted by the convention for ratification to the persons registered under the provisions of this act, at an election to be conducted by the officers or persons appointed or to be appointed by the commanding General, as hereinbefore provided, and to be held after the expiration of thirty days from the date of notice thereof to be given by said convention; and the returns thereof shall be made to the commanding General of the district.

SEC. 5. That if, according to said returns, the constitution shall be ratified by a majority of the votes of the registered electors qualified as herein specified, cast at said election (at least one half of all the registered voters voting upon the question of such ratification), the President of the convention shall transmit a copy of the same, duly certified, to the President of the United States, who shall forthwith transmit the same to Congress, if then in session, and if not in session, then immediately upon its next assembling; and if it shall, moreover, appear to Congress that the election was one at which all the registered and qualified electors in the State had an opportunity to vote freely and without restraint, fear, or the influence of fraud, and if the Congress shall be satisfied that such constitution meets the approval of a majority of all the qualified electors in the State, and if the said constitution shall be declared by Congress to be in conformity with the provisions of the act to which this is supplementary, and the other provisions of said act shall have been complied with, and the said constitution shall be approved by Congress, the State shall be declared entitled to representation, and Senators and Representatives shall be admitted therefrom as therein provided.

SEC. 6. That all elections in the States mentioned in the said "Act to provide for the more efficient government of the rebel States," shall, during the operation of said act, be by ballot; and all officers making the said registration of voters and conducting said elections shall, before entering upon the discharge of their duties, take and subscribe the oath prescribed by the act approved July second, eighteen hundred and sixty-two, entitled "An act to prescribe an oath of office:" *Provided*, That if any person shall knowingly and falsely take and subscribe any oath in this act prescribed, such person so offending and being thereof duly convicted, shall be subject to the pains, penalties, and disabilities which by law are provided for the punishment of the crime of willful and corrupt perjury.

* * * * *

SEC. 8. That the convention for each State shall prescribe the fees, salary, and compensation to be paid to all delegates and other officers and agents herein authorized or necessary to carry into effect the purposes of this act not herein otherwise provided for, and shall provide for the levy and collection of such taxes on the property in such State as may be necessary to pay the same.

* * * * *

Passed March 28, 1867.

Passed both Houses of Congress on March 19. It was vetoed on March 23. On the same day the House repassed it by a vote of yeas 114 (all Republicans), nays 25 (all Democrats), and the Senate by a vote of yeas 40 (all Republicans except Johnson, of Md.), and nays 7 (all Democrats).

THE IRON-CLAD OATH.

This is the oath referred to in section 6 of preceding act:

Be it enacted, etc., That hereafter every person elected or appointed to any office of honor or profit under the Government of the United States, either in the civil, military, or naval departments of the public service, excepting the President of the United States, shall, before entering upon the duties of such office, and before being entitled to any of the salary or other emoluments thereof, take and subscribe the following oath or affirmation: "I, A. B., do solemnly swear (or affirm) that I have never voluntarily borne arms against the United States since I have been a citizen thereof; that I have voluntarily given no aid, countenance, counsel, or encouragement to persons engaged in armed hostility thereto; that I have never sought, nor accepted, nor attempted to exercise the functions of any office whatever, under any authority or pretended authority, in hostility to the United States; that I have not yielded a voluntary support to any pretended government, authority, power, or constitution within the United States, hostile or inimical thereto; and I do further swear (or affirm) that, to the best of my knowledge and ability, I will support and defend the Constitution of the United States against all enemies foreign and domestic; that I will bear true faith and allegiance to the same; that I take this obligation freely, without any mental reservation or purpose of evasion, and that I will well and faithfully discharge the duties of the office on which I am about to enter: so help me God;" which said oath, so taken and signed, shall be preserved among the files of the Court-house of Congress, or Department to which the said office may appertain. And any person who shall falsely take the said oath shall be guilty of perjury, and on conviction, in addition to the penalties now prescribed for that offense, shall be deprived of his office, and rendered incapable forever after of holding any office or place under the United States.

An Act supplementary to an act entitled "An act to provide for the more efficient government of the rebel States;" passed on the second day of March, eighteen hundred and sixty-seven, and the act supplementary thereto, passed on the twenty-third day of March, eighteen hundred and sixty-seven.

Be it enacted by the Senate and House of Representatives of the United States of America in Congress assembled, That it is hereby declared to have been the true intent and meaning of the act of the 2d day of March, 1867, entitled "An act to provide for the more efficient government of the rebel States," and the act supplementary thereto, passed the 23d day of March, 1867, that the governments then existing in the rebel States of Virginia, North Carolina, South Carolina, Georgia, Mississippi, Alabama, Louisiana, Florida, Texas, and Arkansas, were not legal State governments, and that thereafter said governments, if continued, were to be continued subject in all respects to the military commanders of the respective districts, and to the paramount authority of Congress.

SEC. 2. That the commander of any district named in said act shall have power subject to the disapproval of the General of the Army of the United States, and to have effect until disapproved, whenever, in the opinion of such commander, the proper administration of said act shall require it, to suspend or remove from office, or from the performance of official duties, and the exercise of official powers, any officer or person holding or exercising, or professing to hold or exercise, any civil or military office or duty in such district, under any power, election, appointment, or authority derived from, or granted by, or claimed under, any so-called State, or the government thereof, or any municipal or other division thereof, and upon such suspension or removal by such commander, subject to the approval of the General as aforesaid, shall have power to provide from time to time for the performance of the said duties of such officer or person so suspended or removed, by the detail of some competent officer or soldier of the army, or by the appointment of some other person to perform the same, and to fill vacancies occasioned by death, resignation, or otherwise.

SEC. 3. That the General of the Army of the United States shall be invested with all the powers of suspension, removal, appointment, and detaching granted in the preceding section to district commanders.

SEC. 4. That the acts of the officers of the army, already done in removing, in said districts, persons exercising the functions of civil officers, and appointing others in their stead, are hereby confirmed; provided that any persons heretofore or hereafter appointed by any district commander to exercise the functions of any civil office, may be removed either by the military officer in command of the district or by the General of the army, and it shall be the duty of such commander to remove from office, as aforesaid, all persons who are disloyal to the Government of the United States, or who use their official influence in any manner to hinder, delay, prevent or obstruct the due and proper administration of this act and the acts to which it is supplementary.

SEC. 5. That the boards of registration provided for in the act entitled "An act supplementary to an act entitled 'An act to provide for the more efficient government of the rebel States,' passed March 2, 1867, and to facilitate restoration," passed March 23, 1867, shall have power, and it shall be their duty, before allowing the registration of any person, to ascertain, upon such facts or information as they can obtain, whether such person is entitled to be registered under said act, and the oath required by said act shall not be conclusive on such question, and no person shall be registered unless such board shall decide that he is entitled thereto; and such board shall also have power to examine, under oath (to be administered by any member of such board), any one touching the qualification of any person claiming registration; but in every case of refusal by the board to register an applicant, and in every case of striking his name from the list as hereinafter provided, the board shall make a note or memorandum, which shall be returned with the registration list to the commanding General of the district, setting forth the grounds of such refusal or such striking from the list: *Provided,* That no person shall be disqualified as member of any board of registration by reason of race or color.

SEC. 6. *And be it further enacted*, That the true intent and meaning of the oath prescribed in said supplementary act is (among other things), that no person who has been a member of the Legislature of any State, or who has held any executive or judicial office in any State, whether he has taken an oath to support the Constitution of the United States or not, and whether he was holding such office at the commencement of the rebellion, or had held it before, and who has afterward engaged in insurrection or rebellion against the United States, or given aid or comfort to the enemies thereof, is entitled to be registered or to vote; and the words "executive or judicial office in any State" in said oath mentioned, shall be construed to include all civil offices created by law for the administration of any general law of a State, or for the administration of justice.

SEC. 7. *And be it further enacted*, That the time for completing the original registration provided for in said act may, in the discretion of the commander of any district, be extended to the first day of October, eighteen hundred and sixty-seven; and the boards of registration shall have power, and it shall be their duty, commencing fourteen days prior to any election under said act, and upon reasonable public notice of the time and place thereof, to revise, for a period of five days, the registration lists, and upon being satisfied that any person not entitled thereto has been registered, to strike the name of such person from the list, and such person shall not be allowed to vote. And such board shall also, during the same period, add to such registry the names of all persons who, at that time, possess the qualifications required by said act, who have not been already registered; and no person shall, at any time, be entitled to be registered or to vote by reason of any executive pardon or amnesty for any act or thing which, without such pardon or amnesty, would disqualify him for registration or voting.

* * * * *

SEC. 9. *And be it further enacted*, That all members of said boards of registration and all persons hereafter elected or appointed to office in said military districts, under any so-called State or municipal authority, or by detail or appointment of the district commanders, shall be required to take and to subscribe the oath of office prescribed by law for officers of the United States.

* * * * *

Passed both Houses of Congress, on July 13, 1867. It was vetoed by the President on July 19, but on the same day repassed by both Houses over the veto. The vote in the Senate stood—yeas 30 (all Republicans), nays 6 (all Democrats); in the House—yeas 100 (all Republicans), nays 22 (all Democrats).

Open Revolution Attempted by the Radical Majority in the House of Representatives.

The most palpable and direct effort to subvert the Judicial and Executive branches of the Government, and consolidate all their powers by Congress, was embraced in a bill which passed the House of Representatives in the latter part of January; but which has not been deemed necessary as yet by the Senate, where it remains unacted upon to this time. In the final decision every entire Republican voted in favor, while every entire Democrat, and Cary of Cincinnati, unclassified, voted against. Here is the bill as adopted:

SECTION 1. *Be it enacted, etc.*, That in Virginia, North Carolina, South Carolina, Georgia, Alabama, Mississippi, Louisiana, Texas, Florida and Arkansas, there are no civil State Governments, republican in form, and that the so-called civil governments in said States, respectively shall not be recognized as valid or legal State Governments, either by the executive or the judicial power or authority of the United States.

SEC. 2. *And be it further enacted*, That for the speedy enforcement of the act entitled "An Act to provide for the more efficient government of the Rebel States," passed March 2, 1867, and the several acts supplementary thereto, the General of the Army of the United States is hereby authorized and required to enjoin, by special orders, upon all officers in command, within the several military departments within said several States, the performance of all acts authorized by said several laws above recited; is authorized to remove, at his discretion, by his order, from command, any or all of said commanders, and detail other officers of the United States Army, not below the rank of Colonel, to perform all the duties and exercise all the powers authorized by said several acts, to the end that the people of the said several States may speedily reorganize civil governments, republican in form, in said several States, and be restored to political power in the Union.

SEC. 3. *And be it further enacted*, That the General of the Army may remove any or all civil officers now acting under the several Provisional governments within the said several disorganized States, and appoint others to discharge the duties pertaining to their respective offices, and may do any and all acts which, by said several laws above mentioned, are authorized to be done by the several commanders of the Military Departments within said States; and so much of said acts, or of any act, as authorizes the President to detail the Military Commanders to said Military Departments, or to remove any officers who may be detailed as herein provided, is hereby repealed.

SEC. 4. *And be it further enacted,* That it shall be unlawful for the President of the United States to order any part of the army or navy of the United States to assist by force of arms the authority of either of said Provisional governments in said disorganized States, to oppose or obstruct the authority of the United States, as provided in this act, and the acts to which this is supplementary.

SEC. 5. *And be it further enacted,* That any interference by any person, with intent to prevent by force the execution of the orders of the General of the Army, made in pursuance of this act and of the acts aforesaid, or any refusal or willful neglect of any person to issue any order or do any act required by this act, or other of the acts to which this act is additional and supplementary, with intent to defeat or delay the due execution of this act or of either of the acts to which this is supplementary, shall be held to be a high misdemeanor, and the party guilty thereof shall, upon conviction, be fined not exceeding five thousand dollars and imprisoned not exceeding two years.

SEC. 6. *And be it further enacted,* That as much of all acts, and parts of acts, as conflicts, or is inconsistent with the provisions of this act, is hereby repealed.

The revolutionary character of the measure is well shown by the following protest as presented in the House of Representatives:

"The undersigned, a minority of the Committee on Reconstruction, so-called, submit among others the following as some of their reasons in opposition to the bill:

"First.—That a Congress, *ex parte,* is asked in the first section to abrogate and destroy all civil government in ten States; four, viz: Virginia, North Carolina, South Carolina and Georgia, being of the original thirteen that started the Government and created the Constitution; while four others of that thirteen, making eight in all, have just been demonstrating through their popular elections that they recognize their civil governments, and guarantee as far as popular voice can, their preservation, not destruction, as legal governments. Self-government and representation are cardinal principles of a Republic, and solemnly ordained in our Federal Constitution; but this section ignores both, and robs ten States of the Union and their twelve million inhabitants of all protection from the judiciary or executive branches of the Government, while dooming them to a military despotism.

"Second—That a Congress thus representing but a part of the people, and that part now in a minority, even if a full Congress, in the parliamentary sense of that word, would be but one of three great branches of the Government with no right, no power to invalidate or deny the recognition of judicial or executive power as asserted in the bill. The executive or judiciary has as much right to proclaim or adjudicate that Congress shall not be recognized, as Congress has thus to enact for the executive and judiciary. Both are as much the Government and the creation of the Constitution as the House of Representatives or the Senate, and the executive, elected by the whole people, better represents the principle of popular government than a Senate, the mere arbitrary creation of the State.

"Third—That the invalidation or nullification of executive and judicial power in ten States is not only a violation of the Federal Constitution, but, without direct repeal of the great military acts of 1792, 1795 and March 3, 1867, putting the army and navy and militia of the United States, in certain cases, at the disposal of the President; also in conflict with the fundamental judiciary act of 1789; also in conflict with article 4, section 5, of the Constitution, which, while guaranteeing to every State a republican form of government, also guarantees, on application of the civil authorities of States, protection against domestic violence or invasion, such as is contemplated in the bill.

"Fourth—That the second and third sections are in utter violation of the Constitution, Article II, section 2, which declares the President to be Commander-in-chief of the Army of the United States, inasmuch as the General of the Army is there authorized to be Commander-in-chief, and to remove by his order alone any and all officers of the United States Army independent of the Constitution and the people elected Commander-in-chief. This investure of a General of the Army with the supreme dictatorship is, as if in solemn mockery, set forth to be to recognize civil governments republican in form.

"Fifth—That the whole act is revolutionary and incendiary in arraying Congress—but one branch of the Government—against the co-ordinate branches, in all respects the Constitutional equals of Congress, and in some respects the Constitutional superior of that Congress, and thereby calculated, if not intended, to involve the whole country in commotion and civil strife, the end of which no human eye can foresee.

JAMES BROOKS, of New York.
JAMES B. BECK, of Kentucky.

It will be appropriate here to introduce the results of military reconstruction, by a short sketch of the proceedings under it, initiated after the passage of the first Reconstruction Bill. The President made assignments of commanders as follows: To the First District, Virginia, Major-General J. M. Schofield; Second District, North and South Carolina, Major-General Daniel E. Sickles; Third District, Georgia, Alabama, and Florida, Major-General John Pope; Fourth District, Mississippi and Arkansas, Major-General E. O. C. Ord; Fifth District, Louisiana and Texas, Major-General P. H. Sheridan.

From the moment of their assumption of their several commands, these Generals began a system of regulating and controlling all elections in accordance with their view of the desire of the Radical majority in Congress. Elections under the existing State organizations were forbidden everywhere within the military authority, unless by order or sufferance of the commanding Generals. Civil officers were removed, against whom there was no charge but that of an opposition to the Congressional policy, and Radical favorites were installed in their places. Large municipalities, like that of New Orleans, whose city treasuries cover the receipts of millions of money, were placed at the mercy of vagrant white Radicals and ignorant, thriftless negroes. White policemen were removed and negroes put in their places, as if with the incendiary purpose of bringing on a war of races. Particularly was General Sheridan conspicuous in such exercises of power. The police in Mobile were forbidden to wear grey. General Pope placed one negro on each board of registration without reference to qualification. General Schofield appointed military commissioners from the officers of the Army and Freedmen's Bureau, to command, with sufficient military force, all local police or other forces. These commissioners were "clothed with all the power of magistrates," and when they tried a man, the commanding General was to give a decision on report of the case; but till such decision was announced, "the orders of the military commission will be paramount." While each commander was thus placing his own construction upon the acts of Congress, in June the President issued an order that the military commanders should guide themselves, in their interpretation of the Reconstruction acts, by the opinion of the Attorney-General—whereupon General Sickles resigned the command of the Second District. June 4, General Sheridan removed Governor Wells, of Louisiana. Subsequently, the Attorney-General furnished a second opinion, that the district commanders had no right to remove civil officers. Nevertheless, July 30, General Sheridan issued a special order removing Governor Throckmorton, of Texas, and appointing Mr. E. P. Pease in his place.

Generals Pope and Sheridan had inquired whether the opinion of the Attorney-General as to registration, etc., was to be considered binding upon them, and General Grant had replied that it had not been put in the form of an order, and he presumed it was not so intended by the President; the commanders were directed to put their own construction upon the military bills, till ordered to do otherwise. In expressing his dissent from General Ord's views respecting registration in the Fourth District, General Grant says: "The law, however, makes the district commanders *their own interpreters* of their power or duty under it; and, in my opinion, the Attorney-General or myself can no more than give our opinion of the meaning of the law; neither can enforce his views against the judgment of those made responsible for the faithful execution of the law—the district commanders."

President Johnson, August 17, prepared an order removing General Sheridan from the Fifth District. General Grant urged the retention of Sheridan in his command. The President replied at length, stating that Sheridan's rule had been of "absolute tyranny," that his course had even "seriously interfered with a harmonious, satisfactory and speedy execution of the acts of Congress," and that alone was "sufficient to justify a change." General Grant, August 26, issued the President's order removing General Sheridan, and General Hancock was assigned to the command. At the same time the order was issued removing General Sickles from command of the Second District, and assigning General Canby in his place. The President, September 3, issued a proclamation declaring that military officers are sworn to obey the orders of the President, and enjoining all military and civil officers "to render due submission to the laws and decrees of the Courts of the United States," and to "sustain the authority of the law," and "to maintain the supremacy of the Federal Constitution." General Sickles, considering this proclamation a censure of his course as commander of the Second District, addressed to General Grant a vindication of his conduct. He had ordered one of his officers to disregard a certain process issued by the United States District Court; General Grant ordered Sickles to obey the process; but subsequently, upon receipt of Sickles' statement of the case in question, General Grant rescinded his order. Afterward General

Sickles complied with the process of the Court.

Meanwhile, in all the districts, registration was conducted under military supervision—every opportunity being afforded to the negroes, and every restriction being thrown in the way of the great body of whites, by the boards of registration. Subsequent elections in several of the districts were still more under military control, in many instances negroes coming in armed battalions to the polls; and formal charges have been made that in several cases arms and equipments for these negro political organizations were issued from the military commands and from agencies of the Freedmen's Bureau. These elections were to decide for or against calling conventions to frame new State constitutions, and to provide for the appointment of provisional civil officers. Whether or not the conventions were under military control, is sufficiently indicated in the case of the convention convened at Montgomery, Alabama, November 5. Agents and employés of the Freedmen's Bureau are declared to have been "members" of the convention.

Who Builds States Now.

THE CONSTITUTION-MAKERS.

The Conventions in all of the States were made up of a compound of cornfield darkies, city negroes of the hotel-waiting and tonsorial class; officers of the Freedmen's Bureau; ex-officers of United States Army, who, at the ebbing of the war, had been left as worthless drift upon the shores of the South; ex-rebel Officers, and soldiers, who had either been cashiered or had deserted, and had professed adherence to both sides; citizens from Northern States, who were from everywhere but the place at which they were engaged in the indecent manufacture of offices which were to contain themselves; ex-criminals, educated proprieties for the penitentiary, and every species of vagrant scurf and scum that could be well picked by the *chiffoniers* of Radicalism from the dregs and offal of society. A very small minority in each of the conventions was composed of gentlemen, who happened to have been elected from their counties, and who were there, fruitless conservators of the public weal, overpowered by the outlawry, ignorance and venality, which controlled the bodies, and powerless to do anything for their States. In the Virginia convention the prominent white Radical leader was an ex-Baptist preacher, named Hunnicut, who formerly edited an obscure religious paper, called the *Banner*, published at Fredericksburg, Virginia. In its issue of the 3d of March, 1854, he said:

"We are decidedly opposed to any and all African churches south of Mason and Dixon's line. In the present state of things, and at this particular crisis, we think it exceedingly impolitic in the Southern people to allow such organizations to exist in our midst. The time for such unhallowed assemblages is not yet; nor is Virginia the place of rendezvous for such dangerously mischievous, ungodly masses of crude mind and matter to congregate to concoct and execute their nefarious schemes of religious villanies.

"*They are ignorant and superstitious to a proverb. Depravity, ignorance, and superstition form a dangerous compound, and such a compound is the black population of Virginia.*"

Yet this base counterfeit upon the religious currency of the country, became the leader of the Radical party of Virginia, and the High Priest at whose altar the negro voters worshiped.

The grand jury of Charles City County had indicted the reverend rascal for the use of language inciting to murder, arson, and a conflict of races. The language charged in the indictments is as follows:

"You, the colored people, have no property. The white race have houses and lands. Some of you are old and feeble, and can not carry the musket, but can apply the torch to the dwellings of your enemies. There are none too young—the boy of ten and the girl of twelve can also apply the torch."

The New York *Express*, in furnishing a sketch of the Virginia Convention, said:

After Hunnicut and Underwood (white), comes one James Morrissey, a deserter from the British army, who keeps a low groggery supported by negro custom. Joseph Cox, the fourth delegate from the capital, is a black man of good sense and some little education. The next is Lewis Lindsay, formerly a slave of John Minor Botts—who was a defeated candidate for the Richmond Convention. A correspondent of the *World* thus describes Lindsay and others:

"Lindsay is coarse, uneducated and vulgar, but a popular negro orator. He was a paper-carrier of the Richmond *Dispatch*. While thus serving, his employers detected him in the larceny of 1,800 newspapers, which he disposed of to soldiers encamped near Richmond. For this he received a sound thrashing at the public whipping-post. As an orator he made his *debut* April 3, 1867, when, before a large body of negroes, he said: 'Lindsay is as good as any man. Don't tell me I ain't on an equality with any body God made. I want the privilege of going to see any white man, of eating with him, of sleeping with him—and, if I choose to, why should n't I marry his daughter.'"

Since his election, in a speech at Hunnicut Hall, he said:

"Before any of his children should suffer for food, the streets of Richmond should run knee-deep in blood. He thanked God that the negroes had learned to use guns, pistols, swords and ramrods."

This language caused his arrest, and he is now under bond to appear for trial before a military commissioner.

"Dr. Bayne is a perfect specimen of the African; before the war, the servant of a dentist, now following that profession for himself. He is illiterate, but original. Willis Hodges, bacon-colored son of Ham, is from Princess Anne. He is a field-hand, but appears in the convention clad in his Sunday clothes. wears enormous brass-rimmed spectacles, and boasts a suit of glossy, well-greased hair."

All these are but specimen bricks of the Radical Convention of the Old Dominion. Shade of Washington, Jefferson, Madison, Monroe, Marshall and Henry—where are you?

The Lynchburg Virginia *News*, gives the following history of the doings of a dark-complected loyalist and patriot in that vicinity. The niggers begin to show the effects of mixing with Puritan Yankees. The old copy-books used to say that "evil communications corrupt good manners," and here we have a case in point. A likely nigger transformed into a Republican delegate and horse-thief. We quote from the *News*:

"Yankee Allen, a negro elected to the Convention from the county of Prince Edward, has proven himself decidedly a man of business. On the day of election, he stole a horse, rode it to the election, was pursued, captured, and imprisoned for the theft, and is now in jail awaiting his trial for the offense. He has thus stolen the horse, run him off, been pursued, overtaken, captured, incarcerated, and elected a delegate to the Convention to form a constitution for the State, all in the course of one day. Who will say hereafter that the negro delegates have no capacity for business? And yet he is but a 'specimen brick' from the Radical tower of infamy."

What is here shown as to Virginia, is a fair index of the character of a large portion of the ruling party of all of the Southern States. We could fill this book with specimens of these Constitution-makers; but it is unnecessary. We will conclude the samples with a speech of the negro Cromwell, a delegate in the Louisiana Convention, delivered in that body, January 7, 1868. We quote from the New Orleans *Times* of the 8th.

The subject of discussion was a resolution pending, protesting against "the slander that it was the idea of the colored people to 'Africanize the South.'" The speech is given *verbatim*:

MR. PRESIDENT: I hab listend to de readin' ob' de resolutions for de second time. Dey is genuine doctrine. I wants dis, Merican people to know dat to-day my race stands out in bold and graphic relief as de stanchion dat upholds de Government of dis country. I tinks we ar able to take keer ob ourselve. Ebery wind I hear rushin in de leaves proclaims that the blak man who fought for de national honor am de equal of de white. We is able to vindicate our cause. I'se not skeered [Sensation outside the bar and excitement among the police.] This Government has carved out our future. My people has agin and agin been on de battle-field and shed dere blood for it. Dey claim dere rights upon the floor and in dis country, and let me say dat we will rule de rebels—dat loyal blacks must rule dis Government. [Profound sensation in the lobbies] De rebels who hab ruled us shan't rule no longer. *Talk of a war of races—we are ready for it.* We will rule until the last one of us goes down forever. We don't intend to get down on our knees and beg for our rights. Gentlemens, I ask you that you will not deprive us of our rights. This Government is pledged to maintain the rights of negroes. Gentlemens, much is said about anodder rebbelution. I say if we can not gain our rights and be placed on an equality wid de whites, let it come. Let de rebbelution come. Equal rights I demand, and notin else will I have. I will die fust. I acts as a man, I feels as a man, and I asks no more than odder men if dey possess de fine sentiments of manhood as I does. We car nothing for Andy Johnson or any other man in dis Government. We are goin to have our rights if it is to be obtained by rebolution and blood (swaying to and fro of negroes outside the bar). We claim from dis convention equal liberty and equal privileges of de white man. I stand here, sir, to advocate de cause of my race—dat all de rights and privileges be enjoyed that pertains to Andy Johnson or any odder man. We wants all liberties, civil and religious, and dem we shall have. I wants dem for de white man and de black man. Har in dis convention dar are rebels. (Here he pointed to a representative of a New York paper, who wore grey pantaloons and the badge of Thomas' old Army of the Cumberland). Dar are secret blows agin us. *Let us go into secret meetings and prepar for dem.* Let dem hole dere secret meetings at the St. Charles Hotel and udder holes. Let dem telegraph from de St. Charles dat I,

Cromwell, will demand his rights. (Hisses,) Gentlemens, pardon me for dis harangue. Gentlemens, I know my rights—I demand dem. I demand dem for my race, and shall endeavor to have dem embodied in de Constitution. I demand a guaranty. Do you know what dat is? When de proper time comes, you will know what I mean by de guaranty.

The Constitutions they made.

The bogus constitutions of the Southern States, seven of which have already been ratified by Congress, disfranchise from citizenship in those States, not only many thousands of the citizens thereof, but debar hundreds of thousands of Northern voters from citizenship in the same. Here are proofs:

ALABAMA—"All persons before registering must take and subscribe the following oath: 'I, ———, do solemnly swear (or affirm) * * * * * that I accept the civil and political equality of all men, and agree not to attempt to deprive any person or persons, on account of race, color, or previous condition, of any political or civil right, privilege, or immunity enjoyed by any other class of men,'" etc. *Bogus Constitution, Art.* VII, *sec.* 4.

ARKANSAS—"All persons, before registering or voting, must take and subscribe the following oath: 'I, ———, do solemnly swear (or affirm) * * * * * that I accept the civil and political equality of all men, and agree not to attempt to deprive any person or persons, on account of race, color, or previous condition, of any political or civil right, privilege, or immunity enjoyed by any other class of men,'" etc. *Bogus Constitution, Art.* VIII, *sec.* 5.

MISSISSIPPI—"The Legislature shall provide, by law, for the registration of all persons entitled to vote at any election, and all persons entitled to register shall take and subscribe to the following oath or affirmation: 'I, ———, do solemnly swear (or affirm), in the presence of Almighty God, * * * * * that I admit the political and civil equality of all men. So help me God.'" *Bogus Constitution, Art.* VII, *sec.* 3.

VIRGINIA—"All persons, before entering upon the discharge of any functions as officers of this State, must take and subscribe the following oath or affirmation: 'I, ———, do solemnly swear (or affirm) * * * that I recognize and accept the civil and political equality of all men before the law, etc. So help me God.'" *Bogus Constitution, Art.* III, *sec.* 6.

LOUISIANA—"Members of the General Assembly, and all other officers, before they enter upon the duties of their offices, shall take the following oath or affirmation: 'I (A. B)., do solemnly swear (or affirm) that I accept the civil and political equality of all men, and agree not to attempt to deprive any person, or persons, on account of race, color, or previous condition, of any political or civil right, privileges, or immunity enjoyed by any other class of men, etc. So help me God.'" *Bogus Constitution, Title* VI, *Art.* 100.

Commenting on the foregoing, the New York *World* says:

"With this much as to this express condition precedent to citizenship, it may be said that an essentially similar qualification is to be found in the bogus constitutions of Florida, North Carolina, South Carolina and Georgia. All are based on this idea of negro equality, and an oath to support them is made a condition more or less of citizenship under them, the Florida instrument having this most, and the Georgia one least clearly expressed.

"But in all of them it is to be found, and we, therefore, repeat that no Northern man, not in favor of negro equality, can move to any of these Southern States, as reconstructed by Congress, without disfranchising himself. As to the number thus disfranchised we are enabled to give an approximate idea, taking first the Democratic vote as cast in the represented States at the latest elections held therein, and then adding to that the vote against negro suffrage where the issue was made direct, thus:

DEMOCRATIC VOTE.

Maine	45,644	Indiana	155,102
Vermont	11,510	Illinois	147,058
New Hampshire	32,663	Iowa	58,880
Massachusetts	70,890	Missouri	40,958
Rhode Island	3,340	Wisconsin	68,873
Connecticut	47,575	Nebraska	3,948
New York	373,029	Nevada	4,065
Pennsylvania	267,751	West Virginia	13,393
New Jersey	67,468	Tennessee	22,548
Maryland	63,739	Oregon	11,156
Delaware	9,810		
Kentucky	90,225	Total	1,659,000
California	49,905		

VOTE AGAINST NEGRO SUFFRAGE.

Ohio	255,340	Michigan	110,582
Minnesota	28,759		
Kansas	19,421	Total	414,102

RECAPITULATION.

Total Democratic vote..................1,659,000
Total vote against Negro Suffrage.........414,102

Grand Total..........................2,073,102

"We have put in italics the names of those States where the vote given is that of the majority, and it thus appears that these bogus Southern constitutions actually debar from citizenship under them a majority of the people in thirteen of the twenty-seven represented States and large minorities in the others, or, in exact numbers, 2,073,102 voters, more than a majority of the whole Presidential vote at the next election. And yet this rogue Congress approves them, and turns to the North, thus disfranchised, with a smirk, to say 'We have settled the South now, and you may move there, if you will, and live in peace.'"

Social Equality.

WHITE AND NEGRO CHILDREN TO GO TO THE SAME SCHOOLS.

LOUISIANA—The General Assembly shall establish at least one free public school in every parish throughout the State, and shall provide for its support by taxation and otherwise. All children of this State, between the ages of six (6) and twenty-one (21) shall be admitted to the public schools or other institutions of learning sustained or established by the State, in common, without distinction of race, color, or previous condition. There shall be no separate schools or institutions of learning established exclusively for any race by the State of Louisiana. *Article 135, Bogus Constitution.*

NORTH CAROLINA—The General Assembly, at its first session under this constitution, shall provide, by taxation and otherwise, for a general and uniform system of public schools, wherein tuition shall be free of charge to all the children of the State between the ages of six (6) and twenty-one (21) years. *Sec. 2, Art. IX, Bogus Constitution.*

FLORIDA—It is the paramount duty of the State to make ample provision for the education of all the children residing within its borders, without distinction or preference. *Sec. I, Art. VIII, Bogus Constitution.*

The Legislature shall provide a uniform system of common schools, and a university, and shall provide for the liberal maintenance of the same. Instruction in them shall be free. *Sec. 2 of same.*

GEORGIA—The General Assembly, at its first session after the adoption of this constitution, shall provide a thorough system of general education, to be forever free to all children of the State, the expense of which shall be provided for by taxation or otherwise. *Sec. 1, Art. VI, Bogus Constitution.*

SOUTH CAROLINA—It shall be the duty of the General Assembly to provide for the compulsory attendance, at either public or private schools, of all children between the ages of six (6) and sixteen (16) years, not physically or mentally disabled, for a term equivalent to twenty-four (24) months, at least: *Provided,* That no law to that effect shall be passed until a system of public schools has been thoroughly and completely organized and facilities afforded to all the inhabitants of the State for the free education of their children. *Sec. 4, Art. X, Bogus Constitution.*

All the public schools, colleges and universities of this State, supported in whole or in part by the public funds, shall be free and open to all the children and youths of the State, without regard to race or color. *Sec. 10 of same.*

ARKANSAS—A general diffusion of knowledge and intelligence among all classes being essential to the preservation of the rights and liberties of the people, the General Assembly shall establish and maintain a system of free schools for the gratuitous instruction of all persons in this State between the ages of five (5) and twenty-one (21) years. *Sec. I, Art. IX, Bogus Constitution.*

The General Assembly shall require by law, that *every child* of sufficient mental and physical ability, shall attend the public schools during the period between the ages of five (5) and eighteen (18) years, for a term equivalent to *three years,* unless educated by *other means. Sec. 6, Art. IX, Bogus Constitution of Arkansas.*

ALABAMA—It shall be the duty of the board to establish, throughout the State, in each township, or other school district which it may have created, one or more schools, at which all the children of the State, between the ages of five (5) and twenty-one (21) years, may attend free of charge. *Sec. 6, Art. XI, Bogus Constitution.*

Qualifications of Voters.

HOW NEGRO SUPREMACY IS SECURED IN SOME OF THE STATES.

ART. 99. The following persons shall be prohibited from voting or from holding any office: All persons who shall have been convicted of treason, of perjury, forgery, bribery or other crimes punishable in the penitentiary, and persons under interdiction.

"All persons who are estopped from claiming the right of suffrage by abjuring their allegiance to the United States Government, or by notoriously levying war against it, or adhering to its enemies, giving them aid or comfort, but who have not expatriated themselves, nor have been convicted of any of the crimes mentioned in the first paragraph of this article, are hereby restored to the said right, except the following: Those who held office, civil or military, for one year or more, under the organization styled 'The Confederate States of America;' those who registered themselves as enemies of the United States; those who acted as leaders of guerrilla bands during the late rebellion; those who, in the advocacy of treason, wrote or published newspaper articles or preached sermons during the late rebellion; and those who voted for and signed an ordinance of secession in any State. No person included in these exceptions shall either vote or hold office until he shall have relieved himself by voluntary writing and signing a certificate setting forth that he acknowledges the late rebellion to have been morally and politically wrong, and that he regrets any aid and comfort he may have given it; and he shall file the certificate in the office of the Secretary of State, and it shall be published in the official journal: *Provided,* That no person who, prior to the first of January, eighteen hundred and sixty-eight, favored the execution of the laws of the United States popularly known as the Reconstruction Acts of Congress, and openly and actively assisted the loyal men of the State in their efforts to restore Louisiana to her position in the Union, shall be held to be included among those herein excepted. Registrars of voters shall take the oath of any such person as *prima facie* evidence of the fact that he is entitled to the benefits of this proviso."

To enforce the obnoxious legislation that will ensue, whatever be the consequences, the negro has practically secured the organization of the militia, by requiring all its officers to take the "iron clad" oath. *Vide Art.* 144.

ALABAMA.—Sec. 2. Every male person, born in the United States, and every male person who has been naturalized, or who has legally declared his intention to become a citizen of the United States, twenty-one years old or upward, who shall have resided in this State six months next preceding the election, and three months in the county in which he offers to vote, except as hereinafter provided, shall be deemed an elector: *Provided,* That no soldier, or sailor, or marine, in the military or naval service of the United States, shall hereafter acquire a residence by reason of being stationed on duty in this State.

Sec. 3. It shall be the duty of the general assembly to provide, from time to time, for the registration of all electors; but the following class of persons shall not be permitted to register, vote, or hold office: 1st. Those who, during the late rebellion, inflicted, or caused to be inflicted, any cruel or unusual punishment upon any soldier, sailor, marine, employé or citizen of the United States, or who in any other way violated the rules of civilized warfare. 2d. Those who may be disqualified from holding office by the proposed amendment to the Constitution of the United States, known as "Article XIV," and those who have been disqualified from registering to vote for delegates to the Convention to frame a constitution for the State of Alabama, under the act of Congress "to provide for the more efficient government of the rebel States," passed by Congress, March 2, 1867, and the act supplementary thereto, except such persons as aided in the reconstruction proposed by Congress, and accept the political equality of all men before the law: *Provided,* That the general assembly shall have power to remove the disabilities incurred under this clause. 3d. Those who shall have been convicted of treason, embezzlement of public funds, malfeasance in office, crime punishable by law with imprisonment in the penitentiary, or bribery. 4th. Those who are idiots or insane. *Art.* VII, *Bogus Constitution.*

Sec. 4. All persons, before registering, must take and subscribe the following oath: "I, ———, do solemnly swear (or affirm) that I will support and maintain the Constitution and laws of the United States, and the constitution and laws of the State of Alabama; that I am not excluded from registering by any of the clauses in section 3, article 7, of the constitution of the State of Alabama; that I will never countenance or aid in the secession of this State from the United States; that I accept the civil and political equality of all men, and agree not to attempt to deprive any person or persons, on account of race, color or previous condition, of any political or civil right, privilege or immunity enjoyed by any other class of men; and furthermore, that I will not in any way injure, or countenance in others any attempt to injure, any person or persons on account of past or present support of the Government of the United States, the laws of the United States, or the principle of the political and civil equality of all men, or for affiliation with any political party." *Art.* VII, *Bogus Constitution.*

FLORIDA—Sec. I. Every male person of the age of twenty-one years and upward, of whatever race, color, nationality, or previous condition, who shall at the time of offering to vote, be a citizen of the United States, or who shall have declared his intention to become such in conformity to the laws of the United States, and who shall have resided and had his habitation, domicile, home, and place of permanent abode in Florida for one year, and in the county for six months next preceding the election at which he shall offer to vote, shall in such county be deemed a qualified elector at all elections under this constitution. Every elector shall, at the time of his registration, take and subscribe to the following oath:

"I, ———, do solemnly swear that I will support, protect, and defend the Constitution and government of the United States, and the constitution and government of Florida, against all enemies, foreign and domestic; that I will bear true faith, loyalty, and allegiance to the same, any ordinances or resolution of any State convention or legislature to the contrary notwithstanding; so help me God." *Art.* XV.

Sec. 7. The legislature shall enact laws requiring educational qualifications for electors after the year one thousand eight hundred and eighty, *but no such laws shall be made applicable to any elector who may have registered or voted at any election previous thereto.* *Art.* XV.

Sec. 1. Any person debarred from holding office in the State of Florida by the third section of the fourteenth article of the proposed amendment to the Constitution of the United States, which is as follows: "No person shall be a Senator or Representative in Congress, or elector of President or Vice-President, or hold any office, civil or military, under the United States or under any State, who, having previously taken an oath as a member of Congress, or as an officer of the United States, or as a member of any State legislature, or as an executive or judicial officer of any State, to support the Constitution of the United States, shall have engaged in insurrection or rebellion against the same, or given aid and comfort to enemies thereof. But Congress may, by a vote of two-thirds of each house, remove such disability," is hereby debarred from holding office in this State: *Provided,* That whenever such disability from holding office shall be removed from any person by the Congress of the United States, the removal of such disability shall also apply to this State, and such person shall be restored, in all respects, to the rights of citizenship as herein provided for electors. *Art.* XVI.

ARKANSAS—SEC. 2. Every male person born in the United States, and every male person who has been naturalized, or has legally declared his intentions to become a citizen of the United States, who is twenty-one years old or upward, and who shall have resided in the State six months next preceding the election, and who at the same time is an actual resident of the county in which he offers to vote, except as hereinafter provided, shall be deemed an elector: *Provided,* No soldier, or sailor, or marine, in the military or naval service of the United States, shall acquire a residence by reason of being stationed on duty in this State.

SEC. 3. The following classes shall not be permitted to register, or vote, or hold office, viz:

1. Those who during rebellion took the oath of allegiance, or gave bonds for loyalty and good behavior to the United States Government, and afterward gave aid, comfort, or countenance to those engaged in armed hostility to the Government of the United States, either by becoming a soldier in the rebel army, or by entering the lines of said army, or adhering in any way to the cause of rebellion, or by accompanying any armed force belonging to the rebel army, or by furnishing supplies of any kind to the same.

2. Those who are disqualified as electors, or from holding office in the State or States from which they came.

3. Those persons who, during the late rebellion, violated the rules of civilized warfare.

4. Those who may be disqualified by the proposed amendment to the Constitution of the United States, known as Article XIV, and those who have been disqualified from registering to vote for delegates to the convention to frame a constitution for the State of Arkansas, under the act of Congress entitled "An act to provide for the more efficient government of the rebel States," passed March 2, 1867, and the acts supplementary thereto: *Provided,* That all persons included in the 1st, 2d, 3d and 4th subdivisions o this section, who have openly advocated or who have voted for the reconstruction proposed by Congress, and accept the equality of all men before the law, shall be deemed qualified electors under this constitution.

SEC. 4. The general assembly shall have the power, by a two-thirds vote of each house, approved by the Governor, to remove the disabilities included in the 1st, 2d, 3d and 4th subdivisions of section three of this article, when it appears that such person applying for relief from such disabilities has in good faith returned to his allegiance to the Government of the United States: *Provided,* The general assembly shall have no power to remove the disabilities of any person embraced in the aforesaid subdivisions who, after the adoption of this constitution by this convention, persists in opposing the acts of Congress and reconstruction thereunder.

SEC. 5. All persons, before registering or voting, must take and subscribe the following oath : " I, ———, do solemnly swear (or affirm) that I will support and maintain the Constitution and laws of the United States and the constitution and laws of the State of Arkansas; that I am not excluded from registering or voting by any of the clauses in the 1st, 2d, 3d or 4th subdivisions of Article VIII of the constitution of the State of Arkansas; that I will never countenance or aid in the secession of this State from the United States; that I accept the civil and political equality of all men, and agree not to attempt to deprive any person or persons, on account of race, color, or previous condition, of any political or civil right, privilege, or immunity enjoyed by any other class of men; and, furthermore, that I will not in any way injure, or countenance in others any attempt to injure, any person or persons on account of past or present support of the government of the United States, the laws of the United States, or the principle of the political and civil equality of all men, or for affiliation with any political party."

Extraordinary Patronage Bestowed on The Governors of some of the Rotten Boroughs—Popular Choice of Officers Ignored.

MISSISSIPPI—The terms of all county, township and precinct officers are made to expire in thirty days after the constitution shall be ratified. All these offices are to be filled by the Governor, and are to continue in office until the Legislature shall provide by law for an election of the same; but no time is limited within which the Legislature shall perform this duty. In the Judicial Department, the elective system is abolished, and the Judges of the Supreme Court are appointed by the Governor for *nine years* and the Circuit Judges for six years.

FLORIDA—SEC. 17. The Governor shall be assisted by a cabinet of administrative officers, consisting of a secretary of state, attorney-general, comptroller, treasurer, surveyor-general, superintendent of public instruction, adjutant-general, and commissioner of immigration. Such officers shall be appointed by the Governor, and confirmed by the Senate, and shall hold their offices the same time as the Governor, or until their successors shall be qualified. (Art. V.)

SEC. 18. The Governor shall, by and with the consent of the Senate, appoint all commissioned officers of the State militia. (Art. V.)

SEC. 19. The Governor shall appoint, by and with the consent of the Senate, in each county, an assessor of taxes and collector of revenue, whose duties shall be prescribed by law, and who shall hold their offices for two years. * * * * * The Governor shall appoint in each county a county treasurer, county surveyor, superintendent of common schools, and five county commissioners, each of whom shall hold his office for two years. (Art. V.)

SEC. 3. The supreme court shall consist of a chief justice and two associate justices, who shall hold their offices for life, or during good behavior. They shall be appointed by the Governor and confirmed by the Senate. (Art. VI.)

SEC. 6. The supreme court shall appoint a clerk of the supreme court, who shall have his office at the Capitol, and shall be librarian of the supreme court library. He shall hold his office until his successor is appointed and qualified. (Art. VI.)

SEC. 7. There shall be seven circuit judges appointed by the Governor and confirmed by the Senate, who shall hold their office for eight years. (Art. VI.)

SEC. 9. There shall be a county court organized in each county. The Governor shall appoint a county judge for each county, who shall be confirmed by the Senate, and such judge shall hold his office for four years from the date of his commission, or until his successor is appointed and qualified. (Art. VI.)

SEC. 15. The Governor shall appoint as many justices of the peace as he may deem necessary. Justices of the peace shall have criminal jurisdiction and civil jurisdiction not to exceed fifty dollars, but this shall not extend to the trial of any person for misdemeanor or crime. (Art. VI.)

SEC. 19. The Governor, by and with the advice and consent of the Senate, shall appoint a State attorney in each judicial circuit, whose duties shall be prescribed by law. * * * * * The Governor, by and with the advice and consent of the Senate, shall appoint in each county a sheriff and clerk of the circuit court, who shall also be clerk of the county court and board of county commissioners, recorder, and ex-officio auditor of the county. *Art.* VI, *Bogus Constitution of State of Florida.*

Some Startling and Monstrous Constitutional Provisions.

SOUTH CAROLINA—It shall be the duty of the general assembly to provide for the compulsory attendance, at either public or private schools, of all children between the ages of six (6) and sixteen (16) years, not physically or mentally disabled, for a term equivalent to twenty-four (24) months, at least: *Provided,* That no law to that effect shall be passed until a system of public schools has been thoroughly and completely organized, and facilities afforded to all the inhabitants of the State for the free education of their children. *Sec.* 4, *Art.* X, *Bogus Constitution of South Carolina.*

The general assembly shall require by law, that *every child* of sufficient mental and physical ability, shall attend the public schools during the period between the ages of five and eighteen years, for a term equivalent to *three years,* unless educated by *other means. Sec.* 6, *Art.* IX, *Bogus Constitution of Arkansas.*

These are intended to give the general assembly the power to compel white parents to send their children to schools in common with negro children, if unable to educate them otherwise.

SEC. 1. The personal property of any resident of this State, to the value of two thousand dollars, to be selected by such resident, shall be exempted from sale on execution or other final process of any court, issued for the collection of any debt contracted after the adoption of this constitution. *Art. XII, Bogus Constitution of Arkansas.*

SEC. 2. Hereafter the homestead of any resident of this State, who is a married man or head of a family, shall not be encumbered in any manner while owned by him, except for taxes, laborers' and mechanics' liens, and securities for the purchase-money thereof. *Art. XII, of same.*

SEC. 3. Every homestead not exceeding one hundred and sixty acres of land, and the dwelling and appurtenances thereon; to be selected by the owner thereof, and not in any town, city or village; or in lieu thereof, at the option of the owner, any lot in a city, town or village, with the dwelling and appurtenances thereon, owned and occupied by any resident of this State, and not exceeding the value of five thousand dollars, shall be exempted from sale on execution or any other final process from any court; but no property shall be exempt from sale for taxes, for the payment of obligations contracted for the purchase of said premises, for the erection of improvements thereon, or for labor performed for the owner thereof: *Provided,* That the benefit of the homestead herein provided for, shall not be extended to persons who may be indebted for dues to the State, county, township, school or other trust funds. *Art. XII, of same.*

This amounts to exemption of $7000. We should say this is steep. Northern, as well as all honest creditors, would have a sweet show with this $7000 class of rich men.

The odious acts of the Legislature, prescribing a test oath for nearly all kinds of business, we will receive and insert in latter part of book.

Why the United States Forces are Kept in the Southern States.

WHY THE INCREASE OF SOUTHERN GARRISONS WAS RECOMMENDED—A FACT FOR THE CONTEMPLATION OF THE TAX RIDDEN PEOPLE.

On page 25 of General Grant's Annual Report as Secretary of War, there occurs the following extract, which is copied from the report of General Ord, commanding Fourth Military District, but which General Grant adopts as his own recommendation in the report referred to:

"The extension of suffrage to freedmen has evidently aroused a sentiment of hostility to the colored race and to Northern men in many parts of this district which did not exist before, and from information derived from ex officers of the Union army, planting in the interior, I am convinced that a larger force than is now stationed in the States of my district to preserve order and organize conventions will be required hereafter to protect them, and to secure the freedmen the use of the suffrage. In a majority of the counties of my district there are but very few men who can take the test oath, and these are not disposed to defy public opinion by accepting office unless supported by a military force afterward. *The will of the colored people may be in favor of supporting loyal office-holders, but their intelligence is not now sufficient to enable them to combine for the execution of their will.* All their combinations are now conducted by white men under the protection of the military. If this protection is withdrawn the white men now controlling would generally withdraw with it, and some of the Southern people, now exasperated at what they deem the freedmen's presumption, would not be very gentle toward them; so that the presence of a larger military force will be required for some time to maintain the freedmen in the possession of the right of suffrage."

The whole question of negro suffrage is embraced in the sentence we have italicised. The unfitness of the negro for the possession of the elective franchise is admitted. The necessity of a combination of the negro vote to insure Radical success is developed as the purpose for which negro suffrage was instituted. Their want of intelligence to make such combination is confessed. The control of that vote "by white (Radical) men, under the protection of the military," is an abuse, the necessity of continuing which is coolly and officially stated. As if it were a meritorious fact, it is officially heralded by the General commanding the armies. To make this arrangement permanent, tax-payers, you see what is recommended. An increase of the military force at your expense to protect these white Radicals, and induce their stay in the Southern States to carry on the manipulation of these negro voters. A logical appeal to Congress—to shield, with a military force, the cowardly persons of the Radical emissaries in the South. A preservation of the combined negro vote to the Radicals—a military necessity. Was there ever anything more reprehensible embraced in a military recommendation?

How the Military Imperials Ruled their Dominions.

A FEW ORDERS.

HEADQUARTERS FOURTH MILITARY DISTRICT,
MISSISSIPPI AND ARKANSAS,
VICKSBURG, Miss., April 15, 1867.

Hon. Isaac Murphy, Governor of the State of Arkansas, Little Rock, Ark.:

SIR—Will you, through the proper channel and in the most expeditious manner, please inform the members of the Provisional Legislature of the State of Arkansas, lately in session, that their reconvening is incompatible with the act of Congress "To provide a more efficient government for the rebel States," passed March 2, 1867, and that they, therefore, will not reassemble, as may have been appointed by them.

Please acknowledge the receipt of this letter, and state the steps which may have been taken therewith.

I am, sir, with great respect,
Your obedient servant,
E. O. C. ORD,
Brigadier-General Commanding.

Special Orders No. 6.]
HEADQUARTERS SUB-DISTRICT OF ARKANSAS,
LITTLE ROCK, April 25, 1867.

EXTRACT.

II. In compliance with letters of instruction from Brevet Major-General Ord, commanding Fourth Military District, dated Vicksburg, Miss., April 15, 1867, Brevet Colonel Henry Page, A. Q. M. U. S. Vol., will immediately relieve the Hon. L. B. Cunningham, Treasurer of the provisional government of the State of Arkansas, of the duties, bonds, books, papers and all effects appertaining to the office. * * *

By order of   GENERAL SMITH.

SATRAP POPE'S CONFIDENTIAL LETTER TO SWAYNE—THE PATRON SAINT OF RADICALISM SPEAKS FOR HIS PARTY.

HEADQUARTERS THIRD MILITARY DISTRICT,
GEORGIA, ALABAMA AND FLORIDA,
ATLANTA, GA., November 20.

My Dear General:

I write you unofficially, as I do not wish to reply to your telegrams relating to the compensation of the members of the Convention. The reconstruction acts prescribe the manner in which such compensation shall be made, and *I do not know that I have authority to act at all in the matter.*

I am willing, however, to sanction the payment of the Convention from funds now in the State Treasury, under the following conditions:

1. That the Convention provide for the levy and collection of a special tax, in accordance with the requirements of the reconstruction acts to cover the payment, which amount shall be paid in to the State treasury before the end of the fiscal year.

2. That the compensation of the members of the Convention shall be fixed at a reasonable sum.

3. That the payments from the treasury be not made until the Convention has completed its work.

As I have said, I do not know that I have the authority to order this payment, but I will do so on the foregoing conditions.

In this connection I hope you will suggest to the members of the Convention, that if the newspaper accounts are true, the amount of compensation they propose seems to me (as, indeed, it does to everybody I have heard speak of it) excessive; and, if adopted, a very bad effect will be produced upon the friends of the Convention. The Convention should fix the lowest possible compensation for its members, barely enough to pay actual expenses. I can not tell you what an unpleasant impression has been created by the newspaper reports on the subject.

I hope, on every account, that the Convention will finish its work and adjourn at an early day. If they knew how their proceedings are watched, alike by friend and enemy, and how much of their future depends upon their prompt and reasonable action, it seems to me that unless discussions should be avoided and a fair and satisfactory result reached in the shortest possible time, every day they remain in session after the 20th of this month will be used as a reproach against them, and will tend to discourage the friends of reconstruction everywhere.

I hope you will do what you can to urge these or similar views upon those who have influence.

I hold it of the greatest importance that the Constitution be made as soon as possible. *I speak not more for the interests of Alabama than for the interests of the political party upon whose retention of power for several years to come the success of reconstruction depends.*

Truly your friend,   JOHN POPE.

HEADQUARTERS THIRD MILITARY DISTRICT,
GEORGIA, ALABAMA AND FLORIDA,
ATLANTA, GA., January 13, 1868.

Charles J. Jenkins, Milledgeville, Ga.:

SIR—I have received with profound regret your communication of the 10th inst., in which you decline to accede to the request made in mine of the 7th inst. As I can not but consider your action as a failure to co-operate with me in executing the laws known as the Reconstruction laws of Congress, and as I am further advised that you declined to pay the salary of M. S. Bigby,

Solicitor-General on the Tallapoosa Circuit, on the ground that said officer having been appointed by the military commander of the Third Military District, you can not recognize the validity of his appointment, I am forced most reluctantly to view your actions as obstructions to the execution of the Reconstruction laws, and have no alternative but to remove you from your office, as you will see that I have done by the inclosed order. I do not deem myself called upon to answer the arguments of your letter. The issue is very plain between us. I must require the acknowledgment of the validity of the Reconstruction laws, and you plainly deny them as having any binding force on your actions. Both of us are acting from a conscientious sense of duty, but the issue is so plain and direct that all hope of harmonious co-operation must be abandoned.

With feelings of high personal respect, and with sincere regret for the course I feel myself compelled to take, I remain, most respectfully,

Your obedient servant,
GEORGE G. MEADE,
Major-General Commanding.

HEADQUARTERS THIRD MILITARY DISTRICT,
GEORGIA, ALABAMA AND FLORIDA,
ATLANTA, GA., January 13, 1868.

John Jones, Esq., Milledgeville:

SIR—Your refusal to obey the instructions of Brevet Major-General Pope, commanding Third Military District, is viewed by me as an obstruction to the execution of the Reconstruction laws of Congress, and I am, therefore, compelled to remove you from office, as you will see I have done by the inclosed order.

Very respectfully,
Your ob't servant,
GEORGE G. MEADE,
Major-General Commanding.

RICHMOND, September 21, 1867

To Sub-District Commanders:

In the discharge of your duties as military commissioner you are authorized to exercise the jurisdiction given by law to judges of the circuit courts of the State.

The judicial authority of these courts can only be exercised by a military commission, or by the commanding General, but you are authorized to investigate and report for the action of the commanding General any case of which a circuit court may take jurisdiction.

The jurisdiction of military commissioners of counties and cities is limited to that of justices, or police magistrates, but you are authorized to direct them, in any case within your jurisdiction, to investigate and report the facts, with the record of the evidence taken.

You are also authorized to hear appeals from the judgment of a circuit court, and report the facts, with the record in the case, and your opinion thereon, to these headquarters.

The jurisdiction herein conferred is to be exercised only when, in your judgment, it is necessary to a faithful execution of the acts of Congress of March 2 and 23, and of July 19, 1867. By order of
Major-General SCHOFIELD.

HEADQUARTERS CHARLESTON, S. C.
October 18, 1867.

Judge Aldrich has been suspended, and will not be permitted to hold any courts in his circuit. See special order number one hundred and eighty-three (183) of this date.

By command of Brevet Major-General E. R. S Canby.
L. V. CAZIARC.
Aid de-Camp and Act. Ass. Adj.-General.

Financial Aspects of Reconstruction—Plunder and Extravagance the Rule.

LOUISIANA—ART. 55. The Governor shall receive a salary of $8,000 per annum.

ART. 56. The Lieutenant-Governor shall receive a salary of $3,000 per annum.

ART. 75. The Chief-Justice shall receive a salary of 7,500. Each of the Associate Justices (four) a salary of $7,000 annually.

ART. 84. Each of said Judges (meaning seven in the Parish of Orleans, and not less than twelve nor more than twenty in the State), shall receive a salary to be fixed by law which * * * shall never be less than $5,000.

ART. 86. Each Parish Judge (one for each Parish), shall receive a salary of $1,200 per annum.

ART. 92. There shall be an Attorney-General for the State. * * * He shall receive a salary of $5,000 per annum.

ART. 137. A Superintendent of Education. * * * He shall receive a salary of $5,000 per annum.

ART. 71. The Treasurer and the Auditor shall receive a salary of $5,000 per annum each. The Secretary of State shall receive a salary of $3,000 per annum.

ART. 39. The Members of the General Assembly, shall receive from the public Treasury * * * eight dollars per day during their attendance.

FLORIDA—ART. XVI, SEC. 4. The salary of the Governor of the State shall be $5,000 per annum; that of the Chief Justice shall be $4,500; that of each Associate Justice (two) shall be $4,000; that of each Judge of the Circuit Court (seven) shall be $3,500; that of the Lieutenant-Governor shall be

$2,500; that of each Cabinet officer shall be $3,000; the pay of the members of the Senate and House of Representatives shall be $500 per annum, and in addition thereto ten cents per mile for each mile traveled from their respective places of residence to the Capitol, and the same to return; but such distances shall be estimated by the shortest general thoroughfare. All other officers of the State shall be paid by fees, or per diem, fixed by law.

Florida, it must be recollected, is a small State, having but one representative in Congress, of sparse population and few voters. The size of these salaries can then be appreciated.

MISSISSIPPI—The expenses of the bogus Convention, had, up to the 1st of June, already footed up $201,000.

The Convention entailed upon the State three election commissioners in each county, at $6 per day each, or $1,098 for the whole State, without any limit as to time, except their own discretion, which, in the hands of such greedy Radical cormorants, is not governed by any rules of propriety.

It paid its Radical printer $28,000 for a job of printing worth only $2,000.

The Legislature to be assembled under its auspices has no limit upon its sessions, and, it is estimated, will cost over $1,000 per day.

Well does the Jackson (Miss.) *Clarion*, say:

"But the expenses of the Legislature itself, enormous as they would be, will be a mere trifle compared with the sums which would be appropriated to carry into operation the gigantic schemes proposed in the constitution under the head of Public Works, Militia, Common Schools, etc., to pamper and enrich the swarm of hungry vultures who would be privileged to feed upon the substance of the people. It requires no stretch of the imagination to see that an annual tax of MILLIONS OF DOLLARS would be levied to meet these demands. They would necessarily absorb all the revenues of the people. They would bring property of all kinds to the block to be sacrificed under the sheriff's hammer. They would bring those who are in comparatively comfortable circumstances, to penury, and will take the last morsel of bread from the mouths of starving women and children. All classes, and both races, will groan under this afflicting burden."

What is here said of Mississippi, is true of all these Rotten Borough organizations. The whole system is one of device and plunder, to give jobs and places to Radical vagrants and to perpetuate itself by the power of a majority of votes at the polls made up of illiterate and non-taxpaying suffragans of the negro race.

A few Details of what Reconstruction has Cost the National Treasury.

In North and South Carolina, up to Sept. 30, 1867, Gen. Canby reported $54,802.87 already paid out; that outstanding liabilities would exceed the balance of $194,802.87 then on hand. Total, $249,605.74.

In Georgia, Florida and Alabama, Gen. Pope reports expended, $162,325.00.

In Virginia, General Schofield reports as expended, up to Nov. 7, 1867, $169,409.33. Outstanding accounts not yet paid, $70,000. Total $239,409.33.

The compiler of this book has not seen, among the reports of the Secretary of War, any estimate of the expenditures in the Fourth and Fifth Military Districts, but as they were extensive and less possessed of the facilities for economy than the others, we will put them down at $250,000, each making $500,000.00, or a grand total of $1,158,424.40 expended last year out of the Federal Treasury in this matter of Military Reconstruction. Supposing it to have cost 50 per cent. of that amount to have run it since, a period of nine months in some and eight months in others, a moderate estimate of the entire cost up to this time, to the tax-burdened people of the United States, independent of the large amounts it has cost the people of the States embraced in said districts, will not fall short of $1,850,000. This does not include the pay and allowances proper of army officers engaged in it, which are considerably augmented by commutation for quarters in towns, etc.; nor does it embrace any of the expenses of the army garrisoned in the Southern States, which is tremendous.

Act Admitting Arkansas.

The following is the text of the Arkansas bill:

WHEREAS, The people of Arkansas, as in pursuance of the provisions of an act entitled "An act for the more efficient government of the Rebel States," passed March 2, 1867, and the acts supplementary thereto, have framed and adopted a constitution of State Government, which is republican in form, and the Legislature of said State has duly ratified the amendment to the Constitution of the United States, proposed by the Thirty-ninth Congress, and known as Article XIV; therefore,

Be it enacted by the Senate and House of Representatives of the United States of America, in Congress assembled, That the State of Arkansas is entitled and admitted to representation in Congress, as one of the States of the Union, upon the following fundamental condition: That the Constitution of Arkansas shall never be so amended or changed as to deprive any citizen, or class of citizens, in the United States, of the right to vote, who are entitled to vote by the constitution herein recognized, except as a punishment for such crimes as are now felonies at common law, whereof they shall have been duly convicted, under laws equally applicable to all the inhabitants of said State; provided, that any alteration of said constitution, prospective in its effect, may be made in regard to time and place of residence of the voters.*

WASHINGTON, June 20.

The President sent the following Message to Congress to-day:

To the House of Representatives:

I return without my signature a bill entitled an act to admit the State of Arkansas to representation in Congress.

To approve of this bill would be an admission on the part of the Executive that the act "for the more efficient government of the rebel States," passed March 2, 1867, and the acts supplementary thereto, were proper and constitutional.

My opinion, however, in reference to those measures has undergone no change, but, on the contrary, has been strengthened by the results which have attended their execution. Even were this not the case, I could not consent to a bill which is based upon the assumption either that by an act of rebellion of a portion of its people, the State of Arkansas seceded from the Union, or that Congress may, at its pleasure, expel or exclude any State from the Union, or interrupt its relations with the Government by arbitrarily depriving it of representation in the Senate and House of Representatives.

If Arkansas is not a State in the Union, this bill does not admit it as a State. And if, on the other hand, it is a State in the Union, no legislation is necessary to declare it entitled to representation in Congress as one of the States of the Union.

The Constitution already declares that each State shall have at least one representative; that the Senate shall be composed of two Senators from each State; that no State without its consent shall be deprived of its equal suffrage in the Senate; and also makes each House the judge of the election returns, and qualifications of its own members, and therefore all that is now necessary to secure Arkansas in all its constitutional relations to the Government, is a decision by each House upon the eligibility of those who, presenting their credentials, claim seats in the respective Houses of Congress. This is the plain and simple plan of the Constitution, and believing that had it been pursued when Congress assembled in the month of December, 1865, the restoration of the States would long since have been completed; I once again earnestly recommend that it be adopted by each House.

In reference to this legislation, I respectfully submit that it is not only of doubtful constitutionality, and, therefore, an unwise and dangerous precedent, but unnecessary, and that it is not so effective in its operation as the mode prescribed by the Constitution. It involves additional delay, and from its terms will be taken rather as applicable to a territory about to be admitted as one of the United States, than to a State which has occupied a place in the Union for upward of a quarter of a century.

The bill declares that Arkansas is entitled and admitted to representation in Congress as one of the States of the Union, upon the following fundamental conditions:

That the constitution of Arkansas shall never be so amended or changed as to deprive any citizen or class of citizens of the United States of the right to vote who are entitled to vote by the constitution herein recognized, except for punishment for crimes that are now felonies at common law, whereof they shall have been convicted, equally applicable to all the inhabitants of said State; provided, any alteration of said Constitution prospective in its effect, may be made in regard to the time and place of residence of voters.

I have been unable to find in the Constitution of the United States any warrant for the exercise of the authority thus claimed by Congress in assuming power to impose fundamental conditions on a State which has been duly admitted into the Union on an equal footing with the original States in all respects whatever. Congress asserts a right to enter a State as it may a territory, and to regulate the highest prerogative of a free people, the elective franchise. This question is reserved by the Constitution to the States themselves, and to concede to Congress the power to regulate this subject would be to reverse the fundamental principle of the republic, and place in the hands of the Federal Government, which is a

---

*The proviso to the act of March 28, 1867, hereinbefore contained, says, "That such Convention shall not be held unless a majority of all such registered voters shall have voted on the question of holding such Convention." Yet Arkansas is admitted when neither the "Convention" nor the "Constitution" received a majority of the registered vote in Arkansas. We give the figures as found in the official reports:

	Registered Vote.	Vote For.	Less than a Majority.
"CONSTITUTION"	71,734	27,913	8,980
"CONVENTION"	66,831	27,831	5,585

creature of the States, the sovereignty which justly belongs to the States or the people, the true source of all political power, by whom our federal system was created, and to whose will it is subordinate.

The bill fails to provide in what manner the State of Arkansas is to signify its acceptance of the fundamental condition which Congress endeavors to make inalienable or irrevocable; nor does it prescribe the penalty to be imposed should the people of the State amend or change the particular portions of the constitution which it was one of the purposes of the bill to perpetuate; but, as to the consequence of such action, it leaves them in uncertainty and doubt. When the circumstances under which the constitution has been brought to the attention of Congress are considered, it is not unreasonable to suppose that efforts will be made to modify its provisions, especially those in respect to which this measure prohibits any alteration. It is seriously questioned whether the constitution has been ratified by a majority of the persons who, under the act of March 2, 1865, and the acts supplementary thereto, were entitled to registration and to vote upon that issue. Section 10 of the schedule provides that no persons disqualified from voting or registering under this constitution shall vote for candidates for any office, nor be permitted to vote at the polls for the ratification or repudiation of the constitution, which is herein authorized and assumed to be in force before its adoption.

In disregard of the law of Congress, the constitution undertakes to impose upon the electors other and further conditions. The fifth section of the eighth article provides that all persons, before registering or voting, must take and subscribe to an oath which, among others, contains the following clause:

"That I accept the civil and political equality of all men, and agree not to attempt to deprive any person or persons on account of race, color, or previous condition, of any political or civil right, privilege, or immunity enjoyed by any other class of men."

It is well known that a very large portion of the electors in all the States, if not all, a majority, do not believe in or accept the practical equality of Indians, Mongolians, or negroes, with the race to which they belong. If the voters in many of the States of the North and West were required to take such an oath as a test of their qualifications, there is reason to believe that a majority of them would remain from the polls rather than comply with such degrading conditions. How far, and to what extent this test oath prevented the registration of those who were qualified under the laws of Congress, it is impossible to know; but that its effect was to prevent the registration of a number at least sufficient to overcome the small and doubtful majority in favor of the constitution, there can be no reasonable doubt. Should the people of Arkansas, therefore, desire to regulate the elective franchise so as to make it conform to the institutions of a large proportion of the States of the North and West, and should they modify the provisions referred to in the fundamental condition, what is the consequence? Is it intended that a denial of representation shall follow? If so, may we not expect at some future day a recurrence of the troubles which have so long agitated the country? Would it not be the part of wisdom to take for our guide the Federal Constitution, rather than to resort to measures which, looking only to the present, may, in after years, renew in an aggravated form the strife and bitterness caused by legislation which has proved to be so ill-timed and unfortunate?

ANDREW JOHNSON.
WASHINGTON, D. C., June 20, 1868.

The bill passed over the veto of the President.

Southern Satrapies.

DEMOCRATIC PROTEST AGAINST THE ADMISSION OF THE ARKANSAS REPRESENTATIVES.

In the House of Representatives, on Monday, Mr. Brooks, on behalf of the Democratic members, offered the following protest, which was ordered to be printed in the official journal of Congressional debates:

"The recognized presence of three persons on the floor of this House from the State of Arkansas, sent here by military force, acting under a Brigadier-General of the army, but nevertheless claiming to be members of this Congress, and to share with us, the representatives from free States, in the imposition of taxes and customs and other laws upon our people, makes it our imperative duty in this, the first case to remonstrate most solemnly, and to protest as solemnly, against this perilous and destructive innovation upon the principles and practices of our hitherto constitutional self-government. The so-called reconstruction acts which created the military governments in Arkansas, and like governments in other Southern States, to share with us in the legislative power of the Northern and Western free people, we have every reason to believe, have been held to be unconstitutional by the Supreme Court of the United States, the public declaration of which fact was avoided only by the extraordinary and strange device in this Congress in snatching jurisdiction from the court in the McArdle case, when such a public decision was about to be made. Of the three great branches of the Government, it seems, then, that after the Executive vetoed these acts as unconstitutional, the Judiciary adjudicated them to be so, while a Congress—the creation of but twenty-seven of the thirty-seven States of the Union—override these equal and co-ordinate branches of that Government, first, by voting down the vetoes; next, by nullifying the judgment of the court. In an era of profound peace, when not an armed man rises against the Government from the Potomac to the Rio Grande, there, in ten States, our American historical way of creating the organic law has been utterly subverted by the bayonet. Ever since the Declaration of Independence, with scarcely an exception, and even amid the battles of the Revolution, conventions have been convoked through, and constitutions created by electors of the States, the only authorized depositories of the sovereign power of every State, without exterior dictation, as under the existing Federal Constitution, the hardest and harshest test oath required from 1776 to the peace of 1783 was an abjuration oath of allegiance to George the Third; while some of the now so called bayonet-made constitutions from the South, propose absurd and cruel tests—absurd, as in Arkansas, where is interwoven in the organic law a mere party test between the Radical Reconstructionists and the Democratic Conservatives, such as would exclude from voting, if living there, the thousands and tens of thousands and hundreds of thousands of Democrats in the free States (article 8, section 4); or cruel, as in Alabama, where no white man can vote who will not forever forswear his own race and color, and perjure himself by swearing in defiance of the law of God, that the negro is his equal, and forever to be his equal, at the ballot box, in the jury-box, with the cartouch-box, in the school, in the college, in house and home, and by the fire-side, in short, in every way, everywhere. (Article 7, section 4). Now, in these, and the other Southern States, in the midst of war, President Lincoln, in his proclamation December 8, 1863, offered amnesty and pardon to rebels then in arms if they would lay down their arms and take an oath of fidelity; while now not a Union man in Arkansas or Alabama can vote unless, in the first place, he swears allegiance to the majesty of this Congress, and in the next, swears off his Americanism and Africanizes himself. Hitherto constitutions with us have been the outgrowth of popular life, springing from the exuberance of our enterprise and energy in the settlement of the forests or prairies of our country; but here before us now we have nine constitutions, with one, if not three, more yet to come from Texas, which have all been imposed upon the people by five military satraps or pentarchs, in a manner never before known under our law, but borrowed, at best, from imperial Roman colonization, or from the worst precedents of the French Revolution. France is then recorded to have had five constitutions in three years, so frequently made and so frequently changed that they were ironically classed by the French people with the periodical literature of the day. Louisiana, a colony of that France, has had four constitutions in four years, and a constitution there has now become periodical literature, as in France in the agonies and throes of the great Revolution. Laws, mere statute laws, which can never be created by constitutions, are appended, more or less, to all these constitutions; and these bayonet-created, one-branch governments, with no Executive, no Senate, no House of Representatives, no Judiciary, have ordained irrepealable, irreversible laws in the very organism of the State, such as can not thus be created by the Executive, the Senate, and the House of Representatives of legitimate governments, when acting in unison, and all combined. All this has been done without regard to preceding constitutions or precedents, or to the common law of the States, or the law of nations. The military, which under legitimate institutions can only be used in times of peace to conserve or preserve the State, have been used to destroy States. The General of the Army, who represents the sword, and only the sword, of the republic, has been exalted by acts of Congress above the constitutional Commander-in-chief of the army and navy, in order to execute those military decrees, and as the surer way to root out every vestige of constitutional law or liberty. The same General of the army, in order to prolong and perpetuate this military domination North and West, as well as South, has been selected in party convention at Chicago to head the electoral vote for the Presidency in ten of our States, which are as much under his feet as Turkey is under the Sultan, or Poland under the Czar of Russia. But, as if only to add insult to the injury of this military outrage upon the popular government in these ten States, either by act of Congress or by these Congress made State constitutions, at least 250,000 whites have been disfranchised, while 750,000 negroes, inexperienced in all law-making, and more ignorant than our children, have been enfranchised in their stead, and have thus been created absolute masters and sovereigns over the whole white population of the South.

Because of all this, and in opposition to all this, we, representatives of the people from the free States, in behalf of our constituents, and of thousands and tens of thousands of others who would be represented if the popular power without could now constitutionally act here within, earnestly and solemnly protest against this violence upon our Constitution and upon our people, and do hereby counsel and advise all friends of popular government to submit to this force only until at the ballot-box, operating through the elections, this great wrong can be put right. There is no law in the land over the constitutional law. There is no government but constitutional government; and hence all bayonet-made, all Congress-imposed constitutions are of no weight, authority, or sanction, save that enforced by arms—an element of power unknown to Americans in peace, and never required but as it acts in and under the supreme civil law, the Constitution, and the statutes enacted in pursuance thereof. We protest, then, in behalf of the free people of the North and the West, against the right of this military oligarchy, established in Arkansas, or elsewhere in the now re-enslaved States of the South, to impose upon us, through Congress, taxes or customs, or other laws to maintain this oligarchy, or its Freedmen's Bureau. We protest against going into the now proposed copartnership of military dictators and negroes in the administration of this Government. We demand, in the name of the fathers of the Constitution, and for the sake of posterity, not its reconstruction, but the restoration of that sacred instrument which has been to us a pillar of fire from 1787 on to its present overthrow; and in all solemnity, before God and man, under a full sense of the responsibility of all we utter, we do hereby affix our names to this protest against the admission of these three persons, claiming to be members of Congress from Arkansas.

James Brooks, James B. Beck, P. Van Trump, Charles A. Eldridge, Samuel J. Randall, A. J. Glossbrenner, Stevenson Archer, John A. Nicholson, John Morrissey, Thomas Laurens Jones, W. E. Niblack, John W. Chanler, S. B. Axtell, S S. Marshall, W. S. Holman, C. W. P. Haight. Charles Sitgreaves, Lewis M. Ross, H McCullough, J. Proctor Knott, W. Mungen, Stephen Taber, Asa P. Grover, L. S. Trimble, George M. Adams, J. S. Golladay, J. W Humphrey, Fernando Wood, J. Lawrence Getz, F. Stone, M. C. Kerr, John Fox, James A. Johnson, John V. L. Pruyn, W. E. Robinson, B. M. Boyer, George W. Woodward, C. E. Phelps, A. G. Burr, D. M. Van Auken, J. R. McCormick, Demas Barnes, James M. Cavanaugh.

An Act to admit the States of North Carolina, South Carolina, Louisana, Georgia, and Florida, to representation in Congress.

WHEREAS, The people of North Carolina, South Carolina, Georgia, Alabama and Florida, have, in pursuance of the provisions of an act entitled "An act for the more efficient government of the rebel States," passed March 22, 1867, and the act supplemental thereto, framed constitutions of a State government which are republican, and had adopted said constitutions by large majorities of the votes cast at the elections held for the ratification or repealing of the same; therefore,

Be it enacted, That each of the States of North Carolina, South Carolina, Louisana, Georgia, Alabama and Florida, shall be entitled and admitted to representation in Congress as a State of the Union, when the Legislatures of such States shall have duly ratified the amendment to the Constitution of the United States proposed by the Thirty-ninth Congress, and known as Article XIV, upon the following fundamental conditions:

SECTION 1. That the constitutions of neither of said States shall ever be so amended or changed as to deprive any citizen or class of citizens of the United States of the right to vote in said State, who are entitled to vote by the constitutions thereof herein recognized, except as punishment of such crimes as are now felony at common law, whereof they shall have been duly convicted under laws equally applicable to all the inhabitants of said States, provided that any alteration of said constitutions prospective in effect, may be made with regard to the time and place of residence of voters, and the State of Georgia shall only be entitled and admitted to representation upon this further fundamental condition, that the first and third subdivisions of section seventeen, of the fifth article of the constitution of said State, except the proviso to the first sub division, shall be null and void, and that the general assembly of said State, by solemn public act, shall declare the assent of the Sta e to the foregoing fundamental condition.

SEC. 2. That if the day fixed for the first meeting of the Legislature of either of said States by the constitution or ordinances thereof shall have passed, or so nearly arrived before the passage of this act, that there shall not be time for the Legislature to assemble at the period fixed, such Legislature shall convene at the end of twenty days from the time this act shall take effect, unless the Governor elect shall sooner convene the sam .

SEC. 3. That the first section of this act

shall take effect as to each State, except Georgia, when such State shall by its Legislature duly ratify Article XIV of the amendment to the Constitution of the United States, passed by the Thirty-ninth Congress; and as to the State of Georgia, when it shall in addition give the assent of said State to the fundamental condition hereinbefore imposed upon the same, and thereupon the officers of each State duly elected and qualified under the constitution thereof shall be inaugurated without delay, but no person prohibited from holding office under the United States or under any State by the section of the proposed amendment to the Constitution of the United States, known as Article XIV, shall be deemed eligible to any office in either of said States, unless relieved from disability as provided in the said amendment; and it is hereby made the duty of the President within ten days after receiving official information of the ratification of said amendment by Legislature of either of said States, to issue a proclamation announcing that fact.

Passed Senate June 10, 1868.

YEAS—Messrs. Anthony, Cameron, Chandler, Cole, Conklin, Conness, Cragin, Drake, Ferry, Frelinghuysen, Harlan, Howard, Howe, Morgan, Morrill (Vt.), Morrill (Me.), Nye, Patterson (N. H.), Pomeroy, Ramsey, Ross, Sherman, Stewart, Sumner, Thayer, Tipton, Trumbull, Wade, Williams, Wilson, Yates—31.

NAYS—Messrs. Bayard, Buckalew, McCreery, Patterson (Tenn.), Vickers—5.

So the bill passed.

The following Senators were paired off; Saulsbury with Willey, Davis with Morton, and Hendricks with Van Winkle.

It was stated that Mr. Morton was absent from illness.

Against the admission of Alabama into the "omnibus" there were many protests by Senators Trumbull, Edmunds, Hendricks, and Buckalew, but a motion to strike from the bill the section authorizing it, which had been previously adopted in committee, was lost by the following vote:

YEAS—Messrs. Bayard, Buckalew, Conkling, Davis, Edmunds, Frelinghuysen, Hendricks, Howe, McCreery, Morgan, Morrill (of Vermont), Patterson (of Tennessee), Saulsbury, Trumbull, Vickers, and Yates—16.

NAYS—Messrs. Cameron, Chandler, Conness, Corbett, Cragin, Drake, Ferry, Harlan, Morrill (of Maine), Morton, Nye, Pomeroy, Ramsey, Ross, Sherman, Stewart, Sumner Thayer, Tipton, Van Winkle, Wade, Willey, Williams, and Wilson—24.

Senator Conkling, of New York, then called the attention of the Senate to the necessity for legislation for the protection of riparian owners in Alabama, who might under the proposed constitution, be deprived of their right to collect wharfages and to otherwise enjoy the profits of their lands. He offered the following amendment:

"And the State of Alabama shall be entitled and admitted to representation only upon this further fundamental condition: that section twenty-six of the first article of the constitution of said State, except so much thereof as makes navigable waters a public highway, shall be null and void; and that the General Assembly of said State by solemn act shall declare the consent of the State to the foregoing fundamental condition."

On this amendment there followed a spicy debate, Senators Conkling and Hendricks attacking the proviso in the constitution as a violation of vested rights, while Senators Sherman, Williams and Morton defended it. Other Senators had an occasional word to say, and the Alabama Representatives elect on the floor of the Senate prompted their defenders. The case appeared to be clear, but party discipline was invoked, and the amendment was lost by the following vote:

YEAS—Messrs. Anthony, Buckalew, Conkling, Corbett, Edmunds, Frelinghuysen, Hendricks, Howard, Howe, McCreery, Morgan, Morrill (of Maine), Morrill (of Vermont), Nye, Patterson (of Tennessee), Ross, and Vickers—16.

NAYS—Messrs. Chandler, Cole, Conness, Cragin, Drake, Ferry, Harlan, Howard, Morton, Pomeroy, Ramsey, Saulsbury, Sherman, Stewart, Sumner, Thayer, Tipton, Van Winkle, Wade, Willey, Williams, Wilson, and Yates—23.

By which citizens of Mobile will be deprived of the use and occupation, the rents, issues and profits of their lands fronting on the water, which they have improved at a large expense. They have, it was stated, successfully defended their rights in the courts, but now those rights have been stricken down and obliterated at a blow.*

In the House, the bill coming up June 12, 1868, Mr. Farnsworth moved to strike "Florida" out of the bill, and gave his reasons for the motion. He was throughly convinced that Florida ought not to be admitted with its present constitution.

Mr. Paine also argued against the admission of Florida under this bill. He declared that the population and wealth of the State of Florida was less than in the average of Congressional districts in the United States. He argued against the republicanism of the State constitution, particularly in giving to the Governor the appointment of thirty-nine county treasurers, thirty-nine

---

* "A majority of the voters of Alabama did not cast their ballots for the constitution." Then let it be denied now. The total registration at the "election" on that bogus instrument was 170,631, total vote "for the constitution." 70,812, just 14,404 less than a majority. See Meade's report of March 23, 1868.

county surveyors, the superintendent of common schools, one hundred and ninety-five county commissioners, and as many justices of the peace as the Governor may see fit to appoint, each of the latter to hold his office for life at the pleasure of the Governor. He could not consent to fasten such a constitution on the people of Florida, particularly in view of the difficulties of amending it, which can only be done by a two-thirds vote in two successive legislatures, and by the subsequent vote of the people.

Mr. Butler replied to the arguments of Messrs. Farnsworth and Paine and declared that the new constitution of Florida was similar to that under which the people of Massachusetts and of other New England States and of New York had so long lived.

Mr. Washburne (Illinois) remarked that so far as he was concerned he would remand Florida to a territorial condition. He did not want her to come here with two Senators to offset the Senators from Illinois, Pennsylvania or New York, particularly with such a constitution.

Mr Butler—Let me ask whether Florida has not as many inhabitants as Colorado, for which the gentleman voted.

Mr. Washburne—I beg your pardon, sir, I voted against it.

Mr. Butler spoke at some length in favor of the admission of Florida, and was followed by Mr. Hubbard, of New York, on the same side.

Mr. Bromwell asked the gentleman from New York whether he thought it was very safe to trust all the local organizations of the State in the hands of one man, so that, if he should prove recreant to his principles, or die, and be succeeded by the Lieutenant-Governor, the entire organization of the State might not be committed into rebel hands.

Mr. Hubbard replied that Florida had not made the tremendous mistake which was made at Baltimore, in selecting a man as second who could not be trusted in case the principle died.

Mr. Bromwell inquired then whether the whole thing did not depend upon one man, and whether, if he died, his successor would be as good as himself.

Mr. Hubbard replied, the Lieutenant-Governor was a "loyal," true man, as he believed. He added, the whole of this objection arose because a citizen of Illinois had gone down to Florida and had not succeeded, as he expected, in obtaining a majority for the Governorship. That was the trouble. It was because that Illinois man had not succeeded in getting control of the organization of the State. If he had succeeded, there would be no objection to-day to the admission of Florida.

Mr. Bromwell protested, so far as he was concerned, he neither knew nor cared what Mr. Richards' performances were. They and he never had had the least idea that the gentleman's welfare had anything to do with the matter.

Mr. Farnsworth asked Mr. Hubbard whether the Reconstruction Committee approves, even to-day, of the constitution of Florida?

Mr. Hubbard replied it did, and added that he had understood the gentleman from Illinois (Mr. Farnsworth) to say, this morning, in the committee room, that he regarded the constitution of Florida as the very best Constitution that any of the Southern States had.

Mr. Farnsworth—The gentlemen is entirely mistaken. I never made such a remark. I never said anything at all on the subject.

Mr. Hubbard—Will the gentleman tell me what his remark did apply to?

Mr. Farnsworth—I may have spoken about Alabama, but the entire Reconstruction Committee have unanimously and repeatedly declared against the constitution of Florida.

Mr. Hubbard—So it has, Mr. Speaker.

Mr. Farnsworth—And it does so now. But the members say they had better admit the State notwithstanding.

Mr. Hubbard—I deny the gentleman's right to say that.

Mr. Baker remarked that the legislation involved some questions of law and policy, and five minutes was a short time in which to say everything adequate to the subject. He should ask leave to print some remarks, which was granted.

Mr. Bingham desired the action of the House speedily on the bill, and would therefore move the previous question, but first asked his colleague (Mr. Spalding) whether he desired to offer his amendment now.

Mr. Spalding—Yes, I move to strike out "Alabama" from the bill.

In the course of his remarks Mr. Bingham alluded to "the apostle of the White House."

Mr. Brooks called him to order, but withdrew the point, whereupon Mr. Bingham said perhaps he ought not to have said it.

Mr. Shellabarger asked Mr. Bingham whether the committee found that Florida has conformed to the requirements of the acts of Congress. If so, he was willing to leave the details of the matter not affecting the "loyalty" and safety of the Government to the people, and welcome her back as speedily as possible to the Union.

Mr. Bingham replied that Florida had complied with all the requirements of the

Reconstruction acts, and proceeded with his remarks.

Mr. Spalding, in view of the fact that both branches of Congress had voted in favor of admitting Alabama, withdrew his amendment.

After further debate, the motion to exclude Florida from the Omnibus Bill, was defeated—yeas 45, nays 99.

Messrs. Bromwell, Cobb, Eliot, Farnsworth, Harding, Hopkins, Julian, Maynard, Paine, Pike, Price, Sawyer, Taffe and Washburne, of Illinois, Radicals, voting aye. On concurring in the amendments of the Senate, which was virtually voting on the bill as a whole, the yeas were 111 (all Radicals), nays 28 (all Democrats).

The bill then passed without a division.

VETO OF THE OMNIBUS BILL.

To the House of Representatives:

In returning to the House of Representatives, in which it originated, a bill entitled "An act to admit the States of North Carolina, South Carolina, Georgia, Louisiana and Florida to representation in Congress," I do not deem it necessary to state at length the reasons which constrain me to withhold my approval. I will not, therefore, undertake, at this time, to reopen the discussion upon the grave constitutional questions involved in the act of March 2, 1867, and the acts supplementary thereto, in pursuance of which it is claimed in the preamble of this bill these States have framed and adopted constitutions of State Government Nor will I repeat the objections contained in my message of the 20th inst., returning without my signature the bill to admit to representation the State of Arkansas, and which are equally applicable to the pending measure. Like the bill recently passed in reference to Arkansas, this bill supersedes the plain and simple mode presented by the Constitution for the admission to seats in the respective Houses of Senators and Representatives from the several States.

It assumes authority over six States of the Union, which has never been delegated to Congress, or is even warranted by the previous unconstitutional legislation upon the subject of restoration. It imposes conditions which are in derogation of the equal rights of the States, and is founded upon a theory which is subversive of the fundamental principles of the Government. In the case of Alabama it violates the plighted faith of Congress, by forcing upon that State a Constitution which was rejected by the people, according to the express terms of an act of Congress requiring that a majority of the registered electors should vote upon the question of its ratification. For these objections, and many others that might be presented, I can not approve this bill, and therefore return it for the action of Congress required in such cases by the Federal Constitution.

[Signed] ANDREW JOHNSON.
WASHINGTON, D. C., June 25, 1868.

Referring to the first section of this bill, an able writer in the New York World says:

"Such a condition is not worth the paper on which it is written. The Chicago Convention itself had to confess in its platform that in 'the loyal States' Congress has no right to interfere with the elective franchise. But if it does not possess this right in all the States, it has it in none. We will grant, for the sake of the argument, that the unrepresented States are, to all intents and purposes, nothing but Territories; but it can not be disputed that when they shall have been readmitted, they will be States, standing on the same footing and entitled to the same rights as the others. On what legal or constitutional ground, then, can such a condition be enforced?

"If such a condition can stand at all, it must be on the ground of a compact between particular States, each acting for itself, and the Federal Government. But there is a prior compact of superior obligation to which all the States are parties, and the proposed condition is a violation of that compact. The relations of the States to the Federal Government can not be changed by a compact made by them individually and Congress, but only by amendments to the Constitution, in which three-fourths of the States simultaneously concur. If by a compact with a particular State its relations to the Federal Government can be changed, the rights of every State in the Union may in like manner be changed, and every State be put on a different footing from any of the others. Our Federal system may thus be completely altered and the Constitution abolished by supplanting it in one State at a time by a compact between that State and Congress. A bare majority of Congress and one contracting State may do what two-thirds of Congress and three-fourths of the States are not competent to do by amendments to the Constitution; for when the Constitution is amended in the regular way, the change affects all the States alike.

"This doctrine that a State may change its relations to the Federal Government by compact might not, in the end, bear all the fruits the Republican party expects from it. For, if a State may surrender its constitutional rights by a compact, it may by a subsequent compact regain them. Such a condition as Congress attempts to impose is not only legally null, but practically futile. If Louisiana wishes to make, like Michigan, distinctions founded on race and color, it has only to wait until Congress is Democratic, then by joint consent abrogate this compact. Or, the first Democratic Congress can repeal this restriction, and leave the States as free as they ever were. Or, still again, the States, after their readmission, may amend their constitutions and change the rules of suffrage; and then see what steps even a Republican Congress can take to reverse their action. When they are again in the Union their rights as States will depend on the Constitution, and as the Constitution incontestably permits Ohio and Michigan to exclude negroes from voting, every State that chooses may do the same, unless it can be made to appear that the Constitution uses different language in respect to a part of the States from what it does in respect to the rest. But, in good truth, the perfect equality of the States is the clearest and the most fundamental thing in the Constitution."

A Radical Senator on the Admission of Alabama.

Speech of Mr. Trumbull, of Illinois, in the Senate of the United States, June 8, 1868:

We said to the people of Alabama that the constitution would be adopted only in case a majority of the registered voters take part in the election. Now, after having said that, when there are in Alabama one hundred and seventy thousand registered voters, and only sixty-nine thousand have voted for the constitution, you propose to declare that the constitution of the people of Alabama! One hundred thousand voters did not go to the polls at all, sixty-nine thousand only voted for the constitution, and seventy thousand took part in the election under it. They had a right to stay from the polls; you said so by your law. Having published this law to the people of Alabama, under which they were to reconstruct their State government, and said to them that unless a majority take part in the election on this constitution it was not to be transmitted as the constitution, can you turn around now to-day and say, 'It is the constitution of your State; your people should have known better than to have staid away from the polls?' Here may have been loyal men, good men, to whom it was inconvenient to take part in the election; and how did they reason? They said, "If we do not go to the election our vote counts just the same as if we do go." Now, after you have held this out to them, and said to them that their votes should count the same, you propose to turn around and say, " We will put the constitution upon you at any rate." It is the old Lecompton principle over again. We can not stand upon such a position as that before the country.

Mr. Conners. We can.

Mr. Trumbull. No; my friend from California, and nobody else, in my judgment, can stand before the intelligent people of this country on such a proposition. When we have authorized the people of a State to form a constitution and State government, and have said to them that that constitution was to be adopted only in case a majority of their registered voters took part in its formation, I do not think we can afterward turn around and adopt that constitution as the fundamental law of that State, when only a minority, less by thirty thousand than those not voting, have taken part in the formation of the constitution.

It has been repeatedly said on this floor that a larger number in proportion voted for the constitution in Alabama than elsewhere. I will correct that. I have here the official report, which will be found in Executive document No. 53, which is a "letter of the General of the Army of the United States, communicating, in compliance with a resolution of the Senate of December 5, 1867, a statement of the number of white and colored voters registered in each of the States subject to the Reconstruction acts of Congress, with other statistics relative to the same subject." The first State to which I will turn the attention of the Senate is North Carolina. In the State of North Carolina, according to this official report, there were registered 179,653 votes, half of which is 89,826. According to this official report from the General of the Army, it appears that in North Carolina there were cast for the constitution 92,500 votes. More than one-half of all the registered voters voted for the constitution in North Carolina, so that even if the law never had been changed, North Carolina adopted the constitution by those who voted affirmatively in its favor. There were cast against the constitution in North Carolina 71,820 votes, so that one hundred and sixty-four thousand voted on the question, and a majority of all the registered voters in North Carolina voted for the constitution. Now, I ask the Senator from Ohio and the Senator from Nevada, if they are satisfied that a larger proportion voted in North Carolina for the constitution than did in Alabama according to the vote? Do they "give it up" in reference to North Carolina? It was but a moment ago it was stated by both these Senators that there was a larger vote cast for the constitution in Alabama than in any other State. I show you by the official vote, that a majority of all the registered voters voted for the constitution in North Carolina. Now, what becomes of that misstatement?

Mr. Sherman. When the Senator is

through, and does not address himself in that way, I will reply to him. I have the facts before me.

Mr. TRUMBULL. Well, if there is any other official statement, I should be glad to see it. I read from this Executive document. Now I will read as to South Carolina. According to the official report, which I hold in my hand, there were in the State of South Carolina 127,432 registered voters. The half of 127,432 is 63,716. There were cast for the constitution in the State of South Carolina, according to an official report from the General of the Army, made the 12th day of May, 1868, 70,758 votes; so that in South Carolina there were cast 7,042 votes, more than half of the registered voters, in favor of the constitution, and the constitution was therefore ratified by a majority of all the registered voters of South Carolina; so that if the law never had been changed, the constitution would have been adopted by the voters of that State.

I next come to the State of Georgia. In the State of Georgia, according to this same official report made from the headquarters of the Third Military District, by Major General Meade, there were 191,501 registered voters; the half of which is 95,750. There were cast for the constitution in Georgia, according to the same official authority, 89,007 votes, which, deducted from 95,750, half of all the registered voters, shows that less than half voted for the constitution in Georgia by 6,743, but not so great a proportion less as in Alabama. In Alabama the difference between the vote for the constitution and half of the registered voters was 13,099, while in Georgia, with a much larger registered vote, the difference was only 6,743, so that the State of Georgia adopted her constitution by a much larger vote in proportion than was cast for the constitution in the State of Alabama. There were cast against the constitution in Georgia, at the same time, seventy-one thousand votes, so that there voted on the question, in the State of Georgia, one hundred and sixty thousand.

I come next to the State of Louisiana. It appears by this same official report that there were in the State of Louisiana, 129,654 registered voters; one-half of that number would be 64,827. There were cast for the constitution in Louisiana 66,152 votes. A majority of all the registered voters of the State voted for the constitution, a majority of 1,325, so that the constitution of Louisiana was adopted by an actual majority of all the registered votes, leaving out the large vote which was cast against the constitution in that State, being 48,739.

I come next to the State of Florida. In the State of Florida, according to the registration, there were 28,003 votes, one half of which is 14,001; and there were cast for the constitution, according to the report from the General of the Army, 14,511 votes, which is a majority of 510 votes of all the registered voters of the State.

Thus, it is seen, that in every State except Georgia an actual majority of all the registered voters voted for the constitution. In the State of Georgia it only lacked 6,743 of being a majority of all the votes voting for it, and one hundred and sixty thousand voters in Georgia voted on the question. Now, what becomes of the statement made in the Senate, in order to induce the Senate to adopt a constitution for the people of the State of Alabama, which was only carried by a minority vote, that that constitution had more votes in its favor than the constitution in any other of these reconstructed States? The gentlemen have labored under a misapprehension in their zeal and their anxiety to have these States recognized, which is no greater than mine. I am as anxious for the early recognition of these States as any member upon this floor; but I can not consent to violate fundamental principles; I can not consent to force upon the people of any State by a minority vote a fundamental law; I can not consent to break the faith of this nation for the purpose of bringing Alabama into this bill.

With all these facts before us, how is it that the State of Alabama is to be forced in here to embarrass the bill under consideration? We have a bill here embracing five States, North Carolina, South Carolina, Louisiana, Georgia and Florida, each one of which has ratified its constitution in accordance with the law.

What is Sauce for Goose not Sauce for Gander.

"There is associated with Mr. Stevens, on this impeachment, one John A. Bingham, of Ohio. Mr. Bingham is the Member of Congress from Ohio who lately introduced the bill into the House of Representatives declaring the constitution of Alabama adopted, notwithstanding its defeat at the polls, and thereupon admitting the State into the Union.

"Mr. Bingham was a Member of Congress when the Convention of Kansas, at Lecompton, sent a constitution on which they asked admission into the Union.

"Mr. Bingham was a violent opponent of the admission of Kansas, under that constitution, because it did not emanate from the people of Kansas, and its seeming adoption was procured by Federal interference with elections. He declared that:

"'The monstrous proposition is now

made by the President, and by gentlemen on this floor, to establish this instrument as the constitution of Kansas, by act of Congress, and against the will of the people of that territory; so in the first time in the history of the Republic that the attempt has been made to establish, by Federal authority, a State constitution, against the will of the people, and without their consent. State constitutions have been framed and sent to Congress for ratification without any formal submission thereof to the popular vote; but it was only in cases where the people, beyond all question, made the constitution by their legally appointed delegates.'

"In descanting upon Kansas, he describes Alabama now as faithfully as any unreconstructed white man on the spot could do He said:

"'The delegates who framed this instrument were chosen by a body of men not equal in number to one-fourth the whole number of qualified voters in Kansas, and by virtue of an election law passed by usurpers.

"'The constitution thus framed is the joint production of local and Federal usurpation.

"'But for Federal intervention the delegates to the Lecompton Convention would never have been chosen. But for Federal intervention and the presence of Federal bayonets at Lecompton, those delegates would not have thus conspired against the liberties, and insulted the majority of the people.

"'Sir, It is not the first time that acts of tyranny have been dignified with the title of peace measures. The invader has before now destroyed the vintage, enslaved the people, plundered and burnt their habitations, and called the devastation which followed in the train of his conquest, peace.'

"Insert Alabama and Montgomery wherever Kansas and Lecompton occur, and this is the true picture of the Radicalism of Alabama, of which this same Mr. Bingham is the selected champion in Congress in the forcing of a rejected constitution by act of Congress on an unwilling people.

"He then maintained boldly, in language which would now subject any conservative man within these ten States to the peril of military arrest for inciting sedition, that such an action by Congress would justify armed resistance. He grew vehement on this subject, and thus confronted the majority and the Executive, who had shown the desire to force the constitution on a despondent and reluctant people:

"'Sanction this constitution, conceived in sin and brought forth in iniquity, and you can only maintain it by the Federal arm and the Federal bayonet. It can never receive the voluntary support of a free people. Sanction this constitution, and with it sanction, as it sanctions, that code of abominations which the invaders of Kansas enacted, and you would compel *resistance.* Resistance to such legislation would be DUTY, NOT CRIME: PATRIOTISM, NOT TREASON!'"

Senator Doolittle on the Way it will Work.

In a recent speech in New Jersey, Senator Doolittle said:

"What is this constitution that comes up from the State of Arkansas? It contains a clause of disfranchisement of which I will presently speak. It contains something more; it contains a test-oath, which is to be put to every man as he approaches the ballot-box, requiring him to swear that he accepts political equality of all men, civil and political equality of all men, meaning the right of franchise in the negro equally with the white man; in the Chinese, the Coolie, and the Indian, as well as the white man. When he goes to the ballot-box in Arkansas, before he can deposit his ballot he must lay his hands upon the Holy Book and swear that he accepts this dogma of political equality, and swear further that he will never undertake to make any distinction in political rights between the races on account of race or color. Now, fellow-citizens of New Jersey, how does this bear upon you and upon your children? You have the right to emigrate to Arkansas if you please; so have your sons; and if the majority of the people of New Jersey (for I have no doubt that there is a majority of fifteen or twenty thousand, if not more, in the State of New Jersey who reject this doctrine—(applause)—this dogma of the political equality of the races—if you were to emigrate to the State of Arkansas you would be disfranchised. You could never vote at all unless you go to the polls and swear that you accept political equality for the negroes and Indians, and swear that you will never undertake to make any distinction between negroes and Indians. I ask you, is it right? Is it constitutional? Is it just that any such test-oath as that which would exclude from the polls in Arkansas the majority of the electors of New Jersey, or the electors of New York; the majority of the electors of Connecticut—(applause)—the majority of the electors of Ohio—(great applause)—the majority of the electors of Michigan, and a majority, I believe, of ten thousand of the electors of Wisconsin? (Applause.) By this oath in Arkansas they would be excluded from the right to exercise the ballot. Why, fellow-citizens, these Radicals are almost equal to

Napoleon III, when he wanted to be elected Emperor, "You can vote for whom you please, but you must vote for Napoleon." "You may vote for whom you please, but, if you vote at all, you must swear that you believe in our dogma." Now, fellow-citizens, is this just; is it in accordance with the first principles of civil liberty that such a test-oath is to be applied to a man before he is allowed to exercise the right of franchise? You might just as well apply to him a religious test, and make him swear that he is not a Catholic, and never will be a Catholic, or that he is not a Protestant, and never will be a Protestant." (Applause.)

A Glorious Harvest for the Carpet-baggers.

ANTECEDENTS OF THE GOVERNORS, SENATORS AND CONGRESSMEN OF THE ROTTEN BOROUGHS, WITH THEIR NATIVITY—BY WHOM THE SOUTH IS TO BE GOVERNED.

The editor is indebted to the Cincinnati *Commercial* for the greater part of the following information:

STATE OFFICERS.

The seven States which have been re-admitted to representation in Congress have elected Radical Governors and Legislatures, and their principal State officers are as follows:

GOVERNOR.	LIEUT.-GOVERNOR.
Alabama......Wm. H. Smith,	A. J. Applegate.
Arkansas......Powell Clayton,	Jas. M. Johnson.
Florida......Harrison Reed,	Wm. H. Gleason.
Georgia......R. B. Bullock,	[None].
Louisiana......H. C. Warmouth,	Oscar J. Dunn.
North Carolina...Wm. W. Hold-n,	Tod R. Caldwell.
South Carolina...Robert K. Scott,	Lemuel Boozer.

Governors Smith and Holden are natives of their States, and were Union men during the war. Governor Bullock is a native of New York. Governor Clayton is a native of Pennsylvania, and was an officer of Kansas troops. Governor Reed was formerly a Wisconsin editor. Governor Warmouth is a native of Illinois, and was an officer of Missouri troops. Governor Scott is a native of Pennsylvania, and was an officer of Ohio troops.

Of the Lieutenant-Governors, Johnson, Dunn, Caldwell and Boozer are Southern born, and Lieutenant-Governor Dunn is a colored man. Applegate went from Indiana, and Gleason from Wisconsin.

UNITED STATES SENATORS.

Arkansas and Florida, of the seven States, have elected United States Senators.

The Arkansas Senators are Benjamin F. Rice, formerly of Minnesota, elected for the term ending in 1871, and Alexander McDonald, formerly of Kansas, elected for the term ending in 1869.

The Florida Senators are Mr. A. S. Welch, originally from Michigan, where he was a Professor in the University of that State, and subsequently served in the Union army during the war; the other is T. W. Osborn, of New York, formerly of General Howard's staff.

Florida has elected a third Senator to succeed Mr. Welch, on the 4th of March 1869, for the term ending 4th of March 1865. His name is Abijah Gilbert. Gilbert is a New Yorker; nothing known about him—not a citizen (as we infer). Is said to be rich, and supposed to have "come down" handsomely for the post. It was said, among other things, he had engaged to advance $90,000 for $100,000 in Convention scrip to pay the mileage and per diem of the whites and negroes who elected him. Florida (says the *Floridan*) is in the hands of the Philistines, and we wish, for the sake of Florida, it were true; but her case, we fear, is a good deal worse than that.

The South Carolina Senators are likely to be Dr. A. G. Mackey, of Charleston, and Thomas J. Robinson, of Columbia, both old residents and Unionists during the war.

The North Carolina Senators are likely to be General J. C. Abbott, of Wilmington, formerly of New Hampshire and commander of a volunteer regiment from that State; and Mr. Pool, a native of the State.

In Georgia, the names most mentioned are those of Foster Blodgett, Henry P. Farrow, ex-Governor Joseph E. Brown, and J. L. Dunning.

The Louisiana Senators are Colonel William P. Kellogg, Collector of the Port of New Orleans, formerly of Illinois; and J. S. Harris of Michigan.

REPRESENTATIVES IN CONGRESS.

The Representatives elect are twenty-eight Republicans and five Democrats (the latter designated by stars), as follows:

Arkansas—First District, Logan H. Roots, of Duvall's Bluff, a native of Illinois, and officer of volunteers. Second James Hinds, of Little Rock, formerly of Minnesota. Third, Thomas Bolles, of Dardanelle, an old resident and Circuit Judge.

Alabama—First District, Francis W. Kellogg, of Mobile, formerly Representative in Congress from Michigan, 1859 to 1865, and since 1865, Collector of Internal Revenue at Mobile. Second, Charles W. Buckley, of Hayneville, formerly of Freeport, Illinois; Valedictorian at Beloit College in 1860; graduated at Union Theological Seminary; appointed chaplain in the army, and subsequently Assistant Superintendent of Freedmen in Alabama. Third, Benjamin W. Norris, of Montgomery, formerly of Maine, chairman of the Republican Central Committee of Alabama. Fourth, Charles W. Pierce, of Demopolis. Fifth, Joseph W. Burke, of Huntsville. Sixth, Thomas Haughey, of Decatur.

Florida—Charles M. Hamilton, formely of Wisconsin.

Georgia—First District, J. W. Clift, of Savannah, formerly of Massachusetts, and a surgeon of Volunteers. Second, *Nelson Tift. Third, William P. Edwards, of Butler, Taylor county, a native of Georgia and a lawyer. Fourth, Samuel F. Gove, of Griswoldville, Twiggs county, formerly of Massachusetts (born in Weymouth) and an officer of volunteers. Fifth, Charles H. Prince, of Augusta, a native of Buckfield, Maine, and late Captain of volunteers. Sixth, *John H. Christy. Seventh, *P. M. B. Young.

Louisiana—First District, J. Hale Sypher, of New Orleans, a native of Pennsylvania; commanded a Pennsylvania battery and afterward the Eleventh United States colored artillery. Second, *James Mann, of New Orleans, formerly of Bangor, Maine; a paymaster of volunteers, now a special agent of internal revenue. Election contested by Colonel Simon Jones, Radical. Third, Joseph P. Newsham of West Feliciana; member of the convention. Fourth, Michael Vidal, of St. Landry, native born, of French lineage; editor of the St. Landry Progress; member of the convention. Fifth, W. Jasper Blackburn, of Homer, Claiborne county; editor of the Iliad; formerly of Tennessee.

North Carolina—First District, John R. French, of Chowan, a native of Gilmanton, New Hampshire; editor of the Concord Herald of Freedom, the early organ of New Hampshire Free-soilers; subsequently editor of the Painesville (Ohio) Press; paymaster of volunteers; late Tax Commissioner of North Carolina. Second, David Heaton, of Craven, formerly editor of the Middletown (Ohio) Herald; member of the Ohio Senate; subsequently of the Minnesota Senate. Third, Oliver H. Dockery, of Richmond. Fourth, John T. Dewees, of Raleigh; formerly a Colonel of Indiana volunteers, late Second Lieutenant in the Eighth United States Infantry; more recently Register in Bankruptcy for the Raleigh District. Fifth, Israel G. Lash, of Forsyth. Sixth, *Nathaniel Boyden, of Salisbury; native of Massachusetts; resided in North Carolina since 1821, and represented that State in Congress in 1847–49. Seventh, Alexander H. Jones, of Buncombe; editor of the Asheville Progress; a native of Carolina, and Unionist throughout the war; confined in Libby prison.

South Carolina—First District, Benjamin F. Whittemore, of Darlington, formerly of Massachusetts, a clergyman and Freedmen's Bureau agent. Second, C. C. Bowen, of Charleston, a native of Rhode Island; has long resided in the South, and (it is claimed by compulsion) served for a time in the Confederate army. Third, Simon Corley, of Lexington, a native of South Carolina; non-combatant, in the war. Fourth, James H. Goss, of Unionville, a native of South Carolina; non-combatant in the war. At large, two additional Representatives elected by order of the convention, viz.: J. P. M. Epping, of Charleston, a native of North Carolina, now United States Marshal; Elias S. Dickson, of Clarendon, a native of South Carolina.

Mississippi—Constitution defeated in this State. The Radical candidates:

GOVERNOR—Beroth B. Eggleston.
LIEUTENANT GOVERNOR—Andrew J. Jamison.
SECRETARY OF STATE—Robert J. Alcorn.
TREASURER—Duncan McA. Williams.
AUDITOR—William J. Morgan.
ATTORNEY GENERAL—Joshua S. Morris.
SUPERINTENDENT OF PUBLIC INSTRUCTION—Charles W. Clarke.
REPRESENTATIVES IN CONGRESS—Jeff. L. Wofford, Jehiel Railsback, Charles A. Sullivan, George C. McKee, Legrand W. Perce.

For Governor—Eggleston is formerly of Ohio, and was President of the late Constitutional Convention.

Of the other Radical candidates—Jamison is a South Carolinian, and Alcorn a Kentuckian, both resident in Mississippi before the war; Morris is a Mississippian, Morgan is a native of New York, and commanded a Union regiment raised under Fremont's authority in Missouri and Arkansas in 1861. McKee was formerly of Centralia, Illinois, and an officer of the Eleventh Illinois (Ransom's) Regiment. The anomaly exists that while General Wofford, a Confederate officer, is the Republican candidate for Congress in the Corinth District, his Democratic opponent is Lieutenant Townsend, formerly of Wisconsin.

The Virginia election should have begun on Tuesday, June 2, but General Schofield, the then military commander, announced that the reconstruction fund for the First District was exhausted, and by his order the election was postponed until Congress should have made an appropriation to pay expenses.

General Wells the Radical candidate for Governor, is the present incumbent for that office, appointed by General Schofield. He was formerly of Michigan, and as an army officer was Military Governor of Alexandria during the war. Since the war he has resided at Alexandria.

The Kind of Senators and Representatives they send to Congress.

"Oh shame where is thy blush!"

It would be as sensible to send for a lot of accomplished burglars, and give them free access with their "jimmies and picks" to the Treasury vaults, as to send some of the men to the Senate and House, we read of:

A PRETTY PAIR OF SENATORS—ANTECEDENTS OF McDONALD, U. S. SENATOR FROM ARKANSAS.—If other arguments were wanting, the bad character of the carpet-bag Senators foisted upon the people of Arkansas, would condemn the whole Radical policy of reconstruction. The exploits of B. F. Rice, one of those Senators, who left Kentucky under the most disgraceful circumstances, are hereafter narrated. That the other Senator is a proper yoke-fellow for such a creature is evident from the following statements, which we find in the Washington correspondence of the New York *Herald*:

"Hon. A. McDonald, Republican Senator elect from Arkansas, is not altogether unknown to the distinguished body of officials among whom he claims a seat. The honorable claimant was a member of the firm of McDonald, Fuller & Sells, Indian contractors. In the Senate debate upon transferring the Indian Bureau to the Interior to the War Department, Senator Sherman read a portion of the statement showing up some of that firm's operations, little thinking that an embryo United States Senator was in the case. The official records of the first session of the Thirty ninth Congress contain the following — (See *Globe*, part 4, page 3,552). Senator Sherman said:

"'I will read an extract from a memorial, signed by a portion of the Cherokees. I am not responsible for the facts here stated, but as they are presented regularly to us by them in a written memorial, complaining of certain grievances, I read their statements as alleged facts. If they are true, they certainly require some investigation.

"'By the act of March 3, 1865, the Secretary of War was authorized to feed and clothe the pauper Indians in the Indian Territory, from the date of the passage of the law until the end of that fiscal year. On July 1, 1865, when the military authorities ceased to have authority to feed refugee Indians, there was an immense surplus of flour and corn on hand at Fort Gibson, amounting to as much as all that has since been issued to pauper Indians in that country. These stores the commanding officer at Fort Gibson offered to turn over to the Superintendent of Indian Affairs at $8 50 per barrel for flour, and $2 per bushel for corn. Instead of making this purchase, the Superintendent went to Leavenworth and entered into a contract with McDonald, Fuller & Sells (the son of the Superintendent) at $8 per bushel for the corn, and $34 per barrel for flour. This contract was let, as we are informed, and believe, without the requisite advertisement, on the pretence that there was not time to advertise. The most of the flour furnished under this contract was sent by a steamboat from St. Louis, costing the contractors about $12, and the Indian Department $34 per barrel, while a large amount of the flour offered by the War Department to the Interior at $8 per barrel was being shipped down the Arkansas from Fort Gibson to Little Rock. The corn furnished by the contractors under this contract was part bought from the Indians at $2 per bushel, and part bought of the military authorities at Fort Gibson by one McKee, who is understood to have been the agent and partner of McDonald, Fuller & Sells, at eighteen cents per bushel, and turned over to the Superintendent at $8 per bushel. The gross amount of these supplies we are unable to state, but are satisfied that it was several hundred thousand dollars, and we have information that it has all or nearly all been paid.'

"'I do not wish to read any more from the various allegations made by these Indians. I only read this much to show that when the War Department is charged with a certain portion of the duties connected with our intercourse with the Indians, and the Interior Department with another portion, there will necessarily be a conflict of jurisdiction and great complaints of fraud and peculation. This certainly is a very serious charge which is alleged by these Indians. It is that the Government actually being in possession of a large amount of stores and property through the War Department, which offered to turn them over to the Interior Department—corn at $2 a bushel and flour at $8 50 a barrel—the Interior Department, instead of taking them, purchased flour at $34 a barrel and corn at $8 a bushel. It seems to me that if this kind of transactions can go on under this system of mixed responsibility it is time we should put a stop to it.

"I have looked the record through in vain to find any satisfactory explanation or defense against these charges. Senator Doolittle stated that the amount thus purchased was 'for a very small supply, which the superintendent deemed necessary to take with him.' The charge of buying corn of the Government for eighteen cents per bushel, and selling it back again at $8 per bushel, is not even noticed.

"Besides the ability to drive a sharp bargain with Uncle Sam and the Indians, I am not informed of Mr. McDonald's other qualifications; but the War Department records would, if examined, throw a little light. The Leavenworth *Times*, the leading Republican paper of Kansas, has the following, with which I close for the present:

"'We are both astonished and mortified to see some of the Republican presses of Kansas, claiming to occupy a conspicuous place in the ranks of the organization, indulging in fulsome and extravagant adulations of Mr. A. McDonald, who has recently been elected one of the Senators from the State of Arkansas. If any one of the journals referred to know Mr. McDonald at all, they know he is utterly unqualified for the high position of United States Senator. The very proposition is ridiculous, and it lowers the character of the profession, for leading newspapers to hold up a man for what he is not, and can never become. Hon. A. McDonald, United States Senator from Arkansas! If that isn't enough to make a horse laugh, nothing ever was.

McDonald's Colleague.

Benjamin F. Rice, one of the so-called Arkansas United States Senators elect, must be a lovely specimen from a Radical, judging from the following document, which has just come to light:

"Irvine, December 23, 1859.

"Dear Sir: I received your letter inquiring if I was dead or run away. I am neither. I settled all your business in Tennessee and got the money, and intended to be at your court and pay it, but before the time arrived I got on a spree and gambled off over $5,000; and hence can not send you any money at this time, but will make every effort to raise it as soon as possible.

"Yours, etc.,
"BEN. F. RICE."
"Henry Haggard."

Senator Ben. will doubtless make his mark in the Senate—when there are pickings and stealings to be disposed of.

A Specimen Representative.

"Data," the Washington correspondent of the Baltimore *Sun*, tells, as follows, of a specimen "representative" from Arkansas. The creature has not been in the State long enough to know the counties in his district:

"During the debate in the Senate to-day, several of the carpet-bag Representatives from Arkansas and the other States, occupied seats on the floor. One of these gentlemen, an enterprising and indefatigable Yankee, was in this city less than five months ago, and boasted that he was going down to Arkansas to get a good office. He now comes back elected to the House of Representatives, and, with his colleagues, is very anxious to commence the pleasant pastime of drawing $5,000 a year, with nothing to do. There has been quite an influx of the Southern loyalists this week, and Senators have no rest for them."

How a Governor is Ejected by Force.

His Offense, the Exercise of the Freedom of Speech.

At the recent election in Mississippi, Governor Humphreys was nominated for re-election by the Democratic party of the State. He took the stump, and with a becoming temperance and firmness which is characteristic of him, canvassed the State in opposition to the ratification of the rotten borough Constitution. The new military ruler, McDowell, who had just ascended the throne, wishing to recommend himself, without delay, to the esteem of the Radical revolutionists, deemed this exercise of the right of discussion by the Governor a criminal impediment to reconstruction, whereupon he issued the following order:

Headquarters Fourth Military District, (Mississippi and Arkansas,)
Vicksburg, Miss., June 15, 1868.

General Orders, No. 23.]

1. Major-General Adelbert Ames is appointed, temporarily, Provisional Governor of the State of Mississippi, *vice* Benjamin G. Humphreys, hereby removed.

2. Captain Jasper Myers is appointed, temporarily, Attorney-General of the State of Mississippi, *vice* C. E. Hooker, hereby removed.

3. The officers appointed as above will repair without delay to Jackson, and enter immediately upon the duties of their respective offices. They will receive no other compensation than their pay and allowances as officers of the army.

By command of Brevet Major-General McDowell.

JOHN TYLER,
First Lieut. Forty-third Infantry, Brevet Major U. S. Army, Act. Ass't Adjutant-General.

Official: NAT. WOLF,
Second Lieut. Thirty-fourth Infantry, Acting Ass't Adjutant-General.

Upon being officially informed by General Ames, says the Vicksburg *Times* of the 24th, of his removal from office, he promptly refused to surrender the seal and archieves of the State, or to retire from his position as the legal and constitutional Chief Magistrate of Mississippi. The information of his refusal was at once communicated to the headquarters of General McDowell, and orders were immediately transmitted to Colonel Biddle, commandant of the post at Jackson, to eject the Governor from his office by military force! Upon receipt of the order, Colonel Biddle called upon Governor Humphreys and demanded possession of the Executive office, which was again refused. Colonel Biddle then arrested the Governor, while armed men took possession of the Executive office, and now hold it. Governor Humphreys was subsequently released from arrest.

This simple recital needs no words from us to add to the enormity of the crime that has been perpetrated, or to stir the indignation that must swell the heart of every man that was born free! The foul outrage has been consummated, and the chosen chief of the people of Mississippi has been struck down in his high place. The capitol of the State has been polluted by armed soldiers, and the person of its Chief Magistrate outraged. Comment is unnecessary. This last act of wrong and oppression will rouse the whole nation, for if the Governor of Mississippi may be driven from office to-day by bayonets, what shall prevent the same outrage from being perpetrated in New York to-morrow.

At a later date the Governor and his family were expelled by bayonets from the Executive mansion.

Soothing Effects of Radical Restoration.
GENERAL GRANT SNUBBED AND DEFIED—THE BIG GUNS AND THE CAVALRY CALLED OUT.

The Omnibus bill was to give that peace to the States which Grant says, "let us have." To propitiate the favor of all Radicalism, particularly that of those States, he did not wait for the regular birth of the new power; but he sent orders to most of them, installing the elect by military orders to act until they regularly came into official existence, and to hurry up the processes which he fondly hopes will result in the rotten boroughs voting for him for the next Presidency, majority or no majority.

In Louisiana he caught, by his own act, one negro tartar, and incidentally came in possession of another of the same *genus homo.* He ordered the installation in advance of Lieutenant-Governor Dunn, a negro, of Louisiana.

We give the New York *Tribune's* report of what transpired.

"NEW ORLEANS, June 29.

The Louisiana Legislature convened to-day. The Senate was called to order by Lieutenant-Governor Dunn. The temporary Secretary was ordered to read General Buchanan's order promulgating General Grant's order removing Governor Baker and Lieutenant-Governor Voorhees, and appointing Warmouth and Dunn Provisional Governor and Lieutenant-Governor in their stead; also, Governor Warmouth's order convening the Legislature. The roll was called from General Buchanan's order announcing the names of those who had been elected. Thirty-four members answered. The Clerk also read General Grant's order to General Buchanan, approving the action of the latter in relation to the municipal officers, suggesting that only the oath prescribed by the new constitution be required of the newly-elected officers. Lieutenant-Governor Dunn announced that he was not prepared to comply with General Grant's suggestions, but he would require the test oath to be administered. The Democrats appealed. It was argued that the presiding officer had no authority to prescribe any oath whatever; that the Legislature was convened under the new constitution, and that no other oath than the one therein specified, could be demanded. It was moved to refer the question to the commanding General. Lieutenant-Governor Dunn ruled that, until the members had qualified, no appeal could be taken or motion offered, and he ordered the roll-call for the members, who could do so, to come forward and take the test oath as their names were called. The Democratic members entered a protest, and refused to take the oath; several asserting their ability to do so, but denying the right to demand it. Nineteen, a bare quorum, took the test oath; after which the constitutional oath was administered. A Committee on Credentials and Elections was appointed, and several contests for seats were referred to them. An adjournment was then carried, until to-morrow at noon. After the adjournment, a throng of negroes surrounded the presiding officer, to offer their congratulations. Four of the Senators are full negroes, and several are of mixed blood.

The House was called to order by Colonel Bachelder, of General Buchanan's staff, who called the roll. R. H. Isabell, a negro, was elected temporary Chairman. He took the test oath on taking his seat, and announced, in reply to a protest, that no member, who could not take the test oath, could take his seat. Fifty-three, a quorum, took the required oath, the majority of the Democrats retiring. A Committee on Elections was appointed. The Legislature then adjorned until to-morrow. Mr. Millan (Rep.) entered a protest against the recognition of the authority of General Buchanan to interfere in the organization of the House, and made some remarks, concluding as follows:

"And when this House is once organized, then I desire to announce to Colonel Bachelder and to General Buchanan, commanding, and to the United States Army at large, if necessary, that all interference on the part of the army must cease."

The proportion of negroes in the House is greater than in the Senate.

SECOND DAY'S PROCEEDINGS—THE COLORED LEGISLATORS STILL FIRM.

NEW ORLEANS, June 30.

At the meeting of the Senate to-day only the names of those who took the test oath, yesterday, were called. All answered. Dan. Bolly (Dem.) said his name was not called. The Chair replied that other gentlemen were present, whose names were not called, who had not interrupted business during the reading of the minutes. Mr. Jewell, of New Orleans, demanded the reading of a communication, which he knew was in the possession of the presiding officer, relative to the oath to be taken by Senators. No attention was paid to the demand. After some difficulty, order was restored, and the reading of the minutes concluded.

The Committee on Elections reported that Hugh J. Campbell (Radical) was entitled to the seat from the Second District, in place of Anthony. Sam. Bolla was declared elected by Gen. Buchanan. The Committee deny the right of Gen. Buchanan to change the Register's return. Mr. Campbell was sworn in. No Democratic member could obtain recognition from the Chair. On motion of Mr. Allen, the Democratic address to the Senate was tabled.

The Chair then handed a communication to the Secretary, which he directed to be read. It proved to be an order addressed to O. J. Dunn, Lieutenant-Governor, the presiding officer of the Senate, communicating a telegram from Gen. Grant to Gen. Buchanan.

"I have no orders at present to give, but I repeat to you, as heretofore, that the members of the Louisiana Legislature are only required to take the oath prescribed by their constitution, and are not required to take the test oath prescribed in the Reconstruction acts. Generals Meade and Canby are acting on this view of the case. U. S. GRANT."

General Buchanan directs that the oath prescribed by the constitution, and no other, be required.

A copy of Gen. Grant's telegram was read in the House, and referred to a committee.

The Committee on Elections reported adversely to the entire Democratic delegation from Caddo parish, whose names appear in the election order, and the Republican members were accordingly admitted.

Adjourned.

The City Comptroller, Sheriff, and District Attorney elect, have taken possession of their offices, under Gen. Buchanan's order of Saturday, taking the constitutional oath.

Mr. Isabell, negro, temporary Speaker of the House, to-day, after Gen. Buchanan's order was read, said that in his opinion the House could decide what kind of test oath was necessary for the admission of members, and that for his part he would not accept any order from Gen. Grant or Gen. Buchanan upon the subject.

THIRD DAY'S PROCEEDINGS—ORDER PRESERVED BY THE MILITARY.

NEW ORLEANS, July 1.

This morning before the hour for the assembling of the Legislature, a section of artillery and a squadron of cavalry prepared for service occupied Lafayette Square. Two companies of the First Infantry, commanded by Capt. Veile, occupied the sidewalk fronting Mechanics' Institute, and a large body of police were on duty in and around the buildings. No one was allowed to approach who could not give good account of his business. Appearances indicated that trouble was expected. Col. Gentry and Gen. Neil, of Gen. Buchanan's staff, were also present.

Fifteen Democratic Senators took constitutional oaths. Several motions were offered, when Mr. Lynch called attention to article 150 of the constitution, which states that no action of any kind can be taken by the Legislature until action upon the fourteenth amendment has been had.

The Committee on Elections were discharged, that a new one might be appointed, in which the Democratic side might be represented.

Mr. Lambola will probably take his seat to-morrow, and contests for seats will proceed regularly.

The House proceedings were of a similar nature, but showed more oppositon to dispensing with the test oath. Only the names of those who had previously taken the test oath were called on assembling. Subsequently, when the roll was called, of those elected who had not qualified, but three qualified under the constitution, but more will probably do so to-morrow.

The House permanently organized by the election of Chas. W. Lowell (white) for Speaker, and adopted a joint resolution ratifying the fourteenth amendment, by 57 yeas to 3 nays.

A resolution was offered by Pope W. Noble, one of the three Democrats who qualified that the roll of members as returned by

Gen. Buchanan, be called and the members qualified whether their seats are contested or not, was tabled.

It was resolved by the House that those not disqualified by the fourteenth amendment, or article 96 of the constitution, or whose seats are not contested, be allowed to take seats.

How Reconstruction was Worked in the States.

How the Negroes Voted in Alabama.

We copy as follows from a letter to the New York *World*, dated at Montgomery:

"And now to another point. It is generally supposed, and perhaps you, O reader! have the impression that this Alabama 'election' was conducted on the plan of the registration prescribed by 'acts' of Congress. If so, disabuse your mind at once. By the ordinance, hereinbefore alluded to, of the Black Crook Convention, ratified by General Pope, this registration was practically nullified by the following provision:

"'Any registered voter of the State who may have removed from the county in which he was registered, shall be permitted to vote in the county to which he has removed, upon making affidavit before a member of the Board of Registration, or a judge of election, that he was registered, naming the county in which he was registered, and that he has not voted at this election.'

"Something like a third of the entire vote cast in the State was received on no better evidence than these affidavits, and for my own part, I saw several administered. This was the process.

"Enter Timbuctoo:
"'What's your name?'
"'Pomp.'
"'Pomp what?'
"'Pomp Jones, sah.'
"'Show your ticket,' and a great paw would reach out of a ragged sleeve, and thrust a dirty scrap under the judge's nose. No such name as given would be found upon the list, and then would come the balance of the formality. I quote from the printed document:

"'I, ———— ————, do solemnly swear that I am duly registered as a qualified voter in the county of ————, in this State; that I now reside in this county, and that I have not voted at this election, so help me God.'

"Pomp, or Cuff, or Cudjo, would swallow it all, meekly taking off his hat as he was bidden, and holding up his hand and nodding like a toy mandarin at every other word in the oath. In would go his vote; and now take him out and ask him what 'solemnly' meant, or 'qualified,' or 'reside,' and Pomp's big mouth would open and his eyes would stretch, and nine in ten would tell you 'Fore God, mas'r, I dunno nuffin 'bout all dis yer, but dey tole us we mus' come up and put de ting in de box or dey would fine us or put us in de jail.' If this be thought exaggeration, attend, O skeptic! the next 'election' in a Southern State. Don't be afraid of the negroes. Go right among them, talk to them, look at them, watch them vote, and then put them to the question and see where all your preconceived ideas of God's image in ebony would be. Entitled these people are, of course, to the equal protection of the law, and even more than equal protection, just in proportion as they are weak, ignorant and easily deluded; but to give them political power is to intrust the destinies of America to a race with the brawn of gladiators and the brains of little boys."

Negro Rule.

A correspondent asks us, says the New York *World*, to give the vote on the bogus Southern constitutions in detail. We are only able, at this writing, to do so in the case of one State, thus:

	Registered Vote.		For "Constitution."	
	White.	Negro.	White.	Negro.
Alabama	61,295	104,518	5,802	62,089
				5,802

Negro majority 57,287

By which our correspondent will see that the loil constitution is a negro constitution, to the extent of a majority of 57,287.

With regard to six other of the Southern States, we are enabled to give, from official sources, the vote in detail on the question of "convention," a matter having direct bearing on the query put us, since the vote calling these "conventions" is, in effect, the vote creating the "constitutions" framed by them:

	Registered Vote.		"For Convention."	
	White.	Negro.	White.	Negro.
Georgia	96,333	95,168	32,000	70,283
Florida	11,914	16,089	1,220	13,080
North Carolina	106,721	72,932	31,284	61,722
South Carolina	46,882	80,550	2,350	68,418
Texas	59,633	43,497	7,757	36,032
Virginia	120,101	105,832	14,835	92,507
Total	441,584	420,068	89,446	340,942
				89,446

Negro majority 251,496

From these exhibits our correspondent will see how emphatically reconstruction is a rebuilding of the State governments of the South on a basis of absolute negro supremacy.

Registration Figures.

General Grant's communication to the Senate incloses reports from district commanders. General Schofield's report gives the whole number of voters registered in Virginia as 225,933, of whom 120,111 are whites, and 105,832 colored.

Judging from the tax-list and other data, the number of whites who failed to register is 16,343. There is no report of the number disfranchised in Virginia under the Reconstruction laws.

General Canby reports 103,721 white, and 72,932 colored voters in North Carolina, nearly all of whom voted. It is estimated that 19,477 whites, and 3,289 blacks failed to register, and of these 11,686 whites are disfranchised.

In South Carolina there are 46,883 white, and 80,550 black voters registered; 10,992 whites, and 4,167 blacks failed to register. About seventy-five per cent. of the whites are disfranchised.

In Georgia, 96,333 white, and 95,168 colored voters are registered, of whom 60,333 whites, and 24,758 colored, failed to vote; 10,000 whites are disfranchised, and 8,500 refused to register.

In Alabama there are 61,295 white, and 104,518 black voters, of whom 37,158 white, and 32,947 colored, failed to vote. There are no data to show the number disfranchised.

In Florida few are disfranchised, and nearly all are registered, and have voted. The number of whites is 11,914, and blacks 16,079.

General Gillem says there are no data kept from which to ascertain the number of voters of different colors in Mississippi.

In Arkansas, 25,697 failed to vote.

General Houck reports that 45,218 whites and 84,436 blacks were registered in Louisiana; of this number 50,480 failed to vote, but what proportion are whites the General is unable to say, nor can he report how many are disfranchised.

In Texas, 55,633 white, and 49,497 colored voters are registered, of whom 1,757 whites and 36,932 blacks voted. The number disfranchised can not be ascertained.

A PICTURE FOR DISTRIBUTION—SAMPLES OF "RECONSTRUCTION."

[From the Trenton True American.]

Wilmington is the chief city of North Carolina, and Charleston of South Carolina. These two cities are respectively represented in the bogus Legislatures, elected under the Reconstruction swindle:

WILMINGTON, NORTH CAROLINA—SENATE.

A. H. Galloway, negro; Joseph C. Abbott, New Hampshire; L. C. Estes, U. S. A.; G. W. Price, negro.

CHARLESTON, SOUTH CAROLINA—SENATE.

D. T. Corbin, unknown; R. H. Cabin, negro; A. J. Ransier, negro; R. Tomilson, unknown; W. H. H. Gray, negro; B. A. Boseman, negro; George Lee, negro; D. F. Jackson, negro; Joseph H. Jenks, Freedmen's Bureau; William McKinlay, negro; F. J. Moses, junior, S. C; W. J. Brodie, negro; J. B. Dennis, negro; Jno. B. Wright, negro; William Jervey, negro; Abraham Smith, negro; Samuel Johnson, negro; Stephen Brown, negro; Edw'd Mickery, negro.

How IT WAS DONE IN FLORIDA.

An old and respectable citizen of Tallahassee writes the New York *Express*, in which he says:

"We select two counties only as sufficient evidence of the honesty of those who now aspire to lord it over the people of the South. Take the county of Madison and the annexed affidavits conclusively prove: That Daniel Terrants, a carpenter, was employed by one Eagan, an inspector of the election, to construct a box with a slide—yes, a FRAUDULENT BALLOT-BOX; that Katzenberg, a candidate for the State Senate from that county, and *one of the registers, paid for making said box, and that it was used on the days of election*. The affidavits of John Fraser and Peter Wright also show *rascality and fraud!* Katzenberg, a State Senator elect, after the election had progressed one day, opened the registration books at night, in his OWN HOUSE, and assisted by Eagan, *added eighty-seven names to the list!* Orders from headquarters directed that the registration books should be closed on the morning of April 24, ten days prior to the election.

It can be proven by honorable men as any in the State, that about 270 votes more were counted out of the ballot-box in Madison than were actually voted. Where and when did they make their appearance? Why was the ballot-box made with something of a funnel in the top, so that while the top of the funnel was sealed, the funnel itself could be removed?

We have two affidavits in relation to Leon county. As in Madison, so in Leon, the ballot-boxes *were made to order*. Robert Williams says that one O. Morgan, President of the Board of Registration for the county, engaged him to make boxes for Leon and Gadsden. He further states that said boxes could have been easily opened at the bottom Now mark the date that these boxes were made—August, 1867. They were used at the election for the convention, thus showing that not only our recent election for State officers, but the election for the call of a convention was tampered with.

"Rev. James Page, an honorable citizen, whose affidavit before us shows that a slide in the ballot-box dropped out during the election when no one was touching it. Mr. Page will also testify that the box used at the election for State officers was the *same pieces* of the box used at the election for the Convention, which Robt. Williams says was ordered to be made so as to be easily entered. The only difference was, it seems that the *bottom* of the box, which contained the false entrance, was put up on the *side* instead of where it formerly staid.

"As in Madison, so in Leon. It can be proven by those who kept the tally-lists that nearly *three hundred* more votes were counted out of the box than were *honestly* put in. Why, on the second day of the election was the ballot-box moved behind the lid of a desk, so that voters could not see whether their votes were put in the box or not! This election farce lasted three days, and the inspectors took the boxes home with them at night. Who can doubt fraud? The colored people were formed into long double columns and, with attending guards, loud huzzas, etc., were marched to the polls, and free rations were liberally promised just prior to the election, to all who would vote the proper ticket, while those freedmen who chose to exercise the right of deciding for themselves received the cold shoulder. The strikers of Reed & Co. took advantage of the ignorance of the blacks, and made them believe that voting a Reed ticket was necessary to secure rations free."

The Tallahassee *Floridan* states that Harrison Reed, the Governor elect, was sworn into office and delivered his inaugural, and that the Legislature met, but no quorum was present. The military authorities insisted that the Reorganizers should wait till Congress passed the Omnibus bill. Mr. Reed was sworn in by Judge Boynton of the United States District Court.

THE WAY EVIDENCE IS PROCURED TO BE SUBORNED — A HANDY PARTY WITH THE BIBLE.

It is known that General Meade ordered a military commission for the ostensible purpose of inquiring into the alleged frauds of the late Georgia election. The Democratic papers are giving Colonel Hulbert, President of the "Central Grant Club" of Georgia, an enviable notoriety, by bringing to light letters written by him, in which he asks a citizen of Columbus to procure or manufacture testimony to be brought before the commission. "Can't you," he asks, "get up affidavits from the counties of Chattahooche and Marion? Try. Get Dr. Gilbert and other friends at work at once, and send me their affidavits. Can't you send me the affidavits of yourself and Chapman of frauds committed in Columbus, or at least that force and intimidation were used by the rebels against the freedmen?" And again: "We want affidavits proving force, fraud, intimidation, in violation of general orders. We must have them, and plenty of them. Go to work and get them up at once. The names of the parties making the affidavits will not be known to any person except yourself and the board. They need have no fears on that score. You can swear them before Captain Hill. Please go to work, sharp and quick. The election in your county will be contested; defend yourself by attacking the enemy."

The Columbus *Sun* remarks that Hulbert will not dare to deny the authenticity of these letters.

Intelligence of so-called Southern Loyalists.

The intellectual standard of the carpet-baggers—scallywags—and African statesmanship, which is now under Radical auspices to rule the South, and to contribute to a large balance of power which is to control the national legislation, and determine upon grave questions of finance, revenue, and other complicated details of government, is well ventilated by the following official letter from Gen. Schofield, commanding First Military District, to Gen. Grant, contemplating the early ratification of the proposed fourteenth amendment to the Constitution, he writes May 15, 1868:

"In the States not readmitted to representation, the oath prescribed by the act of Congress of July 2, 1862, will still be required of all persons elected or appointed to any office. I have reports which will give the number of officers of various grades in Virginia, who will be displaced by the operation of the constitutional amendment, and will forward the specific information when obtained. For the present I can only state that there will probably be 70,000, and that only a small proportion of the vacancies thus created can possibly be filled by persons with the necessary qualifications, including the ability to take the test oath. To dispense with the test oath men would probably be insufficient for the bar. Nearly all lawyers of sufficient experience to fit them for the bench held some office before the war, and hence are disqualified by the constitutional amendment. I have already appointed in Virginia nearly 500 officers, and would have appointed more if qualified persons could be found. It is important to observe that the large majority of city, town, and county officers receive little or no compensation for their services. Hence, men who possess the necessary qualifications can not be induced to accept such offices, except in places where they reside and own property, and have substantial interests. Reports have been received from several portions of the State that no persons can be found even to fill vacancies that now exist. When the constitutional amendment takes effect a large number of important offices must become vacant and remain so until restoration is completed, unless some relief is afforded by Congress.

"Very respectfully,
"Your obed't ser't.
"J. M. SCHOFIELD."

Effects of Radical Reconstruction.

Says an exchange: "At a late dinner in North Carolina, there sat down to table three ex-Governors, an ex-Justice of the Supreme Court, two ex-members of Congress, and some other men of honorable distinction in their State, and the only person in the room who could vote or hold office was the negro who waited on the table. Such is reconstruction."

In the First District of Mississippi, Townsend, an ex-United States soldier, is the Democratic candidate for Congress, and Wofford, late of the Confederate army, is his Radical opponent. Verily, "times change and men change with them."

An incident occurred in a North Carolina court the other day, which pretty well illustrates the capability of Sambo for the discharge of jury duty. The case involved was a civil suit. One of the parties to the suit had refused, some time previous, to credit a certain negro on the jury for some trifling articles; but he succeeded in obtaining the credit from the other party. At the conclusion of the trial the negro juryman approached the man who had refused him credit, and boasted that he had revenged himself for the refusal by voting against a verdict in his favor!

Thomasville, Ga., was fired by the negroes in fifteen places after it was ascertained that the election had resulted in favor of the Democrats.

The carpet bag doctors at the South tell the negroes they must buy their medicine of them, for they say Southern doctors sell the negroes poison.

In Savannah, Ga., several negroes were supplied by a wag with labels of Costar's Rat and Roach Exterminator, and shoved them in as ballots.

The Man and Brother.

SHOCKING OUTRAGE BY NEGROES—THE RESULT OF RADICAL TEACHING.

About eleven o'clock, Friday night, five negroes came to the store of Mr. M. A. Muldrow, in Darlington district, about nine miles from the court house, and rapping up the clerk, Mr. R. Sugs, asked admittance. Mr. Sugs inquired who they were, and receiving the response that they were friends come to trade with him, opened the door of the store. Four negroes, armed with double-barreled shot guns, entered, and, placing their weapons in the corner of the room, commenced examining goods, remarking that they were in the employ of the railroad, had just been paid off, and desired to make purchases to the extent of ten dollars each. About fifty dollars' worth of goods were selected, when one of the number asked Mr. Sugs if he could change a treasury note of the denomination of one hundred dollars. The wife of Mr. Sugs, who was in the adjoining room, heard the remark, and her suspicions being excited by it, she went out of the back door to the house of a gentleman named Wyndham, and requested him to come to the store, and in case any trouble should occur, to render Mr. Sugs what assistance he could. Mr. Wyndham complied, taking a gun with him, and as he reached the store heard the report of a shot. He threw open the door and was immediately fired upon five times by the negroes. He returned the fire, when they rushed upon him and seized his gun, and a scuffle ensued, during which he managed to effect his escape, and repairing to Mr. Muldrow's house, reported the condition of affairs. As soon as the latter could dress and arm himself, he ran to the store, accompanied by Mr. Wyndham. There all was quiet, and entering, they found the shelves of the store completely stripped, the money desk was robbed, and the clerk, Mr. Sugs, lying dead on the floor, a load of buckshot having passed through his head. From this melancholy scene Messrs. Muldrow and Wyndham went to the house of the latter, where they found that Mr. Wyndham's father-in-law had been dangerously shot twice in the head, and his wife in three different places on the person by the same party of negroes.—*Charleston Evening News.*

A Few More of the Same Sort.

On the 11th of April, the stage, on its way to Selma, some twenty miles from Montgomery, in Tallawossee Swamp, was fired into by two negroes. The stage was full of passengers. The "loyal" newspapers "at a venture," like bows have been drawn before, raised a howl as usual against the "rebel banditti," the disloyal "desperadoes in Alabama," "the Ku Klux Klan." They had "inaugurated the Mexican style of doing things in Alabama!" "Congress must give the Union people of the State a government of some kind, so all this threatening marauding can be put down," etc. When the offending negroes were arrested, the tune was changed. They quietly said, "only a couple of drunken negroes, who, having a prejudice (very pardonable, of course!) against the stage driver, resorted to this outlawry!" (about as legally correct as Mongrel ideas are generally) "to get revenge." On the 13th *idem*, Mr. Binns, in his store, was shot instantly to death by a negro, who escaped to Selma, from the scene of the murder, near Jones' Bluff, in the Bigbee river, and has not been heard of since. Judge Ogden, a venerable citizen of Louisiana, late of the Supreme Court, was dogged three quarters of a mile from Carrolton, to his residence in Greenville, by a powerful negro, who said to him, "I hear you have been running down the carpetbaggers," and immediately, with repeated blows with a club, struck him to the earth, mangled and maimed, and continued the infliction in his prostrate condition, laying bare his arm to the bone from elbow to wrist, crushing his hand, producing severe contusions and opening the scalp to the bone.

Recently a negro foreman on a plantation in Alabama brutally whipped a white boy, aged about fourteen years, who was employed as a laborer on the place. A warrant was issued for the arrest of the negro, but he had made his escape, threatening to kill any one who should attempt to take him. No notice was taken of the affair by the military authorities.

Ben. Welborn, a highly respected colored man of Louisiana, doing business at Tigerville, Terrebonne Parish, was assassinated in his own house on the 20th of June. The shot, which was fired at him by some unknown person, killed him instantly. The Governor has been petitioned to offer a reward for the capture of the murderer. The deceased was a witness for Governor Baker in the trial of the latter before Commissioner Shannon on the ridiculous charge of perjury. This is probably the cause of his death, as it is said there were threats at the time he gave his evidence that he would rue it.

OUTRAGES BY NEGROES IN LOUISIANA.

One night last week, before bed time, several negroes came to the house of Mr. Stewart, a mile and a half in the rear of Franklin, entered his storeroom, and fired upon the family. One shot struck Mr. Stewart's little girl, and several shots struck a negro man. The family retreated to another room for safety, and the robbers took several barrels of corn, a barrel of molasses, flour, meat, etc. The robbers have not yet been apprehended.

A week ago Thursday night, Billy Mayer was returning home accompanied by Louis Fisher, and they were suddenly fired on by a party of negroes, six or seven in number, on horseback, and were compelled to retreat to the woods, they being unarmed. Their guns were loaded with buckshot, and the firing commenced without any provocation or excuse whatever.

Last Saturday the negroes on the Simon plantation refused to work, under the plea that they wanted pay on Saturday morning, instead of Saturday evening or Sunday morning. After a parley they finally agreed to go to work, but, when they started for the field across the bayou, two leading negroes took possession of the bridge, armed with a shotgun and a pistol, and threatened to shoot any negro that attempted to go to the field to work. No labor was done that day, though it was a busy season of the year. Monday morning, Major Simon made affidavit of the facts before Justice McKerall; the two ringleaders were arrested and brought to town by Constable McGregor, tried and put in jail, they being unable to give bonds of two hundred and fifty dollars each to keep the peace.

Last Wednesday week, Mrs. Porter's hands came to Franklin in a mass, armed with sticks and clubs, much excited. They said that one of the hands had been turned off, and they had a club arrangement that if one hand was turned off all would leave the plantation. The Provost Marshal sent them back to the plantation and settled the matter the next day, and the hands went to work. Such are some of the effects of club meetings and incendiary political teachings in the South.—[*Planter's Banner*.

MORE NEGRO OUTRAGES IN ALABAMA.

The following, from the Marion (Alabama) *Commonwealth* of the 12th of April, shows that there is imminent danger of social trouble in that place:

"The *Beacon* of last Saturday infers from a number of circumstances, which it proceeds to state, that the burning of the livery stables in that town, one the 24th ult., was the work of negro incendiaries. Just one week before the stables were burned, it was reported at our residence before sunrise by a freedman, who, to our personal knowledge, had neither left the lot nor received communication from any one living elsewhere (subsequent to 12 or 1 o'clock of the night before), that Greensboro had been burned that night. As soon as our breakfast was over, we started to go to the *Commonwealth* office, and on the way there met Mr. N. R. McElroy, who informed us that he had that morning met a freedman, six miles from

Marion, who told him that Greensboro had been burned the night before.

"Had there been any great light in the direction of Greensboro during the night in question (Sunday night), the concurrent testimony of these two negroes, delivered so nearly at the same moment of time and at such distance from each other (six or seven miles, might have been easily accounted for. But the absence of any such fact renders the circumstance we have named very suspicious, to say the least of it. And when that suspicion is strengthened by the fact that at least two different freedmen in this place had been previously overheard indulging in threats which promised something very like a similar outrage in Marion, on the very same night (*i. e.*, Sunday night, the 17th), and the additional fact that boasting bets were offered here on the morning of Monday, the 18th, to the extent of one thousand dollars, that Marion would be laid in ashes before ten days rolled around, we can not but conclude that the conjectures of the *Beacon* have something more substantial than mere fancy for a foundation. The designs of the incendiaries against Marion were defeated by the well-timed vigilance of our citizens.

"One circumstance, however, was very observable. On the night in which the supposed burning was to have occurred, a most extraordinary number of strange negroes, negroes whom many of our citizens had never seen before, were parading the streets, fully armed and prepared, from daylight down until a very late hour. But the sixty or seventy brave boys who had volunteered for the defense of the town that night, soon showed them that any unlawful demonstration on their part would be promptly suppressed, and the result was, everything passed off without the promised pyrotechnic display."

Negro Defiance of Law in the South.
[From the Charleston News.]

A collision between the civil authorities and the negroes took place at Orangeburg, on Thursday, but owing to the firmness shown by the officer assailed, and by the citizens, no general outbreak occurred. During the afternoon the Sheriff sent his deputy into the interior to arrest three negro men, against whom warrants had been issued for stealing goods from a store in Orangeburg. The deputy found the negroes, arrested them, and set out on his return. On his way he was met by a crowd of negroes, most of whom he knew to be from the vicinity of the place in which he had made his arrests. As he rode up, one of the negroes came forward and demanded that the prisoners be released. The Sheriff asked him very quietly what was his authority. The negro drew a pistol, cocked it, presented it at the Sheriff, and said, "This is my authority." Without further parley the Sheriff fired, wounding the negro mortally. The rest of the negroes made a rush forward and the prisoners made their escape; but the Sheriff stood his ground like a man and did not attempt to make his escape until he had fired every barrel of his pistol, wounding one negro slightly and a second very badly. When the Sheriff reached Orangeburg, he collected his posse and returned. At the place where the attack had been made he found the negro first wounded in the care of a colored man. Both were arrested and left in charge of a citizen named Izlar, while the Sheriff went on and recaptured his escaped prisoners. Soon after the Sheriff left Mr. Izlar's, one of the negroes in Mr. Izlar's custody asked permission to go to the spring for water. Mr. Izlar went with him, and as they approached the spring the negro seized a stick and struck at Mr. Izlar. The blow was parried, and the two had a desperate fight, in which the rammer of Mr. Izlar's pistol was broken off. The negro, seeing he could do no better, broke away and ran off. Mr. Izlar halted him three times and then fired, wounding him in the neck and body. When the news of these events reached the town there was great excitement, and the citizens did not hesitate to charge the negro "Senator" elect, B. F. Randolph, with having instigated the attempted rescue. Randolph had around him a large number of negroes, whom he then told to go home and be quiet. There was some fear of a rising in the night, and arrangements were made that the citizens should assemble when a gun was fired or a bell tolled. Late at night a rapid discharge of fire-arms was heard. The citizens tumbled out on all sides, but found that it was only the *entre* of Herr Lengel into the lion's den during the performance of Ames' circus. Yesterday troops were sent for to Columbia and a detachment of infantry arrived at Orangeburg and was marched to the Sheriff's office. All was then quiet and the danger appeared to be past.

The Reign of Military Terror in the South.

THE TORTUGAS HORROR AND THE OTHER DEVICES OF TORTURE BY MILITARY SATRAPCY.

The blood runs cold at the contemplation of the ridiculous and cruel indifference with which the liberties of the citizen are regarded by the military power which has, ever since the war, governed so large a portion of this boasted free land. The horrors of the Tortugas make the sufferings of the English prisoners, for which England has just wiped out Abyssinia, pale into gentle punishment compared with those that are now daily enacted on that torrid and treeless desert waste known as Tortugas. Except in location, the Bastile of Meade at Atlanta, and those of Ord in Mississippi and Arkansas, are no less cruel and atrocious in all their tyrannical details. We have not documents to refer to the sufferings which Ord made men to endure in Mississippi and Arkansas. Death, in one of which cases, came to the relief of one of his victims before the cruel and inhuman monster would release his wasting frame from the unjust imprisonment which his mandate had imposed. We can not now recall the name. It is known to all Arkansas, and to no one better than Ord himself, and his regime of military tyrants. His imprisonment of the fearless McArdle, of the Vicksburg *Times*, whose only offense was a personal castigation in his columns of Ord himself for his despicable, unmanly and inhuman course of government. The case is the one which has so sensibly affected the weak nerves of our high Supreme Court, so much as to induce its postponement for fear of Congress. The case of Mr. Lusk, who, we believe, is now in prison, was tried by a military commission for the murder of a negro on a boat in the Mississippi river, and sentenced to be hung. Defendant took exceptions to the jurisdiction of the commission, denying its *legality*, under the decision of the United States Supreme Court in the Milligan case, and claimed that he should have been tried by the civil court, which was open within the Fifth Military District. On this exception, and under the Reconstruction law, the case was presented to the President, and is now under advisement upon the points above named. General Grant indorses on the papers his approval of the sentence of Lusk, upon the ground that it is one of the first cases of the kind arising under the Reconstruction acts.

The case of Colonel David C. Cross, one of the most worthy and respectable citizens of Arkansas, who was arrested by a miserable little Captain Williams, who is allowed to exercise regal powers over a large part of Arkansas, and who, upon the complaint of a number of worthless negroes, subjected him to imprisonment and all other kinds of indignities, until the tedious process of an investigation by a superior officer was had, and he was ordered to be released. Williams did this during the progress of impeachment, under the vain delusion that Wade would soon be President, and back him in whatever he did—a boast to that effect being common with him. Hundreds of other cases, which have happened all over the South, might be adduced Indeed. it would be no exaggeration to say over a thousand. We will give a few of the more atrocious.

THE DRY TORTUGAS—THE GREENE COUNTY VICTIMS.

[From the Montgomery Mail.]

*　　　*　　　*　　　*　　　*

At the Dry Tortugas the heads of the prisoners are shaved, and they labor under a torrid sun upon a sandbank in the midst of the ocean, with balls and chains about their limbs. The officers who command at that fortification are amenable to the laws of neither God nor man. Colonel Greutel was tied up by his thumbs, and treated with every species of cruelty and barbarity. No one interfered. The laws were silent. The man that enters there leaves liberty, justice and hope behind.

If we were to write and publish what we think about the sentence of these young men, we would violate the order of General Meade forbidding the use of language calculated to arouse the prejudice and passions of our people. Our free speech would be throttled. Our free press would be suppressed. Our business would be ruined, and our wife and children brought to want. We dare not speak the whole truth. The lips of our Alabama journals are pinned together by the bayonet, and our hands fastened in iron cuffs.

These young men who are condemned to hard labor at the Dry Tortugas, with chained limbs and shaved heads, have had nothing but a drum-head trial. They are condemned for what, in every State of the Union, is considered the least reprehensible and most excusable kind of assault and battery, personal indignities toward a pest of society, a perjured blasphemer, expelled from the pulpit for stealing money committed to his charge, an inhuman thief against whom it is in evidence that he stole the coffin of a dead Federal soldier. This pest of society is caught stealing wood from the land of a neighbor. He is assaulted by the son of the gentleman who is depredated upon. A few thoughtless young men, determined to free the community of the villain, drive him from the country. No serious harm is done the man. The only wish is to get rid of him. He may have been a Radical. It is probable that he was a Radical, since every thief and assassin of the State has joined that party and attempted to cloak villany under the flags of the Loyal Leagues. The villain was run out of the county, not because he was a Radical, but because he was a rascal. How should his assailants have been punished? No jury in a civilized country ever inflicted, in such a case, a harsher punishment than a moderate fine. These military jurymen inflict a most barbarous punishment—the penalty of death. They know that these boys will die at the Dry Tortugas in two years.

Not long ago a Federal officer, cowardly assassin, killed an old gentleman at Mount Vernon, who was a prisoner in his hands. He refused to fight him in honorable combat, but murdered him while a prisoner. Was the officer sent to the Dry Tortugas and compelled to labor two years with shaved head, and with chains upon his limbs? On the contrary, he was so mildly punished that his offense seemed to be recommended as a virtue. A few months' confinement to a fort was a sufficient punishment for a deliberate murder.

Is this justice? Will the people of the North permit such oppression? Will they look calmly on and see military officers, in the name of law and liberty violating both, and crushing down to the dust that feeling of nationality which has been struggling to rise, with all the weight of calumny, injustice and oppression, which has been heaped upon its back?

It is true, General Meade released them after they had been there a few weeks; but does that lessen the odium of a despotism which was permitted to exercise such a power? His very order of release threatens a repetition of the outrage, in similar offenses, for fear that his majestic leniency might be misinterpreted. The gentlemen who were so outraged (William Petigrew, Frank H. Munday, Hugh L. White, Thomas W. Roberts, James Steed, John Cullen, and Samuel Strayhorn), are citizens of as high respectability as there is in the country—as high even as the autocrat who endeavored to disgrace them as felons:

The Revolting Tyranny now Existing in Georgia.
THE ASHBURN CASE.

Not long ago a bad man named Ashburn was killed in a house of ill-fame at Columbus, Georgia. Leading a life of shame and violence, he was at war not only with society, but had also his special friends with those who, like himself, followed a life of crime. Falling thus in a low haunt of vice, the natural presumption that he fell by the hands of some of his own set, was confirmed by the expressions and acts of these parties. To the conservatives of Georgia, the fact that such a man was a prominent Radical leader and agent was a daily argument that was to them invaluable, just as is the character and antecedents of such persons as Hunnicutt, Holden, Matchetts, Conover, Ashley, and others whom this party delight to honor. But it suited the purpose of Radicalism to ascribe this murder or killing (for the exact facts have never transpired), to members of the conservative party at Columbus.

The Columbus (Georgia) *Sun*, of the 16th of June, contains the following article:

"Yesterday morning eight of our citizens—young men—were marched to the depot under military escort and sent to Atlanta. These, added to former arrests of persons already in confinement at Atlanta, make twenty-four parties now in prison. The charges against them are only matters of conjecture—a connection with the killing of Ashburn. From the best information we can gather, the parties have been arrested upon the testimony of negroes, much of it forced, while from others bribery has been the instrument. Immediately after the murder was perpetrated, the Military Governor of Georgia issued a proclamation in which he offered a reward of two thousand dollars for the first, and one thousand dollars for each additional party connected with the assassination, with proof to convict. This is a big sum to place before the eyes of a bad negro as an inducement to bear false witness. It has doubtless had its effect. With such inducements, no citizen of Columbus, however exemplary his walks in life, is exempt from arrest. When these arrests will end, and what number of our citizens are to be incarcerated under the influence of such testimony, no one can even conjecture."

THE EFFECTS OF CONJURY TRIED ON SUPERSTITIOUS NEGROES.

The Columbus (Georgia) *Enquirer*, says. "We knew that the process of Africanizing these Southern States had made considerable progress, and that its chief promoter was the military power. But we were really not prepared for the announcement that the good old African rite of *obeah* had been revived as a substitute for law! This, however, has been done in this city, according to the reports of negroes who have come from the secret military inquisition, after a searching examination. They say that the officer making the examination told them that he had consulted a fortune teller, and that the conjurer had already told him what the negro witness knew about the case in hand. Of course, with this admonition, the negroes had to know *something*, and the presumption is that the revelations of the conjurer were then made to agree with the statements of the witnesses, as it would not do to have a conflict of testimony."

A letter addressed by Mr. Edward T. Shepherd to the *Sun and Times*, of Columbus, Georgia, alluding to the arrest of seven negroes by the military authorities, and the means employed to compel them to give satisfactory evidence, states:

"But when a witness did not tell enough to suit them, the gentlemen examining them would accuse them of lying, saying "they had a fortune-teller who had told them all about it and what they knew," and threatened them with a shaved head, a ball and chain, and being at once sent to Fort Pulaski if they did not tell the truth—asking which they would prefer, Fort Pulaski or Tortugas? Such the evidence, and such the means of obtaining it (of freedmen) with which military despotism is seeking to convict respectable citizens of a most heinous crime—offering rewards of thousands of dollars to the cupidity of one class, and threats of punishment by being sent a long ways from home, shaved heads, and menaces, to the other."

It is by such impressions upon the excessive superstition of the negroes that evidence was procured, no doubt to base the arrest of these citizens, and will be used for their conviction. Well does the *Enquirer* say: "If *conjury* is to take the place of law and testimony, that is his peculiar gift—his ancestors brought it with them from Africa. Throw away the Bible, and erect a Fetisch altar in our temples of justice, and we know no more suitable administrators of law than the most ignorant negro that can be found in the rice-fields of South Carolina or the sugar plantations of Louisiana."

Ashburn supposed to have been Murdered by Radicals.

RESPECTABLE CITIZENS TO BE MADE THE SCAPEGOATS.

The *Sun* gives a brief review of the Ashburn murder, which goes appropriately with the high-handed proceedings of General Meade. It is as follows:

"That there are bad men in our community, as in others, we have not the least doubt. Mr. Ashburn was killed at the dead hour of night, and doubtless by dastardly cowards—men who did not dare to meet him in mortal combat in open day. We have good reason for believing, too, that the assassins were Radicals—black and white—to whom he was a stumbling block in the road to office.

"In proof of the correctness of our suspicions, we will mention a few facts. It will be recollected by many of our citizens that previous to the election of delegates to the Constitutional Convention, and in the temporary absence of Ashburn from Columbus, a hand-bill was issued, signed by fifteen or twenty Radicals—the entire white element of the party in the city—calling a meeting to appoint delegates to a nominating convention at Cusseta. The leader of the movement avowed to us uncompromising hostility to Ashburn, and expressed determination that Ashburn should no longer control the party. Ashburn returned before the day for the meeting, went in and took posession of it, and appointed delegates to his liking—himself among the number. Indeed, so hostile had the feeling become between Ashburn and two leading Federal office-holders in this city, that he threatened in our presence to have them removed. Time sped on—the nominating convention assembled at Cussetta, and put out candidates for the Senatorial District suited to the taste of Ashburn—himself among the number from this county. Ashburn having the ear and confidence of the negroes and full control of the loyal leagues, whipped the fight and proved himself master of the situation. His ticket was elected. Whether his Radical opponents voted for him we can not say.

"The convention met, did its work and adjourned. Ashburn returned to Columbus, avowed his intention to be elected by the Legislature to the Senate of the United States, and set to work to organize his colored friends, and secure the election of such members from this Senatorial district as would support his Senatorial pretensions. On Saturday before he was killed, through his influence, a large number of negroes assembled in the court-house square, and were harangued by him, and a ticket was nominated for the House and Senate, composed, for the House of one of the delegates to the convention, and a negro, and the head of the Freedmen's Bureau, a known friend of Ashburn's, for the Senate. What part, if any, his former Radical opponents took in this meeting, or whether they were present at all, we can not say.

"On the Monday night succeeding the meeting referred to, the career of Ashburn was brought to a close. After he was dead, and had come to his death, too, at the hands of assassins, what was the conduct of the Columbus Radicals? If they had felt any pangs of grief or indignation at this outrageous act, is it not reasonable to suppose they would have interested themselves so much at least, as to have called to see his corpse, and give some assistance toward the final disposition of his remains? Not one, as we were informed, did his remains even the honor of a call. Being a pauper, the expenses of his funeral were borne by the city. His remains were attended to the depot, for shipment to Macon, by only two white men—his son, and a Radical Jew named Coleman."

PETITION OF THE FATHER OF ONE OF THE PRISONERS.

To the Honorable Senate and House of Representatives of the United States:

Your petitioner, Wm. S. Chipley, respectfully states that he is a citizen of the United States, and a resident of the city of Lexington, in the State of Kentucky; that he is the father of Wm. Dudley Chipley, a citizen of Columbus, Georgia, who has been arrested and imprisoned by order of the military authorities of the United States without cause, and in disregard of the provisions of the Constitution of the United States, and carried out of the district in which any offense charged against him was committed, to Atlanta, Georgia, some two hundred miles distant from his home, and is now confined there in a cell which is wholly unfit for the confinement, even as punishment, of a criminal. He is denied the privilege of seeing or consulting with either his family, his friends, or his counsel, and deprived of all information as to the nature of the charge against him, without power to summon or procure the attendance of witnesses in his defense. In short, he is utterly at the mercy of his prosecutors, and deprived of every right which the Constitution and laws secure to the citizen. He is not, and has not been, either in the naval or military service of the United States. He is a commission merchant in Columbus, a married man, and a good citizen, as all who know him will testify. Your petitioner does not know certainly what the charges against his son are, and can only surmise, from the statements of discharged negro witnesses, who were arrested, confined, and examined, touching his connection therewith, that he is imprisoned for complicity in the murder of one G. W. Ashburn, who was killed in a house of ill-fame, kept by a negress, in Columbus, on the night of the 31st of March, 1868. These negroes, since their release, have voluntarily given affidavits as to the mode of examination resorted to—the torture, starvation, and threats against their liberty and lives, to which they were subjected in order to extort false testimony against my son and others, which affidavits are filed herewith, and made part hereof as fully as is copied *verbatim* herein.

Comment on the facts stated in said affidavits is unnecessary—indeed, can only be fitly made under the right of discussion in your honorable bodies. Your petitioner will not venture to make any. The enormous rewards—over $25,000—offered for the conviction of some person or persons as the murderers of Ashburn, have induced spies, informers, detectives and suborners of ignorant and corrupt witnesses to embark in the scheme of procuring conviction, and with the military assistance afforded them, probably by arrangement for division of the spoils, it will be wonderful if they do not buy or coerce some testimony on which they can procure a conviction in the military court organized to convict, etc.

HOW THE PRISONERS ARE TREATED.

The Atlanta *Constitution* concludes the foregoing story with the following account of the treatment which the prisoners receive in the military dungeon of the Gate City:

"The following details of the manner in which these prisoners have been manipulated by the Federal authorities come to us from the mouth of one who has had unusual facilities for obtaining facts. If true, they are a darker stain upon the Government than even the treatment of poor 'Surratt, whose long imprisonment,' says a certain United States District Judge, 'is a disgrace to the Court.'

"We give below the statement, *verbatim et literatim,* as made in our hearing:

"Last Wednesday week the prisoners were brought to McPherson Barracks, near Atlanta, and placed in separate cells six by eight feet, each cell having one diminutive iron-barred hole in the wall for the admission of air. This apology for a window is far beyond the tiptoe reach of the solitary occupant. Within, there were neither bed-clothes, bed or bedstead until the following Saturday, when bed-clothes were kindly(!) permitted to be supplied by friends, and a bedstead to each cell by the Government. On Sunday, General Meade returned from Huntsville, and allowed the prisoners to be transferred to the officers' quarters, upon their giving bonds to the amount of $20,000 not to attempt to escape or communicate with any one except by special permit of the officer in command.

"This bond, signed by prominent citizens of Atlanta, was acknowledged by the proper authorities to be satisfactory. Thursday, without notice or specified charges, Bedell was returned to solitary confinement—on the following Monday Chipley and Kirksey followed suit. These three, with the other prisoners (three in number), from Fort Pulaski, are not allowed to receive anything in the way of rations, except from the Government; nor are they permitted to communicate with their friends or each other. A Government detective, however, goes and comes whenever he sees fit, takes out a prisoner under guard, and tampers with witnesses. But Major M., counsel for the defense, is refused admittance to or communication with his unfortunate clients. Neither he nor they have any knowledge of the charges under which these citizens of Georgia and of the United States have been incarcerated.

The Radical Military Domination in the South.

ANOTHER OUTRAGE.

[From the Augusta (Ga.) Constitutionalist.]

It seems that, about six weeks ago, a Federal soldier was killed at Warrenton, in this State. No clue, so far as we can ascertain, has yet been afforded to detect the perpetrator of this violence. But the military authorities—those fine gentlemen sent here to preserve order and protect the innocent—assumed full knowledge of the case; and, without cognizance of law, and without the feeble show of affidavits from any party or parties whatsoever, arrested a peaceful and inoffensive citizen of Warrenton, by the name of Cody. This gentleman was hustled off to Milledgeville, with manacles on his ankles and wrists.

While thus chained, and in a dungeon, he was brutally attacked by four or five soldiers who had been imprisoned in the same apartment for trivial misdemeanors. These soldiers set upon him because they deemed him to be the slayer of one of their comrades. As their superiors did not give the unfortunate man a chance to exculpate himself, neither did these base underlings allow him the charity of a doubt. One of them kicked him in the mouth, leaving a hideous gash upon his lip, and Mr. Cody was finally saved from fatal consequences through the rescue of a sergeant of the guard.

A military commission was then designated for his trial at Milledgeville, and one day's notice given of the time to Mr. Cody's counsel. Upon repairing to Milledgeville the counsel had been informed that the order for trial had been revoked, and Atlanta substituted for Milledgeville.

The trial took place one hundred and twenty miles from the residence of the prisoner, and occupied twenty-one days, during which time Mr. Cody was marched from his cell to the court, chained like a felon at his ankles and wrists.

Now mark the sequel. After an abrupt seizure; maltreatment, when menacled, by Federal soldiers; transportation and imprisonment remote from his residence; a tedious trial, and the degrading handcuffs of a condemned criminal—he was allowed to go home fully acquitted of the charge against him.

There is not an innocent man in Georgia who is not liable to a similar fate. Will the people of the North abet and encourage the awful humiliation of the South? If so, they may well shudder for their own fate, when tyranny has exhausted itself upon us, and seeks its victims among themselves.

Some of the same Kind of Thing in South Carolina.

[From the Savannah News and Herald, June 3.]

We have before published an account of the arrest of several citizens of Hamburg, S. C., by order of the miserable military satrap, Canby, for refusing to permit the negroes to hold a political meeting in their church.

The citizens in question were arrested at the instance of a carpet-bagger named Arnum, who resides in the neighborhood of Hamburg. This individual induced several negroes to make affidavit that the citizens of Hamburg who were arrested attempted to mob and incite a riot against them, for simply refusing to give their consent to this carpet-bagger, Arnum, and the negroes, to hold one of their midnight orgies in a church.

This constituted the whole offense; and yet, at the instance of an irresponsible character, and some equally worthless and irresponsible negroes, this General Canby arrests and puts to hard labor six respectable citizens of the State, which is now insulted and oppressed by his arbitrary acts and unbridled license.

MORE ARRESTS BY THE MILITARY.—We are informed that a squad of cavalry returned to the city yesterday from Gwinnett county, bringing with them two prisoners charged with the grave offense of attempting to frighten a negro. It is thought the negro has become reconciled since he finds Uncle Sam so ready to back him. One of the prisoners was discharged before the squad arrived in town, but the other was put in the barracks. [*Atlanta (Ga.) Intelligencer*, June 13.

A VOICE FROM FLORIDA.—The Tallahassee *Sentinel*, of the 1st, contains a leader devoted to showing up the villanies of the Radicals, from which we copy the following paragraph:

"In our own State—in this very town—we have seen a man arrested, sent to the military guard-house, released, rearrested on his bed at midnight, dragged again, under a heavy guard, to the military guard-house, and from thence sent a prisoner to Fort Marion—because he wrote a personal insult to an officer who had insulted him! And every effort was made, we hear, to have him sent to Tortugas."

OUGHT SUCH THINGS BE TOLERATED?—The *National Intelligencer*, commenting on these excesses of power, says:

"In a free country, governed by laws, a false accusation against a citizen may be dangerous under special circumstances, but there are very many safeguards to innocence. The citizen is arrested, but he has a right to know at once the nature of the accusation against him, to be present at the examination of the witnesses, to have counsel, to have visits from counsel and relatives, to be tried by a jury, with known rule of evidence; whatever is done against him must be done in the light of day.

"How different is this case! Without any proof four respectable citizens are arrested and confined in separate apartments at Atlanta, denied all communication with friends save under military surveillance, and all opportunity to confer with counsel. Two white men are in Fort Pulaski, confined in cells, and denied all access to friend or counsel. To-day, we believe, these six parties are to be brought out of their dungeons and hurried to trial for their lives before a military commission—one of those institutions which Mr. Webster says "are always organized to convict."

"Such a statement of facts is sufficently horrible, disgraceful to us as a people, damning to every officer and agent concerned in it. It is hardly possible to realize that such a thing can be while we dare to hold up our heads among civilized nations, and claim that this is a land of liberty, to which we have proudly invited the oppressed of all nations.

"But this is only part of this infamous record. While these men are thus immured in dungeons, cut off from access to friends and counsel, their enemies, with artful and incessant malice, have been busy in procuring false testimony. Large and extraordinary rewards are offered for testimony, and lest base men be not found ready to earn this blood-money, the uniform of the nation is degraded by the military apprehension of ignorant and impressible negroes, dragging them by force before a secret military board, and there by threats, curses, starvation and solitary confinement, endeavoring to extort from them the false testimony upon which the lives of innocent men may be taken away. The testimony we publish to-day establishes these facts. It demonstrates the character of the Government under which these people of the South are now living.

"Let every man ask himself, under such a system, what safety there is for the life or liberty of any man, however pure or blameless may be his conduct. Any man is liable to be convicted by these base instrumenalities. No man is safe for one moment And now shall we fold our arms because these things happen to men far off, whom we have not seen, of whose names we have barely heard, and possibly would never have heard but for this dastardly outrage? If we do not make this case our own, if we do not mark it by our own indignant protest and reprobation, then are we by our silence the accomplices of these tyrants. In this matter neither we nor Congress nor the President can escape a just and solemn responsibility if either fails to do his part toward arresting this act of atrocity. While we read, this crime, this incredible shame, this deed of cruelty and cowardice may be pushed to its consummation."

Whilst this book is being printed, the trial by military commission is going on, having begun on the 30th of June.

THE SOURCE OF ALL THESE OUTRAGES—THE RADICAL CANDIDATE FOR THE PRESIDENCY RESPONSIBLE.—Gen. Grant could, by a mere order, stop these things. Three years or more have elapsed since the war. The military commanders of these districts, and those who preceeded them, before the passage of the Reconstruction laws, were all agencies of his selection. He has never checked them by hint, suggestion, request or order. In the Lusk case he approved the sentence of death by a military commission, when the civil courts were in Mississippi, without a just suspicion of incompetency to do justice between the prisoner and his country.

MILITARY ARREST IN TENNESSEE.

Notwithstanding Tennessee has been rehabilitated in the Union by the admission of her Representatives into Congress, the military power of the United States is felt in her territory as much as if there was no pretense of the civil authority being restored. The Governor of that State, noted for his utter contempt for all law and every thing else except the unrestrained exercise of his own malignant and savage will, needs but to telegraph to General Thomas for his aid and that of his forces, upon the fiction of an apprehended domestic insurrection, to receive the accession of that officer's power to awe, by its presence, obedience to some revolutionary construction of the law to prevent a Radical defeat at a pending election. The alliance between these two military functionaries appears complete. General Thomas, in August, 1867, upon a mere charge of assault, preferred by some officer of the Freedmen's Bureau, at La Grange, Tenn., which was then pending in the civil courts, sent an armed guard which seized young Mr. Milliken, not then twenty-one years of age, and charging him with violating his parole, dragged him from his own State into Kentucky, where he was confined 'n a military prison, at Newport, and released upon the interposition of the United States Court. Brownlow made no objection to all this. The alliance between him and Thomas appears to be offensive and defensive.

Freedom of the Press in the South.

On November 15, 1867, a file of soldiers under the command of a Lieutenant, entered the printing office of the Vicksburg *Times*, and arrested the editor, W. H. McArdle, and conveyed him to a military prison, on the ground that he was obstructing the execution of the Reconstruction acts. A writ of *habeas corpus* was granted by Judge Hill, of the United States Circuit Court, and served upon General Ord. The return set forth that the prisoner was held by General Ord, under certain charges, and that he was then undergoing a trial by a military commission. The proceedings of the commission were read, by which it appeared that Col. McArdle had refused to plead, and that a plea of not guilty had been entered for him. The charges preferred were as follows:

1. Disturbance of the public peace. Specification—Substantially in defamation of the character of General Ord, and denunciation of despotism and usurpation of authority.

2. Inciting to a breach of the peace. Specification—Col. McArdle, in an article published in his paper, said that if General Ord removed Governor Humphreys, and appointed Mr. Burwell in his stead, Governor Humphreys would refuse to surrender the State archieves to Ord's appointee; that, probably, General Ord would force him from his office by the bayonet, and then a higher tribunal than Governor Humphrey's or satrap Ord's would decide whether Mississippi was a Poland, and Ord her autocrat.

Charge 3. Libel. Specification—Defaming the character of one Captain Platt, of the Freedmen's Bureau.

Charge 4. Impeding reconstruction. Specification—Advising voters to remain away from the polls.

Judge Hill held that the Reconstruction act of Congress, in virtue of which General Ord had placed Col. McArdle under arrest, was constitutional, and that the powers vested by the law were not transcended by the district commander. It was therefore decided that the prisoner was subject to arrest and to trial before a military commission, and he was remanded to the custody of the military authorities. He took an appeal to the United States Supreme Court and entered into a recognizance for his appearance before that tribunal.

Early on the morning of August 8, a body of thirty or more Federal soldiers, under the command of Capt. George S. Pierce, forcibly entered the office of the *Constitutional Eagle*, published at Camden, Arkansas, and carried off and destroyed the material of the office. Colonel C. C. Gilbert, U. S. A., commanding the post, when remonstrated with, defended the act by saying "that the paper unnecessarily exasperated the soldiers." The exasperating articles were decorous rebukes to the soldiers for a common habit of getting drunk, and indecently exposing their persons in the town. In reporting the matter to General Ord, Colonel Gilbert said:

"The censures of the press directed against the servants of the people, may be endured; but General Ord, and the military force detailed to perform his duties, are not the servants of the people of Arkansas, BUT RATHER THEIR MASTERS, and it is felt to be a great piece of impertinence for a newspaper in this State to comment upon the military UNDER ANY CIRCUMSTANCES WHATEVER.

"C. C. GILBERT."

General Ord wrote a stinging rebuke to Gilbert.

Northern Perils from Reconstruction.

THE SOUTHERN NEGRO TO HAVE THE BALANCE OF POWER.

[From the New York Herald, June 14.]

We desire to invite the attention of every right-thinking man to the way in which Congressional Reconstruction, if allowed to stand, will react upon the North.

In the first place, 715,948 ignorant negroes will be brought in to legislate, not alone for the South but the North too. They will elect twenty (20) Senators and fifty (50) Representatives, and wield in one solid body the entire political weight of ten States. Seventy legislative votes in Congress and seventy electoral votes out, will hold the balance of power in any question of a policy or a President, and the balance of power, when cast, becomes *the* ruling power. In a tie vote, it is the casting vote that wins, and so, on anything like an equal division hereafter, these 715,948 Africans will rule America.

In the next place the "Constitutions" validated by this Congressional Reconstruction, disfranchised many hundreds of thousands of Northern voters by making suffrage dependent on an oath that affiant accepts the civil and political equality of all men. The bogus constitutions of Alabama, Louisiana, Arkansas and Virginia, do this in so many words, and the rest by direct implication. Here, then, is a point to be considered. If the South becomes quiet, and Northern men, who do not believe in negro equality wish to move there, they can not do so without divesting themselves of the highest privilege of American citizenship; they can neither vote nor hold office; they are disfranchised just as the secession leaders are disfranchised, and this, though they may have fought knee deep in blood for the Union.

If these infamous governments are to stand, they will disfranchise from Southern citizenship 255,340 voters in Ohio, 28,759 in Minnesota, 19,421 in Kansas, 110,852 in Michigan—all States where this exact question of negro equality was voted down, not to speak of the further disfranchisement of 1,811,754 other voters in the North, who have, in a less pronounced form, put themselves on record as against the abomination that this infamous Congress is seeking to crystalize into organic law.

Other points there are to be noticed hereafter, but these two in especial, as coming more directly home, are particularly commended to the candid thinker—that Congressional reconstruction will make the negroes the balance of power in this country, and that two, and perhaps nearer three millions of Northern voters are debarred from Southern citizenship unless they believe and will swear they are no better than a negro.

RECONSTRUCTION AND WORKINGMEN.

In the National Labor Congress, held at Chicago, August 4, 1867, Mr. B. E. Green, of Baltimore, delivered a most instructive and important address, which closed as follows:

"A few words more. Have you reflected on what will be the effect of the Reconstruction Act of Congress? The ffect will be to bring back the little State of Florida, controlled by some 25,000 or 30,000 ignorant negroes, with two Senators in Congress to neutralize the votes of the two Senators from the great State of Illinois, and with as much voice in laying taxes on your labor and on your property. It will bring back ten Southern States, with twenty Senators, representing only some 2,000,000 of lazy, ignorant negroes; supported by that great negro-trading monopoly, the Freedmen's Bureau, and controlled by the party of tax consumers, of National Banks, and other privileged and favored classes. Against them the great States of Illinois, Ohio, New York, Pennsylvania, with their 10,000,000 of white inhabitants, can only oppose eight Senators. They, on whom the taxes must fall, to support these privileged classes, including the negroes themselves and their Bureau; you, mechanics and farmers of the great States I have mentioned, will be outvoted in the Senate in the proportion of twenty Senators to eight on every question of taxing you to support them, and in the election of those Senators, one idle, lazy, vagabond negro in the South will weigh as much as ten hard-working, industrious mechanics in the North and East; or as many intelligent farmers in the West."

This subject will be concluded in some subsequent part of the book, in order that other matter pertinent thereto, which is daily occurring, may be presented to the reader. With it, the action of Congress preventing cognizance by the Supreme Court of cases arising under the Reconstruction law and the postponement of the McArdle case by the court, will be presented.

The Question of Veracity between the President and General Grant.

GRANT IN HIS CELEBRATED TWO-HORSE ACT—CRUSHING DEMOLITION OF THE GENERAL COMMANDING THE ARMIES.

Upon the refusal of the Senate to concur in the suspension, by the President, of E. M. Stanton, Secretary of War, the General commanding had to show his hand. "Under which king, Benzonia? speak or die." He could no longer palter with the President and the country "in a double sense." In this way he came to grief, as follows:

"On the Saturday before the action of the Senate," says the *National Intelligencer*, "when Senator Howard's report from the Senate Committee on Military Affairs, in favor of Stanton, was under discussion, General Grant was pointedly asked by the President if he had changed his mind in reference to the course he would pursue if the Senate should refuse to make Stanton's suspension final, when he reiterated the promise previously made, that he would either hand in his resignation as Secretary of War *ad interim* early enough for the President to appoint his successor, or take any other action he might deem requisite, or allow a mandamus to be served upon him for the surrender of the office; adding a promise to the President, that he should hear from him on the subject on Monday.

"Monday passed without the promised communication. On Monday evening, after it was known that the Senate had passed Howard's resolutions refusing to recognize the suspension of Stanton as Secretary of War, General Grant was present at the reception at the Executive Mansion, where he greeted the President, but mentioned nothing of any change in the determination previously declared. The President heard nothing whatever from General Grant upon the subject until twelve o'clock Tuesday, two hours after Mr. Stanton had taken possession of the War Office, when the following communication was delivered to him by Major Comstock, one of General Grant's staff officers:

HEADQUARTERS ARMIES UNITED STATES,
"WASHINGTON, D. C., January 14, 1868.

His Excellency Andrew Johnson, President of the United States:

SIR: I have the honor to inclose herewith copy of official notice received by me last evening of the action of the Senate of the United States in the case of the suspension of Hon. E. M. Stanton, Secretary of War. According to the provisions of section two of "An act regulating the tenure of certain civil offices," my functions as Secretary of War *ad interim* ceased from the moment of the receipt of the within notice.

I have the honor to be, very respectfully, your obedient servant,

U. S. GRANT, General.

IN EXECUTIVE SESSION,
SENATE OF THE UNITED STATES,
January 13, 1868.

Resolved, That having considered the evidence and reasons given by the President, in his report of the 12th of December, 1867, for the suspension from the office of Secretary of War of Edwin M. Stanton, the Senate do not concur in such suspension.

JOHN W. FORNEY, Sec'y,

HEADQUARTERS ARMIES UNITED STATES,
January 14, 1868.

Attest: GEO. K. DENT, A. A. G.

Soon after the delivery of this communication, General Grant called in person upon the President during the meeting of the Cabinet, and upon being reminded by the President of his reiterated promise, and especially of the promise made only on Saturday morning last, General Grant admitted the promise in the presence of members of the Cabinet.

On the 24th of January, 1868, the General called on the President to give him, in writing, his order to disregard all orders from Stanton, unless they were known to have emanated from him, which was complied with as follows:

"As requested in this communication, General Grant is instructed not to obey any order from the War Department, assumed to be issued by direction of the President, unless such order is known by the General commanding the Armies of the United States to have been authorized by the Executive.

"ANDREW JOHNSON."

To this General Grant replied as follows:

HEADQUARTERS ARMY OF THE UNITED STATES,
WASHINGTON, D. C., January 28, 1868.

Sir: On the 24th instant I requested you to give me in writing the instructions which you had previously given me verbally not to obey any order from Hon. E. M. Stanton, Secretary of War, unless I knew that it came from yourself. To this written request I received a message that has left doubt in my mind of your intentions. To prevent any possible misunderstanding, therefore, I renew the request that you will give me written instructions, and, till they are received, will suspend action on your verbal ones.

* * * * * *

Some time after I assumed the duties of Secretary of War *ad interim* the President asked me my views as to the course Mr. Stanton would have to pursue, in case the Senate should not concur in his suspension, to obtain possession of his office. My reply was, in substance, that Mr. Stanton would have to appeal to the courts to reinstate him, illustrating my position by citing the ground I had taken in the case of the Baltimore police commissioners.

In that case I did not doubt the technical right of Governor Swann to remove the old commissioners and to appoint their successors. As the old commissioners refused to give up, however, I contended that no resource was left but to appeal to the courts. Finding that the President was desirous of keeping Mr. Stanton out of office, whether sustained in the suspension or not, I stated that I had not looked particularly into the "Tenure-of-Office bill," but that what I had stated was a general principle, and if I should change my mind in this particular case I would inform him of the fact.

Subsequently, on reading the "Tenure-of-Office bill" closely, I found that I could not, without violation of the law, refuse to vacate the office of Secretary of War the moment Mr. Stanton was reinstated by the Senate, even though the President should order me to retain it, which he never did.

Taking this view of the subject, and learning on Saturday, the 11th instant, that the Senate had taken up the subject of Mr. Stanton's suspension, after some conversation with Lieutenant-General Sherman and some members of my staff, in which I stated that the law left me no discretion as to my action should Mr. Stanton be reinstated, and that I intended to inform the President. I went to the President for the sole purpose of making this decision known, and did so make it known. In doing this I fulfilled the promise made in our last preceding conversation on the subject.

The President, however, instead of accepting my view of the requirements of the "Tenure-of-Office bill," contended that he had suspended Mr. Stanton under the authority given by the Constitution, and that the same authority did not preclude him from reporting, as an act of courtesy, his reasons for the suspension to the Senate; that, having appointed me under the authority given by the Constitution, and not under any act of Congress, I could not be governed by the act. I stated that the law was binding on me, constitutional or not, until set aside by the proper tribunal.

An hour or more was consumed, each reiterating his views on this subject, until getting late, the President said he would see me again.

I did not agree to call again on Monday, nor at any other definite time, nor was I sent for by the President until the following Tuesday.

From the 11th to the Cabinet meeting on the 14th instant, a doubt never entered my mind about the President's fully understanding my position, namely, that if the Senate refused to concur in the suspension of Mr. Stanton my powers as Secretary of War *ad interim* would cease, and Mr. Stanton's right to resume at once the functions of his office would under the law be indisputable; and I acted accordingly. With Mr. Stanton I had no communication, direct nor indirect, on the subject of his reinstatement during his suspension

* * * * * *

At this meeting, after opening it as though I were a member of the Cabinet, when reminded of the notification already given him that I was no longer Secretary of War *ad interim*, the President gave a version of the conversations alluded to already. In this statement it was asserted that in both conversations I had agreed to hold on to the office of Secretary of War until displaced by the courts, or resign, so as to place the President where he would have been had I never accepted the office. After hearing the President through, I stated our conversations substantially as given in this letter. I will add that my conversation before the Cabinet embraced other matter not pertinent here, and is therefore left out.

I in nowise admitted the correctness of the President's statement of our conversations, though to soften the evident contradiction my statement gave, I said (alluding to our first conversation on the subject) the President might have understood me the way he said, namely, that I had promised to resign if I did not resist the reinstatement. I made no such promise.

I have the honor to be, very respectfully, your obedient servant,
U. S. GRANT, General.
His Excellency, A. JOHNSON, President of the United States.

HEADQUARTERS ARMY OF THE UNITED STATES,
WASHINGTON, January 30, 1868.

SIR: I have the honor to acknowledge the return of my note of the 24th inst. with your indorsement thereon, that I am not to obey any order from the War Department, assumed to be issued by the direction of the President, unless such order is known by me to have been authorized by the Executive; and in reply thereto to say that I am informed by the Secretary of War that he has not received from the Executive any order or instructions limiting or impairing his authority to issue orders to the army as has heretofore been his practice under the law and the custom of the Department. While this authority to the War Department is not countermanded, it will be satisfactory evidence to me that any orders issued from the War Department by direction of the President are authorized by the Executive.

I have the honor to be, very respectfully, your obedient servant,
U. S. GRANT, General.
His Excellency, A. JOHNSON, President of the United States.

EXECUTIVE MANSION, January 31, 1868.

GENERAL: I have received your communication of the 28th inst., renewing your request of the 24th, that I should repeat in a written form my verbal instructions of the 19th inst., namely, that you obey no order from Hon. Edwin M. Stanton as Secretary of War, unless you have information that it was issued by the President's direction.

* * * * *

[The President then refers to Gen. Grant's statement of the facts attending his abandonment of the War Department, and goes on to say:]

It is not necessary, however, to refer to any of them, excepting that of Saturday, the 11th instant. mentioned in your communication. As it was then known that the Senate had proceeded to consider the case of Mr. Stanton, I was anxious to learn your determination. After a protracted interview, during which the provisions of the Tenure-of-Office bill were freely discussed, you said that, as had been agreed upon in our first conference, you would either return the office to my possession in time to enable me to appoint a successor before final action by the Senate upon Mr. Stanton's suspension, or would remain as its head, awaiting a decision of the question by judicial proceedings. It was then understood that there would be a further conference on Monday, by which time, I supposed, you would be prepared to inform me of your final decision. You failed, however, to fulfill the engagement, and on Tuesday notified me, in writing, of the receipt by you of official notification of the action of the Senate in the case of Mr. Stanton, and at the same time informed me that, "according to the act regulating the tenure of certain civil offices, your functions as Secretary of War *ad interim* ceased from the moment of the receipt of the notice." You thus, in disregard of the understanding between us, vacated the office without having given me notice of your intention to do so. It is but just, however, to say, that in your communication you claim that you did inform me of your purpose, and thus "fulfilled the promise made in our last preceding conversation on this subject." The fact that such a promise existed is evidence of an arrangement of the kind I have mentioned. You had found in our first conference "that the President was desirous of keeping Mr. Stanton out of office, whether sustained in the suspension or not." You knew what reasons had induced the President to ask from you a promise. You also knew that, in case your views of duty did not accord with his own convictions, it was his purpose to fill your place by another appointment. Even ignoring the existence of a positive understanding between us, these conclusions were plainly deducible from our various conversations. It is certain, however, that even under these circumstances you did not offer to return the place to my possession; but, according to your own statement, placed yourself in a position where, could I have anticipated your action, I would have been compelled to ask of you, as I was compelled to ask of your predecessor in the War Department, a letter of resignation, or else to resort to the more disagreeable expedient of suspending you by a successor.

As stated in your letter, the nomination of Governor Cox, of Ohio, for the office of Secretary of War, was suggested to me. His appointment as Mr. Stanton's successor was urged in your name, and it was said that his selection would save further embarrassment. I did not think that in the selection of a Cabinet officer I should be trammeled by such considerations. I was prepared to take the responsibility of deciding the question in accordance with my ideas of constitutional duty, and, having determined upon a course which I deemed right and proper, was anxious to learn the steps you would take should the possession of the War Department be demanded by Mr. Stanton. Had your action been in conformity to the understanding between us, I do not believe that the embarrassment would have attained its present proportions or that the probability of its repetition would have been so great.

I know that, with a view to an early termination of a state of affairs so detrimental to the public interests, you voluntarily offered, both on Wednesday, the 15th instant, and on the succeeding Sunday, to call upon Mr. Stanton and urge upon him that the good of the service required his resignation. I confess that I considered your proposal as a sort of reparation for the failure on your part to act in accordance with an understanding more than once repeated, which I thought had received your full assent, and under which you could have returned to me the office which I had conferred upon you, thus saving yourself from embarrassment and leaving the responsibility where it properly belonged, with the President, who is accountable for the faithful execution of the laws.

I have not yet been informed by you whether, as twice proposed by yourself, you have called upon Mr. Stanton and made an effort to induce him voluntarily to retire from the War Department.

You conclude your communication with a reference to our conversation at the meeting of the Cabinet held on Tuesday, the 14th inst. In your account of what then occurred you say that after the President had given his version of our previous conversations, you stated them substantially, as given in your letter, that you in no wise admitted the correctness of his statement of them, "though, to soften the evident contradiction my statement gave, I said (alluding to our first conversation on the subject) the President might have understood in the way he said, namely, that I had promised to resign if I did not resist the reinstatement. I made no such promise."

My recollection of what then transpired is diametrically the reverse of your narration. In the presence of the Cabinet I asked you:

First. If, in a conversation which took place shortly after your appointment as Secretary of War *ad interim*, you did not agree either to remain at the head of the War Department and abide any judicial proceedings that might follow non-concurrence by the Senate in Mr. Stanton's suspension; or, should you wish not to become involved in such a controversy, to put me in the same position with respect to the office as I occupied previous to your appointment, by returning it to me in time to anticipate such action by the Senate.

This you admitted.

Second. I then asked you if, at our conference on the preceding Saturday, I had not, to avoid misunderstanding, requested you to state what you intended to do; and further, if, in reply to that inquiry, you had not referred to our former conversation, saying that from them I understood your position, and that your action would be consistent with the understanding which had been reached.

To these questions you also replied in the affirmative.

Third. I next asked if, at the conclusion of our interview on Saturday, it was not understood that we were to have another conference on Monday, before final action by the Senate in the case of Mr. Stanton.

You replied that such was the understanding, but that you did not suppose the Senate would act so soon; that on Monday you had been engaged in a conference with General Sherman, and were occupied with "many little matters," and asked if General Sherman had not called on that day. What relevancy General Sherman's visit to me on Monday had with the purpose for which you were then to have called, I am at a loss to perceive, as he certainly did not inform me whether you had determined to retain possession of the office or to afford me an opportunity to appoint a successor, in advance of any attempted reinstatement of Mr. Stanton.

This account of what passed between us at the Cabinet meeting on the 14th instant widely differs from that contained in your communication, for it shows that, instead of having "stated our conversations as given in the letter" which has made this reply necessary, you admitted that my recital of them was entirely accurate. Sincerely anxious, however, to be correct in my statements, I have to-day made this narration of what occurred on the 14th instant to the members of the Cabinet who were then present. They, without exception, agree in its accuracy.

It is only necessary to add that on Wednesday morning, the 15th, you called on me, in company with Lieutenant-General Sherman. After some preliminary conversation, you remarked that an article in the *National Intelligencer* of that date did you much injustice. I replied that I had not read the *Intelligencer* of that morning. You then first told me that it was your intention to urge Mr. Stanton to resign his office.

After you had withdrawn I carefully read the article of which you had spoken and found that its statements of the understanding between us were substantially correct. On the 17th I caused it to be read to four of the five members of the Cabinet who were present at our conference on the 14th, and they concurred in the general accuracy of its statements respecting our conversation upon that occasion.

In reply to your communication I have deemed it proper, in order to prevent further misunderstanding, to make this simple recital of facts.

Very respectfully, yours,
ANDREW JOHNSON.

General U. S. GRANT, Commanding United States Army.

HEADQUARTERS ARMY OF THE UNITED STATES, }
WASHINGTON, D. C. February 3, 1868. }

SIR: I have the honor to acknowledge the receipt of your communication of the 31st ultimo, in answer to mine of the 28th ultimo.

* * * * * *

I confess my surprise that the Cabinet officers referred to should so greatly misapprehend the facts in the matter of admissions alleged to have been made by me at the Cabinet meeting of the 14th ultimo as to suffer their names to be made the basis of the charges in the newspaper article referred to, or agree in the accuracy, as you affirm they do, of your account of what occurred at that meeting.

You know that we parted on Saturday, the 11th ultimo, without any promise on my part, either express or implied, to the effect that I would hold on to the office of Secretary of War *ad interim* against the action of the Senate, or, declining to do so myself, would surrender it to you before such action was had, or that I would see you again at any fixed time on the subject.

The performance of the promises alleged by you to have been made by me would have involved a resistance to law and an inconsistency with the whole history of my connection with the suspension of Mr. Stanton.

From our conversations and my written protest of August 1, 1867, against the removal of Mr. Stanton, you must have known that my greatest objection to his removal or suspension was the fear that some one would be appointed in his stead who would, by opposition to the laws relating to the restoration of the Southern States to their proper relations to the Government, embarrass the army in the performance of duties especially imposed upon it by these laws; and it was to prevent such an appointment that I accepted the office of Secretary of War *ad interim*, and not for the purpose of enabling you to get rid of Mr. Stanton by my withholding it from him in opposition to law, or, not doing so myself, surrendering it to one who would, as the statement and assumptions in your communication plainly indicate was sought.

And it was to avoid this same danger, as well as to relieve you from the personal embarrassment in which Mr. Stanton's reinstatement would place you, that I urged the appointment of Governor Cox, believing that it would be agreeable to you and also to Mr. Stanton, satisfied as I was that it was the good of the country, and not the office, the latter desired.

On the 15th ultimo, in presence of General Sherman, I stated to you that I thought Mr. Stanton would resign, but did not say that I would advise him to do so. On the 18th I did agree with General Sherman to go and advise him to that course, and on the 19th I had an interview alone with Mr. Stanton, which led me to the conclusion that any advice to him of the kind would be useless, and I so informed General Sherman.

Before I consented to advise Mr. Stanton to resign I understood from him, in a conversation on the subject immediately after his reinstatement, that it was his opinion that the act of Congress entitled "An act temporarily to supply vacancies in the Executive Departments in certain cases," approved February 20, 1863, was repealed by subsequent legislation, which materially influenced my action. Previous to this time I had had no doubt that the law of 1863 was still in force, and, notwithstanding my action, a fuller examination of the law leaves a question in my mind whether it is or is not repealed; this being the case, I could not now advise his resignation lest the same danger I apprehended on his first removal might follow.

The course you would have it understood I agreed to pursue was in violation of law and without orders from you; while the course I did pursue, and which I never doubted you fully understood, was in accordance with law, and not in disobedience of any orders of my superior.

And now, Mr. President, where my honor as a soldier and integrity as a man have been so violently assailed, pardon me for saying that I can but regard this whole matter, from the beginning to the end, as an attempt to involve me in the resistance of law for which you hesitated to assume the responsibility in orders, and thus to destroy my character before the country. I am, in a measure, confirmed in this conclusion by your recent orders directing me to disobey orders from the Secretary of War—my superior and your subordinate—without having countermanded his authority to issue the orders I am to disobey.

With assurance, Mr. President, that nothing less than a vindication of my personal honor and character could have induced this correspondence on my part, I have the honor to be, very respectfully, your obedient servant,
U. S. GRANT, General.
His Excellency, A. JOHNSON, President of the United States.

EXECUTIVE MANSION,
February 10, 1868.

GENERAL.—The extraordinary character of your letter of the 3d instant would seem to preclude any reply on my part, but the manner in which publicity has been given to the correspondence of which that letter forms a part, and the grave questions which are involved, induce me to take this method of giving, as a proper sequel to the communications which have passed between us, the statements of the five members of the Cabinet who were present on the occasion of our conversation on the 14th ultimo, and copies of the letters which they have addressed to me upon the subject are accordingly herewith inclosed. You speak of my letter of the 1st ultimo as a reiteration of the many and gross misrepresentations contained in certain newspaper articles, and reassert the correctness of the statements contained in your communication of the 28th ultimo, adding, and I here give your own words, "anything in your reply to it to the contrary notwithstanding."

When a controversy upon matters of fact reaches the point to which this has been brought, further assertion or denial between the immediate parties should cease, especially when upon either side it loses the character of the respectful discussion which is required by the relations in which the parties stand to each other, and degenerates in tone and temper; and in such case, if there is nothing to rely upon but the opposing statements, conclusions must be drawn from those statements alone, and from whatever intrinsic probabilities they afford in favor of or against either of the parties.

I should not shrink from the controversy, but, fortunately, it is not left to this test alone. There were five Cabinet officers present at the conversation, the details of which were given in my letter of the 28th ultimo. You allow yourself to say that letter "contains many and gross misrepresentations." These gentlemen heard that conversation, and have read my statement. They speak for themselves, and I leave the proof without a word of comment.

I deem it proper before concluding this communication, to notice some of the statements contained in your letter. You say "that a performance of the promises alleged to have been made by you to the President would have involved a resistance to law and an inconsistency with the whole history of my connection with the suspension of Mr. Stanton." You then state that you "had fears the President would, on the removal of Mr. Stanton, appoint some one in his place who would embarrass the army in carrying out the Reconstruction acts, and it was to prevent such an appointment that I accepted the office of Secretary of War *ad interim*, and not for the purpose of enabling you to get rid of Mr. Stanton by my withholding it from him in opposition to the law, or not doing so myself, surrendering it to one who, as the statements and assumptions in your communication plainly indicate, was sought." First of all, you here admit that from the very beginning of what you term "the whole history of your connection with Mr. Stanton's suspension," you intended to circumvent the President.

It was to carry out that intent that you accepted the appointment. This was in your mind at the time of your acceptance. It was not then in obedience to the order of your superior, as has heretofore been supposed, that you assumed the duties of the office. You knew the President's purpose to prevent Mr. Stanton from resuming the office of Secretary of War, and you intended to defeat that purpose. You accepted the office, not in the interest of the President, but of Mr. Stanton. If this purpose so entertained by you had been confined to yourself, if, when accepting the office you had done so with a mental reservation to frustrate the President, it would have been a deception in the ethics of some persons. Each course is allowable, but you can not stand even upon that questionable ground. The history of your connection with this transaction, as written by yourself, places you in a different predicament, and shows that you not only concealed your design from the President, but induced him to suppose that you would carry out his purpose to keep Mr. Stanton out of office, by retaining it yourself, after an attempted restoration by the Senate, so as to require Mr. Stanton to establish his claim by judicial decision.

I now give that part of this story as was written by yourself in your letter of the 28th ultimo:

"Some time after I assumed the duties of Secretary of War *ad interim*, the President asked my views as to the course Mr. Stanton would have to pursue in case the Senate should not concur in his suspension, to obtain possession of the office. My reply was in substance that Mr. Stanton would have to appeal to the courts to reinstate him, illustrating my position by citing the grounds I had taken in the case of the Baltimore Police Commissioners."

Now, at that time, as you admit in your letter of the 3d, you held the office for the very object of defeating an appeal to the courts. In that letter you say that " in accepting the office one motive was to prevent the President from appointing some other person who would retain possession, and thus make judicial proceedings necessary." You knew the President was unwilling to trust the office with any one who could not, by holding it, compel Mr. Stanton to resort to the courts.

You perfectly understood that in this interview. Sometime after you accepted the office, the President, not content with your silence, desired an expression of your views, and you answered him that Mr. Stanton would have to appeal to the courts. If the President had reposed confidence before he knew your views and that confidence had been violated, it might have been said he made a mistake. But a violation of confidence reposed after that conversation, was no mistake of his nor of yours.

The fact only that need be stated is, that after the date of this conversation you did not intend to hold the office with the purpose of forcing Mr. Stanton into court, but did hold it then and had accepted it to prevent that course from being carried out; in other words, you said to the President, that is the proper course, and you said to yourself, I have occupied this office and now hold it to defeat that course.

The excuse you make in a subsequent paragraph of that letter of the 18th ult., that afterward you changed your views as to what would be the proper course, has nothing to do with the point now under consideration. The point is that before you changed your views you had secretly determined to do the very thing which at last you did—surrender the office to Mr. Stanton. You may have changed your views as to the law, but you certainly did not change your views as to the course you had marked out for yourself from the beginning.

I will only notice one more statement in your letter of the 3d inst.: "That the performance of the promise which it is alleged was made by you, would have involved you in the resistance of law." I know of no statute that would have been violated had you carried out your promise in good faith and tendered your resignation when you concluded not to be made a party in any legal proceedings. You add: "I am in a measure confirmed in this conclusion by your recent orders to disobey orders from the Secretary of War, my superior and your subordinate, without having countermanded his authority to issue orders I am to disobey."

On the 24th ult. you addressed a note to the President, requesting in writing an order given to you verbally, five days before, to disregard orders from Mr. Stanton as Secretary of War, until you knew from the President himself that they were his orders. On the 29th, in compliance with your request, I did give instructions in writing "not to obey any order from the War Department, assumed to be issued by the direction of the President, unless such order is known by the General commanding the armies of the United States to have been authorized by the Executive."

"There are some orders which a Secretary of War may issue without the authority of the President. There are others which he issues simply as the agent of the President. For such orders the President is responsible, and he should therefore know and understand what they are before giving such direction;" says Mr. Stanton in his letter of the 4th inst., which accompanies the published correspondence with the President since the 12th of August last. He further says that "since he resumed the duties of the office he has continued to discharge them without any personal or written communication with the President." And he adds, "no orders have been issued from this department in the name of the President with my knowledge, and I have received no orders from him."

It thus seems that Mr. Stanton now discharges the duties of the War Department without any reference to the President, and without using his name. My order to you had only reference to orders assumed to be issued by the President. It would appear from Mr. Stanton's letter that you have received no such orders from him. In your note to the President, of the 13th ult., in which you acknowledge the reception of the written order of the 29th, you say that you have been informed by Mr. Stanton, that he has not received any order limiting his authority to issue orders to the army according to the practice of the department, and state "that while this authority to the War Department is not countermanded, it will be satisfactory evidence to me that any orders issued from the War Department, by direction of the President, are authorized by the Executive." The President issues an order to you to obey no order from the War Department, purporting to be made by direction of the President, until you have referred it to him for his approval; you reply, you have received the President's order, and will not obey it; but will obey an order purporting to be given by his direction if it comes from the War Department. You will obey no direct order of the President, but will obey his indirect order. If, as you say, "there has been a practice in the War Department to issue orders in the name of the President, without his direction," does the precise order you have requested, and have received, change the practice as to the General of the army? Could not the President countermand any such order, issued in the name of the President to do a special act, and an order directly from the President himself not to do the act, is there a doubt which you are to obey? You answer the question when you say to the President in your letter of the 3d inst., "the Secretary of War is my superior and your subordinate," and yet you refuse obedience to the superior out of deference to the subordinate. Without further comment on the insubordinate attitude which you have assumed, I am at a loss to know how you can relieve yourself from the orders of the President, who is made, by the Constitution, Commander in-chief of the army and navy, and is therefore the official superior as well of the General of the army, as of the Secretary of War.

Respectfully yours,
ANDREW JOHNSON.
Gen. U. S. Grant, Com'd'g armies of the U. S., Washington, D. C.

The letter of the President is accompanied by letters from the Secretaries of the Navy, Treasury, Interior, State, and Postmaster General, supporting his position.

THE PRESIDENT TO THE MEMBERS OF CABINET.

EXECUTIVE MANSION, WASHINGTON, }
February 5, 1868. }

SIR—The *Chronicle* of this morning contains a correspondence between the President and General Grant, reported from the War Department, in answer to a resolution from the House of Representatives. I beg to call your attention to that correspondence, and especially to that part of it which refers to the conversation between the President and General Grant, at the Cabinet meeting on Tuesday, the 14th of January, and to request you to state what was said in that conversation. Very respectfully yours,

ANDREW JOHNSON.

FROM GIDEON WELLS.

WASHINGTON, Feb. 5, 1868.

SIR—Your note of this date was handed to me this evening. My recollection of the conversation at the Cabinet meeting on the 14th of January, corresponds with your statement of it in the letter of the 31st ult., in the published correspondence. The three points specified in that letter, giving your recollection of the conversation, are correctly stated.

Very respectfully,
GIDEON WELLES.

FROM HUGH M'CULLOCH.

TREASURY DEPARTMENT, February 6, 1868.

SIR—I have received your note of the 5th instant calling my attention to the correspondence between yourself and General Grant, as published in the *Chronicle* of yesterday, especially to that part of it which relates to what occurred in the Cabinet meeting on Tuesday, the 14th ultimo, and requesting me to state what was said in the conversation referred to. I can not undertake to state the precise language uttered, but I have no hesitation in saying your account of that conversation, as given in your letter to General Grant, on the 31st ultimo, substantially, in all important particulars, accords with my recollection of it.

With great respect,
Your obedient servant,
HUGH McCULLOCH.
To the President.

FROM ALEX. W. RANDALL.

POSTOFFICE DEPARTMENT, WASHINGTON, D. C., February 6, 1868.

SIR—The following extract from your letter of the 31st of January, to General Grant, is according to my recollection of the conversation that took place between the President and General Grant at the Cabinet meeting on the 14th of January last:

[The Postmaster-General here quotes the statement of the President, in the letter referred to, and concludes thus]:

I take this mode of replying to the request contained in the President's letter, because my attention had been called to the subject when the conversation between the President and General Grant was under consideration.

Very respectfully,
Your obedient servant,
ALEXANDER W. RANDALL,
Postmaster-General.
To the President.

FROM O. H. BROWNING.

DEPARTMENT OF THE INTERIOR, WASHINGTON, D. C., February 6, 1868.

* * * * *

At the Cabinet meeting Tuesday, January 14, 1868, General Grant appeared and took his accustomed seat at the board. When he had been reached in the order of business, the President asked him, as usual, if he had anything to present. In reply, the General, referring to a note which he had that morning addressed to the President, inclosing a copy of the resolution of the Senate, refusing to concur in the reasons for the suspension of Stanton, proceeded to say: "He regarded his duties as Secretary of War *ad interim* terminated by that resolution, and that he could not lawfully exercise such duties for a moment after the adoption of the resolution; that the resolution reached him last night, and this morning he had gone to the War Department, entered the Secretary's room, bolted one door on the inside, locked the other on the outside, delivered the key to the Adjutant-General, and proceeded to the headquarters of the army and addressed the note above mentioned to the President, informing him that he was no longer Secretary of War *ad interim*."

The President expressed great surprise at the course which General Grant had thought proper to pursue, and addressed himself to the General, and proceeded to say, in substance, that he had anticipated such action of the Senate, and being very desirous to have the constitutionality of the Tenure-of-Office Bill tested, and his right to suspend or remove a member of the Cabinet decided by the judicial tribunal of the country, he had some time ago, and shortly after General Grant's appointment as Secretary of War *ad interim*, asked the General what his action would be in the event that the Senate should refuse to concur in the suspension of Mr. Stanton, and that the General had then agreed either to remain at the head of the War Department until a decision could be obtained from the Court, or resign the office into the hands of the President before the case was acted upon by the Senate, so as to place the President in the same situation he occupied at the time of Grant's appointment.

The President further said that the conversation was resumed on the preceding Saturday, at which time he asked the General what he intended to do if the Senate should undertake to reinstate Mr. Stanton, in reply to which the General referred to their former conversation upon the same subject, and said, "you understand my position, and my conduct will be conformable to that." He understood that he (the General) then expressed a repugnance to being made a party to a judicial proceeding, saying he would expose himself to fine and imprisonment by doing so, as his continuing to discharge the duties of Secretary of War *ad interim* after the Senate should have refused to concur in the suspension of Mr. Stanton would be a violation of the Tenure-of-Office Bill; that in reply to this the President informed General Grant that he had not suspended Mr. Stanton under the Tenure-of-Office Bill, but by virtue of the power conferred on him by the Constitution, and as to the fine or imprisonment, the President would pay whatever fine was imposed and submit to whatever imprisonment might be adjudged against him.

The General continued the conversation for some time, discussing the law at length, and finally separated without having reached a definite conclusion, and with the understanding that the General would see the President again on Monday.

I reply, General Grant admitted the conversations had occurred, and said that at the first conversation he had given it as his opinion to the President, that in the event of non-concurrence by the Senate in the action of the President in respect to the Secretary of War, the question would have to be decided by the Court; that Mr. Stanton would have to appeal to the Court to reinstate him in office; that the ins would remain in until they could be displaced, and the outs put in by legal proceedings, and that he then thought so, and had agreed that if he should change his mind he would notify the President in time to enable him to make another appointment, but at the time of the first conversation he had not looked very closely into the law; that it had recently been discussed by the newspapers and this had induced him to examine it more carefully, and that he had come to the conclusion that if the Senate should refuse to consent in the suspension, Mr. Stanton would thereby be reinstated, and that he (Grant) could continue thereafter to act as Secretary of War *ad interim*, without subjecting himself to fine and imprisonment; that he came over on Saturday to inform the President of this change in his views, and did so inform him; that the President replied that he had not suspended Mr. Stanton under the Tenure-of-Office Bill, but under the Constitution, and had appointed him (Grant) by virtue of the authority derived from the Constitution, etc.; that they continued to discuss the matter some time. Finally he left without any conclusion having been reached, expecting to see the President on Monday. He then proceeded to explain why he had not called upon the President on Monday, saying that he had a long interview with Gen. Sherman; that various little matters had occupied his time until late, and he did not think the Senate would act, and asked, "did not Gen. Sherman call on you on Monday?"

I do not know what passed between the President and General Grant on Saturday, except as I learned it from the conversation between them at the Cabinet meeting, on Tuesday, and the foregoing is substantially what then occurred. The precise words used on the occasion are not, of course, given exactly in the order which they were spoken, but the ideas expressed and facts stated are faithfully preserved and presented.

I have the honor to be, sir, with great respect, your obedient servant,

O. H. BROWNING.

To the President.

FROM W. H. SEWARD.

DEPARTMENT OF STATE,
WASHINGTON, February 6, 1868.

SIR—The meeting to which you refer in your letter was a regular Cabinet meeting, and while the members were assembling, and before the President had entered the Council Chamber, General Grant, on coming in, said to me that he was in attendance not as a member of the Cabinet but upon invitation, and I replied by the inquiry whether there was a change in the War Department.

After the President had taken his seat business went on in the usual way of hearing matters. When the time came for the Secretary of War, General Grant said he was not there as Secretary of War, but upon the President's invitation, that he had retired from the War Department. A slight difference then appeared about the supposed invitation. General Grant said the officer who had borne his letter to the President, announcing his retirement from the War Department, had told him the President desired to see him at the Cabinet, to which the President answered that when General Grant's communication was delivered to him the President simply replied, he supposed General Grant would be very soon at the Cabinet meeting. I regarded the conversation thus began as incidental. It went on very informally, and consisted of a statement on your part of your views in regard to your understanding of the tenure upon which General Grant had assented to hold the War Department *ad interim*, and of his replies by way of answer and explanation. It was respectful and courteous on both sides in this conversation. As details could only have been presented by verbal report, so far as I know no such report was made at the time—I can give only the general effect of the conversation. Certainly you stated that, although you had reported the reasons for Mr. Stanton's suspension to the Senate, you, nevertheless, held he would not be entitled to resume the office of Secretary of War, even if the Senate should disapprove of his suspension, and that you had proposed to have the question tested by judicial process, to be applied to the person who should be the incumbent of the Department, under your designation of Secretary of War *ad interim*, in the place of Mr. Stanton. You contended that it was well understood between yourself and General Grant that when he entered the Department as Secretary *ad interim* he expressed his concurrence in a belief that the question of Mr. Stanton's restoration would be a question for the courts. That, in a subsequent conversation with the General, you had adverted to the understanding thus had, and that General Grant expressed his concurrence in it. At some conversation which had been previously held, General Grant said he still adhered to the same construction of the law, but said if he should change his opinion he would give reasonable notice of it, so you could in any case be placed in the same position in regard to the War Department that you were while General Grant held it. I did not understand him as denying nor as explicitly admitting these statements in the form and full extent to which you made them. His admission of them was rather indirect and circumstantial, though I did not understand it to be an evasive one. He said, that, reasoning from what occurred in the case of the police in Maryland, which he regarded as a parallel one, he was of the opinion, and so assured you, that it was his right and duty, under your instructions, to hold the War Office until the Senate should disapprove of Mr. Stanton's suspension, and the question should be decided by the courts; that he remained until very recently of that opinion, and on the Saturday before the Cabinet meeting a conversation was held between yourself and him, in which the subject was generally discussed.

General Grant's statement in that conversation, that he had stated to you the difficulties which might arise, involving fine and imprisonment under the civil tenure bill, and that he did not care to subject himself to these penalties. That you replied to this remark that you regarded the civil tenure bill as unconstitutional, and did not think its penalties were to be feared, or that you would voluntarily assume them, and you insisted that General Grant should rather retain the office until relieved by yourself according to what you claimed was the original understanding between yourself and him, or by seasonable notice of change of purpose on his part, put you in the same situation in which you would be if he adhered. You claimed that General Grant finally said in that Saturday's conversation, that you understood his views and his proceedings thereafter would be consistent with what had been so understood.

General Grant did not controvert, nor can I say that he admitted, this last statement. Certainly, General Grant did not at any time in the Cabinet meeting insist that he had, in the Saturday conversation, either directly or finally advised you of his determination to retire from the charge of the War Department, otherwise than that, under your subsequent direction, he acquiesced in your statement that the Saturday conversation ended with an expectation that there would be a subsequent conference on the subject, which he, as well as yourself, understood could reasonably take place on Monday.

You then alluded to the fact that General Grant did not call upon you, as you expected, from that conversation. General Grant admitted that it was his expectation or purpose to call upon you Monday. General Grant assigned reasons for the omission. He said that he was in conference with General Sherman; that as there were many little matters to be attended to, he had conversed upon the matter of surrendering the War Department with General Sherman; he expected General Sherman would call on Monday. My own mind suggested a further explanation, but I do not remember whether it was mentioned or not, namely: it was not supposed by General Grant on Monday that the Senate would decide the question so promptly, as to anticipate a further explanation between yourself and him, if delayed beyond that day. General Grant made another explanation, that he was engaged on Sunday with General Sherman, and I think also Monday, in regard to the War Department, with a hope, though he did not say in an effort, to procure an amicable settlement of the affair of Mr. Stanton, and still hoped it would be brought about.

I have the honor to be, with great respect, your obedient servant,
WM. H. SEWARD.

GENERAL GRANT TO PRESIDENT JOHNSON.

HEADQUARTERS ARMY OF UNITED STATES,
WASHINGTON, D. C., Feb. 11, 1868.

His Excellency, Andrew Johnson, President of the United States:

SIR—I have the honor to acknowledge the receipt of your communication of the 10th inst., accompanied by the statements of five Cabinet ministers of their recollection of what occurred in the Cabinet meeting on the 14th of January. Without admitting anything contained in these statements where they differ from anything heretofore stated by me, I propose to notice only the portion of your communication wherein I am charged with insubordination.

I think it will be plain to the readers of my letter of the 30th of January, that I did not propose to disobey any legal order of the President, distinctly given, but only give an interpretation of what would be regarded as satisfactory evidence of the President's sanction to orders, communicated by the Secretary of War. I will say here that your letter of the 10th instant contains the first intimation I have had that you did not accept that interpretation.

Now, for my reasons for giving that interpretation. It was clear to me, before my letter of January 30 was written, that I, the person having more public business to transact with the Secretary of War than any other of the President's subordinates, was the only one who had been instructed to disregard the authority of Mr. Stanton, where his authority was derived as agent of the President. On the 27th of January I received a letter from the Secretary of War (copy herewith) directing me to furnish an escort to the public treasure from the Rio Grande to New Orleans, at the request of the Secretary of the Treasury to him. I also sent two other articles showing the recognition of Mr Stanton as Secretary of War by both the Secretary of Treasury and Postmaster-General, in all of which cases the Secretary of War had to call upon me to make the orders requested, or give the information desired, and where his authority to do so is derived, in my view, as agent of the President, with an order so clearly ambiguous as that of the President's here referred to, it was my duty to inform the President of my interpretation of it, and abide by that interpretation until I received further orders. Disclaiming any intention now or hereafter, of disobeying any legal order of the President, distinctly communicated,

I remain, very respectfully,
Your obedient servant,
U. S. GRANT, General.

The Niagara Falls Negotiation.

As part of the history of the negotiation, this letter of Mr. Greeley is given:

NEW YORK, July 7, 1864.

MY DEAR SIR—I venture to inclose you a letter and telegraphic dispatch that I received yesterday from our irrepressible friend, Colorado Jewett, at Niagara Falls. I think they deserve attention. Of course, I do not indorse Jewett's positive averment that his friends at the Falls have "full powers" from J. D., though I do not doubt that he thinks they have. I let that statement stand as simply evidencing the anxiety of the Confederates everywhere for peace. So much is beyond doubt.

And, therefore, I venture to remind you that our bleeding, bankrupt, almost dying country also longs for peace—shudders at the prospect of fresh conscriptions, of further wholesale devastations, and of new rivers of human blood; and a wide-spread conviction that the Government and its prominent supporters are not anxious for peace, and do not improve proffered opportunities to achieve it, is doing great harm now, and is morally certain, unless removed, to do far greater in the approaching elections.

It is not enough that we anxiously desire a true and lasting peace; we ought to demonstrate and establish the truth beyond cavil. The fact that A. H. Stephens was not permitted a year ago to visit and confer with the authorities at Washington, has done harm, which the tone at the late National Convention at Baltimore is not calculated to counteract.

I entreat you, in your own time and manner, to submit overtures for pacification to the Southern insurgents, which the impartial must pronounce frank and generous. If only with a view to the momentous election soon to occur in North Carolina, and of the draft to be enforced in the free States, this should be done at once. I would give the safe conduct required by the rebel envoys at Niagara upon their parole to avoid observation and to refrain from all communication with their sympathizers in the loyal States; but you may see reasons for declining it. But whether through them or otherwise, do not, I entreat you, fail to make the Southern people comprehend that you, and all of us, are anxious for peace, and prepared to grant liberal terms. I venture to suggest the following

PLAN OF ADJUSTMENT.

1. The Union is restored and declared perpetual.
2. Slavery is utterly and forever abolished throughout the same.
3. A complete amnesty for all political offenses, with a restoration of all the inhabitants of each State to the privileges of citizens of the United States.
4. The Union to pay four hundred million dollars in five per cent. United States stock to the late slave States, loyal and secession alike, to be apportioned *pro rata*, according to their slave population respectively by the census of 1860, in compensation for the losses of their loyal citizens by the abolition of slavery. Each State to be entitled to its quota upon the ratification by its Legislature of this adjustment. The bonds to be at the absolute disposal of the Legislature aforesaid.
5. The said slave States to be entitled henceforth to representation in the House on the basis of their total instead of their Federal population, the whole now being free.
6. A National Convention, to be assembled so soon as may be, to ratify this adjustment, and make such changes in the Constitution as may be deemed advisable.

Mr. President, I fear you do not realize how intently the people desire any peace consistent with the national integrity and honor, and how joyously they would hail its achievement and bless its authors. With United States stocks worth but forty cents in gold per dollar, and drafting about to commence on the third million of Union soldiers, can this be wondered at?

I do not say that a just peace is now attainable, though I believe it to be so. But I do say that a frank offer by you to the insurgents of terms which the impartial say ought to be accepted, will, at the worst, prove an immense and sorely needed advantage to the national cause. It may save us from a Northern insurrection.

Yours, truly,
HORACE GREELEY.
Hon. A. LINCOLN, President, Washington, D. C.

P. S.—Even though it should be deemed unadvisable to make an offer of terms to the rebels, I insist that, in any possible case, it is desirable that any offer they may be disposed to make should be received, and either accepted or rejected I beg you to invite those now at Niagara to exhibit their credentials and submit their ultimatum.

H. G.

EXECUTIVE MANSION,
WASHINGTON, July 18, 1864.

To whom it may concern:

Any proposition which embraces the restoration of peace, the integrity of the whole Union, and the abandonment of slavery, and which comes by and with an authority that can control the armies now at war against the United States, will be received and considered by the Executive Government of the United States, and will be met by liberal terms on other substantial and collateral points, and the bearer or bearers thereof shall have safe conduct both ways.

ABRAHAM LINCOLN.

The character of this reply of Mr. Lincoln was regarded as a repulse of the proposed negotiations by Messrs. Holcombe and Clay, and with it terminated the effort of Mr. Greeley to bring about a peace. Those gentlemen, though occupying a confidential and diplomatic relation to the Confederate Government, were not authorized, until they heard from Richmond, to act definitely on the subject, though they felt justified to give the assurance that such authority would certainly be vested in them. With a candor that was creditable, they informed Mr. Lincoln's agent of the fact, before accepting the safe conduct which had been guaranteed them to Washington. Whereupon Mr. Lincoln replied with his "To whom it may concern" document, which defeated the purpose contemplated.

These documents are reproduced in this work to show the opinions of Mr. Greeley and Mr. Lincoln as to what was intended to be secured by peace.

"The Union is restored * * * with a restoration of all the inhabitants of each State to the privileges of citizens of the United States," said Mr. Greeley.

—" the restoration of peace, the integrity of the whole Union," said Mr. Lincoln.

Platform of the National Union Convention, held at Philadelphia, August 14, 1866.

This Convention, composed of delegates representing the Conservative sentiment of the country, assembled at Philadelphia, on the 14th of August, 1866. It was one of the largest Conventions ever held in the United States On the 16th of August, it adopted the following

DECLARATION OF PRINCIPLES.

The National Union Convention, now assembled in the city of Philadelphia, composed of delegates from every State and Territory in the Union, admonished by the solemn lessons which, for the last five years, it has pleased the Supreme Ruler of the Universe to give to the American people; profoundly grateful for the return of peace; desirous, as are a large majority of their countrymen, in all sincerity, to forget and forgive the past; revering the Constitution as it comes to us from our ancestors; regarding the Union in its restoration as more sacred than ever; looking with deep anxiety into the future, as of instant and continuing trials, hereby issues and proclaims the following declaration of principles and purposes, on which they have, with perfect unanimity, agreed:

1st. We hail with gratitude to Almighty God the end of the war and the return of peace to our afflicted and beloved land.

2d. The war just closed has maintained the authority of the Constitution, with all the powers which it confers, and all the restrictions which it imposes upon the General Government, unabridged and unaltered, and it has preserved the Union, with the equal rights, dignity, and authority of the States perfect and unimpaired.

3d. Representation in the Congress of the United States and in the Electoral College is a right recognized by the Constitution as abiding in every State, and as a duty imposed upon the people, fundamental in its nature, and essential to the existence of our republican institutions, and neither Congress nor the General Government has any authority or power to deny this right to any State or to withhold its enjoyment under the Constitution from the people thereof.

4th. We call upon the people of the United States to elect to Congress as members thereof none but men who admit this fundamental right of representation, and who will receive to seats therein loyal representatives from every State in allegiance to the United States, subject to the constitutional right of each House to judge of the elections, returns, and qualifications of its own members.

5th. The Constitution of the United States, and the laws made in pursuance thereof, are the supreme law of the land, anything in the constitution or laws of any State to the contrary notwithstanding. All the powers not conferred by the Constitution upon the General Government, nor prohibited by it to the States, are reserved to the States, or to the people thereof; and among the rights thus reserved to the States is the right to prescribe qualifications for the elective franchise therein, with which right Congress can not interfere. No State or combination of States has the right to withdraw from the Union, or to exclude, through their action in Congress or otherwise, any other State or States from the Union. The Union of these States is perpetual.

6th. Such amendments to the Constitution of the United States may be made by the people thereof as they may deem expedient, but only in the mode pointed out by its provisions; and in proposing such amendments, whether by Congress or by a Convention, and in ratifying the same, all the States of the Union have an equal and an indefeasible right to a voice and a vote thereon.

7th. Slavery is abolished and forever prohibited, and there is neither desire nor purpose on the part of the Southern States that it should ever be re-established upon the soil, or within the jurisdiction of the United States: and the enfranchised slaves in all the States of the Union should receive, in common with all their inhabitants, equal protection in every right of person and property.

8th. While we regard as utterly invalid, and never to be assumed or made of binding force, any obligations incurred or undertaken in making war against the United States, we hold the debt of the Nation to be sacred and inviolable; and we proclaim our purpose in discharging this, as in performing all other national obligations, to maintain unimpaired and unimpeached the honor and the faith of the Republic.

9th. It is the duty of the National Government to recognize the servives of the Federal soldiers and sailors in the contest just closed, by meeting promptly and fully all their just and rightful claims for the services they have rendered the Nation, and by extending to those of them who have survived, and to the widows and orphans of those who have fallen, the most generous and considerate care.

10th. In Andrew Johnson, President of the United States, who, in his great office, has proved steadfast in his devotion to the Constitution, the laws, and interests of his country, unmoved by persecution and undeserved reproach, having faith unassailable in the people and in the principles of free government, we recognize a Chief Magistrate worthy of the Nation and equal to the great crisis upon which his lot is cast; and we tender to him, in the discharge of his high and responsible duties, our profound respect and assurance of our cordial and sincere support.

The resolutions were unanimously adopted.

OFFICERS OF THE CONVENTION.

A correct idea of the *personnel* of this body, may be inferred from the list of its various officers. Major-General John A. Dix, of New York, now Minister to France, acted as temporary President.

President—Hon. JAMES R. DOOLITTLE, of Wisconsin.

Vice-Presidents—Leonard Wood, L.L.D., Maine; Daniel Marcy, New Hampshire; Myron Clark, Vermont; Hon. R. B. Hall, Massachusetts; Alfred Anthony, Rhode Island, Hon. O. F. Winchester, Connecticut; Hon. Theodore S. Faxton, New York; Gen. Gershom Mott, New Jersey; Asa Packer, Pennsylvania; Ayres Stockley, Delaware; General George Vickers, Maryland; Hon. John W. Brockenborough, Virginia; Thos. Sweeney, West Virginia; Hon. John A. Gilmer, North Carolina; Judge David Lewis Wardlaw, South Carolina; Richard S Lyons, Georgia; Judge Thomas Randall, Florida; G. A. Sykes, Mississippi; Cuthbert Bullitt, Louisiana; J. M. Tebbetts, Arkansas; D. J. Burnett, Texas; Thomas A. R. Nelson, Tennessee; George S. Houston, Alabama; Hon. J. W. Ritter, Kentucky; Hon. R. P. Ranney, Ohio; Hon. W. S. Smith, Indiana; D. K. Green, Illinois; Hon. O. B. Clark, Michigan; Hon. John Hogan, Missouri; Franklin Steele, Minnesota; General Milton Montgomery, Wisconsin; Edward Johnston, Iowa; J. L. Pendery, Kansas; William T. Coleman, California; Frank Hereford, Nevada; Hon. George L. Curry, Oregon; Joseph H. Bradley, senior, District of Columbia; J. W. Turner, Dakotah; Chas. F. Powell, Idaho; George L. Miller, Nebraska; Hon. B. F. Hall, Colorado; Elwood Evans, Washington Territory.

Secretaries—James Mann, Maine; E. S. Cutter, New Hampshire; George H. Simmons, Vermont; Charles Wright, Massachusetts; James H. Parsons, Rhode Island; James A. Hovey, Connecticut; E. O. Perrin, New York; Colonel Thomas S. Allison, New Jersey; Harry A. Weaver, Pennsylvania; J. F. Tharp, Delaware; Dr. W. W.

Watkins, Maryland; Thomas Wallace, Virginia; Henry S. Walker, West Virginia; S. F. Patterson, North Carolina; Thomas Y. Simmons, South Carolina; J. H. Christie, Georgia; Judge B. D. Wright, Florida; A. G. Mayer, Mississippi; A. W. Walker, Louisiana; Elias C. Boudinot, Arkansas; J. M. Daniel, Texas; John Lellyet, Tennessee; C. S. G. Doster, Alabama; M. H. Owsley, Kentucky; E. B. Eshelman, Ohio; Colonel C. C. Matson, Indiana; John McGinnis, junior, Illinois; General John G. Parkhurst, Michigan; Colonel C. B. Wilkinson, Missouri; Richard Price, Minnesota; George C. Ginty, Wisconsin; J. M. Walker, Iowa; W. A. Tipton, Kansas; Jackson Temple, California; Colonel Jesse Williams, Nevada; A. D. Fitch, Oregon; Jas. R. O'Beirne, District of Columbia; D. T. Bramble, Dakotah; Major L. Lowrie, Nebraska; Charles F. Egan, Washington.

COMMITTEE TO WAIT ON THE PRESIDENT.

Hon. REVERDY JOHNSON, Chairman; Maine, W. G. Crosby, Calvin Record; New Hampshire, J. Hosley, J. H. Smith; Vermont, L. Robinson, General Isaac McDaniel; Massachusetts, E. C. Bailey, Edward Avery; Rhode Island, Amasa Sprague, Gideon Bradford; Connecticut, James E. English, G. H. Hollister; New York, Vivus W. Smith, S. E. Church; New Jersey, T. H. Herring, General Theodore Runyon; Pennsylvania, J. R. Flanigan, George W. Cass; Delaware, Saxe-Gotha Laws, C. H. B. Day; Maryland, J. Morrison Harris, Isaac D. Jones; Virginia, Hon. James Barbour, G. W. Bolling; West Virginia, John J. Thompson, Daniel Lamb; North Carolina, D. M. Barringer, G. Howard; South Carolina, J. L. Manning, James Farrow; Georgia, S. J. Smith, J. L. Wimberly; Florida, J. P. Sanderson, J. C. McKibben; Mississippi, Giles M. Hillyer, H. F. Simrall; Louisiana, T. P. May, William H. C. King; Texas, D. J. Burnett, B. H. Epperson; Tennessee, A. A. Kyle, D. B. Thomas; Arkansas, John B. Luce, E. C. Boudinot; Alabama, Lewis E. Parsons, John Gill Shorter; Kentucky, J. W. Stevenson, A. Harding; Ohio, Henry B. Paine, General A. McD. McCook; Indiana, General Sol. Meredith, David S. Gooding; Illinois, General George C. Bates, Hon. W. R. Morrison; Michigan, General C. O. Loomis, General G. A. Custer; Wisconsin, A. W. Curtis, Robert Flint; Iowa, Colonel Cyrus H. Mackey, B. B. Richards; Kansas, General H. S. Sleeper, Orlin Thurston; California, J. A. McDougall; Colonel Jacob P. Leese; Nevada, Gideon J. Tucker, John Carmichael; Oregon, W. H. Farrar, E. M. Barnum; District of Columbia, Thomas B. Florence, B. T. Swart; Idaho, Hon. H. H. DePuy, S. Cummins; Nebraska, George L. Miller, L. Lowrie; Washington, George D. Cole, C. P. Egan; Minnesota, H. M. Rice, D. S. Norton; Missouri, E. A. Louis, John M. Richardson; Dakotah, D. T. Bramble, L. D. Parmer.

NATIONAL UNION EXECUTIVE COMMITTEE.

Joseph T. Crowell, Chairman; Maine, James Mann, A. P. Gould; New Hampshire, Edmund Burke, E. S. Cutter; Vermont, B. D. Smalley, Colonel H. N. Worthan; Massachusetts, Josiah Dunham, R. S. Spofford; Rhode Island, Alfred Anthony, James H. Parsons; Connecticut, James T. Babcock. D. C. Scranton; New York, Robert H. Pruyn, Samuel I. Tilden; Pennsylvania. S. M. Zulick, J. S. Black; Delaware, J. P. Comegys, E. L. Martin; Maryland, T. Swann, T. D. Pratt; Virginia, J. F. Johnson, E C. Robinson; West Virginia, Daniel Lamb, John J. Jackson; North Carolina, T. S. Ashe, Joseph H. Wilson; South Carolina, J. L. Orr. B. F. Perry; Georgia, J. H. Christie, T. Hardeman, jr.; Florida, Hon. William Marvin, Hon. Wilkinson Call; Alabama, M. H. Cruikshank, C. C. Huckabee; Mississippi, William L. Sharkey, G. L. Potter; Louisiana, Randall Hunt, Alfred Hennen; Arkansas, Lorenzo Gibson, E. H. English; Texas, B. H. Epperson, John Hancock; Tennessee, Hon. David T. Patterson, W. D. Campbell; Kentucky, R. H. Stanton, Hamilton Pope; Ohio, Lewis D. Campbell, George B. Smythe; Indiana. Hon. David S. Gooding, T. Dowling; Illinois, General J. A. McClernand, J. O. Norton; Michigan, Alfred Russell. Byron G. Stout; Missouri, Barton Able, James S. Rollins; Minnesota, H. M. Rice, D. S. Norton; Wisconsin, S. A. Pease, J. A. Noonan; Iowa, George H. Parker, William A. Chase; Kansas, James L. McDowell, W. A. Tipton; New Jersey, Joseph T. Crowell, Theo. F. Randolph; Nevada, John Carmichael, G. B. Hall; District of Columbia, J D. Hoover, J. B. Blake; Nebraska, H. H. Heath, J. S. Morton, Washington Territory, R Willard, Elwood Evans; California, Samuel Purdy, Joseph P. Hoge; Oregon, J. W. Nesmith, B. F. Bonham; Dakotah, W. K. Armstrong, N. W. Miner; Idaho, William H. Wallace, Henry Cummins.

RESIDENT EXECUTIVE COMMITTEE AT WASHINGTON.

Charles Knap, Chairman; Hon. Montgomery Blair, Hon. Charles Mason, Ward H. Lamon, John F. Coyle, A. E. Perry, Samuel Fowler, Colonel James R. O'Beirne, Cornelius Wendell.

COMMITTEE ON FINANCE.

Charles Knap, Chairman; Maine, A. W. Johnson, John Burleigh; New Hampshire, Daniel Marcy, W. N. Blair; Vermont, R. W. Chase, C. L. Davenport; Massachusetts, F. O. Prince, George M. Bentley; Rhode

Island, Amasa Sprague, James Waterhouse; Connecticut, J. H. Ashmead, Freeman M. Brown; New York, Abraham Wakeman, Richard Schell; New Jersey, J. L. McKnight, Francis S. Lathrop; Pennsylvania, R. L. Martin, Henry M. Phillips; Delaware, Charles Wright, T. F. Crawford; Maryland, R. Fowler. W. P. Maulsby; Virginia, Edmund W. Hubbard, George Blow, jr.; West Virginia, Charles T. Beale, Thomas Sweeney; North Carolina, A. H. Arrington, A. McLean; South Carolina, F. J. Moses, W. Pinkney Schingler; Georgia, Lewis Tumlin, William M. Lowry; Florida, George Scott, W. C. Maloney; Alabama, Lewis Owen, J. S. Kennedy; Mississippi, E. Pegues, J. A. Bingford; Louisiana, A. M. Holbrook; Arkansas, M. L. Bell, John R. Fellowes; Texas. M. B. Ochiltree, J. Hancock; Tennessee, W. B. Ferguson, J. Williams; Kentucky, M. J. Durham, W. W. Baldwin; Ohio, T. E. Cunningham, J. H. James; Indiana, Levi Sparks, Moses Drake; Illinois, William B. Ogden, Isaac Underhill; Michigan, G. C. Monroe, William B. McCreery; Missouri, Thomas L. Price, Charles M. Elliard; Minnesota, C. F. Buck, Charles F. Gilman; Wisconsin, J. B. Doe, C. L. Sholes; Iowa, W. D. McHenry, S. O. Butler; Kansas. T. P. Fitzwilliam, G. A. Colton; California, John H. Baird, Henry F. Williams; Nevada, Frank Hereford, L. H. Newton; District of Columbia, Charles Knap, Esau Pickrell; Dakotah, J. B. S. Todd, F. C. DeWitt; Idaho. C. F. Powell, T. W. Betts; Nebraska, James R. Porter, P. B. Becker; Washington, Elwood Evans, Edward Lander; Oregon, J. C. Ainsworth, O. Hummason.

Freedom of the Press.

THE RADICALS' OPPOSED TO IT.

On the 19th of May, 1864, by order of the Secretary of War, the offices of the New York *Journal of Commerce* and the New York *World*—in which papers had appeared a forged proclamation of the President for 400,000 troops—were seized by the military authorities and held several days. This led to these proceedings:

On the 29th of May, 1864, in the House of Representatives, Mr. Pruyn asked consent, on behalf of a portion of the New York delegation, to offer this resolution:

"*Resolved*, That the conduct of the Executive authority of the Government in recently closing the offices and suppressing the publication of the *World* and *Journal of Commerce*, newspapers in the city of New York, under circumstances which have been placed before the public, was an act unwarranted in itself, dangerous to the cause of the Union, in violation of the Constitution, and subversive of the principles of civil liberty, and, as such, is hereby censured by this House."

Several members objected. At a later hour he moved a suspension of the rules for the purpose of offering it, but this motion was rejected—yeas 54, nays 79, as follows:

YEAS—Messrs. James C. Allen, Augustus C. Baldwin, Bliss, Brooks, James S. Brown, Chanler, Coffroth, Cox, Dawson, Denison, Eden, Edgerton, Eldridge, Finck, Grider, Harding, Charles M. Harris, Herrick, Holman, Hutchins, Philip Johnson, William Johnson, Kalbfleisch, Kernan, King, Knapp, Law, Lazear, Mallory, Marcy, McAllister, McDowell, Wm. H. Miller, Morrison, Nelson, Noble, John O'Neill, Pendleton, Pruyn, Radford, Samuel J. Randall, Robinson, James S. Rollins, Ross, Scott, John B. Steele, William G. Steele, Strouse, Voorhees, Wadsworth, Ward, Wheeler, Joseph W. White, Fernando Wood—54.

NAYS—Messrs. Alley, Ames, Arnold, John D. Baldwin, Baxter, Beaman, Jacob B. Blair, Blow, Boutwell, Boyd, Broomall, William G. Brown, Ambrose W. Clark, Freeman Clarke, Cobb, Cole, Cresswell, Henry Winter Davis, Thomas T. Davis, Dawes, Deming, Dixon, Donnelly, Driggs, Eckley, Eliot, Farnsworth, Garfield, Gooch, Grinnell, Higby, Hooper, Hotchkiss, Asahel W. Hubbard, Ingersoll, Jenckes, Julian, Kelley, Francis W. Kellogg, Loan, Longyear, Marvin, McBride, McClurg, Samuel F. Miller, Moorhead, Morrill, Amos Myers, Leonard Myers, Charles O'Neill, Orth, Patterson, Perham, Pike, Pomeroy, Price, William H. Randall, John H. Rice, Edward H. Rollins, Scheuck, Scofield, Shannon, Sloan, Smithers, Smith, Spalding, Stevens, Thayer, Thomas, Upson, Elihu B. Washburne, William B. Washburn, Webster, Whaley, Williams, Wilder, Wilson, Windom, Woodbridge—79.

Every Democrat, it will be seen, voted to suspend the rules to vindicate the liberty of the press. Every Radical voted against it.

The consistency of their opposition to this sacred and constitutional guaranteed franchise of the press is illustrated by General Grant's order on this subject, and his suppression of the Richmond *Enquirer*, referred to in a previous part of this work; as also by the notes in this work to that clause of the Constitution guaranteeing the liberty of the press.

We have not space to give the innumerable instances of assault on the freedom of the press during the war. They would occupy a large part of this work. To afford an idea of its extent, we give a mere index of the cases of this kind of outrage in 1864:

May 18, 1864—New York Journal of Commerce and the New York World suppressed.

Constitution and Union, Fairfield, Iowa, destroyed February 8, 1864.

Crawford Democrat, Meadville, Pennsylvania, mobbed February 5, 1864.

Northumberland Democrat, Pennsylvania, destroyed by mob February 7, 1864.

Volksblatt, Belleville, Missouri, destroyed a second time May 18, 1864.

Democrat, Sunbury, Pennsylvania, mobbed January 18, 1864; office destroyed and property stolen.

Mahoning Sentinel, Youngstown, Ohio, destroyed by a mob, January 28, 1864; attempt to assassinate the editor.

Eagle, Lancaster, Ohio, partially destroyed by a mob February 3, 1864.

Crisis, Columbus, Ohio, saved, by being armed, from a mob, February 15, 1864.

Statesman, Columbus, Ohio, saved by the same means, same day.

Democrat, Laporte, Indiana, destroyed February 15, 1864.

Democrat, Waseon, Ohio, destroyed February 20, 1864.

Advertiser, Lebanon, Pennsylvania, defended successfully March 15, 1864.

Empire, Dayton, Ohio, completely destroyed March 3, 1864.

Picket Guard, Chester, Illinois, totally destroyed August 20, 1864.

Herald, Franklin county, Indiana, demolished March 20, 1864.

Democrat, Greenville, Ohio, demolished March 5, 1864.

Union, Louisiana, Missouri, destroyed March 6, 1864.

St. Mary's Gazette, Leonardtown, Maryland, warned April 12, 1864.

Picayune, New Orleans, suppressed, date unknown.

Courier, New Orleans, suppressed and editors banished May 23, 1864. Order never revoked.

Metropolitan Record, New York, circulation forbidden in the West, March 26, 1864.

Transcript, Baltimore, Maryland, suppressed May 18, 1864, for publishing that the loss of the Army of the Potomac had been not less than 70,000.

Democrat, Cambridge, Maryland, suppressed September 9, 1864.

Freeman's Journal, burned at Nashville, September 12, 1864.

Democrat, Gallatin county, Illinois, editors seized and imprisoned August 19, 1864.

Crisis, Columbus, Ohio, editors seized and imprisoned May 10, 1864.

Register, Wheeling, West Virginia, editors seized, paper suppressed July 20, 1864.

Journal, Belfast, Maine, seized August 18, 1864.

News, Memphis, Tennessee, suppressed July, 1864.

Bulletin, Baltimore, Maryland, suppressed July, 1864.

Gazette, Parkersburg, West Virginia, editor seized by Gen. Hunter, July 27, 1864.

Kentucky, June, 1864—All Democratic papers excluded from the State.

Memphis—All Democratic papers except the Missouri Republican excluded from this place September 16, 1864.

Loyalist, Baltimore, Maryland, September 30, 1864, discontinued by order of General Wallace.

True Presbyterian, Louisville, Kentucky, discontinued November 29, 1864, by General Burbridge.

For cases of violent assault upon the freedom of the press since the war, we refer to Grant's record, and also the history of Reconstruction, both in a previous part of this book, which treats of the more conspicuous objects of outrage in that respect.

A Southern Fire-Eater in the Chicago Convention.

A CONFEDERATE GOVERNOR IN COUNCIL WITH THE RADICALS.

We see from the proceedings of the Convention which nominated Grant and Colfax, that Joe Brown was there, in full feather, the representative of the negroes and carpet-baggers of Georgia. He was not only there, but constituted a prominent figure in that motley conclave of debased politicians and unprincipled conspirators. It is not believed by many that he is the same old Joe Brown, the Sorghum Governor of Georgia, the head and front of the Georgia militia, the life-long disunionist, the treacherous friend of any cause he espouses, the ambitious aspirant who has long since lost all honor in the successful pursuit of office, and who proposes now to sacrifice his country to obtain a new lease on power.

He is the same Joe Brown who seized Fort Pulaski, one of the forts of the United States, for doing which the Convention of Georgia thanked him in the following resolution:

Be it unanimously resolved, by the people of Georgia, in convention assembled, as a response to the resolutions of New York, that we highly approve of the patriotic and energetic conduct of our Governor in taking possession of Fort Pulaski by the Georgia troops, etc. * * * *

He is the same Joe Brown who, on the 21st day of February, 1861, seized the ship Martha J. Ward, bark Augusta and brig Harold, vessels belonging to private citizens of the State of New York, which were then, long before hostilities had begun, in the waters of the Savannah, engaged in the peaceful pursuits of a legitimate commerce; thus assailing the private fortunes of their owners who had done nothing against Georgia, merely because they were residents of the city of New York, whose Police Commissioners had illegally seized some arms belonging to Georgia.

He is the same Joe Brown who, on the 26th day of April, 1861, issued a proclamation forbidding the payment of debts to Northern creditors. The proclamation began thus:

Whereas, by the oppressive and wicked conduct of the Government and people of that part of the late United States, known as the Anti-slavery States, war actually exists between them and the people of the Southern States, etc. * * And I hereby invite each citizen or inhabitant of this State who is indebted to said Government or either of said States, or any citizen or inhabitant thereof, to pay the amount of such indebtedness, whenever due, into the Treasury of Georgia, etc.

That he do not, under any pretext whatever, remit, transfer, or pay to the Government of the United States, or any one of the States composing said Government, which is known as a Free-soil State, including, among others, the States of Massachusetts, Rhode Island, Connecticut, New York, New Jersey, Pennsylvania and Ohio, or to any citizen or inhabitant of any such State, any money, bills, drafts, or other things of value, either in payment of any debt due, or hereafter to become due, or for, or on account of, any other cause whatever, until the termination of hostilities. * *

JOSEPH E. BROWN.

E. P. WATKINS, Sec'y of State.

He is the same Joe Brown who, on the 25th of January, 1861, demanded the surrender of the Augusta Arsenal, and coerced its abandonment by the United States authorities to him as Governor.

He is the same Joe Brown who, on the 2d of November, 1862, issued a call announcing that if a sufficient supply of negroes be not tendered within ten days, General Mercer will, in pursuance of authority given him, proceed to impress, and asking of every planter of Georgia a tender of one-fifth of his negroes to complete the fortifications around Savannah. This one-fifth is estimated at 15,000.

He is the same Joe Brown who became impatient at the delay of the Confederate Government in whipping the Federal forces, and called on the Georgia Legislature to give him the means of cleaning them out at once. In that call be said:

"My own opinion is that it is not now the time to count the cost; but that we should call out as many troops as may be necessary to repel the invader. * * * Whether it may take 10,000 or 20,000 men, or whether it may cost $5,000,000 or $10,000,000. I ask, in the name of the people, that their representatives place at my command the men and money necessary to accomplish this object."

This is the Joe Brown who hobnobbed with Dan Sickles and John Logan at the National Convention of the Radical party. A noble and consistent trio. Logan and Sickles professed to be secessionists before the war, patted the South on the back, and told her to go ahead. Brown, next to the South Carolina authorities, was the first to begin war upon the Federal authority.

Mr. Colfax on the Man and Brother.

MARCH 1, 1861—He voted for an amendment to the Fugitive Slave law, which provided for the return of and the trial of the title to an alleged fugitive slave claiming to be free in the State or district from which he escaped.

He would then trust the white people of those States to be jurors to sit upon the question of the slavery or freedom of a colored loyalist. Now he would make them the political vassals of the race whose title to liberty he would have rested upon their consciences as jurymen.

DEC. 17, 1860—He voted for Mr. Adrain's resolution recommending a repeal of the personal liberty bills, enacted by most of the States of the North. He would not have the Free States then to interpose to prevent his present colored ally from being returned to the chains about which he prates so much and so fervently.

FEB. 11, 1861—Mr. Sherman of Ohio, offered the following:

Resolved, That neither the Congress of the United States, nor the people or governments of the non-slaveholding States have the constitutional right to legislate upon or interfere with slavery in any of the slaveholding States in the Union.

Which was agreed to—yeas 162, nays none. Mr. Colfax voted yea.

If this resolution had been adhered to in good faith, where would the colored loyalists, including the negro delegates to the Chicago Convention, be now? IN SLAVERY.

JUNE 4, 1862—He voted for Mr. Porter's amendment, providing that slaves belonging to certain classes of persons be discharged from service or labor and colonized in Mexico, Central or South America, or the Gulf Islands.

He was not then for political affiliation with them as equals, but for exiling them to foreign lands.

MARCH 10, 1862—He voted for compensated emancipation, as proposed by Mr. Roscoe Conkling.

APRIL 7—He voted for a similar proposition offered by Mr. A. S. White.

JAN 6, 1863—He voted for Mr. Noell's bill appropriating $10,000,000, to purchase emancipation in Missouri.

JAN. 12, 1863—He voted for Mr. Frances Thomas' resolution looking to an appropriation for that purpose in Maryland.

He thus recognized the right of property in slaves, and proposed that the United States should purchase and pay for them.

APRIL 8, 1862—He voted to tax slaves as property.

APRIL 11, 1862—The Senate considered a bill "to remove all disqualification of color in carrying the mails of the United States." It directed that after the passage of the act no person, by reason of color, shall be disqualified from employment in carrying the mails, and all acts and parts of acts establishing such disqualification, including especially the seventh section of the act of March 3, 1825, are hereby repealed.

The vote in the Senate was yeas 24, nays 11, as follows:

YEAS—Messrs. Anthony, Browning, Chandler, Clark, Collamer, Dixon, Doolittle, Fessenden, Foot, Foster, Grimes, Hale, Howard, Howe, King, Lane(of Kansas), Morrill, Pomeroy, Sherman, Simmons, Sumner, Wade, Wilkinson, and Wilson (of Massachusetts)—24.

NAYS—*Davis*, Henderson, *Kennedy*, Lane (of Indiana), *Latham*, *Nesmith*, *Powell*, *Stark*, Willey, *Wilson* (of Missouri), *Wright*—11.

In the House it was laid on the table, yeas 82, nays 45. Mr. Colfax voted in the affirmative. He would not trust his loyal colored brother at that time to carry the mail. He is now in favor of him to be President, Vice-President, United States Senator, Representative, Governor, or anything, high or low.

February 27, 1861.—Voted for the declaratory resolutions reported by the Committee of Thirty-three, embracing one denying any authority, "legally or *otherwise*," to interfere with slavery in the States.

Mr. Colfax now turns up his eyes in holy horror at the bare contemplation that the colored troops who fought so nobly were ever slaves, or less than the equals of the white men of the country. Voted same day for Mr. Corwin's proposed amendment to the Constitution of the United States, which was as follows:

"ART. XII. No amendment shall be made to the Constitution which will authorize or give to Congress the power to abolish or interfere, within any State, with the domestic institutions thereof, including that of persons held to labor or service by the laws of the said State."

He would then preclude by Constitutional amendment, the possibility of a negro ever becoming free. He now declares him to be the peer of the white man, and entitled to all the privileges, civil and political, including those of voting and holding office, possessed by the white man.

CENSURE OF MR. ALEXANDER LONG, OF OHIO—MR. COLFAX v. THE LIBERTY OF SPEECH.

On the 9th day of April, 1864, Mr. Colfax, then Speaker of the House, sought to make himself conspicuous as the most reckless contemner of one of the dearest franchises of the Constitution, by descending to the floor and offering the following preamble and resolution:

"WHEREAS, on the 8th of April, 1864, when the House of Representatives was in Committee of the Whole on the state of the Union, Alexander Long, a Representative from the Second District of Ohio, declared himself in favor of recognizing the independence and nationality of the so-called Confederacy now in arms against the Union; and whereas, the said so-called Confederacy, thus sought to be recognized and established on the ruins of a dissolved or destroyed Union, has as its chief officers, civil and military, those who have added perjury to their treason, and who seek to obtain success for their parricidal efforts by the killing of the loyal soldiers of the nation who are seeking to save it from destruction; and whereas the oath required of all members, and taken by the said Alexander Long on the first day of the present Congress, declares 'that I have voluntarily given no aid, countenance, counsel, or encouragement to persons engaged in armed hostility to the United States,' thereby declaring that such conduct is regarded as inconsistent with membership in the Congress of the United States: Therefore,

"*Resolved*, That Alexander Long a Representative from the Second District of Oh o, having, on the 8th of April, 1864, declared himself in favor of recognizing the independence and nationality of the so-called Confederacy now in arms against the Union, and thereby "given aid, countenance. and encouragement to persons engaged in armed hosti'ity to the United States," is hereby expelled."

April 14—Mr. Broomall, offered this amendment, as a substitute, which Mr. Colfax accepted:

"WHEREAS, Alexander Long, a Representative from the Second District of Ohio, by his open declarations in the national Capitol and publications in the city of New York, has shown himself to be in favor of a recognition of the so-called Confederacy now trying to establish itself upon the ruins of our country, thereby giving aid and comfort to the enemy in that destructive purpose— aid to avowed traitors in creating an illegal government within our borders—comfort to them by assurance of their success, and affirmations of the justice of their cause; and whereas such conduct is at the same time evidence of disloyalty and inconsistent with his oath of office and his duty as a member of this body: Therefore,

"*Resolved*, That the said Alexander Long, a Representative from the Second District of Ohio, be, and he is hereby, declared to be an unworthy member of the House of Representatives.

"*Resolved*, That the Speaker shall read these resolutions to the said Alexander Long during the session of the House."

The second resolution was laid on the table. A rebuke to Colfax who meanly desired the opportunity of administering the censure. The preamble was adopted by almost a like vote to that on the first resolution.

The first resolution was agreed to yeas 80, nays 70, as follows:

YEAS—Messrs. Alley, Allison, Ames, Anderson, Arnell, Ashley, *Bailey*, John D. Baldwin, Baxter, Beaman, Blaine, Boutwell, Boyd, Broomall, Ambrose W. Clarke, Cobb, Cole, Creswell, Dawes, Deming, Driggs, Dumont, Eckley, Farnsworth, Frank, Garfield, Gooch, Grinnell, Higby, Hooper, Hotchkiss, John H. Hubbard, Jenckes, Julian, Kasson, Kelly, Francis W. Kellogg, Orlando Kellogg, Loan, Longyear, Marvin, McBride, McClurg, McIndoe, Samuel F. Miller, Morrill, Daniel Morris, Amos Myers, Leonard Myers, Norton, Charles O'Neil, Orth, Patterson, Perham, Pike, Pomeroy, Price, William H. Randall, A. H. Rice, John H. Rice, Edward H. Rollins, Schenck, Shannon, Sloan, Smith. Smithers, Starr, Stephens, Thayer, Thomas, Upson, Van Valkenburgh, Elihu B. Washburne, William B. Washburn, Webster, Whaley, Wilder, Wilson, Windom, Woodbridge—80.

NAYS—Messrs. *James C. Allen*, *William J. Allen*, *Ancona*, *Augustus C. Baldwin*, *Franc. P. Blair*, *Bliss*, *James S. Brown*, *William G. Brown*, *Chanler*, *Clay*, *Coffroth*, *Cox*, *Cravens*, *Dawson*, *Denison*, *Eden*, *Eldridge*, *Finck*, *Ganson*, *Grider*, *Hall*, *Harding*, *Harrington*, *B. G. Harris*, *Herrick*, *Holman*, *Hutchins*, *P. Johnson*, *W. Johnson*, *Kalbfleisch*, *Kernan*, *King*, *Knapp*, *Law*, *Lazear*, *Mallory*, *Marcy*, *McDowell*, *McKenney*, *William H. Miller*, *James R. Morris*, *Morrison*, *Nelson*, *Noble*, *Odell*, *John O'Neill*, *Pendleton*, *Perry*, *Pruyn*, *Radford*, *Samuel J. Randall*, *Robinson*, *Rogers*, *James S. Rollins*, *Ross*, *Scott*, *Stebbins*, *John B. Steele*, *Wm. G. Steele*, *Strouse*, *Stuart*, *Sweat*, *Voorhees*, *Ward*, *Wheeler*, *Chilton A. White*, *Joseph W. White*, *Winfield*, *Fernando Wood*, *Yeaman*—70.

Similar resolutions were offered with reference to Mr. B. G. Harris, of Md, on the same day, which we have mislaid and are unable to replace in time.

MR. COLFAX V. THE HABEAS CORPUS.

December 10, 1861—He voted to lay the resolution of Mr. Pendleton, of Ohio, on the table, declaring that Congress alone has the power to suspend the writ of *habeas corpus*, and that it is the duty of the President to deliver certain citizens of Maryland to the U. S. Marshall, to the end that they may be indicted, and "enjoy the right of a speedy public trial by an impartial jury," etc.

MR. COLFAX AND GREENBACKS.

February 6, 1862—The act of February 25, 1862, being under consideration, he voted to make the $150,000,000 of notes, authorized to be issued, "*lawful money, and a legal tender in payment of all debts, public and private, within the United States.*"

Mr. Colfax appeared to have a weakness for avoiding to vote on a great many of the questions, financial and political, which arose during and since the war—a not very creditable abstinence to be practiced by a Representative who descended from the Speaker's chair that he might offer a resolution to expel Mr. Long, and who made it to appear conspicuous on the record that he voted to impeach the President of the United States.

The Freedmen's Bureau.

ITS OUTRAGEOUS HISTORY—ITS TREMENDOUS COST—AND ITS CORRUPT AND MISCHIEVOUS USES.

One of the most successful impediments, after the war, to the return of prosperity to the South, was the Freedmen's Bureau. It was a gigantic invention for the expenditure of vast amounts of public treasure, not only for the independent support of its own corrupt and mischievous existence, but was the excuse for the maintenance of large standing armies to quiet unfounded apprehensions of danger, which the consciousness of its own excesses, and its studied aggravation of the white people of the South, excited in its administration. It was the available agency at all times to disturb the labor of the country by encouraging idleness on the part of the laborer, exciting in his mind antagonism to his employer, and inviting complaints against the latter by the former, which were heeded by it, without reference to their verity or gravity, and were used by it for the exercise of its vindictive power, to crush out the hope and spirits of the white agriculturists of the country, and unite the black field-hands into a systematic combination for the annoyance and ruin of their employers. It would seem that it was the fiendish purpose of this organization to annoy to such an extent the land-owners of the country, that an abandonment of their estates to the occupation, abuse, and utter destruction by the negroes, would be resorted to as a welcome riddance from the accumulation of trouble and loss their pursuit as planter's entailed. It exercised judicial, legislative, military and proprietary powers. It would enter judgment against the employer for debt, upon the fraudulent action of the negroes whom he had employed. It would listen to trifling complaints of assault made by negroes against white men, and punish the latter upon no principle of justice or law, according to the ignorant caprice of the officer exercising the power. It would, to gratify any resentment which a negro might cherish, send armed guards to the house of the alleged white offender, drag him into its presence, and either fine or imprison him, as it might see fit. It would make laws to govern the relations between whites and blacks in a business and municipal view which was unknown to the Constitution and laws of the land. It used the military power with all the arrogant and offensive excess that the small minds of the agents could devise. It assumed to be the regulator of the citizen's private business, and dictated the amount of wages he should pay his negro laborers, and coerced him into acquiescence by making his property liable for the execution of their enforced stipulations. This chapter might be made almost endless, if the means of extending it were used to show up the villanous history of this tyrannical and corrupt bureau Agriculture became paralyzed under its auspices, and a large per cent. of the present distress in the South is attributable to its existence and its practices. The general commercial and financial interests of the entire country suffered from its administration, because those interests are all involved in the agricultural prosperity of the South.

The first attempt to establish this monster by law, was the passage of a bill by the House of Representatives on the first of March, 1864, creating it. The bill passed by a vote of sixty-nine to sixty-seven. The entire affirmative vote was Radical. The negative vote, with a few exceptions, was Democratic.

Mr. FRANCIS P. BLAIR voted against it. The bill was amended by the Senate, and. a disagreement taking place between the two Houses, it was postponed.

LAW CREATING THE FREEDMEN'S BUREAU.

A bill, finally, creating the institution, was agreed to on a report of a joint Committee on Conference. It was adopted in the Senate, February 28, 1865. In the House, March 3, 1865, Mr. Cox, of Ohio, moved to lay it on the table, which was lost, yeas 52, nays 77. Every Democrat, except one, voting for the motion, and every Radical, except one, voting against it. The House then passed the bill without a division

CONTINUATION OF THE ABUSE.

The act continuing the Bureau, to prevent its expiration by limitation, passed July 3, 1866, and was vetoed by the President on the 16th of July. On the same day it passed the House over the veto of the President. Every Radical, except Mr. Kuykendall, of Illinois, and Mr. Henry D. Washburn, voted for it. Every Democrat voted against it. It passed the Senate the same day. Every Radical, except Mr. Van Winkle, of Virginia, voting for it. Every Democrat voted against it.

THE PRESIDENT'S VETO.

In his message announcing his veto of the bill, the President says:

"Independently of the danger in representative republics of conferring upon the military in times of peace extraordinary powers—so carefully guarded against by the patriots and statesmen of the earlier days of the Republic, so frequently the ruin of governments founded upon the same free principles, and subversive of the rights and liberties of the citizen—the question of practical economy earnestly commends itself to the consideration of the law-making power. With an immense debt already burdening the incomes of the industrial and laboring classes, a due regard for their interests, so inseparably connected with the welfare of the country, should prompt us to rigid economy and retrenchment, and influence us to abstain from all legislation that would unnecessarily increase the public indebtedness. Tested by this rule of sound political wisdom, I can see no reason for the establishment of the "military jurisdiction" conferred upon the officials of the Bureau by the fourteenth section of the bill.

"By the laws of the United States and of the different States, competent courts, Federal and State, have been established, and are now in full practical operation. By means of these civil tribunals, ample redress is afforded for all private wrongs, whether to the person or the property of the citizen, without denial or unnecessary delay. They are open to all, without regard to color or race. I feel well assured that it will be better to trust the rights, privileges, and immunities of the citizen to tribunals thus established, and presided over by competent and impartial judges, bound by fixed rules of law and evidence, and where the right of trial by jury is guaranteed and secured, than to the caprice or judgment of an officer of the bureau, who, it is possible, may be entirely ignorant of the principles that underlie the just administration of the law. There is danger, too, that conflict of jurisdiction will frequently arise between the civil courts and these military tribunals, each having concurrent jurisdiction over the person and the cause of action, the one judicature administered and controlled by civil law, the other by the military. How is the conflict to be settled, and who is to determine between the two tribunals when it arises? In my opinion, it is wise to guard against such conflict by leaving to the courts and juries the protection of all civil rights and the redress of all civil grievances. * * * * *

"Besides the objections which I have thus briefly stated, I may urge upon your consideration the additional reason, that recent developments in regard to the practical operations of the bureau in many of the States show that in numerous instances it is used by its agents as a means of promoting their individual advantage, and that the freedmen are employed for the advancement of the personal ends of the officers instead of their own improvement and welfare, thus confirming the fears originally entertained by many, that the continuation of such a bureau for any unnecessary length of time would inevitably result in fraud, corruption, and oppression. It is proper to state that in cases of this character investigations have been promptly ordered, and the offender punished whenever his guilt has been satisfactorily established.

"As another reason against the necessity of the legislation contemplated by this measure, reference may be had to the 'Civil Rights bill,' now a law of the land, and which will be faithfully executed so long as it shall remain unrepealed, and may not be declared unconstitutional by courts of competent jurisdiction. * * * *

"By the provisions of the act, full protection is afforded through the district courts of the United States, to all persons injured, and whose privileges, as thus declared, are in any way impaired; and heavy penalties are denounced against the person who wilfully violates the law. I need not state that that law did not receive my approval; yet its remedies are far more preferable than those proposed in the present bill, the one being civil and the other military.

"By the sixth section of the bill herewith returned, certain proceedings by which the lands in the 'parishes of St. Helena and St. Luke, South Carolina,' were sold and bid in, and afterward disposed of by the tax commissioners, are ratified and confirmed. By the seventh, eighth, ninth, tenth, and eleventh sections, provisions by law are made for the disposal of the lands thus acquired to a particular class of citizens. While the quieting of titles is deemed very important and desirable, the discrimination made in the bill seems objectionable, as does also the attempt to confer upon the commissioners judicial powers, by which citizens of the United States are to be deprived of their property in a mode contrary to that provision of the Constitution which declares that no person 'shall be deprived of life, liberty, or property, without due process of law.' As a general principle, such legislation is unsafe, unwise, partial and unconstitutional. It may deprive persons of their property who are equally deserving objects of the nation's bounty, as those whom, by this legislation, Congress seeks to benefit. The title to the land thus to be proportioned out to a favored class of citizens must depend upon the regularity of the tax sales, under the law as it existed at the time of the sale, and no subsequent legislation can give validity to the rights thus acquired, as against the original claimants. The attention of Congress is therefore invited to a more mature consideration of the measures proposed in these sections of the bill.

"In conclusion, I again urge upon Congress the danger of class legislation, so well calculated to keep the public mind in a state of uncertain expectation, disquiet, and restlessness, and to encourage interested hopes and fears that the national Government will continue to furnish to classes of citizens in the several States means for support and maintenance, regardless of whether they pursue a life of indolence or of labor, and regardless also of the constitutional limitations of the national authority in times of peace and tranquillity.

"The bill is herewith returned to the House of Representatives, in which it originated, for its final action.

"ANDREW JOHNSON.

"WASHINGTON, D C., *July* 16, 1868."

THE EXPENSES OF THIS SWINDLE.

The various reports of Gen. Howard, the chief of this immense piece of furniture, are so much mixed that it is hard to derive from them the exact cost of its administration.

To November 1, 1865, its expenditures were $478,363.17.

For year beginning January 1, 1866, the estimates, which always falls below expenditures, were $11,745,050.00.

For the next fiscal year, besides the funds it had on hand, which amounted to $6,513,965.00, he required an additional sum of $3,863,300.00; making a total of $10,350,265.00.

This last amount embraces what it was estimated it would cost to run it up to July 1, 1868.

ITS SALARIES AND ABUSES, WHAT THEY COST.

[From the New York World.]

The Freedmen's Bureau is an outrage upon the tax-payers of the country, which should be suppressed. Ostensibly established to benefit the emancipated blacks, it has been used from the outset as a political machine—first, to provide bread, butter and clothes for a small army of political paupers and nomadic carpet-baggers, and next, to use these nomads as negro-drivers in the Radical interest, as overseers, to see that the blacks deposit Radical tickets in the ballot-boxes. Beyond these objects the bureau has no purpose whatever. The cant about "schools and churches" for the blacks is only to cover the pretended necessity for hundreds of "superintendents of schools" at $1,800, and $1,200, each, and Massachusetts school-marms and missionaries, at from $900 to $1,200 apiece; the stipend for similar services in their own State, where "the Government" does not pay the bills, ranging from $350 to $500, with a "donation party," which generally cost the beneficiary about $50. Even more egregious is the gammon about the Bureau as a means of furnishing employment for the blacks. The planters are suffering for labor, while the negroes are attending political meetings, or are marching in procession to the polls with muskets in their hands to vote as they are directed by their masters, the paid agents of the bureau. This glaring swindle upon Northern tax-payers, apart from the enormous, expensive and useless military establishment in the Southern satrapies, is costing not less than eleven millions of the people's money every year, and this money is taken from the property owners and laborers of the North to purchase black votes for the continuance of the Radical party in power. To show how stupendous this swindle is in the mere item of "salaries" we have collated the following list of Bureau agents and clerks with their pay annexed:

	Agents and Clerks.	Salaries.
Washington	64	$90,460
District of Columbia,	56	53,640
Maryland,	9	11,600
Virginia,	53	61,180
North Carolina,	44	5,800
South Carolina	46	58,880
Georgia,	72	78,500
Florida,	17	19,200
Alabama,	45	51,440
Kentucky,	42	42,000
Tennessee,	34	40,500
Mississippi	57	53,400
Missouri,	2	3,600
Arkansas,	53	64,320
Louisiana,	67	78,400
Texas	42	49,320
Total.	703	$809,340

Besides their salaries, a large number of these agents manage also to swindle their living in Government rations, and they derive other perquisites and pantaloons, which are all set down as "stationery."

How these leeches really regard the value of labor appears curiously, in connection with their own magnificent salaries, in the sums paid to "messengers" and "laborers" who are rewarded for their services at the rate of from $150 to $300 a year. Months ago, when it was shown that this enormous drain on the Treasury was as useless as it is outrageous, the Radicals in Congress voted that it was inexpedient to discontinue it at present, that is, so long as it could be made a political machine for Radical benefit at the tax payers' expense. But it is not less an outrage now than it has been since the day it was established, and the fact that such a swindle should be continued, shows to what straits Radicalism is reduced in its effort to prolong, not merely its power, but its existence as a party.

What a Radical Thinks of the Freedmen's Bureau.

SOCIAL EQUALITY AND AMALGAMATION ADVOCATED BY IT—ITS MANIFOLD CORRUPTIONS.

Under date of June 27, the special Washington correspondent of the Cincinnati *Gazette*, makes the following revelations of the operations of the Freedmen's Bureau in the District of Columbia:

"The bureau may have been administered honestly in the rebel States, but here, in the District of Columbia, its operations would afford Congress valuable information to guide it in the bill it is framing, if the members would take the trouble to inquire into the character of transactions passing under their very eyes.

SOCIAL EQUALITY—AMALGAMATION.

"The outlines of one single operation will suffice. Howard University is an institution for the education of colored men, which is being erected here under the auspices of the Freedmen's Bureau. The money used is a fund retained by military authority from the bounties paid colored soldiers, and is, in all honest senses, Government funds. The land cost $150,000. After purchase, part of it was laid out in city lots and sold. One acre was given to a prominent officer of the bureau. The others interested managed to obtain the most available lots. The buildings now in course of erection are to cost about $100,000. Prominent officers of the bureau purchased the right to use a patent brick machine in this district, and took the contract for the brick-work—a transaction not sanctioned, to say the least, in army regulations. Here then is a property, whose cost price will reach a quarter of a million of dollars, which, under the bill continuing the bureau, can be passed into private hands for a mere song.

"The bureau in this district has been a close corporation, and a very corrupt one. It has so long been considered treason to the Republican party to question the honesty and integrity of those engaged in this organization, that transactions of the most questionable character have been concealed from the public. Now, that Congress has the chance, in the bills concerning the bureau pending before it, to stop some of these operations, it can but do good to institute a slight investigation.

"The doings of those who make up what may well be called the Freedmen's Bureau 'Ring' here, have been a matter of town talk for some months, and Democrats are already chuckling over the advantages which the failure of the Republicans to repudiate some of these things, will give them in the coming campaign. An attempt was the made, when the bill passed the House, by opposition, to expose some of these matters; but those managing the bill, fearing that exposure would greatly modify its provisions, choked off explanation by the previous question, secured the bill, and concealed these glaring objections to it.

"Great dissatisfaction has existed for a considerable time among prominent Republicans at the state of affairs known to exist in the circles referred to; and yet they shrunk from such an exposition as would compel reform. But now all the matters to which allusion has been made have been investigated in a quarter which will inevitably bring the facts before the country during the Presidential campaign, and the part of wisdom is to face them now, and at least avoid the appearance of sanctioning them in bills which are yet open to revision or amendment.

"The publications when made will show that some of the prominent officers in the bureau have gone so far in the attempt to secure political preferment by the negro vote, as to cause them to understand that the bureau advocated complete social equality, even extending to amalgamation. And in this Gen. Howard himself was an active participant. In spite of all denials, this will be made to appear within a short time, and in view of this, several provisions of the bill now pending deserve a more careful attention than they have yet received.."

One of the last allusions in this correspondence to the Freedmen's Bureau, was a warm defense of General Howard against such charges as the above.

In that letter, published in the *Gazette* of January 31, there appeared the following regarding the charge of favoring amalgamation:

"Justice to Gen. Howard requires that the country should know that he is no disciple of this doctrine, and is not administering the affairs of the bureau in a manner to encourage it. His name has been connected with it because the little clique, or most composing it, conducting this battle for amalgamation, happen to be employed in the bureau."

So soon as the paper containing the above reached this city, Gen. Howard addressed the following letter regarding the above extract to the *Gazette* correspondent, which, as will be seen, is in effect a request not to commit him any further against amalgamation:

"WASHINGTON, February 4, 1866.

"I see by a letter of yours that you commit me, together with certain officers and agents of this bureau, on the subject of amalgamation. As I have hardly canvassed the subject, and have expressed no opinion, *pro or con*, it is better not to commit me further. Very truly yours,

"O. O. HOWARD, Maj.-General."

Yet, the evening before this is dated, at an informal discussion of the subject of amalgamation among a part of the trustees of Howard University, Gen. Howard declared himself, in the most emphatic manner, to be in favor of amalgamation, and the statements of at least four of the gentlemen present have been taken in a direction that must shortly lead to their publication in full.

These matters had so far been brought to the notice of members of Congress, as to render the passage of the Freedmen's Bureau bill quite doubtful, and so, to secure its passage, a sweeping denial of all charges by Gen. Howard was agreed upon and read in the House.

These things need little comment. If the insight afforded into Freedmen's Bureau affairs in this district serves to attract the attention of members of the House, the object of this letter will be accomplished. It is better to meet such matters while bills are pending, where a proper remedy can be applied, than to neglect them and meet them on the stump.

STILL FURTHER CONTINUANCE OF THE SWINDLE.

The House, says the New York *World*, of July 14, 1868, has passed the Senate bill for the discontinuance of the Freedmen's Bureau, with an amendment, sent to the Senate for its concurrence, that the discontinuance shall be "absolute" after January 1, 1869. The Senate bill left the matter open to such construction as Congress, or the party, might choose to give the following words: "The Commissioner of the Bureau shall, on the 1st day of January next, cause the said bureau to be withdrawn from the several States, and its operation discontinued, as soon as the same may be done without injury to the Government." It would be quite supererogatory to say that "the Government" means the Radical party. But the barefaced statement that this enormous outrage has been sustained at an annual cost of millions of the people's money, solely to advance the interests of the Radical party, and the admission that its continuance is only to assist in tiding that party over the coming election, is a refined cruelty to the freedmen, for whose benefit the bureau was assumed to have been instituted, and is an utter neglect of the claims of the schoolmarms, carpet-bagging beggars, and other *loil* leeches who have sucked support from this stupendous swindle. If the bureau can be discontinued next January, it can be discontinued to-day. But no; the party needs this valuable assistance till after election, and the white tax-payers of the North, in addition to the millions which this shameful swindle has absorbed already, are called upon to contribute more money to support idle negroes who, in return for such support, are expected only to vote the Radical ticket. If Radicalism cost the country nothing, it would be insupportable; but it requires millions every day in the year to keep alive this recklessly extravagant party, and these millions come from the white tax-payers of the country, and not from the negroes and carpet-baggers who are confessedly the last resort of this party for its continuance in power.

The Supreme Court.

ON TRIAL BY MILITARY COMMISSIONS, DECEMBER 17, 1866.

No. 350.—December Term, 1865.—Ex-parte in matter of Lambdin P. Milligan, petitioner.—On a certificate of division of opinion between the Judges of the Circuit Court of the United States for the District of Indiana.

Mr. Justice Davis delivered the opinion of the Court.

On the 10th day of May, 1865, Lambdin P. Milligan presented a petition to the Circuit Court of the United States for the District of Indiana, to be discharged from an alleged unlawful imprisonment. The case made by the petition is this: Milligan is a citizen of the United States; has lived for twenty years in Indiana, and at the time of the grievances complained of was not, and never had been, in the military or naval service of the United States. On the 5th day of October, 1864, while at home, he was arrested by order of General Alvin P. Hovey, commanding the military district of Indiana, and has ever since been kept in close confinement.

On the 21st day of October, 1864, he was brought before a military commission, convened at Indianapolis by order of General Hovey, tried on certain charges and specifications, found guilty, and sentenced to be hanged, and the sentence ordered to be executed on Friday, the 19th day of May, 1865.

On the 2d day of January, 1865, after the proceedings of the military commission were at an end, the Circuit Court of the United States for Indiana met at Indianapolis and impanneled a grand jury, who were charged to inquire whether the laws of the United States had been violated, and if so, to make presentments. The Court adjourned on the 27th day of January, having prior thereto discharged from further service the Grand Jury, who did not find any bill of indictment or make any presentment against Milligan for any offense whatever, and, in fact, since his imprisonment no bill of indictment has been found or presentment made against him by any Grand Jury of the United States.

Milligan insists that said military commission had no jurisdiction to try him upon the charges preferred, or upon any charges whatever; because he was a citizen of the United States and the State of Indiana, and had not been, since the commencement of the late rebellion, a resident of any of the States whose citizens were arrayed against the Government, and that the right of trial by jury was guaranteed to him by the Constitution of the United States.

The prayer of the petition was, that under the act of Congress approved March 3,

1863, entitled "An act relating to *habeas corpus*, and regulating judicial proceedings in certain cases," he may be brought before the Court, and either turned over to the proper civil tribunal, to be proceeded against according to the law of the land, or discharged from custody altogether.

With the petition were filed the order for the commission, the charges and specifications, the findings of the Court, with the order of the War Department, reciting that the sentence was approved by the President of the United States, and directing that it be carried into execution without delay. The petition was presented and filed in open court by the counsel for Milligan; at the same time the District Attorney of the United States for Indiana appeared, and, by the agreement of counsel, the application was submitted to the court. The opinions of the Judges of the Circuit Court were opposed on these questions which are certified to the Supreme Court:

"1. On the facts stated in said petition and exhibits, ought a writ of *habeas corpus* to be issued?

"2. On the facts stated in said petition and exhibits, ought the said Lambdin P. Milligan to be discharged from custody, as in said petition prayed?

"3. Whether, upon the facts stated in said petition and exhibits, the military commission mentioned therein had jurisdiction legally to try and sentence said Milligan, in manner and form as in said petition and exhibit is stated?"

The importance of the main question presented by this record can not be overstated; for it involves the very frame-work of the Government and fundamental principles of American liberty.

* * * * *

Milligan, in his application to be released from imprisonment, averred the existence of every fact necessary under the terms of this law to give the Circuit Court of Indiana jurisdiction. If he was detained in custody by the order of the President, otherwise than as a prisoner of war; if he was a citizen of Indiana, and had never been in the military or naval service, and the Grand Jury of the district had met, after he had been arrested for a period of twenty days, and adjourned without taking any proceedings against him, *then* the Court had the right to entertain his petition and determine the lawfulness of his imprisonment.

* * * * *

But it is said that this case is ended, as the presumption is that Milligan was hanged in pursuance of the order of the President. Although we have no judicial information on the subject; yet the inference is that he is alive; for otherwise learned counsel would not appear for him and urge the Court to decide his case.

It can never be in this country of written constitution and laws, with a judicial department to interpret them, that any Chief Magistrate would be so far forgetful of his duty as to order the execution of a man who denied the jurisdiction that tried and convicted him, after his case was before Federal Judges, with power to decide it, who, being unable to agree on the grave questions involved, had, according to known law, sent it to the Supreme Court of the United States for decision. But even the suggestion is injurious to the Executive, and we dismiss it from further consideration. There is, therefore, nothing to hinder this Court from an investigation of the merits of this controversy.

* * * * *

Have any of the rights guaranteed by the Constitution been violated in the case of Milligan? and, if so, what are they? Every trial involves the exercise of judicial power; and from what source did the military commission that tried him derive their authority? Certainly no part of the judicial power of the country was conferred on them, because the Constitution expressly vests it "in the Supreme Court and such inferior courts as the Congress may from time to time, ordain and establish," and it is not pretended that the commission was a court ordained and established by Congress. They can not justify on the mandate of the President, because he is controlled by law, and has his appropriate sphere of duty, which is to execute, not to make the laws; and there is "no unwritten criminal code to which resort can be had as a source of jurisdiction." But it is said that the jurisdiction is complete under the "laws and usages of war." It can serve no useful purpose to inquire what those laws and usages are, whence they originated, where found, and on whom they operate; they can never be applied to citizens in States which have upheld the authority of the Government, and where the courts are open and their process unobstructed. This Court has judicial knowledge that in Indiana the Federal authority was always unopposed, and its courts always open to hear criminal accusations and to redress grievances; and no usage of war could sanction a military trial there for any offense whatever, of a citizen in civil life, in nowise connected with the military service. Congress could grant no such power; and, to the honor of our National Legislature be it said, it has never been provoked by the state of the country even to attempt its exercise. One of the plainest constitutional provisions was, therefore, infringed when Milligan was tried by a court not ordained and established by Congress, and not composed of judges appointed during good behavior. * * * *

Every one connected with these branches of the public service (the Army and Navy) is amenable to the jurisdiction which Congress has created for their government, and while thus serving, surrenders his right to be tried by the civil courts. All other persons, citizens of States where the courts are open, if charged with crime, are guaranteed the inestimable privilege of trial by jury. This privilege is a vital principle, underlying the whole administration of criminal justice; it is not held by sufferance, and can not be frittered away on any plea of State or political necessity. When peace prevails, and the authority of the Government is undisputed, there is no difficulty of preserving the safeguards of liberty; for the ordinary modes of trial are never neglected, and no one wishes it otherwise. But if society is disturbed by civil commotion—if the passions of men are aroused and the restraints of law weakened, if not disregarded—these safeguards need, and should receive, the watchful care of those intrusted with the guardianship of the Constitution and laws. In no other way can we transmit to posterity unimpaired the blessings of liberty, consecrated by the sacrifices of the Revolution.

It is claimed that martial-law covers with its broad mantle the proceedings of this military commission. The proposition is this: That in a time of war the commander of an armed force (if, in his opinion, the exigencies of the country demand it, and of which he is to judge,) has the power, within the lines of his military district, to suspend all civil rights and their remedies, and subject citizens as well as soldiers to the rule of his will; and in the exercise of his lawful authority can not be restrained, except by his superior officer or the President of the United States. If this position is sound to the extent claimed, then when war exists, foreign or domestic, and the country is subdivided into military departments for mere convenience, the commander of one of them can, if he chooses, within his limits, on the plea of necessity, with the approval of the Executive, substitute military force for, and to the exclusion of, the laws, and punish all persons as he thinks right and proper, without fixed or certain rules.

The statement of this proposition shows its importance; for, if true, republican government is a failure, and there is an end of liberty regulated by law. Martial-law, established on such a basis, destroys every guarantee of the Constitution, and effectually renders the "military independent of and superior to the civil power"—the attempt to do which by the King of Great Britain was deemed by our fathers such an offense that they assigned it to the world as one of the causes which impelled them to declare their independence. Civil liberty and this kind of martial-law can not endure together; the antagonism is irreconcilable, and in the conflict one or the other must perish.
* * * * * *

It is difficult to see how the safety of the country required martial-law in Indiana. If any of her citizens were plotting treason, the power of arrest could secure them until the Government was prepared for their trial, when the courts were open and ready to try them. It was as easy to protect witnesses before a civil as a military tribunal; and, as there could be no wish to convict, except upon sufficient legal evidence, surely an ordained and established court was better able to judge of this than a military tribunal, composed of gentlemen not trained to the profession of the law.

It follows, from what has been said on this subject, that there are occasions when martial rule can be properly applied. If in foreign invasion or civil war the courts are actually closed, and it is impossible to administer criminal justice according to law, then on the theater of active military operations, where war really prevails, there is a necessity to furnish a substitute for the civil authority thus overthrown to preserve the safety of the army and society; and as no power is left but the military, it is allowed to govern by martial rule until the laws can have their free course. As necessity creates the rule, so it limits its duration; for if this government is continued after the courts are reinstated, it is a gross usurpation of power. Martial rule can never exist where the courts are open, and in the proper and unobstructed exercise of their jurisdiction. It is also confined to the locality of actual war. Because during the late rebellion it could have been enforced in Virginia, where the national authority was overturned and the courts driven out, it does not follow that it should obtain in Indiana, where that authority was never disputed, and justice was always administered. And so in the case of a foreign invasion, martial rule may become a necessity in one State, when in another it would be "mere lawless violence."

The remaining two questions in this case must be answered in the affirmative. The suspension of the privilege of the writ of *habeas corpus* does not suspend the writ itself. The writ issues as a matter of course; and on the return made to it, the court decides whether the party applying is denied the right of proceeding any further with it.

If the military trial of Milligan was contrary to law, then he was entitled, on the facts stated in his petition, to be discharged from custody by the terms of the act of Congress of March 3, 1863.

* * * * *

The provisions of this law having been considered in a previous part of this opinion, we will now re-state the views there presented. Milligan avers he was a citizen of Indiana, not in the military or naval service, and was detained in close confinement, by order of the President, from the 5th day of October, 1864, until the 2d day of January 1865, when the circuit court for the district of Indiana, with a grand jury, convened in session at Indianapolis, and afterward, on the 27th day of the same month, adjourned without finding an indictment or presentment against him. If these averments were true (and their truth is conceded for the purposes of this case), the court was required to liberate him on taking certain oaths prescribed by the law, and entering into recognizance for his good behavior. But it is insisted that Milligan was a prisoner of war, and, therefore, excluded from the privileges of the statute. It is not easy to see how he can be treated as a prisoner of war, when he lived in Indiana for the past twenty years, was arrested there, and had not been, during the late troubles, a resident of any of the States in rebellion. If, in Indiana, he conspired with bad men to assist the enemy, he is punishable for it in the courts of Indiana; but, when tried for the offense, he can not plead the rights of war, for he was not engaged in legal acts of hostility against the Government, and only such persons, when captured, are prisoners of war. If he can not enjoy the immunities attaching to the character of a prisoner of war, how can he be subject to their pains and penalties.

This case, as well as the kindred cases of Bowles and Horsey, were disposed of at the last term, and the proper orders were entered of record. There is, therefore, no additional entry required.

On the Missouri Constitutional Test Oath of Loyalty, January 14, 1867.

Mr Justice Field delivered the opinion of the Court in the case of John A. Cummings v. The State of Missouri.

This case comes before us on a writ of error to the Supreme Court of Missouri, and involves a consideration of the test oath imposed by the constitution of that State. The plaintiff in error is a priest of the Roman Catholic Church, and was indicted and convicted, in one of the circuit courts of that State of the crime of teaching and preaching, as a priest and minister of that religious denomination, without having first taken the oath, and was sentenced to pay a fine of $500, and to be committed to jail until the same was paid. On appeal to the Supreme Court of the State, the judgment was affirmed.

The oath prescribed by the constitution, divided into its separable parts, embraces more than thirty distinct affirmations or tests. Some of the acts against which it is directed constitute offenses of the highest grade, to which, upon conviction, heavy penalties are attached. Some of the acts have never been classed as offenses in the laws of any State, and some of the acts under many circumstances would not even be blameworthy. It requires the affiant to deny not only that he has been in armed hostility to the United States or the lawful authorities thereof, but, among other things, that he has ever, "by act or word," manifested his adherence to the cause of the enemies of the United States, foreign or domestic, or his desire for their triumph over the arms of the United States, or his sympathy with those engaged in rebellion, or that he has ever harbored or aided any person engaged in guerrilla warfare against the loyal inhabitants of the United States, or has ever entered or left the State for the purpose of avoiding enrollment or draft in the military service of the United States, or to escape the performance of duty in the militia of the United States, or has ever indicated in any terms his disaffection to the Government of the United States in its contest with rebellion.

Every person who is unable to take this oath is declared incapable of holding in the State "any office of honor, trust, or profit under its authority, or of being an officer, counselor, director, or trustee, or other manager of any corporation, public or private, now existing or hereafter established by its authority, or of acting as a professor or teacher in any educational institution, or in any common or other school, or of holding any real estate or other property in trust for the use of any church, religious society, or congregation." And every person holding any of the offices, trusts, or positions mentioned, at the time the constitution takes effect, is required within sixty days thereafter to take the oath, and if he fail to comply with this requirement, it is declared that his office, trust, or position shall *ipso facto* become vacant. And no person after the expiration of sixty days is permitted, without taking oath, "to practice as an attorney or counselor at law, nor, after that period, can any person be competent as a bishop, priest, deacon, minister, elder, or other clergyman of any religious persuasion, sect, or denomination, to teach, or preach, or solemnize marriage." Fine and imprisonment are prescribed as a punishment for holding or exercising any of the offices, positions, trusts, professions or functions specified, without having taken the oath, and false swearing or affirmation to the oath is declared to be perjury, and punishable by imprisonment in the penitentiary.

The oath thus required is without any precedent that we can discover for its severity. In the first place, it is retrospective. It embraces all the past from this day, and if taken years hence, it will also cover all the intervening period. In its retrospective feature, it is peculiar to this country. In England and France there have been test oaths, but they have always been limited to an affirmation of present belief or present disposition toward the Government, and were never exacted with reference to particular instances of past misconduct. In the second place, the oath is directed not merely against overt and visible acts of hostility to the Government, but is intended to reach words, desires, and sympathies also; and, in the third place, it allows no distinction between acts springing from malignant enmity and acts which may have been prompted by charity or affection or relationship. If one has ever expressed sympathy with any who were drawn into the rebellion, even if the recipients of that sympathy were connected by the closest ties of blood, he is as unable to subscribe to the oath as the most active and most cruel of rebels, and is equally debarred from the offices of honor and trust and the positions and employments specified.

* * * * * *

The disabilities created by the Constitution of Missouri must be regarded as penalties. They constitute punishment. We do not agree with the counsel of Missouri that "to punish one is to deprive him of life, liberty, or property, and that to take from him anything less than these is no punishment at all." The learned counsel does not use these terms, "life, liberty and property," as comprehending every right known to the law. He does not include under "liberty" freedom from outrage on the feelings as well as restraints on the person. He does not include under "property" those estates which one may acquire in professions, though they are often the source of the highest emoluments and honors.

The deprivation of any rights, civil or political, may be punishment, the circumstances attending and the causes of deprivation determining this fact. Disqualification from office may be punishment, as in cases of conviction upon impeachment. Disqualification from the pursuit of a lawful avocation, or from positions of trust, or from the privilege of appearing in the courts, or acting as executor, administrator, or guardian, may also, and often has been, imposed as punishment.

* * * * * *

Now, the clauses in the Missouri Constitution which are the subject of consideration do not in terms define any crime or declare that any punishment shall be inflicted, but they produce the same result upon the parties against whom they are directed as though the crimes were defined and the punishment declared. They assume that there are persons in Missouri who are guilty of some of the acts designated. They would have no meaning in the Constitution were not such the fact. They are aimed at past acts, and not future facts. They were intended to operate upon parties who, in some form or manner, by action or words, directly or indirectly, had aided or countenanced the rebellion, or sympathized with parties engaged in the rebellion, or had endeavored to escape the proper responsibilities and duties of a citizen in time of war. And they were intended to operate by depriving such persons of the right to hold certain offices and trusts, and to pursue their ordinary and regular avocations. This deprivation is punishment; nor is it any less so because a way is opened for escape from it by the expurgatory oath. The framers of the Constitution of Missouri knew at the time that whole classes of individuals would be unable to take the oath prescribed. To them there is no escape provided. To them the deprivation was intended to be and is absolute and perpetual. To make the enjoyment of a right dependent upon an impossible condition is equivalent to an absolute denial of the right under any condition, and such denial enforced for a past act is nothing else than punishment imposed for that act; it is a misapplication of terms to call it anything else.

* * * * * *

The objectionable character of these clauses will be more apparent if we put them in the ordinary form of a legislative act. Thus, if instead of the general provisions in the Constitution, the Convention had provided as follows: "Be it enacted, that all persons who have been in armed hostility to the United States shall, upon conviction thereof, not only be punished as the laws provided at the time the offenses were committed, but shall also be thereafter rendered incapable of ing any of the offices, trusts, and positions, and of exercising any of the pursuits mentioned in the third article of the Constitution of Missouri," no one could have any doubt of the nature of the act. It would be an *ex post facto* law, and void, for it would add a new punishment to an old offense. So, too, if the Convention had passed an enactment of a similar kind with reference to those acts which do not constitute offenses. Thus, had it provided as follows: "Be it enacted, that all persons who have heretofore at any time entered or left the State of Missouri with intent to avoid enrollment or draft in the military service of the United States, shall, upon conviction thereof, be forever rendered incapable of holding any office of honor, trust, or profit in the United States, or of teaching in any seminary of learning, or of preaching as a minister of the Gospel of any denomination, or exercising any of the professions or pursuits mentioned in the third article of the Constitution," there would be no question of the character of the enactment. It would be an *ex post facto* law, because it would impose a punishment for an act not punishable at the time it was committed.

The provisions of the Constitution of Missouri accomplish precisely what enactments like those supposed would accomplish. They impose the same penalty without the formality of a judicial trial and conviction, for the parties embraced by the supposed enactments would be incapable of taking the oath prescribed. To them its requirements would be an impossible condition.

* * * * * * *

Take the case before us: The Constitution of Missouri excludes, on failure to take the oath we have described, a large class of persons within her borders from numerous offices and pursuits. It would have been equally within the power of the State to have extended the exclusion so as to deprive the parties who were unable to take the oath from any avocations whatever in the State. Suppose, again, in the progress of events, persons now in the minority in the State should obtain the ascendency, and secure the control of the Government; nothing could prevent, if the constitutional prohibition can be evaded, the enactment of a provision requiring every person, as a condition of holding any office of honor or trust, or of pursuing any avocation in the State, to take an oath that he had never advocated or advised or supported the imposition of the present expurgatory oath. Under this form of legislation the most flagrant invasions of private rights in periods of excitement may be enacted, and individuals, and even whole classes, may be deprived of political and civil rights.

A question arose in New York, soon after the treaty of peace of 1783, upon a statute of that State, which involved a discussion of the nature and character of these expurgatory oaths when used as a means of inflicting punishment. The subject was regarded as so important, and the requirement of the oath such a violation of the fundamental principles of civil liberty and the rights of the citizen, that it engaged the attention of eminent lawyers and distinguished statesmen of the time, and among others, of Alexander Hamilton. We will cite some passages of a paper left by him on the subject, in which, with his characteristic fullness and ability, he examines the oath and demonstrates that it is not only a mode of inflicting punishment, but a mode in violation of all the constitutional gaurantees secured by the Revolution of the rights and liberties of the people:

"If we examine it" (the measure requiring the oath), said this great lawyer, "with an unprejudiced eye, we must acknowledge not only that it was an evasion of the treaty, but a subversion of one great principle of social security, to wit: that every man shall be presumed innocent until he is proved guilty. This was to invert the order of things, and instead of obliging the State to prove the guilt in order to inflict the penalty, it was to oblige the citizen to show his own innocence to avoid the penalty. It was to excite scruples in the honest and conscientious, and to hold out a bribe to perjury."

* * * "It was a mode of inquiring who had committed any of those crimes to which the penalty of disqualification was annexed, with this aggravation, that it deprived the citizen of the benefit of that advantage which he would have enjoyed by leaving, as in all other cases, the burden of proof upon the prosecution. To place this matter in a still clearer light, let it be supposed that instead of the mode of indictment and trial by jury, the Legislature was to declare that every citizen who did not swear that he had never adhered to the King of Great Britain should incur all the penalties which our treason laws prescribe, would this not be a palpable evasion of the treaty, and a direct infringement of the Constitution? The principle is the same in both cases, with only this difference in the consequences: that, in the instance already acted upon, the citizen forfeits part of his rights; in the one supposed, he would forfeit the whole. The degree of punishment is all that distinguishes the cases. In either, justly considered, it is substituting a new and arbitrary mode of prosecution for that ancient and highly esteemed one recognized by the laws and the Constitution of the State—I mean the trial by jury.

"Let us not forget that the Constitution declares that trial by jury in all cases in which it has been formerly used should remain inviolate for ever, and that the legislature should at no time erect any new jurisdiction which should not proceed according to the course of the common law. Nothing can be more repugnant to the true genius of the common law than such an inquisition, as has been mentioned, into the consciences of men." * * * "If any oath with respect to past conduct had been made, the condition on which individuals who have resided within the British lines should hold their estates, we should immediately see that this proceeding would be tyrannical and a violation of the treaty; and yet, when the same oath is employed to divest that right which ought to be deemed still more sacred, many of us are so infatuated as to overlook the mischief.

Test Oath as to Lawyers.

The act of Congress of January 24, 1865, prescribed a test oath to be taken by lawyers practicing in the United States Courts, the same as that commonly known as the "Iron Clad," required to be taken by all officers. The Supreme Court amended its second rule in compliance with said act. The Hon. A. H. Garland, of Arkansas, was a Senator in the Confederate Congress during the war. He had been admitted an attorney and counselor of that court at the December term, 1860. For his participation in the rebellion he was pardoned by the President. He then presented his petition to the court, asking permission to appear and continue to practice there under his admission of 1860 and the pardon of the President, without being required to make the oath prescribed by the act of January 24, 1865, and the rule of court made in pursuance of said act. The decision of the court was that his application should be granted.

Mr. Justice Field delivered the opinion of the Court on the 14th of January, 1867, in which he said:

The statute is directed against parties who have offended in any of the particulars embraced by these clauses, and its object is to exclude them from the profession of the law, or at least from its practice in the courts of the United States. As the oath prescribed can not be taken by these parties, the act as against them operates as a legislative decree of perpetual exclusion. An exclusion from any of the professions or any of the ordinary avocations of life for past conduct, can be regarded in no other light than as a punishment for such conduct. The exaction of the oath is the mode provided for ascertaining the parties upon whom the act is intended to operate, and, instead of lessening, increases its objectionable character. All enactments of this kind partake of the nature of bills of pains and penalties, and are subject to the constitutional inhibition against the passage of bills of attainder, under which general designation they are included. In the exclusion which the statute adjudges, it imposes a punishment for some of the acts specified, which were not punishable, or may not have been punishable at the time they were committed; and for other acts it adds a new punishment to that then prescribed, and it is thus brought within the further inhibition of the Constitution against the passage of an *ex post facto* law.

In the case of Cummings v. The State of Missouri, just decided, we had occasion to consider the meaning of a bill of attainder and an *ex post facto* law in the clause of the Constitution forbidding their passage by the States, and it is unnecessary to repeat here what we there said. A like prohibition is contained in the Constitution against enactments of this kind by Congress, and the arguments presented in that case against certain clauses of the constitution of Missouri is equally applicable to the act of Congress under consideration in this case.

The profession of an attorney and counselor is not like an office created by an Act of Congress, which depends for its continuance, its powers, and its emoluments on the will of its creator, and the possession of which may be burdened with any conditions not prohibited by the Constitution. Attorneys and counselors are not officers of the United States. They are not elected or appointed in the manner prescribed by the Constitution for the election or appointment of such officers. They are officers of the court, admitted as such by its order upon evidence of their possessing sufficient legal learning and fair character. Since the statute of Henry IV, it has been the practice in England, and it has always been the practice in this country, to obtain this evidence by an examination of the parties. In this court the fact of the admission of such officers in the highest court of the States to which they respectively belong for three years preceding their application is regarded as sufficient evidence of the possession of the requisite legal learning, and the statement of counsel moving their admission sufficient evidence that their private and professional character is fair. The order of admission is the judgment of the court that the parties possess the requisite qualifications as attorneys and counselors, and are entitled to appear as such and conduct causes therein. From its entry the parties become officers of the court, and are responsible to it for professional misconduct.

They hold their office during good behavior, and can only be deprived of it for misconduct, ascertained and declared by the judgment of the court, after opportunity to be heard has been afforded. Their admission and their exclusion are not the exercise of a mere ministerial power. The court is not in this respect the register of the edicts of any other body. It is the exercise of judicial powers, and has been so held in numerous cases. It was so held by the Court of Appeals of New York in the matter of the application of Cooper for admission. "Attorneys and counselors," said that court, "are not only officers of the court, but officers whose duties relate almost exclusively to proceedings of a judicial nature, and hence their appointment may, with propriety be intrusted to the courts; and the latter, in performing this duty, may very justly be considered as engaged in the exercise of their appropriate judicial functions." In *ex parte* Secomb, a *mandamus* to the Supreme Court of the Territory of Minnesota to vacate an order removing an attorney and counselor was denied by this court on the ground that the removal was a judicial act.

"We are not aware of any case," said the court, "where a *mandamus* was issued to an inferior tribunal commanding it to reverse or annul its decision, where the decision was in its nature a judicial act and within the scope of its jurisdiction and discretion." And in the same case the court observed that "it has been well settled by the rules and practice of common-law courts that it rests exclusively with the court to determine who is qualified to become one of its officers as an attorney and counselor, and for what causes he ought to be removed." The attorney and counselor, being by the solemn judicial act of the court clothed with his office, does not hold it as a matter of grace and favor; the right which it confers upon him to appear for suitors, and to argue causes, is something more than a mere indulgence, revokable at the pleasure of the court, or at the command of the legislature; it is a right of which he can only be deprived by the judgment of the court for moral or professional delinquency. The legislature may undoubtedly prescribe qualifications for the office, with which he must conform, as it may, where it has exclusive jurisdiction, prescribe qualifications for the pursuit of any of the ordinary avocations of life; but to constitute a qualification, the condition or thing prescribed must be attainable, in theory at least, by every one. That which, from the nature of things, or the past condition or conduct of the party, can not be attained by every citizen, does not fall within the definition of the term. To all those by whom it is unattainable, it is a disqualification which operates as a perpetual bar to the office. The question in this case is not as to the power of Congress to prescribe qualifications, but whether that power has been exercised as a means for the infliction of punishments against the prohibition of the Constitution. That this result can not be effected indirectly by a State under the form of creating qualifications, we have held in the case of Cummings *v.* The State of Missouri, and the reasoning upon which that conclusion was reached applies equally to similar action on the part of Congress.

These views are further strengthened by a consideration of the effect of the pardon produced by the petitioner, and the nature of the pardoning power of the President. The Constitution provides that the President "shall have power to grant reprieves and pardons for offenses against the United States, except in cases of impeachment." The power thus conferred is unlimited, with the exception stated; it extends to every offense known to the law, and may be exercised at any time after its commission; either before legal proceedings are taken, or during their pendency, or after conviction and judgment. This power of the President is not subject to legislative control. Congress can neither limit the effect of his pardon, nor exclude from its exercise any class of offenders. The benign prerogative of mercy reposed in him can not be fettered by any legislative restriction. Such being the case, the inquiry arises as to the effect and operation of a pardon. On this point all the authorities concur: a pardon reaches both the punishment prescribed for the offense, and the guilt of the offender; and when the pardon is full, it releases the punishment and blots out of existence the guilt, so that, in the eye of the law, the offender is as innocent as if he had never committed the offense. If granted before conviction, it prevents any of the penalties and disabilities consequent upon conviction, from attaching. If granted after conviction, it removes the penalties and disabilities, and restores him to all his civil rights. It makes him, as it were, a new man, and gives him a new credit and capacity. There is only this limit to its operation: it does not restore offices forfeited, or property or interests vested in others in consequence of the conviction and judgment. The pardon produced by the petitioner is a full pardon for all offenses by him committed, arising from participation, direct or implied, in the rebellion, and is subject to certain conditions which have been complied with. The effect of this pardon is to relieve the petitioner from all penalties and disabilities attached to the offense of treason committed by his participation in the rebellion. So far as that offense is concerned, he is thus placed beyond the reach of punishment of any kind; but to exclude him by reason of that offense from continuing in the enjoyment of previously acquired right, is to enforce a punishment for that offense notwithstanding the pardon. If such exclusion can be affected by the exaction of an expurgatory oath covering the offense, the pardon may be avoided, and that accomplished indirectly which can not be reached by direct legislation. It is not within the constitutional power of Congress thus to inflict punishment beyond the reach of executive clemency.

From the petitioner, therefore, the oath required by the act of January 24, 1865, can not be exacted, even were that act not subject to any other objection than the one just stated. It follows, from the views expressed, that the prayer of the petitioner must be granted.

The case of R. H. Marr is similar in its main features to that of the petitioner, and his petition must be granted; and the amendment to the second rule of the court, which requires the oath prescribed by the act of January 24, 1865, to be taken by attorneys and counselors, having been unadvisedly adopted, must be rescinded, and it is so ordered.*

The Condition of Tennessee.

THE FRUITS OF RADICAL RECONSTRUCTION.

The condition of Tennessee at this time, is but an index of what will be that of the seven Southern States which have been placed by Radical military reconstruction under rotten borough governments, and of the three others which are destined, if the Radicals succeed, to the same terrible doom. Let us see what her down-trodden people have to bear. An Executive, the gratification of whose fierce and cruel resentments is the supreme law of the land, backed by a Legislature without honor or conscience, who do not hesitate to violate their own laws whenever their master or themselves deem it necessary to set aside registration and elections, or do any other act to preserve the unity of their despotic power; a people, three-fifths of the white and law-abiding portion of which are disfranchised, while all of the negroes are enfranchised to an exclusive control of the political power of the State; a system of taxation, State, county and municipal, consuming not only the bulk of the production of capital, but threatening the consumption of the capital itself, to the enrichment of mercenary politicians, most of whom have located recently in the State, and are content to live, not by labor, but by forays upon the people's purse, in which they are upheld by the State Government, with whom they consort, and to the discharge of subsidies which many of the members of the Legislature exact as compensation for each measure of outrage and plunder they impose as law upon the impoverished and heart-sick people of the State; an organized conspiracy of fraud and violence at the polls which makes an election a farce, and imperils the life of all who attempt an independent exercise of suffrage, to the antagonism of the State Government, backed, among other means, by an expensive organization of State militia, such as that which Congress now proposes to arm in the rotten boroughs of the South, called out upon the fancy of the Governor and quartered upon the people of the State for the purpose of upholding violence, intimidating voters, and precluding a free system of elections; in fact every monstrous detail of outrage and wrong which a brutal fiendishness can devise, and a cowardly horde of reckless and unprincipled mercenaries can enforce, is the lot of Tennessee. The circumstances of her condition were well set forth in an address to the recent National Democratic Convention, by a committee from among her ablest and most trusted citizens. Hon. T. W. Brown, Chairman; Messrs. William Clare, J. H. Callender, J. E. Bailey and W. A. Quarles.

THE REPRESENTATION OF TENNESSEE IN CONGRESS.

When the delegation from Tennessee appeared in the House of Representatives to be sworn in as members of the Fortieth Congress, on the 21st of November, 1867, Mr. Brooks, of New York, objected in manner following:

Mr. BROOKS. I object upon the ground that the elective franchise law of Tennessee, under which these gentlemen are said to have been elected, disfranchises a large portion of the white population—a majority of the white population of the State of Tennessee; that these members thus elected

---

* The new order, made by a majority, is as follows:

SUPREME COURT OF THE UNITED STATES. December Term, 1866 — *Monday, January* 14, 1867.

ORDER OF COURT.

It is now here ordered by the Court that the amendment to the second rule of this Court, which requires the oath prescribed by the act of Congress of January 24, 1865, to be taken by attorneys and counselors, be, and the same is, hereby rescinded and annulled.

under that State Franchise law of the State of Tennessee were elected by 55,000 negro votes 45,000 white voters only voting, and that there were disfranchised in the State of Tennessee in that election from forty to forty-five thousand white voters; 100,000 voters controlled that election, 55,000 of whom were negroes; 45,000 whites being voted down, and 40,000 white voters disfranchised, who could not vote at all under the law of the State. I object to them upon the ground that an oligarchy exists and reigns in the State of Tennessee, and that it is not such a republican form of government as the Constitution prescribes and ordains; and, therefore, I object to the swearing in of the whole delegation upon the principles which I have here alleged.

I will not at this time consume the attention of the House by reading the lengthened law of franchise of the State of Tennessee. But what I have to say upon that subject is, that a more oligarchical, monarchical, exclusive, tyrannical law hardly ever existed under any form of government, and does not now exist in Great Britain or in France. That law, in my judgment, with all due respect to the Representatives from the State of Tennessee, or to the State of Tennessee—for she has no Representatives on this floor—that law is a disgrace to a free form of government, a dishonor to civilization, and a reprobation of all forms of republican self-government.

Without proceeding further upon this point, I shall first object to the swearing in of Mr. Butler, from the first district of Tennessee; from East Tennessee, I think, he comes—from the region where Governor Brownlow lives; and I object to him upon many and various points, which I shall proceed to show as good grounds for objection, and which I have but very little doubt will meet with the attention and consideration of both sides of this House when the facts are brought home fully to the consideration of Republican members, because almost all of them are on record in the vote which they gave last July for the exclusion of the Kentucky members; almost all of them are upon a record which excludes Mr. Butler irrevocably from being sworn in, upon the facts which I shall present to the consideration of this House.

I hold in my hand the journal of the extra session of the Thirty third General Assembly of the State of Tennessee, which convened at Nashville on the first Monday of January, 1861, upon the special convocation or order of the then Governor of the State, Isham G. Harris, the declared and avowed object of which, in the message, was to separate or segregate the State of Tennessee from the States of this Union; and of that Legislature Mr. Butler, who is now claiming a right to be sworn in here, was a member.

And before I go further, I shall proceed to read a portion of his record in that Legislature, which I shall show to be the record of one among the most extreme and violent men among the seceding members in this State; not out-done by Isham G. Harris himself, and going as far and as fully as any man did in the Legislature to separate the State of Tennessee from the Union. And I shall proceed to show the active part which he took in that Legislature before I proceed to another and more active part taken by him in the perambulatory Legislature, first convened in Nashville by Governor Harris, and subsequently portable and transferable, after the affair of Fort Donelson, to the city of Memphis, on the Mississippi river. On page 57 of the House Journal of 1861 of the extra session of the General Assembly of Tennessee, Mr. Butler offered a "House resolution, No. 34," as follows:

"*Be it resolved by the General Assembly of the State of Tennessee*, That our Senators in Congress be, and they are hereby, instructed to vote against the confirmation of any man to office who indorsed an infamous libel upon the South, known as the Helper book; and that the Governor is hereby requested to forward a copy of this resolution to each of our Senators in Congress."

I do not blame Mr. Butler so much for that. I read it, not so much for the consideration of this side of the House as for the other side of the House more particularly.

The second resolution was that—

"The people of Tennessee receive the report of the appointment of William H. Seward to a position in the Cabinet of the incoming Administration as further evidence of hostility to the institutions of the South; and if the policy he has advocated in all his speeches upon the subject of domestic slavery shall be inaugurated with said Administration, the South has but little hope of a settlement of existing difficulties between her and the North."

* * * *

The great object of that Legislature was, as I have said, to ordain or order a convention in the State of Tennessee, which convention should, under the doctrine of secession, take the State of Tennessee, as was contended, constitutionally out of the Union. A resolution was offered by Mr. Jones that "the action of the convention shall be submitted to the people, upon reasonable notice, for ratification or rejection, and shall be of no binding force unless it is adopted and ratified by a majority of the qualified voters of the people of Tennessee;"

and upon the final vote on that subject Mr. Butler voted with the seceders to create a convention, to ordain it by law, to make it, as was then contended, a legitimate and constitutional convention. Upon the final vote taken on that subject, the strongest sort of a resolution for the creation of a convention, whose action was to be submitted to the people, was adopted by a vote of sixty-eight ayes and no noes; and the bill for the holding of a convention was then ordered to be transferred to the Senate, Mr. Butler voting in the affirmative.

Another resolution, No. 44, introduced in that Legislature by Mr. Farrelly, provided that "His Excellency the Governor be, and he is hereby, authorized and requested to make inquiry of the different banks of the State whether or not they are willing to loan the State money in the present crisis of affairs, and if so, how much and upon what terms." On that resolution the vote was 47 yeas to 19 nays, Mr. Butler voting in the affirmative.

Mr. Pickett submitted resolution No. 51, on the subject of Federal relations—a long series of resolutions, too long to read, but the purport of which can easily be imagined when I describe them as of the worst kind of the resolutions which were at that time introduced into the "secesh" legislatures of the Southern States. The resolution to which I particularly call the attention of the House is that which was offered by Mr. Jones as an amendment, and which was carried, that—

"Should a plan of adjustment satisfactory to the South not be acceded to by the requisite number of States, to perfect amendments to the Constitution, it is the opinion of the General Assembly that the slaveholding States should adopt for themselves the Constitution of the United States, with such amendments as may be satisfactory to the slaveholding States; and that they should invite into a union with them all States of the North which are willing to abide such amended Constitution and frame of government; severing at once and forever all connections with States refusing such reasonable guarantees to our future safety."

The vote on the adoption of that resolution was—yeas 42, nays 23; Mr. Butler being recorded in the affirmative.

In the same volume I find another long series of resolutions of the same sort, introduced by Mr. Gantt, from the Joint Committee on Federal Relations. The concluding resolution of the series I will read:

"Resolved, That, should a plan of adjustment satisfactory to the South not be acceded to by the requisite number of States to perfect amendments to the Constitution of the United States, it is the opinion of this General Assembly that the slaveholding States should adopt for themselves the Constitution of the United States, with such amendments as may be satisfactory to the slaveholding States; and that they should invite into a union with them all States of the North which are willing to abide such amended Constitution and frame of government, severing at once all connection with States refusing such reasonable guarantees to our future safety; such renewed conditions of federal union being first submitted for ratification to conventions of all the States respectively."

This resolution received the vote of Mr. Butler. There are other points in this book, all going to demonstrate as forcibly, or more forcibly than what I have read, that at all times and on all occasions, without any exception whatsoever, Mr. Butler voted against the Union members of the Legislature of Tennessee, and with the leading "secesh" members of that body.

Secession was ordained, and that ordinance of secession I have before me, but I will not consume the time of the House by having it read. It was adopted May 7, 1861, and ratified June 8, 1861. It was an ordinance of secession professing to take the State of Tennessee out of the Union, and declaring that it thereafter formed an independent State—one of the Confederate States of America.

Of the "secesh" Legislature held in Tennessee after this ordinance took that State out of this Union, Mr. Butler, of East Tennessee, became a prominent and active member; and I have in my hands a variety of motions in which he took an active part, and when they are fully presented to the consideration of the other side of the House, they will bind gentlemen to the mischievous precedent established in this House in the case of the member-elect from the State of Kentucky in July last, and compel them to refuse to Mr. Butler the right to take the oath and become a member of this body.

I have before me, Mr. Speaker, the record of Mr. Butler's votes in the "secesh" Legislature of the Confederate State of Tennessee. I have here where he moved an amendment and voted to amend a bill authorizing the authorities of the Confederate State of Tennessee to confiscate and sequestrate all Northern debts due from people in Tennessee to people in the North, and to sequestrate all Northern property held in Tennessee belonging to any citizen of the North. That bill of confiscation and sequestration not only proceeds to confiscate and sequestrate Northern property, but also declares citizens of the North to be aliens, and entitled to no more rights than aliens from

Great Britain, aliens from France, or aliens from Austria or Turkey. And when the ambulatory or ambulance "secesh" Legislature of the Confederate State of Tennessee was threatened by the irruption of our army after the success at Fort Donelson—when it was threatened at Nashville, Mr. Butler, among others of that ambulatory Legislature, decamped from that city and established the headquarters of that Legislature in the city of Memphis. Among other measures adopted in the city of Memphis, for which Mr. Butler voted, was one for taking care of the invalid soldiers of the South; providing the ways and means for supporting also the families which were left behind. This may have been charity, but it was a charity showing his heart as well as his votes, at that time, to be with the Southern Confederacy.

But, sir, the point to which I wish now particularly to call attention was a motion for removing the incorporated banks of the State of Tennessee from within the Union dominion, from those portions of the State which had been taken possession of after the victory of Fort Donelson, to those portions not in the occupation of our army. And a vote of his is on record in the "secesh" Legislature indorsing that motion, and threatening those banks with a deprivation of their corporate rights if they did not change their places of business to within the Confederate or "secesh" dominion in the State of Tennessee. No more important vote than that could be given; for, next to the sword of the South, was the purse of the South—if indeed the purse was not the most important. By that act of Mr. Butler he voted to take ten million dollars from the then conquered portion of Tennessee, and to transfer that capital to the Confederate government of Tennessee. His vote is on the record. And if this were not enough, he is on the record to give the use of the Tennessee hall of the House of Representatives to the electors for President and Vice-President who elected Jeff. Davis to be President of the Confederate States.

He is also on record as voting to pay for the cavalry horses of the Confederate Government. He is also on record, in the eighty-ninth resolution of the "secesh" Convention, as declaring that no compromise whatsoever should be made with the Northern United States of America, except with the express condition that the Confederate States should be recognized as sovereign, independent States of this Union. The eighth-sixth resolution of this convention, then assembled at Memphis, was to seize all United States property to pay for rebel services during the war, and Mr But-ler is on record as voting for that. He is also on record to build a railroad from Cleveland, Tennessee, under the authority of the Confederate Government, as a great military necessity of the Confederate States of the South.

I might, I presume, stop here, but I hold in my hand some resolutions upon which Mr. Butler voted in the "secesh" Legislature, which I will proceed to read, and to which I ask the particular attention of all sides of the House. Mr. Jones offered the following resolutions in the "secesh" House of Assembly:

"*Resolved*, That it is the sense of this General Assembly that the separation of those States now forming the Confederate States of America from the United States is, and ought to be, final, perpetual, and irrevocable; and that Tennessee will, under no circumstances, entertain any proposition from any quarter which may have for its object a restoration or reconstruction of the late Union on any terms or conditions whatever.

"*Resolved*, That the war which the United States are waging upon the Confederate States should be prosecuted on our part with the utmost vigor and energy, until our independence and nationality are unconditionally acknowledged by the United States.

"*Resolved*, That Tennessee pledges herself to her sister States of the Confederacy that she will stand by them throughout the struggle; that she will contribute all the means which her resources will supply, so far as the same may be necessary, to the support of the common cause, and will not consent to lay down arms until peace is established on the basis of the foregoing resolutions."

These resolutions were carried—ayes 41, nays 19; and among the 41 ayes is the name of Mr. Butler, now claiming to be a Representative on the floor of this House from the State of Tennessee.

I will now refer to the member elect from the Fourth District of the State of Tennessee, Mr. Mullins, who I believe comes from the central part of the State. I object to him, not upon grounds so strong as I have objected to the admission of Mr. Butler, but I object to him upon the ground that he gave aid and comfort to the rebellion; made speeches in behalf of the rebellion, lent it aid and support, and assisted to raise troops for that rebellion. In the year 1861 he made a speech in Bedford county, Tennessee, at a place known as Moore's Springs, near Shelbyville, for the purpose of urging the young men there to join a rebel company to be raised there. In the speech referred to, Colonel Mullins said that he wanted to see all the young men go out and fight for their homes and firesides; that he was old and not able to do much fighting; that he would remain at home and make meat and bread for those to live on who did fight; and whenever it became essential he would himself go into the rebel army. The speech was entirely a rebel speech.

I hold in my hand authority for these declarations, and if this authority is denied hereafter, I shall proceed to submit in a more substantative and official form than I have named here.

In the Fourth District of Tennessee, where lived some eight thousand of the twenty-two thousand white voters who organized the State of Tennessee after the rebellion, Governor Brownlow, under this wicked registry act, in order to elect a man of his own school, and to prevent the election by the Conservative voters of that district, threw out four counties, containing five thousand registered voters, the counties of Coffin, Franklin, Lincoln and Giles. In those counties, where, I say, lived eight thousand of the twenty-two thousand voters who organized the State of Tennessee, five thousand of those white voters were thrown out by the proclamation of the Governor of Tennessee; doing away with the whole registry of these counties. He disfranchised them all by an arbitrary edict of power; and if Mr. Mullins could be maintained in his seat otherwise, this declaration is sufficient here to show that republican self government does not now, and did not exist, in at least the Fourth District of Tennessee.

I have also objections to urge to the admission of Mr. Arnell, of the Sixth District of Tennessee. During the war he was established in the county of Lawrence, Tennessee, where he lives, and had a tannery, which, during no inconsiderable portion of the war, was devoted to the manufacture of shoes. He declared he was unable to supply his neighbors with shoes, because, such were the requisitions of the rebel authorities upon him, that before he could supply the women and children of his neighborhood with shoes, he must supply this foundation and understanding of the rebel army.

I also object to the admission of Mr. Trimble, from the Fifth District of Tennessee, who, I am informed—I have not the authentic information in his case that I have in the others—because, when the ordinance of secession was submitted to the people of Tennessee, in 1861, if he voted at all, as many believe he did vote, he voted to take Tennessee out of the Union.

Mr Trimble says that is not true; I was about to state, when he said so, that if he would rise upon this floor and say that it was not so, I would say no more—but as he has no right to say it to the House, he whispers it to me, and I say to the House for him, that he did not vote at that time. I withdraw my objection, then, to Mr. Trimble, because I have no authentic testimony; none except a mere verbal report, which is not enough for me to make charges respecting him upon the floor of this House.

I now yield the rest of my time to the honorable gentleman from Wisconsin [Mr. Eldridge]. But before I yield I wish to introduce some resolutions, which I will put in form.

The SPEAKER. The Chair would state that a mere objection to the swearing in of a gentleman will not arrest the administration of the oath; but it will require some action of the House.

Mr. BROOKS. I will propose two resolutions, one against the admission of all the members; the other, that the certificates of Messrs. Butler, Stokes and Arnell, previous to their being sworn in, be referred to the Committee of Elections.

Mr. ELDRIDGE. Mr. Speaker, I do not intend to make but a single remark. I was apprehensive at the last session that the precedent which gentlemen were establishing in the case of Kentucky, would come back at some not distant day to torment its inventors; and as I have objected to Mr. Stokes being sworn in as a member of this House, and have moved that his credentials be referred to the Committee of Elections, I now ask to place before the House the ground of my objection.

On the 27th of July, 1866, Mr. Stokes was making a speech in this House, when I asked of him the privilege of introducing and having read at the Clerk's desk a letter purporting to have been written by him. That letter was read, as follows:

LIBERTY, May 10, 1861.

DEAR SIR—I have just learned from a friend that there are some gross misrepresentations going the rounds in your section in regard to my position in this trying crisis, and for the benefit of yourself and others I write this.

I have been a zealous advocate of the Union up to the time of Lincoln's call for seventy five thousand troops; that being in violation of law, and for the subjugation of the South. I commend Governor Harris for his course, and for arming the State and resisting Lincoln to the point of the bayonet, and have enrolled my name as a volunteer to resist his usurpation. I have, in Congress and out, opposed coercion and all forced measures, believing that it was better to recognize the independence of the "Southern Confederacy" than to attempt to coerce them back.

I have always opposed secession, but claim the right of revolution, and the right to resist the oppression of the Federal Government, and to throw off their allegiance to the same when that oppression becomes intolerable. That time has now come. I have been, and I am now, for standing by the border slave States, for they are to be the great sufferers during the conflict. I am opposed to being tacked on to the Southern Confederacy at present (except as a military league). But when peace is restored, if the two nations can not live in peace, let all the fifteen slave States elect delegates, meet in convention, frame their constitution, and submit it to the people for their ratification.

The South ought to be a unit during the war, by all means. I had announced myself as a candidate for re-election, but on seeing Lincoln's proclamation for troops, abandoned the canvass at once, and I am no candidate. I claim to have done my duty in trying to heal our difficulties and restore peace. That having failed, I shall now march forward in the discharge of my duty in resisting Lincoln, regardless of false charges, or what not, by those who are trying to put me down. Time will tell where we all stand, and who have been faithful.

Hoping to hear from you soon, I remain yours truly,
WILLIAM B. STOKES.
Mr. JOHN DUNCAN, McMinnville, Tennessee.

When this letter was read, I inquired of Mr. Stokes, who was then addressing the House, whether it was a genuine letter written by him. His answer was, "Yes, sir, it is." Upon this letter, therefore, I have made the objection to the swearing in of Mr. Stokes, and have moved that his credentials, with this letter, be referred to the Committee of Elections, and the gentleman on the other side will now have the opportunity of following the precedent of the Kentucky case.

At a subsequent stage of the proceedings, Mr. Brooks said: I rise to a question of privilege in the case of Colonel Mullins. As it seems to be required on the other side that in order to make a charge, some affidavit or some specific statement, signed by somebody, should be presented, I ask the Clerk to read the paper which I send to the desk.

The SPEAKER. A resolution must first be offered before any paper can be read.

Mr. BROOKS. I then offer the following resolution, understanding it to be necessary:

Resolved, That the certificate of Mr. Mullins be referred to the Committee of Elections, and that he be not sworn in pending the investigation.

The Clerk read, as follows:

I am well acquainted with Colonel James Mullins of Bedford county, Tennessee. I have known him from my boyhood, and I now make this statement:

In the year 1861—I forget the day and month—I heard Colonel Mullins make a speech in Bedford county, Tennessee. The speech was made at a spring known as "Moore's" Spring, some three or four miles from Shelbyville, Tennessee. The speech was made for the purpose of urging the young men of that locality to join a rebel company then being made up by one Jas. A. Moore, of said State and county. In the speech, Colonel Mullins said that he wanted to see all the young men go out and fight for their homes and firesides; that he was an old man and not able to do much fighting, but that he would make meat and bread for others to live on while they fought, and that whenever it became essential, he too, would go into the rebel army. In fact, the entire speech was an "out and out" rebel speech, and in entire accord with the speeches being then made throughout Tennessee by such men as Governor Harris and other rebel leaders.

In one or two days after hearing this speech, I met Colonel Mullins in Shelbyville, Tennessee, and rebuked him for the speech referred to. He replied that half of the North and all of the South had gone with the rebellion, and that he thought it the duty of every Southern man to take sides with the South in the struggle. I told him if he thought so he could go that way, but as for myself I should "paddle my own canoe."

At the conclusion of the speech referred to, I urged the young men to pay no attention to what Mullins had said, and not to go into the rebel army. A great many took my advice, and remained firm Union men, many of them subsequently becoming Union soldiers.

At the time Colonel Mullins made this speech I regarded him as a "*rebel*," and I am sure his language would have sustained such a belief.

I have been a loyal man from the beginning. On the 17th day of April, 1862, I enlisted as a Union soldier. I was subsequently elected a lieutenant in the First Tennessee United States troops, known as the guard of Governor Andrew Johnson, then Military Governor of Tennessee.

I am now a First-Lieutenant in the Twelfth U. S. Infantry, Regular Army.

The Colonel Mullins referred to is now the Congressman-elect from the Fourth Congressional District of Tennessee.
A. M. TROLUGER,
First-Lieut. Twelfth U. S. Infantry.
WASHINGTON, D. C., Nov. 12, 1867.

All the members of the delegation were, notwithstanding the presentation of these facts, then sworn in, except Mr. Butler, who has since had his political disabilities removed, and an oath fixed up for him to swallow the Constitution of the United States against all enemies, foreign and domestic, and to bear true faith and allegiance to the same; taking the obligation freely, without any mental reservation or purpose of evasion, and swearing faithfully to discharge the duties of the office.

Why there should be any question of the ability of Butler to take any oath, is a good joke, since he has had an experience in that kind of business which is perfect. Notwithstanding his record, so truthfully presented by Mr. Brooks, he took the following candidates' oath, prescribed by the Franchise law of Tennessee, before his election to Congress:

State of Tennessee, Davidson county, ss:

I do most solemnly swear that I have never voluntarily borne arms against the Government of the United States for the purpose or with the intention of aiding the late rebellion, nor have I, with any such intention, at any time, given aid, comfort, counsel, or encouragement to said rebellion, or to any act of hostility to the Government of the United States.

I further swear that I have never sought or accepted any office, either civil or military, or attempted to exercise the functions of any office, either civil or military, under the authority or pretended authority of the so called Confederate States of America, or of any insurrectionary State, hostile or opposed to the authority of the United States Government, with the intent and desire to aid said rebellion; and that I have never given a voluntary support to any such government or authority, so help me God.

[Signed] R. R. BUTLER.

Subscribed and sworn to before me, this 21st day of June, A. D. 1867.

JONATHAN LAWRENCE,
Justice of the Peace for Jefferson county.

I, Andrew J. Fletcher, Secretary of State of the State of Tennessee, do certify that the foregoing is a copy of the oath of R. R. Butler, as a candidate for Congress, under the Franchise law of Tennessee, the original of which is on file in my office.

In testimony whereof, I have hereunto subscribed my official signature, and by order of the Governor affixed the great seal of the State of Tennessee, at the department in the city of Nashville, this 10th day of August, A. D. 1867.

[SEAL.] A. J. FLETCHER,
Secretary of State.

How the Loyal Militia Act.

BROWNLOW'S MILITIA ON THE RAMPAGE—MURDER OF A CITIZEN—OTHER PARTIES SHOT AT—LADIES INSULTED—MEETING OF CITIZENS TO PETITION FOR PROTECTION.

[From the Nashville Union, May 31, 1867.]

The citizens of Franklin county held a meeting at Winchester, on Wednesday night, in reference to the conduct of the militia in that county. F. A. Loughmiller acted as Chairman, and W. J. Slatter as Secretary.

On motion, a committee of twenty citizens was appointed to inquire into and report upon the conduct of the militia, and to make suggestions as to the best course to be pursued.

The committee, after retiring, made a report, and thereupon speeches were made by Jesse Arledge, the chairman of the committee, Colonel Peter Turney, A. S. Colyar and Henry Singleton. The report was then adopted unanimously.

The report is as follows:

Your committee report that, upon examination, they find the following facts to be true: That the militia now located in this county, under one Captain Kirkman, are committing depredations that call for prompt and immediate action. For weeks the conduct of this militia has been such as to deter many of our citizens from engaging in their ordinary pursuits, and in particular parts of the county, farmers particularly have been deterred from making any expenditure, in the purchase or collection of stock to make a crop; and in portions of the county the indications now are that the crop will have to be abandoned, and will be entirely lost.

Several of our citizens have been driven from their homes, and for weeks have been hiding out. Within the last few days, the outrages of this militia have been of a much more serious and alarming character. They have been traveling over the country, pretending to be hunting arms, but they have, in the most violent manner, entered people's houses, insulted the women, alarmed the children, threatening to kill many persons.

Among the families thus outraged are Dr. Abernathy's, E. H. Poe's, Hampton's, and many others.

Only a few days ago they took an inoffensive boy, the son of E. H. Poe, a prisoner, carried him to camp and tied him, and condemned him to be shot, and his life was saved by the intercession of a friend, making the young man promise, on pain of death, not to tell what had taken place.

Yesterday morning, about daylight, a portion of this militia went to the house of a peaceable, quiet citizen, James Brown, and upon a pretended acknowledgment, which they claim to have extracted from him, by falsely personating East Tennessee refugees, as to the part he (Brown) took in the war, they took him into the woods, utterly disregarding the appeals and cries of his wife and father, and put him to death in a most heartless and cruel manner. Leaving him dead, they returned to camp, only sending word to his wife that she could send and get her husband if she wanted him.

Other citizens were shot at, and the lives of many men have been threatened. Several of our citizens have been notified within the last few days that they would be killed. And these things are all done, as is alleged, because of the part said persons took in the war, which has now been over more than two years, and for which the parties have all been pardoned, and have the pledge of the United States Government, through its highest military officers, that they should be protected, having laid down their arms.

We further report that so far as the citizens of this county are concerned, and especially the men who were rebels during the war, the most perfect quiet and order prevails. Everybody, and especially the former rebels, have shown a disposition to obey the laws, no matter how onerous, never before witnessed in this country. It has been the constant remark of our Judges, to wit: Judge Hickerson, Judge Patterson and Judge Steele, all of whom have held court in this district, and all of whom were appointees of Gov. Brownlow, that they never knew a people more disposed to be law-abiding. The truth is, no one pretends that any man who was a rebel has committed any crime or done anything since the war for which he deserves punishment.

Your committee recommend, first, for the immediate protection of men who were in the Southern army and who live in the neighborhood where this militia is located, that they protect themselves by keeping out of the way of this militia for the present, even if they have to abandon their families and give up their crops.

Second. That a committee be appointed to draft a petition to the Federal Government, setting forth our grievances, and asking protection for our lives and property.

Third. If the depredations of this militia are continued, and our people are indiscriminately driven from their homes and murdered, and, after appealing in the most earnest manner to the Federal and State authorities, we can get no protection, we recommend that the people combine and protect themselves.

Jesse Arledge,	Chas. H. Cherry,
Wm. F. Taylor,	J. L. Baugh,
J. J. Williams,	W. T. Faris,
Nathan Frizzell,	John Burrough,
Tilman Arledge,	M. Ransom,
J. C. Garner,	J. W. Bone,
J. M. Pryor,	Henry Singleton,
Wiley S. Embry,	Aleck Smith,
Wiley Sanders,	A. S. Colyar,
E. F. Colyar,	A. D. Trimble.

Yet these are the kind of beasts that Congress proposes to arm with rifle and cannon to inaugurate a like reign of terror, previous to the Presidential election, in the other States of the South.

Brownlow's Militia Extending their Jurisdiction.

The commander of "Company A," Brownlow's army, has issued the following order—which it will be seen involves a question of such rare and delicate subtlety, that the learned Gresham could not decide. Unlike Rickman and Clingan, Gresham seems inclined to call for the assistance of civil officers to participate in his uncivil proceedings. The document is without a precedent in legal or military history:

"Headquarters Company A, First Regiment Tennessee State Guard, Camp near Bristol, Tenn., May 27, 1867.—J. S. Shangle, Esq.—*Dear Sir:* You are hereby notified to appear at these headquarters on tomorrow morning (28th) at 8 o'clock, to set with two other magistrates.

"The case is: A man and his wife have parted recently, and the man takes from his wife a female infant, only seven months old. She applies to have the infant restored to her. You will inform yourself in regard to the points of law which may be involved, and fail not to report at the hour appointed.

"GEO. EDGAR GRESHAM,
"Captain commanding Co."

Negro Office-Holders.

The 16th section of the Franchise act of Tennessee, precluded negroes from holding office. Upon this point the Senators and Representatives of Tennessee in Congress, addressed the following memorial to the Legislature:

"*To the Senate and House of Representatives of Tennessee:*

"The undersigned, citizens of the State, your constituents and personal and political friends, respectfully but earnestly pray that you will repeal the 16th section of the Franchise act, thus giving full effect to the principle on which is based our restored State government, by obliterating from the statute books the last vestige of legislation which imposes disabilities where there has been no blame, and which neither time nor merit can remove. It would gratify us, and we feel sure it would gratify the body of your constituents, to know that you had acted in this manner promptly and unanimously. And, as in duty bound, we will ever pray.

"(Signed)   Jos. S. Fowler,
"Horace Maynard,
"W. B. Stokes,
"Jas. Mullins,
"D. A. Nunn,
"Jno. Trimble,
"Samuel M. Arnell.
"Washington, December 7."

Brownlow's Exercise of the Pardoning Power.

Ex-Attorney General Stubblefield Lets Loose on Radicalism.

In its report of the County Convention at McMinnville, the *New Era*, of June 2, says:

"The Hon. George J. Stubblefield being present was called to the stand, and addressed the large and attentive audience for about one hour. During his remarks Mr Stubblefield attempted to excuse himself from further effort, but the cries of 'go on, go on,' induced him to prolong his remarks to the great satisfaction of the good men present, and to the utter discomfiture of the few Radicals who came within the sound of his voice. His expose of their corruption and avariciousness carried conviction with his earnestness. One statement made by Mr. Stubblefield, as an evidence of the 'law and order' of the Radical party as contrasted with that of the Conservatives, we must be permitted to mention in this connection:

"He said he had labored hard for three years to convict and have punished criminals for every grade of offense—for rape, murder and theft; that during the time he had succeeded in having convicted and confined in the penitentiary some three hundred criminals for the worst grade of offenses; and that in one month's time our most excellent Governor, W. G. Brownlow, had turned the whole batch loose to renew their depredations upon the communities; and asked if such conduct did not exhibit a desire to harrass and goad the people rather than promote good feeling and amity."

Governor Brownlow Desires to Extinguish, and Thus get Rid of the Negro Race.

In the Knoxville *Whig*, published as late as May 28, 1864, Brownlow plainly, freely and without any reserve, tells the colored men that he wants them freed only for the reasons that he, *Brownlow, believes it will be the very means of extinguishing the negro race.* Brownlow says:

"We have never differed with the South upon the abstract question of slavery, and *do not now differ;* and we are free to say, that the condition of the slaves when liberated, *if left in the South, will be worse* than it has been during their servitude. But we are for emancipating every negro in the South notwithstanding all this."

Here Brownlow classes the negro with the rebel, and says he wants the negro punished the same as rebels are punished, and for no other reason than that he is a negro. He says, "for taking this ground we have just *two* controlling reasons." Now, reader, look at the reasons: First, he says, "it will be the severest punishment of Southern rebels that can be inflicted." *Now, see what a noble object he has in view; nothing more or less than the destruction of the negro race.* And next, "it will be the very means of *extinguishing the negro race.*"

Radical Officials in Tennessee.

Tremendous Tax-payers.

The Memphis *Avalanche* says: "The taxable property of Shelby county, for 1867, was returned at forty-eight millions of dollars. On this amount, in 1867, six hundred and fifty-eight thousand dollars was collected. It will be seen from information which we derive from the Tax-Collector's books, that on the forty eight millions of dollars' worth of taxable property, and the six hundred and fifty-eight thousand dollars collected for taxes, the Radical office-holders of this county pay the enormous sum of *one hundred and forty-seven dollars and fifty cents!*"

Brownlow Sustained by Grant.

His Usurpations Encouraged by the Use of United States Troops in their Behalf.

Brownlow's invocations for the aid of the Armies of the United States to back up his excesses, are as potential as that of the order of any general officer in it. The commander of the Department of the Cumberland is as certain to heed his call, as the General commanding is sure to give countenance to whatever may be necessary to uphold the diseased power of the so-called Governor of Tennessee. On the 28th of September, 1867, the regular charter election was to have been held. The Mayor, as was usual, ordered the election, as had always been done in compliance with the terms of the charter. The Governor insisted upon the right and duty of his Commissioner of Registration to hold it in compliance with the Franchise laws. The charter having been established previous to negro suffrage, did not recognize that article, and had never before been claimed to come under any of the proscriptions of the Franchise laws, or to be affected by any extension of the franchise, they provided. Hence the concern of the Governor. A charter, every one knows, can not be affected by the provisions of any subsequent statute unless it is especially, and by terms named in the same, and subjected to the effect of a repealing or amending clause. The Mayor was willing that Brownlow should hold an election in his way, and that he, the Mayor, would hold one in compliance with the charter, the courts to decide the question as between the two elections thereafter. All the Mayor wanted was to be permitted to discharge his duty peaceably. Brownlow, however, was inexorable, and concentrated his loyal militia at Nashville, to prevent by bloodshed, if necessary, the discharge of his duty by the Mayor. He knew his militia were of little concern to the people except in the way of taxes to support them, and they did not fear them. So he gave Gen. Thomas a hint that the services of the United States forces might be needed.

A correspondence ensued on the subject, of which the following is material.

The Mayor, in a letter to General Thomas dated September 24, 1867, announced his purpose to hold the election, which he closed as follows:

Let the courts, the only proper arbiters, decide in the end, if we are wrong, and we will bow to their decision; but we will not be deterred from the free exercise of our rights by any power on earth, except that of the United States.

W. MATT. BROWN, *Mayor.*

On which General Thomas made the following indorsement of transmittal:

HEADQUARTERS DEPARTMENT OF THE CUMBERLAND, }
LOUISVILLE, KY., Sept, 24, 1867. }

Respectfully referred to the Adjutant-General of the Army for the information of the General-in-chief.

As yet no requisition has been made for a military force for service in the case, but I have reason to believe there will be.

Under existing instructions from the honorable Secretary of War to assist the civil authorities in preserving the peace, and the Governor of the State being chief magistrate of the State, and he having announced by proclamation his construction of the law, and his determination to enforce it, I am of the opinion that if called upon I should be compelled to aid him in enforcing his decrees with the forces at my command. Such will be the action taken unless ordered to the contrary, and instructions by telegraph are requested if this is not approved of.

GEORGE H. THOMAS,
Maj.-Gen. U. S. A., Commanding.

General Thomas sent to General Duncan the following instructions:

HEADQUARTERS DEPARTMENT OF THE CUMBERLAND, }
LOUISVILLE, KY., Sept. 24, 1867. }

* * * * *

Governor Brownlow is chief magistrate of the State, and has announced by proclamation his construction of the law. If he needs military force to assist him in enforcing it, you will render him all the assistance in your power.

The Major-General commanding has referred your letters and accompanying documents to the War Department, with advice of the action taken by him, and requested instructions by telegraph if it was not approved of. If such instructions are received you will be advised immediately.

In the absence of any requisition upon you for troops prior to the day of election, you will on that day hold your command in readiness for immediate action, as you may be called upon at any moment to assist in quelling riots.

I am, General, very respectfully,
Your obedient servant,
ALFRED L. HOUGH,
Brevet-Col. U. S. A., A. A. A. G.
Brevet Brigadier-Gen. THOMAS DUNCAN.

HEADQUARTERS TENNESSEE STATE GUARDS, }
NASHVILLE, September 23, 1867. }

GENERAL: Inclosed please find copy of Governor Brownlow's instructions to me as commanding officer of the State forces. I forward you this copy at the request of General Duncan, in order that you may consider it in connection with the documents in the case already referred to you by him.

I am, General, your obedient servant,
JOSEPH A. COOPER,
Brig.-Gen. Com. Tennessee State Guards.
Major-Gen. GEORGE H. THOMAS, *Commanding Dep't of the Cumberland, Louisville, Ky.*

STATE OF TENNESSEE, EXECUTIVE DEPARTMENT, }
NASHVILLE, September 22, 1867 }

SIR: You will bring to Nashville immediately all the troops, infantry and cavalry, you can command, to enable you to protect the judges and clerks appointed by the commissioners of registration, and to enforce the Franchise law.

If need be call on Major-General George H. Thomas for additional force to enable you to keep the peace and enforce the law.

Respectfully, W. G. BROWNLOW,
Governor of Tennessee.
Gen. JOSEPH A. COOPER, *Com'g State Guard.*

Transmitted to the headquarters of the Army with the following indorsement:

HEADQUARTERS DEPARTMENT OF THE CUMBERLAND, LOUISVILLE, KY., Sept. 25, 1867.

Respectfully forwarded to the Adjutant-General of the Army for the information of the General-in-chief.

GEORGE H. THOMAS,
Maj.-Gen. U. S. A. Commanding.

On the morning of the 25th instant, General Thomas received the following telegram from the General-in-chief:

WASHINGTON, D. C., Sept. 24, 1867—3:30 P. M.

Major-General GEORGE H. THOMAS:

The Mayor, City Attorney, and Common Council of Nashville, express great fear of collision at time of charter election on the twenty-eighth.

Go to Nashville to-morrow, to remain until after election, to preserve peace. If you think more troops necessary for that purpose, order them there from the most convenient points in your command. The military can not set up to be the judge as to which set of election judges have the right to control, but must confine their action to putting down hostile mobs. It is hoped, however, by seeing the Governor and city officials here referred to, your presence and advice may prevent disturbances. Please keep me advised of condition of affairs.

U. S. GRANT, *General.*

To which General Thomas replied in the following telegram:

LOUISVILLE, KY., September 25, 1867.

General U. S. GRANT. *Washington, D. C.:*

Your cypher telegram of 3:30 P. M. yesterday received. I forwarded you yesterday a proclamation of the Governor, the chief magistrate of the State, proclaiming any other election than that held under the Franchise law illegal, and directing General Cooper to take measures to preserve the peace and to protect the judges of election in the discharge of their duties; also a proclamation by the Mayor of the city of Nashville, taking adverse grounds to the Governor, and ordering an extra police force to be organized to preserve the peace and to protect the judges of election appointed by the City Council to hold the election for city officers under the charter for your information and instructions. In the indorsement I expressed the belief that, under instructions from the War Department, I should be compelled to take sides with the Governor, he being the chief civil officer of the State, and having proclaimed the law govering elections in the State, should he call upon me for aid. As further expressed in that indorsement, I should have used the troops to aid the civil authorities to enforce the Franchise law, and preserve peace at the election, had I not received your telegram of 3:30 P. M. yesterday.

I start for Nashville this afternoon, and will do what I can to preserve the peace. Please instruct me whether I am to sustain the Governor or the Mayor.

G. H. THOMAS, *Major-General.*

General Thomas reached Nashville that night.

On the morning of the 26th, says General Thomas, I called at the capitol to see the Governor; found he was absent at Knoxville, but I was informed by his private Secretary that Governor Brownlow had determined to have his proclamation carried out, and had reiterated his directions therein embodied to General Cooper, to protect the judges and clerks appointed by the commissioners of registration, and to enforce the Franchise law.

That day the following dispatches were sent:

NASHVILLE, TENN., September 26, 1867.

Gen. U. S. GRANT, *Washington, D. C.:*

If both parties persist in holding their election, there will be great danger of collision. In such contingency am I to interfere and allow both elections to go on, or are my duties simply to prevent mobs from aiding either party?

GEORGE H. THOMAS,
Major-General U. S. Army, Commanding.

MILITARY PREPARATIONS.

NASHVILLE, TENN., September 26, 1867.

Col. A. L. HOUGH, *Assistant Adjutant-General, Louisville, Ky.:*

Order all the companies of the Second Infantry at Louisville, Bowling Green, and Franklin, also two companies from Memphis, the two at Paducah, at Humbolt, and the company at Union City, to proceed to Cumberland barracks, Nashville, at once; and Leih's company, Fifth Cavalry, to Ash barracks.

GEORGE H. THOMAS,
Major-General U. S. A. Commanding.

GRANT IN A TWO-HORSE ACT.

WASHINGTON, D. C., September 26, 1867—5 P. M.

Major-General GEORGE H. THOMAS:

I neither instruct to sustain the Governor nor Mayor, but to prevent conflict. The Governor is the only authority that can legally demand the aid of United States troops, and that must be by proclamation declaring that invasion or insurrection exists beyond the control of other means at his hands.

It is hoped your presence and good judgment and advice will prevent conflict.

U. S. GRANT, *General.*

In his answer Thomas admits, that, to command the peace, is to decide against the Governor and the Franchise law. Read his dispatch:

NASHVILLE, TENN., September 26, 1867—3 P. M.
General U. S. GRANT, *Washington, D. C.:*

Governor Brownlow is in Knoxville. Have seen his instructions to General Cooper not to permit the city authorities to hold their election. The Mayor is determined to hold an election in defiance of the State authority. A collision is inevitable. If I command the peace, my action will be a practical decision against State authority and against the Franchise law. I can not preserve the peace without interfering in case of collision.

GEORGE H. THOMAS,
Major-General United States Army

WASHINGTON, D. C., September 26, 1867—4 P. M.
Major-General GEORGE H. THOMAS:

You are to prevent conflict. If the Executive of the State issue his proclamation declaring insurrection or invasion to exist too formidable to be put down by force at his own command, and calls upon the United States to aid him, then aid will have to be given. Your mission is to preserve peace, and not to take sides in political difference until called out in accordance with law. You are to prevent mobs from aiding either party. If called upon legally to interfere, your duty is plain.

U. S. GRANT, *General.*

WASHINGTON, D. C., Sept. 26, 1867—9 P. M.
Major-General GEORGE H. THOMAS:

I will send you further instructions to-morrow. Nothing is clearer, however, than that the military can not be made use of to defeat the Executive of a State in enforcing the laws of the State. You are not to prevent the legal State force from the execution of its orders.

U. S. GRANT, *General.*

MAYOR'S OFFICE, NASHVILLE, TENNESSEE, September 27, 1867.

SIR—I have had the honor this moment of receiving at your hands in my office the following telegram from Washington City, dated September 26: (Here he quotes the foregoing dispatch from General Grant.)

I do not know precisely what construction to place upon the above telegram. I am certainly not conscious of ever having contemplated a resistance of the laws of the State of Tennessee, nor have I desires to defeat the Executive of the State in his efforts to enforce the laws thereof. I have only designed, if not prevented by armed violence, to hold a strictly legal election, in a perfectly peaceful manner, and in full accordance with the provisions of the charter of this city. You are directed by the telegram received, "not to prevent the legal State force from the execution of its orders." I shall be pleased if you will inform me explicitly whether you deem it your duty, under the order received by you, to uphold General Cooper and his militia in the threatened attempt to prevent the peaceful holding of the election heretofore ordered by the corporate authorities of Nashville? If so, I have no choice left me but to yield to the authority of the Government of the United States, with a respectful but emphatic protest, however, against the signal and deplorable mistake which I must consider to have been made in this case, and with the expression of that profound regret which I can not but feel, in view of the deplorable and ruinous consequences now plainly in store for this devoted city, whose chartered interest I have so long and earnestly labored to protect.

I have the honor to be, very respectfully,
Your obedient servant,
W. MATT BROWN, *Mayor*
Major-Gen. GEO. H. THOMAS, *Commanding, etc.*

P. S.—I have the honor to ask an early response to the above communication.
W. M. BROWN, *Mayor.*

NASHVILLE, TENN., Sept. 27, 1867—11 A. M.
General U. S. GRANT, *Washington, D. C.:*

Your telegram of 9 P. M. yesterday I read to the Mayor this A. M., and explained to him that under it I should sustain the Governor in case of collision.

As a great many of the City Council are opposed to the strong and defiant attitude of the Mayor, he has, upon reconsideration, decided to acquiesce, and will not attempt to hold an election under the city charter, and has this moment so informed me.

GEORGE H. THOMAS,
Major-General U. S. Army.

WAR DEPARTMENT,
WASHINGTON, Sept. 27, 1867—11.10 A. M.
Major-General GEORGE H. THOMAS:

Until afternoon I can give you no further instructions than you have already had. Report by telegraph, immediately on receipt of this, the nature of the difficulty in Nashville, and your view of the best way to meet it.

U. S. GRANT, *General.*

As my telegram of 11 A. M., says Gen. Thomas, had given the information desired, no other answer was made to this. No further instructions, as intimated in that would be sent, ever reached me.

After the receipt of Mayor Brown's letter I returned the following reply:

HEADQUARTERS DEP'T OF THE CUMBERLAND,
NASHVILLE, September 27, 1867.

In reply to your inquiry "whether you (I) deem it your (my) duty under the order you have received, to uphold Gen. Cooper and his militia in the threatened attempt to prevent the peaceful holding of the election heretofore ordered by the corporate authorities of Nashville," I have to say that the proper interpretation of Gen. Grant's telegraphic order is, to sustain the State authorities in the execution of its orders.

It is not left to me to decide the question of legality or illegality of the election ordered by you.

Very respectfully, your obed't serv't,
GEORGE H. THOMAS,
Major-General U. S. Army, Com'g Dep't.
Hon. W. MATT. BROWN, *Mayor, Nashville.*

UNITED STATES TROOPS TAKE POSSESSION OF THE POLLS.

HEADQUARTERS DEP'T OF THE CUMBERLAND, }
NASHVILLE, TENN., Sept. 27, 1867. }

Major General Thomas directs me to say that you will send one of the cavalry companies now under your command to report to Brevet Major-General S. W. Crawford, Lieutenant-Colonel Second Infantry, at six o'clock, on the morning of September 28.

With the remaining troops under your command, you will be expected to protect the polls at all precincts north of Church street. You will cause a guard to be placed near each precinct by seven o'clock, in the morning, with orders to preserve the peace and sustain the judges appointed in accordance with the Franchise law, and under the proclamation of his Excellency, Governor W. G. Brownlow, under date of September 18, 1867. The precincts under your supervision are as follows:

First Ward—Jail, Front street, between the square and Church street.

Second Ward—Goodwin's feed store, Market street, between Square and Locust.

Third Ward—No. 63 North Cherry street.

Fourth Ward—Old theater.

Fifth Ward—New theater.

I have the honor to be, your obedient servant, R. W. JOHNSON,
Brevet Major-Gen. U. S. Army, A. A. A. G.
Brevet Brig.-Gen. THOMAS DUNCAN, *Commanding District, Nashville.*

HEADQUARTERS DEP'T OF THE CUMBERLAND, }
NASHVILLE, Sept. 27, 1867. }

GENERAL: Major-General Thomas directs me to say that General Duncan has been instructed to direct a company of cavalry to report to you at six o'clock in the morning, September 28, and with the troops under your command, you will be expected to protect the polls at all precincts south of Church street. You will cause a guard to be placed near each precinct, by seven o'clock in the morning, with orders to preserve the peace and sustain the judges appointed in accordance with the Franchise law, and under the proclamation of his Excellency, Governor W. G. Brownlow, under date of September 18, 1867. The precincts under your supervision are located as follows:

Sixth Ward—Jones' stable, Market street, south of Broad.

Seventh Ward—Woodfin's grocery, Murfreesboro' Pike.

Eighth Ward—Firemen's Hall, No. 5 South Cherry street.

Ninth Ward—School-house, corner of Cherry and Madison streets.

Tenth Ward—Police station, Broad street, just west of the Nashville and Chattanooga Railroad.

I am, very respectfully, your obedient servant, R. W. JOHNSON,
Brevet Maj.-Gen. U. S. Army, A. A. A. G.
Bevet Maj.-Gen. S. W. CRAWFORD, Lieut.-Col. Second Infantry.

During that evening General Cooper had taken possession of the polls with the militia force under his command, for the purpose of preventing the city authorities from attempting to open the polls under the charter, and late at night General Cooper handed General Thomas in person the following order:

Special Order No. 147.]

HEADQUARTERS TENN. STATE GUARDS, }
NASHVILLE, Sept. 27, 1867. }

Major John T. Robeson, commanding battalion Tennessee State Guards, is hereby ordered to take charge of the different places designated for holding the election on the 28th instant.

Major Robeson will station a sufficient force at each place designated, at 8 o'clock this P. M., to hold said places; and will only deliver them up to the judges and clerks appointed by B. F. Sheridan, Commissioner of Registration for Davidson county, upon the production of their certificates from said Commissioner.

After the polls are opened, Major Robeson will see that the said judges and clerks are protected in the discharge of their duty, and permit no disturbance at the polls.

By order of Brigadier-General Joseph A. Cooper. S. B. GAMBLE,
[Official copy.] Lt. and Aid-de-Camp.

This he had issued to the troops under his command. On the morning of the 28th, the United States troops were posted as directed, and the polls were opened at 9 A. M., by the Commissioner of Registration, and the election commenced, and was continued without any disturbance until the hour of 4 P. M., the time appointed by law for the closing of the same.

Soon after the opening of the polls, General Cooper withdrew the militia, leaving the United States troops in charge.

The following address of the Mayor to the citizens of Nashville, giving his reasons for withdrawing as a candidate, was published in the morning papers of the 28th:

MAYOR'S OFFICE, September 27, 1867.

Governor Brownlow having, through General Cooper, notified the city authorities that he would use force to prevent the holding of an election under the charter and by-laws of the corporation, and by the judges appointed by the the Board of Aldermen, according to law, and General G. H. Thomas having notified me officially, in writing, that he would use the military of the United States in sustaining the Governor of the State in forcibly preventing a peaceable election; and the city authorities having, under solemn protest against this most unjust, illegal, and high-handed course, determined to submit to force, but to refuse to recognize the legality of the election which may, under the circumstances, be held, I do therefore hereby withdraw my name as candidate at the election (so-called), being now unwilling to be understood, by my silence, as in any way, either as an officer or an individual, lending countenance to such gross violations of law and right.

W. M. BROWN, *Mayor.*

Thus ended this contest. The corporate authorities were forced to yield to the superior force of the Army of the United States, and another one of the high-handed outrages of Brownlow was carried out.

Amendment to the Constitution Abolishing Slavery.

Be it resolved, etc., That the following article be proposed to the Legislatures of the several States as an amendment to the Constitution of the United States, which, when ratified by three-fourths of said Legislatures, shall be valid, to all intents and purposes, as a part of the said Constitution, namely:

ARTICLE XIII.

SECTION 1. Neither slavery nor involuntary servitude, except as a punishment for crime, whereof the party shall have been duly convicted, shall exist within the United States, or any place subject to their jurisdiction.

SEC. 2. Congress shall have power to enforce this article by appropriate legislation.

Passed the Senate April 8, 1864.
Passed the House January 31, 1865.

Secretary Seward, on the 18th of December, 1865, issued a proclamation, as follows:

"And whereas, it appears from official documents on file in this department that the amendment to the Constitution of the United States, proposed as aforesaid, has been ratified by the Legislatures of the STATES of Illinois, Rhode Island, Michigan, Maryland, New York, West Virginia, Maine, Kansas, Massachusetts, Pennsylvania, VIRGINIA, Ohio, Missouri, Nevada, Indiana, LOUISIANA, Minnesota, Wisconsin, Vermont, Tennessee, ARKANSAS, Connecticut, New Hampshire, SOUTH CAROLINA, ALABAMA, NORTH CAROLINA and GEORGIA, in all twenty-seven States;

"*And whereas, the whole number of States in the United States is thirty-six;*

"And whereas, the before specially named STATES, whose Legislatures have ratified the said proposed amendment, constitute three-fourths of the whole number of STATES in the United States;

"Now, therefore, be it known that I, William H. Seward, Secretary of State of the United States * * * do hereby certify that the amendment aforesaid has become valid to all intents and purposes as part of the Constitution of the United States."*

PROPOSED FOURTEENTH AMENDMENT TO THE CONSTITUTION.

This amendment will be found on page 47 of this book.

It has been ratified by the States of Maine, New Hampshire, Vermont, Massachusetts, Rhode Island, Connecticut, New York, New Jersey, Pennsylvania, West Virginia, Tennessee, Indiana, Illinois, Michigan, Missouri, Minnesota, Kansas, Wisconsin, Oregon and Nevada.

Ohio and New Jersey ratified at one time, but the Legislatures of those States have since, and before the question is closed, withdrawn their ratification, and rejected the same. Delaware, Maryland and Kentucky, States which have been in unbroken association with the Union, rejected it.

Virginia, North Carolina, South Carolina, Georgia, Florida, Alabama, Mississippi, Louisiana, Texas and Arkansas—States which were not represented in Congress—rejected it.

Rotten boroughs, created by the military power, under the auspices of the Reconstruction legislation of the Radical Congress, and pretending to be the legitimate governments of North Carolina, South Carolina, Georgia, Florida, Alabama, Arkansas and Louisiana, have very recently ratified it.

Virginia, Mississippi and Texas, having not, as yet, adopted the rotten borough form

---

* How is it that the seven Southern States, enumerated above, were in the Union on the 18th day of December, 1865, (the date of the announcement quoted from), and out of the Union, to all intents and purposes, on the 1st of June, 1868?

of government, have not, in that condition, acted upon it.

The Amending Power.

The withdrawal of the assent of Ohio and New Jersey to the ratification of this amendment, after it had once been given, will bring up an exciting question, should the ratification or rejection turn upon the vote of those two States.

The New Orleans *Picayune*, in an article written before New Jersey had withdrawn her assent, and after Ohio had done so, presented the question with great clearness:

"The rescinding, by the present Legislature of Ohio, of the assent given by the previous Legislature to constitutional amendment XIV, has raised new questions in Congress.

"The first is, whether a State Legislature, having in due form ratified an amendment to the Constitution, can, under any circumstances, revoke its assent.

"Of course, if the requisite number of State ratifications has been obtained, and the amendment is adopted in fact and form, there can be no right of change; for that would be equivalent to the conceding of a right by which a single State might change the Constitution itself. The point mooted is, where does the right of a State to object to a change in the Constitution cease to be within its own control? Is there any such period short of the final closing of the question, against all parties, by the full ratification of the amendment proposed?

"Mr. Sumner, of Massachusetts, started up in the Senate to maintain the position that a State can not withdraw its consent, when once given, any more than it could withdraw from the Union.

"This is a very extravagant assumption. Pending a proposition, and before a decision, the right of reconsidering a judgment is as reasonably the privilege of a State as it was for any member of Congress, by whom the amendment was proposed, to change his own vote in any of the preliminary stages; though he could not do so after the result was declared. It is the rational and republican view of the right of judgment, against which no subtleties, drawn from the armory of party warfare, ought to be allowed to prevail.

"But, if Mr. Sumner establishes this point, that States having once voted on the question, are foreclosed forever from reconsidering it, he encounters consequences he is obliged to meet by other and more extraordinary assumptions.

"The number of States in the Union—at least the number recognized by all the other departments of the Government, and even in numerous acts of the Legislature itself—is thirty-seven. Three-fourths of thirty seven States can not be less than twenty-eight. Ten States are more than one-fourth; consequently, the negative vote of ten States, or more, is the final defeat of the amendment—that is, Mr. Sumner's rule would so decide it, beyond reversal.

"The amendment was passed in July, 1866, and on the 16th day of that month it was transmitted by the Executive Department to the Governors of the thirty-seven States.

"During the next six months, and while the Legislatures of all the Southern States were in the full exercise of their functions, and before any of the military or other bills suppressing them were passed, the ten Southern Legislatures rejected the amendment. Besides these, Kentucky, Maryland and Delaware have also rejected it; and now Ohio is added, making fourteen, or more than one-third of the whole number of States, when more than one-fourth is sufficient to defeat.

"If the Sumner theory be conceded to be the true one, the votes of the thirteen are no more subject to revisal to the affirmative, than that of Ohio is to the negative. The position is really stronger, in respect to them, than by the universal rule of Mr. Sumner, which would also deny the right of reconsideration before decision. These votes decided the question, because they constitute more than the constitutional number sufficient to reject. On the most rigid ground, as well as Mr. Sumner's wider rule, the amendment is defeated, and can not become a part of the Constitution, except by a two-thirds vote in both Houses of Congress, and a new submission to all the State Legislatures.

"Therefore, it becomes a necessary part of Mr. Sumner's argument in favor of the vitality of the amendment, to assume that there are not thirty-seven States, but only twenty-seven States entitled to be counted. Three-fourths of twenty-seven, which can not be less than twenty-one, are claimed to be sufficient to ratify. There are, without Ohio, twenty-one ratifying States, and he insists triumphantly that the amendment is ratified, and the action of the Ohio Legislature is impotent to effect the result, even if it were lawful, which he denies.

"Here there arises, in Congress now, and probably before the Judiciary hereafter, the grand question of all—whether there are twenty-seven States or thirty-seven States in the Union; in other words, is the Constitution in force in only twenty-seven States, with the others subject to powers outside of the Constitution?

"The Ohio resolution, which has been sent before the Senate Committee of the

Judiciary, brings this question up directly. On that, a judgment can not well be avoided; and the issue on that question includes all the important issues connected with the Congressional methods of Southern reconstruction.

"Mr. Sumner is certainly a little afraid of the plain issue which his previous course and declarations would make; for, on sending the question to the Judiciary Committee, he accompanied it with the suggestion for a quibbling way of reading the Constitution, for the purpose of escaping the consequences of his own doctrines. He found in the Constitution that constitutional amendments are to be ratified by "the Legislatures" of three-fourths of the States, not by three-fourths of the States, and he implies that there may be States without Legislatures and without functions. The existence of Legislatures is the condition of the right of voting, and where there are no Legislatures to vote, there is no right of a State to be counted at all. There may be States without Legislatures, but if they have no Legislatures, they are not to be counted at all, and the power of these suppressed votes is to be distributed among the others.

"This is a complete swing round the Radical circle. The State Legislatures, while in the exercise of their complete functions, are violently suppressed, and their votes on amending the Constitution are then annulled, because they have no Legislatures. It is as if a military commander should call up a prisoner of war, take away his commission and burn it, and then hang him as a marauder for not having one."

How the Qestion of its Ratification Stands.

On the 16th of July, 1868, the President sent a message to the Senate, including, among other papers, the following letter from the Secretary of State:

To the President:

The Secretary of State having received a resolution of the Senate of the 9th instant, requesting him to communicate to that body without delay, a list of the States of the Union whose Legislatures had ratified the Fourteenth Amendment of the Constitution of the United States, with copies of all the resolutions of ratification in his office, and to communicate to that body all resolutions of ratification of said amendment which he may hereafter receive, so soon as he shall receive the same respectively, has the honor to report to the President that official notice has been received at this department of the ratification of the amendment referred to by the Legislatures of the following States, to-wit: Connecticut, Tennessee, New Jersey, Oregon, Vermont, West Virginia, Kansas, Missouri, Indiana, Ohio, Illinois, Minnesota, New York, Wisconsin, Pennsylvania, Rhode Island, Michigan, Nevada, New Hampshire, Massachusetts, Nebraska, Maine and Iowa. Besides these acts of ratifications, notices and certificates have also been received by the Secretary of State, that the same proposed amendment has been ratified by the Legislatures of the States respectively of Arkansas, Florida and North Carolina, which notices and certificates last mentioned were received from the newly constructed and established authorities assuming to be and acting as the Leigslatures and Governors of the said States of Arkansas, Florida and North Carolina. These acts of ratification are for this reason stated in this report separately and distinctly, and for the more accurate information of Congress, a copy of all the acts and resolutions of ratification of all said Legislatures, is herewith subjoined, together with a copy, also, of certain resolutions of the Legislatures of Ohio and New Jersey, which purport to rescind the resolutions of ratification of said amendment, which had previously been adopted by the Legislatures of those two States, respectively, and to withdraw their consent to the same.

Respectfully submitted,
WILLIAM H. SEWARD.

Military Interference in Elections.

RADICALS AGAINST PROHIBITING IT.

On the 22d of June, 1864, the Senate voted on a bill to prevent any interference by the military forces of the United States at any election to be held in the United States. This bill was made necessary by the flagrant interference of the military in elections which had been held in Kentucky, Missouri, Maryland and Deleware.

It passed the Senate—Yeas 19, nays 13, as follows:

YEAS — Messrs. *Buckalew, Carlile, Davis,* Grimes. Hale, Harlan, *Hendricks, Hicks, Johnson,* Lane (of Kansas), *McDougall,* Pomeroy, *Powell, Richardson, Riddle, Saulsbury,* Trumbull, Wade, Willey—19.

NAYS—Messrs. Anthony, Chandler, Clark, Collamer, Dixon, Foot, Foster. Harris, Howard, Morgan, Sumner, Ten Eyck, Wilson—13.

Democrats in Italics, Radicals in Roman.
The Radical House did not act upon it, thus justifying military interference in elections.

How Boldly it was Done.

General Thomas, in 1863, issued the following special order:

WAR DEPARTMENT, ADJUTANT-GENERAL'S OFFICE,
WASHINGTON, March 13, 1868.
Special Order No. 19.]

By direction of the President, the following officers are hereby dismissed from the service of the United States: Lieutenant A. J. Edgerly, Fourth New Hampshire Volunteers, for circulating COPPERHEAD TICKETS, *and doing all in his power to promote the success of the rebel cause.*

By order of the Secretary of War.

L. THOMAS, Adjutant-General.

To the Governor of New Hampshire.

The Blasphemy and Irreligious Tone of the Radical Leaders.

THADDEUS STEVENS ON THE BIBLE.

The Lancaster (Pennsylvania) *Intelligencer*, published at the home of Thaddeus Stevens, thus alludes to a phase in his character, which will be exceedingly gratifying to the pious preachers of the Gospel who have been his special enemies and antagonists. It says:

"During all his life Thaddeus Stevens has openly scoffed at the Christian religion. A few years since, while trying a case at a town in another part of the State, he and some other lawyers were conversing one evening, when one of the party adduced the Bible as authority for some statement he had made. 'Oh,' said Mr. Stevens, 'the Bible is no authority. It is nothing but the obsolete history of a barbarous people!'"

The Man whom it is Proposed to make President for Nine Months.

The following is a striking comment upon the fact that on Monday the Senate adjourned in consequence of Senator Howard's illness:

"About two years ago, upon a motion to postpone action (upon a message of the President vetoing the Civil Rights bill) because of the illness of Senator Dixon and the late Senator Wright, Mr. Wade made one of his characteristic speeches, which drew from Senator McDougal a reply which was characterized, by all who heard it, as one of the happiest impromptu oratorical efforts of the age.

"Senator Wade then said some shockingly blasphemous things, and among them the following: 'I feel myself justified in taking every advantage which the Almighty has put into my hands to defend the power and authority of this body, of which I claim to be a part. I will not yield to these appeals of comity on a question like this, but I will tell the President and everybody else, that, if God Almighty has stricken one member so that he can not be here to uphold the dictation of a despot, I thank him for his interposition, and will take advantage of it if I can.'"

What a contrast to the action of the Senate of the 11th inst.

Blasphemous Old Thad. Stevens.

This old miscreant, whose decaying legs are already sinking into the grave; not in the heat of *spoken* words, but in a document written and printed, which he caused to be read for him by the mouth of Beast Butler, speaking of President Johnson's attempted removal of Stanton, uttered the following atrocious blasphemy:

"Baser than the betrayal by Judas Iscariot, who betrayed *only a single individual*, Johnson sacrificed a whole nation, and the *holiest of principles!*"

It is horrible to repeat such words of blasphemy, even to execrate them, and the concoctor of them, and the *Beast* that consented to read them for the rotten wretch. The "*only a single individual*" that, being God, became man, and died for love of man, is "an individual" for whom Thad. Stevens has no love, and of whom he expects no salvation. But it is a mournful fact that a Chief-Justice, in his robes, and Senators, in their places, sat and listened to so horrible a blasphemy, without one of them crying out, and calling the blasphemer to stop!

The gods of Radicalism are all profane. Witness Wade with his mouth stuffed with abuses of the Almighty name; Thad. Stevens, who alluded to Jesus as "that single individual;" Karl Schurz, who, a few years since, spoke of the Redeemer as "the ideal gentleman beyond the skies, called by some people God!" The divinities of Radicalism shock the religious as well as political sense of the people. Radicalism, in its last analysis, is infidelity — infidelity to man and God.—*Augusta* (Ga.) *Constitutionalist*.

The American Inquisition.

BEN. BUTLER'S SYSTEM OF ESPIONAGE.

[Correspondence of the New York World].

WASHINGTON, May 19.

The Board of Managers, now resolved into a Board of Inquisitors by authority of the House, continued to-day the investigation of charges trumped up against Senators who voted for the acquittal of the President. The charges and insinuations which Butler and his gang are hopelessly trying to sustain, are, in effect, that the votes of certain Senators were purchased with money, or procured by other improper means. Of a verity, Butler, as will be seen in this narrative, neglects and refuses to solicit or accept testimony in support of the rumors that votes were bought on the side of conviction. The pachyderm from Massachusetts is not quite thick-skinned enough to listen to anything of this sort with patience. The inquisitors proceeded to-day with the examination of Mr. Charles W. Woolley, of Cincinnati, a lawyer who has been for some time engaged here on business intrusted to him by his clients. Mr. Woolley, one of the bitterest enemies of the so called "whisky ring," was, as it seems, conveniently suspected by the impeachers of sympathizing with that delectable body; so when Mr. Woolley entered the miniature Star Chamber where Butler now presides, the latter at once began to question him, upon the supposition that he had had the impudence to offer money to doubtful Senators. Before proceeding to relate Mr. Woolley's experience, I wish to make your readers aware of how closely he, his friends and everybody else in Washington whom the managers choose to make a note of, had been watched. Innumerable letters, both anonymous and signed, were in possession of the managers, bearing dates all the way up from a week after the beginning of the trial until the present time. The hints thus conveyed are presumed to have guided the detectives, who are in some instances known to have dogged certain Senators for days previous to Saturday, when the verdict was rendered upon the eleventh article. Chief-Justice Chase was tracked incessantly. Nobody entered his house without observation. The persons with whom he dined were marked. So with respect to Senators Fessenden, Trumbull, Grimes, Henderson, Van Winkle, Fowler and Ross.

The espionage was so strict on Friday night that some of the detectives employed missed and mistook their men. I am informed to-day that one Senator, one of the most violent impeachers in the chamber, was tracked that evening by a detective, who labored under the impression that his man was a doubtful one! This detective had a long chase, which ended at a house of ill-fame. The hostess, as it is said, agreed, for a consideration, to open the door of the apartment to which the prey of the detective had hied. The spy peeped, beheld the Senator, a bottle of wine, several glasses, and three damsels in decidedly negligent attire, and vanished, overcome with disappointment and disgust. The Senator thus apprehended is said to be a "man of prayer."

The Fort Pillow Libel on General Forrest.

For years, indeed, ever since it happened, it has pleased the Radical press to charge the Confederate General N. B. Forrest with the responsibility of what they call the Fort Pillow negro massacre in 1863. He has been exonerated from this aspersion in a late book issued in New Orleans, entitled "The Campaigns of General Forrest," written by General Thomas Jordan.

In noticing this book the New York *Times* (Republican) has the honesty to say:

"General Forrest's connection with the Fort Pillow massacre has been the black spot upon his reputation as a soldier. Upon this episode and Forrest's connection with it, General Jordan throws much new light. He shows from Federal documents and the testimony taken before the Congressional Committee, that General Forrest himself not only took no part in the massacre, but, being absent from the spot at the time, hastened forward with all possible speed, and put an immediate stop to the misdeeds of that part of his command which had captured the fort. The proofs he furnishes on this matter are numerous and abundant, and will, no doubt, lead many to new views of General Forrest's conduct at Fort Pillow."

Nevertheless, the Radical press will continue, we predict, to denounce General Forrest for the Fort Pillow massacre. They believe that a lie well stuck to is as good as the truth. At any rate, they always act upon that principle.

The Radical Candidate for Governor of New York.
[From the New York World.]

When Griswold, the Radical candidate for Governor, was elected to Congress in 1862, he had, like a good many other "loil" men, heavy contracts with the Government for building war vessels. During the summer of that year the materials entering into the construction of iron-clads largely and rapidly advanced in price, and Griswold's fellow-contractors, filled with patriotic emotions in behalf of their own pockets, appeared before Congress and asked "relief." The *Tribune* then came to their rescue by announcing that the iron-clad builders were "menaced with ruin." Griswold with characteristic modesty and propriety, secured a place on the Naval Committee before which his own and his partners claims were discussed and finally adjudicated. The resolution affording the "relief" asked for passed Congress—ayes, 85; noes, 36—the reserved and patriotic Griswold, of course, voting in favor of the measure. Thus Griswold, his partners and sureties, were released from their contracts, and thereby enabled to get out of the Government several hundred thousands of dollars. This is he whom the Radicals have nominated for Governor of the State of New York.

Mr. Pendleton and Governor Seymour.

The following manly and generous private letter addressed by Mr Pendleton to Washington McLean, of the Ohio delegation, before that delegation left Ohio, was handed to John A. Green, Jr., on their arrival in New York:

"CINCINNATI, Thursday, June 25, 1868.

"MY DEAR SIR: You left my office this morning before I was aware of it. I seek you at home but you are not here. I must say what I want by note.

"As soon as you get to New York see Governor Seymour. You know well my affection and admiration for him. You know well what was my feeling before and after I heard from him last fall. He is to-day the foremost man in our party in the United States. His ability, cultivation, and experience put him at the head of our statesmen. He commands my entire confidence—I would rather trust him than myself with the delicate duties of the next four years. You know I am sincere.

"Make him feel this, and that he can rely on me and my friends. I have a natural pride—an honest pride, I believe—in the good-will of my countrymen; but you, better than any one else, know that it is neither egotistical nor overruling, and that I am ready—anxious to give up the nomination to anybody who can get one single vote more than myself.

"Express all this frankly to the Governor, but delicately, and let him understand my views of men and measures as I have frequently given them to you. Good bye! God bless you!

"Very truly,
"GEORGE H. PENDLETON.
"To WASHINGTON MCLEAN, Esq."

The Rump Congress as Pictured by a Radical Pen.

The dishonesty of the Radical Congress is well depicted by the following, written to one of their leading organs:

"After the vote to tax Government bonds, in the House, last Monday, many sagacious Republicans feel that there is greater risk in remaining than in the postponement of many important bills. The grand difficulty of legislation just now is the fact that a Presidential campaign is opening. The members cast their votes almost solely with reference to that. If a measure affecting the rights of colored people were brought up in either House at this time, it is quite probable that it would be kil ed outright, or be kicked unceremoniously to one side till next winter.

"The Republican members who come from the Middle and some of the Western States are very much afraid of the 'negro question,' in some of its aspects, *just now*. They will vote right enough *next winter, when the election is passed;* but would rather be excused at this moment. This is but a sample. On all the great questions before Congress there is more or less of this feeling, and on the little ones too. The Twenty-per-cent-bill will pass next winter, or certainly would do so, if it had not been brought up now and defeated, because members did not care to face their constituents after voting for it. It would not have hurt the consciences of gentlemen, whose pay has been raised from three to five thousand dollars, to give the departmental clerks 20 per cent. more than they had when paid in gold. However, it can not be done *now.* This, as well as other things, must wait."—*Washington (D. W. B.) Correspondence N. Y. Independent.*

Congressional Indignity to the Memory of Mr. Buchanan.

LETTER FROM THE HON. THAD. STEVENS.

The following letter from Mr. Stevens was addressed to Dr. Henry Carpenter, of Lancaster, Pennsylvania:

"WASHINGTON, June 23, 1868.

"DEAR SIR: I learn there was a report in Lancaster that I opposed paying due honors to Mr. Buchanan at his funeral.

"On the other hand, I attempted twice to introduce resolutions laudatory of Mr. Buchanan's private character and personal history, and asked the House to adjourn to attend his funeral. A single objection would prevent its being introduced that day. Mr. Van Wyck, of New York, constantly objected. I earnestly appealed to him to withdraw the objection. He persisted until I left the House. He then permitted a very tame resolution, barely appointing a committee, to be passed. I am anxious that this mistake should be corrected, for I should be ashamed of such prejudice against the dead. I have no such prejudice. I would be glad if you could have this statement in some way communicated to the public, through Democratic organs, as I do not wish Mr. Buchanan's friends to believe so mean a thing.

"THADDEUS STEVENS."

The above, says the Cincinnati *Enquirer,* is creditable to Mr. Stevens. The shameful manner in which the House of Representatives, under its Radical leaders, behaved in relation to the death of an ex-President of the United States, was one of the many incidents which show the malignant temper and character of that organization, which carries its political animosities beyond the grave, and like hyenas, prey upon a corpse to gratify its hates.

By reference to the proceedings of the House of Representative it will be seen that Mr. Stevens' statement is verified, and how disreputably that body acted at the grave, as it were, of Mr. Buchanan.

Mr. WOODWARD. I offer the following resolution, and ask the unanimous consent of the House for its consideration at this time:

The House having received with becoming sensibility intelligence of the death of James Buchanan, ex-President of the United States, at his country-seat at Wheatland, on the 1st instant, does hereby resolve:

1 That whatever diversities of opinion may prevail in respect of the administration of Mr. Buchanan as President of the United States, the members of this House can cordially unite in honoring the purity of his private character, the ability and patriotic motives which illustrated his long career of public service, and the dignity which marked the retirement of the latter years of his life.

2. That, as a token of honor to the many virtues, public and private, of the illustrious sage and statesman whose death, in the ripeness of his age, has arrested the attention of the nation, the Speaker of the House is requested and authorized to appoint a committee of seven members to attend the funeral of Mr. Buchanan on behalf of the House, and to communicate a copy of these resolutions to the relatives of the deceased.

The SPEAKER. If there is no objection, the resolutions are before the House

MR. FARNSWORTH. I suggest to the gentleman from Pennsylvania that he modify those resolutions a little. He certainly can not expect to get a unanimous vote of the House commending the "patriotic motives" which animated Mr. Buchanan at all times in his public career. For one, I certainly can not vote aye.

Mr. MULLINS. Neither can I.

Mr. FARNSWORTH. I move to lay the resolutions upon the table, unless the gentleman will modify them. I am willing the grave shall bury the man's faults, and to speak only well of him, now that he is dead; but when the gentleman asks me to vote that the motives or Mr. Buchanan were always patriotic and pure, he asks me to vote what I believe to be a falsehood, and I can not do it.

Mr. BLAINE. Will the gentleman from Pennsylvania allow me to have read a substitute, which I think would obviate the very disagreeable scene of contending over the body of a dead man? I have a resolution in my hand which I think would secure the unanimous consent of the House.

Mr. ELDRIDGE. I think this scene corresponds with the usual action of this House in such matters.

Mr. MULLINS. Especially on the other side of the House.

The Clerk read as follows:

The House having received, with becoming sensibility, intelligence of the death of James Buchanan, ex-President of the United States, at his country-seat at Wheatland, on the 1st instant, it is hereby

Resolved, That, as a mark of honor to one who has held such eminent public station, the Speaker of the House is requested to appoint a committee of seven members to attend the funeral of Mr. Buchanan, on behalf of the House, and to communicate a copy of this resolution to the relatives of the deceased.

Mr. WOODWARD. I can not accept that amendment. I call the previous question upon my resolution.

Mr. BLAINE. I suppose if the call for the previous question is voted down, then my resolution would be in order as a substitute.

Mr. FARNSWORTH. I move that the resolutions be laid upon the table.

Mr. ELDRIDGE. Upon that motion I call for the yeas and nays.

The yeas and nays were ordered.

Mr. STEVENS (of Pennsylvania). I ask unanimous consent to make a suggestion.

Mr. VAN WYCK. I object. [Cries of "Oh, no!"] I withdraw the objection.

No further objection being made,

Mr. STEVENS (of Pennsylvania), said: I ask my colleague [Mr. Woodward] to consent to strike out the words "the ability and patriotic motives which illustrated his long career of public service," and let the resolution be adopted without that in it.

Mr. FARNSWORTH. That is what I proposed.

The SPEAKER. The Clerk will read that portion of the resolution as proposed to be modified.

The Clerk read as follows:

That whatever diversities of opinion may prevail in respect to the administration of Mr. Buchanan as President of the United States, the members of this House can cordially unite in honoring the purity of his private character, and the dignity which marked the retirement of the latter years of his life.

Mr. WOODWARD. If the House will strike out the general allusion to the patriotic motives of Mr. Buchanan they can do so, but I can not consent to do it myself.

The question was then taken upon the motion to lay the resolutions on the table; and it was decided in the affirmative—yeas 74, nays 46, not voting 69; as follows:

YEAS—Messrs. Allison, Arnell, James M. Ashley, Baldwin, Beaman, Beatty, Benton, Blaine, Blair, Bromwell, Broomall, Buckland, Cake, R ader W. Clarke, Sidney Clarke, Cobb, Coburn, Cornell, Covode, Cullom, Delano, Dixon, Donnelly, Driggs, Eckley, Eggleston Farnsworth, Ferry, Fields, Garfield, Halsey, Harding, Hill, Hopkins, Hunter, Julian, Kitchen, William Lawrence, Logan, Loughridge, Mallory, Maynard, McClurg, Mercur, Miller, Moore, Morrill, Mullins, Myers, Newcomb, O'Neill, Paine, Perham, Polsley, Pomeroy, Price, Raum, Schenck, Selye, Starkweather, Aaron F. Stevens, Stokes, Taffe, Trowbridge, Upson, Van Aernam, Burt Van Horn, Robert T. Van Horn, Van Wyck, Ward, Cadwalader C. Washburn, Henry D. Washburn, William B. Washburn, and William Williams—74.

NAYS—Messrs. Adams, Delos R. Ashley, Barnes, Beck, Boyer, Brooks, Burr, Butler, Eldridge, Getz, Golladay, Griswold, Haight, Higby, Holman, Hotchkiss, Chester D. Hubbard, Richard D. Hubbard, Ingersoll, Johnson, Jones, Kerr, Knott, Koontz, George V. Lawrence, Marshall, McCormick, Moorhead, Niblack, Nicholson, Phelps, Plants, Randall, Ross, Sawyer, Scofield, Sitgreaves, Smith, Stewart, Taylor, Thomas, Lawrence S. Trimball, Van Auken, Van Trump, Wood, and Woodward—46.

From this it will be seen that but 14 Radicals, viz: Messrs. D. R. Ashley, Butler, Griswold, Higby, Chester D. Hubbard, Ingersoll, Koontz, G. V. Lawrence, Moorhead, Plants, Sawyer, Scofield, Smith and Taylor, had decency sufficient to oppose this effort to scandalize the grave of Mr. Buchanan.

So the resolutions were laid on the table.

Mr. PAINE. I rise to make a privileged report from the Committee on Reconstruction.

Mr. STEVENS (of Pennsylvania). I ask unanimous consent to be allowed to offer a resolution in relation to the death of Mr. Buchanan.

Mr. VAN WYCK. I object.

Mr. BLAINE. I ask leave to offer a resolution on that subject.

MR. STEVENS (of Pennsylvania). I trust I will be allowed to offer the resolution.

Mr. VAN WYCK. I insist upon my objection.

Mr. PAINE. I have been requested to yield to the gentleman from Maine [Mr. Blaine] to offer a resolution. I will do so if it gives rise to no debate.

Mr. RANDALL. I object to the gentleman from Maine [Mr. Blaine] offering the resolution. I will not object to my colleague, the gentleman from Pennsylvania [Mr. Stevens], offering the resolution, for I think he is the proper person to present it.

The SPEAKER. The gentleman from Pennsylvania [Mr. Randall] objects to the resolution proposed by the gentleman from Maine [Mr. Blaine], and the gentleman from New York [Mr. Van Wyck] objects to the one proposed by the gentleman from Pennsylvania [Mr. Stevens].

Mr. BLAINE. I desire it to be noted that if any mark of respect upon the death of ex-President Buchanan is prevented in this House, it is prevented by the gentleman from Pennsylvania [Mr. Randall].

Mr. RANDALL. I withdraw the objection.

Mr. WARD. I renew it.

A few hours afterward the following resolution was passed—a constrained effort to be decent, the natural impossibility of which was palpable. This resolution was introduced by Mr. Blaine, of Maine, to get which through, as will be seen by comparison with the original substitute offered by him, he had to strike out the words, "with becoming sensibility;" also the word "honor," and insert "respect" instead. Was there ever such low-down sporting for terms at a funeral:

"The House of Representatives having received intelligence of the death of James Buchanan, ex-President of the United States, at his country seat at Wheatland, on the 1st instant, do hereby resolve, that, as a mark of respect to one who has held such eminent public station, the Speaker of the House is requested to appoint a committee of seven members to attend the funeral of Mr. Buchanan on behalf of the House, and to communicate a copy of this resolution to the relatives of the deceased."

A Convict in the Penitentiary retained in Office by the Senate.

A CONVICT AND RADICAL OFFICE HOLDER AT ONE AND THE SAME TIME.

In a previous chapter a notice of the arrival at the New York Penitentiary of ex-Radical Speaker of the New York Assembly, Callicott, and late Collector of Internal Revenue at Brooklyn. Some six months since the President sent to the Senate the reasons for the suspension of Callicott from the latter office, and notwithstanding that Callicott was indicted upon the charges alleged against him in the President's order of suspension, and was, about two months ago, convicted upon this indictment, and sentenced thereon to imprisonment in the penitentiary, it was not until the 16th of July, 1868, that the Senate concurred in the President's reasons for Callicott's suspension—thus keeping Callicott in office two months, while he was in the discharge of his duties as a convict at the New York Penitentiary.

Seizure of Private Papers.

RADICALS INDORSE THE UNCONSTITUTIONAL OUTRAGE.

In the House of Representatives, the following resolutions came up for consideration:

"*Resolved*, That it was not the purpose or intention of this House to authorize the committee of managers, and it hereby denies the power or authority of said managers, under the Constitution, to require persons called before them, as witnesses to produce or give evidence with reference to their personal and private papers; and that, in the opinion of this House, private and personal telegrams are within the provision of article four of the amendments to the Constitution, which provides that—

"'The right of the people to be secure in their persons, houses, papers, and effects, against unreasonable searches and seizures, shall not be violated, and no warrants shall issue but upon probable cause, supported by oath or affirmation, and particularly describing the place to be searched, and the persons or things to be seized.'"—

"And that any violation of the rights intended to be secured by said article is an outrage upon personal liberty, which no free people can tolerate or submit to."

The SPEAKER. The question is on suspending the rules.

Mr. ELDRIDGE. On that question I demand the yeas and nays.

The yeas and nays were ordered.

The question was taken; and there were —yeas 27, nays 95, not voting 67; as follows:

YEAS—Messrs. Barnes, Beck, Boyer, Burr, Cary, Eldridge, Getz, Glossbrenner, Golladay, Haight, Holman, Hotchkiss, Johnson, Jones, Kerr, Knott, Marshall, McCormick, McCullough, Niblack, Phelps, Ross, Sitgreaves, Stone, Lawrence S. Trimble, Van Trump, and Woodward—27.

NAYS—Messrs. Allison, Ames, Arnell, Delos R. Ashley, Baldwin, Beaman, Beatty, Benton, Blaine, Blair, Bromwell, Buckland, Churchill, R. W. Clarke, Cobb, Coburn, Cornell, Covode, Cullom, Dawes, Dixon, Donnelly, Driggs, Eckley, Eggleston, Ela, Farnsworth, Ferriss, Ferry, Fields, Garfield, Griswold, Harding, Higby, Hill, Hooper, Hopkins, Chester D. Hubbard, Hunter, Jenckes, Judd, Julian, Kelley, Ketcham, Kitchen, Koontz, Laflin, George V. Lawrence, William Lawrence, Lincoln, Loughridge, Maynard, McCarthy, McClurg, Miller, Moore, Moorhead, Mullins, Myers, Newcomb, Nunn, O'Neill, Orth, Paine, Perham, Pike, Poland, Polsley, Pomeroy, Price, Raum, Robertson, Sawyer, Schenck, Scofield, Selye, Smith, Starkweather, Aaron F. Stevens, Thaddeus Stevens, Stokes, Taffe, Taylor, Thomas, John Trimble, Trowbridge, Upson, Burt Van Horn, Robert T. Van Horn, Cadwalader C. Washburn, Henry D. Washburn, William B. Washburn, Welker, John T. Wilson, and Windom—95.

The motion to suspend the rules was a test vote. Yeas, all Democrats, except General Cary, Independent. Nays, all Radicals. Thus the Radicals announce boldly their indorsement of the right to seize private papers, in violation of Article IV of the amendments to the Constitution.

National Democratic Convention, Held at New York, July 4, 1868.

For *President*—HORATIO SEYMOUR, of New York.

For *Vice-President*—FRANCIS P. BLAIR, Jr., of Missouri.

The Convention was called to order by Hon. August Belmont, of New York, Chairman Democratic National Convention, in an eloquent and well-timed speech, which elicited the greatest applause.

Mr. Belmont nominated for temporary Chairman, the Hon. Henry S. Palmer, of Wisconsin, which was agreed to.

Mr. Palmer, on taking the chair, returned his acknowledgments for the compliment conferred upon him, and, after a short speech, closed by introducing the Rev. Dr. Morgan, of New York, who offered prayers.

Edwin O. Perrin, Esq., of New York, was appointed Secretary.

The rules of the last convention were adopted as the rules of this, until otherwise directed. The Secretary then read the following:

The National Democratic Committee, by virtue of the authority conferred upon them by the last National Democratic Convention, at a meeting held this day at Washington, D. C., voted to hold the next Convention for the purpose of nominating candidates for President and Vice-President of the United States, on the 4th day of July, 1868, at twelve o'clock M, in the city of New York.

The basis of representation, as fixed by the last Democratic Convention, is double the number of Senators and Representatives in Congress in each State under the last appointment.

Each State is invited to send delegates accordingly.

S. R. Lyman, Josiah Minot, H. B. Smith, Wm. M. Converse, Gideon Bradford, W. G. Steel, W. A. Gailbraith, John A. Nicholson, Odin Bowie, James Guthrie, L. S. Trimble, Rufus P. Ranney, W. E. Niblack, Wilber F. Storey, W. L. Bancroft, Lewis V. Bogy, George H. Paul, D. O Finch, Isaac E. Eaton, Thomas Hoynes, William McMillan, William Aiken, Absalom H. Chappell, George A. Houston, Joseph A. Rozier, A. B. Greenwood, John W. Leftwich, Thomas Sweeney, John Patrick, Jas. W. McCorckle, W. L. Sharkey, John Hancock, John H. McKinney.

AUGUST BELMONT, Chm'n.

FREDERICK O. PRINCE, Sec'y.

WASHINGTON, February 22, 1868.

Mr. Clymer (Pennsylvania) offered the following:

"*Resolved*, That there shall now be two committees appointed, each committee to consist of one delegate from each State, to be selected by respective delegates thereof, one committee to act as a Committee on Permanent Organization, and the other as a Committee on Credentials."

The Chair put the question, *viva voce*, and declared the resolution adopted.

The roll of the delegates was then called, and the following gentlemen were selected as members of the Committee on Credentials:

Alabama, W. H. Barnes; Arkansas, E. C. Boudinot; California, A. Jacoby; Connecticut, M. Bulkley; Delaware, C. W. Wright; Florida, A. Huling; Georgia, E. H. Potter; Illinois, T. A. Hayne; Indiana, Charles H. Reeves; Iowa, J. D. Test; Kansas, W. Shannon; Kentucky, J. B. McCreary; Louisiana, D. D. Duponte; Maine, J. S. Drew; Maryland, G. F. Maddox; Massachusetts, George W. Gill; Michigan, B. G. Stout; Minnesota, W. A. Gorman; Mississippi, P. M. Brown; Missouri, S. Sawyer; Nebraska, J. Black; Nevada, J. E. Doyle; New Hampshire, J. Proctor; New Jersey, J. R. Moullany; New York, J. A. Hardenburg; North Carolina, General W. R. Cox; Ohio, W. Griswold; Oregon, O. Joynt; Pennsylvania, General W. H. Miller; Rhode Island, W. Hale; South Carolina, W. D. Simpson; Tennessee, J. F. Morse; Texas, H. Broughton; Vermont, W. Brigham; Virginia, George Blow; West Virginia, H. S. Davis; Wisconsin, S. A. Pease.

THE COMMITTEE ON ORGANIZATION.

The following gentlemen were selected a Committee on Organization:

Alabama, J. H. Clanton; Arkansas, J. S. Dunham; California, E. Steele; Connecticut, J. A. Hovey; Delaware, C. Beasten; Florida, A. J. Seeier; Georgia, C. Peeples; Illinois, W. R. Morrison; Indiana, S. A. Burkirk; Iowa, W. F. Braman; Kansas, T. P. Fenlon; Kentucky, W. B. Machen; Louisiana, G. W. McCranie; Maine, J. E. Maddigan; Maryland, A. K. Sylster; Massachusetts, John R. Briggs; Michigan, John Moore; Minnesota, E. A. McMahon; Mississippi, B. Matthews; Missouri, W. H. D. Hunter; Nebraska, G. L. Miller; Nevada, G. G. Berry; New Hampshire, J. Adams; New Jersey, H. C. Little; New York, Gen. J. A. Green, jr.; North Carolina, W. N. H. Smith; Ohio, F. C. Leblonde; Oregon, N. B. Bell; Pennsylvania, H. Clymer; Rhode Island, S. Pierce; South Carolina, Carlos Tracey; Tennessee, Gen. W. B. Bate; Texas, J. M. Burroughs; Vermont, J. D. Deavett; Virginia, J. Barbour; West Virginia, H. S. Walker; Wisconsin, S Clark.

Mr. Henry C. Murphy (New York)—I move that a committee of two from each State be selected by the delegates thereof to be appointed a Committee on Resolutions, and that all resolutions relating to the Platform of the Democratic party be referred to that committee without debate. Adopted.

The Secretary then received from the chairmen of the different delegations the names of the Committee on Resolutions and Platform, as follows:

THE COMMITTEE ON RESOLUTIONS.

Alabama, C. C. Langdon; Arkansas, A. H. Garland; California, J. H. Rose; Connecticut, T. E. Doolittle; Delaware, James A. Bayard; Florida, W. Call; Georgia, Henry S. Fitch; Illinois, Wm. J. Allen; Indiana, J. E. Macdonald; Iowa, J. H. O'Neill; Kansas, Geo W. Glick; Kentucky, Wm. Preston; Louisiana, J. B. Eustis; Maine, R D. Rice; Maryland, Stephenson Archer; Massachusetts, Edward Avery; Michigan, Charles E. Stuart; Minnesota, J. J. Green; Mississippi, E. Barksdale; Missouri, Chas. Mauson; Nebraska, Charles F. Porter; Nevada, J. A. St. Clair; New Hampshire, J. M. Campbell; New Jersey, Jacob R. Wortendyke; New York, Henry C. Murphy; North Carolina, R. Strange; Ohio, Wm. J. Gilmore; Oregon, R. D. Fitch; Pennsylvania, T. W. Hughes; Rhode Island, Thomas Steere; South Carolina, Wade Hampton; Tennessee, E. Cooper; Texas, George W. Smith; Vermont, Charles M. Davenport; Virginia, Thos. S. Bocock; West Virginia, John Davis; Wisconsin, James A. Mallory.

SECOND DAY'S PROCEEDINGS.

Mr. Clymer, of Pennsylvania, from the Committee on Permanent Organization, reported as follows: For President, Hon. Horatio Seymour, of New York [great cheering]; and one Vice-President and Secretary from each State.

The following are the Vice-Presidents and Secretaries of the Democratic Convention:

Alabama, Reuben Chapman, Wm. A. Lowe; Arkansas, B Turner, John W. Wright; California, Hon. A. H. Rose, M. J. Gillett; Connecticut, H. A. Mill, George D. Harding; Delaware, George W. Cummings, Custis W. Wright; Florida, Thos. Randall, C. H. Smith; Georgia, Hon. A. R. Wright, W. A. Reid; Illinois, D. M. Woodson, W. T. Dowdell; Indiana, J. A. Craven. W. R. Bowls; Iowa, W. McClintock, P. H. Bowsquet; Kansas, Andrew J. Mende, Isaac Sharp; Kentucky, Lucius Desha, Hart Gibson; Louisiana, Louis St. Martin, J. H. Kennard; Maine, Isaac Reed, J. A. Truscott; Maryland, Geo. R. Dennis, Outerbridge Horsey; Massachusetts, Peter Harvey, Chas. G. Clark; Michigan, A. N. Hart, Fred'k V. Smith; Minnesota, Winthrop Young, Isaac Staple; Missouri, Thos. L. Price, A. J. Reed; Mississippi, E. C. Walthall, Felix Labauve; Nebraska, Geo. N. Crawford. Peter Smith: Nevada, D. C. Buel, George H. Willard; New Hampshire, Geo. H. Pierce, Gilbert R Hatch; New Jersey, Francis S. Lathrop, Charles E. Hendrickson; New York, Wm. M. Tweed, Henry A. Richmond; North Carolina, Bedford Brown, Dr. R. B. Haywood; Ohio, Edson B. Olds, John Hamilton; Oregon, E. L. Bristow, A. D. Fitch; Pennsylvania, John L. Dawson, Ginery M. Reilly; Rhode Island, Amasa Sprague, E. B. Bronson; South Carolina, B. F. Perry, W. S. Mullins; Tennessee, A. O. P. Nicholson, Henry C. McLaughlin; Texas, Ashbel Smith, Daniel A. Veitch; Vermont, Henry Keyes, George H. Simmons; Virginia, Robert Y. Conrad, Wm. D. Coleman; West Virginia, Joseph W. Gallagher, Carlos A. Sperry; Wisconsin, ex-Governor Nelson Dewey, E. T. Thorn.

For Recording Secretaries—E. O. Perrin, of New York; Moses M. Strong, of Wisconsin; V. A. Gusken, of Georgia; F. M. Hutchinson, of Pennsylvania; Robert B. Tanney, of Illinois.

For Sergeant-at-Arms—Edward A. Moore, of New York.

RULES.

It was also recommended that the rules of the Democratic Convention of 1864 be adopted for the government of this Convention. Carried.

The Chairman appointed Mr. Bigler, of Pennsylvania, and Mr. Hammond, of South Carolina, a committee to conduct the permanent Persident to the chair.

SPEECH OF MR. SEYMOUR.

"GENTLEMEN OF THE CONVENTION—I thank you for the honor you have done me in making me your presiding officer. [Cheers.] This Convention is made up of a large number of delegates from all parts of our broad land. To a great degree we are strangers to each other, and view the subjects which agitate our country from different stand-points. We can not at once learn each other's mode of thought, or grasp all the facts which bear upon the minds of others. Yet our session must be brief, and we are forced to act without delay upon questions of an exciting character and of deep import to our country. To maintain order, to restrain all exhibition of passion, to drive out of our minds all unkind suspicions, is at this time a great duty. [Cheers.]

"I rely upon your sense of this duty, and not upon my own ability, to sustain me in the station in which I am placed by your kind partiality. Men never met under greater responsibilities than those which now weigh upon us. [Applause.]

"It is not a mere party triumph we seek. We are trying to save our country from the dangers which overhang it. We wish to lift off the perplexities and the shackles which, in the shape of bad laws and of crushing taxation, now paralyze the business and labor of our land. [Loud cheers.]

"We hope, too, that we can give order, prosperity and hapiness to those sections of our country which suffer so deeply to-day in their homes and in all the fields of their industry from the unhappy events of the last eight years. I trust our actions will show that we are governed by earnest purposes to help all classes of our citizens. Avoiding harsh invectives against men, we should keep the public mind fixed upon the questions which must now be met and solved. [Cheers.]

"Let us leave the past to the calm judgment of the future, and confront the perils of the day. [Cheers.] We are forced to meet the assertions in the resolutions put forth by the late Republican Convention. I aver there is not in this body one man who has it in his heart to excite so much of angry feeling against the Republican party as must be stirred up in the minds of those who read these declarations in the light of recent events, and in view of the condition of our country. In the first place, they congratulate the perplexed man of business, the burdened tax-payer, the laborer, whose hours of toil are lenghtened out by the growing costs of the necessaries of life, upon the success of that reconstruction policy which has brought all these evils upon them by the cost of its military despotism and the corruption of its bureau agencies. In one resolution they denounce all forms of repudiation as a national crime. Then why did they put upon the statute books of the nation the laws which invite the citizens who borrow coin to force their creditors to take debased paper, and thus wrong him out of a large share of his claim, in violation of the most solemn compact? [Loud cheering.]

"If repudiation is a national crime, it is a crime to invite the citizens of this country thus to repudiate their individual promises. [Applause.] Was it not a crime to force the creditors of this and other States to take a currency, at times worth no more than forty cents on the dollar, in repayment for the sterling coin they gave to build roads and canals, which yield such ample returns of wealth and prosperity? [Applause.] Again, they say it is due to the laborer of the nation that taxation should be equalized;

then why did they make the taxation unequal?

"Beyond the injustice of making one class of citizens pay for another the shares of the costs of schools, of roads, of the local laws, which protected their lives and property, it was an unwise and hurtful thing. [Cheers.] It sunk the credit of the country, as unusual terms always are hurtful to the credit of the borrower.

"They also declare the best policy to diminish our burden of debt is so to improve our credit, that capitalists will seek to loan us money at lower rates of interest than we now pay, and must continue to pay, so long as repudiation is threatened or suspected.

"Then why have they used full five hundred millions of the taxes drawn from the people of this country to uphold a despotic military authority, and to crush out the life of States, when, if this money had been used to pay our debts, capitalists would now seek to lend us money at lower rates of interest? But for this covert repudiation our national credit would not be tainted in the markets of the world. [Applause.]

"Again, they declare that, 'of all who were faithful in the trials of the late war, there were none entitled to more especial honor than the brave soldiers and seamen, who endured the hardships of campaign and cruise, and imperiled their lives in the service of the country. The bounties and pensions provided by the laws for these brave defenders of the nation, are obligations never to be forgotten. The widows and orphans of the gallant dead are the wards of the people—a sacred trust bequeathed to the nation's care.' Have these sacred trusts been performed? They pay to the maimed man, to the widow or to the orphan, a currency which they have sunk one-quarter below its rightful value by their policy of hate, of waste, and of military despotism, the pittance to the wounded soldiers is pressed down twenty-five per cent. below the value of that coin which he had a right to expect. [Loud cheering.] Is there no covert repudiation in this? [Applause.]

"Again, they say foreign immigration, which in the past has added so much to the wealth, development, and resources, and increase of power to this Republic, the asylum of the oppressed of all nations, should be fostered and encouraged by a liberal and a just policy. Is this foreign immigration fostered by a policy which, in mockery of laws just passed declaring eight hours to be a legal day's labor, by the cost of Government and of swarms of officials, so swells the costs of living that men must toil on to meet these exactions? [Cheers.]

"The time was when we could not only invite the Europeans to share with us the material blessings of our great country, but, more than this, we could tell those who fled from oppression that we lived under a government of laws administered by the judiciary which kept the bayonet and the sword in due subordination. [Cheers.] We could point to a written Constitution, which not only marked out the powers of government, but with anxious care secured to the humblest man the rights of property, of person, and of conscience. Is immigration encouraged by trampling that Constitution in the dust, treating with contempt and shackling the Judiciary, insulting the Executive, and giving all the world to understand that the great guarantees of political and civil rights are destroyed? [Great applause.]

"But the crowning indictment against the follies and crimes of those in power is in these words:

"'That we recognize the great principles handed down in the Declaration of Independence as the true foundation of democratic government, and we hail with gladness every effort toward making these principles a living reality on every inch of American soil.'

"If within the limits of ten States of this Union an American citizen, stung by a sense of his wrongs, should publicly and truthfully denounce the men in power, because, in the very language of this Declaration of Independence, they 'have erected a multitude of offices, and sent hither swarms of officers to harass our people and eat out their substance,' he would, in all human probability, be dragged to a prison. Or, if in the indignant language of our fathers he should exclaim: 'They have affected to render the military independent or superior to the civil power; they have abolished the free system of English laws, and established here an arbitrary government'—for the offense of asserting these principles he would be tried and punished by a military tribunal. [Great cheering.]

"Having declared that the principles of the Declaration of Independence should be made a living reality on every inch of American soil, they put in nomination a military chieftain who stands at the head of that system of despotism that crushes beneath its feet the greatest principle of the Declaration of Independence. [Cheers.] To-day, in some States, it is held by military order to be a crime to speak out the indignation and contempt which burn within the bosoms of patriotic men. If to-morrow a military order should be put forth in that State where the ashes of Washington are entombed; that it be an offense to declare that the military should ever be subordinate to the civil authority; to speak the sentiment that it was a disgrace to our country to let hordes of officials eat up the substance of the people, he who uttered these words could be dragged to prison, from the very grave where lie the remains of the author of the Declaration of Independence. [Loud cheering.] From this outrage there could be no appeal to the courts; and the Republican candidate for the Presidency has accepted a position which makes the rights and liberties of a large share of our people dependent on his will. [Applause.]

"In view of these things, can there be one man in this Convention who can let a personal ambition, a passion, a prejudice, turn him aside one hair's breadth in his efforts to wipe off the wrongs and outrages which disgrace our country? [Cheers.] Can there be one man, whose heart is so dead to all that is great and noble in patriotism, but that he will gladly sacrifice all other things for the sake of his country, its liberty and its greatness? Can we suffer any prejudices, growing out of past differences of opinion, to hinder us uniting now with all who will act with us to save our country? [Cheers.]

"We meet to-day to see what measures can be taken to avert the dangers which threaten our country, and to relieve it from the evils and burdens resulting from bad government and unwise counsels. I thank God that the strife of arms has ceased, and that once more, in the great conventions of our party, we can call through the whole roll of States and find men to answer for each. Time and events, in their great cycles, have brought us to this spot to renew and invigorate that constitutional government which, nearly eighty years ago, was inaugurated in this city. [Loud cheers.]

"It was here that George Washington, the first President, swore to preserve, protect and defend the Constitution of these United States [cheers]; and here this day we as solemnly ourselves swear to uphold the rights and liberties of the American people. Then, as now, a great war, which had desolated our land, had ceased. Then, as now, there was in every patriotic breast a longing for the blessings of a good government for the protection of lives, and for sentiments of fraternal regard and affection among the inhabitants of all the States of this Union.

"When our Government, in 1789, was inaugurated in this city, there were glad processions of men, and those manifestations of great joy which a people show when they feel that an event has happened which is to give lasting blessings to the land. [Cheers.] To-day, in this same spirit, this vast assemblage meets, and the streets of this city are thronged with men who have come from the utmost borders of our continent. They are filled with the hope that we are about, by our actions and our policy, to bring back the blessing of a good government. It is among the happiest omens that inspire us now, that those who fought bravely in our late civil war are foremost in their demands that there shall be peace in our land. The passions of hate and malice may linger in meaner breasts, but we find ourselves upheld in our generous purposes by those who showed true courage and manhood in battle. [Cheers.]

"In the spirit, then, of George Washington and of the patriots of the Revolution, let us take the step to reinaugurate our Government, to start it once again on its course to greatness and prosperity. [Cheers.] May Almighty God give us the wisdom to carry out our purposes—to give every State of our Union the blessings of peace, good order and fraternal affection."

Mr. Seymour closed amid great cheering.

Mr. Nelson, of Tennessee, moved the admission of delegates from the Democratic Convention of that State who were appointed to memorialize this body in reference to grievances of the people there under Radical rule. Adopted.

Resolutions from the National Labor Convention were sent up and read, favoring the payment of the public and private debts in greenbacks.

It was received with great cheering, as also was one against further grants of public lands to private corporations, and favoring their reservation for distribution to actual settlers.

Mr. Tilden, of New York, offered a resolution admitting delegates from the Territories to honorary seats in the Convention. Agreed to.

The Chairman of the Committee on Credentials reported that full delegations were present from every State in the Union, and recommended that three delegates from each Territory, and from the District of Columbia, be admitted to the floor without the privilege of voting.

Mr. Cox, of New York, moved to amend so as to admit the entire eleven delegates from the District. Lost.

A delegation from California moved the admission of delegates from the Territories to all the privileges of the Convention, except that each Territory shall have but one vote, which was rejected, and the committee's report was then adopted.

Mr. Phillips, of Missouri, offered the following:

"*Resolved*, That the delegates to this Convention pledge themselves, in advance, to support the nominees."

Numerous resolutions were then offered and referred.

DELEGATION FROM THE SOLDIERS' CONVENTION.

The President—The Secretary will read to the Convention a letter just received by the Chair.

The Secretary read the following:

"NEW YORK, July 6, 1868.

"MY DEAR SIR—A Committee of Conservative Soldiers and Sailors, from the Convention now in session at this place, desires to present itself to the Convention of which you are President, with an address in answer to the invitation to the privileges of the floor, and it will be glad to learn at what time you will receive it. We will be glad to be received as soon as it is convenient to the Convention.

"Very respectfully yours,

"W. B FRANKLIN, *President.*

"To Hon. HORATIO SEYMOUR, President National Democratic Convention."

Mr. Woodward (of Pennsylvania)—I move that a committee of five be appointed to wait upon the Committee of the Soldiers' and Sailors' Convention, and invite them to come upon the floor. Adopted.

The following were appointed said Committee: Mr. Woodward, of Pennsylvania; General McCook, of Ohio; Mr. Miller, of Nebraska; General Richardson, of Illinois; and Mr. Steele, of California.

General McCook asked to be excused from serving on the committee, as he was about to leave the hall, and suggested that General G. W. Morgan be appointed in his place, which suggestion was adopted.

The Soldiers' and Sailors' Committee, headed by the flag borne by Sergeant Bates, was received with loud cheers, the delegates rising.

THE SOLDIERS INTRODUCED.

Mr. Woodward, of Pennsylvania, presented the Committee from the Convention of Soldiers and Sailors. They were requested to take positions upon the platform.

The President—The Chair has the honor to present to the Convention, General Franklin, as one who represents here now the Conservative soldiers and sailors of our country, who desire peace, union and fraternal regard.

General Franklin—I have been deputed by the Conservative Soldiers' and Sailors' Convention, sitting in this place, to present you their committee. This committee has for its Chairman, General H. W. Slocum, of this State, and it has prepared an address, which it desires now to make known to the members of this Convention.

Colonel O'Bierne read the address, as follows, to the Convention:

"*Mr. President and Gentlemen of the Convention*—We are instructed by the unanimous vote of the Convention of Union Soldiers and Sailors, now in session at Cooper Institute, to return to you our thanks for extending to us the privileges of the floor of your Convention. The objects for which we are assembled are clearly set forth in the address of our presiding officer. Our Convention is composed of two thousand delegates, elected to represent every State and Territory in the Union, who have served in the Union army and navy, every one of whom believes that in co-operating at this time with the Conservative party of the country, he is still engaged in the same cause for which he risked his life during the war, viz: To preserve the Union and maintain the supremacy of the Constitution.

"We believe that the crimes now being perpetrated in the name of Republicanism and loyalty, are not less alarming than were those committed by the armed foes of the Government during the war. The party now in power has destroyed the equality of the States, has forced Southern States to submit to have their constitutions and laws framed by ignorant negroes, just released from servitude, while at the North it has denied the negro, although comparatively educated, the right of suffrage.

"It has attempted to influence the highest tribunal of the land by calling meetings of excited partisans to condemn all members of the court who might refuse to act in accordance with their dictation, while all the leading journalists of the party, since the close of the impeachment trial, have denounced and villified, in the most unmeasured terms, the once chosen leaders of their own party, going so far, in some instances, as to threaten personal violence, and for no other reason than that they were unwilling to perjure themselves at the behest of party.

"It has freely removed political disabilities from men of the South, who, before and during the war, were the most violent and malignant rebels, but have since become the sycophants of the party in power, while it persecutes those in the same localities who have always been true to the Union, but are unwilling to be ruled by their recently emancipated slaves.

"At the North it has denied official positions to hundreds of the veterans of the war, most of whom are disabled by wounds received in battle, while it has foisted into place partisans of its own, having no claims on the Government, many of whom, fortunately for the country, have, during the past few months, become inmates of our penitentiaries.

"It has placed the General of the armies beyond the control of the President of the

United States, to whom the Federal Constitution makes him subordinate; has nominated him for the Presidency, and the events of the last four months indicate that, by the use of the army under his supreme control, there is a determination to cause the electoral votes of the Southern States to be cast for himself through force and fraud.

"We solemnly declare our convictions, that the free institutions of the country have never been in greater jeopardy than at this time, and we look to the deliberations of the Democratic party now assembled in convention, with the deepest anxiety, feeling that on its action depends the future prosperity of our country. We earnestly trust and believe that no devotion to men, or adherence to past issues, will be permitted to endanger the success of the great party to which the country now looks with anxious eye for permanent peace and the perpetuity of our institutions. We believe that there are living half a million of men, who served in the Union army and navy, who are in sympathy and in judgment opposed to the acts of the party in power, and at least another half million who have heretofore acted with the Republican party, but who, viewing with alarm the recent acts of that party, are now anxious for a change of administration.

"With a platform of principles reviving no dead issues, and looking only to the arrest of existing evils, and with candidates whose fidelity to the Constitution and devotion to the country can not be questioned, we shall co-operate with you in this campaign with the enthusiasm and confidence that will bring victory and salvation to the country."

At the conclusion of the reading of the address, three cheers were given for the soldiers and sailors, and calls were made for Thomas Ewing, jr., of Ohio, who was introduced to the Convention, and was greeted by a round of applause.

Mr. Ewing said: "Gentlemen of the Convention—If it were appropriate for me, it would be impossible, for lack of voice, to express to this Convention the thankfulness which I and the members of the committee feel for the enthusiastic manner of this reception. We feel that the members of the two conventions, however separate their paths may have been in the past, will march henceforth in one line. [Applause.] We earnestly wish to accomplish the purposes of the war as we understood them— [applause]—the truly cordial and unconditional restoration of this Union. [Applause.] We have no sympathy for those purposes that have been falsely and dishonestly substituted by the Republican party for the avowed objects of the war. [Applause.] We care not for their dogmas of negro suffrage; we abhor their measures of white disfranchisement. [Applause.] We look upon them as enemies of the Republic, when we see them endeavoring, by means of that power which a great, confiding people intrusted to them, to undermine and overthrow the settled foundations of our government. [Applause.] We can not, we will not associate with them longer [applause]; we earnestly wish to associate with the great body of the Democracy, North and South [applause]; with thousands against whom we fought during the war [applause]; with thousands who felt, perhaps, coldly in the North toward the Union cause, while the war went on; with all those who maintain cordially, as the established theory of the Constitution, that the Union is irrevocable, and who will stand by and defend the Constitution as interpreted by the Government and the Supreme Court. [Applause.]

"Since our meeting here we have had the pleasure of friendly intercourse with many of the most prominent Generals of the Confederate Army. [Applause.] Knowing them to be men of honor, comparing views with them, and feeling that their views and our views as to the present and future policy of this Government coincide, we will take them by the hand as brothers. [Applause.] Forgetting past issues and passions, we will recognize political enemies only in those who are plotting to overthrow the Union of the States and our constitutional form of government, and we will recognize political friends in all those who will sustain us in endeavoring to overthrow that party. [Applause.]

"I thank you, gentlemen, for the very unexpected honor of being called upon to address you, and beg you will excuse me for this extempore effort."

[Cries of "go on." Three cheers were given for General Thomas Ewing, jr.]

W. D. Burrer, of Illinois, proposed three cheers for the soldiers and sailors of the army and navy, represented by the Convention at Cooper Institute. Three cheers were given.

Mr. Dowdle, of California, offered the following resolution, which was adopted:

"*Resolved*, That the address of the Soldiers' and Sailors' Convention, just read by their Secretary, be received and entered upon the Minutes of our proceedings, and become a part of the proceedings of this Convention."

The names of the delegates from Territories admitted to seats on the floor, in pursuance of the resolution adopted, were: Thomas W. Betts, of Idaho; Thomas E Evershed, of Arizona; and James M. avananagh and Green Clay **Smith, of Montana**.

The Convention, after a long debate, adopted the following resolution of Mr. Bigler, of Pennsylvania:

"*Resolved,* That candidates for President be now placed in nomination; and that no second balloting be had until the platform is adopted."

THIRD DAY'S PROCEEDINGS.

The Hon. Horatio Seymour, the President, being slightly indisposed (though present on the platform), the Convention was called to order by Gen. Thomas L. Price, of Missouri, who introduced Dr. Plummer, who opened the proceedings with prayer.

Mr. Murphy (N.Y.), Chairman of the Committee on Resolutions—I am directed by the Committee on Resolutions to report the platform, and I hold it in my hand, and ask to read it to the Convention. [Applause.]

THE PLATFORM.

The Democratic party in National Convention assembled, reposing its trust in the intelligence, patriotism, and discriminating justice of the people, standing upon the Constitution as the foundation and limitation of the powers of the Government, and the guaranty of the liberties of the citizen, and recognizing the questions of Slavery and Secession as having been settled for all time to come by the war, or the voluntary action of the Southern States in constitutional conventions assembled, and never to be renewed or re-agitated, do with the return of peace demand;

First. Immediate restoration of all the States to their rights in the Union, under the Constitution, and of Civil Government to the American people.

Second. Amnesty for all past political offenses and the regulation of the elective franchise in the States by their citizens.

Third. Payment of the public debt of the United States as rapidly as practicable, all moneys drawn from the people by taxation, except so much as is requisite for the necessities of the Government economically administered, being honestly applied to such payment, and where the obligations of the Government do not expressly state upon their face, or the law under which they were issued does not provide that they shall be paid in coin, they ought, in right and in justice, be paid in lawful money of the United States. [Thunders of applause.]

Fourth. Equal taxation of every species of property according to its real value, including Government bonds and other public securities. [Renewed cheering and cries of "read it again."]

Fifth. One currency for the Government and the people, the laborer and the office-holder, the pensioner and the soldier, the producer and the bondholder. [Great cheering and cries of "read it again." The fifth resolution was again read and again cheered.]

Sixth. Economy in the administration of the Government, the reduction of the standing army and navy, the abolition of the Freedmen's Bureau [great cheering] and all political instrumentalities designed to secure negro supremacy; simplification of the system and discontinuance of inquisitorial modes of assessing and collecting Internal Revenue, so that the burden of taxation may be equalized and lessened, the credit of the Government, and the currency, made good, the repeal of all enactments for the enrolling the State Militia into National forces in time of peace, and a tariff for revenue upon foreign imports, and such equal taxation under the Internal Revenue laws as will afford incidental protection to domestic manufactures, and as will, without impairing the revenue, impose the least burden upon and best promote and encourage the great industrial interests of the country.

Seventh. Reform of abuses in the Administration, the expulsion of corrupt men from office, the abrogation of useless offices, the restoration of rightful authority to and the independence of the Executive and Judicial Departments of the Government, the subordination of the military to the civil power, to the end that the usurpations of Congress and the despotism of the sword may cease.

Eighth. Equal rights and protection for naturalized and native-born citizens at home and abroad, the assertion of American nationality which shall command the respect of foreign powers and furnish an example and encouragement to people struggling for national integrity, constitutional liberty, and industrial rights; and the maintenance of the rights of naturalized citizens against the absolute doctrine of immutable allegiance and the claims of foreign powers to punish them for alleged crime committed beyond their jurisdiction. [Applause.]

In demanding these measures and reforms we arraign the Radical party for its disregard of right and the unparalleled oppression and tyranny which have marked its career. After the most solemn and unanimous pledge of both Houses of Congress to prosecute the war exclusively for the maintenance of the Government and the preservation of the Union under the Constitution, it has repeatedly violated that most sacred pledge under which alone was rallied that noble volunteer army which carried our flag to victory. Instead of restoring the Union, it has, so far as in its power, dissolved it, and subjected ten States in time of profound peace to military despotism and negro supremacy. It has nullified there the right of trial by jury; it has abolished the *habeas corpus*, that most sacred writ of liberty; it has overthrown the freedom of speech and the press; it has substituted arbitrary seizures and arrests, and military trials, and secret star-chamber inquisitions for the constitutional tribunals; it has disregarded in time of peace the right of the people to be free from searches and seizures; it has entered the post and telegraph offices, and even the private rooms of individuals, and seized their private papers and letters without any specific charge or notice of affidavit, as required by the organic law; it has converted the American Capitol into a bastile; it has established a system of spies and espionage to which no constitutional monarchy of Europe would now dare to resort; it has abolished the right of appeal on important constitutional questions to the supreme judicial tribunals, and threatens to curtail or destroy its original jurisdiction which is irrevocably vested by the Constitution; while the learned Chief-Justice has been subjected to the most atrocious calumnies merely because he would not prostitute his high office to the support of the false and partisan charges preferred against the President. Its corruption and extravagance have exceeded anything known in history; and by its frauds and monopolies it has nearly doubled the burden of the debt created by the war. It has stripped the President of his Constitutional power of appointment, even of his own Cabinet. Under its repeated assaults the pillars of the Government are rocking on their base, and should it succeed in November next and inaugurate its President, we will meet as a subject and conquered people amid the ruins of liberty and the shattered fragments of the Constitution; and we do declare and resolve, that ever since the people of the United States threw off all subjection to the British Crown the privilege and trust of suffrage have belonged to the several States, and have been granted, regulated, and controlled exclusively by the political power of each State respectively, and that any attempt by Congress, on any pretext whatever, to deprive any State of this right, or interfere with its exercise, is a flagrant usurpation of power which can find no warrant in the Constitution; and, if sanctioned by the people, will subvert our form of government, and can only end in a single centralized and consolidated government, in which the separate existence of the States will be entirely absorbed, and an unqualified despotism be established in place of a Federal Union of coequal States; and that we regard the Reconstruction acts (so called) of Congress, as such, usurpations and unconstitutional, revolutionary and void; that our soldiers and sailors who carried the flag of our country to victory against a most gallant and determined foe, must ever be gratefully remembered, and all the guarantees given in their favor must be faithfully carried into execution. That the public lands should be distributed as widely as possible among the people, and should be disposed of either under the preemption or homestead laws, and sold in reasonable quantities, and to none but actual occupants, at the minimum price established by the Government. When grants of the public lands may be allowed necessary for the encouragement of important public improvements, the proceeds of the sale of such lands, and not the lands themselves, should be so appled.

15

That the President of the United States, Andrew Johnson [applause], in exercising the power of his high office in resisting the aggressions of Congress upon the constitutional rights of the States and the people, is entitled to the gratitude of the whole American people, and in behalf of the Democratic party we tender him our thanks for his patriotic efforts in that regard. [Great applause.] Upon this platform the Democratic party appeal to every patriot, including all the Conservative element, and all who desire to support the Constitution and restore the Union, forgetting all past differences of opinion, to unite with us in the present great struggle for the liberties of the people; and that to all such, to whatever party they may have heretofore belonged, we extend the right-hand of fellowship, and hail all such co-operating with us as friends and brethren. [Applause.]

At the conclusion of the reading of the platform, Mr. Murphy said: As might have been expected, in the preparation of this platform, there were differences of opinion, which, however, upon consultation, have vanished. I say to this Convention that this platform has received the unanimous approval of the Committee. [Great applause]. And, sir, in view of this fact, I move the previous question.

The Secretary — Mr. Murphy, of New York, Chairman of the Committee on Resolutions, moves the previous question on the Platform. The question now before the Convention is: Shall the previous question be ordered?

Cries of "Question, question."

The previous question was seconded, and the main question ordered.

A Delegate—I should like to hear those resolutions read again.

Cries of "No," "no," and "Question."

The question was then put upon the adoption of the Platform, and it was unanimously adopted, amid enthusiastic cheering, the entire body of delegates and spectators rising and waving their hats and handkerchiefs.

A NOMINATION CALLED FOR.

Mr. Bigler (Pa.)—I offer the following resolution:

"*Resolved*, That the Convention do now proceed to nominate a candidate for President of the United States."

Great applause, and cries of "Question, question."

The question was put and carried unanimously.

THE TWO-THIRDS RULE.

The President (who here resumed the Chair)—Before the Committee proceeds to ballot, to avoid all possible misunderstanding, it is proper that this Convention should understand and clearly define what the two-thirds rule is. The Chair is exceedingly anxious that no question shall be decided by it after a ballot that can by any possibility lead to any misunderstanding, or any disappointment. The Chair holds itself ready in the construction of the two-thirds rule to be governed by the directions of this Convention. We have adopted the rules which governed the Convention in 1864. The Convention of 1864 adopted the rules that governed the Convention of 1860. I see before me a number of eminent gentlemen, one from Illinois, another from Michigan, and others from other States, who were conspicuous and prominent members of that Convention. I was not a member of that body. I have read through its proceedings with a view of understanding what that rule is. I will direct the Clerk to read the decision of the Convention in Charleston in 1860, and the decision of the Convention when it met again at Baltimore, under another Chairman, after the unfortunate disruption of that body.

Here a long debate ensued on a motion of Mr. Richardson, of Illinois, that two-thirds of all the members voting be the requisite number to make a nomination.

Mr. Clymer (Pa.)—I believe it was the unanimous judgment of that Committee, when it reported the rule that it required not two thirds of the votes cast, but two-thirds of the vote of the entire Electoral College. [Cries of "Good," and applause.] Therefore, I move, sir, to substitute for the resolution of the honorable gentleman from Illinois (Mr. Richardson) the following, which I send to the Chair.

Mr. Richardson withdrew his motion.

The Chair advises this Convention that they adopt the construction which was put upon this resolution in 1860, by the President of the Convention at Charleston, and by the President of the Convention at Baltimore. The Chair understands that the decision at Charleston (which decision was assented to afterward at Baltimore) was that it required two-thirds of the electoral vote. In order that the Convention may understand this, I will ask the Secretary to read it. The only wish of the Chair is to prevent any possible misunderstanding from arising here as the rule under which we act.

Mr. White (Md.)—Inasmuch as the decision of the Chair contains exactly what my resolution contained, I will withdraw it.

The Secretary, by direction of the President, then read from the report of the decision of the Chair made at the Democratic Convention of 1860, as follows:

"The resolution passed at Charleston, as understood by the President of this Convention, as understood by the present occupant of the Chair, was not a change in the rule requiring a two-thirds vote to be given to nominate, but merely a direction given to the Chair by the Convention not to declare any one nominated until he had received two-thirds of the votes of the Electoral College, and the present occupant of the Chair will not feel at liberty, under that direction, to declare any one nominated until he gets 202 votes, unless the Committee shall otherwise instruct him."

Mr Bigler (Pa.)—Moved that the roll of States be called, and that the delegates of the several States proceed to the nomination of candidates for the Presidency. Which was carried.

Mr. Eaton, on behalf of Connecticut, nominated Gov. James E. English, of Connecticut.

When Illinois was called, Mr. Richardson (Ill.) said we will cast our vote for Mr. Pendleton [applause]; but we leave it to the Ohio delegation to make the nomination.

When Indiana was called, Mr. Fitch said: The gentleman for whom the delegation of Indiana designs to cast their vote has been already named to the Convention.

When Iowa was called, the Chairman of the delegation said: Iowa makes no nomination, but expects to sustain the nomination made by the State of Ohio.

Mr. H. J. Anderson on the part of a majority of the Maine Delegation, nominated Gen. Winfield S. Hancock.

Mr. Emory (Maine)—In behalf of the minority of the Maine delegation, nominated, as their choice, the Hon. George H. Pendleton.

Nebraska makes no nomination, but will cast her vote for George H. Pendleton.

Mr. Little (of N. J.)—The State of New Jersey nominates ex-Governor Joel Parker.

Mr. Tilden (of N. Y.)—On behalf of the New York delegation, nominated Sanford E. Church, of New York.

Gen. McCook (of Ohio)—By the unanimous voice of the Democratic Convention of Ohio, nominated George H. Pendleton, of Ohio.

Mr. Bristow (of Oregon)—Oregon will cast its vote for George H. Pendleton.

Judge Woodward (of Penn.)—On behalf of the Pennsylvania delegation, nominated the Hon. Asa Packer, of Pennsylvania.

Mr. T. A. R. Nelson (of Tenn.)—On behalf of the Tennessee delegation, nominated Andrew Johnson.

Mr. Smith (of Vt.)—Nominated the only Democratic Governor of New England, Jas. E. English.

Mr. Baldwin (of Va.)—Indorsed, as its first and only choice, the nominee of this Convention.

Mr. Clark (of Wis.)—On behalf of a majority of the delegation, nominated James R. Doolittle.

Mr. Palmer (of Wis.)—For the minority of the delegation, seconded the nomination of George H. Pendleton.

Six ballots were then had for President, without result.

Soldiers and sailors indorse the platform.

HON. HORATIO SEYMOUR DECLINES.

On the fourth ballot, North Carolina voted for the Hon. Horatio Seymour.

The President (Mr. Seymour)—I trust I may be permitted now to make a single remark. Very much to my surprise, my name has been mentioned. I must not be nominated by this Convention, as I could not accept its nomination if tendered, which I do not expect. My own inclinations prompted me to decline at the outset; my honor compels me to do so now. I am grateful for any expression of kindness. It must be distinctly understood, it is impossible, consistently with my position, to allow my name to be mentioned in this Convention against my protest. The Clerk will proceed with the call.

The Secretary read the following communication to the Convention:

Resolved, That the Declaration of Principles adopted by the Democratic National Convention be, and the same are hereby approved.

Ordered, That the Secretary communicate to the Democratic Convention a copy of the above resolution forthwith.

JAMES P. O'BIERNE,
Sec'y Soldiers' and Sailors' Convention.
To the Democratic Convention.

Mr. Richardson (Ill.)—I move that the document just received from the Soldiers' and Sailors' Convention be put upon the record of the Convention and made a part of the proceedings. Carried.

The Convention then adjourned.

FOURTH DAY'S PROCEEDINGS.

THE NATIONAL EXECUTIVE COMMITTEE.—The following list of the National Executive Committee was read:

Alabama—John Forsyth, Mobile.
Arkansas—John M. Harrell, Little Rock.
California—John Bigger.

Connecticut—W. M. Converse, Franklin.
Delaware—Saml. Townsend, Newcastle.
Florida—Chas. E. Dyke, Tallahassee.
Georgia—A. H. Colquitt, Albany.
Illinois—Wilbur F. Strong, Chicago.
Indiana P. O.—William E. Niblack.
Iowa—Daniel O. Finch, Des Moines.
Kansas—Isaac E. Eaton, Leavenworth City.
Kentucky—T. C. McCreery, Owensboro.
Louisiana—Jas. McClosky, New Orleans.
Maine—Sylvanus R. Lyman, Portland.
Maryland—Odey Bowie, Prince George.
Massachusetts—Fred. O. Prince, Boston.
Michigan—William A. Moore, Detroit
Minnesota—Charles W. Nash, St. Paul.
Mississippi—Charles E. Hooker, Jackson.
Missouri—Charles A. Swarts, St. Louis.
Nebraska—G. L. Miller, Omaha.
Nevada—J. W. McCorkle, Virginia City.
New Hampshire—H. Bingham, Littleton.
New Jersey—John McGregor, Newark.
New York—August Belmont.
North Carolina—Thos. Bragg, Raleigh.
Ohio—John G. Thompson, Columbus.
Oregon—J. C. Hawthorn, Portland.
Pennsylvania—Isaac Eskister, Lancaster.
Rhode Island—G. Bradford, Charleston.
South Carolina—Charles H. Simonton, Charleston.
Tennessee—Jno. W. Leftwick, Memphis.
Texas—John Hancock, Austin.
Vermont—H. B. Smith, Milton.
Virginia—John Goode, Norfolk.
West Virginia—John Hall, Port Pleasant.
Wisconsin—Fred. W. Horn, Cedartown.

Mr. G. N. Fitch (of Ind.)—In behalf of a majority of the delegation from Indiana, put in nomination Hon. Thomas A. Hendricks, of Indiana.

Mr. R. J. Reeves (of Ind.)—Felt under obligations to regard the preference of his State, expressed by her convention for Geo. H. Pendleton.

Twelve more ballots were had, making eighteen in all, without result.

The Hon. T. W. Brown, chairman of the committee appointed by the Democratic Convention of Tennessee, then read the address to the Convention prepared by the committee.

The Convention then adjourned.

FIFTH DAY'S PROCEEDINGS.

Mr. Broadhead (of Missouri)—Put in nomination General Francis P. Blair, Jr., of Missouri.

Mr. Rose (of California)—Put in nomination Judge Stephen J. Field, of California.

MR. PENDLETON WITHDRAWS.

Mr. Vallandigham (Ohio)—I have a communication in writing to make to this Convention. By permission of the Chair I will read it from the stand. [Applause, during which Mr. Vallandigham made his way to the rostrum.]

The Chair—Mr. Vallandigham, of Ohio, will make a communication to the Convention.

Mr. Vallandigham—The following is the communication to which I refer:

MR. PENDLETON'S LETTER.

CINCINNATI, July 2, 1868.
WASHINGTON MCLEAN, Fifth Avenue Hotel, N. Y.:

My Dear Sir—You know better than any one the feelings and principles which have guided my conduct since the suggestion of my name for the Presidential nomination. You know that while I covet the good opinion of my countrymen, and would feel an honest pride in so distinguished a mark of their confidence, I do not desire it at the expense of one single electoral vote [great applause], or of the least disturbance of the harmony of our party. I consider the success of the Democratic party in the next election of far greater importance than the gratification of any personal ambition, however pure and lofty it might be. [Loud cheers.] If, therefore, at any time, a name shall be suggested which, in the opinion of yourself and those friends who have shared our confidences, shall be stronger before the country, or which can more thoroughly unite our own party, I beg that you will instantly withdraw my name, and pledge to the Convention my hearty, and zealous, and active support for its nominee.

Very truly yours,
GEO. H. PENDLETON.

[Great cheering.]

Mr. Vallandigham—At the request of the gentleman to whom this letter is addressed, I submit it to this Convention. It was his desire that it should have been done very early in the afternoon of yesterday, but the earnest zeal and fidelity of the Ohio delegation to the distinguished son of Ohio, whom they had presented to the Convention for the office of President, precluded their consent to any such proposition. This morning his request has been reverenced, and in conformity with it I have produced and read the letter, and submit that the spirit of magnanimity, unselfishness, and of patriotic devotion to the interests of the country, speak in terms of far higher eulogy in behalf of this distinguished gentleman than any words I could utter. [Great applause.] Pursuant, therefore, to the authority of Mr. McLean, and acting under the advice of Mr. Pendleton, I withdraw his name, with hearty thanks to the multitude of earnest, zealous and devoted friends who have adhered to him with so great fidelity. [Applause, and long-continued cheers for Pendleton.]

The Convention then proceeded to ballot.

NOMINATION OF HORATIO SEYMOUR ON THE TWENTY-SECOND BALLOT.

When Ohio was called, General McCook (Ohio) said: Mr. Chairman—I arise at the unanimous request and the demand of the delegation from Ohio, and with the consent and approval of every public man in the State, including the Hon. George H. Pendleton, to again place in nomination, against his inclination, but no longer against his honor, the name of Horatio Seymour, of New York. [Rousing cheers, and long-continued applause.] Let us vote, Mr. Chairman and gentlemen of the Convention, for a man whom the Presidency has sought, but who has not sought the Presidency. [Applause.] I believe in my heart that it is the solution of the problem which has been engaging the minds of the Democrats and Conservative men of this nation for the last six months. ["Good, good."] I believe it will have a solution which will drive from power the vandals who now possess the Capitol of the nation. [Applause.] I believe it will receive the unanimous assent and approval of the great belt of States from the Atlantic—New York, New Jersey, Pennsylvania, Ohio, Indiana, Michigan, Illinois, Missouri, and away West, for quantity—to the Pacific Ocean. I say that he has not sought the Presidency; and I ask—not demand—I ask that this Convention shall demand of him that, sinking his own inclination and the well-known desires of his heart, he shall yield to what we believe to be the almost unanimous wish and desire of the delegates to this Convention. [Great applause, and three cheers.] In my earnestness and enthusiasm, I had almost forgotten to cast the twenty-one votes of Ohio for Horatio Seymour. [Tremendous excitement, and nine cheers for Horatio Seymour.]

The President, the Hon. Horatio Seymour, here advanced to the front of the stage, and, as soon as the enthusiasm would permit of his being heard, addressed the Convention.

SPEECH OF MR. SEYMOUR.

GENTLEMEN OF THE CONVENTION [cheers]: The motion just made by the gentleman from Ohio excites in my mind the most mingled emotions. [Applause.] I have no terms in which to express my gratitude [cheers] for the magnanimity of his State and for the generosity of this Convention. [Cheers.] I have no terms in which to tell of my regret that my name has been brought before this Convention. God knows that my life and all that I value most in life I would give for the good of my country, which I believe to be identical with my own. [Applause, and cries of "Take the nomination, then."] I do not stand here as a man proud of his opinions or obstinate in his purposes; but upon a question of honor I must stand upon my own convictions against the world. [Applause, and a voice, "God bless you, Horatio Seymour."] Gentlemen, when I said here at an early day that honor forbade my accepting a nomination by this Convention I *meant* it. When, in the course of my intercourse with those of my own delegation and my friends, I said to them that I could not be a candidate, I *meant* it. And now permit me here to say that I know after all that has taken place, I could not receive the nomination without placing, not only myself, but the great Democratic party in a false position. [Great Applause.] But, gentlemen of the Convention, more than that, we have had to-day an exhibition from the distinguished citizen of Ohio that has touched my heart, as it has yours. [Cheers.] I thank God, and I congratulate this country, that there is in the great State of Ohio, whose magnificent position gives it so great a control over the action of our country, a young man rising fast in the estimation of his countrymen, and whose future is all glorious, who has told the world that he could tread beneath his feet every other consideration than that of duty; and when he expressed to his delegation, and expressed in more direct terms, that he was willing that I should be nominated, who stood in such a position to his own nomination, I should feel a dishonored man if I could not tread the same honorable path which he has marked out. [Great applause.] Gentlemen, I thank you, and may God bless you for your kindness to me; but your candidate I can not be. [Three cheers for Horatio Seymour.]

SPEECH OF MR. VALLANDIGHAM.

Mr. Vallandigham (Ohio): Mr. President—In times of great public exigency, and especially in times of great public calamity, every personal consideration must be yielded to the public good. [Applause.] The safety of the people is the supreme law, and the safety of the American Republic demands the nomination of Horatio Seymour of New York. [Cheers.] Ohio can not, Ohio will not accept his declination, and her 21 votes shall stand recorded in his name—[cries of "good, good," and cheers]—and now I call upon the delegations from all the States represented on this floor; upon the delegations from all the States of this Union, from the Atlantic to the Pacific, from the great Lakes to the Gulf, disregarding those minor considerations which, justly it may be, properly I know, tend to sway them in casting their ballots to make this nomination unanimous; and, before God, I believe that in November the judgment of this Convention will be confirmed and ratified by the people of all the United States. [Applause.] Let the vote of Ohio stand recorded then— 21 votes for Horatio Seymour. [Applause.]

SPEECH OF MR. KIERNAN.

Mr. Kiernan (New York): Mr. President —Belonging to the delegation from the State of New York, and coming from the district where the President of this Convention lives, I can not, as an individual delegate, refrain from asking the indulgence of this Convention in making one or two observations; and in order that we may relieve everybody, in order that we may relieve our Chairman from every bit of sensitiveness on the question of honor, I desire to say, on behalf of the delegation from the State of New York, that they have had neither lot nor part in the motion, which in our hearts we yet rejoice to hear, from the State of Ohio. [Applause.] We heard but recently that some such movement was thought, by wise and good men, necessary for the safety of our country; but our hearts were coerced, out of deference to the sensitiveness of the gentleman who presides over this Convention, and we told them we could have neither lot nor part in it, unless others would overcome that which we had never been able to do. Now, Sir, let me say another word. We have balloted two or three days. We have balloted, thank God, in the best of temper and of spirits. We have resolved, and we required the judgement of two-thirds of the delegates of this Convention for our nominee to the end that we might be sure, for the sake of our country, that we would have a majority of the electors next November. And after striving hard, after striving long, and after consulting as well as we could in reference to the various names brought before us, we have not been able yet to convince the judgment of two-thirds of the Convention for the candidates we have supported. New York has steadily voted her judgment, with kind feelings to other candidates. We have pronounced, as our second choice, for a distinguished citizen of Indiana. But it seems to me that after this long struggle, and in this crisis of our affairs, and in view of what is so important to every man, woman and child in this Union, that we should succeed in November—it seems to me now, in reference to our distinguished Chairman, that his honor is entirely safe. No one can doubt that he has steadily and in good faith declined; but now his honor is safe, and his duty is to his country, his duty to his fellow citizens, to all that shall come after us, requires that he shall let the judgment of the delegates of this Convention prevail; and if it should select him as the standard bearer, most certain, in their opinion, to win a triumph for the country next November. [Applause]. We leave it in the hands of others, as we are constrained to do; but I give it as my judgment, for the past, the present and the future, that if we should select him as the man, in our judgment, upon whom we can all unite, New York will fall in and give a majority of a hundred thousand without a canvass. [Great cheers].

When Wisconsin was called, Mr. H. L. Palmer, of Wisconsin, said: "The delegation from Wisconsin have steadily supported a distinguished citizen of that State for the position of President of the United States, but I am now instructed by the delegation of that State to change that vote, and in making this change I am instructed to second the State of Ohio [applause], and to cast their eight votes for Horatio Seymour.". [Loud applause].

When Massachusetts was called, Mr. Abbott, of Mass., said: "The State of Massachusetts instructs me to cast her vote for one whom Massachusetts, whom all the East, so far as I know, has regarded for years past as the leader of the Democracy, Horatio Seymour, of New York." [Great applause].

Mr. Wright (of North Carolina)—I am instructed by the delegation from North Carolina to change their vote and to cast it as they originally cast it—for Horatio Seymour, of New York. [Applause].

Mr. Featherstone (of Mississippi)—I am instructed to change the vote of Mississippi from General Hancock to Horatio Seymour.

The announcement was received with uproarious applause, and the rising of delegates to their feet and calling for recognition by the Chair. The Chairman insisted upon gentlemen taking their seats.

Mr. Woodward (of Pennsylvania)—The State of Pennsylvania, having voted uniformly, thus far, for two of her distinguished sons, had instructed him, through her delegation, to transfer her entire twenty-six votes to Horatio Seymour.

The wildest confusion here ensued. Nothing was heard but cheers from the galleries and floor, and cries of "Mr. President" from delegates standing in their seats.

The Secretary successively recognized the Chairmen of the delegations from Missouri and Virginia, announcing that they had changed their votes to Horatio Seymour.

A scene of still greater confusion and tumultuous discord followed. All the delegations were standing in their places, and striving for the recognition of the Chair by gesture and by voice. A perfect babel reigned, in the midst of which the announcement was made that Maryland, Illinois, Texas and Deleware had transferred their united votes to Horatio Seymour.

The announcement of the vote of each State added, if possible, to the tumult.

At this point the cannon outside the building commenced firing, and the discharges were answered by those inside the hall rising to their feet with vociferous cheers and the waving of handkerchiefs.

Mr. Smith (of Vermont)—Vermont was the first State in this Convention to cast its vote for the distinguished citizen of Indiana (Mr. Hendricks). She now yields to the evident wish of the Convention, and she finds in the distinguished gentleman from New York all she desires as a candidate. She therefore changes her vote from Thomas A. Hendricks to Horatio Seymour.

New Jersey, West Virginia, Alabama, Tennessee, Arkansas, Maine and Georgia, here changed their votes to Seymour, receiving the approval of all who heard the Secretary declare the change.

The Chairman of the Kansas Delegation—Kansas casts her three votes for Horatio Seymour.

Mr. Bigler—California casts her five votes for Horatio Seymour. [Applause].

Mr. Lawson (of Pennsylvania)—I am requested to say that it is the unanimous voice of this Convention that the nomination of Horatio Seymour be made by acclamation.

The Chairman—It can not be done until all the States have voted on this ballot.

The Chairman of the Florida Delegation—Florida wishes to cast her three votes for Horatio Seymour. [Applause].

The Chairman of the Minnesota Delegation—Minnesota, following the lead of Ohio, casts her entire vote for Horatio Seymour.

The Chairman of the New Hampshire Delegation—The State of New Hampshire changes her vote, and casts it entire for Horatio Seymour.

The Chairman of the Georgia Delegation—The State of Georgia has indicated her choice by casting her vote for the most accomplished soldier of the Union Army—he who, when the war was ended, yielded to the supremacy of the Constitution of his country. But, sir, we came here to abide t'e choice of the Democratic party, and now join our voice with that of the Democracy from one end of the country to the other for Horatio Seymour. [Applause].

Mr. Jones (of Louisiana)—Louisiana asks leave to change her vote, and vote for Horatio Seymour. And, Mr. Chairman, although we have twenty-five thousand of our white population disfranchised, and although we have fifty thousand voters who are unknown to our Constitution and to our laws, yet, Mr. Chairman, I pledge the vote of the State of Louisiana to the nominee. [Applause].

Mr. Stuart (of Mich.)—Mr. Chairman: The delegates from the State of Michigan came to this Convention of all the States in this Union, with but one single purpose in view, and that was to nominate a candidate for the office of President of the United States who could certainly be elected. That position we occupy to-day; and, sir, when we look around in this Convention, and see here, for the first time in eight years, the assembled wisdom of the Democracy of the country, bounded only upon the Atlantic and upon the Pacific, because, on the north and on the south America acknowledges as yet no boundary whatever. When, therefore, sir, so much wisdom as is here to-day, with a voice so united as this, speaks for the distinguished son of New York, the greatest statesman, in my judgment, now living [applause], Michigan can not consent to withhold her voice in this general expression of confidence; but, sir, unites it with this expression of patriotic determination to rescue this country from the grasp of the most desperate rebel that ever seized upon the reins of the Government. [A voice: "Good, good."] It is a question of Constitution, it is a question of country; it is a question of whether our blessed Union and the freedom of these millions is to live, or whether it is to be buried down in everlasting oblivion and infamy. [A voice: "Good, go on!"] Sir, under these circumstances, it is with infinite pleasure that Michigan casts her vote for Horatio Seymour, of New York. [Great applause].

Mr. James B. Campbell (S. C.)—Mr. President: I rise to answer for that State of the Union which bears at this time most heavily the chains and weight of Radical misrule. I did not suppose, sir, that my voice or that of any of my colleagues would be heard in this assembly, except in the discharge of the routine business. In the words of the Convention that sent us here, we were instructed to behave with the proprieties which belong to the well-bred guest, and not to assume any of the functions of symposiac of the feast. We came here, Mr. President, and gentlemen of the Convention, having no favorite candidate—going not for men, but for measures. We have been more than grateful for the declaration of principles, and the prospective measures that have been announced by this Convention, not only with unanimity, but with unsurpassed enthusiasm. We were instructed, and the instructions were coincident with the feelings of every honest heart in South Carolina, to accept the nomination of that man who seemed to have the voice of this Convention. Obeying these instructions, South Carolina, with an invocation of God's blessing, and upon this party wherein is centered the last hopes of the Republic of Washington, nominates and votes for Horatio Seymour of New York. [Great applause.]

A delegate from California moved that Horatio Seymour be tendered the unanimous nomination of the Convention. [Voices—"No," "no;" let the vote be finished. Great confusion.]

The Chairman of the Delegation—Delaware would change her vote, if not too late, and cast all her votes for Horatio Seymour. [Applause and laughter.]

Samuel J. Tilden—Mr. Chairman—

A Delegate from New York—See if any other State wants to change its vote first.

Mr. Tilden—If there is any State which has not yet voted, or that wishes to change its vote, I will yield the floor for that purpose.

Delegate—"No, no; go on."

Mr. Tilden—It is fit that on this occasion New York should wait for the voice of all her sister States. Last evening I should not have believed—did not believe—the event which has just happened to be possible. Not because I had not seen here that the underlying choice of almost all of this Convention was that we should do what we have now done. There was but one obstacle, and that was in the repugnance, which I take upon myself the whole responsibility of declaring to have been earnest, sincere, deep felt, on the part of Horatio Seymour to accept this nomination. I did not believe that any circumstance would make it possible, except that Ohio, with whom we have been unfortunately dividing our votes, herself demanding it, and to that I thought New York ought to yield. We were without any connection or any combination that bound our faith or our honor, and I was anxious that when we should leave this Convention that there should be, underlying our action, no heart-burnings, no jealousy, no bitterness of disappointment, and I believe that in this result we have lifted this Convention far above every such consideration [cries of "order," "order"]; and I believe further, after having surveyed the ground for a long time, and meditated most carefully what we ought to do, influenced, I am sure, by no personal partiality, by no other thing than the deliberate conviction of my judgment, I believe that we have made the nomination most calculated to give us success in the election which approaches. And, sir, having made these observations in behalf of the New York delegation, I now ask that our vote be changed, and be recorded for Horatio Seymour. [Cheers.]

The Secretary—The State of New York changes her vote, and casts her unanimous vote for Horatio Seymour. [Loud and long-continued applause.]

Mr. White (of Maryland)—I now propose, Mr. President, that a committee of one from each State shall be appointed to call upon—[Loud cries of "No, no," "Better wait until the vote is taken" "Too soon," and great noise.]

The Chairman—The vote has not yet been announced.

Mr. White—I understood that the chairman of the New York delegation asked if all the States had voted, and it was announced that they had; that they had all voted for Horatio Seymour, and that he was unanimously nominated.

The Chairman—The vote has not been announced.

Mr. White—I withdraw my motion.

THREE CHEERS FOR SEYMOUR.

Mr. S. Clark (of Wis.)—I have a proposition to make to this Convention for myself, and it is in order to announce it before the vote is announced. I see around me, on the floor and in the galleries, ladies and gentlemen who desire also to be heard, and who should have some voice in this Convention, in ratifying the nomination by acclamation. I therefore move that they ratify it by giving three cheers for Horatio Seymour.

The suggestion was immediately acted upon. Every one rose, and amid the waving of hats, handkerchiefs, fans, canes and parasols, three tremendous cheers were given, which fairly made the building rock. Loud cries of "order," "order."

The Chairman—The Convention will come to order.

EX-GOVERNOR SEYMOUR NOMINATED.

The Secretary—The following is the result of the 22d ballot: All the States have voted, and the vote of the full electoral college having been given, the roll stands for Horatio Seymour 317 votes.

Renewed cheering, the Convention and audience again rising, and another scene of enthusiasm prevailing for five minutes.

The Chairman—The Convention will come to order. All business will be suspended until order is restored.

Mr. Dawson (Penn.)—Mr. President—

The Chairman—General Price in the Chair—The official announcement has not yet been made. Gentlemen of the Convention will sit down.

Order having been restored, the Chairman said: "The Hon. Horatio Seymour having received the unanimous vote of this

Convention, I, therefore, declare him the candidate, and the standard-bearer of the Democratic party in the ensuing election

The Convention then proceeded to the nomination of Vice-President. Illinois nominated General John A. McClernand, of Illinois.

General McClernand, on rising, was greeted with loud applause. He said: Mr. President—The State of Illinois, through her delegation to this Convention, has done me the honor to present my name for the high office of Vice-President of the United States. This compliment is far above any merit which I possess. I beg in return to offer my sincerest thanks, and in doing so I beg that the delegates of Illinois will withdraw my name from the consideration of the Convention. [Cries of "no," "no."] I am here, Mr. President and gentlemen, seeking no office, but to contribute my humble efforts to liberate the country from the thraldom which now binds her and degrades her. [Applause.] I have given my efforts as a delegate to the Soldiers' and Sailors' Convention in a very humble way in this Convention. As a Democrat and as a citizen I approve the nomination for President which has been made to-day. [Applause.] I can say, in behalf of the numerous and distinguished body of soldiers and sailors assembled in this city a few days since, that the nomination will meet with their hearty response; and the coming election will determine the fact that all the soldiers and sailors of this country are not for a sham hero—a mere fatuity—a mere compromise between abler and better men; that they are not to have a plagiarism of other and better men's deserts; but that they are to have Horatio Seymour of New York—an eminent statesman, an orator and a gentleman, a man every way qualified to administer the Executive office of this country. They will prove, I say, in the approaching election, that one-half, and more than one-half of the patriotic soldiers and sailors are for Horatio Seymour. [Applause.] And now a word to my friends, and against whom I was so lately arrayed in battle. I say to them by-gones are by-gones—[cries of "Good," "good," and cheers]—let the dead bury the dead. I stretch to them the hand of fellowship, and say to them let us co operate to arrest disunion and usurpation. We have a common interest in it; we have a common stock in it; and unless we do it, the Government will be overthrown It is even now a despotism. I have said much more, Mr. President, than I intended to say when I arose. I am in earnest in what I have said; and I ask, I appeal to my delegation to withdraw my name as a candidate before this Convention. [Cries of "no," "no."] There are other gentlemen in this Convention whom I had rather support than have my name presented.

Mr. Sparks (Illinois)—It is believed, by me at least, that when a gentleman declines a nomination we ought to consult his wishes. At the request of General McClernand, whom Illinois would take great pleasure in supporting, I now withdraw his name.

Iowa nominated Hon. Augustus C. Dodge.

Kansas nominated Gen. Thos. Ewing, Jr.

Kentucky being called, General Preston (Kentucky) said: Mr. President, I am instructed unanimously by the State of Kentucky, by its delegates here assembled, to place in nomination a gentleman of great distinction in his State and in the country; one in the prime of manhood; distinguished by his devotion to the Union, having served it both in a civil and in a military capacity with the utmost honor, and obtained a reputation in the army second to no man of his grade. Kentucky feels that this nomination is due the great West, and no Southern State has presented any nominee for any place, as you will observe here, but I feel that it is appropriate—for we having entertained different opinions from him—to state that I am instructed now to nominate him, in order to testify that we, the soldiers of the South, stretch forth our hands to the soldiers of the North [applause] in the spirit of noble amity that your resolutions have inculcated. [Applause.] It is with that view, sir, after consultation with the Northern delegations, and one of the most powerful, that the duty is devolved upon me of making this nomination. I now have the privilege, therefore, of nominating as a candidate for Vice-President of the United States, General Francis P. Blair, of Missouri. [Applause.]

LOUISIANA—General James B. Steedman of Louisiana: Mr. President: I rise, sir, as one of the humble representatives of the United States Army in the late war, holding a seat in the Convention, to second on behalf of Louisiana the nomination of my comrade in arms, Major-General Frank P. Blair. [Applause.] When the Convention adjourned I went immediately to the headquarters of the Soldiers' and Sailors' Executive Committee, on Union square. I met there some ten or twelve gentlemen who were distinguished in the army, and consulted them in regard to their choice as a candidate as a Vice-President of the United States, and by a unanimous vote of all who were present, I was requested to say to this Convention, without disparagement to the name of any other soldier that has been presented here, or that may be presented, that General Frank P. Blair would be acceptable to the soldiers of the United States army. [Applause.] In the exhibition of magnanimity that has been made in this Convention by the soldiers of the Confederate army, in coming up and giving a contradiction to the charge of the Radical party that they did not accept sincerely the situation in casting their votes as they did in this Convention for that distinguished soldier of the United States army, Major-General Winfield Scott Hancock, they have given renewed assurances of their devotion to the Union, of their willingness to accept the issues of the war, by presenting to this Convention, through General Preston, whom I met on the bloody field of Chickamauga, the name of Major-General Francis P. Blair. [Loud applause.] I therefore feel authorized to say that if General Blair is nominated, his nomination will meet with a response from every brave and true man that fought on either side, who desires to see peace and prosperity restored to our common country. [Applause.]

MARYLAND—Maryland makes no nomination, but heartily concurs in the nomination made by the State of Kentucky. [Applause.]

MISSISSIPPI—Mr. President, the State of Mississippi makes no nomination, but most cordially seconds the nomination of General Blair.

MISSOURI—The Chairman of the Delegation: Missouri makes no nomination, but seconds the nomination of General Blair. [Applause.]

NEBRASKA—Nebraska makes no nomination, but seconds the nomination of General Frank P. Blair. [Applause.]

NEVADA—Nevada makes no nomination, but seconds that of Frank P. Blair.

NORTH CAROLINA—The Chairman of the Delegation: Mr. President—North Carolina makes no nomination for Vice-President, but in order to show the people of the United States that we have no prejudice against a gallant soldier who fought for his section of the country, we desire to second the nomination of General Francis P. Blair. [Applause.]

OHIO—No nomination.

OREGON—Oregon makes no nomination, but seconds the nomination of General Francis P. Blair.

PENNSYLVANIA — Mr. Woodward — Mr. President: The State of Pennsylvania makes no nomination, but I am instructed by the delegation of Pennsylvania to second the nomination of that brave soldier and judicious statesman, General Frank P. Blair. [Applause.]

RHODE ISLAND—No nomination.

SOUTH CAROLINA—Mr. Campbell, Chairman: The State of South Carolina answers her call, not by her chairman, but by her best beloved son, a soldier, who knows better than I do how to interchange the courtesies which belong to enemies in war and friends in peace. I have the honor to introduce to this Convention Mr. Wade Hampton. [Loud cheers.]

Mr. Chairman: The only reason I can give why my State has done me the honor to ask me to speak for her on this occasion is, I suppose, that I met the distinguished gentleman whose name has been presented by Kentucky, on more than one field. Our State wishes me to say to the soldiers, and in reply to the remarks of the gentleman from Illinois, the distinguished soldier from Illinois, that the soldiers of the South cordially, heartily, and cheerfully accept the right hand of friendship which is extended to them. [Cries of "Good," and cheers.] We wish to show that we appreciate the kindness and cordiality that has been extended to us by all classes. We wish particularly to make an acknowledgment to the Federal soldiers who have met us so cordially and so friendly. It is due to them, I think, that they should have the second place upon the ticket. It is due to that Convention which so cordially approved your platform; it is due to the South; and I, for my State, most heartily and cordially second the nomination of General Blair.

On the conclusion of his remarks, Mr. Hampton was congratulated personally by General McClernand, amid the applause of the Convention and the spectators.

The call of States was then proceeded with, as follows:

When Tennessee was called, the Chairman of the delegation said—Mr. Chairman: It is the pleasure of the Tennessee delegation that the vote of the State of Tennessee shall be cast by a distinguished Southern soldier, whom I have the honor to present to the Convention—the well known General N. B. Forrest. [Great applause.]

General Forrest—I have the pleasure, sir, to cast the vote of Tennessee for General Blair. And I here wish to take this occasion to thank the delegates and people here for the kind and uniformly courteous treatment that the Southern delegates have received during their attendance upon this Convention. [Great cheering.]

The Chairman of the Texas Delegation—Mr. President: The Texas delegation desires that a distinguished soldier from that State should respond for it.

General Smith (Texas)—Mr. President: I esteem it a great honor that I have been requested by the Chairman of the Texas delegation and the members of that delegation on this occasion to cast the six votes of the State of Texas for Major-General

Frank P. Blair. It is an evidence that the soldiers of Texas, who fought through the Confederate war, will give, when they come to vote, as warm a reception in the support of General Frank P. Blair, as we did on the field of battle from the commencement of the war to the end of it. [Cheers.]

VIRGINIA—General Kemper: As a son of the old Commonwealth of Virginia, I am instructed to strike hands with the soldiers of the army of the North, and, in the name of Virginia, to accept and ratify, as a token of the perpetuity of the Union, the nomination of Major-General Frank P. Blair of Missouri.

NEW YORK—Mr. Tilden: The State of New York, following Ohio and the other great States of the North-west, concurs in the nomination of General Frank P. Blair.

General Charles W. Blair (Kansas)—Mr. Chairman: As I had the honor to present to this Convention the name of Thomas Ewing, jr., of Kansas, I now desire, on behalf of his friends, and at his instance, to withdraw his name, and move that the nomination of Francis P. Blair be made by acclamation.

Mr. O'Neil (Iowa)—In view of the almost unanimous sentiment of this Convention, I beg leave, in the name of the Iowa delegation, to withdraw the name of Gen. Dodge, and to second the nomination of General Francis P. Blair. [Cheers.]

The Secretary then proceeded with the call of States.

The Secretary—The vote stands, upon Vice-President, as follows: Whole vote of the Electoral College, 317; which were given unanimously for Frank P. Blair, of Missouri.

Three hearty cheers greeted this announcement, and another scene of noise and confusion ensued.

The Chairman—The unanimous vote having been cast for Francis P. Blair, of Missouri, for Vice President, he is declared the candidate of the Democratic party for Vice-President. [Loud cries of "Seymour," "Seymour."]

Mr. Cox (of N. Y.)—I move, sir, that our nomination for Vice-President be made unanimous by both delegations and audience. [A voice in the gallery, "With a will."]

Another scene of intense enthusiasm and excitement followed, delegates and audience rising to their feet, and joining in cheer after cheer.

Mr. McDonald (of Ind.) offered a resolution for a committee of one from each State, to inform the nominees of the action of this Convention, and to tender them the nominations.

The resolution was adopted.

LABOR MOVEMENT OF THE COUNTRY INDORSED.

Mr. Vallandigham offered the following resolution:

Resolved, That this Convention sympathize cordially with the workingmen of the United States in their efforts to protect the rights and promote the interests of labor and of the laboring classes of the country.

The resolution was adopted.

The Chair announced the following as the names of the committee to inform the nominees of this Convention of their selection:

Alabama, Michael J. Bulger; Arkansas, P. O. Thewett; California, Joseph Roberts; Connecticut, James A. Hovey; Delaware, Thomas B. Bradford; Florida, Wilkinson Call; Georgia, B. H. Hill; Illinois, William C. Gormley; Indiana, M. D. Manson; Iowa, Hon. A. C. Dodge; Nebraska, George L. Miller; Nevada, D. E. Buell; New Hampshire, Albert W. Hatch; New Jersey, H. S. Little; New York, Francis Kernan; Kansas, Isaac Sharpe; Kentucky, General William Preston; Louisiana, Thos. Allen Clarke; Maine, R. D. Rice; Maryland, Wm. Pinckney White; Massachusetts, J. G. Abbott; Michigan, Hon. C. E. Stuart; Minnesota, Willis A. Gorman; Mississippi, W. H. McArdle; Missouri, General Thomas L. Price; North Carolina, M. Ransom; Ohio, General George W. Morgan; Oregon, R. E. Bell; Pennsylvania, Colonel William C. Patterson; Rhode Island, Thos. Steere; South Carolina, J. P. Campbell; Tennessee, General W. B. Bate; Texas, F. S. Stockdale; Vermont, P. S. Benjamin; Virginia, General J. S. Kemper; West Virginia, John A. Martin; Wisconsin, George Reed; Montana, General Green Clay Smith; Idaho, Thomas W. Betts; New Mexico, Robert B. Mitchell; Arizona, Thomas E. Evershed; Colorado, General William Craig.

Mr. Kiernan (N. Y.) offered the following:

Resolved, That the thanks of this Convention be tendered to Chief-Justice Salmon P. Chase, for the justice, dignity and impartiality with which he presided over the Court of Impeachment on the trial of President Andrew Johnson.

[Applause, and cries "We have already done that."]

The motion was put and carried by acclamation.

General McCook (of Ohio)—I move, sir, that this Convention, having performed its important duty, do now adjourn.

[Voices—"*Sine die.*"]

General McCook—*Sine die.*

The motion was put by the Chair and carried, and, at 3:50 the Convention adjourned *sine die*, amid enthusiastic cheers for Seymour and Blair.

VOTE FOR PRESIDENT IN DEMOCRATIC NATIONAL CONVENTION IN 1868.

TABULAR STATEMENT OF VOTES RECEIVED BY EACH CANDIDATE ON EACH BALLOT.

CANDIDATES.	First	Second	Third	Fourth	Fifth	Sixth	Seventh	Eighth	Ninth	Tenth	Eleventh	Twelfth	Thirteenth	Fourteenth	Fifteenth	Sixteenth	Seventeenth	Eighteenth	Nineteenth	Twentieth	Twenty-first	Twenty-second
Adams, J. Q., Massachusetts					1																	
Blair, Frank P., Missouri	½	10½	4½	2	14½	5	½	½	½	½	½	½	½						13½	13		
Chase, Salmon P., Ohio												½	½				½	½	½		4	
Church, Sanford E., New York	34	33	33	33	33	33	33															
Doolittle, James R., Wisconsin	13	12½	12	12	15	12	12	12	12	12	12½	12½	13	13	12	12	12	12	12	12	12	
English, James E., Connecticut	16	12½	7½	7½	7	6	6	6	6										6	16	19	
Ewing, Thomas L., jr., Kansas		½	1	1																		
Field, Stephen J., California																			13	9	8	
Hancock, W. S., Pennsylvania	33½	40½	45½	43½	46	47	42½	28	34½	34	33	30	48½	56	79½	113½	137½	144½	136½	142½	139½	
Hendricks, Thomas A., Indiana	2½	2	9	11½	19½	30	39½	75	89½	82½	88	89	81	89½	82½	70½	80	87	107½	121	132	
Hoffman, J. T., New York																	3	3				
Johnson, Andrew, Tennessee	65	52	34½	35	24	21	12½	6	5½	6	5½	4½	4½		5½	5½	6	10	5			
Johnson, Reverdy, Maryland	8½	8	11	8	9½																	
McClellan, George B., New Jersey												1									½	
Pierce, Franklin, New Hampshire													1									
Packer, Asa, Pennsylvania	26	26	26	26	27	27	26	26	26½	27½	26	26	26	26					22			
Parker, Joel, New Jersey	13	15½	13	13	13	13	7	7	7	7	7	7	7	7	7	7	3½					
Pendleton, George H., Ohio	105½	106½	119½	118½	122	122½	137½	156½	144	147½	144½	145½	134½	130	129½	107½	70½	56½				
Seymour, Horatio, New York				9																		317½
Seymour, T. H., Connecticut																			6	2		

VOTE IN CONVENTION FOR PRESIDENT.

VOTE IN DETAIL OF THE MOST IMPORTANT BALLOTS IN CONVENTION.

These are the most important ballots that transpired in the Convention, therefore the vote in detail is given.

[Large tabular data showing state-by-state vote counts across multiple ballots — Third day's proceedings (First ballot), Fourth day's proceedings (Eighth ballot), Fourth day's proceedings (Eleventh ballot), and Fifth day's proceedings (Twenty-first ballot) — for candidates including R. Johnson, Blair, Hendricks, Doolittle, A. Johnson, Packer, Parker, English, Church, Hancock, Pendleton, Hoffman, McClellan, Chase, Field, Parker, and others. States listed: Alabama (8), Arkansas (5), California (5), Connecticut (6), Delaware (3), Florida (3), Georgia (9), Illinois (16), Indiana (13), Iowa (8), Kansas (3), Kentucky (11), Louisiana (7), Maine (7), Maryland (7), Massachusetts (12), Michigan (8), Minnesota (4), Mississippi (7), Missouri (11), Nebraska (3), Nevada (3), New Hampshire (5), New Jersey (7), New York (33), North Carolina (9), Ohio (21), Oregon (3), Pennsylvania (26), Rhode Island (4), South Carolina (6), Tennessee (10), Texas (6), Vermont (5), Virginia (10), West Virginia (5), Wisconsin (8). Total 317.]

On the twenty-second ballot Horatio Seymour, of New York, received all the votes (317), and was unanimously nominated.

Speeches of the Nominees.

Their Signification of Acceptance.

Tammany Hall, New York, was crowded from pit to dome on the night of July 10, to witness the ceremony of notification, by the Committee of the Convention, to the candidates of their selection as the standard-bearers of the National Democracy. Speaking of the crowd in attendance, the New York *Tribune* says:

Gov. Seymour and General Blair can have no fault to find with the measure of their reception. It might have been of a more refined quality, and perhaps, then, it would have lost none of its merit for the ears of the Governor and the General.

The Hon. Samuel J. Tilden opened the meeting as follows:

Fellow-Citizens—I congratulate you on this spontaneous assemblage of the Democracy of our State. I did not know of this meeting until a few hours ago. There does not seem to be any organization for carrying it on, and therefore I have been invited to accept the duty of presiding on this occasion. As I came through the hall I saw a vast mass of people, many times more than are here assembled. I feel how strongly the meeting is here, and the meeting outside indicates the spontaneous uprising of the mass of the people to rescue our land. [Cheers.] For my part, I have not entertained any gloomy apprehensions of the result of the contest on which we are about entering. I believe in God, and in the people. [Applause.] I believe that we are destined to preserve and restore the great frame-work of American constitutional Government; that we are to refound that Government on the liberties of the people, and that we are to restore in every part of this continent over which we exercise dominion, local self-government to every integral portion of the American people [Applause.] You know, my fellow-citizens of New York, that I am not very sanguine in the anticipations which I form of political results, but I venture to predict, and I call upon our adversaries to second that prediction, that if the Democracy gather, as I believe they will gather to this contest, they will bear our standard to certain and assured victory. [Applause.] On the whole, I believe we have made the strongest and the best nomination which we could make after much anxious deliberation. I am willing, myself inviting all conservative citizens to join with us in the movement to rescue our country—I am willing to accept the gauge of battle that is before us. I am willing, under the standard-bearers that we have chosen, to go forward and place upon the issues of the day the destinies of the Democratic party, as also the destinies of our country and of mankind. Aye, fellow-citizens, I say of mankind, because if this beautiful and proud specimen of constitutional government that our fathers regarded as an experiment, and that we afterward made to be perfectly assured—if it shall fail now, there is no hope for mankind of any effective participation of the popular masses in their own government. It will not fail, it can not fail, and this contest in which we are now engaged will give us, I verily believe, a political revolution as great, as momentous in its results as that political revolution which brought Thomas Jefferson in the Presidential chair in 1801, and founded the Democratic party that prosperously governed the country for sixty years. [Cheers.] It is our mission to restore that party, to restore its principles in the administration of the Government, to restore a liberal policy to all the systems, and to give to our people everywhere the assurance of complete peace after war is over, the pacification of every part of our broad land, of local self government, of individual rights and individual safety, of the re-establishment of the great guarantees of personal freedom and constitutional rights everywhere upon this continent. Fellow-citizens, I now present to you Gen. Morgan, of Ohio, and also Horatio Seymour.

Gov. Seymour was received most enthusiastically, and it was several minutes before order was sufficiently restored for the Chairman of the Committee, Major-General Geo. W. Morgan, of Ohio, to formally tender the nomination, which he did in these words:

SPEECH OF GENERAL MORGAN.

Gov. Seymour: On behalf of the committee appointed for that purpose, I have the honor to present to you this communication, announcing your unanimous nomination as candidate for the office of President of the United States by the National Democratic Convention; and on behalf, sir, of the Conservative people of the United States I have the honor to represent, I here pledge their united and cordial efforts in securing the relief of the country from the thraldom which now oppresses it, and in placing you, as the chosen Chief Magistrate of the nation in the Executive chair.

Amid great applause, Mr. Seymour stepped forward, and replied as follows:

SPEECH OF GOV. SEYMOUR.

Mr. Chairman and Gentlemen of the Committee: I thank you for the courteous terms in which you have communicated to me the decision of the Democratic National

Convention. Its nomination, by me, was unsought and unexpected. I meant to take part in the great struggle which is now to take place for the restoration of peace, order, and good government to our land. But I have been caught by the great tide that is swelling our party on to victory, and I am unable to resist the pressure. [Applause.] You have also communicated to me the resolutions adopted by that Convention. As its Chairman, I am familiar with its language, and as a member of that Convention, I am a party to its terms. [Applause.] I accord with its views, I stand upon its position in this contest; and I shall strive hereafter, whether in public or private life, to carry them into effect. Our opponents hoped, when this Convention assembled, that there would be discord in its councils. They mistook the great anxiety felt by each of its members that we should do nothing that was not marked out by wisdom and by prudence; they mistook the intense anxiety to do all things aright, for a spirit of doubt, a spirit of discord. But during its lengthened session, during all the excitement of its proceedings, there was uttered no word of unkindness, but there was shown through all its proceedings that spirit of courtesy, patient forbearing, and self-sacrifice that is the sure omen of the great victory which awaits us. [Applause.] Mr. Chairman, in a few days I will reply to your communication, in writing or by letter, in the customary forms. In the mean time, sir, accept for yourself and your colleagues, my best wishes for your future happiness and future welfare.

Gen. Morgan then addressed the nominee for the Vice-Presidency as follows:

GEN. BLAIR—The committee appointed by the Convention have made it my pleasing duty, sir, to announce to you your unanimous nomination as the Democratic candidate for the office of Vice-President of the United States. In tendering to you this nomination, we feel assured that it will not only be hailed by acclamation by your fellow-citizens throughout the United States, but thousands of your gallant comrades on many a well-fought field under your lead will once again rally to the Stars and Stripes in defense of free institutions. [Applause.]

After the applause had subsided, Gen. Blair made reply as follows:

SPEECH OF GEN. FRANK P. BLAIR.

I accept the platform and the resolutions passed by the late Democratic Convention, and I accept their nomination with feelings of the most profound gratitude. [Applause.] And, sir, I thank you for the very kind manner in which you have conveyed to me the decision of the Democratic Convention. I accept the nomination with the feeling that your nomination for the Presidency is one which will carry us to certain victory [Applause], because I believe the nomination is the most appropriate that could be made by the Democratic party. The contest which we wage is for the restoration of constitutional government. [Applause and cheers.] And it is proper that we should make this contest under the lead of one who has given his life to the maintenance of constitutional government. We make this contest for the restoration of those great principles of government which belong to our race, and, my fellow-citizens, it is most appropriate that we should select for our leader, a man, not from military life, but one who has devoted himself to the civil pursuits, one who has given himself to study and the understanding of our Constitution and its maintenance, with all the force of reason and judgment. [Applause.] My fellow-citizens, I have said the contest before us was one for the restoration of our Government. It is also for the restoration of our race. [Prolonged applause, and cheers.] It is to prevent the people of our race from being exiled from their homes. [Hear, hear, and applause.] Exiled from the Government which they created for themselves and for their children, and to prevent them from being driven out into exile, or trodden under foot by an inferior and semi-barbarous race. [Applause.] In this contest we shall have the sympathy of every man who is worthy to belong to the white race. What civilized people on earth would refuse to associate with themselves under all the rights, honors and dignities of their country, such men as Lee and Johnston? [Cries of "No one."] What civilized country on earth would fail to do honor to those who, fighting for an erroneous cause, yet distinguished themselves by a gallantry never surpassed. In that contest in which they were sought to be disfranchised, and to be exiled from their homes; in that contest they proved themselves worthy of themselves. [Applause.] My fellow-citizens, it is not my purpose to make any address, but simply to express my gratitude for the great and distinguished honor which has been conferred on me. And now, from my heart, I reiterate the words that fell from my lips when I began. [Applause.]

LIST OF DELEGATES TO THE DEMOCRATIC NATIONAL CONVENTION, 1868.

Alabama.
DELEGATES AT LARGE.

Reuben Chapman,	Lewis E Parsons,
John A Winston,	James H Clanton.

240   DEMOCRATIC SPEAKER'S HAND-BOOK.

DISTRICT DELEGATES.
1. C C Langdon,   4. Samuel Ruffin,
   R G Scott, Jr.   John J Jolly.
2. J T Holtzclaw,   5. Wm M Lowe,
   W C Oates.   James L Sheffield.
3. W H Barnes,   6. R O Pickett,
   M J Bulger.   Thos J McClellan.

Arkansas.
DELEGATES AT LARGE.
Robert A Howard,   A H Garland,
B D Turner,   E C Boudinot.
DISTRICT DELEGATES.
1. Robert Smith,   3. J S Dunham,
   Jacob Frolich.   R C Davis.
2. John W Wright,
   S A Saunders.

California.
DELEGATE AT LARGE.
Thomas Hayes (deceased).
DISTRICT DELEGATES.
1. R C Page,   3. C Steele,
   A Jacoby,   Chas S Fairfax,
   Joseph Roberts.   W Woodward.
2. John Bigler,
   Richard Heath,
   A H Rose.

Connecticut.
DELEGATES AT LARGE.
Wm W Eaton,   Benjamin Stark,
Tilton E Doolittle,   James H Hoyt.
DISTRICT DELEGATES.
1. Henry A Mitchell,   3. James A Hovey,
   Geo D Hastings.   Marvin H Sanger.
2. John Kendrick,   4. Matthew Buckley,
   Isaac Arnold.   Donald D Warner.

Colorado.
DELEGATES AT LARGE.
Hugh Butler,   Captain Craig,
H B Morse,   T J Campbell,
M Anker,   S Blayton.

Delaware.
James A Bayard,   Thos B Bradford,
Charles Beesten,   James Ponder,
Geo W Cummins,   Curtis W Wright.

District of Columbia.
J D Hoover,   T A Tolson,
Dr. Charles Allen,   Esau Pickerell,
Colonel J G Berret,   B T Swart.

Florida.
F R Cotton,   Thomas Randall,
Wilkinson Call,   S Fairbanks,
J P Sanderson,   Charles Davis,
C E Dyke,   S H Owens,
W D Barnes,   A F Smith,
C H Smith,   A Hewling,
J C McLean,   J B Brown,
H Wright,   E C Love,
James McKay,   R L Campbell,
W H Robinson,   W W Van Ness,
E M L Engle,   J J Williams.

Georgia.
DELEGATES AT LARGE.
A H Chappell,   H S Fitch,
B H Hill,   J B Gordon.
DISTRICT DELEGATES.
1 W T Thompson,   5. A R Wright,
  P C Pendleton.   E J Pottle.
2. A H Hood,   6. Phil R Simmons,
   B G Lockett.   Wm P Price,
3. H Buchanan,   7. J D Waddell,
   J L Mustain.   F Toumlin.
4. W A Reid,
   C Peeples.

Illinois.
DELEGATES AT LARGE.
W J Allen,   W R Morrison,
George W Shutt,   W T Dowdal,
W F Story,   W A Richardson.
DISTRICT DELEGATES.
1. Thomas Hoyne,   8. Dr R B M Wilson,
   W C Gormley.   Charles A Keyes.
2. R S Malony,   9. Henry L Bryent,
   A M Harrington.   Lyman Lacy.
3. William P Malburn, 10. Edw Y Rice,
   B H Truesdale.   D M Woodson.
4. Charles Buford,   11. Samuel K Casey,
   George Edmunds.   Joseph Cooper.
5. W H O'Brien,   12. Timothy Grearye,
   James S Eckles.   W A J Sparks.
6. Charles E Boyer,   13. William H Green,
   J H McConnell.   George W Wall.
7. John Donlon,
   Thomas Brewer.

Indiana.
DELEGATES AT LARGE.
D W Voorhees,   Graham N Fitch,
J E McDonald,   William E Niblack.
DISTRICT DELEGATES.
1. A T Whittlesey,   7. W D Manson,
   W S Turner.   Harris Reynolds.
2. James A Cravens,   8. R P Effinger,
   David Hoffstetter.   J M Dickson.
3. H W Harrington,   9. E Sturgis,
   W T Pate.   Adam Wolf.
4. Lafe Devlin,   10. James R Slack,
   J W Carleton.   S W Sprott.
5. W H Talbott,   11. T J Merrifield,
   D G Vawter.   C H Reeve.
6. Samuel H Buskirk,
   C G Patterson.

Iowa.
DELEGATES AT LARGE.
A C Dodge,   D O Finch,
John H O'Neil,   George H Parker.
DISTRICT DELEGATES.
1. John Rhinehart,   4. Samuel H Fairall,
   Patrick Gibbon.   P H Bousquet.
2. T S Bardwell,   5. J D Test,
   W E Brennan,   J N Udell.
3. William McClintock, 6. H E J Boardman,
   Ray B Griffin.   E B Holbrook.

Kansas.
George W Glick,   Charles W Blair,
Andrew D. Meed,   Isaac Sharp,
Wilson Shannon, jr.   Thomas P Fendon.

Kentucky.
DELEGATES AT LARGE.
R H Stanton,   William Preston,
L A Spalding,   J G Carlyle.
DISTRICT DELEGATES.
1. W B Machen,   6. Lucius Desha,
   J A Flournoy.   F A Boyd.
2. Gano Henry,   7. B F Buckner,
   C B Vance.   J Warren Grigsby.
3. J P Bates,   8. Edward Turner,
   A J Ray.   James B McCreery.
4. E A Graves,   9. George Hamilton,
   C B Mattingly.   A L Martin.
5. T L Jefferson,
   Lyttleton Cooke.

Louisiana.
DELEGATES AT LARGE.
James McCloskey,   Duncan S Cage.
DISTRICT DELEGATES.
1. Durant Daponte,   4. E M Willard,
   Louis St. Martin.   M Ryan.

DELEGATES TO THE DEMOCRATIC NATIONAL CONVENTION.

2. R L Gibson,
   James B Eustis.
3. Scott Duncan,
   D F Kenner.
5. M S Ponham,
   Geo W W Craney.

Maine.
DELEGATES AT LARGE.
Richard D Rice, David R Hastings,
Samuel J Anderson, James C Madigan.
DISTRICT DELEGATES.
1. Ira T Drew,
   Sylv C Blanchard.
2. J A Linscott,
   Moses Biggs.
3. James A Creighton,
   Isaac Reed.
4. Henry Hudson,
   Marcellus Emory.
5. P J Carleton,
   J C Talbot.

Maryland.
DELEGATES AT LARGE.
Richard B Carmichael, Montgomery Blair,
George R Dennis, Charles J McGwin.
DISTRICT DELEGATES.
1. Hiram McCullough,
   Edw Floyd.
2. Stephenson Archer,
   William Byrnes.
3. W Pynkney White,
   George W Benson.
4. Andrew R Syester,
   Outerbridge Horsey.
5. John D Bowling,
   Geo Fred Maddox.

Massachusetts.
DELEGATES AT LARGE.
Josiah G Abbott, Reuben Noble,
Josiah Bardwell, G W Gill.
DISTRICT DELEGATES.
1. Edward Merrill,
   N Hathaway.
2. S B Thaxter,
   Ed Every.
3. James M Keith,
   Michael Doherty.
4. Peter Harvey,
   Thos Whittemore.
5. Charles G Clark,
   A O Moore.
6. D W Lawrence,
   George Johnson.
7. W W Warren,
   Gardner Prouty.
8. George L Chesbro,
   James E Estabrook.
9. Frank Pratt,
   L B Jaquith.
10. A W Springfield,
    John R Briggs.

Michigan.
DELEGATES AT LARGE.
John Moore, Robert McClelland,
Byron G Stout, Charles E Stewart.
DISTRICT DELEGATES.
1. Wm A Moore,
   Mich A Patterson.
   Fred V Smith,
   Walter G Beckwith.
3. John L Butterfield,
   A M Hart.
4. John F Godfrey,
   John C Blanchard.
5. E B Winans,
   Seymour Brownell.
6. S M Axford,
   Clarence E Eddie.

Minnesota.
DELEGATES AT LARGE.
A G Chatfield, W A Gorman,
James J Green, Winthrop Young.
DISTRICT DELEGATES.
1. E A McMahon,
   George D Snow.
2. Isaac Staples,
   Thomas N Sheehey.

Mississippi.
DELEGATES AT LARGE.
W S Featherston, W T Martin,
E C Walthall, E M Yerger.
DISTRICT DELEGATES.
1. Orlando Davis,
   F B Irby.
2. R M Brown,
   S A Jonas.
3. G P M Turner,
   H L Jarnagin.
4. T A Marshall,
   E Barksdale,
5. J S Holt,
   T R Stockdale.

Missouri.
DELEGATES AT LARGE.
James O Broadhead, Thomas L Price,
A J Garesche, Bernard Schwartz.
DISTRICT DELEGATES.
1. Erastus Wells,
   Stillson Hutchins.
2. Carl Deanger,
   David Murphy.
3. Thomas H Bird,
   J W Everson.
4. O S Fahnestock,
   Nathan Bray.
5. Adam E Smith,
   Van Pelt.
6. Samuel L Sawyer,
   John B Dale.
7. Wm A Ridenbaugh,
   Charles A Mansur,
8. John M Glover,
   Thomas B Reed.
9. W H D Hunter,
   A T Reed.

Nebraska.
G L Miller, J Sterling Morton,
G N Crawford, John Black,
Chas F Porter, Peter Smith.

New Hampshire.
DISTRICT DELEGATES.
1. Anson S Marshall,
   Albert R Hatch.
2. George H Pierce,
   Isaac Adams.
3. James M Campbell,
   John Rector.
4. Horatio Cylony,
   H W Parker.
5. John G Sinclair,
   E D Rand.

New Jersey.
DELEGATES AT LARGE.
Jacob R Wortendyke, Richard F Stevens,
Thomas McKeen, F D Lathrop.
DISTRICT DELEGATES.
1. Samuel Still,
   Isaac M Smalley.
2. Henry S Little,
   C D Hendrickson.
3. Ryneas H Vechtes,
   Miles Ross.
4. David Dodd,
   Thomas Kays,
5. John R Mullaney,
   George Peters.

New York.
DELEGATES AT LARGE.
Horatio Seymour, Samuel J Tilden,
Sanford E Church, Henry C Murphy.
DISTRICT DELEGATES.
1. Erastus Brooks,
   John Armstrong.
2. James B Craig,
   William Marshall.
3. Alex McCue,
   James Murphy.
4. Joseph Dowling,
   Michael Norton.
5. Wm M Tweed,
   John Morrissey.
6. Emanuel B Hart,
   Oswall Ottendorffer.
7. Chas G Cornell,
   Chas E Loew.
8. Augustus Schell,
   A Oakey Hall.
9. Albert Cardozo,
   Edw Jones.
10. Colin Talmie,
    Robert Cochran.
11. Jas D Decker,
    Enoch Carter.
12. Henry A. Tilden,
    Chas Wheaton.
13. Jacob Hardenbergh,
    Geo Beach.
14. Wm Cassidy,
    Chas Goodyear.
15. Moses Warren,
    Emerson E Davis.
16. Timothy Hoyle,
    Halsey R. Wing.
17. Samuel B. Gordon,
    Darius W Lawrence.
18. Cornelius A Russell,
    Col S Sammons.
19. Luther J. Burdett,
    John F Hubbard, jr.
20. Allen C Beach,
    Lorenzo Caryl.
21. Francis Kiernan,
    George H Sandford.
22. Wm F Allen,
    Chas Stebbins, jr.
23. Jas P Haskins,
    John A Green, jr.
24. Elmore P Ross,
    Chas L Lyon.
25. Joseph L Lewis,
    Lester B Faulkner.
26. Hiram A. Beebe,
    Jeremiah McGuire.
27. M B Champlain,
    Daniel C Howell.
28. Geo W Miller,
    Henry J Sickles.

29. Sherburn B Piper, 31. Chas H Lee,
Henry A Richmond. Jonas Button.
30. Joseph Warren,
Wm Williams.

Nevada.
W G Monroe, L P Drexler,
George G Berry, John E Doyle,
D E Buell, W M Seawell.

North Carolina.
DELEGATES AT LARGE.
W N H Smith, William A Wright,
W L Cox, John F Hoke.
DISTRICT DELEGATES.
1. M W Ransom, 4. W J Green,
   D M Carter, R B Haywood,
   P H Winston, 5. Bend Brown,
   R H Smith. J M Leach.
2. M E Manly, 6. Z B Vance,
   George Howard. J M Long.
3. Robert Strange, 7. Thomas L Clingman.
   N A McLean.

Ohio.
DELEGATES AT LARGE.
George W McCook, John G Thompson,
Washington McLean, W W Armstrong.
DISTRICT DELEGATES.
1. Joseph C Butler, 11. John Hamilton,
   J C Collins. J W Collins.
2. Theodore Cook, 12. E B Olds,
   H C Lord. Wayne Griswold.
3. Granville Stokes, 13. Frank H. Hurd,
   Wm G Gilmore. William Veach.
4. John E Cummings, 14. T J Kenny,
   Dr J E Matchett. Neal Power.
5. R R McKee, 15. Jere Williams,
   F C LeBlond. Wylie S Oldham.
6. David Tarbill, 16. Wm Lawrence,
   J M Trimble. J C Boyles.
7. Jacob Rheinhard, 17. James B Estep,
   John H. Blose. James Quinn.
8. H T Van Fleet, 18. Morrison Foster,
   W M Randall. H H Dodge.
9. Thomas Beer, 19. R O Bate,
   John A Williams. D C Coleman.
10. John Maidlom,
    J G Haley.

Oregon.
E L Bristow, W W Page,
N M Bell, Judge P Bruin,
O Joynt, J C Avery.

Pennsylvania.
DELEGATES AT LARGE.
Isaac E Hiester, George W Woodward,
Asa Packer, William Bigler.
DISTRICT DELEGATES.
1. William McMullen, 10. Francis W Hughes,
   W C Cassidy. David S Hammond.
2. William Reilly, 11. E W Hamlin,
   Wm C Patterson. Henry S Mott.
3. H R Linderman, 12. Jasper B Star,
   John E Faunce. Ralph P Little.
4. Jer. McKibben, 13. Michael Meylert,
   John McDidden. David Lowenburg.
5. Charles M Hurley, 14. David M Crawford,
   H P Ross. William H Miller.
6. B M Boyer, 15. John A. Magee,
   John D Stiles. John Gibson.
7. John H. Brinton, 16. George W Brewer,
   Jackson Larkins. John R. Donahue.
8. Heister Clymer, 17. James Burns,
   Jer Hagenman. Owen Clark.
9. William Patton, 18. Geo A Auchenbach,
   A J Steinman. William Brindle.

19. Byron D Hamlin, 22. John A Strain,
    William L Scott. John B Guthrie.
20. William L Corbett, 23. R H Kerr,
    Gaylord Church. John T Bard.
21. John L Dawson, 24. A A Purman,
    James B Sansom. David S Morris.

Rhode Island.
Charles S Bradley, Thomas Steere,
Alfred Anthony, Edward B Brunsen,
Lyman Pierce, William H Allen,
Edward Newton, Amasa Sprague.

South Carolina.
Appointed by the April Convention.
DELEGATES AT LARGE.
B F Perry, J A Inglis,
James Chesnut, A P Aldrich.
DISTRICT DELEGATES.
1. W S Mullins, 3. J S Preston,
   J B Kershaw. W B Stanley.
2. C Macy, 4. A Burt,
   W L Bonham. W D Simpson.
Appointed by the June Convention.
DELEGATES AT LARGE.
Wade Hampton, C M Furman,
S B Campbell, J P Carroll.
DISTRICT DELEGATES.
1. A L Manning, 3. M W Gary,
   R Dozier. A D Frederick.
2. C H Simonton, 4. To be appointed.
   John Huuckel.

Tennessee.
DELEGATES AT LARGE.
T A R Nelson, A O P Nicholson,
N B Forrest, Edmund Cooper.
DISTRICT DELEGATES.
1. James White, 5. W B Bate,
   W C Kyle. I D Walker,
2. John Williams, 6. John F House,
   R M Edwards. Dorsay B Thomas.
3. P H Marbry, 7. Wm Conner,
   W J Ramage. W T Caldwell.
4. H C McLaughlin, 8. A W Campbell,
   Joseph H Thompson. J W Leftwich.

Texas.
DELEGATES AT LARGE.
Horace Boughton, Ashbel Smith,
Stephen Powers, Gustavus Schleicher.
DISTRICT DELEGATES.
1. James M Burroughs, 3. J D Giddings,
   Daniel A Veitch. E J Gurley.
2. H R Runnels, 4. G W Smith,
   George W Wright. George Ball.

Vermont.
DELEGATES AT LARGE.
H B Smith, Henry Keyes,
Isaac McDaniels, P S Benjamin.
DISTRICT DELEGATES.
1. E R Wright, 3. Waldo Brigham,
   Geo H Simmons. J J Deavitt.
2. Geo H Weeks,
   C N Davenport.

Virginia.
DELEGATES AT LARGE.
T S Bocock, J B Baldwin,
F McMullen, J M Kemper,
Geo. Blow, jr. T S Flournoy.
DISTRICT DELEGATES.
1. B B Douglass, 3. James Barbour,
   H S Neal. Rob't Ould.
2. John Goode, 4. Rob't Ridgeway,
   John R Kilby. Thos F Goode.

5. R H Glass,   7. John R Tucker,
   Wm Martin.   Ro Y Conrad.
6. J C Southall,   8. Joseph Kent,
   Samuel W Coffman.   Wm B Aston.

West Virginia.
DELEGATES AT LARGE.
John Hall,   Henry S Walker.
John W Kennedy,
DISTRICT DELEGATES.
1. D D Johnson,   3. C A Sperry,
   J N Camden.   B H Smith.
2. H G Davis,
   J A P Martin.

Wisconsin.
DELEGATES AT LARGE.
H L Palmer,   Nelson Dewey,
S Clark,   Gabriel Bouck.
DISTRICT DELEGATES.
1. Jas A Mallory,   4. F O Thorp,
   John Mather.   F W Horn.
2. E B Dean, jr.,   5. Geo Reid,
   S T Thorn.   S A Pease.
3. Jas G Knight,   6. Thos B Tyler,
   Chas G Rodolph.   Allen Dawson.

Soldiers' and Sailors' Convention.

The National Convention of Soldiers and Sailors met at New York, on the 4th of July, 1868, the same day of the Convention of the National Democracy.

At half past 11 the meeting was called to order by General McQuade, Chairman of the National Executive Committee, who nominated Major-General John A. McClernand, of Illinois.

General McClernand, of Illinois, was unanimously elected.

General McClernand, upon taking the chair, expressed his thanks in graceful terms.

General McQuade proposed the following list of Secretaries: General John R. Slack, of Maryland; General Hugh Cameron, of Kansas; Colonel O'Beirne, of Washington; Colonel Lynch, of New York; Colonel G. Stoddard, of Connecticut; Captain Thomas Brigham, of Maine; Captain O. G. Chase, of West Virginia; and private J. Haldreth, of Illinois.

General Campbell, of Ohio, desired to offer a preamble and resolution. It had been deemed important by that committee that there should be harmonious action between this Convention and the National Democratic Association. There had been an effort to make this Convention appear in a false position. There had been some talk of its being intended for the purpose of dictation, and some foolish speeches of its being a mere side-show. To put the Convention right in this respect, he offered a preamble and resolution which express the full harmony of the Convention with the purposes and objects of the National Democratic Convention.

The resolution was then temporarily withdrawn by General Campbell; and, upon motion of General McQuade, the respective delegates were requested to name members for each of the regular standing committees.

A call of the States was thereupon made, and committees then retired.

General Thomas Ewing, jr., of Kansas, being loudly called for, made his appearance on the platform, and was received with cheers. He spoke as follows:

Mr. President and gentlemen of the Convention: I heartily thank you for the honor of being called upon to address this vast assemblage of soldiers and sailors—the largest ever gathered on the continent since the grand review in Washington, at the close of the war, of the victorious armies of the Potomac, of the Tennessee, and of Georgia. Of the comrades who separated then, and went each to his home and civic occupation, almost every regiment has here its representative. Why have we, soldiers and sailors, who are proud of our service for the Union, assembled here in delegate convention to plan the overthrow of that political party which administered the Government through the war, and the defeat of the Presidency of him who was erst the leader of the Union armies? [Applause.] With your indulgence, I will endeavor briefly to give the reasons for our meeting, and our intended action. [Cries of "Go on."]

On the 4th of July, three years ago, the war for the suppression of the rebellion had wholly ended. General Lee had surrendered to General Grant the Army of Northern Virginia, and its officers and men were plowing the fields of the Old Dominion, drenched with the blood and scorched with the fires of four years of devastating war. Joe Johnston had surrendered to Sherman [applause] the daring and stubborn troops which our Western army had driven inch by inch from Belmont to Raleigh; and Shelby's frontier command was scattered over the hemisphere from Montana to Brazil. [Laughter.] There was not in arms a Confederate soldier, mounted or on foot; not a dockyard, fort or arsenal, in which there was a rebel ship, cannon or musket; not a rood of land on earth, or a foot of deck on sea, over which the Confederate banner waved. The last rebel privateers were being dragged for condemnation from the Indian Ocean and the North Pacific; and the haughtiest leaders of the rebellion were wandering outcasts over the earth, or seeking pardon of a President who was a noble type at once of the loyal Southerner they had hated, and the laboring white man they had despised. [Applause.] Never was there a rebellion more utterly overthrown, or a cause more hopelessly lost.

The people of the Southern States, with wonderful promptness, quiet and unanimity, submitted to the result. You all know it was commonly predicted and believed, North and South, that when the great armies of the Confederacy were conquered, dispersing, they would fill the land with guerrillas, and wage a Bendean warfare more destructive and irrepressible than the regular war out of which it grew. But this prediction was not in the smallest degree verified. Within sixty days after the last great battle of the war, the Federal marshals and tax-gatherers executed their processes unarmed and unattended throughout the Southern States, in the jungles lately swarming with guerrillas and over fields lately shaken with the roar of rebel artillery. The whole people of the South *bowed to the authority of the nation*, with hearts in which, as they were human, there were yet doubtless revenges and sorrows, humiliations and bereavements, and undying attachments to the cause they had dearly loved and bravely maintained, but which yielded implicitly all that the people, the President, or the war party had ever told them were the purposes of the war. And by the constitutional conventions and Legislatures, chosen by the electors of the Southern States the year the rebellion ended, their several constitutions and their State laws were amended, abolishing slavery and the harsh codes founded on it, abandoning the doctrine of secession, repudiating the rebel debt, recognizing the National debt, and, in short, giving every guarantee which men could give, that in a spirit of concord they recognized and accepted, as accomplished, each avowed object of the war.

Now the Republican party was bound in loyalty, honor, and good conscience to accept this submission, and at once restore the Union by admitting the Southern States to representation, so far as they presented Senators and Representatives personally qualified. [Applause.] It was bound to do it, out of obedience to the Constitution, in the sacred name of which the war was waged, and which, while allowing each House to judge of the qualifications of its own members, prohibits the exclusion from representation of any State *as a State*. And it was bound to do it, because the war was avowedly waged for the sole purpose of effecting the unconditional restoration of the Union, immediately upon the unconditional submission of the Southern people, through amendments of their constitutions and laws, to the National authority. Said Sherman to the South, in his Atlanta letter: "We don't want your negroes or your horses, your houses or your lands, or anything you have; we only want, and will have, a just obedience to the Constitution and laws of the United States." [Applause.] And in that declaration he expressed the sole purpose of the war as declared by the Government, and understood by the army and navy and people of the Union.

The Republican party in its National Convention in 1864—just after Horace Greeley had tried to effect a dishonorable peace through George N. Sanders and Beverly Tucker (hisses and laughter)—declared that the war was, and should be waged only, to force "an unconditional surrender of hostility by the rebels, and a return to their just allegiance to the Constitution and laws of the United States." And from the beginning to the close of the war, there stood, and still stands, on our statute book, a law declaring that the war should be waged "in no spirit of oppression, but solely to restore the Union with all the dignity, equality, and rights of the several States unimpaired." [Applause.] That law was the pledge of the Republican party made in 1861, and reiterated in National Convention in 1864, that the tremendous powers confided to it by the people, without regard to party, for the vindication of the National authority, should never be used for party or sectional dominion. And on the faith of that pledge were given every dollar of money and every drop of blood spent in the war. [Applause.]

But the Republican party had not the wisdom or patriotism to accept this submission of the Southern people, and promptly restore the Union. It recollected that before the war it was a minority party, and came into power in 1861 through a division of the Democratic party by much less than half the popular vote. Yet, with the prestige and moral power resulting from a successful prosecution of the war, and a prompt and cordial restoration of the Union, it could have retained power until this generation of voters had passed away or had forgotten the anti-war follies of the Democratic party. But it took counsel of its fears, doubted its own destiny, forgot the inextinguishable love in the hearts of the Northern people for the Constitution and the Union, and therefore refused to take what the war was alone waged to get—a prompt and cordial pacification and reunion under the Constitution. It did this in the vain hope of controlling the Southern States by making voters of the negroes, and proscribing all the intelligent white men whom Congress and the Freedmen's Bureau could not bribe, coax, or kick, or cuff into Republicanism. But while destroying the ten Southern States, and building in their stead ten rotten boroughs, to be represented in Congress in the interests of the Northern Radicals by white adventurers and plantation negroes, the party is losing its strong hold on the Northern States, and, like the dog in the fable, drops the substance to snatch at the shadow. [Laughter and applause.]

The first step toward postponing reunion until the Southern States could be subjugated by the Radical party, was the offer, in 1866, of the Constitutional amendment. It contained declarations of the results of the war, which the Southern States had already inserted in their constitutions and codes, under the advice of President Johnson, and to which they freely assented, and an alternative of negro suffrage or reduction of representation, and also important additions to the power of the Federal Government, to which they would have assented reluctantly for the sake of reunion. But, inseparably coupled with these, and making with them one proposition, which had to be accepted or rejected as a whole, was the clause of disfranchisement, which they could not accept without dishonor. It disqualified from holding any office, petty or exalted, *State or Federal*, in effect, every man who was of age when the war broke out and was fit to hold any office. So sweeping was the proposed proscription, that, after it was adopted into the reconstruction acts, Generals Meade, Schofield and Canby successively reported that it was impossible to administer the governments of the Southern States while enforcing it, because, in many communities, there was really not a man fit to hold any office who was not disqualified by it. The Southern people did as the Radical leaders wished and knew they would—rejected the amendment. They acted like men in doing so. [Applause.]

Let us ask ourselves, gentlemen, whether, if the North had rebelled and been conquered, and the South had offered us reunion on condition that we should ourselves vote to disfranchise and degrade every Northern man who could read and write and cypher to the rule of three, as punishment for the rebellion in which all had participated, and to commit the Government and destinies of our States to the hands of only the most ignorant of our people, or to the campfollowers of the conquering army, we would have voted for our own disgrace and disfranchisement ? [Voices, "No, no."] No people who are fit to be free would thus, with their own hands, put on their own necks the yoke of political slavery. [Great applause.] And so far from the rejection of that clause and the proposed amendment of the Constitution, with which it was inseparably connected, being a just cause of complaint against the Southern people, they would have merited the scorn and contempt of all high-minded men had they accepted it.

But the amendment served its purpose in the campaign of 1866. It was, to the careless or superficial observer, an effort in good faith, by the Radical party, to effect reunion. The Southern Legislatures, unanimously and promptly, but respectfully, declared that they could not accept it, and were therefore violently denounced by the Radical press and orators, as still defiant and rebellious. Just then, the most mischievous men of both parties in New Orleans contrived to bring on a bloody riot; and the Radicals rode the tempest it created, and swept the North.

Since then, with three-fourths of both Houses of Congress on their side, and animated by a thorough contempt of the Constitution, the Radical party has been omnipotent. It has protracted disunion nearly as long as the rebels did, and done more to destroy our form of Government than all the parties that ever controlled its destinies.

On the 8th of July, 1863, in a debate in the House of Representatives, Old Thad. Stevens [hisses] bluntly and boldly announced the doctrine that the Southern States were not States of the Union, and that Congress could legislate over them as over conquered territory. If this doctrine be true, it is because the acts of secession were constitutional, and in legal effect took the States out of the Union—that is, that under the Constitution, the States had a right to secede, and therefore the United States had no right to make war on them for seceding. This rebel doctrine, when thus announced by Stevens, was violently assailed by Owen Lovejoy, and other fierce Radicals of the House, and repudiated in the name of the war party.

In the year following, in the National Union Convention at Baltimore, Stevens again proclaimed this doctrine, declaring that Tennessee was but a subject province, and Andrew Johnson an alien enemy. But the Convention contemptuously repudiated his theory, and gave emphasis to its declaration by nominating Mr. Johnson for Vice-President, and indorsing Mr. Lincoln's reconstruction policy. All this, however, was while the war was going on, and while soldiers were being called for to fight in the holy cause of the Constitution and the Union, and not for conquest. [Applause.] But when the rebellion ended, and the elections of 1866 gave the Radicals a new lease of power, this infamous dogma, which, if true, makes the war for secession constitutional and just, and the war for the Union a wicked and unprovoked conquest—a doctrine which, three years before, had been, like the hateful Richard—

"Sent before its time
Into this breathing world, scarce half made up,
And that so lamely and unfashionable,
That dogs barked at it as it halted by them,"

was now adopted by the Republican party as the fundamental theory of reconstruction and the shibboleth of loyalty.

Having fully adopted this rebel theory that the Southern States were out of the Union, and unsheltered by the broad ægis of the Constitution, Congress declared invalid the Governments chosen by the electors of these States under the advice of Presidents Lincoln and Johnson, in conformity with State constitutions and laws, and established over them military dictatorships through which to inaugurate the rule of the negroes and their Northern allies. But here a new rent in their programme was discovered, requiring to be patched by a newly invented dogma. The Calhoun-Stevens theory of the validity of secession was good as far as it stretched; but, like a shelter tent, was neither broad nor long enough. It took the States out, and made them conquered Provinces, but did not increase the power of Congress, nor deprive the inhabitants of the conquered territory of those guarantees of life, liberty and property which the Constitution extends *to citizens and aliens alike* on every foot of ground within the jurisdiction of the United States—the right of exemption from punishment by *ex post facto* laws; the liberty of speech and of the press; the right to keep and bear arms; the right to be free from unreasonable searches and seizures, and from deprivation of life, liberty or property, without due process of law; the right of trial by jury; and above all, the privilege of the writ of *habeas corpus*—that shield of liberty in possession of which the people of a monarchy are free, and without which a Republic is a despotism. [Great applause.]

These constitutional guarantees were in the way of coercive reconstruction; and Congress was forbidden, in peace, to touch any one of them. Unless these ancient and sacred liberties could be destroyed, vigorous military despotisms could not be established, and without such despotisms, Radical reconstruction was impossible. While these guarantees remained in the Constitution, and were obeyed, the whole governing talent of the South could not be disfranchised by a sweeping *ex post facto* law; Governors of States duly chosen by the electors in accordance with State Constitutions and laws could not be removed by district commanders as impediments to reconstruction; State Legislatures could not be prorogued at the point of the bayonet; State treasuries could not be robbed, and widow and orphan creditors defrauded of their dividends to pay plantation negroes eight dollars a day for making constitutions. [Applause.]

New codes of laws, framed by Solons and moralists like Dan. Sickles (hisses), could not be proclaimed and enforced over the Carolinas; a judge, conducting a murder trial, could not be pushed from the bench, and the trial carried on to conviction, sentence, and execution, by a colonel in uniform; American citizens, of one of the original thirteen States, charged with no crime, could not be arrested by scores, on *lettres de cachet*, signed by a post adjutant, immured in loathesome dungeons, and tortured to the point of death with the boot and sweat-box, to make them swear to what a military commander *suspected* they knew touching the murder of some wretch like Ashburn (applause); and military commissions, those courts organized to convict, at whose doors no man can lay a charge of uncertainty as to the law, or doubt or delay, or undue clemency in its execution, which adopt the efficient rule that it is better that ninety-nine innocent men should be punished, than one guilty man escape, could not inspire respect for the Radical party and its measures by being prepared at a moment's warning to try any citizen for any act which, in the opinion of the officer convening the court, was a "crime against reconstruction," and to sentence him for months, or years, or life, to the dungeon or the Dry Tortugas, beyond the reach of Executive pardon or reprieve.

It was indispensable, therefore, to get rid of these constitutional provisions, which are at once guarantees of the liberties of the people, and prohibition of power to Congress. To avoid an avowal of a purpose to trample on the Constitution the party, with decent hypocrisy, claimed a new derivation of Congressional power. They said that a formidable rebellion was never contemplated by the framers of the Constitution, and no powers were conferred in anticipation of such an emergency. Congress, therefore, was compelled, in the matter of reconstruction, to act *outside of the Constitution*.

The framers of the Constitution were the sons and grandsons of the Puritans and the Cavaliers, who kept England smoking with civil wars for half a century [applause]; and who knew, by personal experience, how despotic was power when inflamed by the passions of domestic war—whether that power were the legitimate Sovereign, the Pretender, or Parliament. And with recollections of this recent English history, and tradition of family persecutions, fresh in their minds—anticipating that the bold spirits of their sons would be transmitted to their children, and break out in occasional revolts against the National authority—the framers of the Constitution not only withheld from Congress the power of inflicting, in peace, punishments at will for political offences, but also inserted those guarantees of personal liberty *ex industria*, as express prohibitions, in order to prevent a Congress driving the people to renewed war, or to flight by measures of revenge such as sent their forefathers from England to our shores. [Great applause.]

As to Congress deriving power in any contingency outside of the Constitution, it is enough to say that Congress gets all its powers from the Constitution, and outside of it has no powers, and *is no Congress* [applause]; and that all its acts not authorized by the Constitution are mere usurpations, whether against express prohibitions or not. If you present this argument to Radicals, they will reply that the Constitution, in not giving Congress such authority, is therein defective, and Congress needs, and must exercise it. A French philosopher once propounded to Professor Faraday a new theory of the transmission of light, which the English philosopher heard patiently, and then objected to it; that the theory was inconsistent with certain established facts of natural science. "So much *ze* worse for *ze facts,"* was the ready answer of the confident Frenchman. So, if you prove the reconstruction plan unconstitutional, the Radicals, in effect, answer, "So much the worse for the *Constitution.* [Great applause.]

Thus, to secure a reconstruction giving the Radicals of the North absolute control of the ten States of the South, not only were the State governments abolished and military despotisms built on their ruins, but every revered guarantee of life, liberty and property, which the Southern people and ourselves inherited from a free ancestry, and which our forefathers and their forefathers placed in the Constitution to be beyond the reach of the rude hand of faction, was boldly destroyed. No civilized people on this earth are as wholly without legal protection from the capricious oppression of their rulers as the Southern people under these military despotisms. It is amazing how passively the people, North and South, have borne this gross, dangerous, insolent usurpation. But it has been quietly submitted to because of the belief—now, thank God! almost certainty—that the Northern people will, in November, seize this Radical party and its half executed usurpations, and dash them to pieces (prolonged cheering); and because many of the military commanders have tempered the harsh rule they were sent to inflict out of that love for our ancient liberties which is born in every true American, and which so shone through the administration of at least one of those commanders as to cover with new and fadeless glory the twice illustrious name of Hancock. (Tumultuous cheering and waving of hats.)

Gentlemen, I do not understand how any white American, proud of our race and of our free systems of government, can behold, without mingled disgust and indignation, the methods and results of Congressional reconstruction, and the pretenses by which it is sustained. It is claimed to be in the interests of *peace*—while fomenting deadly strife and rancor between the two races, arraying them into conflicting parties, subjecting the superior to the inferior, and then leaving them to struggle for dominion! In the interest of *liberty* and *progress*—while tearing down ten free, enlightened States, four of the old thirteen that founded the Republic, and establishing in their stead ten despotisms, in which the intelligent and cultivated white man is made subject to the ignorant and brutal negro—despotisms mitigated only by the fact that the negroes are but the *ostensible* rulers of the Southern whites, while the Northern Radicals are the *real* ones—that the negro acts only the part of the automaton chess-player, while the Northern Radical party is the unseen intellect which directs the senseless hand that fingers the pawns. It is claimed to be in the interests of *National prosperity*—while wasting the wealth and paralyzing the industries of the South on the one hand, and doubling the burdens of the Northern tax-payers, and destroying the eager markets for their manufactures and breadstuffs on the other.

What a spectacle for gods and men does not this reconstruction present! See the black laborers of the South, fed in idleness out of money wrung from the toil of Northern white men [applause], filled with ambition to rule the whites, and to grow rich by confiscations, and becoming each year more utterly and irreclaimably idle and thriftless. The splendid sugar, cotton and rice plantations, at once the evidence and the product of a century of civilization, overgrown with weeds; idle machinery rusting in the sugar-houses; the floods of the Mississippi sweeping over neglected levees and abandoned plantations, and the boorish negro field-hands sitting in conventions! Behold Virginia, the Niobe of States, the mother of Presidents and illustrious statesmen—her at whose call our great Republic was formed—her by whose free gift the Republic acquired the territory of the six great States of the North-west! See the civil government founded by her Washington [applause] Madison [applause], Jefferson [applause], Lee [applause], the foremost statesmen of their day on the earth, destroyed, supplanted by a military despotism, and that, in turn, about to be supplanted by a civil government framed by infamous whites like Hunnicutt, and a rabble of half-civilized negroes [hisses]. If this be prosperity, progress and liberty, God send us misfortune, reaction and despotism forever! [Applause.]

The radicals endeavor to smooth the

hideous visage of this reconstruction by asserting that it is indispensable to prevent the Democracy getting power and repudiating the National debt. In other words, to prevent repudiation, some device must be arranged by which a majority of the legal electors of ten States shall not be permitted to rule them. If that necessity really exists, the dire event can not be long postponed by devising, in the interest of the National creditors, a scheme of reconstruction which violates the Constitution and the fundamental theory of our Government; breaks pledges of infinitely more sacred obligation than the money debt; cripples every industry of the land, and while reducing one-half every man's ability to pay taxes, doubles his share of the public burden—the essential condition of which scheme is to the perpetuation of the rule of a party which now represents not one-third of the white people of the nation. But thank God, that necessity does not exist! The credit of the Republic, as the Union of the States, rests secure—*secure in the hearts of the people.* [Applause.] A vast majority of all parties will preserve and defend it, as they did the Union. But, if the National credit could be shaken, it would be by the public creditors flocking into one party, and under the panoply of the National honor, scheming to perpetuate the power of that party at the cost of the established Constitutions and liberties of the State and the nation. [Great applause, and cries of "That's so."]

To accomplish this scheme of reconstruction, the Constitution is not only abrogated so far as the Southern States are concerned, but the form of our Government is being destroyed by the absorption by Congress of the chief powers of the National Executive. Congress has assumed to take from the President the control of the army, which the Constitution gives him, and to commit that part of it employed in the South to General Grant and five district commanders [hisses] independent of the orders of the President. By this bold assumption of power, it has converted many high officers in the regular army to Radicalism, and made them zealous instruments of its usurpations.

It has usurped the pardoning power, which the Constitution gives solely to the President, and by sweeping bills of pains and penalties, proscribed the intelligent white men of the South, notwithstanding the pardons of the President. And it now shamelessly avows that it will give *Congressional pardon* only to those who eat the leek of Radicalism. [Hisses.] All such are *loyal*, though, like Governor Brown, of Georgia, they drove and dragged their people into rebellion, and, coward like, seized our arsenals and navy-yards while yet wearing the mask of loyalty; while men like George W. Jones, of Tennessee, who stood by the Union from the first, but who opposed negro suffrage and white disfranchisement, are stigmatized as "*heart malignants,*" deserving only proscription at the hands of the Sumners, and Kellys, and Butlers, of Congress—[Great hisses. Cries, "who stole the spoons?" "Dutch Gap."]

"Those pseudo privy-counselors of God,
Who write down judgments with a pen hard-nibbed,"

It took, too, from the President, the power of removal, thus fomenting insubordination in the civil service as it had done in the military—prohibiting even the removal of his own Cabinet officers, the adjutants through whom he gives orders and receives reports.

And it crowned its usurpations by an impeachment founded on a statute it had passed enacting the glaring and flagitious lie that it is a high crime for the President to discharge the duties of removal imposed on him by the Constitution, as interpreted by the uniform usage of Government from the administration of Washington down [applause]; or even to so far attempt to exercise it, as to bring the question of his Constitutional power of removal to decision by the Supreme Court—that high arbiter fixed by the Constitution to settle every conflict over boundaries of power between the States and the United States, or between departments of the General Government. And after having impeached him, and while giving him a lynch-law trial, the party, with a ferocity unparalleled even in the violent controversies of the day, brought its almost irresistible power to bear through its leading men, its press, and its conventions, to force Republican Senators to commit moral perjury by an insincere verdict. So foul an act was never before attempted by a party in this nation.

Had Andrew Johnson consulted his own interests, and become the instrument of a lawless faction, these essential executive powers would not have been disturbed, nor he arraigned as a criminal at the bar of the Senate. But, to his eternal renown [applause], he stood by the Constitution when it was assailed by his party, as boldly and grandly as he had stood by the Union when the storm of war burst over and around it:

"Unshaken, unseduced, unterrified,
His loyalty he kept, his love, his zeal;
Nor number nor example with him wrought,
To swerve from truth or change his constant mind."

[Three cheers for Andrew Johnson. Three cheers for President Johnson. Tumultuous cheering.]

Gentlemen, in any Government but ours, usurpation so flagrant and fundamental would result in revolution; in ours they can be overthrown by the people at the ballot-box. The appeal to the people this fall will decide whether the Radicals shall retain or surrender the power they have thus used, and are using, for the destruction of the Union and of our form of National Government.

If we could so take our appeal as to present to the people the living issues between the parties, free from the rubbish of past issues, who could doubt the result? If the Democracy could give us a candidate who would unite as thoroughly the opponents of Radical rule as Grant unites its supporters, that candidate would carry nine-tenths of the electoral college. [Applause.] The strength of the Radicals is not in their cause, but in the divisions of their adversaries.

The war was a success—not a failure. [Applause.] It therefore settled the disputed and doubtful question of secession against the right to secede. It settled, too, the subject of slavery. These, however, were unsettled questions in 1864, and were thought to be involved in the political contest of that year. Now, the passions of war and of that political controversy are not as dead as those issues in which they played their part. From them came all the hopes of the Radicals, and all the fears of the friends of the Constitution and the Union. Rousing these slumbering passions of the war, and led on by one of its foremost Generals, the Radicals hope to fight over again the political battle of 1864. Shall they do it? ["No, no."] Ah, gentlemen, I wish this Convention could decide that question—but it is for the Democratic Convention to decide. By its choice of leader it will determine the battle-ground, and decide whether the Democracy shall triumph on living issues or be routed on dead ones [applause]; whether the Radicals shall be arraigned and tried for what they are doing, or the Democracy for what they did or failed to do four years ago.

Of a million and a half of present voters who served in the Union army or navy, this Convention represents at least a half. [Voices, "More than one-half." "Two-thirds." "Three fourths."] Of these so represented, a half or more (among whom I wish to be reckoned as one) will support any of the Democrats whose names have been mentioned for the Presidency; but the remainder, numbering several hundred thousand voters, will be won or lost to the cause, as the nomination proves wise or *otherwise*. [Laughter and applause.] This Convention has assembled in no spirit of dictation, but animated by devotion to the Constitution and the Union, and kindness to all who would preserve them to aid in securing an harmonious nomination, and organizing a certain victory. I can not suffer myself to doubt that the Democratic party has assembled this day in the same patriotic spirit, and will present a candidate who, whether he fought for the Union or not, thoroughly sustained the war [great applause], and whom all the soldiers and sailors of the Union can support without even seeming inconsistency.

The Republican party represents no principle for which we fought. We thought not of negro suffrage [applause, and cries of "No, no"], or of white disfranchisement; of forcing on the Southern States unequal fellowship in the Union ["Never, never"], or of changing our beneficent form of government ["No, never"], or of perpetuating the Republican party ["Never, never."] Out of the five hundred thousand of Union soldiers, Democrats and Republicans, who sleep on fields washed by the waters of the Atlantic and the Gulf, not one laid down his life for any such end. Of the fifteen hundred thousand of their surviving comrades, not one will say he would have risked his life for either of these objects. And these measures of the Republican party are not only not the objects of the war, but are so prosecuted as to defeat those objects, and to inflict on the nation evils as great as those the war was waged to prevent. [Shouts, "That's so."]

The Democratic party is now the only party true to the Constitution and Union. [Applause.] If we would accomplish the purposes of our service and sacrifice, if we would save the Union, the States, their liberties and laws, we must unite with the Democracy. [Long-continued applause.] We must not ask what men have been, but what they are; not who lately defended the constitution, but who now defend it. [Great applause.] In the path which the Democratic party treads, we see the footprints of Washington, Jefferson, Madison, Adams, and all the heroes of the Revolution; of Webster, Jackson, Clay, Wright, and all the giants of the generation just gone before us; and while it keeps that line of march, and bears the flag of the Constitution and Union, we can follow it with pride and unfaltering trust. [Immense applause, cheers, and waving of hats, followed by the band playing "Rally round the Flag."]

At the conclusion of General Ewing's address the band struck up the air "Rally round the Flag boys," the chorus being sung by the audience.

PERMANENT OFFICERS.

The Committee on Permanent Organization then reported the following list of regular officers: For permanent Chairman, Major-General Wm. B. Franklin, of Connecticut. Vice-Presidents and Secretaries—Maine, Major D. R. Hasting, Colonel H. G. Staples; New Hampshire, General M. T. Donohue, Captain Coggswell; Massachusetts, General Luther Stephenson, Major H. G. Waymouthe; Connecticut, Colonel L. G. Kingsberry, Captain Schlutter; Rhode Island, General J. G. Hazard, Colonel T. Ford Brown; New York, General J. W. Blanchard, Col. J. C. Bronson; District of Columbia, Colonel P. H. Allabach, Colonel Jno. R. O'Bierne; California, General J. W. Denver (no secretary); South Carolina, Lieutenant S. Medary (no secretary); West Virginia, Dr. R. A. Vance, Captain O. G. Chene; Iowa, General J. M. Tuttle, Lieutenant R. H. Eddy; New Mexico, General R. B. Mitchell, Captain G. W. Cook; Illinois, Colonel R. A. Schartz, Private J. N. Hildreth; Missouri, General J. S. Fullerton, Colonel S. M. Jewell; Michigan, Major J. Wixan, Major Foster Pratt; Kentucky, Major W. H. White, Colonel W. C. Starr; Florida, Colonel J. C. McKibben (no secretary); Wisconsin, General M Montgomery, Lieutenant G. W. Bird; Tennessee, General Theo. Francevenicht, Lieutenant D. Walker; Alabama, Colonel A. Edwards, Colonel Rutter; Arkansas, Captain C. L. Cameron, Captain William McMahony; Minnesota, Major J. C. Rhodes, Major George A Clark; Indiana, General John Love, Colonel H. S. Crowie; Dakotah, General J. B. S. Todd (no secretary); New Jersey, General Theodore Runyon, Lieutenant-Colonel J. J. Crapen; Nebraska, Colonel John Patrick, Captain A. B. Smith; Pennsylvania, General Pleasant, Colonel J. P. Linton; Kansas, Colonel G. H. English, Dr. J. H. M. Savage; Ohio, General A. Wiley, Captain J. R. Santmeyer; Maryland, Major Leopold Blumenberg. Major A. C. Williams; Louisiana, General J. B. Steedman, Captain R. A. Dennis; Texas, General Horace Walden.

This list of officers were elected by acclamation.

General Franklin was escorted to the chair amid cheers.

General McClernand introduced General Franklin as a favorite of the volunteers.

GENERAL FRANKLIN'S SPEECH.

General Franklin thanked the Convention, and alluding to his want of civil experience, hoped no very difficult questions of order would arise. Secret military organizations were justly looked on with distrust. They were dangerous, and soldiers had no right to use their positions as a political power. What, then, were they doing in forming an organization of soldiers? First, it was not a secret organization; but there was a secret organization thoroughly organized throughout the West and probably the South—the Grand Army of the Republic—organized for political purposes, and opposed to it another, and those two might at any time fly at each other's throats, and thus deluge the country with blood. To declare that Conservatives would not enter into such organizations was one purpose, and to show the country that the Chicago Soldiers' and Sailors' Convention, so-called, did not represent them. The Radical party pretended to be friends of soldiers, but the Radical Senate rejected the soldiers' nominations. He instanced the cases of General McClellan, Slocum and others. No less than 2,000 soldiers and sailors had been nominated to the Senate and been rejected.

The Conservative soldiers felt that certain things had been settled by the war. They had been in favor of conciliation toward their former opponents. The Radicals had been animated with enmity and hate, and judging the future by the past, the only hope for peace was in the success of the Conservative party. They must be prepared to make sacrifices for peace. What they asked of the convention was, a man whom the soldiers and sailors could, without sacrifice of principle, support.

NATIONAL EXECUTIVE COMMITTEE.

The Committee on Finance announced the following as the National Executive Committee: Michigan, Colonel M. Shoemaker; Kentucky, Colonel A. D. Pennebaker; New Hampshire, General M. Y. Donohue; District of Columbia, Colonel J. R. O'Bierne; West Virginia, O. G. Chase; New York, General James McQuade; Tennessee, Colonel F. R. Cahill; Minnesota, Colonel C. S. Uline; Delaware, Captain J, N. Barr; Connecticut, Major J. B. Cost; Maine, Colonel W. W. Bradbury; Pennsylvania, General S. N. Sonlecke; Wisconsin, Brigadier-General E. S. Bragg; Nebraska, Major J. W. Paddock; New Mexico, General B. C. Cutler; Illinois, Brigadier-General G. C. Rogers; Ohio, General L. D. Campbell; Massachusetts, Colonel E. C. Kinsley; Indiana, Colonel B. C. Shaw; Iowa, Captain P. W. Cross; Maryland, Major F. Dorsey Herbert; Rhode Island, General J. G. Hazard; Arkansas, Captain C. S. Cameron; Alabama, Major W. H. F. Randall; Kansas, General Hugh Cameron; Mississippi, Captain B. A. Burns; New Jersey, General Theodore Runyon.

SECOND DAY'S PROCEEDINGS.

Precisely at noon the chairman, Major-General William B. Franklin, of Connecticut, called the Convention to order by vigorous raps upon the Speaker's stand.

General Slocum, of New York, from the Committee on Resolutions, then addressed the Convention, and stated that the committee was not yet prepared to report a platform, but that, by reason of the resolution of the National Convention tendering to this Convention the privilege of the floor, the committee had prepared the following:

ADDRESS TO THE NATIONAL DEMOCRATIC CONVENTION.

Mr. President and Gentlemen of the Convention: We are instructed by the unanimous vote of the Convention of Union Soldiers and Sailors now in session at Cooper Institute, to return to you our thanks for extending to us the privilege of the floor of your Convention. The objects for which we are assembled are clearly set forth in the address of our presiding officer. Our Convention is composed of two thousand delegates, elected to represent every State and Territory in the Union, who have all served in the Union army or navy, every one of whom firmly believes that in co-operating at this time with the Conservative party of the country he is still engaged in the same cause for which he risked his life during the war (cheering), viz: to preserve the Union and maintain the supremacy of the Constitution. We believe that the crimes now being perpetrated in the name of Republicanism and loyalty are not less alarming than were those committed by the avowed foes of the Government during the war. The party now in power has destroyed the equality of the States, has forced the Southern States to submit to have their constitutions and laws framed by ignorant negroes just released from a condition of servitude, while at the North it has denied the negro (although comparatively well educated) even the right of suffrage. It has attempted to influence the decision of the highest judical tribunal of the land by calling public meetings of excited partisans to condemn in advance all members of the court who might refuse to act in accordance with their dictation, while the leading journalists of the party since the close of the impeachment trial have denounced and vilified in the most unmeasured terms the once chosen leaders of their own party, going so far as to threaten them with personal violence, and for no other reason than that they were unwilling to perjure themselves at the behest of party. It has freely removed all political disabilities from men at the South who before and during the war were the most violent and malignant rebels, but who have since become the sycophants of the party in power, while it continues to persecute those in the same localities who have always been true to the Union, but are unwilling to be ruled by their emancipated slaves. At the North it has denied official positions to hundreds of the veterans of the war, most of whom are disabled by wounds received in battle, while it has foisted into place partisans of its own, having no claims upon the Government, many of whom, fortunately for the country, have during the past few months become inmates of our penitentiaries. It has placed the General of our armies beyond the control of the President of the United States, to whom the Federal Constitution makes him subordinate; has nominated him for the Presidency, and the events of the last few months indicate that by the use of the army thus under his supreme control there is a determination to cause the electoral votes of the Southern States to be cast for himself through force and fraud. We solemnly declare our conviction that the free institutions of our country have never been in greater jeopardy than at this time, and we look to the deliberations of the Democratic party now assembled in convention with the deepest anxiety, feeling that upon its action depends the future prosperity of our nation. We earnestly trust and believe that no devotion to men or adherence to past issues will be permitted to endanger the success of this great party to which the country looks with anxious eyes for permanent peace and the perpetuity of our free institutions. We believe that there are living half a million men who served in the Union army and navy who are in sympathy and in judgment opposed to the acts of the party in power, and at least another half million of men who have heretofore acted with the Republican party, but who, viewing with alarm the recent acts of that party, are now anxious for a change of administration. With a platform of principles reviving no dead issues, and looking to the arrest of existing evils, and with candidates whose fidelity to the Constitution and devotion to the country can not be questioned, we shall co-operate with you in this campaign with a degree of enthusiasm and confidence that will bring victory to our standard and salvation to the country.

The address was adopted unanimously, and the following were appointed a committee to present it to the National Democratic Convention: Generals Slocum, Gordon Granger, J. W. Denver, J. J. Peck, W. McCandless, John Love, James McQuade, W. H. Smith, C. E. Pratt, Thomas Ewing, R. B. Mitchell, W. W. Averill, E. B. Browne, T. Kilby Smith, J. A. McClernand, D. Y. Walker, E. C. Kingsley, E. W. Bradbury, S. N. Drake, Colonel J. R. O'Bierne and Lieutenant-commanding James Parker.

A number of resolutions were read and referred, when the Convention adjourned.

THIRD DAY'S PROCEEDINGS.

General Franklin being indisposed, General J. W. Denver, of California, the first Vice President. occupied the chair.

General Slocum (New York), the Chairman of the Committee on Resolutions, came forward and said:

Mr. President and Gentlemen of the Convention—The Committee on Resolutions have found a great deal of difficulty in getting the body together, and it has been deemed prudent that a conference should be had with the members of the Democratic Committee on Resolutions. A great deal of our time has been spent in this way, but we have not prepared a platform on which we could stand. It has been suggested by some of the members of the Convention that the address that was adopted yesterday avows the principles that govern us. It is platform enough for us to stand upon, and I am instructed unanimously by the Committee on Resolutions to report the following for your consideration:

" WHEREAS, A mutual interchange of views between the members of this Convention and the delegates to the Democratic National Convention has fully confirmed us in our previously entertained opinion of the purity and patriotism of that body, and fully justifies the belief that in the selection of candidates and in the construction of a platform, the Convention will be governed by the spirit of the address adopted by this body on the 6th instant; therefore, relying upon this belief,

" *Resolved*, That we will support its nominees for President and Vice-President of the United States, and that on our return home we will induce our late comrades in arms to unite with us in yielding to them an earnest support." [Protracted cheers.]

A Delegate—I move the report be accepted and the committee discharged.

After a long debate the resolution was adopted as follows:

Alabama, yes; Arkansas, yes; Connecticut, yes; Colorado, yes; Georgia, yes; Illinois, no; Indiana, yes; Iowa, yes; Kansas, yes; Kentucky, yes; Maine, yes; Maryland, yes; Massachusetts, yes; Michigan, yes; Minnesota, yes; Mississippi, yes; Nebraska, yes; Nevada, yes; New Hampshire, yes; New Jersey, yes; New York, yes; Ohio, yes; Oregon, yes; Pennsylvania, yes; Rhode Island, yes; Tennessee, yes; Texas, yes; Virginia, yes; Wisconsin, yes; District of Columbia, yes; Colorado, yes; Idaho, yes; Montana, yes; Dacotah, yes; Arizona, yes; Washington Territory, yes.

The platform of the Committee on Resolutions was accordingly declared adopted.

At this moment the result of the first ballot for the Presidency, made by the National Convention then sitting at Tammany Hall, was received, and was read to the Convention. Great interest was manifested in the result, and the announcement of the vote for Pendleton was greeted with mingled cheers and hisses, while that for Hancock was received with wild applause.

GENERAL EWING'S SPEECH.

General Thomas Ewing, jr., said: Gentlemen—This is a political Convention representing three-quarters of a million or a million of returned soldiers and sailors now engaged in the pursuits of civil life, almost all belonging to the industrial classes. They are represented here chiefly by their officers; for the laboring masses of our comrades are not largely represented in this assembly. And in my opinion we should so act here as we know that they and ourselves would act if they were equally represented in this Convention to-day. The address of this Convention, sent to the Democratic Convention, faithfully and cogently represents the views of the Conservative soldiers and sailors on the question of Reconstruction and on Congressional usurpation. But in the address there is not one word on those other questions, which, if they do not touch the liberty or form of government of our people, yet bear upon them with a weight that makes them groan with the burden. Can we afford to ignore those great questions of finance? [No, no.] Can we afford, when the Republican party has, as we know in fact, the support of the great mass of the moneyed interest in this country, to turn upon the laboring men of the country the cold shoulder that was turned upon them at Chicago? We are soldiers, apt to speak what we think; not inclined to dodge great questions. Let us then meet this great question which every man knows is foreshadowed in the political contest before us. Let us meet it, and by our free action determine the position of the Convention. [A voice: The Convention has already determined it.] If another gentleman has the right to speak, I will retire: or if I have it, I can not tolerate interruption. Gentlemen, we, and those we represent, bore the heat and burden of the war. Those who bought the Government securities did it from a patriotic spirit that I admire and bow to. They risked for the cause of their country their money, while we were risking our lives. [Cheers.] Far be it from me or from any delegate in this Convention of Soldiers and Sailors to deny the claims of those men of high public spirit who came to the relief of the General Government in its hour of financial distress. I am animated by no such spirit. But they got—what I admit they amply deserve—a most munificent return for their patriotic investments. The soldiers got broken limbs; they got their estates swept away in judgments during their absence in the field; they got nothing but the honor of risking their lives in the service of the country. Let us, then, fairly balance the accounts between these two parties. Let us give to our patriotic men all that the most exacting honor demands; but, gentlemen, let us avoid the extreme of undertaking to be liberal—to be more than just. They have a right to ask for exact justice; they have no right to ask liberality of those groaning, suffering laboring people. Give them what their contract claims for them; give them strict justice; but not generosity. Now, gentlemen, I am fully aware that there have been discussions on the questions of law which are involved in one of the paragraphs of that resolution; the question whether the five-twenty bonds are redeemable in gold or in legal-tender notes. I say there have been questions raised on that point; but I frankly assert, in the light of recent investigations and discussions that have been made, that there is no longer a question at all about it. The law is plain that they are to be redeemed in the legal-tender of the country. [Great applause.] And no man can rise here and successfully controvert the proposition. But it has been said that this is a question for the courts to decide. If it belongs to the courts to decide it, why haven't those courts decided it before? I will tell you why. Because they who have control of the finances of the country have exerted despotic power in determining this question. They have assumed that the Government was bound by some publications of the Jay Cooke brokers; they have assumed that the Government is bound by some talk of a secretary as to what Government would do, and which talk was not in any way authorized by law. The assurances were such as Jay Cooke was not authorized to make, and by which the public of this country is not bound. Now, although this is a question that does affect the interests, I admit that it does not deeply affect the liberties of ourselves or of our comrades. But let this Convention, and that which now sits in Tammany Hall, beware that the political contest in which we are about to be engaged is to be decided by those questions of reconstruction alone. The people of this country are deeply interested in the question whether the financial policy announced in the resolutions, or before announced, shall prevail in the coming demonstration. And as our comrades are deeply affected by it, and feel the influence of the question on every day of their labor, we ought to meet it like a Convention assembled to consider great political themes—to meet these questions manfully and boldly. I beg the Convention fairly to consider this question. Whatever may be the decision at which the Convention shall arrive, I shall cheerfully bow to its verdict. I beg leave to offer the following resolution:

Resolved, That the faith of the Republic to its creditors, as pledged in its laws, is inviolable, and the public burdens should be lightened by vigilant economy in expenditures, and never by repudiation; that all the bonds of the United States issued after the passage of the Legal-Tender Act, and not by law expressly payable in coin, should be paid, when redeemable, in legal-tender notes, but without undue inflation of the currency, or, at the option of the holders, converted into bonds bearing a low rate of interest; that the National Bank currency should be retired, and its place supplied by legal-tenders, so as to save to the Government interest upon the amount of that circulation, and that the policy of permitting banks to supply nearly half of the national currency—allowing the five-twenty bonds, bearing, as they do, interest at the rate of nearly nine per cent. per annum, to run beyond the date when they become redeemable, and of contracting the currency until it shall rise to the value of gold, is a policy which favors the few against the many, is oppressive to the laboring and the debtor classes, and tends to bring upon the country the dishonor of repudiation.

After a long debate the resolution was withdrawn.

General McQuade announced that he had the original manuscript of the platform just adopted by the National Democratic Convention, and asked that permission be accorded to read it to the Convention. This announcement was received with immense applause, and loud calls were made for the reading of the platform. This admirable document is given at length in the report of the National Democratic Convention; but it may be remarked that its reading was interrupted by frequent bursts of applause. The resolution which calls for the "immediate restoration of all the States," was received with a burst of enthusiasm which shook the building. The demand for amnesty for all past political offenses was also warmly cheered. "We don't want any Poland here," said a delegate. "Faix, no, nor we don't want no Saxon oppression nayther," said another gem from Erin's bright green isle. The resolution relating to the payment of the public debt drew forth a demonstration of rather a mixed and undecided character; but ultimately the principles enunciated appeared to commend themselves to the majority; and finally the article passed with an unanimous roar of applause. One delegate immediately cried out: "The National debt ought to be paid in the lawful coin of the United States." The other resolutions, up to the eighth, were received without much comment, except those in relation to the rights of naturalized citizens, which, of course, raised a round of cheers from the citizens of Irish descent. The grand and stirring rebukes to the Radicals, which succeed these resolutions, awakened the highest enthusiasm of the audience; round upon round of applause interrupted the reading; and at the conclusion, "three times three" were called for and given with indescribable force and effect.

Colonel Lew Campbell (of Ohio), said: For forty years, gentlemen, I have been making war on those Democratic platforms [Laughter and applause]. They never entirely satisfied me. But, I am free to add, it gives me unbounded satisfaction, for the first time in my life, to say that a National Democratic Convention has enunciated a declaration of principles that has elicited my cordial approbation. In early life how I have worshipped those great men that adorn our history—our Webster, our Clay, and others; and I recognize in the very able paper that has been read to us the principles which those great men enunciated. I beg leave to offer the following resolution:

Resolved, That the declaration of principles adopted by the National Democratic Convention be, and the same is hereby received and approved.

The resolution was carried unanimously. It was further ordered that the Secretary communicate a copy of this resolution to the National Democratic Convention forthwith.

Gen. Buckner, of the ex-Confederate army, was introduced, and was cordially received. After some introductory words, which were not distinctly heard, he said:

"Like yourselves, I have been a soldier. Like yourselves, I have, in everything that I have done, evinced my sincerity and my truthfulness. Like yourselves, I am here to-day actuated by the same spirit which moves you, to bury past issues, to raise with you a standard which shall represent the Constitution of our restored country, to oppose with you those revolutionary elements now brought prominently forward by the Radical party; by a party which, while not in profession opposed to the Government, is more inimical to the principles of the Constitution of the country than ever were the Southern armies. [Hear.] When I came, Mr. President and gentlemen, as a spectator of your deliberations, and animated by the feelings I have expressed, I did not expect to be presented to you, nor anticipate the warm reception I have met with. It is an evidence to me of what I had before been ready to believe, that the soldiers and sailors of this country who have fought each other and who have evinced their sincerity by risking their lives and property, can, when the issues upon which they differed have been brought out to the end, better agree upon a common platform than mere politicians who pushed others forward where they did not care to go themselves. I have not, as a Confederate soldier, met with a soldier of the Union armies since the war closed with whom I could not in some way come into agreement on general principles, and I am here to speak for myself and with a knowledge of the views of others to pledge to you for myself and for all other Confederate soldiers harmony of action—support to those general constitutional principles which you are now endeavoring to carry into effect. [Applause.] Mr. President and gentlemen of the Convention, I am, like most of yourselves, a mere soldier, and I therefore close by simply returning my warmest acknowledgments for the kind reception I have met. [Renewed applause.]

General Slocum presented a resolution as follows:

Resolved, That the President of the Convention appoint a committee of five to wait upon General George B. McClellan and assure him that although we are called upon by duty to support the nominee for the Presidency of the National Democratic party now in Convention, our confidence in him is unimpaired, and that our love for him is as ardent as ever (great cheering), and that the highest honor that this Convention could confer upon him would but poorly express our esteem for him. Also, that the said committee be requested to ask him to come and assist us with all his ability during the coming campaign.

[Enthusiastic cheering].

The General said that no soldier who had ever served under McClellan needed a word of argument in favor of the resolution. [Renewed cheering.] The rule of reference was then suspended, and the resolution was unanimously carried.

A delegate from Illinois offered the following resolution:

Resolved, That the thanks of this Convention, and of all patriotic and right-minded citizens are due to the President of the United States for the removal of E. M. Stanton from the War Department of the

Government, a position which the said Stanton has disgraced and dishonored ever since his appointment to that office, by his many acts of cruelty—both to the Union and Confederate soldiers—and by his official acts of tyranny; and that the soldiers and sailors should, on all occasions, meet him with the same feelings of outraged dignity and patriotism that he was received with on an ever-memorable occasion, in the City of Washington, from that great and glorious soldier—General William Tecumseh Sherman.

The rules were suspended as before, and the resolution unanimously adopted.

The Chair appointed the following delegates to form the committee to wait upon General George B. McClellan: Private Higgins, Generals Franklin, Slocum, Pratt and Williams.

A committee of three was appointed to wait upon the National Democratic Convention to inform them that their platform had been unanimously adopted in this Convention.

The Secretary read a dispatch received from General Durbin Ward, of Ohio, congratulating the Convention upon its action, and regretting that he could not be present with them on this occasion.

The Chairman made a brief address to the Convention, thanking them for their courtesy, and expressing a firm belief in the success of the Democratic ticket.

Votes of thanks were accorded to the officers of the Convention, which then adjourned *sine die.*

Letter of Senator Doolittle, of Wisconsin.

THE DUTY OF CONSERVATIVE MEN—THE POSITION OF GOVERNOR SEYMOUR.

WASHINGTON, July 13, 1868.

O. H. OSTRANDER, ESQ., Danville, Pa.:

Dear Sir: I am in receipt of your letter of the 10th instant, in which, speaking for yourself and forty-eight other Conservative Republicans of your town, you express a "sense of disappointment and regret that no better names had been offered by the Democratic party to lead the conservative and patriotic masses of the people to victory, and the Radical Republican party to deserving and merited defeat. As a gentleman and a statesman, Mr. Seymour holds our respect, but as a Peace Democrat, we are indisposed to vote for him;" and, you are pleased to say, that if my name, among others, had been placed at the head of the ticket, "all would have gone well, and victory would have been certain." You desire my opinion upon the situation and "the prospects of a third party."

I thank you for the confidence thus reposed in me, and shall not shrink from the responsibility of stating frankly my opinion.

I do not think the organization of any third party is wise, or can work any practical good to the great cause in which we are engaged. In the very nature of things, when great principles are at stake, there are, and there can be, but two effective political parties. "He that is not for me is against me," in politics as well as in religion, is a truth upon which every wise man is compelled to act.

What, then, is the great and paramount issue? What is that great and unpardonable wrong for which the Radical party is now arraigned and should be overthrown?

It is substantially this:

In violation of the Constitution—in violation of pledges made and often repeated, from the first battle of Bull Run to the end of the war: pledges to the North to get men and money; pledges especially made to the Democracy to get their support in the field and in the elections; pledges made to the South to induce them to lay down their arms and to renew their allegiance; and pledges to foreign powers to prevent intervention—in violation of all these solemn pledges, upon which we invoked the blessings of Almighty God upon our cause, and by which alone we gained strength to master the rebellion—in violation of the natural and inalienable right of the civilized men of every State to govern themselves, and in violation of the clear provisions of the Constitution which leaves to each State for itself the right to regulate suffrage, this party has, without trial, by *ex post facto* laws, disfranchised hundreds of thousands of the most intelligent of their citizens, and has forced upon ten States and six millions of our own Anglo-Saxon race the universal and unqualified suffrage of seven hundred thousand ignorant, and, in the main, half-civilized negroes.

This is the great wrong for which that party is arraigned at the bar of public judgment, and for which it should be overthrown.

To consummate that great wrong, they have abolished all civil government, and civil liberty, even in these ten States;

They have established five absolute military despotisms, wherein all rights to life, liberty, and property are subject to the will of one man;

They have kept the Union divided;

They have prevented the restoration of industry;

They have kept down the credit of the Government, during three years of peace, to a point so low that, to the shame of every American, the six per cent. bonds of the United States sell for only seventy-three in gold, while the bonds of Brazil, bearing only four per cent. interest, bring over ninety in gold.

They have encroached upon the just rights of the Executive;

They have threatened the independence of the Supreme Court;

They have unjustly, and without cause, impeached and put upon trial the President himself, and, by every species of denunciation, and even by threats of assassination, have endeavored to force the Senate to convict him, in order to place in the Executive chair one who will use all his power to consummate that gigantic wrong against the Constitution, against our plighted faith, against civilization, and against our own race and kindred.

The Convention in New York met for the purpose of organizing to overthrow the party in power for this great wrong, and to restore the Union and the Constitution, and the rights of the States and of all the States under it. Now, I do not say the nominations made at New York are the very best that could have been made for that purpose.

The elements to be organized into a victorious army were four fold. To use a military figure, there were four army corps to be organized into one grand army:

1. The great Democratic Corps;
2. The War Democratic Corps;
3. The Conservative Republican Corps;
4. The Civilized Southern Corps.

The first, or Democratic Corps, was fully organized, with ranks well filled, but not in sufficient numbers to secure the victory.

There was the War Democratic Corps, which supported Lincoln in 1864; but which in consequence of the great wrong above mentioned, was ready to sever itself from the Radical army under General Grant; and there was the Conservative Republican Corps, of which you are pleased to speak of me as a leader, who, for the same reasons, were ready to join the Grand Army, and do all in their power to bring success to our cause.

The two last are the recruiting corps. They hold the balance of power. As a matter of policy, had the first office been given to a chief of the one or of the other, it would have made our victory more easy, if not more certain.

Every body knows that the result of this contest is to depend upon the important question, whether we shall be able to recruit these two corps in sufficient numbers, and carry them to the hearty support of Mr. Seymour. If we can, victory is with us. If we can not, victory is against us.

In my judgment it is our duty to do so. The very life of the Constitution is involved, and with it the rights of the States and the liberties of the people.

I can not hesitate for one moment; my judgment is for it; my whole heart is in it. So far from relaxing, we should redouble our efforts. Bear in mind that the war was ended three years ago, when a new era was opened in political affairs; that Mr. Seymour is a man of high character, of unquestioned patriotism, of great ability and experience, wholly with us upon the living and paramount issue; and that, if elected, he will make a most able and dignified President; and certainly no Pennsylvanian will forget that, but for his promptness and energy in forwarding the forces of New York to Gettysburg, that great battle might have been lost and Pennsylvania overrun. While in General Blair we have a civilian and a soldier whose promptness and indomitable resolution seized Camp Jackson, and saved Missouri from secession, who always stood among the foremost of the War Republicans, in council and in the field, while the war lasted; and, when it was over, was among the first to demand that for which the war was prosecuted—the Union of the States under the Constitution, with their rights, equality and dignity unimpaired.

Let us unite for a victory! Let us have peace—a peace which comes not from a violated Constitution and the despotism of the sword, but a peace which comes from a restored Union and the supremacy of constitutional law, by which alone liberty is secured.

Respectfully yours,
J. R. DOOLITTLE.

A Workingman's Champion on the Democratic Platform.

LETTER FROM HON. SAM. F. CARY, OF OHIO.

The following letter from Gen. Cary to one of his constituents, defines his position and his relations to the Labor movement:

HOUSE OF REPRESENTATIVES,
WASHINGTON, D. C., July 11, 1868.

T. J. WHITE, ESQ.:

Dear Sir: I have received your flattering letter of the 9th instant, and hasten to reply. Whatever the Workingmen may think, or however they may feel about the nominations in the National Conventions, or the influences which were brought to bear by bondholders, bankers, gold-gamblers and the moneyed aristocracy to secure the known results, I suppose the situation must be accepted It seems to me that in the present emergency we must make our fight in the Congressional districts, leaving each man to make his own choice in the Presidential canvass. If we can elect enough members of Congress who are true to the principles of the Workingmen, as announced in the platform at Chicago by the Labor Congress in August, 1867, to hold the balance of power, we may secure such legislation as will relieve labor from unjust exactions. There are two planks in the Democratic National platform which must meet the approval of all our workingmen. I refer to the one in regard to finance, and the one on the public lands. My own position is easily defined. I am committed fully to the principles elaborately stated in the platform of the Labor Congress, and I propose to fight it out on that line without regard to the success of any party, or any Presidential candidate. I do not propose to make any entangling alliances, and will make no pledges to any political party. My name is at the disposal of the Workingmen of my district, and I beg to assure you that if they can agree upon a name more acceptable than mine, it will gratify me to unite with them in electing the man of their choice to the place I now have the honor to occupy. In office or out of office, I shall not cease to denounce the contrivances to rob labor of its just rewards, and to demand that the producers of all the wealth shall have a fair share of their earnings.

Your assurances that my course in Congress meets with the hearty indorsement of the great majority of my constituents, affords me great satisfaction.

Doubtless, I have made mistakes, but in every instance where I have been called upon to act, I have done so with sole reference to what I believed to be the public good. With great respect, etc.,

S. F. CARY.

BRITISH OPINION OF THE DEMOCRATIC PLATFORM.

By cable telegram from London, the New York *Herald* is informed that the platform of principles adopted by the National Democratic Convention in this city was received in London—whether complete or in synopsis is not reported—on Wednesday, and that the journals of that city commented on it yesterday. The London *Times* asserts that the financial portion of the instrument lays down a "partial repudiation," and hence the London *Times* "forewarns" the Democrats of the loss of the Presidential election, their permanent exclusion from office, and, it may be, the "complete disruption" of the party.

Of course, the London *Times* does not like the Democratic Platform. The *Times* is in the interest of the Foreign nabobs, who are luxuriating abroad, on the gold interest drawn from our tax-burdened people upon bonds purchased with greenbacks at a tremendous discount on their face. The *Times* would like to see the complete disruption of the Democratic party. It is composed, to a large extent, of the Irish refugees from the terrible slavery of British despotism. The *Times* does not like our Irish fellow-citizens. They are prone to disturb British repose, and John Bull has no fancy for them, or any party that sympathizes with them. The *Times* is like some newspapers and people in this country, in its antagonism to the Irish voters and the great party of which they constitute a large and influential fraction: the Radical newspapers and people, who clothe at once the Southern negro with suffrage, but deny it to the Irish citizen until he has been five years a resident.

Military Arrests.

ARREST, TRIAL, BANISHMENT AND RETURN OF C. L. VALLANDIGHAM, OF OHIO.

For nothing has the Radical party, since its advent to power, shown so much disregard as the personal liberty of the citizen. During the war, no one was safe from the espionage of its unprincipled detectives, and a victimization to the cruel suspicions and heartless remedies of its villainous and criminal discipline. Well did Mr. Seward describe the situation when, on the 14th of December, 1861, he said to the British Minister, Lord Lyons, "*My Lord, I can touch a bell on my right hand and order the arrest of a citizen in Ohio. I can touch the bell again and order the arrest of a citizen of New York. Can the Queen of England in her dominions do as much?*" The victims of this boasted and shameless power were numerous. The public forts were converted into bastiles, and the apprehension of imprisonment and torture so filled the public mind that the free American citizen spoke with bated breath, and the community fast was revolutionized into a populace of timid and muzzled time-servers. There were honorable exceptions to the yielding influences of this blighted state of the public courage, but they became the victims of the licentious caprices of the ruling power. This book could be filled with instances of the personal courage, suffering, and, in many cases, of the cruel torture, of the manly victims of this worse than despotism: a few cases, however, will suffice.

That fearless tribune of the people, C. L. Vallandigham, of Ohio, delivered a public address on the 1st of May, 1863, at Mount Vernon, Ohio, for which Major-General Burnside, the present Radical Governor of Rhode Island—more distinguished as the individual whose tonsorial taste gave name to the Burnside whiskers—seized and imprisoned him, and ordered him to be tried before a military commission. All this in Ohio, where the civil courts were supposed to be intact. He was sentenced to be placed in close confinement in some fortress of the United States, to be designated by the commanding officer of that department, there to be kept during the continuance of the war. General Burnside designated Fort Warren, Boston harbor.

The President directed that Mr. Vallandigham be taken, under secure guard, to the headquarters of General Rosecrans, to be put by him beyond our military lines; and that, in case of his return within our lines, he be arrested and kept in close custody for the term specified in his sentence.

This order was executed, but Mr. Vallandigham very soon ran the blockade at Wilmington, N. C., and went to Canada, remaining at Windsor.

On the 15th of July, 1863, Mr. Vallandigham returned to Ohio, and that day spoke at Hamilton, Ohio. He was nominated as the Democratic candidate for Governor.

Early in July, 1865, after the war had closed, the Hon. Emerson Etheridge, a distinguished (Union) citizen of Tennessee, and for many years a prominent Representative in Congress from that State, opposing to the last all schemes which might culminate in disunion; who had been chosen by the Republican majority in the House of Representatives, during the Thirty-seventh Congress, to the clerkship of the House, but who had separated from that party because of its excesses— this gentleman, with this record, was arrested by the satrap Gen. Geo. C. Thomas, commanding Department of Kentucky and Tennessee, for no other purpose than that, at a public meeting at Dresden, Tennessee, he denounced Governor Brownlow and the State government of Tennessee—the former as an usurper, and the latter as an usurpation. He was seized and dragged from his home, in Tennessee, and carried to Paducah, within the jurisdiction of Kentucky, and there incarcerated in a loathsome prison under a military guard, and kept by said Thomas, in contempt of a writ of *habeas corpus* issued by Judge Marshall, Judge of the First Judicial District of Kentucky. He was afterward released, at the pleasure and convenience of said Thomas, acting professedly under the authority of the President of the United States.

We might refer to the cases of Dr. E. B. Olds, of Ohio; Hon. Geo. W. Jones, of Iowa; Lieut. Gov. Jacobs, of Kentucky, banished into the lines of the Confederacy, a power against which he had been actively warring, both in the field and forum; the case of Col. Frank Woolford, of Kentucky, a most distinguished officer of the army, who was a McClellan elector, and who, during his race, was seized and imprisoned; and numerous other instances of conspicuous prominence—all without the merit of the slightest constitutional provocation; but in a book like this it is impossible to indulge in more than a general reference to these gross violations of the personal liberty of the citizen and the prerogatives with which the Constitution was intended to guard him.

The Latest Popular Vote.

We publish herewith two tables of statistics, giving the vote for President in 1864, and the latest popular vote in each State. In 1864 the total votes of the several States for President were as follows, the majorities being all for Lincoln, except in Delaware, Kentucky, and New Jersey:

States.	Lincoln. Rep.	McClellan. Dem.	Maj.	Electoral votes.
California	62,134	43,841	18,293	5
Connecticut	44,691	42,285	2,406	6
Delaware	8,155	8,767	612	3
Illinois	189,496	158,730	30,766	16
Indiana	150,422	130,233	20,189	13
Iowa	80,075	49,596	39,479	8
Kansas	10,111	2,303	12,759	3

States.	Lincoln. Rep.	McClellan. D. m.	Maj.	Electoral votes.
Kentucky	27,786	64,301	36,515	11
Maine	63,114	46,992	21,122	7
Maryland	40,163	32,739	7,414	7
Massachusetts	126,743	48,745	77,997	12
Michigan	91,521	74,604	16,917	8
Minnesota	25,060	17,375	7,685	4
Missouri	72,750	31,678	41,072	11
Nevada	9,826	6,594	3,232	3
New Hampshire	36,400	32,881	3,599	5
New Jersey	60,723	68,024	7,301	7
New York	368,735	361,986	6,749	33
Ohio	265,154	205,568	59,586	21
Oregon	9,888	8,450	1,431	3
Pennsylvania	296,891	276,316	20,075	26
Rhode Island	14,349	8,718	5,631	4
Vermont	42,419	13,321	29,098	5
West Virginia	23,152	10,438	12,714	5
Wisconsin	83,458	65,884	17,574	8
Totals	2,223,035	1,811,754		
		1,811,754		
Majority	411,281			

The vote in each State, as cast at the last popular election, as far as it can at present be ascertained, is given in the following table:

States.	Rep. vote.	Dem. vote.	Maj.	
Alabama	70,812	1,005	6,807 R	Const'n, '68.
Arkansas	27,913	26,597	1,316 R	Const'n, '68.
California	44,584	47,969	3,385 D	Lt.-Gov., '67.
Connecticut	48,779	50,557	1,772 D	Gov., '68.
Delaware	8,598	9,810	1,212 D	Gov., '68.
Florida	14,520	9,491	5,029 R	Const'n, '68.
Florida	14,170	18,144	4,026 R	Gov., '68.
Georgia	88,123	69,750	18,373 R	Const'n, '68.
Georgia	83,146	76,099	7,047 R	Gov., '68.
Illinois	203,015	147,058	55,987 R	Congress, '66.
Indiana	169,601	155,390	14,202 R	Sen. State, '66.
Iowa	90,789	58,880	31,909 R	Su. Judge, '67.
Kansas	19,370	8,151	11,219 R	Gov., '68.
Kentucky	33,939	103,392	69,453 D	Gov., '67.
Louisiana	66,152	48,739	17,413 R	Const'n, '68.
Louisiana	60,901	41,614	25,287 R	Gov., '68.
Maine	57,649	46,035	11,614 R	Gov., '67.
Maryland	21,890	63,602	41,712 D	Gov., '67.
Massa'setts	98,306	70,300	27,946 R	Gov., '67.
Michigan	80,810	55,865	24,954 R	Su. Judge, '67.
Minnesota	34,870	29,543	5,327 R	Gov., '67.
Missouri	62,187	40,590	20,859 R	S. Schools, '66.
Nebraska	4,820	4,072	748 R	Congress, '66.
Nevada	5,047	4,295	752 R	Congress, '66.
N. Hamp're	39,778	37,260	2,518 R	Gov., '68.
New Jersey	65,402	63,971	1,491 R	Congress, '66.
New York	325,099	373,029	47,930 D	S. State, '67.
N. Carolina	93,084	74,015	19,069 R	Const'n, '68.
Ohio	243,605	240,622	2,983 R	Gov., '67.
Oregon	9,350†	10,659†	1,300 D†	Congress, '68.
Pennsylv'a	266,824	267,746	922 D	Su. Judge, '67.
Rhode Isl'd	10,038	5,731	4,307 R	Gov., '68.
S. Carolina	70,758	27,288	43,470 R	Const'n, '68.
Tennessee	71,484	22,548	51,936 R	Gov., '67.
Texas	44,689	11,440	33,249 R	Conv'n, '68.
Vermont	31,694	11,510	20,184 R	Gov., '67.
Virginia	107,342	61,887	45,455 R	Conv'n, '67.
W. Virginia	23,802	17,158	6,644 R	Gov., '66.
Wisconsin	73,637	68,873	4,764 R	Gov., '67.

The vote of Mississippi has not yet been announced, but the Constitution is believed to be defeated by a very large vote. In Alabama the Constitution received a majority of the votes cast, but not a majority of those registered. The Texas Convention is still in session.

---

* Including scattered and independent.
† Estimated.

Presidential Electoral Vote Since 1788.

The following table gives the electoral vote, and in some cases the popular, since the first election of George Washington:

YEAR.	NAMES OF CANDIDATES.	BY WHAT PARTY.	POPULAR VOTE.	ELECTORAL VOTE.
1788	George Washington	Unanimously		69
1792	George Washington	Unanimously		132
1796	John Adams	Federalist		71
1796	Thomas Jefferson	Republican		68
1800	Thomas Jefferson	Republican		73
1800	John Adams	Federalist		64
1804	Thomas Jefferson	Democrat		162
1804	Charles C. Pinckney	Federalist		14
1808	James Madison	Republican		152
1808	Charles C. Pinckney	Federalist		45
1812	James Madison	Republican		127
1812	De Witt Clinton			83
1816	James Monroe	Republican		183
1816	Rufus King			34
1820	James Monroe	Opp. 1 vote		218
1824	Andrew Jackson	Democrat	152,899	99
1824	John Q. Adams	Federalist	105,321	84
1824	W. H. Crawford	Caucus Dem.	47,265	41
1824	Henry Clay	Republican	47,037	37
1828	Andrew Jackson	Democrat	650,028	178
1828	John Q. Adams	Federalist	512,158	83
1832	Andrew Jackson	Democrat	687,532	219
1832	Henry Clay	Whig	550,189	49
1832	John Floyd	Whig		11
1832	William Wirt	Whig		7
1836	Martin Van Buren	Democrat	771,968	170
1836	W. H. Harrison	Whig		73
1836	Hugh L. White	Whig	769,350	26
1836	Daniel Webster	Whig		14
1836	Willie P. Mangum	Whig		11
1840	Martin Van Buren	Democrat	1,128,369	60
1840	W. H. Harrison	Whig	1,274,263	234
1844	James G. Birney	Liberty	7,609	
1844	James K. Polk	Democrat	1,329,013	170
1844	Henry Clay	Whig	1,231,643	105
1844	James G. Birney	Liberty	66,304	
1848	Zachary Taylor	Whig	1,362,242	163
1848	Lewis Cass	Democrat	1,223,795	127
1848	Martin Van Buren	Free Soil	291,378	
1852	Winfield Scott	Whig	1,383,537	43
1852	Franklin Pierce	Democrat	1,585,545	254
1852	John P. Hale	Free Soil	157,296	
1856	John C. Fremont	Republican	1,341,812	114
1856	James Buchanan	Democrat	1,834,337	174
1856	Millard Fillmore	"American"	373,055	8
1860	Abraham Lincoln	Republican	1,857,601	180
1860	S. A. Douglas	Democrat	1,365,976	12
1860	J. C. Breckinridge	Democrat	847,953	72
1860	John Bell	"Union"	590,631	39
1864	Abraham Lincoln	Republican	2,223,035	216
1864	G. B. McClellan	Democrat	1,811,754	21

Presidential Electors.

The following shows the number of Presidential electors to which each State is entitled:

STATES REPRESENTED IN CONGRESS.

California	5	Nebraska	3
Connecticut	6	Nevada	3
Delaware	3	New Hampshire	5
Illinois	16	New Jersey	7
Indiana	13	New York	33
Iowa	8	Ohio	21
Kansas	3	Oregon	3
Kentucky	11	Pennsylvania	26
Maine	7	Rhode Island	4
Maryland	7	Tennessee	10
Massachusetts	12	Vermont	5
Michigan	8	West Virginia	5
Minnesota	4	Wisconsin	8
Missouri	11		
Total			247

STATES NOT REPRESENTED IN CONGRESS.

*Alabama	9	Mississippi	7
*Arkansas	4	*North Carolina	10
*Florida	3	*South Carolina	8
*Georgia	9	Texas	4
*Louisiana	6	Virginia	10

Total... 70
Whole number....................................317
Necessary to elect...............................159

By the President of the United States of America.
A PROCLAMATION.

[This proclamation would have appeared in an appropriate place in an earlier part of this book but for the difficulty in obtaining a copy.]

I, Abraham Lincoln, President of the United States of America, and commander-in-chief of the army and navy thereof, do hereby proclaim and declare that hereafter, as heretofore, the war *will be prosecuted for the object of practically restoring the constitutional relation between the United States and each of the States and the people thereof,* in which States that relation is or may be suspended or disturbed.

That it is my purpose, upon the next meeting of Congress, to again recommend the adoption of a practical measure tendering pecuniary aid to the free acceptance or rejection of all slave States, so-called, the people whereof may not then be in rebellion against the United States, and which States may then have voluntarily adopted, or thereafter may voluntarily adopt, immediate or gradual abolishment of slavery within their respective limits; and that the effort to colonize persons of African descent with their consent upon this continent or elsewhere, with the previously obtained consent of the governments existing there, will be continued.

That on the First day of January, in the year of our Lord one thousand eight hundred and sixty-three, all persons held as slaves within any State or designated part of a State, the people whereof shall then be in rebellion against the United States, shall be then, thenceforward and forever free; and the Executive Government of the United States, including the military and naval authority thereof,

---

* Alabama, Arkansas, Florida, Georgia, Louisiana, North and South Carolina, have since been admitted to a bogus representation.

will recognize and maintain the freedom of such persons, and will do no act or acts to repress such persons, or any of them, in any efforts they may make for their actual freedom.

* * * * * *

And the Executive will in due time recommend that all citizens of the United States who shall have remained loyal throughout the rebellion shall (upon the restoration of the constitutional relation between the United States and their respective States and people, if that relation shall have been suspended or disturbed) be compensated for all losses by acts of the United States, including the loss of slaves.

In witness whereof, I have hereunto set my hand, and caused the seal of the United States to be affixed.

Done at the city of Washington, this twenty-second day of September, in the year of our
[L. S.] Lord one thousand eight hundred and sixty-two, and of the Independence of the United States the eighty-seventh.

ABRAHAM LINCOLN.
By the President:
Wm. H. Seward,
    Secretary of State.

Decisions of the Supreme Court on Reconstruction.

THE MISSISSIPPI AND GEORGIA INJUNCTION CASES.

Opinion of the Supreme Court on the Mississippi Application for an Injunction against the President and other Officers, April 15, 1867:

Chief-Justice Chase delivered the opinion of the Court, as follows:

A motion was made some days since on behalf of the State of Mississippi, for leave to file a bill in the name of the State, praying this court perpetually to enjoin and restrain Andrew Johnson, President of the United States, and E. O. C. Ord, General commanding in the District of Mississippi and Arkansas, from executing or in any manner carrying out certain acts of Congress therein named.

The acts referred to are those of March 2 and March 25, 1867, commonly called the Reconstruction Acts.

By the first of these acts the President is required to assign Generals to command in the several military districts and to detail sufficient military force to enable such officers to discharge their duties under law. By the supplementary act other duties are imposed on the several commanding Generals, and their duties must necessarily be performed under the supervision of the President, as Commander-in-chief. The duty thus imposed on the President is in no just sense ministerial. It is purely executive and political.

An attempt on the part of the judicial department of the Government to enjoin the performance of such duties by the President might be justly characterized, in the language of Chief-Justice Marshall, as "an absurd and excessive extravagance."

It is true that in the instance before us, the interposition of the court is not sought to enforce action by the Executive under constitutional legislation, but to restrain such action under legislation alleged to be unconstitutional.

But we are unable to perceive that this circumstance takes the case out of the general principle which forbids judicial interference with the exercise of executive discretion.

It was admitted in the argument that the application now made to us is without a precedent; and this is of much weight against it. Had it been supposed at the bar that this court would in any case interpose to arrest the execution of an unconstitutional act of Congress, it can hardly be doubted that applications with that object would have been heretofore addressed to it. Occasions have not been infrequent.

The constitutionality of the act for the annexation of Texas was vehemently denied. It made important and permanent changes in the relative importance of States and sections, and was by many supposed to be pregnant with disastrous results to large interests in particular States. But no one seems to have thought of an application for an injunction against the execution of the act by the President.

And yet it is difficult to perceive upon what principle the application now before us can be allowed, and similar applications in that and other cases could have been denied.

The fact that no such application was ever before made in any case indicates the general judgment of the profession that no such application should be entertained.

It will hardly be contended that Congress can interpose, in any case, to restrain the enactment of an unconstitutional law, and yet how can the right to judicial interposition to prevent such an enactment, when the purpose is evident and the execution of that purpose certain, be distinguished in principle from the right to such interposition against the execution of such a law by the President?

The Congress is the legislative department of the Government; the President is the executive department. Neither can be restrained in its action by the judicial department, though the acts of both, when performed, are in proper cases subject to its cognizance.

The impropriety of such interference will be clearly seen upon consideration of its probable consequences.

Suppose the bill filed and the injunction prayed for allowed. If the President refuse obedience, it is needless to observe that the court is without power to enforce its process. If, on the other hand, the President complies with the order of the court, and refuses to execute the act of Congress, is it not clear that a collision may occur between the executive and legislative departments of the Government? May not the House of Representatives impeach the President for such refusal? And in that case could this court interpose in behalf of the President, thus endangered by compliance with its mandate, and restrain by injunction the Senate of the United States from sitting as a court of impeachment? Would the strange spectacle be offered to the public wonder of an attempt by this court to arrest proceedings in that court?

These questions answer themselves. It is true that a State may file an original bill in this court; and it may be true, in some cases, such a bill may be filed against the United States. But we are fully satisfied that this court has no jurisdiction of a bill to enjoin the President in the performance of his official duties, and that no such bill ought to be received by us.

It has been suggested that the bill contains a prayer that if the relief sought can not be had against Andrew Johnson as President, it may be granted against Andrew Johnson as a citizen of Tennessee. But it is plain that relief against the execution of an act of Congress by Andrew Johnson is relief against its execution by the President. A bill praying an injunction against the execution of an act of Congress by the incumbent of the Presidential office can not be received, whether it describes him as President or simply as a citizen of a State. The motion for leave to file the bill is therefore denied.

In the case of the State of Georgia against certain officers, the Attorney-General makes no objection to the policy of the bill, and we will, therefore, grant leave to file that bill.

Mr. Sharkey—If the court please, the objection to the bill which I attempted to file seems to be that it is an effort to enjoin the President. The bill is not filed, and I can reform it to suit the views of the court, and present it again.

The Chief-Justice—Leave to file the bill is refused. When another bill is presented it will be considered.

Mr. Sharkey—Do I understand the court to say that the application can be made on Thursday?

The Chief Justice—On Thursday.

The bill was filed, and a subpœna was issued in the case, April 16, 1867.

Georgia Injunction in Supreme Court.

CASE DISMISSED FOR WANT OF JURISDICTION—OPINION OF THE COURT.

In the Supreme Court at Washington, February 10, 1868, Associate-Justice Nelson announced the opinion in the case of the State of Georgia against Hon. E. M. Stanton, Secretary of War, General Grant and General Pope. The last named, at the time the bill was filed, was commanding the Third Military District, composed of Georgia, Florida and Alabama, designated by the act of Congress, approved March 2, 1867, entitled "An Act to provide for the more efficient government of the rebel States" and the act supplemental thereto, passed on the 23d of the same month. The bill filed by the State of Georgia prayed for an injunction for the purpose of restraining defendants from carrying into effect the several provisions of these acts, and set forth the existence of Georgia as one of the States of the Union; and further, that on the surrender of the Confederate army in 1865, at the close of the civil war, that State was in possession and enjoyment of all the rights belonging to a State in the Union under the Constitution and laws of the United States, and as such was entitled to representation in both Houses of Congress.

Associate-Justice Nelson having set forth the premises at great length, said in substance, that a motion had been made by counsel for defendants to dismiss the case for want of jurisdiction; and as one without precedent, it was claimed the court had no jurisdiction in the case either of the subject in the bill, or over the parties presented. The first ground was supported by the argument that it was a political and not a judicial question; therefore, it was not a subject of cognizance by this court. The distinction between judicial and political questions resulted from the organization of the Government as executive, legislative and judicial, and from the limitation of the powers of each under the Constitution. The judicial power was vested in the Judicial department, and the political power in the two other departments. The distinction between judicial and political power was so generally admitted, that the court deemed it necessary to do nothing more than to refer to some of the authorities on the subject.

Here Judge Nelson referred to the Rhode Island and Massachusetts case, the Florida and Georgia case, and the Cherokee Nation and Georgia case.

Judge Nelson here showed that political power did not belong to the Judiciary, and that the court could have no right to pronounce merely on an abstract opinion of the Constitution or of State laws. It might, however, decide on all statutes properly falling under judicial authority. By the second section of the third article of the Constitution of the United States, it is provided that the judicial power shall extend to all cases in law and equity arising under this Constitution, the laws of the United States and the treaties made, or which shall be made, under their authority; to all affecting ambassadors, other public ministers and consuls; to all cases of admiralty, maritime jurisdiction; to controversies to which the United States shall be a party; to controversies between two or more States; between a State and citizens of another State; between citizens of different States; between citizens of the same State, claiming lands under grants of different States, and between a State or the citizens thereof and foreign States, citizens or subjects. The bill filed by the State of Georgia, prays for an injunction to restrain defendants from executing certain parts of the acts of Congress, being apprehensive that injury to the State would thereby result. But, according to law and precedent, in order to entitle the parties to relief, a case must be properly presented for the exercise of judicial power, and the case must refer to the rights of persons and property, and not to political questions merely, which do not belong to the judiciary, either in law or equity. In view of the principles which, under the Constitution and statutes, the court had endeavored to explain, the question was whether the court could take cognizance of the question now before it. The court was called on to restrain the defendants, who represented the Executive Department, from putting into execution certain acts of Congress which, it was claimed, would overthrow the existing State government of Georgia and establish a different one in its stead—in other words, destroy the corporate existence of the State. Such is the substance of the bill. It called for the judgment of the court on a political question, and not one involving persons and property. No question of person or property, or threatened danger to them, was presented in the bill in a form justifying judicial action by the court. It was true this bill set forth political rights, as in danger, and among other things that Georgia owned certain property, the State Capitol, Executive Mansion, and other real and personal property, and that putting those acts of Congress into execution, the State would be deprived of the possession of such property. But it was apparent this reference was only incidental and not specific matter of remedy. The relief asked would call for a bill different from the one now before the court.

Having for the reasons stated arrived at a conclusion, it was unimportant to examine the question of jurisdiction in connection with the defendant. The court dismissed the bill for want of jurisdiction.

This decision, the judge remarked, also disposed of the case of the State of Mississippi against Secretary Stanton, Gen. Grant and Major-Gen. Ord, involving a similar question.

Chief-Justice Chase said he did not concur in all the reasons, but assented to the conclusion, believing the court had no jurisdiction in the case.

A Blow at the Supreme Court.

A DECISION IN THE McARDLE CASE ARRESTED BY ACT OF CONGRESS—A SNEAKING PIECE OF LEGISLATION.

On the 14th of March, 1868, the Democratic members of the House of Representatives, discovered that an amendment had been sneaked into a bill which passed both Houses two days before, which prohibited any action of the Supreme Court upon a certain class of cases, including the celebrated McArdle case, which involved the constitutionality of the military reconstruction legislation of Congress. This piece of parliamentary swindling was the more to be deplored in view of the fact that the Supreme Court was understood to have reached a decision in that case in favor of McArdle, and against the constitutionality of the Reconstruction laws. The means by which this trick was carried out is fully exposed in the following proceedings, which transpired in the House of Representatives, on the 14th of March, 1868:

Mr. BOYER. I desire to call the attention of the House, and especially the attention of the country, to a measure of legislation which was passed through this House the day before yesterday, and which passed without any objection solely because it was introduced in a manner calculated to deceive and to disarm suspicion of its real design and effect. I shall refer in this place to the proceedings as published in the *Globe*, and I shall afterward make such brief comments as I may deem proper to the occasion.

There was a resolution pending, introduced by the gentleman from Missouri (Mr. Pile), when the gentleman from Ohio (Mr. Schenck) rose and said:

"I ask leave to take from the Speaker's table Senate Bill No. 213, to amend the Judiciary act. It came from the Finance Committee of the Senate, and I desire the House to pass it now."

"The SPEAKER. That would require unanimous consent, as the morning hour has not yet expired.

"Mr. SCHENCK. There can be no possible objection to it."

Then some proceedings intervened upon a motion of the gentleman from Missouri (Mr. Pile), when Mr. Schenck again rose:

"Mr. SCHENCK. I now ask unanimous consent to take from the Speaker's table the bill to which I referred a few moments since."

Mr. MAYNARD. I suggest to the gentleman from Pennsylvania (Mr. Boyer) that the gentleman from Ohio (Mr. Schenck) is not in his seat, and if he is going to animadvert upon that gentleman he had better wait until he is present.

Mr. BOYER. I do not think that I shall have another opportunity of saying what I desire to say. I am sorry the gentleman is not here. I should be very glad to see him in his place.

A privileged motion then intervened. When the subject was again resumed:

"The SPEAKER. The bill referred to by the gentleman from Ohio (Mr. Schenck), Senate Bill No. 213, to amend an act entitled "An act to amend the Judiciary act, passed September 24, 1789," will now be read."

The bill was then read. It provides that there should be extended to the Supreme Court certain appellate jurisdiction in cases of custom-house and revenue officers. I read from the report:

"Mr. SCHENCK. I desire to make a word or two of explanation, which I think will be perfectly satisfactory. As the law now stands, these appeals or writs of error can be taken in any case where one of the officers of customs is concerned. But by some inadvertence of the law-making power, that can not be done in the case of an internal revenue officer. This bill proposes to put those officers on the same footing in that respect; that is all there is in it. I hope there will be no objection to its consideration at this time."

All objection was accordingly withdrawn. At this stage the gentleman from Iowa

(Mr. Wilson), the honorable chairman of the Judiciary Committee, rose:

"Mr. WILSON (of Iowa). Will the gentleman from Ohio (Mr. Schenck) yield to me to offer an amendment to this bill?

"Mr. SCHENCK. I will hear the amendment

"Mr. WILSON (of Iowa). I desire to move to amend the bill by adding to it the following:

"SEC. 2. *And be it further enacted*, That so much of the act approved February 5, 1867, entitled 'An act to amend an act to establish the judicial courts of the United States, approved September 24, 1789,' as authorizes an appeal from the judgment of a circuit court to the Supreme Court of the United States, or the exercise of any such jurisdiction by said Supreme Court on appeals which have been or may hereafter be taken, be, and the same is hereby repealed.

"Mr. SCHENCK I am willing to have the amendment received, and now I call the previous question on the bill and amendment.

"The previous question was seconded and the main question was ordered."

The amendment of Mr. Wilson was then agreed to, without any objection being made; nor, as will be perceived, was any opportunity for inquiry afforded

Now, sir. it will become perfectly evident when I refer to the character of the act which is repealed by the amendment, that had it been known what the real nature of the amendment was, and to what it actually did refer, it could never have been passed in the manner in which it was suffered to pass at that time, without opposition. The act of February 5, 1867, provides—

"That the several courts of the United States, and the several justices and judges of such courts, within their respective jurisdictions, in addition to the authority already conferred by law, shall have power to grant writs of *habeas corpus* in all cases where any person may be restrained of his or her liberty in violation of the Constitution, or of any treaty or law of the United States; and it shall be lawful for such person so restrained of his or her liberty to apply to either of said justices or judges for a writ of *habeas corpus*, which application shall be in writing and verified by affidavit, and shall set forth the facts concerning the detention of the party applying, in whose custody he or she is detained, and by virtue of what claim or authority, if known; and the said justice or judge to wu m such application shall be made shall forthwith award a writ of *habeas corpus*, unless it shall appear from the petition itself that the party is not deprived of his or her liberty in contravention of the Constitution or laws of the United States."

It further provides:

"The said court or judge shall proceed in a summary way to determine the facts of the case by hearing testimony and the arguments of the parties interested; and if it shall appear that the petitioner is deprived of his or her liberty in contravention of the Constitution or laws of the United States, he or she shall forthwith be discharged and set at liberty."

And it provides further—and this is the important part repealed by the amendment of the gentleman from Iowa (Mr. Wilson):

"From the final decision of any judge, justice, or court, inferior to the circuit court an appeal may be taken to the circuit court of the United States for the district in which said cause is heard, and from the judgment of said circuit court to the Supreme Court of the United States. on such terms and under such regulations and orders, as well for the custody and appearance of the person alleged to be restrained of his or her liberty as for sending up to the appellate tribunal a transcript of the petition, writ of *habeas corpus*, return thereto, and other proceedings, as may be prescribed by the Supreme Court, or, in default of such, as the judge hearing said cause may prescribe."

It is well known to this House and to the country that it was under this provision of the act of February 5, 1867, that the McArdle case has arisen and is now pending before the Supreme Court of the United States. It is now very plain that the object of the amendment introduced by the gentleman from Iowa (Mr. Wilson) was to repeal the jurisdiction of the Supreme Court in such cases. It was, doubtless, intended to operate upon the very case which is now pending before the Supreme Court and which has been argued by counsel and submitted; for the amendment expressly relates to appeals which have been taken, as well as those which may hereafter be taken in such cases

This House, and especially the minority, were disarmed by the remarks with which the gentleman from Ohio (Mr. Schenck) prefaced the introduction of the bill. After we had been told by the gentleman who had charge of the bill that there could possibly be no objection to it, that it related only to revenue officers; and after the House had been asked, as a matter of courtesy, to allow it to be introduced for action at that time, we had reason to think that he would not accept as an amendment to that bill that which was not germane to its subject-matter, which related to an entirely different thing, and which the gentleman must have known, if he understood the nature of the amendment, would never have been suffered to pass without objection if its real character had been explained. The gentleman must have known it would not have passed without objection if, by the title of the bill, by the subject-matter of the bill, and by the remarks of the gentleman by which its introduction was prefaced, we had not been given to understand that it was a matter which related entirely to appeals to the Supreme Court in the cases of revenue officers, and that it was not intended to apply to anything else.

I have already said that the minority were disarmed by the manner in which this measure was introduced. I admit that, occupied by other matters, and trusting to the good faith of the gentleman who introduced this matter into the House, the minority never suspected that in that way the majority would attempt to affect their escape from what they must believe to be a pending judgment of condemnation against them at the hands of the highest judicial tribunal of the land. It must be because they fear that their acts of legislation have been unconstitutional; it must be because they are afraid to submit them to the test of judicial inquiry that, in that covert way, by artful approaches and by disguises not easily seen through at the moment, a measure was smuggled through, which, if it produces the effect for which it was intended, will, perhaps, prevent the constitutionality of the Reconstruction acts from being tested in the manner in which the question is now being tested in the McArdle case, now pending before the Supreme Court of the country. It must proceed, therefore, from a consciousness on the part of the majority that their acts are illegal and outside of the Constitution, that they feel compelled to resort to the passage of such an act as the one I have described.

But if the majority in this House were determined to pass such an act as that, to escape from the judgment of the court, it would have been more worthy in them to have done it openly. It would have been more manly to have introduced it in such a way that it might have been fairly discussed; and then, if by overwhelming numbers they had power enough to pass an act for the purpose of obstructing the administration of justice, they could still have insisted upon it. What I take occasion especially to complain of is the manner in which the attempt was so successfully made to disarm the suspicions of the minority by an appearance of fair dealing. This much is due to the minority, who, I admit, were not "wide enough awake," using the language of the gentleman from Maine (Mr. Blaine), to anticipate that there would come from such a source and in such a manner anything so entirely different from what they had been led to expect by the nature of the introduction of the bill and the remaks by which it was accompanied.

A long debate was had, in which there was nothing practical elicited except an exibition of pride on the part of the Radicals of the sharp practice they had indulged. There was one ordeal through which the law had to pass, and that was the office of the President. On the 25th of March he vetoed the bill as follows:

To the Senate of the United States:

I have considered, with such care as the pressure of other duties has permitted, a bill entitled "An act to amend an act entitled 'An act to amend the judiciary act passed the 24th of September, 1789.'" Not being able to approve all of its provisions, I herewith return it to the Senate, in which House it originated, with a brief statement of my objections.

The first section of the bill meets my approbation, as, for the purpose of protecting the rights of property from the erroneous decisions of inferior judicial tribunals, it provides means for obtaining uniformity by appeal to the Supreme Court of the United States in cases which have now become very numerous and of much public interest, and in which such remedy is not now allowed. The second section, however, takes away the right of appeal to that court in cases which involve the life and liberty of the citizen, and leaves them exposed to the judgment of numerous inferior tribunals. It is apparent that the two sections were conceived in a very different spirit, and I regret that my objection to one imposes upon me the necessity of withholding my sanction from the other.

I can not give my assent to a measure which proposes to deprive any person "restrained of his or her liberty in violation of the Constitution, or of any treaty or law of the United States" from the right of appeal to the highest judicial authority known to our Government. To "secure the blessings of liberty to ourselves and our posterity" is one of the declared objects of the Federal Constitution. To assure these guarantees are provided in the same instrument, as well against "unreasonable searches and seizures" as against the suspension of the privilege of the writ of *habeas corpus*, unless when, in cases of "rebellion or invasion, the public safety may require it." It was, doubtless, to afford the people the means of protecting and enforcing these inestimable privileges that the jurisdiction which this bill proposes to take away was conferred upon the Supreme Court of the Union. The act conferring that jurisdiction was approved on the 5th day of February, 1867, with a full knowledge of the motives that prompted its passage, and because it was believed to be necessary and right. Nothing has since occurred to disprove the wisdom and justness of the measure; and to modify it, as now proposed, would be to lessen the protection of the citizen from the exercise of arbitrary power and to weaken the safeguards of life and liberty, which can never be made too secure against illegal encroachments.

The bill not only prohibits the adjudication by the Supreme Court of cases in which appeals may hereafter be taken, but interdicts its jurisdiction on appeals which have already been made to that high judicial body. If, therefore, it should become a law, it will, by its retroactive operation, wrest from the citizen a remedy which he enjoyed at the time of his appeal. It will thus operate most harshly upon those who believe that justice has been denied them in the inferior courts.

The legislation proposed in the second section, it seems to me, is not in harmony with the spirit and intention of the Constitution. It can not fail to affect most injuriously the just equipoise of our system of Government; for it establishes a precedent which, if followed, may eventually sweep away every check on arbitrary and unconstitutional legislation. Thus far during the existence of the Government the Supreme Court of the United States has been viewed by the people as the true expounder of their Constitution, and in the most violent party conflicts its judgments and decrees have always been sought and deferred to with confidence and respect. In public estimation it combines judicial wisdom and impartiality in a greater degree than any other authority known to the Constitution; and any act which may be construed into or mistaken for an attempt to prevent or evade its decisions on a question which affects the liberty of the citizens and agitates the country can not fail to be attended with unpropitous consequences. It will be justly held by a large portion of the people as an admission of the unconstitutionality of the act on which its judgment may be forbidden or forestalled, and may interfere with that willing acquiescence in its provisions which is necessary for the harmonious and efficient execution of any law.

For these reasons, thus briefly and imperfectly stated, and for others, of which want of time forbids the enumeration, I deem it my duty to withhold my assent from this bill, and to return it for the reconsideration of Congress.

ANDREW JOHNSON.

WASHINGTON, D. C., March 25, 1868.

On the 26th of March, the following proceedings took place in the Senate:

The PRESIDENT *pro tempore*. The question is, "Shall the bill pass notwithstanding the objection, of the President of the United States?" On this question the Secretary will call the yeas and nays.

Mr. WILLIAMS. I wish to state that Mr. Grimes and Mr. Johnson are paired on this question. Mr. Grimes, if here, would vote for the bill; Mr. Johnson against it. Mr. Corbett and Mr. Vickers are also paired. Mr. Corbett, if here, would vote for the bill, and Mr. Vickers against it.

The question being taken by yeas and nays, resulted—yeas 33, nays 9; as follows:

YEAS—Messrs. Cameron, Cattell, Chandler, Cole, Conklin. Cragin, Edmunds, Ferry, Frelinghuysen, Harlan, Henderson, Howard, Howe, Morgan, Morrill (of Maine), Morrill (of Vermont), Morton, Nye, Patterson (of New Hampshire), Pomeroy, Ramsey, Ross, Stewart, Sumner, Thayer, Tipton, Trumbull, Van Winkle, Wade, Willey, Williams, Wilson, and Yates–33.

NAYS—Messrs. Bayard, Buckalew, Davis, Dixon, Hendricks, McCreery, Norton, Patterson (of Tennessee), and Saulsbury—9

ABSENT — Messrs. Anthony, Conness, Corbett, Doolittle, Drake, Fessenden, Fowler, Grimes, Johnson, Sherman, Sprague, and Vickers—12.

The PRESIDENT *pro tempore*. Two-thirds of the members present having voted for the bill, it is passed notwithstanding the objections of the President; and it will be transmitted, with the objections, to the House of Representatives.

In the House, on the 27th of March, the question came up. During the debate on it, Mr. Woodward, of Pennsylvania, said:

I have therefore no complaint to make of the act of 1867. It never could have been necessary, however, if your Reconstruction laws, and your Freedman's Bureau acts had not been passed. It grew out of a necessity of your own creation; and when so violent measures as those were forced upon the people, it was wise and salutary to accompany them by such an act as the act of 1867.

Now, it so happened that an individual of Mississippi, of whom I know nothing, but whose name has become familiar to the public ear as McArdle, fell a victim to the military tyranny which has been sent into those States. As I understand, his offense consisted in criticising in a public print some measures of the commanding General. It was the exercise of the right of freedom of speech and of the press for which he was restrained of his liberty, and thrown into jail. He applied for *habeas corpus*. It was denied him in the local court. He took his appeal to the Supreme Court of the United States. The case came into that court under this act of 1867—this very law that you passed for the purpose of securing to people their liberty. Mr. McArdle came into the Supreme Court of the United States pleading that law. After an argument by counsel, who denied that the case came within that law, the Supreme Court decided that they had jurisdiction in the case under the law; and they decided it unanimously. I read the argument of Mr. Trumbull upon that question as reported in the papers. I have not read the opinion of the court as delivered by the Chief-Justice; but I understand it was a unanimous decision. And what was it in legal effect? It was a decision that that court was entitled to take jurisdiction of McArdle's case, that jurisdiction had attached in the case, and that the argument should proceed. In pursuance of that decree, the argument did proceed by distinguished counsel on the one side and on the other.

Now, I call the attention of the House to the fact that by all this, Mr. McArdle acquired certain rights in that court, rights just as well defined as his right to life. He acquired the right of taking the judgment of that court on his case. It was a right which vested by the circumstances to which I have adverted, and not one of which will be controverted. It was a vested right. It was a vested right in respect to one of the highest interests of the man—his liberty. It was a vested right which the act of 1867 showed you were ready to respect when asserted by a negro. It was a vested right which, I say, is just as worthy of respect when asserted by a white man as when asserted by a negro.

Mr. ELDRIDGE. Do you go that far?

Mr. WOODWARD. Yes, sir; I will go that far? I say that the vested rights of this man are just as worthy of the respect of this Congress as if he were a negro.

Now, sir, what happens? This House having allowed the chairman of the Committee of Ways and Means to take up, by unanimous consent, a bill relating to the revenues of the country, to which nobody had any objection, the gentleman from Iowa [Mr. Wilson], the chairman of the Judiciary Committee, offered as an amendment this section, which takes away the jurisdiction of the Supreme Court under the act of 1867, and takes away the vested, attached jurisdiction of the Supreme Court in McArdle's case. Such is not only the legal effect of it; but upon interrogation, on this floor, the gentleman from Iowa declared that such was his intention in offering that amendment. I asked the question myself; and the gentleman made that distinct declaration. Nay, more, he not only admitted that that was his intention, but, with infinite bad taste, seemed to be proud of it—seemed to be proud that he had slipped in this amendment to rob a fellow-citizen of his vested rights in the Supreme Court of the United States. It was the first time I ever saw a lawyer, not to say a chairman of a Judiciary Committee, plume himself both upon the thing done and the mode of doing it, when both were so questionable. I was shocked last Saturday, in the running debate we had here, at the spirit and manner of my friend from Iowa. When my friends around me here complain of that which I did not feel disposed to complain of—the manner in which this amendment was introduced—it was evident from the tone of the gentleman's remarks, as it had been evident from the tone of the remarks of the gentleman from Ohio [Mr. Schenck], a few days before, that they were proud of what gentlemen on this side called a trick.

I did not call it a trick. I would be sorry to call it so. They talked of their superior vigilance, of their being always "wide-awake," and advised us on this side to keep awake and not confide in them to the extent that we had done—advice, this last, which will probably not be lost on this side of the House. I say all this seemed to be in exceedingly bad taste. For what was the gentleman doing? He was trampling upon the rights of a fellow-citizen. I tried last Saturday to make him see the position in which he was placing himself. I cared nothing about this minor question as to the manner of doing it. I tried to fix the gentleman's eyes upon the real nature of the thing he was doing, the essential quality of the enactment. But he was so much occupied with self-admiration of the manner of doing the thing that I succeeded badly. I could not get him to contemplate the essence and quality of the thing itself, so much enamored was he of that which honorable gentlemen did not hesitate to call a trick. [Laughter.]

But let that matter pass. The thing was done. The bill was passed without a word of debate or explanation. It was afterward justified, and even boasted of; and now these desultory thoughts that I am expressing are the first words of debate upon the measure that have been heard in this hall.

Now, sir, I have said that the act of 1867 was a law in favor of human liberty. This bill proposes the repeal of the law, which has not been asked for by the people of those States in whose behalf the law was passed, not demanded by any great public necessity, but dictated, according to the confession of the gentleman from Iowa himself, merely by a desire to prevent the Supreme Court of the United States from deciding McArdle's case. And the reason of this desire was a fear that the Supreme Court would declare the Reconstruction laws unconstitutional and void.

Sir, in former times, candid and wise legislators were most anxious that questionable legislation should be brought to judicial test at the earliest possible moment. If anybody doubts the constitutionality of an enactment for which I vote while I may have the honor of a seat on this floor, I will facilitate the judicial investigation of the question by all the means in my power. I shall consider it a valuable privilege to bring a questionable measure for which I may cast my vote before the judicial tribunals of the country; and such, I believe, has generally been the prevailing sentiment in legislative bodies in this country until the present time.

But it was rumored that the Supreme Court were likely to declare the Reconstruction laws unconstitutional; and this bill was reported and passed, says the gentleman from Iowa, for the purpose of preventing that. Mr. Speaker, when the country understands that the act of 1867 was a law in favor of human liberty—that a citizen restrained of his liberty had availed himself of this law for the purpose of obtaining the decision of the Supreme Court of the United States—what will they think of the Chairman of the Judiciary Committee of this House, coming in with such a section at such a moment for such an avowed purpose? And what will they think of the action of this House in sustaining such a bill over a veto from the President? Will they not see that it is a deadly blow at the liberties of a citizen? That it is an unworthy device to prevent a review of most questionable legislation? That it amounts in effect to a confession on the part of the House that their legislation can not stand the ordinary judicial tests to which all laws are subjected?

I desire that the people shall understand this matter. If there is honor in it, gentlemen are entitled to it; if there is responsibility in it, gentlemen must expect to bear it. The people of the country shall have their attention riveted upon the facts of this case, if I can rivet it.

There is another point which I trust will not be overlooked by the public. The Government under which we live happily distributes its powers in three separate coordinate departments. The legislative is one of them, but the judiciary is also one of them. And the judicial power is vested in the Supreme Court of the United States, and in such inferior courts as Congress may establish. Now, McArdle's case was a judicial case. It presented a question for judicial inquiry. Jurisdiction had attached. The rights of McArdle had vested. And I deny that the legislative department has any power to meddle with the co-ordinate department, the judiciary, while the latter is performing its appropriate functions in respect to jurisdiction of a particular case that has attached.

* * * * *

The SPEAKER. The question, under the Constitution, is, "Will the House, on reconsideration, agree to the passage of the bill?" The question will be taken by yeas and nays.

The question was taken, and there were yeas 114, nays 34, not voting 41; as follows:

YEAS—Messrs. Ames, Anderson, Arnell, Delos R. Ashley, James M. Ashley, Bailey, Baker, Baldwin, Banks, Beaman, Beatty, Benjamin, Benton, Bingham, Blaine, Boutwell, Bromwell, Broomall, Buckland, Cake, Churchill, Reader W. Clarke, Sidney Clarke, Coburn, Cook, Covode, Cullom, Dawes, Dixon, Dodge, Driggs, Eckley, Eggleston, Eliot, Farnsworth, Ferriss, Ferry, Fields, Gravely, Halsey, Hill, Hooper, Hopkins, Chester D. Hubbard, Hulburd, Hunter, Ingersoll, Jenckes, Judd, Julian, Kelley, Kelsey, Ketcham, Kitchen, Koontz, Laflin, William Lawrence, Lincoln, Loan, Logan, Loughridge, Mallory, Maynard, McClurg, Mercur, Miller, Moore, Moorhead, Morrell, Mullins, Myers, Newcomb, O'Neill, Orth, Paine, Perham, Peters, Pike, Pile, Plants, Poland, Polsley, Pomeroy, Price, Raum, Sawyer, Schenck, Scofield, Selye, Shanks, Smith, Spalding, Aaron F. Stevens, Thaddeus Stevens, Taffe, Taylor, Thomas, John Trimble, Twichell, Upson, Burt Van Horn, Robert T. Van Horn, Van Wyck, Ward, Cadwalader C. Washburn, Elihu B. Washburne, William B. Washburn, Welker, Thomas Williams, James F. Wilson, John T. Wilson, Stephen F. Wilson, Windom, and Woodbridge—114.

NAYS—Messrs. *Adams, Archer, Axtell, Barnes, Beck, Brooks, Burr,* CARY, *Chanler, Eldridge, Fox, Getz, Glossbrenner, Golladay, Holman, Hotchkiss, Richard D. Hubbard, Humphrey, Johnson, Kerr, Knott, Marshall, McCormick, Mungen, Niblack, Nicholson, Pruyn, Ross, Sitgreaves, Stone, Taber, Lawrence S. Trimble, Van Auken,* and *Woodward*—34.

NOT VOTING—Messrs. Allison, Barnum, Blair, Boyer, Butler, Cobb, Cornell, Donnelly, Ela, Finney, Garfield, Griswold, Grover, Haight, Harding, Hawkins, Higby, Asahel W. Hubbard, Jones, George V. Lawrence, Lynch, Marvin, McCarthy, McCullough, Morgan, Morrissey, Nunn, Phelps, Randall, Robertson, Robinson, Shellabarger, Starkweather, Stewart, Stokes, Trowbridge, Van Aernam, Van Trump, Henry D. Washburn, William Williams, and Wood —41.

The SPEAKER. Two-thirds having voted in the affirmative, I do declare that, notwithstanding the objections of the President, the bill (S. No. 213) to amend an act entitled "An Act to amend the Judiciary Act, passed the 24th of September, 1789," has become a law.

Not one Radical voted to prevent this outrage. Every Radical present in both Houses voted for it.

The Effect upon the Court.

THE MCARDLE CASE POSTPONED — JUDGE GRIER PROTECTS HIS OWN JUDICIAL CHARACTER.

In the Supreme Court, on the 31st of March, 1868, it was decided to postpone further argument in the McArdle case (the objective point of the preceding action of Congress) until the next term, which commences on the first Monday in December.

When the case was alluded to in the court, the day before, the venerable Judge Grier, of Pennsylvania, produced a profound sensation by reading the following protest:

"*Ex parte William H. McArdle.*—This case was fully argued in the beginning of the month. It is a case which involves not only the liberty and rights of the appellant, but of millions of our fellow-citizens. THE COUNTRY HAD A RIGHT TO EXPECT IT WOULD IMMEDIATELY RECEIVE THE SOLEMN ATTENTION OF THE COURT. By the postponement of this case, this court will subject themselves, whether justly or unjustly, to the imputation that we have evaded the performance of a duty imposed on us by the Constitution, and waited for legislative interposition to supersede our action, and relieve us from our responsibility. I can only say, '*Pudut hæc opprobria nobis et potuisse dici et non potuisse repeli.*'

"R. C. GRIER."

Popular Vote on Negro Suffrage.

In 1860 a vote was had in the State of New York on a proposition to permit negro suffrage without a property qualification. The result in the city was—yeas 1,640, nays 37,471. In the State—yeas 197,503, nays 337,984. In 1864 a like proposition was defeated—yeas 85,406, nays 224,336.

In 1862, in August, a vote was had in the State of Illinois, on several propositions relating to negroes and mulattoes, with this result:

For excluding them from the State	171,593	
Against	71,306	
		100,587
Against granting them suffrage or right to office	211,920	
For	35,649	
		176,271
For the enactment of laws to prohibit them from going to or voting in the State	198,938	
Against	44,414	
		154,524

In Ohio, at the election in October, 1867, the Constitutional Amendment included negro suffrage, and the disfranchisement of deserters was voted on. The vote was as follows:

For negro suffrage	216,957
Against negro suffrage	255,340
Majority against	38,358

In Kansas, in 1867, a vote was had as follows:

For negro suffrage	10,483
Against negro suffrage	19,421
Majority against	8,938

In Minnesota, in 1867, a vote was had on negro suffrage, as follows:

Against negro suffrage	28,759
For negro suffrage	27,461
Majority	1,298

In Wisconsin, in 1865, a vote was had on equal or negro suffrage, as follows:

Against negro suffrage	55,591
For negro suffrage	46,588
Majority against	9,003

The soldiers' vote, embraced in the above, was:

Against	1,287
For	279
Majority against	1,009

In Connecticut, in 1865, a vote was had:

Against negro suffrage	33,489
For negro suffrage	27,217
Majority against	6,272

In Michigan, a vote was had on the first Monday of April, 1868. The new Constitution, embracing negro suffrage, was defeated by 38,000 majority. It was not submitted as a separate question, though other matters of amendment were so submitted; the Radicals hoping that the people would swallow negro suffrage rather than defeat the new Constitution. The people, however, killed the new organic law because of its institution of negro suffrage, by the large majority we have stated.

The Civil Rights Bill.

COPY OF THE BILL.

AN ACT to protect all persons in the United States in their civil rights, and furnish the means of their vindication.

Be it enacted, etc., That all persons born in the United States, and not subject to any foreign power, excluding Indians not taxed, are hereby declared to be citizens of the United States; and such citizens, of every race and color, without regard to any previous condition of slavery or involuntary servitude, except as a punishment for crime whereof the party shall have been duly convicted, shall have the same right in every State and Territory in the United States to make and enforce contracts; to sue, be parties, and give evidence; to inherit, purchase, lease, sell, hold and convey real and personal property; and to full and equal benefit of all laws and proceedings for the security of person and property, as is enjoyed by white citizens, and shall be subject to like punishment, pains and penalties, and to none other, any law, statute, ordinance, regulation, or custom, to the contrary notwithstanding.

SEC. 2. That any person who, under color of any law, statute, ordinance, regulation, or custom, shall subject, or cause to be subjected, any inhabitant of any State or Territory to the deprivation of any right secured or protected by this act, or to different punishment, pains, or penalties, on account of such person having at any time been held in a condition of slavery or involuntary servitude, except as a punishment for crime whereof the party shall have been duly convicted, or by reason of his color or race, than is prescribed for the punishment of white persons, shall be deemed guilty of a misdemeanor, and, on conviction, shall be punished by fine not exceeding one thousand dollars, or imprisonment not exceeding one year, or both, in the discretion of the court.

SEC. 3. That the district courts of the United States, within their respective districts, shall have, exclusively of the courts of the several States, cognizance of all crimes and offenses committed against the provisions of this act, and also, concurrently with the circuit courts of the United States, of all causes, civil and criminal, affecting persons who are denied, or can not enforce in the courts or judicial tribunals of the State or locality where there may be, any of the rights secured to them by the first section of this act; and if any suit or prosecution, civil or criminal, has been or shall be commenced in any State court against any such person, for any cause whatsoever, or against any officer, civil or military, or other person, for any arrest or imprisonment, trespasses, or wrongs done or committed by virtue or under color of authority derived from this act or the act establishing a bureau for the relief of freedmen and refugees and all acts amendatory thereof, or for refusing to do any act upon the ground that it would be inconsistent with this act, such defendant shall have the right to remove such cause for trial to the proper district or circuit court in the manner prescribed by the "Act relating to *habeas corpus*, and regulating judicial proceedings in certain cases," approved March 3, 1863, and all acts amendatory thereof. The jurisdiction in civil and criminal matters hereby conferred on the district and circuit courts of the United States shall be exercised and enforced in conformity with the laws of the United States, so far as such laws are suitable to carry the same into effect; but in all cases where such laws are not adapted to the object, or are deficient in the provisions necessary to furnish suitable remedies and punish offenses against law, the common law, as modified and changed by the constitution and statutes of the State wherein the court having jurisdiction of the cause, civil or criminal, is held, so far as the same is not inconsistent with the Constitution and laws of the United States, shall be extended to and govern said courts in the trial and disposition of such cause, and, if of a criminal nature, in the infliction of punishment on the party found guilty.

SEC. 4. That the district attorneys, marshals, and deputy marshals of the United States, the commissioners appointed by the circuit court and territorial courts of the United States, with powers of arresting, imprisoning, or bailing offenders against the laws of the United States, the officers and agents of the Freedmen's Bureau, and every other officer who may be specially empowered by the President of the United States, shall be, and they are hereby, specially authorized and required, at the expense of the United States, to institute proceedings against all and every person who shall violate the provisions of this act, and cause him or them to be arrested and imprisoned, or bailed, as the case may be, for trial before such court of the United States or territorial court as by this act has cognizance of the offense. And with a view to affording reasonable protection to all persons in their constitutional rights of equality before the law, without distinction of race or color, or previous condition of slavery or involuntary servitude, except as a punishment for crime, whereof the party shall have been duly convicted, and to the prompt discharge of the duties of this act, it shall be the duty of the circuit courts of the United States and the superior courts of the Territories of the United States from time to time, to increase the number of commissioners, so as to afford a speedy and convenient means for the arrest and examination of persons charged with a violation of this act. And such commissioners are hereby authorized and required to exercise and discharge all the powers and duties conferred on them by this act, and the same duties with regard to offenses created by this act, as they are authorized by law to exercise with regard to other offenses against the laws of the United States.

SEC. 5. That it shall be the duty of all

marshals and deputy marshals to obey and execute all warrants and precepts issued under the provisions of this act, when to them directed; and should any marshal or deputy marshal refuse to receive such warrant or other process when tendered, or to use all proper means diligently to execute the same, he shall, on conviction thereof, be fined in the sum of one thousand dollars, to the use of the person upon whom the accused is alleged to have committed the offense. And the better to enable the said commissioners to execute their duties faithfully and efficiently, in conformity with the Constitution of the United States and the requirements of this act, they are hereby authorized and empowered, within their counties respectively, to appoint, in writing, under their hands, any one or more suitable persons, from time to time, to execute all such warrants and other process that may be issued by them in the lawful performance of their respective duties; and the persons so appointed to execute any warrant or process as aforesaid shall have authority to summon and call to their aid the bystanders or the *posse comitatus* of the proper county, or such portion of the land and naval forces of the United States, or of the militia, as may be necessary to the performance of the duty with which they are charged, and to insure a faithful observance of the clause of the Constitution which prohibits slavery, in conformity with the provisions of this act; and said warrants shall run and be executed by said officers anywhere in the State or Territory within which they are issued.

SEC. 6. That any person who shall knowingly and wilfully obstruct, hinder, or prevent any officer, or other person charged with the execution of any warrant or process issued under the provisions of this act, or any person or persons lawfully assisting him or them, from arresting any person for whose apprehension such warrant or process may have been issued, or shall rescue, or attempt to rescue, such person from the custody of the officer, other person or persons, or those lawfully assisting as aforesaid, when so arrested pursuant to the authority herein given and declared, or shall aid, abet, or assist any person so arrested as aforesaid, directly or indirectly, to escape from the custody of the officer or other person legally authorized as aforesaid, or shall harbor or conceal any person for whose arrest a warrant or process shall have been issued as aforesaid, so as to prevent his discovery and arrest after notice or knowledge of the fact that a warrant has been issued for the apprehension of such person, shall, for either of said offenses, be subject to a fine not exceeding one thousand dollars, and imprisonment not exceeding six months, by indictment and conviction before the district court of the United States for the district in which said offense may have been committed, or before the proper court of criminal jurisdiction, if committed within any one of the organized Territories of the United States.

SEC. 7. That the district attorneys, the marshals, their deputies, and the clerks of the said district and territorial courts, shall be paid for their services the like fees as may be allowed to them for similar services in other cases; and in all cases where the proceedings are before a commissioner, he shall be entitled to a fee of ten dollars in full for his services in each case, inclusive of all services incident to such arrest and examination. The person or persons authorized to execute the process to be issued by such commissioners for the arrest of offenders against the provisions of this act, shall be entitled to a fee of five dollars for each person he or they may arrest and take before any such commissioner as aforesaid, with such other fees as may be deemed reasonable by such commissioner for such other additional services as may be necessarily performed by him or them, such as attending at the examination, keeping the prisoner in custody, and providing him with food and lodging during his detention, and until the final determination of such commissioner, and, in general, for performing such other duties as may be required in the premises, such fees to be made up in conformity with the fees usually charged by the officers of the courts of justice within the proper district or county, as near as may be practicable, and paid out of the Treasury of the United States on the certificate of the judge of the district within which the arrest is made, and to be recoverable from the defendant as part of the judgment in case of conviction.

SEC. 8. That whenever the President of the United States shall have reason to believe that offenses have been, or are likely to be committed against the provisions of this act within any judicial district, it shall be lawful for him, in his discretion, to direct the judge, marshal and district attorney of such district to attend at such place within the district, and for such time as he may designate, for the purpose of the more speedy arrest and trial of persons charged with a violation of this act; and it shall be the duty of every judge or other officer, when any such requisition shall be received by him, to attend at the place and for the time therein designated.

SEC. 9. That it shall be lawful for the President of the United States, or such person as he may empower for that purpose, to employ such part of the land or naval forces of the United States, or of the militia, as shall be necessary to prevent the violation and enforce the due execution of this act.

SEC. 10. That upon all questions of law arising in any cause under the provisions of this act, a final appeal may be taken to the Supreme Court of the United States.

The President vetoed this bill. It passed over his veto in the Senate on the 6th of April, 1866. Yeas 33—all Radicals; nays 10—all Democrats except Messrs. Lane (of Kansas), and Van Winkle. It passed the House April 9. Yeas 122—all Radicals; nays 41—all Democrats except Messrs. Latham, W. H. Randall, Raymond, Smith and Whaley.

A Constitutional Warrior.

NOBLE ORDER OF GENERAL HANCOCK.

HEADQUARTERS FIFTH MILITARY DISTRICT,
NEW ORLEANS, LA., NOV. 29, 1867.

General Orders No. 40.]

1. In accordance with General Orders No. 81, Headquarters of the Army, Adjutant-General's Office, Washington, D. C., August 27, 1867, Major-General W. S. Hancock hereby assumes command of the Fifth Military District and of the Department composed of the States of Louisiana and Texas.

2. The General commanding is gratified to learn that peace and quiet reign in the Department. It will be his purpose to preserve this condition of things. As a means to this great end, he regards the maintenance of the civil authorities in the faithful execution of the laws, as the most efficient under existing circumstances.

In war it is indispensable to repel force by force, and overthrow and destroy opposition to lawful authority. But when insurrectionary force has been overthrown, and peace established, and the civil authorities are ready and willing to perform their duties, the military power should cease to lead, and the civil administration resume its natural and rightful dominion. Solemnly impressed with these views, the General announces that the great principles of American liberty still are the lawful inheritance of this people and ever should be. The right of trial by jury, the *habeas corpus*, the liberty of the press, the freedom of speech, and the natural rights of persons and the rights of property must be preserved.

Free institutions, while they are essential to the prosperity and happiness of the people, always furnish the strongest inducements to peace and order. Crimes and offenses committed in this district must be referred to the consideration and judgment of the regular civil tribunals, and those tribunals will be supported in their lawful jurisdiction.

Should there be violations of existing laws which are not inquired into by the civil magistrates, or should failures in the administration of justice by the courts be complained of, the cases will be reported to these headquarters, when such orders will be made as may be deemed necessary.

While the General thus indicates his purpose to respect the liberties of the people, he wishes all to understand that armed insurrections or forcible resistance to the law will be instantly suppressed by arms.

By command of Major-General W. S. Hancock. W. G. MITCHELL,
Brevet Lieut.-Colonel, Acting A. A. G.

Sympathy for Ireland.

In the House of Representatives, March 8, 1867, Mr. Fernando Wood (Dem.), of New York, offered the following resolution:

Resolved, That this House extends its sympathy to the people of Ireland in their pending struggle for constitutional liberty. If the despotic governments of Europe shall be allowed to establish monarchical institutions in America, so should the United States foster and promote the extension of republican institutions in Europe.

Mr. BROOMALL (Rad). I object.

Mr. WOOD. I move to suspend the rules to enable me to offer the resolution.

Mr. ELDRIDGE. Upon that motion I demand the yeas and nays.

The yeas and nays were ordered.

The question was taken, and there were: Yeas 104, nays 14, not voting 42.

[The negative vote was as follows: Messrs. Delos R. Ashley, Blair, Broomall, Cake, Covode, Cullom, Driggs, Garfield, Laflin, Noell, Shellabarger, Trowbridge, C. C. Washburn and Winslow—ALL RADICALS but one.]

After a great deal of finessing on the part of the Radicals, to prevent a direct vote on the resolution, a motion to refer it was made by Mr. Banks (Radical), by yeas and nays as follows:

YEAS—Messrs. Allison, Ames, Anderson, Delos R. Ashley, Baker, Baldwin, Banks, Beaman, Benjamin, Bingham, Blaine, Blair, Boutwell, Bromwell, Broomall, Buckland, Cake, Churchill, Reader W. Clarke, Sidney Clarke, Cobb, Cook, Coburn, Cornell, Covode, Cullom, Dawes, Dodge, Driggs, Eckley, Eggleston, Eliot, Farnsworth, Ferris, Ferry, Fields, Finney, Garfield Gravely, Griswold, Hopkins, Chester D. Hubbard, Hulburd, Hunter, Julian, Ketcham, Kitchen, Koontz, Laflin, George V. Lawrence, Lincoln, Loan, Lynch, Marvin, McCarthy, McClurg,

Mercur, Miller, Moore, Moorhead, Morrell, Myers, O'Neill, Orth, Paine, Perham, Peters, *Phelps*, Plants, Poland, Polsley, Pomeroy, Raum, Robertson, Schenck, Scofield, Shanks, Shellabarger, Smith, Spalding, Stevens, Taffe, Thomas, Trowbridge, Twitchell, Upson, Burt Van Horn, Van Wyck, Cadwalader C. Washburn, Henry D. Washburn, Wm. B. Washburn, Welker, Wm. Williams, James F. Wilson, John T. Wilson, Windom and Woodbridge—97.

NAYS—Messrs. Archer, Boyer, Brooks, Burr, Butler, *Chanler*, Dennison, Donnelly, *Eldridge*, Fox, Getz, Glossbrenner, *Haight*, Harding, *Humphreys*, Ingersoll, Judd, *Kerr*, Wm. Lawrence, Logan, *Marshall*, *McCullough*, Morgan, *Morrissey*, *Mungen*, *Niblack*, *Nicholson*, *Noell*, *Pruyn*, *Robinson*, *Ross*, *Stewart*, *Stone*, *Taber*, *Van Auken*, Robert T. Van Horn, *Van Trump*, Ward, Stephen F. Wilson and *Wood*—40.

Every vote, but one, in the affirmative, Radical.

Every vote in the negative, but ten, Democrat.

On the 27th of March, 1867, Mr. Banks, from the Committee on Foreign Affairs, reported the following resolution:

Resolved, That this House extend its sympathy to the people of Ireland and of Candia in all their just efforts to maintain the independence of States, to elevate the people, and to extend and perpetuate the principles of liberty.

An amendment offered by Mr. Washburne (Radical) of Wisconsin, discouraging Fenianism, was lost.

The resolution passed without a division, after the following protest against its evasiveness by Messrs. Wood and Eldridge, Democrats.

Mr. WOOD. Mr. Speaker, the amendment is virtually a nullification of the resolution itself. The country well knows, as the House knows, that the present agitation in Ireland looks to the establishment of free government in that island as the result of this same Fenian movement. We all know it is this Fenian movement that has effected military organization in Ireland, and that every rebel in arms in Ireland, and all the preparatory arrangements looking to the establishment of an independent government in Ireland have been promoted, if not originally prompted, by this Fenian movement.

It may be true that it will cost lives, aye, of hundreds and thousands of men in the prosecution of the Fenian movement. All revolutions cost blood before they become successful. In our own revolutionary war oceans of blood were spilled before we were able to establish our independence of the mother country. Therefore, when we say by this resolution we sympathize with the people of Ireland in their present struggle, we say well and properly, but when we succeed it by saying that we are against the Fenian movement, we nullify the resolution reported from the Committee on Foreign Affairs. I call for the yeas and nays on the amendment.

Mr. ELDRIDGE. I ask the gentleman to yield to me for a moment?

Mr. BANKS. Certainly, sir.

Mr. ELDRIDGE. I hope the amendment submitted to the resolution reported from the Committee on Foreign Affairs will not be adopted. I look upon it as does the gentleman from New York, as an evasion or nullification of the original resolution. It seems to me that it is idle for us to express sympathy with the cause of Ireland and at the same time deprecate every measure which the people of Ireland take for their alleviation. It is worse than mockery to tell them in their degradation and suffering that we sympathize with them, and yet advise against every effort they make to throw off the oppression which weighs upon them.

It is not for me to determine at the outset, and I desire not to do it, that the effort they are making through the Fenian organization may not result to their good. Ireland's nationality is a cause worthy of Irishmen. What shall be done to achieve it is for them to judge. Submission and inaction will certainly not save them. If they will as a nation be free, they must strike the blow themselves; they must wrench their freedom from their oppressors by their own strong arms. It may seem a desperate struggle, but who can say that the liberties of that brave and generous people are not worth all their efforts. Who of us can determine what may or may not be accomplished. If their cause be just and our sympathies with them, in the name of God, in the name of liberty, let us not disparage any effort or discourage any enterprise which to them may betoken success. Any blow which the oppressed may aim at the oppressor to regain his rights and liberty, has my heart's best prayer for its success.

Negro Testimony.

Pending the Confiscation bill, June 28, 1862, Mr. Sumner moved these words as an addition to the fourteenth section:

"And in all proceedings under this act there shall be no exclusion of any witness on account of color."

Which was rejected as follows:

YEAS—Messrs. Chandler, Grimes, Harlan, Howard, King, Lane (of Kansas), Morrill, Pomeroy, Sumner, Trumbull, Wade, Wilkinson, Wilmot—13.

NAYS—Messrs. Anthony, Browning, *Carlile*, Clark, Collamer, Cowan, *Davis*, Dixon, Doolittle, Fessenden, Foot, Foster, Harris, Henderson, Lane (of Indiana), *Nesmith*, *Pearce*, *Powell*,

Sherman, Simmons, *Stark,* Ten Eyck, Willey, Wilson (of Mo.), *Wright*—25.

Pending the consideration of the supplement to the Emancipation bill for the District of Columbia, on the 7th of July, 1862, Mr. Sumner moved a new section: "That in all judicial proceedings in the District of Columbia, there shall be no exclusion of any witness on account of color."

Which was adopted—yeas 25, nays 11, as follows:

YEAS—Messrs. Anthony, Chandler, Clark, Collamer, Doolittle, Fessenden, Foot, Foster, Grimes, Hale, Harlan, Harris, Howe, King, Lane (of Kansas,) Morrill, Sherman, Simmons, Sumner, Ten Eyck, Trumbull, Wade, Wilkinson, Wilmot, Wilson (of Massachusetts)—25.

NAYS—Messrs. Browning, *Carlile,* Cowan, *Davis,* Henderson, *Kennedy, McDougall, Powell, Rice,* Willey, *Wright*—11.

The bill then passed.

July 9—The bill passed the House—yeas 69, nays 36. There was no separate vote on the above proposition. The NAYS were:

NAYS—Messrs. *William Allen, Ancona, Baily, Biddle,* Jacob B. Blair, Clements, *Cobb, Corning, Cox, Crisfield, Dunlap, English, Fouke, Grider, Harding, Knapp, Law, Lazear, Mallory,* Maynard, *Menzies, Morris, Nugen, Pendleton, Perry, Richardson, James S. Rollins, Shiel, John B. Steele, Wm. G. Steele, Stiles,* Francis Thomas, *Voorhees,* Ward, *Webster, Wood*—36.

Pending the consideration in the Senate of the House bill in relation to the competency of witnesses in trials of equity and admiralty,

July 15, 1862—Mr. Sumner offered this proviso to the first section:

Provided, That there shall be no exclusion of any witness on account of color.

Which was rejected—yeas 14, nays 23, as follows:

YEAS—Messrs. Chandler, Grimes, Harlan, Howard, Howe, King, Lane (of Kansas), Pomeroy, *Rice,* Sumner, Wade, Wilkinson, Wilson (of Massachusetts)—14.

NAYS—Messrs. Anthony, *Bayard,* Browning, Clark, Cowan, *Davis,* Doolittle, Foster, Hale, Harris, Henderson, *Kennedy,* Lane (of Indiana), *Powell, Saulsbury,* Sherman, Simmons, *Stark,* Ten Eyck, Trumbull, Willey, *Wilson* (of Missouri), *Wright*—23.

The disposition of the Radicals at that time to "palter" with this question "in a double sense," is well illustrated by the preceding votes. Only thirteen of them are found in the Senate, on two occasions, to vote for Mr. Sumner's amendment involving the admission of negro testimony in the United States Courts in their own States, as well as in other places; but when a proposition is made about the same time to introduce it in the District of Columbia, twenty-four of them are found ready to give it their support.

June 25, 1864—Pending the civil appropriation bill, in Committee of the Whole, Mr. Sumner offered this proviso:

Provided, That in the courts of the United States there shall be no exclusion of any witness on account of color.

Mr. Buckalew moved to add:

Nor in civil actions because he is a party to or interested in the issue tried.

Which was agreed to; and the amendment as amended was agreed to—yeas 22, nays 16, as follows:

YEAS—Messrs. Anthony, Brown, Chandler, Clark, Collamer, Conness, Foot, Foster, Grimes, Hale, Harlan, Howard, Howe, Lane (of Kansas), Morgan, Morrill, Pomeroy, Sprague, Sumner, Wade, Wilkinson, Wilson—22.

NAYS—Messrs. *Buckalew, Carlile,* Cowan, *Davis,* Harris, *Hendricks,* Hicks, Johnson, *Nesmith, Powell, Richardson, Saulsbury,* Sherman, Trumbull, Van Winkle, Willey—16.

In the House, June 29th, the amendment of the Senate was agreed to—yeas 68, nays 48, as follows:

YEAS—Messrs. Allison, Ames, Arnold, Ashley, *Baily,* John D. Baldwin, Beaman, Boutwell, Boyd, Broomall, Cobb, Cole, Thomas T. Davis, Dawes, Deming, Dixon, Donnelly, Driggs, Eckley, Eliot, Farnsworth, Fenton, Frank, Garfield, Gooch, Higby, Hooper, Hotchkiss, Hulburd, Ingersoll, Jenckes, Julian, F. W. Kellogg, Orlando Kellogg, Knox, Littlejohn, Loan, Longyear, McBride, McClurg, Moorhead, Morrill, Daniel Morris, Amos Myers, Leonard Myers, Norton, Charles O'Neill, Patterson, Perham, Alexander H. Rice, John H. Rice, Edward H. Rollins, Schenck, Scofield, Shannon, Smithers, Sloan, Spalding, Stevens, Thayer, Upson, Van Valkenburgh, Ellihu B. Washburne, William B. Washburne, Williams, Wilder, Wilson, Windom—68.

NAYS—Messrs. *Wm. J. Allen, Ancona, Augustus C. Baldwin,* Jacob B. Blair, *Bliss, Brooks,* Wm. G. Brown, *Chanler, Coffroth, Dawson, Denison, Eden, Edgerton, Eldridge, Finck, Harding, Benjamin G. Harris, Charles M. Harris, Herrick, Holman, William Johnson, Knapp, Le Blonde, Mallory, Marcy, James R. Morris, Morrison, Noble,* John O'Neill, *Pendleton, Perry, Samuel J. Randall, Robinson, Ross,* John B. Steele, *William G. Steele, Stiles, Strouse, Stuart,* Thomas Tracy, *Wadsworth, Ward,* Webster, *Whaley, Wheeler, Chilton A. White, Joseph W. White*—48.

Bogus Ratification of an Amendment to the Constitution.

On the 20th of July, 1868, Mr. Seward, Secretary of State, issued the following proclamation:

[Here the Secretary quotes the proposed fourteenth article, as contained on page 117 of this book.]

And whereas, By the second section of the Act of Congress, approved the 20th of April, one thousand eight hundred and eighteen, entitled "An act to provide for the publication of the laws of the United States, and for other purposes," it is made the duty of the Secretary of State forthwith to cause any amendment to the Constitution of the United States, which has been adopted according to the provisions of the said Constitution, to be published in the newspapers authorized to promulgate the laws, with his certificate specifying the States by which the same may have been adopted, and that the same has become valid to all intents and purposes as a part of the Constitution of the United States.

And whereas, neither the act just quoted from nor any other law expressly or by conclusive implication authorizes the Secretary of State to determine and decide doubtful questions as to the authenticity of the organization of State Legislatures, or as to the power of any State Legislature to recall a previous act or resolution of ratification of any amendment proposed to the Constitution;

And whereas, It appears from official documents on file in this Department that the amendment to the Constitution of the United States, proposed as aforesaid, has been ratified by the Legislatures of the States of Connecticut, New Hampshire, Tennessee, New Jersey, Oregon, Vermont, New York, Ohio, Illinois, West Virginia, Kansas, Maine, Nevada, Missouri, Indiana, Minnesota, Rhode Island, Wisconsin, Pennsylvania, Michigan, Massachusetts, Nebraska, and Iowa;

Whereas, It further appears, from documents on file in this Department, that the Legislatures of two of the States first above-enumerated, to wit: Ohio and New Jersey, have since passed resolutions respectively withdrawing the consent of each of said States to the aforesaid amendment;

And whereas, It is deemed a matter of doubt and uncertainty whether such resolutions are not irregular and invalid, and therefore ineffectual for withdrawing the consent of the said two States, or of either of them, to the aforesaid amendment;

And whereas, The whole number of States in the United States are thirty-seven, to wit: New Hampshire, Massachusetts, Rhode Island, Connecticut, New York, New Jersey, Pennsylvania, Delaware, Maryland, Virginia, North Carolina, South Carolina, Georgia, Vermont, Kentucky, Tennessee, Ohio, Louisiana, Indiana, Mississippi, Illinois, Alabama, Maine, Missouri, Arkansas, Michigan, Florida, Texas, Iowa, Wisconsin, Minnesota, California, Oregon, Kansas, West Virginia, Nevada, and Nebraska;

And whereas, The twenty-three States hereinbefore named, whose Legislatures have ratified the said proposed amendment, and the six States next thereafter named as having ratified the said proposed amendment by newly constituted and established legislative bodies, together constitute three-fourths of the whole number of States in the United States;

Now, therefore, be it known, That I, William H. Seward, Secretary of State of the United States, by virtue and in pursuance of the second section of the act of Congress, approved the twentieth day of April, eighteen hundred and eighteen, hereinbefore cited, do hereby certify that if the resolutions of the Legislatures of Ohio and New Jersey, ratifying the aforesaid amendments, are to be deemed as remaining of full force and effect, notwithstanding the subsequent resolutions of the Legislatures of these States, which purport to withdraw the consent of said States from such ratification, then the aforesaid amendment has been ratified in the manner hereinbefore mentioned, and so has become valid to all intents and purposes as a part of the Constitution of the United States.

In testimony whereof, I have hereunto set my hand and caused the seal of the Department of State to be affixed.

Done at the City of Washington, this twentieth day of July, in the year of our Lord one thousand eight hundred and sixty-eight, and of the independence of the United States of America the ninety-third.

WM. H. SEWARD, Sec'y of State.

What the Radicals Propose to Do.

The purpose of the Radicals in hurrying up this pretended ratification, is evident. In a speech at Cincinnati, July 24, 1866, the Hon. George E. Pugh shows it up. Said Mr. Pugh:

They now deny the right of the State of Ohio to withdraw her previous assent to the Fourteenth amendment to the Constitution, as you have heard. No lawyer will deny that right. But will any Republican who is not a lawyer deny it? If he does, then I tell him that his party did that very thing in Ohio. For, in the winter of 1860–61, the Legislature of Ohio, and a Republican Legislature, did give the assent of this State to what is known as the Corwin-Seward Amendment, and a Republican Legislature withdrew that assent; and that is of record.

And yet, although Congress has no business with that question, although Congress never heretofore has concerned itself with the question of declaring whether an amendment was adopted or not, these gentlemen have undertaken to put themselves into the breach and declare that it has been ratified. And how? By resolution passed through both Houses of Congress? No, indeed.

They have got tired of Andrew Johnson's vetoes, and they have now decided not to let him have a chance to veto. Have they concluded to dispense with the Constitution altogether? They tell us that it passed both Houses, but that it need not be sent to the President. Let us see what the Constitution says:

"Every order, resolution or vote, to which the concurrence of the House of Representatives and Senate may be necessary, except on the question of adjournment, shall be presented to the President of the United States, and before the same shall take effect, shall be approved by him, or, being disapproved by him, shall be repassed by two-thirds of the Senate and House of Representatives according to the rules and limitations prescribed in the case of a bill."

And yet in defiance of that plain sentence in the Constitution, they have undertaken, without consulting the President, without even giving him a chance to approve or disapprove, to trample under foot, not merely the rights of the Southern States, but the sovereignty of our own good State of Ohio.

And how does the Fourteenth amendment operate? A year or two ago it was supposed to operate upon the people of the Southern States. Now it operates upon us. It says that a State which denies to the negro the right of voting shall be sheared of its representation in Congress, and in the Electoral College to the extent of the whole negro population of that State. And, therefore, this Fourteenth amendment, which they have hustled through Congress in the last two days in violation of the Constitution, is intended to punish you, my fellow-citizens, for having, by 50,000 majority, refused this negro suffrage last fall. It is you who are the sufferers. It is not a question of imposing it upon the Southern States, for they have crammed the negro question on them. It is an insult put on us. It is the rebuke we have for exercising our right to decide whether or not we will permit negroes to vote in our State.

RIGHT OF A STATE TO WITHDRAW ITS RATIFICATION—CHARLES O'CONNOR'S OPINION.
[From the New York World.]

By the terms of the Reconstruction act the carpet-bag governments are excluded from representation in Congress until the Fourteenth amendment is ratified. It reads, "and when said article shall have become a part of the Constitution said State shall be declared entitled to representation in Congress, and Senators and Representatives shall be admitted therefrom on their taking the oaths prescribed by law."

It should be plain that no amendment to the Constitution can be made except by the *simultaneous* assent of three-fourths of the States. Counting in even the carpet-bag governments, three-fourths of the States have *not* given their simultaneous assent to the Fourteenth amendment. Ohio and New Jersey are here, and now in the attitude of refusing their assent at the moment when twenty-one other Northern States, and the six carpet-bag governments, are in the attitude of giving their assent. No amendment is valid till "*when* ratified by the legislatures of three-fourths of the several States," *i. e., where* being and standing ratified; a precise instant of time and a like coexisting condition of things being thus sharply prescribed as the two indispensable requirements. Said Mr. O'Connor, in the letter to which we have alluded: "During its progress to maturity this process of amendment is strictly analogous to a proposal for a compact made to parties who are competent to accept or decline as they think fit. It is an universal rule admitting of no exception that such a proposal is revocable until accepted. Judicial authorities numberless might be cited in support of this proposition. The decisions and elementary works all concur. Indeed it is a rule dictated by the simplest perceptions of justice and right reason. No one has ever been found silly or hardy enough to question it. It may be pronounced a maxim that until all are bound none are bound. This doctrine can not be less applicable to States or public corporate bodies than to individuals. * * * Every consent, while it remains unaccepted, is naturally ambulatory. No sound, unprejudiced thinker will ever question the right of a rejecting State to revoke its rejection, or of an assenting State to withdraw its assent until the amendment shall have become part of the Constitution" by the *simultaneous* assent of three-fourths of the States.

If anything reasonable could be hoped for from the Rump Congress we might expect it to conform to the requirements of its own reconstruction legislation, but it makes as little of stultifying its own enactment as of disregarding the supreme law; and is now merely adding another stone to the bulwarks about its own powers which the people with their ballots will blow to atoms next November third.

THE THIRTEENTH OR FOURTEENTH AMENDMENT—WHICH?
[From the New York World.]

It is said that Arkansas and North Carolina have ratified the proposed Fourteenth amendment. It is asserted that they have rejected it. The dates are given:

	Rejected.	*Ratified.*
Arkansas	Dec. 17, 1866	April 6, 1868
North Caorlina	Dec. 13, 1866	July 4, 1868

Here's a coil. If the rejection is a good rejection, there has been no ratification. And if the ratification is a good ratification, the Constitution of the United States does not prohibit slavery. The same governments in Arkansas and North Carolina that rejected the Fourteenth, ratified the Thirteenth (or Emancipation) amendment. If the rejection is illegal, then the ratification is illegal too. But it was this ratification that put the Thirteenth amendment in the Constitution, and if illegal that amendment isn't there.

The Public Finances—Government Receipts and Expenditures.

How the 5-20 Bonds are Redeemable.

In this chapter we have endeavored to embrace everything bearing upon the important subject of finance that will aid the intelligent voter in making up his judgment.

LEGAL TENDERS.

The act of February 25, 1862, authorized the issue of $150,000,000 in Treasury-notes, of which $50,000,000 should be in lieu of so many of the "Demand notes"—to be receivable for all duties, imposts, excises, debts, and demands of every kind due to the United States, and all salaries, etc., from the United States, "*and shall also be lawful money, and a legal tender in payment of all debts, public and private, within the United States*," to be exchangeable for twenty-year six per cent. bonds, interest payable semi-annually, or five-year seven per cent. bonds with interest payable semi-annually in coin. Such United States notes to be received the same as coin in payment for loans. Five hundred millions of bonds authorized, payable after twenty years, at six per cent. interest, payable semi-annually.

YEAS—Messrs. Aldrich, Alley, Arnold, Ashley, Babbitt, Goldsmith F. Bailey, *Joseph Baily*, Baker, Beaman, Bingham, Francis P. Blair, Jacob B. Blair, Samuel S. Blair, Blake, Buffinton, Burnham, Campbell, Chamberlain, Clark, Colfax, Cutler, Davis, Delano, *Delaplaine*, Duell, Dunn, Edgerton, Edwards, Ely, Fenton, Fessenden, Fisher, Franchot, Frank, Gooch, Granger, Gurley, *Haight*, Hale, Hanchett, Harrison, Hickman, Hooper, Hutchins, Julian, Kelley, Francis W. Kellogg, William Kellogg, Killinger, Lansing, Leary, Loomis, McKean, McKnight, McPherson, Marston, Maynard, Mitchell, Moorhead, Anson P. Morrill, *Nugen*, Olin, Patton, Timothy G. Phelps, Pike, *Price*, Alexander H. Rice, John H. Rice, Riddle, *James S. Rollins*, Sargent, Shanks, Shellabarger, Sherman, Sloan, Spaulding, *John B. Steele*, Stevens, Trimble, Trowbridge, Upson, Van Horn, Van Valkenburgh, Van Wyck, Verree, Wall, Wallace, Charles W. Walton, Whaley, Albert S. White, Wilson, Windom, Worcester—93.

NAYS—Messrs. Ancona, Baxter, *Biddle*, George H. Browne, *Cobb*, Frederick A. Conkling, Roscoe Conkling, Conway, *Corning*, *Cox*, *Cravens*, Crisfield, *Dunlap*, Diven, Eliot, *English*, Goodwin, Grider, Harding, Holman, Horton, Johnson, Knapp, *Law*, Lazear, Lovejoy, Mallory, May, Menzies, Justin S. Morrill, *Morris*, Nixon, Noble, *Norton*, Odell, Pendleton, *Perry*, Pomeroy, Porter, *Richardson*, Robinson, Edward H. Rollins, Sedgwick, Sheffield, Shiel, William G. Steele, Stratton, Benjamin F. Thomas, Francis Thomas, Train, *Voorhees*, *Vallandigham*, Wadsworth, E. P. Walton, Ward, Webster, Chilton A. White, Wickliffe, Wright—59.

In the Senate. February 12, the Committee on Finance recommended instead of making these notes receivable for all demands due to, and all demands owing by, the United States, this substitute:

"And such notes herein authorized shall be receivable in payment of all public dues and demands of every description, and of all claims against the United States of every kind whatsoever, except for interest upon bonds and notes, which shall be paid in coin."

Mr. Sherman moved to include with these notes, "the notes authorized by the act of 17th of July, 1861," which was agreed to. The amendment to the amendment was agreed to

On the 13th of February, Mr. Collamer moved to strike out these words:

"And such notes herein authorized and the notes authorized by the act of July 17, 1861, shall be receivable in payment of all public dues and demands of every description, and of all claims and demands against the United States of every kind whatsoever, except for interest upon bonds and notes, which shall be paid in coin, and shall also be lawful money and a legal tender in payment of all debts, public and private, within the United States, except interest as aforesaid."

Which was rejected—yeas 17, nays 22, as follows:

YEAS—Messrs. Anthony, *Bayard*, Collamer, Cowan, Fessenden, Foot, Foster, *Kennedy*, King, *Latham*, Nesmith, *Pearce*, Powell, *Saulsbury*, Simmons, *Thomson*, Willey—17.

NAYS—Messrs. Chandler, Clark, *Davis*, Dixon, Doolittle, Harlan, Harris, Henderson, Howard, Howe, Lane (of Indiana), *McDougall*, Morrill, Pomeroy, *Rice*, Sherman, Sumner, Ten Eyck, Wade, Wilkinson, Wilson of (Massachusetts), *Wilson* (of Missouri)—22.

The bill was then passed—yeas 30, nays 7, as follows:

YEAS—Messrs. Anthony, Chandler, Clark, *Davis*, Dixon, Doolittle, Fessenden, Foot, Foster, Grimes, Hale, Harlan, Harris, Henderson, Howard, Howe, Lane (of Indiana), *Latham*, McDougall, Morrill, Pomeroy, *Rice*, Sherman, Sumner, Ten Eyck, Trumbull, Wade, Wilkinson, Wilson (of Massachusetts), *Wilson* (of Missouri)—30.

NAYS—Messrs. Collamer, Cowan, *Kennedy*, King, *Pearce*, Powell, Saulsbury—7.

Feb. 20—In the House, the question being on concurring in the amendment of the Senate making the interest upon bonds and notes payable in coin.

Mr. Stevens moved to include also "payments to officers, soldiers, and sailors, in the Army and Navy of the United States, and for all supplies purchased for the said Government;" which was rejected—yeas 67, nays 72.

The amendment of the Senate, making interest payable in coin was then concurred in—yeas 88, nays 55, as follows:

YEAS—Messrs. *Ancona*, Arnold, Ashley, Baxter, Beaman, *Biddle*, Jacob B. Blair, *George H. Browne*, William G. *Brown*, Burnham, *Calvert*, Clements, *Cobb*, Frederick A. Conklin, Roscoe Conklin, Conway, Covode, *Cox, Cravens, Crittenden*, Diven, *Dunlap*, Dunn, Eliot, *English*, Goodwin, *Grider*, Gurley, *Haight, Hall, Harding, Holman*, Horton, *Johnson*, Kelley, *Knapp, Law*, Leary, *Lehman*, Loomis, Lovejoy, McKnight, *Mallory*, May, *Menzies*, Justin S. Morrill, Nixon, Noble, *Norton, Nugen, Odell*, Patton, *Pendleton, Perry*, Timothy G. Phelps, Pike, Pomeroy, Alexander H. Rice, Riddle, *Robinson*, Edward H. Rollins, *James S. Rollins*, Sargeant, Sedgwick, *Sheffield*, Sherman, *Shiel, Smith, John B. Steele, William G. Steele*, Stratton, Benjamin F. Thomas, Francis Thomas, Train, Trimble, *Vallandigham, Vibbard, Voorhees*, Chas. W. Walton, E. P. *Walton, Ward*, Washburn, Webster, Whaley, Wheeler, *Wickliffe, Woodruff, Wright*—88.

NAYS—Messrs. Aldrich, Alley, Babbit, *Joseph Baily*, Baker, Bingham, Francis P. Blair, Samuel S. Blair, Blake, Buffinton, Campbell, Chamberlain, Clark, Davis, Dawes, Duell, Edwards, Ely, Fenton, Fessenden, Fisher, Franchot, Frank, Granger, Hale, Hanchett, Harrison, Hickman, Hooper, Julian, William Kellogg, Killinger, Lansing, McPherson, Marston, Maynard, Moorhead, Anson P. Morrill, *Noell*, Olin, John H. Rice, Shanks, Sloan, Spalding, Stevens, Trowbridge, Van Horn, Van Valkenburgh, Verree. Wall, Wallace, Albert S. White, Wilson, Windom, Worcester—55.

Other amendments were non-concurred in, and a Committee of Conference agreed upon the bill as it became a law.

One feature of this report was to provide that the Treasury-notes issued under the bill should not be a legal tender in payment of duties, and the duties on imports, made payable in coin, should be pledged for the payment of interest on the bonds.

The report was agreed to in the House—yeas 98, nays 22. The nays were:

Messrs. Baker, *Biddle*, Buffinton, *Cox*, Edwards, *English, Haight*, Hooper, *Johnson*, Justin S. Morrill, *Odell, Pendleton, Perry*, Pike, *Robinson, Sheffield*, W. G. *Steele*, Van Wyck, *Voorhees, Wickliffe*, Wood, *Woodruff*.

The Senate concurred without a division.

TAXING BONDS.

On the 28th of June, 1862, the Loan Bill being under consideration, on concurring in Senate amendments, Mr. Holman moved to add this provision to one of them:

Provided, That nothing in this act shall impair the right of the States to tax the bonds, notes, and other obligations issued under this act.

Which was rejected—yeas 71, nays 77, as follows:

YEAS—Messrs. *William J. Allen, Ancona, Bliss, Brooks, James S. Brown, Chanler, Coffroth, Cox, Cravens*, Dawes, *Dawson, Denison, Eden, Edgerton, Eldridge, English*, Finck, *Ganson, Grider, Griswold, Harding, Harrington, Charles M. Harris, Herrick, Holman*, Hotchkiss, *Hutchins, Philip Johnson, William Johnson, Kalbfleisch, Kernan, Knapp, Law, Lazear, Le Blonde, Long, Mallory, Marcy, McDowell, McKinney, Middleton*, Samuel F. Miller, *William H. Miller, Jas. R. Morris, Morrison, Noble, John O'Neill, Pendleton, Perry*, Pomeroy, *Pruyn, Radford*, Samuel J. *Randall, Robinson*, Ross, John B. *Steele*, Wm. G. *Steele, Stiles, Strouse, Stewart, Sweat*, Thomas, Tracy, Van Valkenburgh, *Wadsworth, Ward*, Whaley, *Wheeler, Chilton A. White, Joseph W. White, Winfield*—71.

NAYS—Messrs. Alley, Allison, Ames, Anderson, Arnold, John D. Baldwin, Baxter, Beaman, Blaine, Blair, Blow, Boutwell, Boyd, Broomall, William G. Brown, Cobb, Cole, Creswell, Henry Winter Davis, Thomas T. Davis, Deming, Dixon, Donnelly, Driggs, Eckley, Eliot, Fenton, Garfield, Gooch, Hale, Higby, Hooper, Asahel W. Hubbard, John H. Hubbard, Hulburd, Ingersoll, Jenckes, Julian, Kelley, Francis W. Kellogg, Orlando Kellogg, Littlejohn, Loan, Longyear, Marvin, McBride, McClurg, McIndoe, Moorehead, Daniel Morris, Amos Myers, Leonard Myers, Norton, Charles O'Neill, Perham, Pike, Alexander H. Rice, John H. Rice, Edward H. Rollins, Schenck, Scofield, Shannon, Sloan, Smith, Smithers, Spalding, Stevens, Thayer, Upson, Elihu B. Washburne, Wm. B. Washburne, Webster, Williams, Wilder, Wilson, Windom—77.

NATIONAL BANKS.

In the Senate, February 12, 1863, the bill commonly known as the National Currency Act passed—yeas 23, nays 21, as follows:

YEAS—Messrs. Anthony, Arnold, Chandler, Clark, Doolittle, Fessenden, Foster, *Harding*, Harlan, Harris, Howard, Howe, Lane (of Kansas), Morrill, *Nesmith*, Pomeroy, Sherman, Sumner, Ten Eyck, Wade, Wilkinson, Wilmot, Wilson (of Massachusetts)—23.

NAYS—Messrs. *Carlile*, Callamer, Cowan, *Davis*, Dixon, Foot, Grimes, Henderson, Hicks, *Kennedy*, King, *Latham, McDougall, Powell, Rice, Richardson, Saulsbury, Trumbull, Turpie, Wall, Wilson* (of Mo.)—21.

The bill passed the House, February 20.

YEAS—Messrs. Aldrich, Alley, Ashley, Babbitt, Beaman, Bingham, Jacob B. Blair, Blake, Buffinton, *Calvert*, Campbell, Casey, Chamberlain, Clements, Colfax, Conway, Covode, Cutler, Davis, Delano, Dunn, Edgerton, Eliot, Ely, Fenton, S. C. Fessenden, T. A. D. Fessenden, Fisher, Frank, Goodwin, Granger, Hahn, *Haight*, Hickman, Hooper, Hutchins, Julian,

Kelley, F. W. Kellogg, W. Kellogg, Lansing, Leary, Lovejoy, Low, McIndoe, McKean, McPherson, Marston, Maynard, Moorhead, Anson P. Morrill, *Noell*, Olin, Patton, T. G. Phelps, Potter, A. H. Rice, J. H. Rice, Sargent, Sedgewick, Segar, Shanks, Shellabarger, Sherman, Sloan, Spalding, Stevens, Trimble, Trowbridge, Van Horn, Van Wyck, Verree, Wall, Wallace, Washburne, Albert S. White, Windom, Worcester—78.

NAYS—Messrs. *W. Allen, Ancona, Baily,* Baxter, Baker, *Biddle,* Cobb, F. A. Conkling, R. Conkling, *Cox, Cravens, Crittenden,* Dawes, Edwards, *English,* Gooch, *Grider, Hale, Harding,* Harrison, *Holman,* Horton, *Johnson, Kerrigan, Knapp, Law, Lazear,* Loomis, *Mallory, May, Menzies,* J. S. Morrill, *Morris,* Nixon, *Noble, Norton, Nugen,* Odell, *Pendleton, Perry,* Pike, Pomeroy, Porter, *Price, Robinson, J. S. Rollins, Sheffield, Shiel,* J. B. Steele, W. G. Steele, *Stiles,* Stratton, B. F. Thomas, F. Thomas, *Vallandigham, Wadsworth,* Wheeler, Whaley, C. A. *White, Wickliffe,* Wilson, *Woodruff, Wright* —64.

The act of 1864, while under consideration in the House of Representatives, was subjected to the following proceedings, involving the question of taxing bonds. On the 6th of April, Mr. Stevens offered a substitute for the whole bill, which he explained as differing from the amended bill in these respects only:

"The substitute provides for a uniform rate of interest at seven per cent., and withdraws these National banks from State taxation, and leaves them to be taxed by the National Government."

Which was rejected—yeas 59, nays 78, as follows:

YEAS—Messrs. Alley, Allison, Ames, Anderson, Ashley, John D. Baldwin, Baxter, Beaman, Blow, Boutwell, Boyd, Broomall, Ambrose W. Clark, Cobb, Cole, Thomas T. Davis, Dixon, Donnelly, Driggs, Eckley, Eliot, Frank, Garfield, Gooch, Grinnell, Hale, Hooper, John H. Hubbard, Jenckes, Julian, Kasson, Kelly, Francis W. Kellogg, Loan, Longyear, Marvin, McBride, McClurg, Morrill, Daniel Morris, Leonard Myers, Charles O'Neill, Patterson, Perham, Alexander H. Rice, Edward H. Rollins, Schenck, Scofield, Shannon, Spalding, Starr, Stevens, Thayer, Thomas, Upson, William B. Washburn, Wilder, Windom, Woodbridge—59.

NAYS—Messrs. *James C. Allen, Wm. J. Allen, Ancona, Baily,* Aug C. Baldwin, Blaine, *Bliss, Brooks, James S. Brown,* William G. Brown, *Chanler, Clay, Cox, Cravens, Dawson, Dennison, Eden, Eldridge, English, Finck, Ganson, Grider,* Griswold, *Hall, Harrington,* Benjamin G. Harris, *Herrick, Holman, Hotchkiss,* A. W. Hubbard, *Philip Johnson,* William *Johnson, Kalbfleisch,* Orlando Kellogg, *Kernan, Law, Long, Mallory, Marcy, McKinney, Middleton, William H. Miller, James R. Morris, Morrison, Amos* Myers, *Nelson,* Odell, *John* O'Neill, Orth, *Pendleton,* Pike, Pomeroy, *Price, Pruyn, Radford, Samuel J. Randall,* William H. Randall, John H. Rice, *Robinson, Rogers, James S. Rollins, Scott,* Smithers, John B. Steele, W. G. Steele, *Strouse, Stuart,* Tracy, Van Valkenburgh, *Ward,* Elihu B. Washburne, Wheeler, *Chilton A. White, Joseph W.* White, Wilson, *Winfield, Benjamin* Wood, Yeaman—78.

Previous to this vote a vote was had on the following proposition:

"That nothing in this act shall be construed to prevent the taxation by States of the capital stock of banks organized under this act, the same as the property of other moneyed corporations, for State or municipal purposes; but no State shall impose any tax upon such associations or their capital, circulation, dividends, or business, at a higher rate of taxation than shall be imposed by such State upon the same amount of moneyed capital in the hands of individual citizens of such State."

The affirmative vote on this was the same as the negative vote on that of Mr. Stevens, and the negative vote on that was the same as the affirmative vote on this with these exceptions: Messrs. Scofield, Starr and Windom voted for both propositions. Messrs. Blaine, A. W. Hubbard, Price, Smithers and E. B. Washburne, voted against both. Messrs. Garfield, Patterson, Thomas and Woodbridge, who voted for Mr. Stevens', did not vote on this. Messrs. Wilson and *J. S. Rollins,* who voted against Mr. Stevens', did not vote on this. Messrs. Whaley, *Lazear* and S. F. Miller, who did not vote on Mr. Stevens', voted for this.

This bill, as amended, having been laid on the table, a new bill was considered, April 16th, containing the following *proviso:*

"*Provided,* That nothing in this act shall be construed to prevent the market value of the shares in any of the said banking associations, held by any person or body corporate created by State law, being included in the valuation of the aggregate personal property of such person or State corporation in assessing any tax imposed by any State or municipal authority on the aggregate personal estate of all persons subject to the authority of such State or municipality."

Mr. Fenton moved to substitute this:

"And that nothing in this act shall be construed to prevent the taxation by States of the capital stock of banks organized under this act, the same as the property of other moneyed corporations for State or municipal purposes; but no State shall impose any tax upon such associations or their capital, circulation, dividends, or business, at a higher rate of taxation than shall be imposed by such State upon the same amount of moneyed capital in the hands of individual citizens of such State: *Provided,* That no State tax shall be imposed on any part of the capital stock of such association invested in the bonds of the United States, deposited as security for its circulation."

Which was agreed to—yeas 70, nays 60, as follows:

YEAS—Messrs. Alley, Allison, Ames, Arnold, Ashley, *Baily*, John D. Baldwin, Baxter, Beaman, Blaine, Boutwell, Broomall, Wm. G Brown, Ambrose W. Clark, Freeman Clarke, *Clay*, Cobb, Cole, Dawes, Driggs, Dumont, Eckley, Farnsworth, Fenton, Frank, Gooch, Grinnell, Higby, Hooper, Hotchkiss, John H. Hubbard, Jencken, Julian, Kasson, Francis W. Kellogg, Orlando Kellogg, Loan, Longyear, Marvin, McClurg, McIndoe, Samuel F. Miller, Moorhead, Morrill, Daniel Morris, Amos Myers, Charles O'Neill, Orth, Patterson, Perham, Pike, Pomeroy, Price, William H. Randall, Alexander H. Rice, John H. Rice, Edward H. Rollins, Shannon, Sloan, Smith, Tracy, Upson, Van Valkenburgh, Elihu B. Washburne, William B. Washburn, Webster, Wilder, Wilson, Windom, Woodbridge—70.

NAYS—Messrs. *James C. Allen, Wm. J. Allen, Augustus C. Baldwin, Brooks, James S. Brown, Chanler, Cravens,* Creswell, *Henry Winter Davis, Dawson, Eden, Eldridge, Finck, Gunson, Hall, Harding, Harrington, Benjamin G. Harris, Herrick, Holman,* Asahel W. Hubbard, *Hutchins, Wm. Johnson, Kalbfleisch,* Kelley, *Kernan, King, Knapp, Law, Lazear, Long, Marcy, McBride, McDowell, McKinney, Wm. H. Miller, James R. Morris, Morrison, Nelson, Noble, Odell, Pendleton, Pruyn, Radford, Samuel J. Randall, Robinson, James S. Rollins, Ross, Scott, John B. Steele, Strouse, Stuart,* Thayer, Thomas, *Wheeler, Chilton A. White, Joseph W. White,* Williams, *Winfield, Fernando Wood*—60.

The bill was then passed.

The Senate amended it, and the House non-concurred, when a Committee of Conference was appointed, who reported, June 1. The tax question was settled by adding these words to the thirty-second section:

And nothing in this act shall be construed to prevent all the shares in any of the said associations, held by any person or body corporate, from being included in the valuation of personal property of such person or corporation, in the assessment of taxes imposed by or under State authority, at the place where such bank is located, and not elsewhere; but not a greater rate than is assessed on other moneyed capital in the hands of individual citizens of said States: *Provided further,* That the tax so imposed under the law of any State upon the shares of any of the associations authorized by this act shall not exceed the rate imposed on shares in any of the bank organizations under the authority of the State where such association is located.

The bill provides for a tax of one per cent. on the circulation of National banks, one-half of one per cent. on their deposits, and one per cent. on their capital above the amount invested in United States bonds

The report was concurred in, without a division in either house

Receipts and Expenditures of the United States Government.

[From a Radical Exhibit.]

Mr. Schenck, of Ohio (Radical), Chairman of the Committee of Ways and Means, in a speech, in the House of Representatives, made the following exhibit:

Revenue Receipts and National Expenditures for the fiscal year June 3, 1867.

RECEIPTS.

The receipts of the National Revenue for the fiscal year ending June 30, 1867, were as follows:

Currency	$314,109,156 01
Coin	176,417,810 88
Total, coin and currency	$490,525,947 49

EXPENDITURES.

The expenditures for the fiscal year ending June 30, 1867, were as follows:

Legislative, Judiciary, Executive and Diplomatic	$ 51,110,027 27
Pensions	20,936,551 71
Indians	4,642,531 77
Navy	31,034,011 04
War—exclusive of bounties	83,841,555 80
Total ordinary expenditures	$191,564,677 59
Interest	143,781,591 91
Bounties	11,382,859 83
Total expenditures	$346,729,129 33

The balance of receipts over expenditures for the fiscal year ending June 30, 1867, was $143,797,818 16

By the acts of July 13, 1866, and of March 2, 1867, Internal Revenue taxes were repealed or abated to an extent sufficient to occasion an annual loss of revenue from internal sources, taking the returns of the preceding year as a precedent, of at least $90,000,000, of which amount some $60,000,000 to $70,000,000 were made applicable for the reduction of taxes during the fiscal years ending June 30, 1866, 1867; the balance taking effect during the succeeding or present fiscal year.

National Receipts and Expenditures for the current fiscal year, ending June 30, 1868—actual and estimated.

RECEIPTS.

For the three quarters, from July 1, 1867, to March 31, 1868—actual:

Customs	$121,208,374 37
Lands	866,337 31
Internal Revenue	140,086,426 44
Direct Tax	1,419,960 46
Miscellaneous	35,019,361 71
Total	$294,194,459 29

Fourth quarter, from March 1, 1868, to June 30, 1868—estimated:

Customs	$ 44,000,000 00
Lands	40,000 00
Internal Revenue	50,000,000 00
Direct Tax	500,000 00
Miscellaneous	12,000,000 00
Total	$106,000,000 00

Total revenue for fiscal year ending June 30, 1868—actual and estimated:

Customs	$165,208,374 37
Lands	1,166,337 31
Internal Revenue	190,686,426 44
Direct Tax	1,713,960 46
Miscellaneous	47,019,360 71
Total	$405,794,459 29

EXPENDITURES.

For the three quarters from July 1, 1867, to March 31, 1868—actual:

Civil, Legislative, Executive, and Foreign intercourse	$ 39,554,175 32
Interior, Pensions and Indians	24,733,337 29
War	88,858,496 82
Navy	19,113,673 53
Interest on the Public Debt	109,418,383 87
Total	$280,678,066 83

For the fourth quarter ending June 30, 1868—estimated:

Civil, Legislative, Executive and Foreign intercourse	$ 13,000,000 00
Interior, Pensions, and Indians	4,000,000 00
War	35,000,000 00
Navy	6,500,000 00
Interest on the Public Debt	40,000,000 00
Total	$ 98,500,000 00

Total expenditures for the fiscal year ending June 30, 1868, actual and estimated:

Civil, Legislative, Executive, and Foreign intercourse	$ 51,554,175 32
Interior, Pensions, and Indians	28,733,337 29
War	123,858,496 82
Navy	25,613,673 53
Interest on the Public Debt	149,418,383 87
Total	$379,178,066 83

RECAPITULATION.

Receipts and expenditures for the fiscal year ending June 30, 1868:

Total Receipts	$405,794,459 29
Total Expenditures	379,178,066 83
Estimated balance of Receipts over Expenditures for the fiscal year ending June 30, 1868	$ 26,616,392 46

National Receipts and Expenditures for the fiscal year ending June 30, 1869.

Under this heading it is proposed to first consider the necessary and probable expenditures of the Government for the next fiscal year; and, secondly, the revenue which may be legitimately expected during the same period.

The appropriation bills for the next fiscal year, which have passed or are now pending, are as follows:

Deficiency bill (Senate, No. 32), passed	$12,839,196 21
Deficiency bill (Senate, contingent, No. 402), passed	82,000 00
Deficiency bill (Reconstruction, No. 1,014), passed	87,710 50
Relief bill (District of Columbia, March 10), passed	15,000 00
Military Academy, passed	284,004 50
Consular and diplomatic (passed)	1,206,431 00
Postoffice, passed	1,545,000 00
Pensions—pending	30,350,000 00
Army—pending	33,081,013 00
Navy—pending	17,500,000 00
Legislative, executive, and judiciary—pending	16,880,672 00
Sundry civil expenditures—pending	6,020,376 32
Indian—pending	2,500,000 00
River and harbor—pending	6,000,000 00
Deficiency bill—pending	1,912,960 00
Total	$130,304,366 53
Miscellaneous, including appropriations for New York City Postoffice, private bills, and judgments of Court of Claims, estimated	10,000,000 00
Permanent appropriations for collecting the revenue, etc	9,969,000 00
Total	$150,273,366 53
Interest on the public debt	129,678,078 50
Total	$279,951,445 03

EXTRAORDINARY EXPENDITURES.

Bounties, estimated	$40,500,000 00
Alaska	7,200,000 00
Total	$327,651,445 03
To this aggregate there should also be added overlapping appropriations heretofore made that will not be extended till next year, viz. :	24,669,174 00
Making a total *probable* expenditure during the next fiscal year, for which revenue must be provided, of	$352,320,629 03

Revenue to meet the above Estimate for Expenditures.

The following receipts may be estimated:

Customs	$165,000,000 00

Mr. Schenck, assuming the passage of the new tax bill as reported by the committee, which afterward became a law in a somewhat modified form, estimates the receipts from internal revenue for the next fiscal year as follows:

Fermented liquors	$6,000,000
Gas and refined petroleum (reduced)	3,500,000
Incomes and salaries	36,000,000
Gross receipts	7,500,000
Stamps	17,000,000
Legacies and successions	2,000,000
Bank dividends, circulation, and deposits	10,000,000
Fines and penalties	1,400,000
Miscellaneous schedule, etc	2,100,000
Special taxes, exclusive of the special taxes on the sales of distillers and rectifiers, and inclusive of taxes on sales	25,000,000
Total	$115,500,000

With the passage of the amended law, it seems impossible, even with the continuance of a defective administration, that the receipts from distilled spirits for the next fiscal year can fall short of $70,000,000, or from tobacco of $25,000,000. Assuming the correctness of the latter estimates, we have, then, the gross sum of $210,500,000 as the receipts from internal revenue which may be reasonably anticipated for the fiscal year ending June 30, 1869. On the other hand, if we fail to secure any increase of revenue from distilled spirits and tobacco beyond what was received during the last fiscal year, the receipts of the next fiscal year can not be estimated at less than $164,000,000.

From the sale of public lands, the revenue, Mr. Schenck estimates, will be $1,000,000.

For the revenue receipts from miscellaneous sources, *i. e.*, premium on gold, sales of property, consular fees, etc., Mr. Schenck adopts the estimate of the Secretary of the Treasury, in his last annual report, viz.: $30,000,000.

A recapitulation of the foregoing estimates gives the following as the total anticipated revenue for the next fiscal year:

Customs	$165,000,000
Internal revenue	210,560,000
Public lands	1,000,000
Miscellaneous	30,000,000
Total	**$406,560,000**

Supposing no increase of receipts from distilled spirits and tobacco over the receipts for the fiscal year ending June 30, 1867—

The above estimate would be reduced to	$360,560,000
Estimate of expenditures for next fiscal year, before submitted	332,320,629
Balance to account of surplus revenue	$28,239,371

This balance to account of surplus revenue prognosticated by Mr. Schenck must be taken *cum grano salis*. Under Radical legislation, balances on that side are unknown. Deficiencies calling for more! more! are more fashionable and more probable.

The Public Debt.

The following is the statement of the public debt of the United States on the 1st of June, 1868:

DEBT BEARING COIN INTEREST.

5 per cent. bonds	$220,812,400 00	
6 per cent. bonds of 1867 and 1868	8,582,641 80	
6 per cent. bonds, 1881	283,677,200 00	
6 per cent. 5-20 bonds	1,494,755,600 00	
Navy Pension Fund	13,000,000 00	
		$2,020,827,841 80

DEBT BEARING CURRENCY INTEREST.

6 per cent. bonds	25,902,000 00	
3-year compound interest notes	21,604,890 00	
3-year 7.30 notes	105,610,650 00	
3 per cent. certificates	50,000,000 00	
		203,117,540 00

MATURED DEBT NOT PRESENTED FOR PAYMENT.

3-year 7.30 notes, due August 15, 1867	947,500 00	
Compound int. notes, matured June 10, July 15, August 15, Oct. 15, and Dec. 15, 1867	8,012,360 00	
Bonds, Texas indem'y	256,000 00	
Treasury notes, acts July 17, 1861, and prior thereto	155,211 64	
Bonds, April 15, 1842	6,000 00	
Treas'y notes, March 2, 1863	555,492 00	
Temporary loan	883 39	
Certificates of indebtedness	18,000 00	
		10,834,202 64

DEBT BEARING NO INTEREST.

U. S. notes	356,144,212 00	
Fractional currency	32,531,589 94	
Gold certificates of deposit	20,298,180 00	
		408,973,981 94
Total debt		$2,643,753,566 38

Am't in Treas'y, coin	90,228,559 31
" currency	43,279,120 33
	133,507,679 64
Am't of debt, less cash in Treasury	$2,510,245,886 74

The foregoing is a correct statement of the public debt, as appears from the books and Treasurer's returns in the Department, on the 1st of June, 1868.

HUGH McCULLOCH,
Secretary of the Treasury.

REVIEW OF THE ABOVE.

[From the Missouri Republican, June 15, 1868.]

The statement made by Secretary McCulloch of the public debt of the United States, on the first day of June, 1868, shows the total debt to be $2,643,753,565. At the same time there was in the Treasury $90,228,559 in coin, and $43,279,120 00. Total in the Treasury of $133,507,679 00. Deducting this from the debt given above, shows an absolute debt of $2,510,245,886 00. For all practical purposes, however, the larger sum, $2,643,753,565 00 is the real debt. The amount in the Treasury does not go at all in diminishing the indebtedness. The large sum of *thirty-two millions of dollars in gold* must be taken from the Treasury to pay the interest on the five-twenty bonds during the present month. Then there are large requisitions from the War Department, which it was contemplated would be made in May, which were deferred till this month, that must come out of the amount in the Treasury.

It appears that, instead of the enormous debt pressing upon the country being in process of diminution, it is increasing. The total debt, less cash in the Treasury at the close of April, was $2,500,528,827. At the close of May it was $2,510,245,886, showing an increase in one month of $9,717,059. Or, if we take the actual debt, irrespective of cash in the Treasury, it was $2,639,612,622 at the end of April, and $2,643,753,566 at the end of May, showing an actual increase of $4,140,944 in one month.

Of the crushing debt resting upon the people, to meet which the large sum of *one hundred and forty-nine millions of dollars* must be paid annually by the people to meet the interest, $1,494,755,600 is in five-twenty bonds. In addition to this large sum, there are two other classes of six per cent. bonds, and one of five per cent., which, with the navy pension fund, bring up the total debt bearing coin interest to the sum of $2,020,827,841, upon which about $120,249,670 is payable annually in hard gold. This the people are heavily taxed to pay.

The total debt bearing currency interest is $203,117,450. The amount of debt bearing no interest is $408,973,981, of which

$356,144,212 is greenbacks, and $32,531,589 fractional currency. The gold certificates of deposit are a little over $20,000,000, making the total given above of $408,973,981.

The question presents itself: What are our Radical rulers doing to relieve the people of the heavy burdens pressing upon them? Nothing—absolutely nothing. They are in no manner diminishing the debt? Everything is in their own hands. No one outside of the Radical party can be held responsible for the condition of financial affairs, for the reins of Government are in their own hands, and all power is in their hands. But instead of there being a diminution of debt, it is increasing—and that too at the very beginning of the Presidential campaign, when they are appealing to the people to give them a new lease of power.

FINANCES AND THE NATIONAL BANKING SYSTEM.

[From the Memphis Appeal.]

The Government of the United States owed, on the first day of the present month, an *acknowledged* debt of over twenty-six hundred and forty-three millions of dollars, less one hundred and thirty-three millions in its Treasury. The amount of *unacknowledged* debt, claimed of the Government in the Court of Claims and before Congress, we can not even guess at; but it is unquestionably very large.

The interest on the acknowledged debt is very nearly one hundred and fifty millions per annum. On the unacknowledged debt no interest accrues, because the Government has always dishonestly refused, with now and then an exception, to pay interest on any claims against it.

The Pension list calls for over thirty millions per annum.

Thus, apart from the current expenses of carrying on the Government, and without paying any part of the principal of the public debt, the Government must pay one hundred and eighty millions per annum; and the necessary cost of carrying on the Government and the Federal taxes amount to at least three hundred millions per annum.

The burthen of taxation which was at first patiently and even cheerfully borne by the people, begins to press more and more hardly upon them, because it exacts too large a percentage of their earnings and incomes, and is unjust and unequal in its operation: and the exemption from taxation of wealth invested by individuals and corporations in Government bonds, as it makes the burden of taxation heavier on those less able to pay, increases the discontent.

Financial embarrassments begin seriously to threaten the Government, which Congress seems to be utterly incapable to avert. The reduction of the debt has ceased. The last report shows an increase of debt of ten millions; and it is certain that there has been no reduction since the 1st of January.

While additional revenue was needed to prevent an increase of the debt, taxes on manufactures, producing sixty millions per annum, were repealed, in order to secure the support of the manufacturing interest for the Radical candidate for the Presidency. It was simply a huge bribe to purchase votes.

The reserve of coin in the Treasury has begun to decline. It has exceeded one hundred millions net: it is now but seventy millions in excess of the outstanding gold certificates; and this will soon be reduced by the payment of eight millions of Mexican war debt, thirty millions of interest, and seven millions of purchase money for Alaska: so that there will probably not be fifty millions of coin in the Treasury on the 4th of July next, over and above the amount deposited there by private owners and balanced by gold certificates of deposit; and the debt will certainly be larger four months hence than it is now.

We take these figures and statements from the New York *Tribune;* and the source from which they come gives assurance that they are not exaggerated. It is evident that there is not the least likelihood of any diminution of the burden of taxation which presses so heavily on the farmer, the merchant and the mechanic, or of the public debt.

The currency in circulation is in amount about seven hundred millions, of which some three hundred millions are National Bank paper. This is represented, founded upon and secured by about three hundred and fifty million dollars in Government bonds, deposited by the Banks, and on which the Government pays these Banks interest at six per cent. per annum in gold; the amount so paid being about twenty one million dollars per annum, equivalent to nearly or quite thirty millions in currency, at present rates.

The banks deposit their three hundred and fifty millions in bonds, and receive in return permission to issue three hundred and fifteen million dollars of their own notes, for the payment of which the deposited bonds are the only security. These notes are loaned to persons who become borrowers on interest. The banks thus make a large profit on their own promises to pay, besides the interest on the bonds. With $110,000, a National Bank purchases $100,000 in bonds, and receives in exchange for these some $90,000 in notes to be issued by itself. On the bonds it receives annually

$6,000 in gold, or its equivalent in specie, as interest; and loans the notes at eight per cent. or more, besides; thus really receiving double interest on the currency at first invested.

This interest is paid by the people, the working and producing classes. Why should not the National currency be retired, and greenbacks substituted for them? This would retire the bonds on which the paper is issued, and stop the payment of thirty millions of interest per annum in currency, an amount larger than the whole expenses of the Government, under the administration of John Quincy Adams.

Under the present system, the National Bank bondholder receives from the Government nearly nine per cent. interest in currency on his bonds, loans the paper represented by it at eight per cent. more, *or employs outside agents* to loan it on mortgage of real estate at from three to five per cent. a month, and is relieved from about three per cent. tax on his bonds. His aggregate profits are thus about twenty per cent. per annum.

The load of taxation on the people is enormous enough, without this in favor of the stockholders of the National Banks. Other Governments have their income tax; but none imposes a burthen at all comparable with our five per cent. It is excessive and unconscionable and, like the whisky tax, does much to defeat itself. To tax a salary, or a professional income, barely sufficient for a man's support, at such a rate, when he expends every dollar as soon as he receives it, and may perhaps at the end of each year be in debt, is little less than cruelty. By our law, the income of a mechanic, an editor, a lawyer or a physician, requiring in each skill and labor, which ill-health or other causes may at any moment suspend or terminate, is taxed at the same rate as the income of a capitalist, with means invested beyond the reach of any probable accident. If he is sick and earns nothing half the year, expending in that time all he has earned during the other half, his income is taxed all the same; and a thousand dollars is the exemption for all men alike, no matter what may be the expenses of living.

The evil day may be postponed for a time; but the sure result of the present condition of things must be a financial convulsion, and probably repudiation.

A Contrast—The Public Debt of England and the United States Compared—The Expenditures Contrasted—Read, Tax-Payers.

[From the New York World.]

Perhaps in no other way can the iniquity of Republican financiering be more plainly shown than by instituting a comparison between the expenditures of our own Government, under Republican control, and those of the kingdom of Great Britain. Such a comparison naturally suggests itself. The population of the two nations is about the same. The amount of the public debt of Great Britain is much larger than that of the United States—in 1861 the amount being $4,700,000,000, and no very material reduction having since occurred. The regular army of Great Britain—that portion of it, we mean, of which the expense is maintained by the Home Government—is at present 213,000 men; while our regular army during 1867 was ostensibly composed of about 70,000 men, and for this year is said to be only about 53,000 men; although every one knows that these figures are grossly exaggerated, and that nothing like this number of effective men are or have been on the rolls. Great Britain has 120 ships on squadron duty in her navy, and in her fleet and coast guard and the other branches of her naval service, are 67,120 men; while we have only 56 vessels on squadron duty, and our whole naval and marine force numbers only 11,900 men. The highest salary paid to any public servant in the United States is that of the President, $25,000 per year, while Great Britain not only supports the expense of a Queen and a royal family so numerous that not many people can remember the names of all its members—maintains them in excellent style, finds pocket-money for the boys and marriage portions for the girls, and provides liberally for their husbands; keeps up several palaces for their accommodation; provides a viceroyal establishment for Ireland, and does not stint the Lord Lieutenant in his expenditures; not only does all this, we say, but pays all its principal public servants, in civil, military, or naval service, much higher salaries than are given to the corresponding functionaries in the United States. Many a British subject receives a much larger pay than our President does, and their retiring pensions are liberal—the Lord-Chancellor, for example, always retiring with a pension of £5,000 per year—a sum equal to the annual pay of the President of the United States; and when ex-Lord-Chancellors live to be 90 years old, as Lord Brougham did, these little drafts on the Treasury come to be no small sum. Bearing all these things in mind the reader may naturally suppose that the governmental expenses of Great Britain are enormous, and that we are about to illustrate the extravagant incompetency of the Republican party in the United States by showing that under its management our expenditures have been almost as great. What will they say when we show that they have been vastly more, and that the "bloated aristocracy" of Great Britain conduct their Government, with all its useless and costly pageantry and show, and with its formidable army and immense navy, upon a more economical scale and with an infinitely greater regard to the interests of the tax-payers than that of the men who have managed the finances of this republic for seven unhappy years, and who now ask the people to continue them in power? We will proceed to show that this is true by the figures of the Republican Chairman of the House Committee on Ways and Means, and by the official reports of the Chancellor of the Exchequer of Great Britain; and even the courteous editor of the *Tribune* will be unable to confute the statement by any other argument than by applying to Mr. Schenck and Mr. Ward Hunt the epithet which he hurled at Mr. Seymour.

The amount paid for interest upon the public debt of Great Britain in the fiscal year 1867, was $128,807,270, the pound sterling being reckoned at $4.84 in our money. The amount paid for interest upon the public debt of the United States during the same year, the principal of the debt being something more than $2,000,000,000 *less* than that of Great Britain, was $143,781,691—that is upon a debt almost one-half less than that of Great Britain, we paid as interest $14,974,321 more than she did. If it be urged in mitigation of this that the rate of interest was unavoidably high, we ask what excuse can the Republican party offer for its failure to accomplish anything toward making the rate less? Does any one believe that had the financial department of the Government been properly managed, and had peace been restored when the war ended, that three years of tranquillity and prosperity would not have enabled the Treasury to refund the debt upon terms as easy as those under which the consolidated debt of Great Britain is arranged? But this is only one item. The civil service of Great Britain in 1867, according to the report of the Chancellor of the Exchequer, cost $41,098,095, while in the same year the civil service of the United States, according to the statement of Mr. Schenck, cost $51,110,027—"republican symplicity" costing more than the pomps of royalty and the pageantry of aristocracy. What excuse or explanation of this can possibly be given? From what arsenal of sophistry and deceit can be drawn a weapon with which to repel this charge? But worse remains behind. The army of Great Britain, numbering 213,000 men, cost in 1867, $74,383,946. This sum embraces every item of military expenditures—pensions, half-pay, transportation, subsistence, bounties, pay, clothing, ordnance, etc. In the same year the expenses of our army, numbering on paper not more than 70,000 men, and in reality much less than this, were $83,841,555, for "strictly ordinary expenditures"—being $9,457,609 more than Great Britain paid for an army of three times its size. This does not tell all the truth—for if we adopt the British plan of classification, and place the expenditures for pensions and bounties in the item of "Army Expenses," the sum is $116,160,965, which is $41,777,019 more than the whole military expenditure of Great Britain for the year named. One pauses in astonishment to contemplate these officially "cooked," yet astounding figures. That the lesson which they teach may be comprehended at a glance, we reproduce them in a tabular form. In reducing the English money to Federal money we have counted the pound sterling at its proper value, $4.84.

Comparative statement of some of the expenditures of the United States and Great Britain, for the year 1867, made up from the report of the British Chancellor of the Exchequer and the statement of Mr. Schenck, Chairman of the House Committee on Ways and Means:

	United States.	Great Britain
*Interest on debt	$143,781,691	$128,807,270
Civil service	51,110,027	41,098,095
†Army—		
War proper. 83,841,555		
Pensions.... 20,936,551		
Bounties..... 11,382,859	116,160,965	74,383,946
¶Navy	31,034,011	53,912,513
Totals	$342,086,594	$298,201,824
Excess against the United States		43,884,767

There are three other items of British expenditure for which we have no equivalent here, and there is one item of our expenditure for which there is no equivalent in the British budget, so that between these no comparison can be made. But adding the amounts of these—namely, the expenditure for the consolidated fund, the Revenue Department and the packet service to the British budget, and the expenditure for Indians to our own, and we have as the total cost of the British Government for 1867, $335,303,418, and as the total cost of our own Government for the same year, $346,729,125. In other words the Government which should be very much the cheaper was $11,426,706 the dearer.

This is the past. With this record behind them, what does this virtuous and thrifty party promise for the future? It is well known that all the estimates made by the Republican managers for the expendi-

*Principal of U. S. debt, January 1, 1867, $2,675,062,505; principal of English debt, about $4,700,000,000.

†Strength of U. S. army, nominally, 70,000 men; strength of British army, 213,000 men.

¶Strength of U. S. navy, 11,900 men; of British navy, coast guard and marine force, 67,120 men.

tures of the coming year are fallacious and deceptive—being cooked up to present a fair show. The sums estimated for are notoriously below the present expenditures, and the deficiency that is sure to arise is to be provided for—after the election. But even these estimates are bad enough, and are enough to condemn the men who make them beyond all redemption. Mr. Ward Hunt states that the total expenditures of the British Government for the financial year 1868 will be $340,968,320. The carefulness with which these estimates are made may be judged of by the fact that the expenditures for 1867 exceeded the estimates only by £1,102,000; and that the English press complained bitterly of this slight error, as showing an unusual carelessness. But with Schenck's loudly trumpeted retrenchment and reform, and notwithstanding his estimates are much below what the expenditures are certain to be if his party remains in power, he is unable to figure them down below $352,320,629, which is $11,352,309 more than those of Great Britain. If they do not turn out to be five times that much more, experience is valueless and the history of the last seven years has been written in vain.

How the People's Tax-Money Goes—A Fat Office.

The official report to the House of Congress of the expenses of its investigating committees gives the whole sum paid for *this session, up to January 6*, at $49,509 85.

More than one-quarter of that sum was paid to the Sergeant-at-arms of the House for his fees and expenses—subpœnaing witnesses and "sundry expenses." He has charged for subpœnaing L. C. Baker twice, $190 20; for subpœnaing J. M. Wells, $317 90; Gen. Hamlin $317 90; W. Jones, $166 40; J. S. Fullerton, $219 20; C. G. Halpin, $49; E. J. Cougher, $227 20; Buck Lewis, $190; E. F. Ferry, $190; T. C. Wetherby, $114 20, and so on. These sums do not include the witness fees and mileage of witnesses; for the witnesses are paid for attendance and mileage. The office of Sergeant-at-arms of the House is a fat berth, under the extravagant propensities of the Radical managers of Congress. It is made fat, however, out of the substance of the people, and while they are growing poor.

Taxation of United States Bonds.

In the House of Representatives, June 28, 1868, Mr. Cobb (Radical, of Wis.) offered the following resolution, and moved the previous question:

Resolved, That the Committee of Ways and Means be and are hereby instructed to report, without unnecessary delay, a bill levying a tax of at least 10 per cent. on the interest of the bonds of the United States, to be assessed and collected annually by the Secretary of the Treasury, and such of his subordinates as may be charged with the duty of paying interest on the bonded indebtedness of the United States.

The House refused to second the previous question—55 to 57.

Mr. MILLER (Republican, Penn.), moved to table the resolution, but, on the remonstrance of several members who wanted it simply referred to the Committee of Ways and Means, he withdrew the motion.

Mr. BUTLER (Republican, Mass.), renewed the motion to lay on the table.

The resolution was not tabled—Yeas, 28, nays, 107.

The following is the affirmative vote:

Arnell, Baily, Banks, Boutwell, Cake, Churhill, Cornell, Dixon, Driggs, Eckley, Eliot, Harding, Higby, Jenckes, Mallory, Mercur, Miller, Moorhead, Myers, O'Neill, Perham, Plants Pomeroy, Spalding, Starkweather, Stevens (of Penn.), Washburn (Mass.), Woodbridge—28.

The question was taken on Mr. Garfield's motion to refer the resolution to the Committee of Ways and Means, and the motion was rejected—yeas, 61; nays, 80.

The following are the yeas:

Allison, Ames, Arnell, Bailey, Baldwin, Beatty, Bingham, Blaine, Boutwell, Cake, Churchill, Cornell, Delano, Dixon, Driggs, Eckley, Eliot, Ferris, Garfield, Griswold, Halsey, Higby, Hooper, Hulburd, Jenckes, Ketcham, Loan, Lynch, Mallory, Marvin, Maynard, McCarthy, Mercur, Moorhead, Myers, Miller, O'Neill, Paine, Perham, Peters, Plants, Poland, Pomeroy, Price, Sawyer, Shellabarger, *Sitgreaves*, Smith, Spalding, Starkweather, Trowbridge, Twichell, Upson, Van Aernam, Washburne (Ill.), Washburn (Mass.), Washburn (Wis.), Williams (Penn.), Wilson (Iowa), Wilson (Penn.), Woodbridge—61.

Democrats in *italic*.

The question recurred on agreeing to the resolution, and it was agreed to—yeas, 92; nays, 55.

YEAS—*Adams, Archer, Ashley* (Nev.), *Axtell, Baker, Barnes, Beck, Benjamin, Benton, Bingham, Boles, Boyer,* Buckland, Butler (Mass.), Butler (Tenn.), *Cary, Clarke* (Kansas). Cobb, Coburn, Cornell, Covode, Cullom, Donnelly, Eggleston, Ela, *Eldridge,* Farnsworth, Ferris, *Ferry, Getz, Golladay,* Gravely, *Grover, Haight, Hawkins,* Hinds, *Holman, Hotchkiss,* Hubbard (W. V.), *Humphrey,* Ingersoll, *Johnson, Jones, Julian, Kerr,* Lawrence (Penn.), Lawrence (Ohio), Logan, Loughridge, *Marshall,* McClurg, *McCormick,* McKee, Mercur, Mullins, *Mungen,* Newcomb, *Niblack,* Orth, *Phelps,* Pike, Polsley, *Pruyn, Randall,* Raum, *Robinson,* Roots, Ross, Scofield, Shanks, Stevens (N. H.), *Stewart,* Stokes, *Stone, Taber,* Taffe, Taylor, Thomas, Trimble (Ky.), Van Auken, Van Horn (N. Y.), *Van Horn* (Mo.), *Van Trump,* Washburn (Wis.), Washburne (Ill.), Washburn (Ind.), Welker,

Williams (Ind.), Wilson (Ohio), Wilson (Penn.), Windom, *Woodward*—92.

NAYS—Allison, Ames, Arnell, Bailey, Baldwin, Banks, Beatty, Blaiue, Boutwell, Bromwell (Ill.), Cake, Delano, Dixon, Driggs, Eckley, Eliot, Garfield, Griswold, Harding, Halsey, Higby, Hooper, Hulburd (N. Y.), Jenckes, Kelsey, Loan, Lynch, Mallory, Marvin, Maynard, Miller, Moorhead, Myers, O'Neill, Paine, Perham, Plant, Poland, Pomeroy, Price, Sawyer, Shellabarger, *Sitgreaves*, Smith, Spalding, Starkweather, Trowbridge, Twichell, Upson, Van Aernam, Washburn (Mass.), Williams (Penn.), Wilson (Ohio), *Wood*, Woodbridge—55. Democrats in *italic*.

Mr. BINGHAM (Republican, Ohio), voted in the affirmative, with the object of moving to reconsider, but was anticipated by Mr. Cobb, who moved to reconsider the vote adopting the resolution, and moved to table the motion to reconsider.

The motion to reconsider was tabled.

On the 2nd of July, the Committee of Ways and Means reported to the House, to-day, the following bill, in obedience to the order of the House, saying, however, it is contrary to their own best judgment, and they reserve to themselves their rights, as members of the House, to oppose, in every possible way, the adoption of a measure which they regard as hostile to the public interest, and injurious to the national character.

"A bill to authorize an internal tax on the interest on bonds and other securities of the United States.

"Be it enacted, etc., that from and after the passage of this act, there shall be levied, collected, and paid a tax of 10 per cent. on the amount of interest hereafter due and payable on all the bonds and other securities of the United States.

"To secure the collection of said tax, the amount of interest hereafter paid on any bonds or other securities of the United States bearing interest at 6 per cent. shall be at the rate of only 5½ per cent. and those bearing interest at the rate of 5 per cent. shall be at the rate of only four and five-tenths per cent. per annum, and those bearing interest at the rate of 3 per cent. shall be at the rate of only two and seven-tenths per cent. per annum. No higher rate of interest than is herein perscribed shall be paid on any bond or other security of the United States, now outstanding or authorized to be issued, all conditions of such bonds or other securities, and all laws and parts of laws to the contrary notwithstanding."

Taxing Bonds.

WHAT THE NEW YORK HERALD THINKS OF IT.

Taxing the interest of the bonds ten per cent. is equal to reducing the interest on the debt more than a half per cent. Butler was the boldest champion of this resolution, and, though we do not see the name of Thad. Stevens among the rolls of yeas or nays, he would probably have voted with Butler had he been present. There are, however, a number of the names of leading Radicals recorded for the resolution. This would be called by the Radical press here, repudiation in Pendleton or any other Democrat. What does it say of Butler, Bingham, Farnsworth, Covode, the Washburns, and the rest of the Radicals who go for taxing the interest on bonds? The Committee of Ways and Means may be able to smother this proposition, or the Senate might refuse to concur in it, but the action of the House is nevertheless very significant. The Chicago platform does not appear to have much influence, or to be much respected by its framers. We shall undoubtedly see some curious developments by and by with regard to the course of Congress and the political parties on financial questions.

THE PAYMENT OF THE BONDS IN GREENBACKS—A REAL CASE IN POINT.

[From the Louisville Courier.]

A great public question was elucidated in a striking manner the other day during the progress of a private conversation. The details of a transaction then alluded to, are stated below with strict accuracy, and the transaction itself illustrates the connection between the Government and a large class of its creditors.

A glass manufacturer from Pittsburg was, a few days since, in the counting-room of a Louisville house with which he has done a large business for twenty years past. In a conversation with his old friend, the Louisville merchant, he remarked that he was not pleased with the nomination of Grant, and would not support him unless Pendleton should be the opposing candidate.

"In that case," said he, "I shall vote for Grant, because I contributed to the support of the Government in the hour of its distress, and Mr. Pendleton would compel me to accept greenbacks for the bonds which I hold. That would be repudiation."

"I remember that investment of yours," said the Louisville merchant. "You sold $10,000 in gold at 282 in 1864, and bought gold-bearing United States bonds, for which you paid 94 in greenbacks."

"Exactly so," said the Pittsburg gentleman.

"Then," said his friend, "you exchanged your $10,000 in gold for $28,200 in greenbacks, and these you exchanged for $30,000 in United States bonds. On these bonds the Government has annually paid you an interest of $1,800 in gold, which is 18 per cent. per annum on the sum you invested in Government securities. Your interest in four years has returned into your pockets 7,200 of your 10,000 gold dollars, and you claim that the Government owes you $30,000 more in gold! If in four years you receive $37,200 in return for $10,000, your patriotism will be well rewarded indeed."

"I am not responsible for the bad management of the Government," said the Pittsburg gentleman. "I was financiering for myself and not for the Government, and I only ask it to keep its engagements as I keep mine."

"But while you were financiering for yourself," said his friend, "you should have observed the striking fact that while the bonds promised gold for the interest they did not specify the money in which the principal was to be paid. Moreover the greenbacks with which you bought those bonds bore this legend:

"*This note is a legal-tender for all debts, public and private, except duties on imports, and the interest of the public debt.*"

"Every one of those notes which has passed through your hands before you bought the bonds, and since, has been a notice served on you by the Government that the principal of your bonds is payable in greenbacks. Accordingly, you see the Government paying its other debts in greenbacks. So it paid the soldier for enduring toils, and braving dangers. Even the pitiful pension of the disabled private is paid in greenbacks; and the widow is paid in greenbacks for the lost labor of the husband, who lies moldering in a soldier's grave. What have you done that the Government shall make an exception in your favor?"

"I hold its bonds," replied the glass manufacturer, "and though the bonds may fail to specify anything of the sort, yet there is an implied obligation, whenever a government issues such bonds, that the principal shall be paid in gold."

"But," rejoined the merchant, "that implied obligation is directly negatived by the inscription on the greenbacks, and negatived also by the wording of the bonds, which carefully specifies gold for the interest and carefully omits any specification as to how the principal is to be paid; thus leaving that point optional with the Government. Moreover, the greenbacks themselves are notes, bonds, 'promises to pay,' which the Government is as much obligated to pay in coin as any other description of bonds whatever. If the Government substitutes its greenback notes for its bonds in your possession, you hold against it as valid an obligation as you held before, and have no right whatever to cry 'repudiation.'

"The government will be able to redeem the greenbacks in coin as soon as it will be able to pay your bonds in coin. Its necessities compel it to give its creditors *promises* instead of *pay*. It is for you to show why it should give you interest-bearing notes and compel other creditors to accept notes which draw no interest. It is for you to show why the people shall be taxed to pay interest on what the Government owes you, while they get no interest on the notes which they hold against the Government. In what respect is your claim more just or sacred than theirs?

"Now, suppose the Government takes your bonds at their face and pays you $30,000 in greenbacks. You can exchange that sum for $21,400 in gold. You will then receive more than double the sum you invested four years ago, and upon which the Government has paid you usury at the rate of 18 per cent. per annum! My friend, you have no good reason for calling this 'repudiation.' When so liberal a settlement is proposed you have no right to demand that $9,000 more gold than is 'nominated in the bond' shall be wrung from the labor of the country for your private emolument. As a just business man you would not set up such a claim against a private individual, and you could not legally collect it. The obligation of your bonds, as you construe it against the public, would convert them and the Government itself into instruments of extortion and inordinate oppression.

"This implied obligation with which you propose to piece out the actual obligation of the Government, applies with far more force and justice to the claims of the soldiers who rendered personal service and devoted their lives to the public defense. But you and the party with which you act do not call it repudiation to pay *them* in greenbacks for the blood they shed and the limbs they lost. You prefer the least meritorious class of the public creditors; and for those who have already grown rich off of the necessities of the Government you demand an exhorbitant, additional gold premium. The scant wages and rewards of the poor, who have toiled for the Government, and who have bled and suffered for it, you would pay in greenbacks!"

STARTLING FACTS.

In a speech at Mansfield, Ohio, Hon. A. G. Thurman, United States Senator elect, stated some facts which are well calculated to impress the people of the North with the direct interest which they have in restoring the peace and prosperity of the South. Speaking of the taxes derived from internal revenue alone, Mr. Thurman says that the amount paid by the whole ten of the Southern States for the last fiscal year was $19,693,749; in the same year Ohio paid $25,081,409, so that the Southern States, which formerly paid their full share, if not more, of the taxation of the country, are now so reduced that, in the last fiscal year, Ohio paid $5,387,000 more than them all. Senator Thurman then undertakes to demonstrate that the taxation of the people of this country is far greater than ever was imposed upon any people. In the last fiscal year, five hundred millions were collected in taxes by the General Government alone. The taxes collected by the States amount to not quite two hundred millions more, making the entire taxation, in round numbers, seven hundred millions of dollars. The gross annual production of the industry of the United States according to the census of 1860, was two thousand millions of dollars. Allowing for the diminished production of the South, and for increased prices, it is not supposed to be greater now. Thus more than one third of the whole annual product of the industry of the country is absorbed by taxation. Mr. Thurman then proceeds to inquire what is the net profit of the production of this country, and taking as a standard the average rate at which money is loaned and borrowed, that being a rule laid down by every writer on political economy to obtain an approximate idea of the net profits of the production of a country, and assuming ten per cent. as the average rate of interest in the United States, which is certainly high enough, the net profits of the industry of the United States, as the productions of agriculture and manufactures of all kinds, would be two hundred millions of dollars. Thus taxation draws from the people five hundred millions a year more than the net profits of all the producing industry of the United States—a great portion of the taxation, however, being of course upon non-productive employments, those engaged in buying commodities and selling them again, who, though securing large individual gains, do not increase the wealth of the country a particle. Yet the startling fact remains that one-third of the gross annual product of the industry of the country is absorbed in taxation. Such is the price which the people must continue to pay so long as a policy is pursued which renders necessary large military establishments and Freedmen's Bureaus, and which hands over one of the largest and formerly most productive sections of the country to increasing impoverishment and the prospect of ultimate ruin.

THE STATUS OF NATIONAL BANKS.

Judge Ingraham, of New York, has just given an important opinion as to the status of National banks. Mr. Pitt Cooke, having a claim against the State National Bank, of Boston, commenced a suit by attachment, that writ having been issued on the ground that the bank was a foreign corporation. The bank moved to vacate the order, mainly on the ground that the act of Congress creating the National banks provided that they may be sued in the United States Courts of the district in which they are located, and that, being Government agents, they are free from the jurisdiction of all other courts. Judge Ingraham decides that their incorporation does not make them United States agents, and, if it did, would not alter their position except as to the particular transaction in which they were agents, being in this respect in the position of any bank; that the word "may" in the act was promissory, not restrictive, and that State courts had jurisdiction, and that the United States was foreign to the State of New York, within the meaning of the code, and therefore the attachment must stand.

Condition of the United States Treasury.

The Cincinnati *Enquirer* publishes the annexed communication which, at this time, possesses very great public interest:

The impeachment of the President is somewhat diverting the attention of the people from the financial villanies of the Treasury Department. This it was intended to do.

If we are true to ourselves, this trick will not succeed well.

There has been no time heretofore when so much wrong has been unpunished; when so much villany has gone by undiscovered and unexposed.

The people of the country must look from the mercenary press under the surveillance of bondholders and capitalists to the independent press of the Western States, and the independent statesmen of the country for help against our oppressors.

The duty, and indeed the only hope of the Western States, is an immediate move for a change in our financial condition.

I know of nothing that will facilitate this change more readily than a fair and fearless expose of the crimes of the Treasury Department, which has been growing, year after year, more corrupt, dangerous and despotic.

The banking system is essentially fraudulent and organized for the purpose of fraud upon the people.

The President of the Continental Bank Note Company, Edward E. Dunbar, remonstrated with Secretary Chase, when the latter proposed the establishment of a Bank Note Engraving and Printing Bureau in the Treasury building, and offered as a reason for his objection that there was "no accountability or responsibility" to any one, and that "no adequate checks could be imposed upon the unlimited facilities of a Government manufactory of paper money in the Treasury Building."

This was apparent to every sensible man who had any knowledge of the ease with which paper money might be surreptitiously issued to the public through every avenue of business and trade. The whole scheme was the foundation of the most gigantic public fraud ever perpetrated in the history of finances since the days of John Law, of France, or the assignate and mandate of Mirabeau and Robespierre.

This opportunity was improved by the men appointed for the purpose of overseeing and managing the department. They never allowed an opportunity to escape them. The plan adopted ostensibly to avoid counterfeit issues was the very one which they well knew would facilitate it most readily, and indeed made counterfeiting easy and safe. Electrotyping always produces in the duplicate such a perfect *fac simile* as defies detection. These electrotype plates are easily reproduced, and were used at the limitless discretion of the operators, who were held to no responsibility whatever. The dangers of this system were well known to every intelligent bank-note engraver in the country; had been thoroughly tested more than a quarter of a century ago, and were employed to give pretext for and cover up the frauds necessary for the plunder of the Treasury contemplated by the managers. The details of the manner in which this fraud has been often done has been duly exposed by Mr. Dunbar.

To prevent the people from understanding the magnitude and monstrous character of these villanies, every trace has been covered up, and only now and then a whisper is heard, while the people are robbed wholesale.

In the report to the Secretary of the Treasury, Mr. Chase, on the 26th of November, 1864, it was stated by the Chief of the Bureau of Currency that there was a deficiency of $54,000,000 in bonds, so Mr. Dunbar says, and it is incontrovertible that the "Bureau did not account for the amount of bonds it had manufactured within that sum, and no explanation of what became of these bonds has ever been given."

"The suppressed reports" give amounts, and seem indifferent to mistakes, frauds and robberies.

The wasteful extravagance in the mechanical management of the Bureau was the pretext for extortions, peculations, corruptions, briberies and conspiracies between contractors of every kind of material and machinery, operators, managers and *employes*.

These things were believed to be well known to the Secretaries of the Treasury. Every fair investigation was suppressed, and where the frauds were made known they attracted but little attention from the Secretaries of the Treasury, who seemed to have no further business in their office than to plunder the country, oppress the people, and amass enormous fortunes.

There is no doubt but that these electrotypes have been duplicated, triplicated, and quadruplicated *ad libitum* in all of the bonds. Treasury notes and fractional currency, So loosely, carelessly, profligately and corruptly were these plates employed by all concerned, that these duplicate plates passed into the hands of persons in nowise connected with the Government, and are now beyond its control. Such was the natural results of the irresponsibility of the management of the printing establishment. No one feature worse than this, that no person seems responsible for what is done.

The amount of the taxes of the people of the United States is astoundingly greater than anything in the history of modern nations. Yet the debt grows no less, but is in fact increasing every month, the report of the Secretary of the Treasury to the contrary notwithstanding

The duplicate coupons, notes and currency are redeemed at the Treasury because the Treasurer can't tell the difference between the quadruplicates, triplicates, duplicates and original issues of these testimonials of our degradation, bankruptcy and ruin.

The amount of the taxes levied upon the people to pay the coupons, bonds and notes issued outside of the Treasury are even greater than those issued by the order of the department itself to pay the peculations, speculations, false and fraudulent accounts and official robberies of its clerks, waiters and chief of department.

Mr. Dunbar says that "the duplicate coupons of the five-twenties and seven-thirties, redeemed and sent to the Treasury, are known to be from the original plates in the department.

"Extra coupons of the five-twenty bonds, third and fourth series, have been issued separate from the bonds, and no descriptive record ever made of them, thus rendering it easy to issue millions of duplicates of the same and have them redeemed without detection. Large amounts of duplicate seven-thirty coupons have already been redeemed by the Treasury, while their corresponding originals were never issued."

To amplify upon the frauds, forgeries and false issues of the Currency Bureau, would require a closely printed volume of small type to serve as an index of the individual cases. I cite from Mr. Dunbar's *Globe*.

ONE ITEM, INVOLVING FROM SIXTY MILLIONS TO ONE THOUSAND FIVE HUNDRED MILLIONS OF DOLLARS.

"The Currency Printing Bureau has not accounted for the excess of sheets in packages in excess of the number authorized, an aggregate of 150,000 sheets of bond Treasury note paper. These sheets, if manufactured into bonds and notes, as was doubtless the case—judging from developments bearing on this matter hereinafter made—would, according to the denomination of the bonds or notes issued, throw upon the country from sixty to one thousand five hundred millions of dollars, which does not appear in the statement of the public debt, but which must ultimately be redeemed by the Government."

Mr. Dunbar says:

COSTLY AND DANGEROUS EXPERIMENTS BY WHICH DISCREDIT IS CAST ON ALL ISSUES OF THE GOVERNMENT.

The following are some of the costly and dangerous experiments made in the Currency Printing Bureau. The facts are contained in the report made to Secretary McCulloch, January, 1867:

A bond plate was sent to New York, and suffered to remain there for two weeks in the hands of an expert for experimental purposes in electrotyping.

There were employed for weeks in the Treasury department, at first surreptitiously, parties to experiment in the making of electrotype plates—duplicates of fractional currency, bonds, notes, etc. The name of the principal expert engaged in this business was not to be found on any official pay-roll in the department.

There were made in the department a variety of electrotyped plates—duplicates of the Government plates of fractional currency, bonds, etc. Also the matrix of moulds of fractional currency notes, bonds and coupons.

How was it possible that such things were done, and the persons not bear away with them the molds in which they were cast, and be as well prepared to make money outside of the department as inside of it? What restraint was there upon them? How could they be detected when their names were not to be found on any official pay-roll in the department at the very time that these frauds were perpetrated against the public Treasury.

A Senator, formerly very poor, now grown rich with the crimes, frauds and taxation of the people, to prevent the exposure of the wickedness of the Treasury Department, arose in his place, breathing cold, deliberate perjury. He, whose duty it was to protect the public Treasury, declares that everything is right when he knew of these very frauds, and arose only to quiet investigation.

Another Senator makes millions through the legerdemain of the Treasury Department; while a member of the lower House of Congress, who swindles the whole community in which he lives, is indicted and pleads privilege of arrest, because he was a member of Congress, using his position to defraud his constituents.

Mr. Dunbar says:

THE PUBLIC DEBT.

We assert that the annexed statement of the total amount of the public debt is not correct, and that on the strength of evidence in the possession of the Treasury Department officials, they must be conscious of the fact.

Always relying on evidence to be found in the Treasury Department, we assert that the Secretary of the Treasury is unable to give a correct statement of the Government pecuniary obligations afloat.

We call for a publication of the suppressed reports, and an investigation.

The following is a statement of the public debt of the United States on the 1st of August, 1867:

DEBT BEARING COIN INTEREST.

Five per cent. bonds	$ 198,431,350 00
Six per cent. bonds of 1867 and 1868	14,932,141 80
Six per cent. bonds of 1881	283,746,400 00
Six per cent. five-twenty bonds	1,168,796,800 00
Navy pension fund	13,000,000 00
Total	$1,678,906,691 80

DEBT BEARING CURRENCY INTEREST.

Six per cent. bonds	$ 15,402,900 00
Three year compound interest notes	108,329,430 00
Three year seven-thirty notes	451,233,425 00
Total	$ 574,964,855 00
Matured notes not presented for payment	$ 15,636,815 87

DEBT BEARING NO INTEREST.

United States notes	$ 369,164,844 00
Fractional currency	28,554,729 72
Gold certificates of deposit	19,457,960 00
Total	$ 417,177,533 72
Total debt	2,686,685,896 39

AMOUNT IN TREASURY.

Coin	$ 102,905,174 00
Currency	72,474,296 38
Total	$ 175,379,470 38
Amount of debt less cash in treasury	2,511,306,426 01

The foregoing is a correct statement of the public debt, as appears from the books and Treasurer's returns in the department, on the first of August, 1867.

HUGH McCULLOCH,
Secretary of the Treasury.

Thaddeus Stevens declares that the public debt is $4,000,000,000, and admits that the whole financial management of the country is essentially corrupt and rotten.

Large amounts of duplicates have been already redeemed. So uncertain was the report of the Secretary of the Treasury that Stevens made his report independent and regardless of it. It is currently stated that these fraudulent bonds are afloat in large amounts in Europe, and are now floating upon that market.

Every facility has been afforded the perpetrators of these frauds, who are very generally and justly believed to be in close partnership with the chief managers.

[The following facts were taken from the *suppressed reports* of the Treasury Department:]

NO RECORD KEPT OF PARTIALLY SPOILED IMPRESSIONS.

The Chief of the Currency Printing Bureau, to whom have been regularly returned the partially spoiled impressions of bonds and notes, or bonds or coupons, as the case might be, has failed to keep a record of the partially spoiled impressions so delivered to him, and has not accounted for the perfect notes, bonds and coupons thereon, which in the aggregate must, at a moderate estimate, amount to a total of many millions of dollars, since not less than 1,000,000 of such sheets were returned to him. (Testimony of M., December 18, 1866.

TEN THOUSAND DOLLARS CONCEALED IN A CUPBOARD.

Ten thousand dollars in fractional currency were found stowed away in the cupboard of the Chief of the Currency Printing Bureau. This amount had been delivered to him some months before it was discovered, and he had failed to hand it over to the Treasurer, or otherwise account for it. (Affidavit of M.)

DISAPPEARANCE OF BANK-NOTE PAPER.

Thirty thousand strips, each capable of printing two notes of the denomination of one hundred, one thousand or five thousand dollars, clipped from the paper prepared for the first series of interest-bearing notes, were suffered to lie about the Printing Department until they mysteriously disappeared. These strips would print six millions, sixty millions or three hundred millions of dollars. (Testimony of G. G. and T., pages 2, 3 and 4.)

ALTERATION OF BOOKS.

In May, 1864, the Chief of the Currency Printing Bureau caused his official books to be so altered as to show a liability to the Government of two thousand dollars less than it actually was. (Testimony of A., page 5.)

SQUANDERING OF PUBLIC MONEY.

Two individuals in the Currency Printing Bureau have squandered some three hundred thousand dollars of the public moneys in furtherance of their private interests, while the same was ostensibly spent for public service. (Suppressed reports to Mr. Fessenden by a clerk specially charged with the investigation of the affair).

DEFICIENCY OF FIFTY-FOUR MILLIONS OF DOLLARS.

On the 26th of November, 1864, the Chief of the Currency Printing Bureau made a false return to the Secretary of the Treasury, in which he failed to account for fifty-four millions of dollars of Government securities that had been manufactured by him. (Testimony B., page 89.)

A DEFICIT OF SIXTY MILLIONS FRACTIONAL CURRENCY.

In addition to the fifty-four millions of bonds hereinbefore mentioned as unaccouted for, the accounts of the Chief of the Currency Printing Bureau with the Treasurer, showed a deficit in November, 1866, of sixty millions fractional currency.

ELECTROTYPING PLATES.

A bond plate was sent to New York, and suffered to remain there two weeks in the hands of an expert for experimental purposes in electrotyping.

There were employed for weeks in the Treasury Department, at first surreptitiously, parties to experiment in the making of electrotype plates—duplicates of fractional currency, bonds, notes, etc. The name of the principal expert engaged in this business was not to be found on any official pay-roll in the department.

There were made in the department a variety of electrotyped plates—duplicates of the Government plates of fractional currency, bonds, etc.—also, the matrix or molds of fractional currency, notes, bonds and coupons.

REDEMPTION OF DUPLICATE COUPONS FROM ORIGINAL PLATES.

Coupons from the original plates have, to the amount of millions of dollars, been presented and redeemed at the Treasury. The exact amount and the denominations of these duplicates may be readily ascertained upon investigation at the proper departments of the Treasury.

ISSUE OF EXTRA COUPONS, AND NO RECORD KEPT.

Extra coupons of the five-twenty bonds, third and fourth series, have been issued separate from the bonds, and no descriptive record ever made of them, thus rendering it easy to issue millions of duplicates of the same, and have them redeemed without detection; large amounts of duplicate seven-thirty coupons, have already been redeemed by the Treasury, while their corresponding originals were never issued.

The duplicate coupons of five-twenty bonds and the seven-thirties redeemed and sent to the Registry, are known to be from the original plates in the department.

CONFUSED CONDITION OF THE PAPER ACCOUNT—OVER-ISSUE OF TWENTY-FIVE MILLIONS OF FRACTIONAL CURRENCY.

Of the vast amount of "membrane" paper for fractional currency manufactured *ad libitum* in the division of the Currency Printing Bureau, no account whatever has been kept, the Chief of the Bureau refusing to allow the book-keeper to do so, saying, whenever requested, that he himself would keep it; thus no record of the amount of money printed on said paper further than a return made by him in November, 1864, acknowledging that he printed one hundred and forty-nine thousand nine hundred and ninety-four sheets, amounting to nine hundred and seventy-four thousand and eleven dollars and twenty-five cents, ($974,011.25). How much more than the amount so returned has been printed may be conjectured, but never known. Since 1864 no return whatever has been rendered of this paper, and these startling facts may explain in a satisfactory manner the otherwise inexplicable over-issue of twenty-five millions of fractional currency that has been discovered.

In the same condition is the "National paper," no record having ever been kept of either the quantity manufactured or the quantity used. Indeed, no general ledger is kept by the Currency Printing Bureau, nor has there been a regular settlement between it and the Secretary of the Treasury. (Testimony of D., E. and F., pages 8 and 10.)

INSECURE MANNER OF KEEPING STOCK PACKAGES.

Packages known as "stock packages," containing five hundred sheets of every class and denomination of Government securities issued, whether of notes or bonds, and complete save as to seal and number, are constantly kept in a place accessible to all, with permission to supply themselves with whatever number they may require to replace the ones they may have spoiled. No record has been kept of these "stock packages," nor has the Chief of the Bureau ever made a return of the number consumed. On one occasion a large number of said sheets were extracted from the cupboard in which they were deposited and their disappearance never explained.

In connection with these circumstances, it is worthy of mention that the superintendent of the numbering division has, on returning to his duties Monday morning, found the rollers and types inked over and the numbering changed, showing conclusively that they had been used during his absence on the Sabbath. But it is not surprising when it is known that the keys of the numbering division are left, not with its superintendent, but, by order of the Chief of the Currency Printing Bureau, with one of the watchmen of the building. (Testimony marked B.)

Moreover, one hundred and twenty-seven thousand eight hundred and sixty two sheets for the same purpose have been received by the Chief of the Currency Printing Bureau from the bank-note companies. These sheets represented a value of four millions and fifty-eight thousand dollars, and were complete save as to Treasury seal. This seal, the chief of the bureau alone was authorized to have put on, and he has never rendered an account of the way in which he has disposed of these sheets. (*Ibid.*)

To pass hurriedly over the facts, notorious in the Treasury Department, that the "standing press" of the superintendent of plate printing has more than once been opened by order of the Chief of the Currency Bureau, and its contents amounting to millions taken out, with no other acknowledgment than a memoranda in pencil that it had been the custom to pass into the hands of the bronzers, sealers and numberers, and receive from these without counting, the paper in its various stages toward completion into bonds and notes; that no account was kept of the third series of five-twenties, and of the fractional currency printed on similar paper, until many million had been issued; in consequence of which no settlement ever has been or can be made; that bonds and notes have been delivered many times by the plate printer in excess of the paper charged to him; that legal-tenders and interest notes, by reason of the fact that these classes of money, being printed in series, and there being eight hundred notes of each and every number, may flood the country to any extent without the possibility of detecting a *duplicate*, until its particular series are redeemed; that the five-twenty bonds are in like manner issued in series; and of the billion of dollars of bonds, notes, etc., redeemed at the Treasury Department, and ordered to be canceled and destroyed, it is easy, on account of the system in operation, to appropriate, and circulate, as in the case of Cromwell, an indefinite amount, we come to the fact, extraordinary as it may appear, that there has not been kept in the Currency Printing Bureau any regular accounts, such as bankers and merchants keep, or from which a balance sheet can be prepared, showing either as to the particular kind or as to the aggregate of the various bonds, the actual amount of paper purchased or manufactured for the printing of currency or bonds; and no record has been kept of even the amount of money that has been printed and delivered to the Treasurer.

Their most ardent friends admit that the Treasury Department at Washington has power to print without any restraint whatever. That the paper money is issued without limitation or check; that the authors are accountable to nobody, responsible to nobody, and reckless of their obligations.

This very condition of things would induce repudiation and hasten financial rebellion in any country. Is there any government that could stand this irresponsible issue of its obligations?

There are no facts in the present system of American Government better established than this, that the people can place no reliance upon the Treasury report, which is intended to deceive them; that an army of public officers are engaged in public robbery; that there is no reliable record of the condition of the public Treasury.

The crimes of the Treasury Department alone would destroy any Government.

It is alleged by those cognizant of the crimes of the Treasury Department—

1. That millions upon millions of dollars have been issued and reissued without authority of law.

2. That the Government is paying interest upon the surplus coupons thus issued, notes and currency, which have in like manner come to the light of the public eye.

3. That discrepancies are constantly occurring, and are passed over as if it were no crime to defraud the public. These gentlemen who are destroying us seem to forget that the public means the people, and that a fraud upon the public is none other than a robbery of the freezing and starving poor of their firewood and bread, raiment and shelter, for the benefit of the rich, idle and pampered capitalist.

The condition of the Treasury and our finances is horrible. Business opens dull in the East. Everything looks gloomy—Sherman's sensation announcement in the Senate, Logan's *expose* in the House—everything tends to show the deplorable condition of our affairs.

It was to keep the Western people from inquiring into our finances that the impeachment imbroglio has been revived. It is intended, as soon as Johnson is removed, to adopt a system of terror similar to that which reigned in 1864, to make it impossible that the people inquire after their finances.

Having seen and conversed with the ablest men in the East, they all concur in these simple principles as a basis of action:

1. That the financial system of the country must be entirely and radically changed at once, or ruin will close in upon us.

2. That for this purpose we must not rely upon a national organization, but must proceed at once to call meetings in every county to consider our financial condition and wants, and organize our forces to resist the whole funding system. This I proposed three years ago, but am more than ever satisfied of the necessity of it. The Eastern fanatics are using Western men to destroy us and build up their monopolies.

Western men like John Logan, of Illinois; John Bingham, of Ohio; and Jas. Wilson, of Iowa, who represent the labor of the West, are used as the cat's paw of Thaddeus Stevens, who represents the iron monopoly of Pennsylvania, and Boutwell, who represents the capital of New England, to impeach the President to avert inquiry into the frauds, villanies and thefts of the Treasury Department

While these Western men are cutting the throats of their constituents, the same docile people are quiet as lambs, and offer not one word of resistance to the system of crime organized to destroy them. The country verges revolution, and if the people would at once commence to organize, and not await the excitement of the campaign, the defeat of the Radicals will be overwhelming.

Universal dissatisfaction pervades the public mind at the present condition of affairs. The country is at the turning point, and will follow the determination of the people. If we organize thoroughly and stand with our lives upon the platform of principle, we will sweep the mongrels from the field. If, upon the other hand, we suffer the moneyed capital to buy up Western Representatives, and fail to meet them like men—the fault will be ours.

What a Radical Bondholder's Organ Thinks of Senator Sherman—Funding.

[From the Cincinnati Gazette, July 1, 1868.]

We funded the currency-payable debt into five-twenty bonds. Senator Sherman, the Chairman of the Finance Committee, said these were gold bonds, and that anybody who was for paying them in greenbacks was a repudiator. In his campaign speech last fall, at Carson's Grove, in this county, he gave a full financial exposition, as was fit for our leading legislative financier, and the principal part of it was an argument showing that the public faith was committed to the payment of the 5-20s in gold. After reviewing the laws under which the bonds and greenbacks were issued, to show the legal pledge, he cited Secretary Chase's letter of May 18, 1864, affirming the payability of the 5 20s in gold, and then, with a solemn oath, he thus declared that he would sacredly keep his pledge:

"That declaration was made by the Secretary of the Treasury, with the sanctions of both Houses of Congress. Upon the faith of that, money was lent by all classes of people to the United States. That policy has prevailed from the foundation of the Government to this time. It has never been violated, and, so help me God, I would never aid in its violation, whatever might be the consequences. [Applause.] The same sacred pledge was made by Mr. Fessenden, when he was Secretary of the Treasury, and the same pledge was made by Hugh McCulloch, the present Secretary of the Treasury."

In another part of the same speech, after arguing against the proposition to pay the bonds in greenbacks, because, he said, "it would be unjust to the bondholders to do so—to give them in exchange for an interest-bearing security, a security that bore no interest, and take away from them all the income from the property or money they loaned to the Government;" and this, he said, "would be as unjust as for a man to undertake to take from you a mortgage note with interest, and to give you in its place a due bill without interest," he concluded that branch of his argument against the greenback scheme of payment, with this fine burst of denunciation:

"The whole proposition is a Utopian, demagogical, mean, dirty, nasty scheme, which no party but the Copperhead party in the United States could invent."

Now, the funding bill which Mr. Sherman launched upon the Senate this Session, on his own responsibility—not having been able to get the Committee to approve it—provides for funding the 5-20s into bonds payable specifically in gold; and that, in consideration of giving gold bonds for those which last year he said were sacredly payable in gold—and "so help him God" he would so keep the faith—the new bonds shall reduce the interest from six to five per cent. And to that end, he said in his speech on introducing this bill, that the declaration of the Secretary of the Treasury as to the payability of the 5-20s in gold, could not bind Congress, and that "Congress never acquiesced in it." And he argued that really the Government was under no legal obligation to pay these bonds in anything but greenbacks.

Thus we see we have got hold of the financial philosopher's stone It consists in funding a debt which was payable in depreciated currency notes, into gold bonds, at a low rate of interest, and then declaring these payable in the same currency, and repeating the operation. And Mr. Sherman told the Senate what he would do in case the bondholders rejected this funding offer. Said he: "I repeat that if this offer is rejected, I will not hesitate to vote to redeem maturing bonds in the currency in existence when they were issued, and with which they were purchased." Mr. Sherman did not add to this declaration that he would pay the bonds in nothing but greenbacks, the solemn "so help me God," with which he swore last fall, that he would never break the obligation to pay them in gold; but a lesser affirmative will serve for the breaking of faith than for the keeping of it. He might have fitly invoked the Devil for the latter oath.

And this financial process will by no means be exhausted by another funding, nor by putting it in words in the bond, that we will pay them in money, this time positively "and without mental reservation"—as Johnson's iron-clad oath said—and not in a new note. We funded the notes bearing 7-30 interest, and those bearing compound interest. into six per cent. five-twenties, by holding out that these were payable in gold. Mr. Sherman now proposes to fund these into five per cent. bonds, specifically payable in gold. That being done, we can fund again in four per cents. by the same process For we have found that a law can make the lightest specific gold bond payable in legal-tender paper. We can make the requisite inducement to the bondholder, by putting into the new four per cent. bond something like the Johnson iron-clad oath, declaring that this gold obligation is positively without any mental reservation, or any intention of availing ourselves of the legal-tender law, and that we rejoice when the public faith is maintained, and grieve when it is hurt, and so on.

By that time the bondholders will have got used to it, as eels do to being skinned, and will not have the disposition to resist another Shermanizing of the bonds. And thus our great debt will all be removed by smart financiering. And yet the measure that is to inaugurate this, fell dead in the Senate, and can get no support in the Finance Committee; and there is a prospect that nothing will be achieved toward shuffling the public debt by funding, and that it will fall back on the honest but oppressive process of paying. That is a line in which our congressional financial genius does not seem to run.

WHO ARE THE REPUDIATORS—SENATOR SHERMAN'S LETTER.

Senator Sherman is Chairman of the Committee on Finance in the Senate. He is, therefore, well acquainted with all the bond laws. We ask our Republican friends to read his letter; and, after doing so, to remember that Grant and Colfax are the bondholder candidates, and are in favor of paying the five-twenty bonds in gold. Here is Senator Sherman's letter:

"*United States Senate Chamber, Washington, March 20, 1868*—DEAR SIR: I was pleased to receive your letter. My personal interests are the same as yours, but, like you, I do not intend to be influenced by them. My construction of the law is the result of careful examination, and I feel quite sure an impartial court would confirm it if the case could be tried before a court. I send you my views as fully stated in a speech Your idea is that we propose to repudiate or violate a promise when we offer to redeem the 'principal' in legal-tenders.

"I think the bondholder violates his promise when he refuses to take the same kind of money he paid for the bond. If the case is to be tested by the law, I am right; if it is to be tested by Jay Cooke's advertisements, I am wrong. I hate repudiation or anything like it, but we ought not to be deterred from doing what is right by fear of undeserved epithets. If, under the law as it stands, the holder of five-twenties can only be paid in gold, then we are repudiators if we propose to pay otherwise. If, on the other hand, the bondholder can legally demand only the kind of money he paid, then he is a repudiator and an extortioner to demand money more valuable than he gave.

"Truly yours,   JOHN SHERMAN.
"Hon. A. MANN, Jr., Brooklyn Heights."

That puts the repudiation saddle upon the right horse—the horse rode by the bondholders.

BEEF AND TAXES—A BOVINE BIOGRAPHY.
[From the Nebraska City News.]

I was born in Nebraska. The farmer to whom I belonged paid a tax upon me as a part of his income during my vealhood. He sold me when I was three years old, and paid an income tax upon what I brought. I was nicely fatted until I weighed nearly a ton, by a Democrat on Weeping Water, who paid the Government eighteen cents for the privilege of selling me to a butcher, who pays a tax of ten dollars for the privilege of selling meat to the public. The butcher sold my tallow to a chandler, who made me, by paying a license as manufacturer, into candles for the poor people, who pay a five per cent. tax on candles to read by. My horns and hoofs are made into combs and glue, and pay another tax. My hide goes to the tanner, who pays a manufacturer's license, and is made into leather, upon which is an *ad valorem* tax of five per cent. The tanner will sell the leather to a wholesale dealer, who pays a mercantile license and an income tax, and he will sell it to the shoemaker, and the shoemaker will get up boots for the laborer, farmer and mechanic, and charge enough for them to cover all the taxes enumerated together, with his own manufacturer's tax.

"CONTINGENCIES"—WHAT THE PEOPLE ARE TAXED TO PAY FOR.

The New York *World* says: "That to the already published works of J. W. Forney—the Jamieson Letter, and Letters from Europe, without which no (Radical) gentleman's library is complete, must be added an interesting volume of eighty-seven pages, edited by 'J. W. Forney, Secretary of the Senate,' who certifies to the entire correctness of certain payments from the contingent fund of the Senate for a single year, amounting in the aggregate to the trifling sum of $164,892 04." The editor says:

"This money was laid out in penknives, for which two thousand dollars were paid to a single dealer. It required seventeen hundred pairs of scissors to merely cut at the Gordion knot of 'Reconstruction' in the Senate. Another lot of penknives cost $67 66; two and one half dozen more were procured at the expense of $98, and still more knives brought the second bill for cutlery up to $487. Of whole pages of individual bills, the following is a fair sample: 'For B. F. Wade, Harper's Magazine, $4; Eclectic, $5; Westminster, $5; Le Bon Ton (indispensable to Wade), $9.' Five dollars for a 'scrap book' was undoubtedly for Senator Sumner's benefit. The frequently occurring item 'one gallon of alcohol, $5 50,' can best be explained in connection with such other items as 'Corkscrews, $24;' 'Lemon-squeezers, $2;' 'Four boxes of lemons, $40;' '168 pounds of sugar, $33 60.' These items for substantials; lesser luxuries appear in the charges of $512 50 for seventeen and a half dozen kid gloves; $2 25 for a gallon of bay rum; $5 for a half gallon of cologne, and $2 for toilet powder. What a sumptuous thing it is to be a Senator, to be sure, with such a secretary as Forney, and such a contingent fund as Radical recklessness draws from the public Treasury and the people's pockets."

On the same subject the Chicago *Times* says: "Thad. Stevens says that, under the name of stationery, some members of Congress have been in the habit of procuring 'pantaloons, shirts and shaving soap enough to last them for years,' and that many have run up an account for stationery to nearly $1,000. Just at this time, when economy in every branch of the public service is so essential, it would be interesting to have a list of the members, and the respective amounts they have drawn for stationery. Perhaps some enterprising newspaper correspondent could procure such a document, and give us the items."

A statement prepared by the Secretary of the Treasury from the official records of his department, has been published in the *National Intelligencer*, and also sent to the public through the Associated Press, in which it is stated that in 119 collection districts removals were made, during the year 1867, upon the recommendation of the Commissioner of Internal Revenue, in which districts the average falling off of internal revenue, as compared with the year 1866, was $160,942 81 per district, and that the same year (1867) removals were made in twenty collection districts by the President, without the recommendation of said Commissioner, in which the falling off of revenue is only $46,470 37 per district.

At the time the war broke out, Nashville had eight millions of banking capital; to-day she has a banking capital of only $700,000.

The tax of one cent a box on matches last year netted to the Government a revenue of $1,500,000. Matches, before the war, retailed at one cent per box.

What is the reason times are hard and money scarce? The Government bonds are swallowing every dollar in the country —that's what's the matter.

Tennessee Free Bank notes were predicated on State bonds; did any holder of the notes of one of these *broken* banks ever get paid in full? National banks are the same family on a large scale.

The interest of the Government debt of the United States amounts to more every forty eight hours than all the taxes levied by the State of Tennessee in a *whole year*.

Members of Congress, and others living on fat salaries, owners of National bank stock, loaning deposits at one per cent. a month, and trading in United States bonds, and the bondholders drawing gold interest and paying no taxes on them, are *all opposed* to paying off the bonds in the kind of money the people have to take for their work.

Senator Hendricks, of Indiana, stated in Congress that at present the expense annually of each soldier in the army was $2,000, and nearly $2,000,000 for each regiment; the total cost being about $100,000,000 a-year for an army of 50,000 men. He argued that, with proper management, the army expense could be cut down forty millions a-year.

The people have not forgotten Jay Cooke's handbill, that was thrown broadcast over the country, to prove that a national debt is a national blessing. A recent letter of the Secretary of the Treasury explains why Jay Cooke was so taken with a national debt. The Secretary says that in ten months of the year 1865 the commissions paid to a broker for selling 5-20 bonds amounted to *ninety-four thousand one hundred and ninety-four dollars!* That is pretty well for peace loyalty. We suppose Jay Cooke would not refuse to issue another handbill in favor of a national debt on like terms—so pure is his patriotism.

A question which we have never yet seen answered: "If bonds are to be paid in greenbacks, in what are the greenbacks to be paid?"—*Indianapolis Journal.*

ANSWER.—*Taxes!* Nothing plainer. But there is none so blind as those who won't see, except those whose eyes are so blinded by the glitter of gold. MECHANIC.

Yes, they are to be paid in taxes, remarks the Cincinnati *Enquirer*, but with this difference: The bonds draw $150,000,000 a-year interest; greenbacks draw no interest. Which is the easiest paid? In twelve or fifteen years we could take up the bonds, if they were in the shape of greenbacks, with the interest money we would otherwise pay on the bonds. To use Mr. Lincoln's favorite remark, "a large debt is easier paid than a larger one!" Did the questioner in the *Journal* ever think of that?

WHAT THAD. STEVENS THINKS OF HIS RADICAL COLLEAGUES.

A young lady, who writes to an Adams County (Penn.) paper, describing an interview with Thad. Stevens, reports that gentleman as saying:

"No honest office-holder that comes here, if he does right, can get one dollar ahead; yet I marvel to see men, poor when they came here, go out of that Senate worth half a million."

A MERE TRIFLE.

The other day Congress voted away the little sum of one hundred and eight millions eight hundred and eighteen thousand four hundred and forty-seven dollars to pay current expenses. Congress acts on the idea of the French showman: "You pays your price and you takes your choice." The people pay, and they can have an economically administered Government or an extravagant one. They can take their choice. They pay their money.

EXPENSES OF WAR AND NAVY DEPARTMENT.

Notwithstanding the war ended in 1865, the expenses of the War and Navy Department during 1867, two years after the war closed, were $5,500,000 more than during the first year of the war. Where does all this money go? The expenses of these two departments in 1867 were over $44,000,000 more than in 1866, and from all accounts the increase of 1868 will be double that sum. Again we ask, where does all this money go?

EXPENSES OF MR. POLK'S ADMINISTRATION.

During the four years of President Polk's administration, which included the Mexican war, the expenses of the War Department were $90,540,788. The expenses of that same Department for the year ending the 1st of July, 1868, the third year of peace, are $128,858,494, or over $38,000,000 more during one year of peace than they were during four years of Democratic rule with the Mexican war on their hands. Is there any wonder that the cost of living remains at an oppressive figure to the mechanics and laboring classes of the country.

REDUCTION OF THE REGULAR ARMY POSTPONED—WHY?

But the authors of the Chicago platform have just, at Washington, deliberately postponed *till next year the reduction of the regular army, thereby entailing upon the taxpayers of this country an admittedly superfluous outlay of nearly fifty millions of dollars, or more than two-thirds of the whole expense of the Federal Government before the war.* Superfluous, we say, this expense is admitted to be, for honest and admissible objects. It is *not* superfluous, however, if the Radicals, who have made the "General of the Armies" their candidate propose to use him, and with him the army, for interfering with the will of the people when they find themselves beaten at the polls next November.

THE AMOUNT OF TAXATION.

In order to bolster up his charge of extravagance against the Republican party, he says that the taxation of 1866 amounted to $590,000,000. Now, Mr. Pendleton must have known that this statement was untrue. * * * The largest sum ever received was during the fiscal year ending June 30, 1866, which reached $490,248,219, almost $100,000,000 less than the figures given by Mr. Pendleton.—*Indianapolis Journal.*

We have once before corrected the *Journal* in this matter. Why does it still continue to blunder? Don't it know that $176,000,000 which we have collected from customs per year was collected in gold, and that, reduced to currency, it amounts to $253,000,000? This, added to $314,000,000 collected from the internal revenue in greenbacks, makes $567,000,000 of taxes. Mr. Pendleton was, therefore, much nearer exact figures than his corrector of the *Journal.* He was $23,000,000 too high. It is $77,000,000 to low!—*Cincinnati Enquirer.*

COST OF RADICAL RULE.

Since the surrender of Lee's army the Radical Government at Washington have borrowed about eight hundred millions of dollars, and have collected in addition thereto from the people during the same period, by way of taxes and custom duties, fourteen hundred millions, which make two thousand two hundred millions that they have expended since the close of the rebellion. This is one half of the entire debt of Great Britain, and more than the entire amount expended by the National Government from the time that George Washington was first inaugurated President up to the close of Buchanan's administration, during which time the country went through two successful foreign wars, and any number of wars with the Indians, and also acquired all the territory of the United States west of the Mississippi river. These facts speak for themselves. What has been done with the money? It is larger than ever. It has gone to support idle negroes at the South; it has been used to maintain a huge standing army in time of peace, for the sole purpose of keeping the white citizens in ten States under the law of the bayonet; it has gone into the pockets of the loil "rings." In November the people will dispose of these public plunderers at the polls, and will put them out of power.—*N. Y. World.*

EXPENDITURES SINCE THE WAR.

Since the close of the war in 1865, the Radicals have expended, over and above the amount paid for interest on the public debt, over one thousand millions of dollars. This is more than one-third of our national debt. Is there any wonder that the Radical papers are anxious to cover this up, and prevent the people seeing these facts, by constantly harping about the questions at issue during the existence of the war?

FINANCES OF THE GOVERNMENT.

Striking Contrast.

The war has been over for nearly four years, and the Radical party has kept the expenses of the Government and the taxes at war rates and enormously high figures. The Government under the management of their party has cost the people more since the war closed than it did from the time Washington was inaugurated to the close of Buchanan's administration in 1861.

Cost of the Navy before the War.

Before the war the cost of the Navy Department was less than thirteen millions per year. Then the shipping interests of the country were fully protected on every sea on the globe. The average cost of that Department for the three years since the war has closed has been over forty millions per year, and that, too, with our shipping interest under Radical rule swept from the ocean by taxation and tariffs. The same parties who have been guilty of this, now that they want a new lease of power, are hypocritically talking about economy.

Public Debt under Democratic and Radical Administration.

In 1860 a Democratic administration left the Government with a debt of about $70,000,000 in round numbers. From 1861 to 1865, being four years of war, the Radicals increased that debt to $2,000,000,0 0. From 1865 to 1868, being three years of peace, the Radicals added to the debt $900,000,000, so that after all the efforts at reducing the national burdens we find ourselves to-day, after three years of peace, making up, with four years of war, seven years of Radical supremacy, more than *two thousand millions* of dollars worse off as a nation than we were in 1860.

Gold Used in New York in 1867.

The amount of duties, in gold, of course, received in the district of New York during the year 1867, stands:

For the month of January, 1867	$ 9,550,451 05
For the month of February, 1867	11,546,396 96
For the month of March, 1867	12,066,421 83
For the month of April, 1867	9,460,328 49
For the month of May, 1867	9,396,739 42
For the month of June, 1867	7,783,383 94
For the month of July, 1867	9,550,343 92
For the month of August, 1867	12,657,754 05
For the month of September, 1867	11,740,019 28
For the month of October, 1867	8,788,017 03
For the month of November, 1867	6,951,886 70
For the month of December, 1867	3,204,516 92
Total	$114,786,259 59

What a pity the voice of the great city pouring all this gold into the Treasury, and of the great State which backs the yellow tide with greenback millions, should be neutralized in the Senate by any two surreptitious Senators from the South.

Grant's Economy.

The Radical papers are publishing huge puffs of General Grant's economy; but, strange to relate, they don't include in his economical doings his recommendation to *increase* the pay of the officers of the army *thirty-three and one-third per cent.*

Cost of Radical Rule in the South.

Wilson, of Massachusetts, from the Senate Military Committee, has the coolness to get up in the Senate and say that the reason why this people must go on paying *eleven millions of dollars a month* is, that it requires "fourteen thousand men in the South alone" to keep the Republican party in power. *In 1860 our whole army was not so large*, and its annual expenses were but little more than the sum now spent every month to make "carpet baggers" Senators and members of Congress.

Our National Bonds.
[From the Chicago Tribune.]

The law of February 25, 1862, which authorizes the issue of five twenties of that year, was the first of the series which attracted general attention. That act authorized the issue of $500,000,000 in six per cent. bonds, redeemable after five years and payable in twenty years from date. About two years later a supplemental law was passed authorizing the issue of $11,000,000 additional five-twenty bonds. The object of this fresh issue was to meet subscriptions already made and paid for. The first of these acts also made greenbacks legal tender, except for interest on bonds and for import duties. In order to crush the rebellion it was necessary for our people to consent to the use of a depreciated currency in the ordinary transactions of business. But it was supposed that, before the bonds became either redeemable or payable, specie payment would have been resumed, and therefore nothing was said in the laws themselves about the currency in which the five-twenties were to be paid.

The next bonds issued were of a temporary character, made payable on ten days' notice, bearing interest at four, five and six per cent. The amount authorized was $150,000,000. The amount now outstanding is not far from $20,000,000.

The bonds of 1863 were ten-forties. The question of paying the debt in gold or greenbacks had then begun to be agitated, and, to allay all fears, the act of March 3, 1863, specifically states that both interest and principal should be payable only in coin. About two hundred and fifty millions of these bonds were issued and are still outstanding. Some of them bear interest at six per cent., but the greater portion of our ten forties draw only five per cent. interest.

In June of the next year an additional issue of five twenties was authorized, amounting to fifty millions. This loan was followed by another of a similar nature, in March, 1865, the last of the five-twenties, and amount, both together, to about two hundred and twenty-five millions.

There were, beside these bonds and the temporary loans already mentioned, authorized certificates of indebtedness running from one to three years, the particulars of which are unessential to the object of this article. The Goverment also authorized the issue of several special bonds, such as the Union Pacific Railroad Company bonds, but these do not form a part of the war debt of the nation.

AMOUNTS OF THE SEVERAL ISSUES OF GOLD-BEARING BONDS.

The subjoined letter from the Secretary of the Treasury shows the amount of the several gold-bearing loans of the United States outstanding July 1, 1868:

TREASURY DEPARTMENT, July 15, 1868.

GENTLEMEN: In reply to your letter of the 13th inst., inquiring the amount outstanding of the various loans, I would respectfully state that on July 1, 1868, there was of

Five per cent. bonds due 1871, outstanding	$ 7,922,000
Five per cent. bonds due 1874, outstanding	20,000,000
Five per cent. ten-forties outstanding	198,440,800
Six per cent. bonds of 1847-48, outstanding	6,878,442
Six per cent. bonds of 1881 outstanding	283,677,200
Six per cent. five-twenties, February 25, 1862, outstanding	514,771,600
Six per cent. five-twenties, June 30, 1864, outstanding	125,561,300
Six per cent. five-twenties, 1865, May and November, outstanding	197,777,250
Six per cent. five-twenties, 1865, consuls, outstanding	334,972,950
Six per cent. five-twenties, 1867, outstanding	364,123,900
Six per cent. five-twenties, 1868, outstanding	17,648,950

The 1865 consuls, 1867's, and 1868's, can not be definitely given, as these loans are being continually increased on account of the exchange of seven-thirty notes.

Very respectfully,
H. McCULLOCH, Secretary.

To Messrs. Henry Clews & Co., New York.

BROWNLOW ON REDEEMING THE BONDS IN GREENBACKS.

Brownlow's letter to the Radical State Convention of Tennessee, dated Knoxville, January 20, 1868, closes as follows:

"If I were a member of your Convention I would endeavor to have incorporated into the platform you adopt a plank to the following effect:

"That the bonds and obligations of the general Government, which do not expressly stipulate for payment in coin in the acts authorizing their issuance, or in their face, should be paid in greenbacks or legal-tenders. and that our delegates to the National Convention be instructed to vote for a resolution in the National Platform embracing this proposition.

"I have the honor to be, etc.,
"W. G. BROWNLOW."

—

Mr. Maynard, in a letter dated Washington, January 19, 1868, to the same body, says:

"The strength of a Government, State or National, is its credit. To sustain this is the primal work of intelligent administration. Public credit depends solely upon the willingness and the ability of the people to meet the public obligations. Repudiation in any and every form is a deadly blight, and any measure that tends logically to repudiation, however slightly, excites instant alarm, and exerts a depressing influence. No people on earth have a greater horror at a breach of the public faith than the Union people of Tennessee; indeed, I may say the Union people all over the country. If their resources are judiciously and economically used, so as to exact from them only a portion of their profits, without encroaching upon the capital, they can respond to every obligation assumed in their name. Let the taxes be so imposed that the industry shall not, by reason of their payment, be any poorer at the end of the year than at the beginning. With honesty and official integrity to enforce these maxims, those who know how to live by the sweat of the face, and are willing to do it, will have but little trouble in making the ends meet. No others can hope to succeed except by some of the phases of bad government, which, at bottom, is simply a contrivance to enable one man to live in idleness upon the fruits of another man's labor."

—

KEEP THE FACTS BEFORE THE PEOPLE.

The cost of the War and Navy Departments since the Republicans have been in power is as follows:

	War Dept.	Navy Dept.
1861	$160,157,794	$29,889,176
1862	479,425,277	47,548,103
1863	680,143,230	88,526,101
1864	815,549,292	112,313,305
1865	848,292,733	103,554,317
1866	114,211,351	46,897,283
1867	156,177,563	49,345,022

THE NATIONAL DEBT AND TAXES.

We take the following from the New York *Journal of Commerce*:

"Our Forrestville correspondent is informed that the highest point of the public debt was on the 31st of August, 1865, when it amounted to $2,757,689,571 43. It has since been reduced to a little below twenty-five hundred millions, *but is now on the increase again, the receipts falling below the current expenses, including payments for interest*. On the 1st of June, 1868, the date of the last official statement, it stood at $2,643-753,566 38, from which, deducting $133,-507,679 64 coin and currency in the Treasury, the net debt beyond available means, amounted to $2,510,245,886 74. Unless something is done looking toward greater economy, or some plan is devised to make up the large deficiency (over one hundred millions) arising from the repeal of duties on domestic manufactures, there will be a further considerable increase of the debt during the current fiscal year. The politicians have cut off the taxes for effect, and will do nothing to restore them until after the fall election."

Mark the language, that "the politicians have cut off the taxes for effect, and will do nothing to restore them until after the fall election." This is true. Then, if the Radical party succeeds, they will be put back, and more added to make up the deficiency! In the mean time, they hope to blind the people by this little stratagem of temporary relief. But it is too apparent to succeed.

RADICAL FINANCIERS.

[From the New York World.]

One good and sufficient reason for putting an end to the Radical influences in this country is the monstrous ignorance of its leaders in regard to the most important questions which can occupy the attention of a national legislature. Not to speak of Sumner's notorious nonsense on financial topics, or of the profound geographical debate which took place some weeks ago in the House between two members of the Committee on Foreign affairs on the question whether Tuscany formed a part of the Kingdom of Italy, here we have Nye in the Senate estimating the "domestic trade of this "country for the year 1867 at $10,000,000,-000, "*and the foreign trade at but a little less ;*" and Garfield in the House averring that England "does not now tax and never did tax the principal or interest of her public debt, whether in the hands of foreigners or of her own people."

It is firing a sixty-pounder at a shrimp, perhaps, to dwell even for a moment upon the financial drivel of Nye, but it is worth noting as an illustration of the almost inconceivable imbecility of the class to which he belongs, that the whole amount of the import trade of this country, from the year 1790 to the year 1863, was not equal by many millions to the sum which the preposterous Senator cited as a single year's exchanges. In these seventy-three years the United States imported $9,450,760,003, while the average annual amount of foreign trade, imports and exports together, since the Radicals came into power in 1861, has been but a little over $500,000,000, against an average annual value of over $700,000,000 during the last four years of Union under a Democratic administration.

Garfield's blunder, if less hilariously absurd than Nye's, is not much less discreditable. It is so far from being true that England has never taxed her public debt in foreign or domestic hands, that in 1842 Sir Robert Peel did not hesitate to impose an equal tax upon the funds, whether held by foreigners or by British subjects, and the British funds have ever since that date been taxable by law. The drift of such loose and unpatriotic talkers on these matters as Garfield, goes to show that Americans who propose to lay a tax upon the American funds, or make foreigners pay a part of that tax, are unprecedented monsters of bad faith, no parallel for whom can be found even in the annals of Spanish or of Italian repudiation. This is of a piece with the general disposition of the Radicals to glorify foreign, and especially British history, at the expense of the character and reputation of our own people. The truth is that it has long been a popular doctrine in England that foreign holders of the funds ought to be specifically taxed, and the strongest language which such a man as Mr. Gladstone, when Chancellor of the Exchequer, in 1853, felt himself at liberty to use in opposing this doctrine was this, that he was "persuaded the House would agree with him in thinking that it would be very impolitic to lay an exceptional tax of this kind upon the foreigner."

Not one word, mark you, of all the gabble in which the Radical ignoramuses of of our own House and Senate indulge about the "moral degradation" and the "despicable meanness" of this or that measure of financial policy. Butler (to give the Devil his due) rebuked the ignorance of Garfield on this subject, and declared, with his usual politeness, that Garfield "knew no more than a Choctaw what he was talking about." Butler has rarely stumbled so nearly into the truth ; but, as it is a necessity of his nature to do injustice to somebody, he did injustice here to the Choctaws. No Choctaw would have talked as Garfield talked; for the Indians, as a race, have an admirable habit of holding their tongues when they have nothing to say.

Are the 5-20s Redeemable in Coin?

RADICAL AND OTHER TESTIMONY THAT THEY ARE NOT.

In the House of Representatives, November 29, 1867, Mr. Brooks (Dem.), of New York, said:

I do not rise to enter at all into this debate, or to express any opinion, one way or the other, upon the subject which the gentleman from Maine (Mr. Blaine) and the gentleman from Massachusetts (Mr. Butler) have been discussing.

I rise to set the gentleman from Maine right—I will not say upon the written history of this legislation, but upon the unwritten history of the act of June, 1864, creating the securities known as "five-twenties." The unwritten history of a country, particularly in connection with finance, is often quite as important as its written history, especially when there is any doubt as to the true meaning of the act.

During the session of 1864 there were two propositions emanating from the Committee of Ways and Means: one from the honorable gentleman from Pennsylvania (Mr. Stevens), the other from the honorable gentleman from Massachusetts (Mr. Hooper). The gentleman from Pennsylvania being in the minority of that committee, and the gentleman from Massachusetts being in the majority, the gentleman from Massachusetts was called upon to report the bill from the Committee of Ways and Means for the consideration and action of the House. The bill which the gentleman from Pennsylvania introduced before the House was a bill making the principal of this debt payable in coin, the debt having a long time to run. He argued that it was wise for the Government to pay a large interest in paper—eight per cent. he named—while it agreed to pay the principal of the debt in coin. That was his bill.

The bill which the Committee of Ways and Means reported through the gentleman from Massachusetts (Mr. Hooper) was a bill which, notwithstanding the warning which the gentleman from Pennsylvania (Mr. Stevens) gave in his bill, omitted, apparently purposely, the provision that the principal should be payable in coin. I called the attention of the committee to this and many other defects in that bill, as they appeared to me at that time. If gentlemen will take the trouble to examine the report of the discussions which took place upon that subject, they will find that I, among others, forewarned the House of the perilous course it was pursuing in reference to the national finances and of the difficulties which would ensue. Unfortunately, I was at that time, as I am now, in the minority in this House, and on account of the political passion and excitement then prevailing I was less heeded at that time than I and others of the minority are likely to be hereafter. I called the attention of the House to the silence of that bill as to the payability of those bonds, whether in paper or in specie. Let me read from the report in the *Globe*:

"Mr. BROOKS. I withdraw my amendment"—

That was the previous amendment, a matter of some importance; but I did not divide the House upon it, because I did not wish to put myself in a false position. I was not responsible for the bill. All I could do was to call the attention of the majority to the point. I withdrew my amendment without a division—

"Mr. BROOKS. I withdraw my amendment and move to insert in the ninth line the words "payable in coin." Those words are not in this bill, although they are in the bill of the gentleman from Pennsylvania (Mr. Stevens).

"Mr. HOOPER. The bill of last year—the $900,000,000 bill—contained these words, but it was not deemed necessary or considered expedient to insert them in this bill. I will send up to the desk and ask to have read, as a part of my reply to the gentleman, a letter from the Secretary of the Treasury, which was published sometime ago, giving his views upon that point."

The gentleman from Maine (Mr. Blaine) read that letter yesterday; and I will read only the sentence which relates particularly to this subject. It will be found to exhibit the same evasion of the point—I mean nothing offensive by this language—as was found in the remarks of the gentleman from Massachusetts. Mr. Chase says:

"It has been the constant usage of the Department to redeem all coupon and registered bonds forming part of the funded or permanent debt of the United States in coin, and this usage has not been deviated from during my administration of its affairs."

This letter was dated May 18, and this discussion was on the 22d of June, more than a month afterward. It will be observed that in this letter there is no pledge of the Secretary of the Treasury directly applicable to this act under consideration. His language is carefully guarded. He says: "It has been the constant usage of the Department to redeem all coupon and registered bonds forming part of the funded or permanent debt of the United States in coin," of which usage there was no manner of dispute, because it had always been the usage. But at that time we were enacting a new law, and the use of the words "payable in coin" was, as I show, purposely avoided, the attention of the House being called to the matter by the gentleman from Pennsylvania (Mr. Stevens), and also by myself in the amendment which I proposed.

The House at that time acted considerately upon the subject, and refused to make a direct pledge for the payment of these bonds in coin. I deeply regretted it at the time. But I should not have made these remarks now if the gentleman from Maine (Mr. Blaine) had not said that I was "apparently satisfied" with the explanation which was then given. I was very much dissatisfied; for I foresaw all this difficulty, all this misunderstanding upon the part of the public, and the doubt which might be thrown upon the honor and character of the Government. What is our duty now, in view of the subsequent letters of the Secretaries of the Treasury, the advertisements which have been put forth upon the part of the Government, the declarations which have been made semi-officially and officially, it is not for me to say. All that I have to say upon the subject is that, as appears by the record here before me, the House did not act inconsiderately or with its eyes shut; that its attention was directed to the subject when this act was before the House for consideration and discussion.

Thad. Stevens' Recollection of the Bond.

In the House, July 17, 1868, in the debate on the "Funding Bill"—

Mr. STEVENS (Pa.) declared himself in favor of a funding bill which should reduce interest. If no person should choose to fund under it, no harm was done; if any person did choose to fund at a lower rate of interest, the Government would profit by it. He thought, however, that the lowest rate of interest should be four per cent.; he did not think they could get money cheaper. He thought it the duty of the Government, with the accumulating gold, to expend one-half in redeeming the five twenties in advance of their falling due. No one could object to their redemption. He had understood the gentleman from Illinois (Mr. Ross) to say that the bonds should be paid according to the New York Platform. What was that platform?

Mr. Ross. To pay the five-twenties in lawful money.

Mr. STEVENS. What do you call lawful money?

Mr. Ross. Greenbacks; that is your doctrine and mine, you know. [Laughter].

Mr. STEVENS. I hold to the Chicago platform, *and as I understand it, on that point, to the New York platform*—that those bonds shall be paid just according to the original contract.

A MEMBER. The law, Mr. Stevens, according to the law.

Mr. PIKE. The spirit and letter of the contract.

Mr. STEVENS. What was that law? That the interest should be paid up to a certain time at 6 per cent. in coin. After the bonds fell due they would be payable in money, just as the gentleman from Illinois [Mr. Ross] understood it; just as he [Mr. Stevens] understood it; just as all understood it when the law was enacted; just as it was explained on the floor a dozen times by the Chairman of the Committee on Ways and Means. *If he knew that any party in the country would go for paying in coin that which was payable in money, thus enhancing the debt one-half; if he knew there was such a platform and such a determination on the part of his own party,* HE WOULD, WITH FRANK BLAIR AND ALL, VOTE FOR THE OTHER PARTY. *He would vote for no such swindle on the tax-payers of the country. He would vote for no such speculation in favor of the large bond-holders and millionaires. He repeated (though it was hard to say it),* THAT EVEN IF FRANK BLAIR STOOD ON THE PLATFORM OF PAYING ACCORDING TO THE CONTRACT, AND IF THE REPUBLICAN CANDIDATE STOOD ON THE PLATFORM OF PAYING BLOATED SPECULATORS TWICE THE AMOUNT AGREED TO BE PAID TO THEM, AND OF TAXING HIS CONSTITUENTS TO DEATH, HE WOULD VOTE FOR FRANK BLAIR, EVEN IF A WORSE MAN THAN SEYMOUR WAS ON THE TICKET. [Much excitement and sensation.]

Mr. Ross. *The Democratic doors are still open, and the gentleman can be taken in.*

On the 24th of July, 1868, Mr. Stevens, rising to a personal explanation, said: I desire to say a few words relating to what I observe reported in the *Globe* of the remarks of General Garfield and others with regard to what I said on the passage of the five-twenty bill. I find that it is all taken from the report of Secretary McCulloch, which I had never read. I am, therefore, free to presume that what those gentlemen quoted, rather than said, is a total perversion of the truth. Had it not been introduced from so respectable a quarter in this House, it would not be too harsh to call it an absolute falsehood. I do not know that I should have taken any notice of what various papers are reporting; some of them half secession, and more of them, I suppose, in the pay of the bondholders. I shall not now undertake to explain the whole of this matter, as I am so feeble; but I shall take occasion hereafter to expose the villany of those who charge me with having said, on the passage of five-twenty bill, that its bonds were payable in coin. The whole debate from which they quote, and all my remarks which they cited, were made upon an entirely different bill, as might be seen by observing that I speak only of the payment of gold after twenty years, when the bill I was speaking of, as well as all the liabilities, were payable in coin, as no one doubted the resumption of specie payment. My speech was made on the introduction of the Legal-Tender bill, on which the interest for twenty years was to be paid in currency. No question of paying interest in gold arose till some time after, when the bill had been passed by the House, and sent to the Senate, returned and went to a Committee of Conference, where for the first time the gold-bearing question was introduced, and yet all these wise and thoughtful gentlemen have quoted from me what took place in debate some weeks before the gold question, either principal or interest, had arisen in the House. I only now want to caution the public against putting faith in the fabrications of demagogues, and they will find that every word which I have asserted with regard to myself is true and to the letter.

Horace Greeley Reads Thad. Stevens out of the Grant Party.

Thad. Stevens having declared in Congress that he would vote the Democratic ticket if the Radical platform, or the Radical party, contemplated the payment of the bonds in gold, Greeley invites him to do so, in the following courteous language, which we quote from the *Tribune* of July 21:

"That those who hated the war and deplore its issue should seek to swindle those who lent the money which insured its success, is deplorable, but not unnatural. That Mr. Stevens should be found in their company is deplorable and *very* unnatural. He, of all men, ought to be found on the side of honesty and good faith; for he drafted and engineered the bills which dragged us into the slough whence he seems determined that we shall never be extricated. If he should succeed in his present effort, no swindler that the world has known ever perpetrated a fraud so gigantic as that he meditates.

* * * * * * *

Mr. Stevens is a fit ally for the Pendletons, Rossees, and Blairs, whom he threatens to join, unless the Republican party can be made the accomplice of the gigantic crime he meditates. That, we can assure him, will never be. If he wishes to swindle efficiently, let him join the party to which swindling is natural—that which will gratify by repudiation its partisan malignity as well as its innate rascality. Mr. Ross courteously opens the doors of the Democratic church for his reception. He says he will enter if the Republicans will not help him defraud the National creditors. That, we will tell him, they will never do. Let him therefore,

"Stay not on the order of his going,
But go at once."

Speech of Senator Morton.

On Monday, the 6th of July, 1868, the Senate debated the Funding bill. In the course of the discussion, Senator Morton, of Indiana, said:

Mr. President, the question as to whether the five-twenties are payable only in coin or may be paid in legal-tender notes, has been brought prominently into this debate. The Chairman of the Committee on Finance, who has had much to do with the financial affairs of this country for six or seven years past, insists that the Government has a right to pay the five-twenties in existing legal-tender notes. I say "existing" as contradistinguished from notes yet to be issued. The distinguished Senator from Massachusetts [Mr. Sumner], on Saturday, in a very elaborate speech, argued at length that the Government was compelled by law to pay these bonds in coin. An argument of great ability and length was made to the same effect by the Senator from Vermont early in the session. This question is not important beyond the time that the Government shall resume specie payments. Whenever we make the legal-tender note as good as gold then this question is settled. But it is an important question, and may be an important and troublesome question until that time occurs. I, for one, believe that the true policy for the Government is to take steps first and foremost to bring about the resumption of specie payments. I believe that that lies at the foundation of our financial troubles, and there is where we should begin.

I will remark that this question is entirely distinct from the question of the right of the Government to make a new issue of legal-tender notes and pay off the five-twenties in that new issue. As I shall speak of the question, I shall speak of the right of the Government to redeem the five-twenties in existing legal-tender notes.

Mr. President, I believe that the law—and it is to the law we must look in regard to this question after all—is with the Senator from Ohio on this question. When it is asserted that the Government is bound to redeem the five-twenties in coin, I say it is not only without the law, but it is in express violation of at least four statutes.

The law authorizing the ten-forties declares that principal and interest shall be paid in coin. The several laws creating the five-twenties declare that the interest shall be paid in coin, but are silent as to the principal of the debt, and do not say in what kind of money the principal shall be paid. This silence is very significant.

But it is said by the Senator from Massachusetts and the Senator from Vermont that the Government is as much bound to pay the principal of the five-twenties in coin as if it was so expressed in the several acts authorizing and creating those bonds, and that there is no difference between the legal obligation of the Government in regard to the five-twenties and in regard to the ten-forties. Let me say to the Senator from Vermont and the Senator from Massachusetts that if they desire to ascertain the qualities and capacities of the legal-tender notes, what debts they will pay, and what debts they will not pay, they must look to the laws creating the legal-tender notes, and not to the statutes authorizing the five-twenty bonds.

The act of February 25, 1862, by its second section authorized the first issue of five-twenty bonds, and by its first section the first issue of legal-tender notes; and in said first section declares such notes herein authorized shall be received in payment of all taxes, internal duties, excise, debts and demands of every kind due the United States, except duties on imports, and all claims and demands against the United States of any kind whatsoever, except for interest upon bonds and notes, which shall be paid in coin, and shall also be lawful money and a legal-tender in payment of all debts, public and private, within the United States, except duties on imports and interest as aforesaid.

The declaration is that such notes shall be receivable in payment "of all claims and demands against the United States of every kind whatsoever, except for interest upon bonds and notes, which shall be paid in coin." More comprehensive language could not be employed, and you can not conceive of any debt against the United States left out of this phrase save that which is specially excepted. It comprehends all claims and demands of whatsoever kind. A bond is a claim; a bond is a demand. The very exception proves that bonds were comprehended in the phrase, for if they were not, there was no necessity for excepting the interest upon them. But the statute does not stop here. It goes on to say, tautologically, that such notes "shall also be lawful money and a legal-tender in payment of all debts, public and private, within the United States, except duties on imports and interest as aforesaid." Every debt which the United States owes is a public debt; it has no private debts, and a five-twenty bond is a public debt in the fullest sense of those words for which the law declares such notes shall be lawful money and a legal-tender. Was ever a statute more comprehensive, unequivocal or plainly written? If the effect of this language can be varied or destroyed by argument, then no statute can be drawn which can withstand the lawyer's ingenuity. But there are three other statutes to the same effect with the one I have just considered.

The act of the 11th of July following, provided for the issue of another $150,000,000 of legal-tender notes, and declared, like the former, that they should be legal-tender in payment of all claims and demands of whatsoever kind against the United States, except interest on notes and bonds, and further declared that these notes

"Shall also be lawful money and a legal-tender in payment of all debts, public and private in the United States, except duties on imports and interest as aforesaid."

There are but two exceptions stated in the law, but it is sought by argument to establish a third, compared with which the two stated in the law are mere trifles.

This statute is unconnected with any provision for the issue of bonds, and was passed before any bonds were sold, authorized by the preceding act of February.

Again, in January, 1863, Congress passed a joint resolution authorizing the issue of another $100,000,000 of legal-tender notes, in which it was again declared that they should be received as "legal-tender in payment of all claims and demands against the United States of whotsoever kind, except interest on notes and bonds," and this joint resolution was unconnected with any provisions for the issue of bonds.

And again, in February, 1863, an act was passed authorizing the issue of another $150,000,000 of legal-tender notes, including the $100,000,000 authorized by the joint resolution just referred to, in which it is declared in language somewhat different from the other acts, but in substance the same, that "these notes so issued shall be lawful money and a legal-tender in payment of all debts, public and private, within the United States, except for duties on imports and interest on the public debt."

Here are four plain, unequivocal, and emphatic declarations of the law, declaring that these notes shall be a legal-tender in payment of every conceivable species of indebtedness against the United States. And whether the fact be agreeable or disagreeable it is one that can not be overcome by argument or ingenuity.

But it is argued that Secretary Chase, and

perhaps one or two Assistant Secretaries or chief clerks of the Treasury, gave it out in letters and speeches that these bonds would be paid in coin, and that the bonds were sold upon such an understanding. It is to be noticed that in giving these opinions by the Secretary and the Assistant Secretaries or chief clerks, that it was predicated entirely upon the practice of the Government heretofore, and not upon any construction of the law authorizing the issue of the bonds or creating the legal-tender notes. In none of these opinions is there any reference made to these statutes, and what was said seemed to have been said in ignorance or indifference toward them, and the opinions were predicated entirely upon what had been the practice of the Government heretofore. These several acts creating the legal-tender were public laws, of which every man in the country was bound to take notice at his peril. Every man in the country purchasing a bond is presumed to know the character of the law creating the bond or the existence of any other law affecting the bond either as to time, manner, or mode of its payment.

In matters of such immense magnitude the nation can only be bound by the law. Its rights must be defined by the law, and by the law only. It can not be bound by the opinion of public officers given either in ignorance or in violation of the law.

The Government of the United States, which has the power to borrow money and create a new loan, has put the terms of that loan into the law, and they can not be varied by the opinion or the action of any public officer.

It would be a monstrous doctrine that the rights of the nation and of future generations, in matters of such immense importance, could be varied or changed by the illegal or unwarranted declaration of a public officer, who has no power to say or do anything, except that which is conferred upon him by law. Nor can it be said that the good faith of the nation can be affected by its refusal to comply with the representations of a public officer when those representations are made in direct conflict with a public statute of which he and everybody else is bound to take notice. Even in matters of private right and of the smallest importance men are presumed to know the law, and their rights are determined accordingly, and no man is bound by the act of his agent when that agent is acting outside of the authority or the presumed authority conferred upon him. Every man buying a bond of the Government must know that the liability of the Government could not be fixed or changed by a declaration of the Secretary of the Treasury, but that the liability of the Government must be determined absolutely and only by the law creating the bond or making regulations for its payment.

The good faith of the nation in a matter of this kind can only be measured by the promise given by the law-making power, which promise must be in the form of a law. The Constitution declares that Congress shall have power to borrow money, from which it must be inferred that Congress, and Congress only, can prescribe the terms, limits and conditions of the loan. The attempt, therefore, to erect a standard of good faith for the nation, not only outside of the law, but in violation of its express provisions, does the nation great injustice by contributing to place it in a false position before the people of other countries.

That is all I have to say on that question. If you prove that the Government is bound to pay the bonds in coin, you do it in the face of four direct and plain statutes, as unequivocal as any statutes that ever were written.

There is the statute, plain, direct, even tautological, upon this subject, declaring in not less than six or seven places that these notes shall be received in payment, and as a legal-tender, in discharge of every claim and demand of whatsoever kind against the United States, except interest upon notes and upon bonds, and then going on to say, as I remarked before, tautologically, that those notes shall be received as lawful money and as legal-tender in payment of all debts, public or private, in the United States, except the interest on notes or bonds as aforesaid. And yet in the face of language so plain, language that can not be misunderstood, it is argued, from day to day, in this Senate that the Government is bound to pay the five-twenties in coin.

Now, Mr. President, this question is important or unimportant as Congress shall make it so. When we return to specie payments it is unimportant, as long as we fail to return to specie payments it is important. As I took occasion to say, some weeks ago, in the Senate, the first duty of Congress and the first great thing to do, in my opinion, is to take some direct step toward the return to specie payments.

I will say further, that it is in the existing legal-tender notes that the Government has a right to pay those five-twenty bonds. There was a limit of $400,000,000 fixed by law to the issue of those notes. I believe that to pass that limit would be a violation of public faith; but that the Government has the right to pay the five-twenty bonds out of the existing legal-tender notes, is as clear, in my opinion, as any right that is defined by any statute of the United States.

Mr. WILSON. I should like to ask the

Senator what practical importance there is in maintaining that doctrine if we have got no greenbacks to pay the bonds with? I take it there is not anybody here who supposes, if we are limited to the present amount of greenbacks, that we have got any greenbacks to redeem the bonds with. Therefore the question is not a practical one in any sense of the word, it seems to me.

Mr. MORTON. I think I can answer that question. The Senator has kindly called my attention to a point that I had forgotten for the moment, and that right in connection with this funding bill. Four hundred million dollars of currency is enough in which to invest all the bonds authorized by this bill. It is not done at once. The Government sells fifty million dollars of these new bonds to-day, and receives pay in existing legal-tender notes. Those notes are paid out to-morrow in the redemption of an equal number of existing five-twenty bonds; and so the process goes on. The Government can redeem the five-twenty bonds in the existing legal-tender notes without issuing a new note, simply by selling the new bonds for legal-tender notes, and applying those legal-tender notes in the redemption of the existing five-twenty bonds.

That comes right down to this funding bill. This bill provides that the proceeds of the sale of these bonds "shall be exclusively used for the redemption, payment, or purchase of, or exchange for, an equal amount"—that is a very important phrase right there—"of the present interest bearing debt of the United States." If you exchange them, it must be done for par. If you sell these new bonds you must sell them for par. Then you can not buy up the five-twenty bonds in the market. You can not buy them unless you buy them for par, because you make the proceeds of these bonds take up and cancel an equal amount of the outstanding bonds. We will suppose that the Secretary of the Treasury has sold $100,000,000 of these five per cent. bonds at par. He has got $100,000,000 of greenbacks in the Treasury of the United States. How is he going to apply that to the extinguishment of an equal amount of the outstanding debt? The holders of the five-twenty bonds will not sell them to the Government on the market for par, because they are commanding a large premium. He can not exchange bond for bond, because the bonds to be exchanged for command a premium, whereas the new bond can only be sold at par; there is no premium on that. He can not obtain the five-twenties by exchange; he can not obtain them by purchase, because the law would require him to purchase the old bonds at par, and they are at a premium. Therefore he can not use the proceeds of the new bonds unless he avails himself of the right of the Government to redeem the old bonds in these legal-tender notes.

Mr. SHERMAN. The Senator is a little mistaken in regard to the legal effect. The plain meaning is that he shall only sell the bonds as he can redeem an equal amount. He would not sell these bonds at a less price than the market value of the five-twenties; but he can do that or make the exchange.

Mr. MORTON. I presume the chairman of the committee is entirely right upon that point; but the practical difficulty is that the Secretary can not sell them for more than par; that will not be pretended, and he can not buy the existing five-twenty bonds at par. So there can be nothing done in the way of buying them on the market. Then there can be nothing done in the way of exchange, because the old bonds command a premium, while the new ones do not. Therefore the holders of the old bonds would lose by the exchange. Then there can be nothing done with these bonds, unless he avails himself of the lawful right of the Government to take in these five-twenty bonds by paying them off in legal-tender notes. I have often heard it said that unless you issue more greenbacks, you can not redeem the five-twenties in greenbacks. I have shown that that is a mistake; that by selling the new bonds at par, to be paid for in the existing legal-tender notes, those notes, when thus received, can be applied in redeeming and absolutely paying off a portion of the existing five-twenty bonds.

I am in favor myself of passing the first section of this bill. I am in favor of trying to give an additional value to these bonds by the length of time that has been fixed in the bill for them to run. That is the only advantage they will have over the old bond.

One word in regard to the amendment of the Senator from Maine, which is to make these bonds all redeemable at the pleasure of the Government after ten years. He takes away the inducement to buy these bonds. He says, however, that these bonds can be made available by the existence of a doubt in the public mind as to how they shall be paid, whether they shall be paid in gold or in greenbacks. I should like to ask that distinguished Senator if it is very broad statesmanship to hang a great measure of this kind simply upon a doubt existing in the public mind? I very much prefer making a frank statement of this question to the whole country. As the law is written, so it must remain; you can not help it; you can not rub it out; you can not argue the seal off the bond; and the distinguished

Senators to whom I have referred, with all their ability and ingenuity, can not take a single word from these four statutes.

I am in favor of tendering this Funding bill to the country. I hope it will be accepted; I hope it may be received; but, sir, to make a candid confession, I have very little faith in any funding bill until such time as we have returned to specie payments. I believe we could return to them in a very short time by legislation in that direction. With a surplus of over eighty million dollars of gold in the Treasury, and with an accruing surplus from month to month, if we were simply to say that the gold we now thus hold and the gold we shall receive in surplus shall be applied to the redemption of these legal-tender notes, it would send the premium on gold down one-half at the very beginning. The very existence of that gold standing in the shadow behind these legal-tender notes, although the Government has declared no purpose in holding that gold, has given strength and value to these notes, simply from the impression upon the part of the people of the United States that, some time or other, that gold will be applied to the redemption of these notes. I believe that the accumulation of surplus gold in the Treasury with what we now have, even for a year or a year and a half, would be sufficient to enable us to begin the work of redemption, and place the legal-tender notes at par, and then all these troublesome questions will disappear; but, sir, until that is done, they will remain to plague us.

The Issue Fairly Stated.
THE POPULAR VERDICT CLAIMED BY THE DEMOCRATIC PARTY.
[From the N. Y. World, July 1, 1868.]

The Democratic party also ask the verdict of the people on the exemption of the wealthy bondholders from taxation. The party expects the Government to keep its engagements, but it wants the question decided, whether such engagements are right, and whether in future issue of bonds, such unjust exceptions shall prevail. It is conceded by everybody, that the public debt can not long remain in its present shape. The present bonds must, as rapidly as possible, be replaced by others. Shall the owners of the new bonds be taxable like other owners of property? The Democratic party want this question decided, and demand that it shall be decided in the affirmative. It has been said that the Supreme Court has given an opinion that Government bonds can not be taxed by State authority. But nobody ever pretended that they can not be made taxable by Congressional permission. The Democratic party demand that the new bonds which must be issued, shall be issued under a law authorizing their taxation at the same rates as other property, but at no higher rates, in order that the public burdens may be equitably distributed according to the ability of tax payers. We ask the people to condemn the unjust laws under which the present bonds are issued, that their representatives may be instructed to disregard this bad precedent in future, and subject the new bonds to the same burdens as other descriptions of property. This is fair and equitable, and the people will give it their indorsement.

The Democratic party also ask the verdict of the people on the present disordered currency. They condemn the Republican policy which has introduced a good currency for the rich, and a bad currency for the poor. The Democratic party can perceive no distinction between the morality of public and the morality of private transactions. Justice is absolute and immutable. If paying the public debt in greenbacks is repudiation, then the payment of private debts in greenbacks is also repudiation. The Republican party, by its outcry against repudiation, condemns itself. Even the private debts which were incurred before the legal-tender act was passed, have been made payable in greenbacks, and there is certainly less injustice in paying in greenbacks the public debts incurred since the legal-tender act was passed. Even the interest on the public debt of the State of New York, a debt incurred before the war, has been paid in greenbacks against the protest of Governor Seymour, by the direction of a Republican Legislature. The Democratic party maintains that public debts and private debts, Federal debts and State debts, stand upon the same footing. The real repudiators are the party which has forced the payment of private debts and State debts, contracted on a gold basis, in depreciated paper. The Democratic party contends that the rights of public creditors are no more sacred than those of private creditors; that the owners of Federal bonds have no rights superior to the owners of State bonds; that, in the eye of justice, and sound morals, all obligations are alike. We ask the Country to indorse this equitable principle; a principle so righteous and incontestible that we can not doubt the popular verdict.

HOW THE NATIONAL BANKS WORK IT—BEN BUTLER'S EXPOSE OF THEIR TRICKS—CLAIM THAT THE BANKS PAY LARGE TAXES.

In his speech in the House of Representatives, November 27 and 28, 1867, General Butler (Radical) said:

If Mr Jay Cooke, or any one else, will tell me of any business in this country that is not taxed, and does not pay a large amount of taxes, then I will agree that the Banks are not favored. Take a single case, only two years ago, in the State of Massachusetts, of a manufacturing corporation of $750,000, and of $1,500,000 annual product of manufactured goods. It exactly divided profits with the United States. Its stockhold rs received two dividends of 5 per cent. each on $750,000, and it paid 5 per cent. tax on the entire amount of production, $1,500,000; so that they in fact took the United States into partnership, only the United States got all the profits; but the stockholders bore all the loss. Now, if there is any greater or more onerous burden of taxes on the banks than that, I have yet to learn where it is.

HOW A NATIONAL BANK GOT INTO EXISTENCE.

Let me state the way a National bank got itself into existence in New England during the war, when gold was 200, and five-twenties were at par, in currency, or nearly that. A company of men got together $300,000 in National bank bills, and went to the Register of the Treasury, with gold at 200, and bought United States five-twenty bonds at par. They stepped into the office of the Comptroller of the Currency and asked to be established as a National bank, and received from him $270,000 in currency, without interest, upon pledging these bonds of the United States they had just bought with their $300,000 of the same kind of money. Now, let us balance the books, and how does the account stand? Why, the United States Government receives $30,000 in National bank bills more from the banks than it gave them in bills; in other words, it borrowed of the bank $30,000 in currency, for which, in fact, it paid $18,000 a year in gold interest, equal to $36,000 in currency, for the use of this $30,000 Let me repeat. The difference between what the United States received and paid out was only $30,000, and for the use of that the Government pay on the bonds deposited by the company, bought with the same kind of money, $18,000 a year interest in gold, equal to $36,000 in currency.

But the thing did not stop there. The gentlemen were shrewd financiers; their bank was a good one; they went to the Secretary of the Treasury and said, "Let our bank be made a public depository." Very well; it was a good bank; the managers were good men; there was no objection to the bank. It was made a public depository, and thereupon the commissaries, the quartermasters, the medical director and purveyor, and the paymasters, were all directed to deposit their public funds in this bank. Very soon the bank found that they had a line of steady deposits belonging to the Government of about a million dollars, and that the $270,000 they had received from the Comptroller of the Currency would substantially carry on their daily business, and as the Government gives three days on all its drafts, if the bank was pressed it was easy enough to go on the street if they had good security. They took the million of Government money so deposited with them and loaned it to the Government for the Government's own bonds, and received therefor $60,000 more interest in gold for the loan to the Government of its own money, which in currency was equal to $120,000. So that when we come finally to balance the books the Government is paying $156,000 a year for the loan of $30,000. And this is the system which is to be fastened forever on the country as a means of furnishing a circulating medium!

ANOTHER WAY OF RUNNING A NATIONAL BANK.

Let me state another case, which might be called an actual case, and perhaps I could call the name of the man. A very shrewd man takes his $100,000, and goes to the Treasury and obtains bonds; he then gets a banking charter, and receives his bills, amounting to $90,000; then he buys with those same bills $90,000 worth of bonds, and comes home and sits in his office, and that is his bank, and his money is all in circulation. Says he: Why should I trouble myself to lend my money to the farmers around me on sixty-day notes, when I can lend it at from ten to twelve per cent. on long twenty-year Government bonds, and Mr. Blaine says I am to be paid in gold for them; that is as good banking as I want to do: the bills never come home; they are going all over the West and South, and I am getting $22,800 interest on my original $100,000: what do I want more: I am comfortable and happy; I think this "banking system is the wisest one the world ever saw, and that it ought to be adopted all the world over."

IMMENSE PROFITS OF THE NATIONAL BANKS— FROM WHOM DO THEY COME?

But let us take the banks' own exhibit of themselves. I hold in my hand the abstract of reports of National banking associations for the 1st of October last. Let us see their condition. They have $419,000,000 of capital stock paid in; they have been in operation on an average of less than four years; they have divided from twelve to twenty per cent., about twelve in New England, and from fifteen to twenty per cent. where money is scarcer and the rate of interest rules higher. In addition to these dividends, take their own statement. "Surplus fund, $66,000,000; undivided profits, $33,000,000;" showing that they have got, after all these dividends, near twenty-five per cent. surplus of that capital stock laid away. What other business, taxed or untaxed, if any untaxed business can be found in this country, will allow a yearly dividend of from fifteen to twenty-five per cent., and a surplus accumulation in four years of twenty-five per cent. on the capital? And from whom and from where do these profits come? They come ultimately from where all taxation, all profits, all productions must come—the labor of the country, and nowhere else; and we are asked here to perpetuate a system which takes these immense profits from the labor of the country and puts them into the hands of capitalists, without a pretense of adequate benefit received by the people.

Why, sir, it is an axiom in finance, if there are any axioms in finance, that any business which is safe should have small profits, and business that is hazardous should have large profits; but here the state of things is reversed; the banking business, which, if well conducted, is the safest business on earth, and which heretofore has always been content with small profits, is now the most profitable of all businesses, and has the largest returns without any risks.

Every member of this House can argue these propositions for himself better than I can argue them for him. It is my part only to suggest the topics upon the question of currency. I insist, as my first proposition, that there should be this change in bank circulation, and by that means we would diminish our interest-bearing debt $300,000,000, by redeeming it with the greenbacks we should thus issue.

WITHDRAWAL OF THE NATIONAL CURRENCY, VOTE IN THE HOUSE ON.

On the 26th of November, 1867, Mr. Ross, (Democrat), of Illinois, introduced the following:

Resolved, That the Committee on Banking and Currency be, and they are hereby, instructed to report at an early day a bill providing for withdrawing from circulation the national currency, and to supply the place with Treasury notes, usually known as "greenbacks."

After some skirmishing, Mr. Ross, to get a test vote on it, moved to lay the resolution on the table.

It was decided in the negative—yeas 52, nays 101, not voting 28; as follows:

YEAS—Messrs. Ames, Arnell, Delos R. Ashley, James M. Ashley, Baldwin, Banks, Beaman, Bingham, Blaine, Blair, Boutwell, Bromwell, Broomall, Churchill, Covode, Dawes, Driggs, Eckley, Eliot, Garfield, Halsey, Hooper, Hotchkiss, Hulburd, Ketcham, Laflin, George V. Lawrence, Lincoln, Lynch, Marvin, Miller, Morrill, O'Neill, Perham, Plants, Poland, Pomeroy, Price, Sawyer, *Sitgreaves*, Smith, Spalding, Starkweather, Trowbridge, Twichell, Ward, Cadwalader C. Washburn, Elihu B. Washburne, William B. Washburn, James F. Wilson, John T. Wilson, and Woodbridge—52.

NAYS—Messrs. *Adams*, Allison, Anderson, Archer, *Axtell*, Baker, *Barnes*, Benton, *Boyer*, *Brooks*, Buckland, *Burr*, Butler, CARY, *Chanler*, Reader W. Clarke, Sidney Clarke, Cobb, Coburn, Cook, Cullom, Dodge, Donnelly, Eggleston, *Eldridge*, Farnsworth, Ferriss, Ferry, Fields, *Getz*, *Glossbrenner*, *Haight*, Hamilton, Harding, Hawkins, Hill, Higby, Hopkins, Asahel W. Hubbard, Chester D. Hubbard, *Richard D. Hubbard*, Hunter, Ingersoll, *Johnson*, Judd, Julian, Kelley, Kelsey, *Kerr*, William Lawrence, Loan, Logan, Loughridge, Mallory, *Marshall*, Maynard, McCarthy, McClurg, *McCullough*, Mercur, Moore, *Morgan*, Mullins, *Mungen*, Myers, Newcomb, *Niblack*, Nicholson, Nunn, Orth, Paine, Peters, Pike, Pile, Polsley, *Pruyn*, *Randall*, *Robinson*, *Ross*, Schenck, Shanks, Shellabarger, Aaron F. Stevens, *Stewart*, Stokes, *Taber*, Taylor, Thomas, *Trimble*, Upson, *Van Aernam*, *Van Auken*, Robert T. Van Horn, *Van Trump*, Henry D. Washburn, Welker, Thomas Williams, William Williams, Stephen F. Wilson, Windom, and *Woodward*—101.

NOT VOTING—Messrs. *Barnum*, Benjamin, Cake, Cornell, Dixon, Ela, Finney, *Fox*, Gravely, Griswold, *Holman*, *Humphrey*, Jenckes, Kitchen, Koontz, Moorhead, *Morrissey*, *Phelps*, Raum, Robertson, Scofield, Selye, Thaddeus Stevens, *Stone*, Taffe, Burt Van Horn, Van Wyck, and *Wood*—28.

So the House refused to lay the resolution on the table, and it was adopted.

Speech of the Hon. Geo. H. Pendleton, of Ohio, at Grafton, West Virginia, July 16, 1868.
[From the Cincinnati Commercial's Report.]

Mr. Pendleton opened his speech with a happy reference to the support which the delegates from West Virginia had given his name in the late National Democratic Convention:

I came to assure you, he said, that no sentiment of personal regret lingers in my bosom, or can abate for one moment the fervor of my zeal in behalf of our party. [Cheers.] I came to assure you that far above all personal considerations I rate the success of those principles to which I am attached, and that, whoever shall bear the flag upon which those principles are inscribed, I will be found, close by his side, in the thickest of the fight, to cheer him with my voice, and to aid him with my arm. [Cheers and cries of "Good."]

After referring in eloquent and approbatory terms to the course of that Convention and the noble Platform which it had adopted, he said:

The assertion of these principles, so dear to every American heart, has been committed to the hands of one who is worthy of that trust. By his age, his experience, his intellect, his cultivation; by his honesty, his patriotism, the integrity of his character; by the possession of every virtue that can adorn a public life, or make beautiful a private one, Horatio Seymour deserves to stand in the front rank of American statesmen; and by his declaration, emphatically made, that he approves every line of those resolutions; that they are in accord with his wish; that he will, in public and in private life, endeavor to carry them out, he has given to us the fullest guarantee that they will be the controlling principles of his administration. [Cheers.]

Associated with him on the ticket is an able and experienced statesman; a brave and patriotic soldier; a man of large heart and large views, who quails not in the presence of any adversary. He comes of a stock that has been celebrated in American politics. His father was the nearest friend of Andrew Jackson; his brother was the confidant and confidential adviser of Abraham Lincoln, and he himself the pupil and *protege*, brought up at the feet of Thomas H. Benton himself.

Gentlemen, with such a platform, and with such candidates, can your hearts fail to be filled with the enthusiasm that marked their nomination at the Convention?

Mr. Pendleton, after denouncing the policy of the Radical party on the subject of Reconstruction, and thoroughly exposing the dangers to the Government which are threatening its utter subversion, proceeded to say:

But, gentlemen, not only is this Republican party the party of usurpation, it is the party of corruption also. ["That's so."] Read the report of the Commissioner of Revenue. Count the number of clerks who are seeking in vain to discover the amount of peculation in the Treasury Department. Go to the War Department and see the mutilated archives, and ask why they were destroyed? Visit the penitentiary and count the public plunderers who are confined there.

It is not only the party of corruption, it is the party of extravagance also. [A voice, 'Now you are coming to it.'] The war ended in May, 1865. During the three years, from July 1, 1865, to July 1, 1868, the expenditure of the Federal Government, independent of interest on the public debt, was $820,000,000. These were years of peace. The army and navy of the war had been reduced; their back pay had already been made up to them; immense sales of Government property, consequent upon the close of the war, had been made, and yet in these three years the Republican administration expended $820,000,000—$270,000,000 a year.

The whole expense of the Government of the United States for four years preceding the war was two hundred and fifty-six millions of dollars. These eight hundred and twenty millions do not include the interest upon the public debt. If this be added, the expenditure of each one of these three years will amount to at least four hundred and thirty millions of dollars. The taxation of the year 1866 amounted to five hundred and ninety millions of dollars. The taxation of the last year of Mr. Buchanan's administration amounted to eighty millions of dollars. The expenses of the War Department during the whole of Mr. Polk's administration, including the Mexican war, were $90,540,000; the expenses of the War Department for 1868 were $128,850,000. In one year of Republican administration, in time of peace, the War Department spent $30,000,000 more than a four years Democratic administration did in time of war. ["Butler was in that family." Laughter.] The Navy Department for four years before the war, cost $62,910,000. Then our commerce was prosperous, our ships sailed on every sea and landed in every harbor. To-day we have no commerce; a foreign flag covers all the trade to our seaports. The ship-builders of Maine are starving for want of occupation, and yet the actual expenditures and the estimates for the navy, for the current four years, is $117,470,000.

I have said that the taxation of 1866 amounted to $590,000,000. I am told that this year it will be less. The securities of the Government are not subject to taxation. The capital invested in the securities reaches $2,500,000,000. All the property, real and personal, of every kind, in the United States, amounted, in 1860, to $16,000,000,000. Fourteen thousand millions, Judge Thurman reminds me. If it were sixteen thousand million dollars, as I said, then you find that there is to-day exempt, in this country, from taxation, one-sixth of all the property, real and personal, in the United States.

But they tell us, my friends that the taxation this year will be less than it was in 1866. Why is this?

Why is it that the amount realized from taxation in 1860 will be less than the amount realized in 1866? The rate of taxation is substantially the same. It is true that this Republican Congress has diminished, in whole or in part, the taxes on the manufactures of New England; it is true that they will diminish, or say they will diminish, somewhat the taxes upon whisky [cheers and laughter], but the amount collected from either of those sources would not materially change the aggregate. Why, then, I ask again, will the amount realized from taxes this year be less than in 1866? The rate of taxation is substantially the same. The burden upon those who do pay is just as great as it was then. The difficulty of making the payment is even greater than it was then.

A cry of distress, when the day for the payment of taxes comes around, arises from every part of the country. It is because the business of the country is stagnant; it is because your workshops are idle [voices, "That's so;]"; it is because labor finds no occupation; it is because the produce of the farmer remains on his hands instead of going to the market; it is because your stores are overcrowded with abundant stocks; it is because energy and enterprise are paralyzed, and capital remains inactive; it is because labor is without employment. And why is this? Why is all this? It is because the Republican party insists upon pursuing its policy of contracting the currency, and thus unsettling all prices, paralyzing all energy, checking all enterprise, throwing out of employment all labor, or reducing it to diminished wages. The tradesman is caught with a large stock on hand, and declining prices. The farmer fears the fall which may overtake him before his wheat reaches the market. The manufacturer fears that the price of his raw material to-day will be greater than the price of his manufactured goods to-morrow; and the capitalist will not take his money out of Government bonds and invest it in houses, or lands and stocks, lest the rents and dividends will not yield him simple interest. In the mean time labor is without employment, and poverty stalks through homes where comfort has always been before.

And yet this work of contraction is steadily pushed. Look at every monthly report of the Secretary of the Treasury; you will find that every month the debt that bears interest in gold is increased; you will find that every dollar which bears no interest at all, or which bears interest in currency, is converted as rapidly as possible into the bonds which pay interest in gold. And why is this? Is there too much currency in the country? Is there a plethora of money? Is speculation rife? No one will dare affirm it. And yet this work of contraction still goes on, and value is coined for the bondholder out of the sweat and tears, the blood and bones and muscle of the laboring man. When we ask the reason for this policy we are answered by the declaration of the Republican Convention at Chicago, that the bonds must be paid in gold, according to the spirit and letter of the contract; by a declaration of the president of that Convention, that the debt of the bondholder is as sacred as the grave of the soldier.

I deny that it is, according either to the spirit or the letter of the contract under which the five-twenty bonds were sold. I say that neither the spirit nor the letter of the law under which those bonds were issued, nor good faith, nor good morals, nor exact justice to the bondholder, requires that they should be paid in gold. They are payable in legal-tender notes of the country [tremendous cheers], and in this opinion I am sustained by the resolution of the Democratic Convention in New York, which declares that "where the obligations of the Government do not expressly state upon their face—or the law under which they were issued does not provide—that they shall be paid in coin, they ought, in right and justice, to be paid in the lawful money of the United States." [Cheers.]

When the Legal-tender act was passed, the private indebtedness of the country amounted to a very large sum. It was contracted to be paid in gold, but was in fact discharged in paper. The public necessity was alleged to be sufficient reason for this wholesale confiscation. Is there no public necessity now to demand the payment of the bonds in the money which was paid for them?

And yet, my friends, the Republican party is pledged to the policy of paying all these bonds in gold; to convert all the currency now outstanding, and all the indebtedness of the United States into these bonds; to pay interest in gold for this enormous amount, whatever it may be, and to extend the time within which the bonds shall be paid. In the mean time the bonds are to be exempt from taxation and the interest is to be paid semi-annually, in gold. ["And tax our children forever."]

What the enormous amount of indebtedness under that system will be, I can not say. We know that the public debt to-day, the acknowledged debt, reaches $2,500,000,000. Less than that it certainly will not be. The interest upon that sum will be $150,000,000 in gold, and this amount is to be drawn annually from the labor of the country, during all your lives, and the lives of your youngest children, in order to carry out the dogmas of the Republican creed.

Upon this whole subject the Democratic party has spoken with no uncertain sound. It declares that the debt shall not be extended, but must be paid as rapidly as possible; all the money collected from the people shall not be squandered on freedmen's bureaus and standing armies, but shall be applied to the payment of this debt and the reduction of the interest. [Loud applause.] It declares that the five-twenty bonds shall be paid in legal-tender, and until they be paid, they shall be subjected to the same rate of taxation as all other property. It declares there shall be "one currency for the Government and the people; for the laborer and the office-holder; the pensioner and the soldier; the freedman and the bondholder."

Now let me ask you a practical question. How soon can that debt be paid? That is all-important; the sooner it is paid the sooner your interest stops, the sooner your taxation stops, and the sooner this burden, which settles like a cloud upon the interests of the country, will be lifted up.

Three hundred and thirty millions of bonds are held in the Treasury Department as a security for the National Bank circulation. Redeem them the very instant you have the option to do so, with legal-tender notes, and let them supply the place of the bank paper. This measure alone, with very little inflation of the currency, and without any addition to the taxation, will reduce the debt and save the twenty millions of dollars in gold, annually, which are now paid as a bonus to the National Banks, for the great privilege they have of charging you 20 per cent. for money. [Ironical cheers.]

Five hundred million dollars of the first issue of five-twenties are already, or will this year, be payable at the option of the Government. Redeem these also, in legal-tender notes. "Where will these notes come from?" asks some friend. Stop this contraction at the Treasury Department; reverse its whole policy; give stability to the money market; let it be understood that fortunes are not held at the whim of any Secretary, and trade will revive and business will become active. Investments will be made; the rate of taxation will yield a larger return, and these notes will flow into your treasury. Let economy be practiced; let corruption be banished; let peculation of public funds be punished; let the army be reduced; let the Freedmen's Bureau be broken up; the impoverishment of the South cease, and notes will be abundant. [Cheers and cries of "Amen."]

But, gentlemen, if these measures will not supply funds, speaking for myself alone, having no desire, as I have no authority, to bid anybody else except those I can persuade to agree with me, and therefore to join me—[A voice, "You are right, go ahead"]—speaking for myself alone, if these measures fail to bring notes into the Treasury, I would judiciously, wisely and gradually expand the currency of the country. I would correct the evils which have been produced by such extraordinary and unprecedented contraction. The business of the country has become adjusted to a larger volume of currency than we now have. The demands of the South and West require a greater amount of currency. They are begging for money, and are willing to pay from ten to twenty per cent. During the war, when the currency was at its largest amount, gold touched 290 per cent., and yet, upon the declaration of peace, when the Southern country—impoverished as it had been—with 10,000,000 of people, who had been shut out from the use of our currency, ready to strain every nerve to repair the wastes of war—was opened to our business, gold stood only at a fraction over 128.

The system of contraction was immediately commenced, and with a currency of at least two hundred millions less than it was then, gold stands to-day at 141. The volume of the currency then was not too large for the demands of the business of the country. I do not believe that it would be necessary or advisable to expand the currency to that extent, but if it should prove to be so, I would not hesitate to restore the currency to the amount at which it stood when gold touched 128. [Applause.] I tell you, gentlemen, if this were done it would be as grateful to the people of the West and South as the dews of Heaven to the parched earth; as the quails and manna which God in his mercy vouchsafed to the children of Israel in the wilderness. By these two measures alone your debt would be reduced $830,000,000, and the interest would be reduced more than $50,000,000 in gold, annually, and the accruing revenue would enable you, without further expansion, to pay off the residue of the five-twenties as they mature, and thus to diminish still further the amount of interest, and, consequently, the taxes. If, then, the currency were found redundant, gradual contraction could be effected, as it would come when the debt had been paid—when the necessity for large sums of money on the part of the Government had passed away—when taxes were low; it could be accomplished without the oppression and disaster which now attend it.

I have been represented as inimical to the bondholder. Gentlemen, you shall be my judges. I am hostile to no class or interest in the country. It would be as wicked as it would be unwise. I simply desire to be just—just to the bondholder—just to the people, also. [Cries of "Good, good."] I would live up, with scrupulous fidelity, to the terms of our contract. I would pay the interest of the five-twenties in gold, because the Government has promised to do so. I would pay both principal and interest of the ten-forties in gold, because the Government has promised to do so. I would pay the principal of the five twenties in legal tender notes, because the bondholders agreed to receive them in payment. [Applause.] And as I would not repudiate an honest bargain to make money for the people, so will I not repudiate an honest bargain to make money for the public creditor.

I know it has been said that this system I propose would depreciate the currency. I do not think so. I think it would appreciate it. I think that just in proportion as the bonded debt is in this way discharged, will the certainty of the ultimate redemption of the legal tender notes become more apparent, and their value be steadily increased. These bonds operate as a mortgage upon the real and personal property and labor of the country. There are two thousand million of them. Pay off that mortgage, discharge that lien, cancel that debt, and every bond you pay makes it more certain that the greenbacks will be ultimately redeemed, and makes their value more appreciated in the market. Instead of depreciating the currency, this system would increase its value, and by the time the bonds were paid, instead of standing as to-day at 141, they would stand at par with gold.

I am no friend of a depreciated currency; I know what its evils are; I know how it oppresses industry; I know how labor suffers from it. Mr. Webster has depicted the evils arising from it in language which I remember, but can not emulate. I would not depreciate the currency. I resisted it when the Republicans introduced this legal-tender act in Congress; I was in favor of keeping our currency pure, and of standing by the gold and silver standard. But they refused to listen to my appeal. They depreciated the currency. They sold bonds for this depreciated currency, and bondholders agreed to take the depreciated paper in payment of their bonds; and I, for one, am in favor of standing by that system until the people, who have borne all the evils, can reap every possible benefit that can be derived from it.

But, gentlemen, I have detained you longer than your patience would warrant or my strength, under the circumstances, will permit. [Cries of "Go on," "go on."] I have sought to bring before you these parties and their policy in direct contrast, in order that I might say to you as was said to the children of Israel of old: "Choose ye this day whom ye will serve." Upon you rests the responsibility of a choice, as you will have to bear the good or evil which that choice will entail. Mark what the struggle is. It is law against power. It is Constitution against revolution. ["That's the doctrine."] It is constitutional government against tyranny; it is purity against corruption; it is economy against extravagance; it is civil law against military despotism. [Voices, "That's so."] It is intellect, patriotism, cultivation, refinement, capacity for government, against———

No, gentlemen, I will forbear. [Great laughter and cries of "Let her out," "go on."] I will not utter one disparaging word against the chosen leader of a great party in my country. [Applause.]

Choose ye, gentlemen, whom ye wil serve; choose wisely and labor diligently, and when the sun shall go down on the first Monday in November, the American people can rejoice that they have achieved a victory which will bring to them that happiness and prosperity which can only be secured by liberty, regulated by law, and by law inspired by the genius of virtuous liberty. And, gentlemen, in all this struggle that is before us, in all this supreme struggle for the mastery of these contending forces, let us remember that the only polar star by which our course can be guided is the Constitution of the United States. [Tremendous cheers.] It secured to us seventy years of unparalleled prosperity and happiness. It will secure to us seventy years more.

Our opponents say that they would overthrow it; that they would overturn it; that they would amend it; that they can make a better government and a better Constitution than our fathers ever made. [A voice—"Have they done it?"] Gentlemen, do not let us emulate this example. I charge it upon you, in this contest on which we are entering—which you in West Virginia inaugurate to-day—I charge it upon you to study the Constitution of the United States. I charge it upon you to revere it, and obey it. Do not seek to amend it. Do not seek to change it. Live up to it, live by it, and it will produce for your children the benefits which it has showered upon you. [Applause.] Take it, gentlemen, to your hearts. Let it go with you in all your walks in life as an ever-living presence; take it to your homes; read it to your wives, teach it to your children, put it upon your family altar, that it may be there when you bow your knees in prayer. Remember, gentlemen, that this is the only ark of safety in the midst of the flood which is upon us. It may be tossed for many a weary day amid the blackness of darkness upon these wrathful waters, but the sun will shine at last, the ark will rest upon the mountain top, and the dove, the emblem of purity, and peace, and love, will go forth never to return; it will rebuild its habitation here in the midst of its former life. [Applause.] I do not despair; I have faith in the aspirations of man—I have hope in the Providence of God. [Loud and enthusiastic applause.]

SPEECH OF HON. S. S. MARSHALL, OF ILLINOIS, IN THE HOUSE OF REPRESENTATIVES, JANUARY 9, 1868.

We are alarmed, Mr. Speaker; and honorable gentlemen seem surprised at the cry of distress that comes up to us from all parts of the land. A once happy, free, and prosperous people find themselves upon the very brink of financial and commercial ruin, while trembling between the Scylla of anarchy and the Charybdis of despotism that threaten to engulf our brightest prospects and fondest hopes forever. But why should we be surprised at our present condition? The experience of all ages, the lessons of all history would have warned us of the rocks against which we are madly dashing if we had but listened to their voices. No people on earth could long exist without utter ruin under the system of misrule, profligacy, and debauchery inaugurated by the men who now, unhappily, control the destinies of our country. Even if the system of peculation and robbery of which I have been speaking could be stopped, the expenditures actually authorized by law would crush any people. The hard-earned money of our people is recklessly voted away and squandered, as if our resources were endless, and the means and patience inexhaustible.

Nearly three long years have passed since the surrender of the last army of the Confederates brought gladness and hope to the hearts of our people. If the men who had control of our Government had permitted the Constitution of our fathers to extend its protection and benign influences to every part of the land, and had at the same time inaugurated a system of strict economy in the administration of the Government, we would to-day be the happiest and most prosperous people on earth. But this would not answer the ends or purposes of the Radical faction. The founders of their sect had denounced the Constitution as a "covenant with death and an agreement with hell;" and now, drunken and debauched with their ill-gotten power, our rulers trampled that sacred instrument under their feet, and inaugurated their most wretched and wicked system of revolution and subversion. And this wicked scheme naturally and inevitably led to the adoption of measures that have quadrupled the expenditure of the Government. A bureau, at an enormous expense, to feed, clothe, and proselyte to Radicalism a horde of lazy, vagabond negroes; a large standing army; an extensive military despotism in the South, extending its withering and blighting influences to every part of the land; a horde of Federal office-holders spread all over the land to spy out and seize upon the substance of the people; these were all appropriate sequences of this wicked purpose to destroy the Constitution, and establish a Radical despotism in its stead.

We have had profound peace, Mr. Speaker, for nearly three years. From the surrender of the Confederate armies in April, 1865, to the present time, there has not been an arm raised anywhere against the power of the Federal Government. Why, then, these enormous expenditures, that are crushing the very life out of the people? Why should the ordinary expenses of the Government now greatly exceed those of the years immediately preceding the war? Mr. Buchanan's administration has always been characterized by the party now in power as most reckless and extravagant. I am not here now for the purpose of defending it. But let us compare for a moment the last and most extravagant year of Buchanan's administration with the expenses now inaugurated under Radical rule. Men may mislead the ignorant by frothy declamation, but figures are stubborn things, and, when used fairly, never mislead. In the figures I now give I do not include the public debt or the interest thereon, nor the pensions and bounties to soldiers and their families, all of which the people will cheerfully pay.

The Secretary of the Treasury asks for appropriations for this year as follows:

For the War Department, exclusive of bounties and pensions.................... $95,000,000
For the Navy Department................ 36,000,000
For the Civil Service.................... 51,000,000

Total.............................. $182,000,000

There can be no doubt that the actual demands and expenditures of the Government, under existing legislation, will greatly exceed even this enormous sum. For who ever heard of a Congress in these days without a series of deficiency bills? The expenditures invariably exceed greatly the estimates.

The whole expenditures of the Government for the same service in 1860 (the last year of Mr. Buchanan's administration) were:

For Civil List...................... $6,077,000
For the War Department............... 16,563,000
For the Navy Department.............. 11,514,000

Total............................. $34,154,000
Difference between the estimates for 1868 and actual expenditures for the same items in 1860 .... $147,817,000

Thus it is demonstrated that the ordinary expenditure of the Government, under Radical rule, is more than five times as great as it was under the much-abused administration of Buchanan.

We have been accustomed to call ours a free and happy and prosperous people. But, sir, no people can be properly called free or prosperous, whatever may be the form of government, whose daily earnings are wrung from them by the tax-gatherer to feed a horde of hungry vultures, who are preying upon them. We now pay in taxes nearly twice as much *per capita* as any other people in the world. And it will be seen from the foregoing figures that, even if our national debt were wiped out as with a sponge, we would still, under our present rulers, be the worst taxed and worst governed people on earth. The people should, in thunder tones, demand of this Congress: "Why does this country, in time of peace, with no prospect of war, require five times more expenditures, in proportion to its population, for the army or the navy or the civil list, than it ever required at any time before the Republican party came into power?" Your wretched, unconstitutional, and most wicked policy—your negro bureaus, your large standing army, your military despotism, your hordes of hungry vultures, sent all over the land to devour the substance of the people—furnish the answer. Sir, the Republican party has been trusted by the people as no party was ever trusted before, and their generous confidence has, in every respect, been most shamefully abused. I know it is easy to indulge in loose and idle declamation and censure; and, lest I might be accused of sinning in this direction, I will furnish here for the consideration of the House and of the country some tables compiled from the archives of our Government, upon which I wish to base a few additional remarks, and which will demonstrate, beyond all possibility of contradiction, the folly, recklessness, and extravagance of the party that now most unfortunately, controls the expenditures of our Government:

Table giving the entire expenditures of the Federal Government, exclusive of the Public Debt, from the foundation of the Government to the close of the last British war.

From March 4, 1807, to December 31,

1791	$1,910,509 52
1792	1,877,903 68
1793	1,710,070 26
1794	3,500,546 65
1795	4,350,658 04
1796	2,531,930 40
1797	2,833,590 96
1798	4,623,223 54
1799	6,480,166 72
1800	7,411,366 97
1801	4,981,669 90
1802	3,737,079 91
1803	4,002,824 24
1804	4,452,858 91
1805	6,357,234 62
1806	5,080,209 36
1807	4,984,572 89
1808	6,504,338 85
1809	7,414,672 14
1810	5,311,082 28
1811	5,592,604 86
1812	17,829,498 70
1813	28,082,396 92
1814	30,127,606 38
Total	$172,697,779 00

Thus it is seen that the entire expenditures of our Government, from the foundation thereof to the 1st day of January, 1815, including the expenses of the last British war, does not equal, by over eleven million dollars, what is now required for the mere ordinary expenses of the Government for the present year under Radical rule. I say ordinary, as I do not in the estimates given include the amount required for bounties, pensions, and interest on the public debt. But these expenditures which I have given are, in fact, most extraordinary, and enough to cause the very clods of our mother earth to rise in mutiny against the further rule of such a party.

It will be seen, by looking at the foregoing table, that the whole aggregate expenditures of the Government during the three years (1812, 1813, and 1814) of our last great struggle with Great Britain, in which we met and grappled in the death struggle on land and sea with the greatest power on earth, amounted only to $76,039,502, which is $105,960,498 less than it now costs to run the Government, in a time of profound peace, for one year, under Radical rule; and that, too, without counting the frauds and robberies perpetrated under our revenue system, and which may be estimated at, at least, fifty millions more, that never reaches the Treasury, but every dollar of which is wrung from the pockets of the toiling millions.

But it may be urged that these comparisons are not fair, and are calculated to mislead, as the population was much less in the early days of the Republic than now, and the expenditures necessarily less than now. Admit all that can be fairly claimed from this fact, and yet it does not weaken the startling character of the facts I have given. Surely no one will contend that it ought to cost more, or at least much more, *per capita*, to administer our Government as we increase in population than it did during the early and struggling days of the Republic. If it does necessarily have this result, we should, in self-defense, immediately put a stop to immigration, and go back as speedily as possible to our original boundaries. But it can not possibly produce this result if the Government were now administered on the principles on which it was founded. Taking this as indisputable, will now furnish another table, that will place in a still stronger light the enormities of our present system:

A table showing the expenses of the General Government, exclusive of Public Debt, and the population shown by the Census during each decennial year, from the foundation of the Government to the year 1850.

Year.	Expenses.	Popula'n.	Rate per Inhab'nt.
1789-90 and 1791..	$1,919,589 52	3,928,827	$0 48
1800................	4,981,669 90	5,305,925	0 90
1810................	5,311,082 28	7,239,814	0 73
1820................	13,134,530 57	9,638,131	1 36
1830................	13,229,533 33	12,866,020	1 03
1840................	24,139,920 11	17,079,453	1 41
1850................	37,165,990 09	23,191,876	1 60

It will be seen from this table that, while during Washington's administration the expenses of the Government amounted to but forty-eight cents *per capita*, in 1840, the last year of Van Buren's administration, but to one dollar and forty-one cents *per capita*, and in 1850 but one dollar and sixty cents *per capita*, they now, in a time of profound peace, under Radical rule, estimating our population at thirty millions, amount to six dollars *per capita*, or about forty dollars annually for each head of a family, for what are called the ordinary expenditures of the Government!

Sir, these facts are in themselves sufficiently alarming, and I do not see that I can now add to their force by dwelling further thereon. If they do not arouse the people from Maine to California to demand an immediate change in our rulers, and in our system of administration, then, indeed, may we say, with a sad heart, farewell forever to all hopes of a restoration of our poor bleeding country to prosperity and happiness.

Mr. Speaker, in these remarks I do not intend to misrepresent, or, if I can avoid it, to be misrepresented; and therefore I must repeat that in this indictment against the Radical party I have not included those expenses and expenditures which are the necessary result of the war through which we have just passed. I have not included the estimates for paying bounties and pensions, or the sums necessary to pay the interest on our public debt. I have left these out, that the people might see whither we are tending under Radical rule, even if these sacred but most burdensome debts were canceled forever.

SPEECH OF HON. GEO. W. MORGAN, OF OHIO.

In the House of Representatives, May 30, 1868, the Hon. Geo. W. Morgan, of Ohio, said: I charge that the aggregate debt of the United States to-day amounts to six thousand five hundred million dollars.

Mr. LAWRENCE, (of Ohio.) As the statement of the amount of the debt of the United States made by my colleague is vastly larger than that stated by the Secretary of the Treasury, I would be glad to know of him how he makes up his statement of the debt.

Mr. MORGAN. I thank my colleague for his question. The debt reported by the Secretary of the Treasury is the liquidated, the audited debt of the country. The liquidated debt of the country amounts to two thousand five hundred millions, while the floating debt, and the gentleman will not deny that, amounts to $4,000,000,000.

Mr. LAWRENCE (of Ohio.) That last remark of my colleague might be misunderstood. He says I will not deny that. I must say that I think he is entirely mistaken, unless he takes into the estimate, as a part of the debt, the value of the slaves emancipated in all the Southern States, and unless he proceeds upon the idea that that is a valid debt which we are to pay.

Mr. MORGAN. I am glad that my colleague has again taken the floor; but he is mistaken. When I say the floating debt is four thousand million dollars I do not embrace in the estimate the former value of the freed slaves.

But I charge this, that the outstanding claims which constitute the floating debt of this Government amount to four thousand million dollars. And I regret that the honorable chairman of the Committee on Claims of this Congress [Mr. Bingham] is not present to confirm what I say. As the honorable gentleman from Ohio [Mr. Lawrence] seems to doubt the correctness of my statement, and as the present chairman of the Committee on Claims is not here to confirm it, I call the attention of the honorable gentleman to the statement made by the chairman of the Committee on Claims of the Thirty-ninth Congress, Hon. Columbus Delano, now of my district. I send it to the Clerk to be read. [Pages 2,189 and 2,190 of Congressional Globe, first session Thirty-ninth Congress.]

The Clerk read as follows:

"Mr. SPEAKER, I know very well that there are reasons why these considerations should be expressed. Our nation now groans with the weight of public debt and necessary taxation, and our credit must be maintained. I know that there are now floating claims against this nation not less in amount than $4,000,000,000, according to my estimate; and these claims, if admitted at all, will never be settled with less than $2,000,000,000. I do not believe they will be settled for that."

* * * * * * *

"Mr. BOUTWELL. Will the gentleman let me ask him a question?

"Mr. DELANO. Certainly, sir.

"Mr. BOUTWELL. I would ask the gentleman whether, when he refers to this floating debt which can not be liquidated without an expenditure of $2,000,000,000, he refers to claims that may be brought by persons in the eleven States lately in rebellion?

"Mr. DELANO. I refer only to claims of loyal persons.

"Mr. BOUTWELL. I would ask him whether he includes claims that may be brought by persons in the eleven States recently in rebellion?

"Mr. DELANO. I refer to such claims as will be made by loyal people in all the States, and none others. When I say it will take $2,000,000,000, I do it on the assumption that we shall compound these claims in some manner without settling up to the full amount.

"Mr. BOUTWELL. Is that to be one of the effects of reconstruction?

"Mr. DELANO. I did not say so; but the nation will ultimately have to meet this question and settle it in some form, either by compounding or refusing to pay it. I do not know that it will necessarily follow reconstruction. I have not got that disease upon the brain.

"Mr. BOUTWELL. Nor upon the heart either."

Mr. MORGAN. It will be observed, Mr. Chairman, that Mr. Delano, chairman of the Committee on Claims of the Thirty ninth Congress, with a better opportunity, perhaps, than any other citizen of the Republic to know what really was the amount of the floating debt, after due investigation, in his official capacity, states that that debt amounted to four thousand million dollars.

Mr. LAWRENCE (of Ohio.) Will my colleague allow me to interrupt him at this point?

Mr. MORGAN. Certainly.

Mr. LAWRENCE (of Ohio.) I desire to state that the claims to which Mr. Delano referred in the extract, which has just been read, are claims for the destruction of and damage to the property of the loyal people of this country by the Union forces and rebel forces during the war. Now, does not my colleague know that it never has been, and never can be, the practice of this nation to pay claims of that character? This nation has never done it; no other nation has ever done it. And, besides that, if these are claims which are to be paid, does not my colleague know that it is only another evidence of the huge proportions of the great Democratic rebellion which afflicted this country through more than four years of war, and in putting down which I am proud to say my colleague did his duty with fidelity and ability while in the service of the Union Army!

Mr. MORGAN. I find, Mr. Chairman, that the honorable gentleman from Ohio [Mr. Lawrence] is in favor of compounding this floating debt of four thousand million dollars, which Mr. Delano declared to be a just debt, by repudiating one-half the amount. I am surprised, sir, to hear my honorable colleague [Mr. Lawrence] say "that neither this nor any other nation ever paid such claims." Why, sir, does not the honorable gentleman know that Congress made a very large appropriation to meet the losses sustained by the citizens of Ohio by the raid of John Morgan? Does not he know that similar appropriations have been made for the benefit of citizens of other States for similar claims, and that the journals of Congress sustain me in what I say?

Sir, it can be truly said of the Republican party, as was once said by a learned historian of England, that it is a party of "false pretenses." The leaders of that party are, at this moment, attempting to raise the cry of repudiation against the Democratic party. And yet my colleague [Mr. Lawrence], here in his seat, avows his anxiety, or willingness, to do that which is equivalent to the repudiation of the outstanding claims against this Government. This is Republican consistency. This, sir, is an illustration of the conduct of that party from the hour that its leaders inaugurated the war, in the spring of 1861, down to the present moment.

* * * * * * * *

In 1860 the true value of all the property of every description in the United States was sixteen thousand three hundred and twenty-nine million six hundred and sixteen thousand and sixty-eight dollars; and this sum included two thousand million dollars, the value of slave property which was destroyed by the war, and which amount must be deducted from the aggregate wealth of the nation as returned in the report of the eighth census, thus making the actual value of all the land, of all the cities, of all the towns, of all the houses, of all the ships, of all the steamers, of all the railroads and their material, of all the manufactured goods and raw material, of all the grain, and of all the cattle in the land, fourteen thousand one hundred and fifty-nine millions six hundred and sixteen thousand and sixty-eight dollars, showing, according to Mr. Delano, that the aggregate Federal debt is nearly equal to one-half of the actual wealth of the entire country.

Mr. LAWRENCE (of Ohio.) Will my colleague allow me?

Mr. MORGAN. Certainly.

Mr. LAWRENCE (of Ohio.) If the Democratic party should get into power, would they regard the claim of Southern slaveholders for compensation for emancipated slaves as a just and valid claim to be paid by the Government? [Cries of "No," on the Democratic side of the House.]

Mr. MORGAN. I renew the expression of my obligations to my colleague for again propounding questions to me; and, in answer to his question, I say undoubtedly not. I have already remarked, sir, that the policy of the Democratic party was at once wise, just, and patriotic. We have nothing to do with the dead carcass of slavery. The loss of slave property was the forfeit paid by the people of the South for allowing their leaders to join the bad men of the Republican party in the North in involving our country in civil war. The loss was theirs; let it remain theirs. That, sir, is my answer.

And now, Mr. Chairman, I will return to the question of the Federal debt; for although an unpleasant subject, yet it is one which we are compelled to consider. We have seen, according to the chairman of the Committee on Claims in the Thirty-ninth Congress, that the aggregate audited and floating debt of the United States amounts to the fearful sum of six thousand five hundred million dollars. And how, sir, is that enormous debt—the handiwork and creation of the Republican party—to be paid?

Let us try, sir, and measure that monster debt by some standard which will convey to the mind some idea of its magnitude. By the returns in the report of the eighth census, it appears that the actual wealth of the great States of New York, Pennsylvania, Ohio and Indiana, including every dollar's worth of property owned by each citizen, amounted to the sum of five thousand eight hundred and fifty-four million four hundred and thirty-four thousand four hundred and ten dollars; so that if the leaders of the Republican party had the power to drive the citizens of those States from their homes, send them penniless among strangers, sell all the property they had left behind, and apply the proceeds of the sales upon the payment of the debt, the Federal Government would still owe the enormous sum of six hundred and forty-six million ninety-four thousand four hundred and seventeen dollars. And for all this are the people indebted to Republican domination.

* * * * * * *

Let me now call attention to the fact that the ordinary expenses of the Government for 1867-8 are estimated at more than one hundred and forty-eight millions over the expenditures of 1861. Why this great excess in the ordinary expenditures of the Government? Where does the money go to? Whose pockets does it fill? Why, sir, the leaders of the Republican party have become so accustomed to handling millions upon millions that the greater the amount proposed to be appropriated the more ready is this House to vote the appropriation. Not only that, but the leaders of that party are guilty of an offense which amounts to a political crime. It was but a few days ago that a resolution was introduced into this House by my colleague [Mr. VAN TRUMP] calling for a statement of the amount of money that had been taken from the Treasury of the people to pay for the publication of a book containing what is called the tributes of all nations to Abraham Lincoln.

The letters contained in this book had already been published in book form, and had been circulated by thousands at the cost of the people. But that was not sufficient. A resolution was introduced by some loyal member of the Thirty-ninth Congress, ordering the same book to be printed in the most expensive style, in full gold, and bound in Turkey morocco. Well, sir, did the resolution of my colleague pass? No, sir; it was strangled at its birth by being referred to a committee; the committee-room intended to be its grave. The cost of this wicked and foolish expenditure is said to be two hundred thousand dollars; but the true amount will never be known until the dominant party shall have been driven from power, and until the people send new agents to investigate the great wrongs which have been perpetrated against them by those who have been acting in their name. Will not every farmer in the land understand, will not every merchant and mechanic and laboring man in the land understand, that the abuses which exist in this Government can only be corrected by driving the men from power who have been for eight long years to their arm-pits in the national Treasury.

Now, sir, why should the expenditures of this Government for the year 1867-68 amount to $148,000,000 more than when the Democratic party was in power during the year 1860? Why, sir, during the decade from 1850-51 to 1860-61 the average expenditures of the Government amounted to only $52,000,000, and yet this audacious party, this party of false pretenses, when the representatives of the people rise in their places in this House and ask for an investigation, dare to refuse to allow an investigation to be had.

Now, sir, these are facts the people wish to know; these are facts the people have a right to know, and if I know my countrymen, as I think I do know them, they are facts which will be investigated by the Forty-first Congress, to which body I will have the honor to belong.

Now, I desire to call your attention to another startling fact. We are told, in the report of the Special Commissioner of Revenue sent to the Senate of the United States on the 3d day of January, 1867, that—

"Assuming the value of the real and personal property of the United States to have increased since 1860, the date of the last census, sufficient to compensate for all the losses and depreciations growing out of the war, the ratio of taxation to property the last fiscal year, was three and ninety-three hundredths per cent."

Nearly four cents on the dollar, or four dollars on every hundred dollars of property, while—

"During the same year the estimated ratio of taxation to property in Great Britain was nine-tenths of one per cent."

Which is nine mills on the dollar, or only ninety cents to every one hundred dollars on the general valuation of property. This estimate is not based upon the taxes directly collected from the people, but it is the general amount raised from all the sources of taxation, direct and indirect.

It has been truly said:

"We are taxed for our clothing, our meat and our bread,
On our carpets and dishes, our table and bed,
On our tea and our coffee, our fuel and lights,
And we're taxed so severely that we can't sleep o' nights.
"We are stamped on our mortgages, checks, notes, and bills,
On our deeds, on our contracts, and on our last wills;
And the star-spangled banner in mourning doth wave,
O'er the wealth of the nation turned into the grave.
"We are taxed on our offices, our stores, and our shops,
On our stoves, on our barrels, on our brooms and our mops,
On our horses and cattle, and if we should die
We are taxed on our coffins in which we must lie.
"We are taxed on all goods by kind Providence given;
We are taxed for the Bible that points us to Heaven;
And when we ascend to the heavenly goal,
You would, if you could, stick a stamp on our soul."

It is an astounding fact that in proportion to the wealth of the two nations, the taxes in the United States to-day are more than four times as great as they are in Great Britain. And yet, sir, England supports the largest navy the world has ever seen. In England there is a monarchy; in England there are princes of the royal blood whose pensions amount to millions; in England there is a proud and haughty aristocracy. And all this disadvantage on our part has been the result of the reckless profligacy of the Republican party. I beg the masses of the Republicans to pardon me for saying the Republican party, for it is the leaders who are alone responsible. And when they shall leave their seats, after the adjournment of this Congress, and go back to the people, it will behoove the people to call them to a stern account; it will behoove the people to require these gentlemen to say why it was that when resolutions were introduced into this body by the minority to investigate fraud and speculation and profligacy, that investigation was denied. I will say further, Mr. Chairman, that I hold in my hand the report of the Special Commissioner of the Revenue, and that the facts that I have stated upon the subject of taxation and the expenditures of the Government are official, and if any gentleman doubts their accuracy, I challenge him now to say so. Why, sir, who ever heard, when the Democratic party was in power, of a man being compelled to pay a tax and put a stamp upon his promissory note when executed by him? Who ever heard, when the Democratic party was in power, of there being a threefold tax on every pair of boots? Who ever heard, when the Democratic party was in power, of every article, worn by every citizen, male and female, old and young, paying a threefold tax?

Sir, for all these evils the Republican party is responsible. It is the result of their maladministration of the affairs of the Government. They have been looking after their own individual interests, to the neglect of the best interests of the country. From being poor, many of them have suddenly become enormously rich. In every large town, and in every city, men who were not worth ten thousand dollars in 1866, are now worth their millions. And where do their millions come from? From the toil and sweat and labor of the people.

These are the abuses which afflict our country; these are the abuses which demand redress; these are the abuses which oppress our people, and cause them, when they lay their heads upon their pillows at night, to doubt how the tax-gatherer will be paid when he comes around in the morning.

Speech of Ex-Governor Seymour.

REVIEW OF THE FINANCIAL CONDITION OF THE NATION.

[From the New York Herald, June 26.]

The Cooper Institute was densely crowded last evening in response to an invitation tendered by the Jackson Club—a young men's Democratic organization—to listen to an address from ex-Governor Horatio Seymour upon the political situation. The stage was tastefully festooned with national flags and portraits of Jackson and Seymour.

At 8 o'clock Governor Seymour arrived; and, as he was approaching the platform, the whole audience rose *en masse*, and cheered him with great enthusiasm.

Senator Creamer, the President of the club, introduced the orator.

Upon rising to address the audience, Governor Seymour was again loudly applauded. He spoke as follows:

We see in every part of our land proofs of a widespread change in political feeling. As the evils of misgovernment unfold themselves, the best men of the Republican party are driven from its ranks. At its late convention its policy was shaped in a great degree by those who are most violent in their passions, and most brutal in the policy they urge upon our people. While the ablest Republicans refuse to go on with a party which tramples upon the judiciary, usurps power, and is unsettling all ideas of political morality, and unhinging all the business machinery of our land, we are laboring under some embarrassments from the great volume of the change in our favor. Those who are rallying around the standard of constitutional rights have heretofore held conflicting views with regard to the events of the past eight years; and the question is, how can we set this great majority in the field so arrayed that they can drive out of place the disciplined and desperate horde of office-holders who now misgovern our country? This is the only problem to be settled. The American people are disgusted with the conduct of the Congressional party. Can we mark out a policy which will unite the majority under our standard? This can only be done by a thoughtful, forbearing, unselfish course. [Cheers.] At the same time we must be outspoken, and must confront all the questions which perplex us. Men look forward with hope and with fear to the action of the

FOURTH OF JULY CONVENTION.

I shall not speak of candidates. Let the claims of each one be considered in a courteous and kindly spirit, and let us take care that no personal partisanship shall draw us aside from our duty to our country. We should support with hearty zeal every upholder of constitutional rights. It is upon discord in our ranks that our opponents build their hopes. A party born of strife naturally looks to selfish passions to keep it alive. Let this hope be crushed out by our action. It will, in the present state of our country, be an unholy thing to go into the July Convention with any purpose which shall not have in view the rescue of our Government from the men who now have it in hand.

HOW THE NEXT ELECTION WILL BE CONDUCTED.

The next election will be controlled by thoughtful business and laboring men. No party can gain their support unless its tone and temper show that it seeks to get our country out of its troubled condition. Appeals to prejudice and passion will have no weight. These were tried at the late Republican Convention. I need not say with what cold indifference they have been received by the public. The quiet, watchful citizens, who seek for the protection of a wise administration of government, now turn their eyes upon us. We must look to it that we take no position which will not bear the closest scrutiny.

THE FINANCIAL CONDITION OF THE COUNTRY

Forces itself upon our attention. Among the evil results of our moneyed and tax policy, the most hurtful is the jealousies it has made between sections of our country. It has divided our Union into debtor and creditor States. It builds up favored interests and crushes out the industry of other classes. It taxes toil and lets some form of wealth go free from the cost of the government. It gives to labor and business a debased money, and to the untaxed bondholder sterling coin. These curses upon honest industry have grown up like ill weeds among the sacred interests of contracts, trusts and the fruits of labor, until we are troubled how to root out the tares sown by evil spirits, without killing the crop planted and tilled by honest industry.

THE NEW YORK DEMOCRATS IN 1862.

Lest it should be felt that what I have to say on this point springs from any views about the candidates or action of the National Convention, I will go back to the first years of the civil war, when the Democratic party of New York took its position upon the financial policy of the Government. In the election of 1862, it was discussed before our people. We then pointed out the great evils which now trouble us as the sure results of the errors of those who were shaping our moneyed system. To show clearly how we then tried to avoid these dangers, let me read some passages from the Message of a Democratic Governor to the Legislature, in January, 1863. In his position he spoke, after a general consultation, for the great party which had just placed him in the Executive chair.

Positions taken many years ago could have no reference to the personal wishes or purposes of this day. I will speak of the questions which now agitate our country in the light of the warnings we then uttered. In the Convention of 1862 the nominee of the Democratic party of the State of New York for the office of Governor used these words:

"The vast debt growing out of this war will give rise to new and angry discussions. It will be held almost exclusively in a few Atlantic States. Look upon the map of the

Union and see how small is the territory in which it will be owned. We are to be divided into creditor and debtor States, and the last will have a vast preponderance of power and strength. Unfortunately there is no taxation upon this national debt, and its share is thrown off upon other property. It is held where many of the Government contracts have been executed, and where, in some instances, gross frauds have been practiced. It is held largely where the Constitution gives a disproportional share of political power."

THE GOVERNOR'S MESSAGE IN 1863.

In his message to the Legislature in 1863 the Democratic Governor, speaking of the public credit, foreshadowed our dishonored condition at the time in these words:

"Extravagance and corruption are violations of the faith pledged to the public creditors. The money loaned to the national treasury was not brought forward at a time of peace, but in a time of doubt and danger. These claims are held by the rich and poor. The amount held by corporations represents the interests of women and children, the aged and infirm. The right of our soldiers to demand integrity is of the most sacred character. A fearful crime will be done by those who suffer national bankruptcy to turn into dust and ashes the pensioners' bounties thus gained at the cost of blood and health and exposure. It is worse that a government should be overturned by corruption than by violence. A virtuous people will regain their rights if torn from them, but there is no hope for those who suffer corruption to sop and rot away the frabric of their freedom."

These are the positions we took years ago, in the darkest hour of the war; these are the positions we hold now, and they cover every question of public and party agitation.

THE GOVERNOR IN 1864.

To show the anxiety we felt to avoid all sectional controversies, and our sense of the value of intercourse with the Western States, I will quote from the message of the same Democratic Governor, in 1864:

"A deep interest is felt with regard to our commerce with the Western States. Its growing value, and the loss of our trade with the Southern States, make us dependent for commercial prosperity upon that section of our country which sustains our domestic and foreign commerce, and which adds so largely to the imports and business prosperity of the city of New York. This State will be untrue to itself if it fails to control this great source of wealth by a vigorous and generous policy. Rather than suffer its diversion into other channels, we should strike off all tolls upon Western produce. New York should exhibit that degree of interest in all measures designed to benefit the West which will show our purpose to keep up the most intimate commercial relationship with that portion of our Union."

These words are quoted, not because the words of any one man are of consequence, but to show the record of the great party which inspired them. The Democratic party saw the evil in the beginning; they are the party to cure it. They have always kept our public finances out of confusion when in power.

THE DEMOCRACY AGAINST INJUSTICE DONE THE WEST.

Years ago we pointed out the wrong done to the West by making them send nearly twice as many soldiers to the war from each Congressional war district as were demanded from Vermont or Massachusetts, while the currency given to them under the banking system was not one quarter as great, although the Western States needed currency the most. The act authorizing the banks of New York to organize under a general banking law was not signed because the currency was unjustly divided and because the system made a useless tax upon our people of eighteen millions of dollars in gold each year. Thus we tried at an early day to save our country from sectional questions. In vain we warned the East and West against an unwise policy.

THE WEST TAXED WITHOUT AN EQUIVALENT RETURN.

The East and the West upheld the policy of the Administration, and we have now to deal with the results. What are some of them? All of the States are heavily taxed, but some of them get back as much, some more, than they pay out, while others get but little. In the case of the heaviest item of expense—the military and naval system—the Western States get nothing back except the cost of Indian war, while large sums are spent at the South. The next heaviest item is the interest on the debt. The West gets but a small sum back; most of it is paid to the Northern Atlantic States. The indirect taxes, tariffs, etc., are still more hurtful to the West, as they are practically premiums given to Eastern manufacturers.

BONDHOLDERS AND THE NATIONAL CURRENCY.

The division of the favors of Government in distributing banking currency is startling in its injustice. They are made more glaring by the way the burdens of war were put on different States. But the most offensive distinction is that of having two kinds of currency—good money for the bondholder and bad money for the laborer, the pensioner and the business man. Every paper dollar now put out is a Government falsehood, for it claims to be worth more than its real value, and it goes about the country defrauding the laborer, the pensioner, the mechanic and the farmer. An indignant chief of one of the tribes from whom we bought land at an early day by a pledge of moneyed annuity, said this Government was a cheat. It got land from the Indians by promising them so many dollars each year; that now it paid them in money which was a lie—which said on its face it was a dollar when it was but little more than a half dollar. The red man told the simple truth. Of all the devices to cheat honest labor, to paralyze industry, to degrade public morals and to turn business pursuits into reckless gambling, none have been so hurtful as a shifting standard of value, a debased and lying currency. I have not thus set forth the condition of our country for the purpose of indulging in invective against the party in power, but for another object. Many Republicans, who admit the wrong-doing of their leaders, say that we have no plans for the relief of our country; that pointing out wrongs is of no use unless we can point out remedies. This we propose to do, and we probe the ulcers to the quick because we mean to meet the case and cure the malady. Among other things which have caused anxiety in the disordered state of our Union, is the fact that our Government bonds are mainly held in one section of our country. The labor of the West puts its earnings, in a large degree, into lands, which are tax-burdened. The labor of the East puts its earnings into savings banks, life insurance, or in other forms of moneyed investment. Thus they are deeply interested in Government bonds The amount in savings banks in this State alone is $140,000,000. This shows that there must be at least $500,000,000 of money thus deposited in all the States. The average of the deposits in 1867 in the State of New York was $270. The number of depositors in the State of New York is about five hundred thousand (487,479), and in the city they number more than one-third of the population. This will make the number of depositors in the Union more than 1,800,000. In the State of Connecticut in 1865 one-quarter of its population had deposits in savings banks. It is now usual for men of small property to insure their lives. The number of policies given out by all the life insurance companies is about 450,000 and the amount of insurance about $1,250,000,000. The money invested is held as a sacred trust, as it is a fund laid aside for their families when the insurers die. All of the funds of savings banks and life-insurance companies are not put in Government bonds, but they hold an amount which would cripple or ruin them if the bonds are not paid, or if they are paid in debased paper. If we add the trusts for widows and orphans, we find that fully two million five hundred thousand persons are interested in Government bonds, who are not capitalists, and who are compulsory, owners at present prices, under the operations of our laws. There is a fear that this state of things will make a clashing of interests between the labor of the East and the labor of the West. It is clear that our opponents hope that it will hinder us from going into the contest with compact ranks and with one battle cry. However alarming this aspect may be, I am sure there is a policy to be marked out which will harmonize all jarring interests. It can be shown that the dangers spring from an unwise conduct of public affairs. They have come up like fogs of night from foul fens; they rise from unwholesome, darkened counsels, and will fade away before the light and life of a clear and honest policy. Is it true that the laborer, the pensioner, the tax-payers and the bondholders have conflicting interests which will hinder them from acting together in upholding constitutional right? Why are the tax-payers laboring under a debt which bears an interest of six per cent., while other governments can borrow money at three per cent., and at this low interest their bonds sell for better prices than ours? Why are the laborer, the farmer, the mechanic, and the pensioner paid in bad money, so that they get one-quarter less than they are entitled to on every paper dollar paid to them? Why is the bondholder wronged by the tainted credit of the Government so that he can not sell his bond for as much by one-third as the citizen of Great Britain gets for the bond of his Government, which bears a lower interest? And why is his claim made odious in the eyes of the people by the fact that his interest is paid in specie, while they are compelled to take debased paper?

UNIFORMITY OF CURRENCY—HOW TO OBTAIN IT.

It is clear to every thoughtful man that public safety and honor will not admit of our having two kinds of currency for any length of time. We must have a uniform currency for all classes. There is but one question to be settled. Shall our currency be uniformly good or uniformly bad? Are we to force the bondholder to take bad money, or are we to give to labor and business good money? Are we to have an honest standard of value for all, or are industry, enterprise and morality to be perplexed and disordered by a shifting and dishonest standard? If it can be shown that all these evils under which we labor spring from a common source, then it is clear that all classes should join in a common effort to root out the policy which sheds such widespread curses. There are two ways of making our paper money as good as coin. One is to contract its volume by calling in the legal-tenders. This will make them scarce and will force a specie standard, but it will carry ruin and bankruptcy into every part of our country. It will bear down the prices of property and of labor. It is a policy which can not be carried through, for the country will not consent to it. There is another way of lifting up our greenbacks to par, which will not harm any, but will help all; which will bring back confidence, will revive business and enterprise, will lighten taxation, will give to labor honest money, and will do justice to the public creditor. And that way is to give to all the world full faith in the honor and wisdom of the American Government. Our paper money is not at par in coin because the national credit is dishonored. How can the notes of our Government which pay no interest be worth their face in gold or silver, when the bonds of the Government, which pay six per cent. interest, are worth only eighty cents on the dollar? You can not make the notes put out by banks worth more than the bonds which secure these notes. It is a sad thing to say that our credit is dishonored in the markets of the world, but it is true, and it must be said if we are to find a remedy. It is humiliating to find that when Great Britain borrows $1,000 for twenty years it pays the lender but $1,700, when, if we make the same loan, we have to pay $2,700 to the lender. If we wish to help the taxpayer, if we wish to get at the cause of debased currency in the hands of the laborer, we must first find out why our credit is dishonored, for it is a tainted credit that sinks alike the value of bonds, of greenbacks and bank-notes. Make the credit of the United States as good as that of Great Britain, or of a merchant in good standing, or of a mortgage on a farm, and our troubles would disappear. If we make our paper money good by a harsh system of contraction, we shall cripple the energies of the country, and make bankruptcy and ruin. If, on the other hand, we debase the currency by unwise issues, we shall equally perplex business and destroy sober industry, and make all prices mere matters of gambling, tricks and chances. This will end as it did in the Southern Confederacy. At the outset the citizens of Richmond went to market with their money in their vest pockets and brought back their dinners in their baskets; in the end they took their money in their baskets and took home their dinners in their vest pockets. Make our money good by an honest and wise course, and when this is done it will be worth twenty-five per cent more than it is now, which will be equal to an increase of one-quarter in the amount of currency. Business will be strengthened, industry will be encouraged, prices will be regular, and men will then dare to go on with useful enterprises. We find right here the cause of our troubles, perplexities and national disgrace. Our credit is tainted. But for that we could borrow money, as Britain does, at three per cent., and cut down taxation. But for that, our paper money would be good, and gold and silver would glitter in the hands of labor. But for that fact, there would be no question how the bonds are to be paid, and we never should have heard of the greenback issue. But for the national discredit, business men would not be perplexed, and the disquiet and fears which now disturb the public mind would not exist. Now, if this dishonor can not be helped, we must bear it in the best way we can, and we must get on with the sectional and social and political troubles growing out of it, until time and events shall bring some cure. But if it can be shown to be the work of those in power, then all sections, all classes, and all interests should unite and turn them out. Fortunately we have official statements to guide us in our inquiries. We take the showing of the very parties under impeachment to show where guilt lies. To show the waste of those in power let us compare the cost of government during the four years of peace before 1861 and the four years of peace following the 1st of July, 1865. For the fiscal year ending July 1, 1869, I will take the estimate just made by the Committee on Ways and Means. Bear in mind that this is the best promise the Republicans can make on the eve of a Presidential election. It will prove to be many millions short of what they will spend, but we will give them the benefit of their own statements. After the close of the war, and up to the 1st of July, 1865, the War Department paid $165,000,000; which is $75,000,000 more than was spent by the same department in the four years of Mr. Polk's administration, and which included the cost of the Mexican war. It took nearly twice as much to stop a war under Republican policy as it did to carry on a war under Democratic management. But I will not take this $165,000,000 into the account. Let that close the war. Since July 1, 1865, about three months after the surrender of Lee, up to July 1, 1868, the cost of government will be, by official reports and estimates, $820,390,208. Up to July 1, 1869, by the estimate of the chairman of the Committee on Ways and Means, it will be $197,973,366, making the cost of government for four years $1,018,363,574. This does not include one cent paid, or to be paid, for interest or principal of the debt. The cost of government during the four years before the war (leaving out interest on debt) was $256,226,414. This shows that the Republicans have spent, in a time of peace, four dollars where the Democrats spent one. But the cost of government grows greater, and we will allow them to spend two dollars where the Democrats spend one. This will make $512,452,828. But they spent $505,910,646 beyond this. What did they do with the money? During the four years of Mr. Polk's term, which included the Mexican war, the cost of the War Department was only $90,540,788 21. We find that the cost of the War Department, taking their own statements and estimates, will be, in these four years of peace, $541,613,619; and this follows an expenditure of more than $3,000,000,000 during the war. The cost of the Navy Department, in the four years ending July 1, 1869, will be by the Republican statements and estimates, $117,471,802; and this follows an expenditure of $314,186,742 during the war. In the four years before the war the navy cost only $62,910,534. We then stood in the front rank of commercial Powers. Our ships were on every sea, and were to be found in every port. American shipping is now, by our tariff policy, swept from the ocean, but the cost of the navy is nearly doubled. The year ending July 1, 1868, is the third year of peace; but the War Department cost $128,858,494, which is more than it cost during the four years of Mr. Polk's term, which covered the expenses of the Mexican war. Not only does one year of peace cost more than four years of war then did, but the third year of peace costs more than the second; for the year ending July 1, 1867, the War Department spent only $95,224,415. In these statements we have given the Republicans the full benefit of their promises for the fiscal year, ending July 1, 1869; but we should like to ask a few questions. If $38,081,013 is enough for the War Department in that year, why and how did you spend $123,858,490 this year? If $17,500,000 is enough for the navy in 1869, why did you spend upon it $43,324,111 in 1866, and $31,034,011 in 1867? You have not cut down the numbers of the army. Did you waste money this year, or are your statements for next year untrue? We ask Republicans to read the estimates for the future, for they show the profligacy of the past.

WHAT A WISE USE OF THE PUBLIC FUNDS WOULD HAVE ACCOMPLISHED.

If five hundred millions of dollars of the money paid for military, naval and other expenses, had been used to pay the debt to-day the credit of the United States would have been as good as that of Great Britain This rapid payment, and the proof it would have given of good faith, would have carried the National credit to the highest point. The bonds would be worth much more in the hands of the holders, and yet the tax-payer would be better off, for the cost of the Government would be cut down as its credit rose. We could put out new bonds, bearing less interest, which would not have the odious exemption from taxation. Our debt would have been less, our interest lower and our taxes reduced. The hours of labor would be shortened. What now lengthens the time of toil? If we were free from any form of taxation, direct or indirect, six hours of work would earn as much as ten do now. One hour more of work ought to meet a laborer's share of the cost of government; another hour should pay his share of the National debt. He now works two hours more each day than he ought to pay for the military and negro policy of Congress and its corrupt schemes. It has just passed a law that eight hours make a day's labor, while it piles up a load of taxation which forces the laborer to work ten hours or starve. But the wise and honest use of this $500,000,000 would not have stopped here. When it carried our bonds to the level of specie value, it would have carried up our currency to the value of specie. The plan of making our currency as good as gold by contracting its volume carries with it great distress and suffering. But if we lift up its value, by getting rid of the taint upon the National credit, it harms no one, it blesses all. Now, our legal-tenders and bank currency must be debased while our National bonds stand discredited. They must rise and fall together. They are all based upon the National credit. Bank notes can not be worth more than the bonds which secure them. If, then, the five hundred millions of dollars had been duly and honestly used to pay our debt, to-day the tax-payers would have been relieved, the mechanic, laborer and pensioner would be paid in coin or money as good as coin, and would not be cheated out of one-quarter of their dues by false dollars. The holders of bonds in savings banks or life insurance would be better off, as their securities would be safer and worth more. There would be no question how they should be paid, for this question grows out of the follies of those in power, and will disappear when they disappear from the places they now hold. The bond-holder would no longer stand in an odious light. He would not be charged with the taxation which has been used to hurt, not to help, his claim.

THE CHICAGO CONVENTION PLEDGED TO THE NEGRO AND MILITARY POLICY.

If a wise, an honest use of the public money would have done this good in the past, it will do it in the future. But the Republican party, at Chicago, pledged itself, by its nominations and resolutions, to keep up its negro and military policy. It is impossible to give untutored Africans at the South uncontrolled power over the Government, the property and laws of the people of ten States, by excluding white votes, without military despotism. You can not give to three millions of negroes more Senators than are allowed to fifteen millions of white men living in New York, Pennsylvania, Ohio, Illinois, Indiana, Wisconsin, Iowa, Kentucky, Missouri and Michigan, without keeping up great standing armies. Without a general amnesty and a restoration of suffrage to all the whites in the South, a great standing army must be a permanent institution. In order to curse the South with military despotism, negro rule and disorganized labor and industry, they cursed the farmers of the North with taxation, the mechanics with more hours of toil, the laborers and pensioners with debased paper, the merchant with a shifting standard, and the public creditor with a dishonored and tainted National faith. Are these classes to turn and to see how each can push the burdens upon each other, or are they to make common cause and do away with the curses of the bad government? If the Republican policy prevails, this struggle must begin. Either the laborer or the capitalist must go down. Both can not live under it, and men must choose between. If, on the other hand, the policy of selfish ambition and of sectional hate is put down, our country will start upon a new course of prosperity, and all classes will reap in common the fruits of good government. [Great applause.]

THE QUESTION TO BE DETERMINED AT THE NEXT ELECTION.

The next election will turn upon this question: Can the Congressional party succeed in their efforts to excite and array the industrial and moneyed interests against each other, or will these unite and turn out the authors of the mischief under which they are all suffering? The only hope of our opponents is discord, where there should be harmony and concert of action.

APPEAL OF THE DEMOCRATIC PARTY.

In our State, at the last election, we appealed to all classes to help us save New York from misgovernment, and all came up to the rescue, and we made a change of seventy thousand. Let us again appeal to all classes of interests throughout the Union; let us go before the people with these facts, and we will make a change which will sweep the wrong-doers from their places. We say to the bondholder and the laborer who has put his money into the savings bank, we do not wish to harm you, we do not seek to give you bad money, but to get a good currency for all. It will not help us to break down the credit of your bonds; it hurts us; it keeps up our taxes by making us pay high interest; but we ask you to help save us as tax-payers from the cost of the negro and military policy at the South. It is hard for us to pay you if you let men in power take the money we give in taxes to reduce your claims and you support them while they use it to uphold military despotism. We see clearly that a state of affairs which will compel you to take a debased currency, will force every laborer, farmer, mechanic and creditor to take a debased currency as well. If your claims were all wiped out to-morrow by an issue of greenbacks, it would not relieve the fear of patriots. Labor would still be cheated by false dollars; our standard of value would still be shifting. Taxation would be kept up by the Reconstruction policy; for it is despotism more than debt that makes taxation so heavy. Nothing would be settled. The judiciary would still be trampled under foot; the Executive would still be manacled so that it could not punish crime nor protect innocence. But strike down the Congressional policy, and all will be set right.

EXTRAVAGANCE OF THE RADICALS.

Since the war closed, in 1865, the Government has spent for its expenses, in addition to payments on principal or interest of the public debt, the sum of more than one thousand million dollars. Of this sum, there has been spent nearly eight hundred million dollars on the army and navy, and for military purposes. This is nearly one-third of the national debt. This was spent in time of peace. The cost of our navy before the war, was about thirteen million dollars each year. Since the war, when our shipping has been swept from the ocean by taxation, the annual average cost has been thirty million dollars, although we have now no carrying trade to protect. While money is thus wasted without scruple upon the army and navy, if any aid is sought to lessen the cost of transportation for the farmers of the West, or to cheapen the food for the laborers of the East, we are at once treated with Congressional speeches upon the virtues of economy. If from this amount there had been saved, and paid upon the debt, the sum of five hundred million dollars, how changed would our condition have been. With this payment, which would have cut down the debt to about two thousand million dollars, our credit would, at least, have been as good as that of Great Britian. It is because we did not thus apply this money to this purpose, but spent it upon the negro policy, the military despotisms, and other abuses of government, that our credit is so low. The world saw we were violating our faith with the public creditors and the tax payers alike, when the money was used for the partisan purpose of keeping the South out of the Union until sham governments could be manufactured by military violence and Congressional action. The world not only saw this monstrous perversion of the money wrung from the people by taxation, but it also saw, that it made through a long series of years still greater annual expenses unavoidable. When the entire control of the Southern States is given over, unchecked by the intelligence of the white race, to untutored negroes whom the people of the North have said to be unfit for voters; when the unfortunate African, drunk with unusual power, and goaded on by bad and designing men, shall make life and property unsafe, and shall shock and disgust the world with outrages, we shall be forced to raise and pay still greater armies. Up to this time the South has had at least an intelligent tyranny in military officers. Every man who is not blinded by hate or bigotry looks forward with horror to the condition of the South under negro domination. The bad faith to the public creditor and tax-payer in thus unsettling our Union, of keeping the South in a condition where it can not help the national prosperity, but is made a heavy load upon the country, is the real cause of our debased credit. The tax-payer was told the burdens put upon him were to pay the debt; but the money was not used in good faith to him, for the debt still stands; nor in good faith to the creditor, for he was not paid what he should have been; but it was used in a way which harmed both—in a way that tainted the Nation's credit, kept up taxation by keeping up the rate of interest, while it sank the value of the bonds, and with them carried down the paper currency, and thus wronged the laborer and pensioner. But for the policy of bad faith, of partisan purposes, and folly we could to-day borrow money as cheaply as Great Britian; but we have cursed the tax-payer, the laborer, the pensioner, the public creditor, for the sake of cursing the people of the South with military despotism and negro domination. Every one must see, if we had paid off one-fifth of our debt, had kept down the cost of government, given peace to our Union, had built up industry and good order in the South, not one of the evils which now afflict us could have existed. Our whole condition would have been changed. ("That's so," and applause.) We demand that our currency shall be made as good as gold, not by contracting the amount, but by contracting the expenses of government. We are against measures which will pull down business credit, and call for those which shall lift up the National credit. When we stop the waste which forces us to pay a usury of ten per cent. and take a course which will enable us to borrow money upon the rates paid by other nations, we shall add to the dignity and power of our Union. When we give value to our bonds by using the money drawn by taxation to the payment of our debt, and not to the military and negro schemes, we shall relieve the tax-payer, the bill-holder, and give strength and value to the claims of the public creditor. We have seen the mischief wrought out by the policy of the past three years. It will be as hurtful in the future as it has been in the past. Yet the Republican party has approved it, and is pledged to uphold it. We have shown how the policy of using our money to pay our debts would have helped us in the past. It will do the same for us in the future. To that policy we are pledged. There is not one man of our party in this broad land who doubts upon this point. It has never been charged that a single Democrat in these United States ever favored the military and negro policy, upon which the credit of the country has been wrecked. Our remedy is to use the public money to pay the public debt. It is a simple, brief, but a certain remedy, for our National malady. Our ailment is debt aggravated by despotism.

TAXATION INCREASED BY THE NATIONAL DEBT.

In another way the Republicans do a constant wrong to the bondholders. In answer to complaints of heavy taxation, they say it can not be helped with our heavy debt, and thus throw the whole odium on the debt. Why do they not tell the truth and say one-third of our taxation is made by our debt? Then they will be asked, what makes the two-thirds? This question they do not want to have asked, and they do not want to answer. When they do answer, the eyes of all classes will be opened. They will be forced to say that last year they spent, by reports of Committee on Ways and Means, $379,178,066. and this in the third year of peace. Well, say our well-meaning Republican friends, we suppose the interest of the debt took most of it. Oh no; that took $149,418,383, not quite as much as was spent by the War and Navy Departments, which was $149,472,165; and besides this we spent

$80,292,513 for other things. Why, that is $20,000,000 more than the Democrats spent for army and navy, and all the expenses of Government put together. But why do you spend $25,613,673 on the navy, when it formerly cost $10,000,000 annually? Has American shipping grown so much that we have to keep up vast navies to protect it? Oh, no. Our tariffs have swept American ships from the ocean; we have lost the carrying trade; the British have got that. Then why don't you give the builders of merchant ships the money spent on the navy by way of drawback on duties? Would that start work at our ship-yards? Oh, yes, half the cost would do it. Then why is it not done? We did not think of it, really; we have been so busy with the impeachment and negro questions that we forgot our sailors and mechanics. But we see that the War Department spent this year $128,858,466, when the year before it spent only about $95,000,000. The longer we have peace the more the army costs. How is this? Well it costs a great deal to keep soldiers and Freedmen's Bureau agents, and to feed and clothe negroes at the South. But why do you do it? Let the negroes support themselves as we do. You make the laborers of the North work to feed and clothe these idle Africans. True; but by so doing we get their votes, and they will send our traveling agents to Congress; we shall get twenty Senators in this way, while a majority of the people of the United States, living in nine States, have only eighteen. The people may vote as they please, but they can not get the Senate nor repeal any of the laws we got through for our advantage; we have managed it so that one-quarter of the people have more power in the Senate than the three quarters. We now own the negroes of the South. Did we not buy them with your blood and money? We now see where the money goes; we now see why the credit of our country is so tainted; we now see why the the value of our paper money is sinking. It was only at twenty-one per cent. discount in 1866; it is now at a discount of about twenty-nine per cent.; we now see why our laborers and pensioners are cheated by false dollars. If the mechanic cares to know why he works so many hours let him study the reports of the Secretary of the Treasury. It is clear why business is hindered and business men perplexed. We now know why the public creditor is harassed by our dishonored credit, and the tax-payer is hunted down by the tax-gatherer. The negro military policy of the Republican party is at the bottom of all these troubles. We now get at the real issues between parties. The Republicans, by their nominations and resolutions, are pledged to keep up the negro and military policy, with all its cost and taxations. These will be greater hereafter. The government of the South is to go into the hands of the negroes. We have said they are unfit to be voters at the North. The Republicans say they shall be governors at the South. We are clearly opposed to this policy. We have seen how much it cost the tax-payer, the bondholder, and the laborer in the past three years. It will be as hurtful in the future. We have also seen how our policy of using the money to pay our debts would have helped the tax-payer, the bondholder and the laborer in the past. It will do as much in the future. The whole question is brought down to this clear point—shall we use our money to pay our debts, relieve the tax payer, make our money good in the hand of the laborer or pensioner, and help the bondholder; or shall we use it to keep up military despotism, feed idle negroes, break down the judiciary, shackle the Executive and destroy all constitutional rights?

THE PRESIDENCY.

I have said nothing in behalf of or against the views of any one who is spoken of as a candidate for the Presidency on the Democratic side. I have said only what each one agrees to and is in favor of. No man has been named who is not in favor of reducing expenses, and thus making our paper as good as gold. No man has been named who is not in favor of cutting down military expenses. No man has been named who is not in favor of using the money drawn from the tax-payers to pay the public debt. No man has been named who is not in favor of a general amnesty to the people of the South. No man has been named who is not an upholder of constitutional rights. No man has been named by the Democratic party whose election would not help the tax-payer, the pensioner, the laborer, and the bondholder. On the other hand, the candidates of the Republican party are pledged to their past policy, which has sunk the value of our currency more than eight per cent. in the past two years. The discount upon our paper money was twenty per cent. in April, 1866; it is now about twenty-nine per cent. It will continue to go down under the same policy. As it sinks it will increase taxes, it will curse all labor and business, it will endanger still more the public credit; for the greater the premium on gold, the harder it becomes to pay specie to the bondholder, and his claims become more odious.

PERORATION.

What claim have the Republicans upon our soldiers? They take away from him one-quarter of his pension by paying him in false money, which is worth less than seventy-five cents on the dollar. A wise and honest administration would have made it worth its face in gold. What right have they to call upon the mechanic and laborer? They have lengthened out the hours of their toil to feed swarms of office-holders at the North, and to support armies and hordes of negroes at the South. How can they look the tax-payers in the face when they have wrung from them so many millions upon the pretext that the debt compelled them to do so, while they were using the money thus collected to support standing armies and to trample upon the rights and liberties of the American people? Can they with decency appeal to the bondholder after tainting the national credit and sinking it to the level of the Turks', and endangering their securities by throwing upon them the whole odium of taxation? Then let the East and the West, the North and the South, the soldier, the toiler in ships or in fields, the tax-payer and the bondholder, by one united effort, drive from power the common enemies of liberty, honesty, honor, rights and constitutional laws.

At the conclusion of Governor Seymour's speech, loud calls were made for S. S. Cox and Captain Rynders, both of whom responded briefly in characteristic denunciation of the negro.

Funding Bill.

The following is the Funding Bill, as agreed to by Congress the last night of the session. The President has not signed it as yet:

An Act providing for the payment of the National Debt, and for the reduction of the rate of interest thereon.

Be it enacted, etc., That the Secretary of the Treasury is hereby authorized to issue coupon or registered bonds of the United States, in such form as he may prescribe, and of denominations of one hundred dollars, or any multiple of that sum, redeemable in coin, at the pleasure of the United States, after thirty or forty years respectively, and bearing the following rates of yearly interest, payable semi-annually in coin; that is to say: The issue of bonds falling due in thirty years shall bear interest at $4\frac{1}{2}$ per centum; and bonds falling due in forty years shall bear interest at 4 per centum; which said bonds, and the interest thereon, should be exempt from the payment of all taxes or duties to the United States, other than such income tax as may be assessed on other incomes, as well as from taxation in any form, by or under State, municipal, or local authority; and the said bonds should be exclusively used for the redemption of, or in exchange for, an equal amount of any of the present outstanding bonds of the United States known as the five twenty bonds, and may be issued to an amount, in the aggregate, sufficient to cover the principal of all such five-twenty bonds and no more.

SEC. 2. And be it further enacted, That there is hereby appropriated out of the duties derived from imported goods, the sum of $135,000,000 annually, which sum, during each fiscal year, should be applied to the payment of the interest, and to the reduction of the principal of the public debt, in such a manner as may be determined by the Secretary of the Treasury, or as Congress may hereafter direct; and such reduction shall be in lieu of the sinking fund contemplated by the fifth section of the act entitled, "An act to authorize the issue of United States notes, and for the resumption or funding thereof, and for funding the floating debt of the United States," approved February 25, 1862.

SEC. 3. And be it further enacted, That from and after the passage of this act no percentage, deduction, commission, or compensation, of any amount or kind shall be allowed to any person for the sale, negotiation, redemption, or exchange of any bonds or securities of the United States, or of any coin or bullion disposed of at the Treasury Department, or elsewhere on the account of the United States. And all acts and parts of acts authorizing or permitting, by construction or otherwise, the Secretary of the Treasury to appoint any agent other than some proper officer of his department to make such sale, negotiation, redemption, or exchange of bonds and securities, are hereby repealed

More about Reconstruction.

RECENT EVIDENCES OF ITS OPERATION.

The late Governor Orr, of South Carolina, in his message to the first Legislature of the Rotten Borough, reports the debt of the State, October 1, 1867, at over eight millions, the annual interest on which, at 6 per cent., exceeds the entire appropriation for the State government before the war. Add to this the expenses of the bogus Convention and a four months' session of the present Legislature, and an idea of what it costs to run these Radical bogus States can be formed. The Convention cost South Carolina $110,000, and ex-Governor Orr estimates that the new Legislature will be in session four months, at an expense of $250,000.

The Generals commanding the several Military Districts have submitted the following estimate of the amounts required for the execution of the Reconstruction acts in these States *up to June* 30, 1869:

In the First Military District (State of Virginia) to June 30, 1869, $100,000.

In the Second Military District (States of North Carolina and South Carolina) to June 30, 1869, $24,000.

In the Third Military District (States of Georgia, Alabama, and Florida) to June 30, 1869, $150,000.

In the Fourth Military District (States of Mississippi and Arkansas) to June 30, 1869, $108,400.

In the Fifth Military District (States of Louisiana and Texas) to June 30, 1869, $80,000.

This verifies our estimate in a previous part of this book.

THE TWO LOUISIANA BOGUS SENATORS.

William Pitt Kellogg, of Illinois, who has been elected United States Senator by the hybrids of Louisiana, was appointed Chief-Justice of Nebraska by President Lincoln, and Colonel of an Illinois cavalry regiment by Governor Yates; and, for a long time, regularly drew the pay of both offices, without discharging the duties of either.

John S. Harris, Kellogg's colleague, was formerly a resident of Milwaukee, Wisconsin, and at one time actively identified with the Know Nothing party, and a speculator by trade. His career as President of the Marine Bank, at Milwaukee, was very short. He was elected to that position at the close of the year 1858, as the successor of Mr. Hoover, and in the following year the bank failed. It did not take him quite a year to ruin a prosperous bank.

A SOUTH CAROLINA BOGUS CONGRESSMAN.

On the 20th of July, 1868, says the *World's* Washington correspondent, two more carpet-baggers were sworn in the House, one of them being a C. C. Bowen, of South Carolina. The latter's life was happily sketched by his Radical colleague, Mr. Mullins, of Tennessee, to the following effect. He said, that Mr. Bowen was born in Ohio, and went to South Carolina ten or fifteen years ago. When the rebellion broke out he voluntarily went into the Confederate service and accepted the commission of a Captain, and was subsequently promoted to be a Major, probably for his gallantry in shooting down Union men. While a Major, he (Mullins) was reliably informed that Bowen had killed his rebel Colonel. For this act Bowen was incarcerated and put in irons, but was released when the Federal troops advanced. He then had one of two things to do, either to be hung or else to join the Federal forces. He did the latter, and he (Mr. Mullins) was informed by General Sickles himself that in the Federal army Bowen acted so badly that he had to be incarcerated by Federal authority. When the war was over he became a Radical, and adopted the faith of franchise for the black men, and, Mr. Mullins might have added, became a "trooly loil" man according to Radical dictum. Bowen, of course, was sworn in. He professed to be a Radical, and that was enough.

A Negro Incendiary in the Georgia Bogus Senate.

A Boston negro lawyer, named Bradley, has been a prominent Radical leader in Georgia since the war. He was a member of the Convention which framed the present Rotten-Borough Constitution, and was such a villain in his antecedents as a convict, and his then incendiary course, that even the stomach of that body revolted at his excesses, and he was expelled from his seat. His constituency, to rebuke the Convention and vindicate Bradley, elected him to the State Senate as the representative of that great commercial center and refined community of the South, the city of Savannah. He made a speech in the Senate a few days since. We quote from the New York *Herald's* report:

"During a debate caused by the introduction of a resolution relative to the eligibility of negroes to hold office, he was unusually blasphemous and violent. This insolent mulatto declared that if the doctrine of ineligibility of negroes for office-holding came from the 'spiritual mind of God' himself, his race would not submit to it. He further warned his hearers that if the negroes were not given full and equal privileges with the whites there would be another rebellion within the next ten years, and that it would be a greater and more successful one than the last. Here, then, we have another outcropping of the animus of those negroes who possess sufficient influence over the masses of their race to be elected to office. It is certainly a pretty commentary upon the age we live in, when the representatives of a half-barbarous people can thus threaten their superiors."

A SOUTHERN RADICAL JOURNAL.

A paper called the *Missionary Record*, published in Charleston, S. C., has an editorial article under the caption of "The Whirlwind Cometh—Beware," inciting the negroes to acts of violence. A number of incendiary fires have lately occurred. General Canby has not yet suppressed the sheet.

THE RAZOR-USING SUFFRAGANS.

In the Freedmen's village opposite Washington, a few days ago, quite a riotous demonstration was made by the negroes against the white superintendents of the village, because they had ordered the removal of the numerous hogs which the negroes had collected about them. Razors were freely used. One or two white persons were gashed, and a military force was sent over to maintain order, but the hogs were removed.

SOUTHERN RADICAL LEGISLATURES.

In the so-called Legislature of the Grant and Colfax party of South Carolina, are eighty negroes who can neither read nor write.

A SPEECH BY A NEGRO LEGISLATOR.

COLUMBIA, S. C., July 6.—The Legislature organized to-day.

In the House, Mr. Wheppen, a Northern negro, nominated a colored man for Speaker, and said the time had come for a change to be made in the party. Heretofore the Republicans had denied the black man every thing, and showed hostility toward them. Hereafter he would assert his own rights, and protect them, too, and the consequences must be with his enemies. He was severe upon ignorant white men who had been elevated to office by colored voters. He said that thing must stop or go to pieces. Considerable excitement was created by the speech.

HUNTING UP THE RECORDS.

The Jackson *Clarion* publishes copies of two bills of indictment found by the grand jury of Chickasaw county against one A. H. Jamison, who was a Radical nominee in the late State election. The indictments are for stealing cotton, three bales from one and one bale from another gentleman of the county, in October, 1865.

BLOODY NEGRO RIOTS IN 1868.

GALVESTON, TEXAS, July 17.—On the evening of the 15th inst., a serious riot commenced at Millican, on the Central Railroad. It appears that a mob of about twenty-five negroes, led by a white school-teacher, and a negro preacher, named Brooks, attempted to hang a man named William Halliday, but the white citizens interfered to prevent the execution, and, headed by the sheriff and the agent of the Freedmen's Bureau, attempted to suppress the mob. The result was the death of ten or twelve negroes. On the 16th inst., the numbers increased on both sides, and skirmishing occurred during the day, the estimated number of casualties being twenty-five. A small body of troops arrived late last night and dispersed the rioters after killing three negroes. The latter, numbering between three and five hundred persons, had fortified themselves three miles from Millican, and refused to lay down their arms until the troops dispersed them. The entire loss was between fifty and sixty persons. The difficulty is said to have arisen from a suspicion that a negro member of the loyal league had been hung; but he has since been found.

NEW ORLEANS, July 19.—Later accounts from Millican, Texas, report that the disturbance there is not yet ended. The negroes sent defiant replies to orders from the civil officers and the agents of the Freedmen's Bureau to disperse; there is but a small squad of soldiers on the ground.

SAVANNAH, GA., July 22.—A difficulty occurred last night, in a drinking saloon, between William Robert Hopkins, Tax-receiver, and Isaac Russell, a Deputy-Sheriff, resulting in the shooting of Hopkins, killing him instantly. Russell claims that he fired in self-defense. The affair caused great excitement among the negroes, *who at a signal of a drum assembled several hundred strong, armed with guns and clubs*, threatening to lynch Russell, and demolish his house. On learning that Russell had been taken to jail they proceeded to attack it, but were dispersed by the police. The excitement was somewhat abated this morning. *The prompt obeyance of the signal shows that the negroes are fully organized in this city.*

MEADE REIGNS IN GEORGIA.

The first bogus Legislature of Georgia assembled in the early part of July. It was found to be closely balanced in its party division, with the indication of a Democratic majority. This alarmed all Radicalism. To overcome it, was thought to be a work of easy achievement in the hands of the military commanders of that district. Notwithstanding the members elected possessed all the qualifications prescribed by the bogus constitution, from which alone the Legislature derived its existence, and could take the oath required by that so-called Constitution, Meade, to defeat this Democratic majority, addressed an order to the Legislature, dated July 8, 1868. requiring it to purge itself of all members who did not possess the qualifications prescribed by section three of the proposed Fourteenth

Amendment to the Federal Constitution. The Legislature declared all of its members qualified under that section, whereupon, on the 21st of July, Meade graciously recognizes the Legislature, and permits it to go on, by a communication to the Governor, in which he says:

I now advise and instruct you that each House, having complied with the requisitions of my communication of the 8th inst., by examining into and deciding on the eligibility of their members under the fourteenth article. I have no further opposition to make to their proceeding to the business for which they were called together, and consider them legally organized from the 18th inst.

In this connection, Brick Pomeroy asked the following pertinent question:

Will the magnificent Meade please to inform an inquiring person how it is that a Legislature that is not to be recognized as *legal* until it has expelled certain members, has the power to do that expelling. And if it's legal enough to expel members, isn't it legal enough to go right on with the business?

The Official Result in Mississippi.

WASHINGTON, July 21—Gen. Gillem has submitted to Gen. Grant the report of his action as regards the condition of Mississippi under the Reconstruction acts. He states the result of the late election—for the constitution, 56,231; against it, 63,830; being a majority against the constitution of 7,629. Gen Gillem says:

"As is generally the case in elections, fraud is charged by both parties. All reports and complaints bearing on the subject are herewith transmitted for the consideration of the proper authorities, merely remarking that I am satisfied the election was as fair and free from intimidation or the influence of fraud as it would be possible to receive under existing circumstances, and that no undue influence was exercised at the polls. If intimidation was used at all it was beyond the military power to reach it. As the defeat of the constitution renders it possible that the State may for a time remain under military control, I consider it my duty to call attention to the almost impossibility of finding persons to fill vacancies in civil offices who possess the necessary attainments, and who can qualify under existing laws. I would therefore recommend that section nine, of the act of July 19, 1867, be so modified as to render eligible to office, persons on the list of registered and qualified voters to fill vacancies which exist, or may occur in civil offices, State or municipal."

Expulsion of Gov Humphreys and His Family from the Executive Mansion of Mississippi.

Gen. Ames, the military satrap who forcibly superseded Governor Humphreys, of Mississippi, did not at first propose to possess himself of the residence of the Governor occupied by the family of the deposed Executive. He afterward conceived a desire to live under the same roof with the Governor and his family—an intrusion upon his domestic circle the Governor was not disposed to saction, whereupon he addressed the satrap the following manly response to his demand:

EXECUTIVE DEPARTMENT, STATE OF MISSISSIPPI, }
JACKSON, MISS., July 7, 1868. }

GENERAL A. AMES—*Sir:* Your letter of the 6th inst., informing me that I would oblige you by vacating the "mansion" at as early a day as convenient, was duly received through the Post-office of this city. The Governor's mansion was built by the tax-payers of Mississippi, only for the use and occupancy of their constitutional Governors and their families. They elected me to that office in 1865, and I, with my family, have been in peaceable, quiet and legal possession ever since. At the recent election the qualified voters of the State, both white and colored, have, by the largest popular vote ever cast in this State, unmistakably expressed their desire for my continuance in the use and occupancy of the mansion as their constitutional Governor. In view of this expressed desire of the just and lawful owners that this property remain in the continuous possession of their own chosen custodian, and from the further fact that the mere occupancy of the mansion by my family can not operate as an impediment to the just administration of the Reconstruction laws of Congress, I must respectfully decline to oblige yourself or others by vacating the mansion until a legally qualified Governor is elected under the constitution of the State.

Very respectfully,
B. G. HUMPHREYS.

Ames protested pitifully in reply that he only wanted half the house. To use a popular phrase, the Governor "could not see it;" whereupon Ames brought bayonets to the rescue, and, expelling him and his family, took possession.

More of the Ashburn Conspiracy—Negro Spies and Vagabond Detectives.

[Special Dispatch to the Cincinnati Enquirer.]

Washington, D. C., July 13, 1868.

No attention was paid to the death of Ashburn. At the time it occurred he was a wretched outcast, forced to seek a home in a negro brothel. When the report of his death reached Washington, the party machinery was set in motion to manufacture political capital, and to prove Southern barbarity which would justify Radical tyranny. General Meade, being applied to, dispatched Major Smythe, of his staff, to Columbus, to examine and report the facts, offering $40,000 reward for the apprehension of the murderers.

Major Smythe caused the arrest of a large number of citizens, but failed to obtain a clue. The Washington Directory, not satisfied, dispatched Reed, a detective, to Atlanta, who had been working up impeachment. Curious facts are stated touching the pay of the detective while making up Butler's impeachment case. Reed reported every day to Hosmer, a claim agent here, who had in service at one time forty negro spies through this city. Hosmer drew checks on which Reed and his co-workers received pay. Butler's report fails to explain Hosmer's connection with the investigation, and how it happened. Hosmer was paymaster for his detectives and spies, but the explanation will come from quarters least expected. Reed reported to Meade, who referred him to Major Smythe, who explained the examination had, and the results reached. In the mean time General Howard telegraphs to Kansas for Major Whitley, a detective who had figured prominently in the service of the War Department with Baker.

These two worthies procured testimony in the trial of Mrs. Surratt. Whitley has arrived, and he hurried into the new field of labor with the incentive of $40,000.

How well he has succeeded in the manufacturing of witnesses, is shown by the published testimony. Its infamy will soon appear from another quarter that the witnesses were all subpœnaed, and a plan concocted in Washington for a political effect, will be proven by Reed, who, becoming disgusted with the foul proceedings, has returned here to expose the whole scheme.

A private citizen of high standing was dispatched to Atlanta to ascertain if it were possible this could be true. The report has been submitted to the President, and, if necessary, Executive interference will be had to protect innocence, as access to the Chief Magistrate is not so difficult as on former occasions, when Mrs. Surratt was under sentence.

How a Helpless and Honest Negro was Treated.

This fellow, Whitley, was tolerated by General Meade to use the following infamous means to make a perjured witness out of an honest negro named John Stapler:

This poor negro, on the 13th of July, 1868, made oath as to the devices used to make him a witness about the killing of Ashburn, of which he knew nothing. In his affidavit before Notary Public John King, he describes how he was taken from Columbus to Fort Pulaski, near Savannah, and subjected to all kinds of torture. But we will let him tell his own story.

Captain Cook ordered the barber sent for to shave deponent's head in one hour! Deponent was then put back in cell. In about an hour he was brought out, blindfolded, carried down into a room, seated in a chair and the bandage taken from his eyes. Then he was asked by Whitley "if he ever was discoursed by a minister before he was put through," and he said he had an order from General Meade "to put him through," and then asked Captain Cook to allow him a little while before he put deponent through, to which Captain Cook replied he would not do it. Whitley insisted, and at last Captain Cook consented to give Whitley fifteen minutes by his watch to "put deponent through."

When the bandage was taken from deponent's eyes, he saw a soldier standing near a brass cannon with a string from the cannon to his hand, and wherever deponent turned, the cannon was ranged upon him. Deponent's head was then lathered with two scrubbing brushes. There were two or three razors lying on the table. Deponent was made to stand up and be measured against the wall. During this time he was asked by Whitley if he knew, or had ever heard the people say anything about the Ashburn murder. He said he did not know anything and had not heard anything about it; Whitley replied, "you need not tell me a lie; the rebels have been posting you, but it is no use;" Whitley then gave deponent till the next day to consult and study and see if it would not bring some good. Deponent was then put back in his cell and there remained in solitary confinement, never seeing Whitley again for four or five days, when he came there, took him out of his cell, carried him to another part of the fort, and showed "the sweat-box," and told him if he didn't up and tell all he knowed about it he would put deponent in that sweat-box and keep him there thirty days. Deponent told him he didn't know nothing, and couldn't tell anything without it was a lie;

but he must tell him all he knew! He then put deponent in the sweat-box, which is a closet in the walls of the fort, a little wider than deponent's body; the door closes within three or four inches of the breast; the only air admitted is through a few auger holes in the door. He was left in this condition under the belief that he was to remain there thirty days, unless he told about the Ashburn murder. He remained in this position about thirty-three hours, when Mr. Reed and Captain Cook came and took him out. Whitley came up and said he allowed they had taken deponent out too soon, and he would have deponent back unless he told what he knew. When deponent was taken out his limbs were swollen and painful, and to this day he suffers from the confinement. He was then turned loose and allowed to walk about the fort, where he remained until the 9th of June; he was then put under guard and carried to Atlanta. During all this time he was strictly forbid to talk to any one. About the 10th of June he was put in McPherson barracks, where he was very well treated, except that he was under orders not to talk to any one without permission. On Saturday, the 11th of July, in the afternoon, Whitley came to deponent, and other colored persons who had been detained in prison, and told us to go to Major Smythe's office. When we got there Major Smythe gave him an order for $146, which he supposed was for witness fees and transportation. Deponent further says that he was never used as a witness, and never knew anything to witness about. Deponent further says that Stevens and Barber both knew that he had been put in the sweat-box, and how he had been treated.

his
JOHN ⋈ STAPLER.
mark.

Sworn to and subscribed before me, July 13, 1868. JOHN KING,
Notary Public.

After a vain, futile effort to erect testimony in this way, to convict the prisoners falsely charged with the murder of Ashburn, General Meade issues the following:

HEADQUARTERS THIRD MILITARY DISTRICT, } July 21.

To General Sibley, President of Commission:

"GENERAL: In view of the action of the Legislature to-day, and the probable admission of Georgia, and the cessation of military authority, the Commanding General directs that the Commission, of which you are the President, suspend proceedings in the trial of the prisoners charged with the murder of Ashburn."

The prisoners will be retained in custody until further orders. The court adjourned until Friday. All the witnesses for the prosecution have left for the North.

A Specimen of the Laws the Bogus Legislatures Enact.

THE KEEPER OF A STALLION MUST TAKE THE ARKANSAS TEST OATH.

An act prescribing electors' oath for certain cases.

Be it enacted, etc.—SECTION 1. No person in the State of Arkansas, without having previously taken the oath prescribed for electors in the Constitution of the State, shall engage in any of the lines of business hereinafter enumerated, viz.: practice law or medicine, preach the Gospel, teach school, act as steamboat captain, pilot, engineer, or mate, edit or publish a paper, run a ferry-boat, keep a toll-bridge, keep a saloon or restaurant, or billiard saloon, act as auctioneer, mail conductor, do no mercantile business, shall not carry arms, shall not keep a stallion.

SEC. 2. Any person violating Section 1 hereof shall be deemed guilty of felony, and shall be punished by imprisonment in the penitentiary not less than two nor more than ten years.

SEC. 3. This act is to be in force from and after its passage.

In the House of Representatives, May 28, 1866, Mr. Bond gave notice that he would at some future day introduce a bill to adopt the gray uniform of the so called Confederate States to be the uniform of the convicts in the penitentiary, and that persons convicted of manslaughter be entitled to wear the insignia of rank of a colonel, and so on down to the lowest grade of crime.

The constitutional test oath, and exemption of persons liable to militia duty by reason of furnishing a uniform, will cut the class of white persons in the State who will be qualified to sit as jurors down to not more than three thousand in the entire State. This, of course, is a hasty estimate, but it is believed to be true.

Arm the Loyal Radical Melish.

A THREATENED REVOLUTION — LET US HAVE PEACE.

Subjoined is the text of the Peace bill now before Congress:

A bill to provide for the Issue of Arms for the use of the Militia.

Be it enacted by the Senate and House of Representatives of the United States of America in Congress assembled, That the Secretary of War be, and he hereby is, authorized and required to deliver to the Governor of each State and Territory represented in the Congress of the United States, at the seat of government of such State or Territory, for the use of the militia thereof, as many serviceable Springfield rifled muskets of caliber fifty-eight, with accoutrements and equipments, and serviceable field pieces, with carriages, caissons, equipments, and implements, as the Governor of such State or Territory shall require for the use of the loyal militia therein, not exceeding two thousand rifled muskets, with accoutrements and equipments, and two field pieces, with carriages, caissons, equipments, and implements, for each Congressional district and Territory so represented, upon the certificate of the Governor of such State or Territory, showing to the satisfaction of the General of the Army that the regiments and companies for which such ordnance and ordnance stores are required are duly organized of loyal citizens of State or Territory, under the laws thereof, and such ordnance and ordnance stores shall thereafter remain the property of the United States, subject to the control of Congress.

Its intention is to give the bogus Governors of the rotten boroughs Federal arms to place in the hands of a brutal and cowardly militia, like that of Brownlow in Tennessee, to intimidate voters, and carry the Presidential election in those States by bayonets and bloodshed.

The substance of this measure was embraced in the bill to reduce "the military peace establishment." Upon the merits of the bill, on the 20th of July, 1868, Mr. Hendricks, of Indiana, said that he considered this a most dangerous bill, because it proposed to arm one political party against the other. It placed the control of the arms to be distributed with the Governors of the States designated; and this, too, immediately before the Presidential election. In regard to the ratio of distribution, he asked what Maine wanted with seven thousand muskets, Massachusetts with twelve thousand, and Indiana with thirteen thousand? And, in order to illustrate his argument, he referred to the fact that the Governor of Indiana, being a candidate for re-election, these arms placed at his disposal could be used according to his design and pleasure. And so with the other States. He commented upon the action of the Senate, last night, in rejecting Mr. Vicker's amendment, providing that the distribution of arms, etc., shall not take place prior to the 1st of January, unless the President shall deem it necessary for the prevention of disturbance in the Southern States. This fact, he remarked, was significant of the design of the bill. Arms were to be distributed to all the States, with the exception of Virginia, Mississippi, and Texas; and these States were omitted because there was to be no election there. Therefore he argued that *the only purpose of this distribution of arms before the election was to make a military force out of one party to overawe the other, and thus control the election.* All he asked was a fair election, and that the people may vote without hindrance, governed by their own judgment. General Grant had said, in the last sentence of his letter accepting the nomination for the Presidency, "We want peace. Let us have peace." All parties should desire this, and quiet in the country. After this expression of the desire for peace on the part of the candidate of the Republican party, *we find here a fire-brand—a measure calculated to excite passion and produce strife, and perhaps bloodshed.* With a measure so threatening and dangerous in its character, *the people would be slow to believe that the party desired peace.* He hoped the President would exercise the power he possessed to prevent this bill from becoming a law. The President owed this not only to his constitutional duty, but to the peace and quiet of the country. He should defeat *a measure so full of peril to the country, and which invited a conflict between the whites and blacks.*

In the House, on the 23d of July, the concurrent resolution of the Senate for adjournment from the 27th of July to the third Monday in September was discussed at length, the debate involving the topics of the Presidential election, impeachment, funding bill, tax bill, and bill to distribute arms to the South.

Mr. STOKES said that unless the people have arms in the Southern States, the Union whites and blacks will be overrun. "And I say it is the duty of Congress to stay here until this measure is put through. My people are expecting every moment that Forrest and his rebel Democratic crew will commence making war upon them. They are entitled to ten thousand stand of arms in my district, and the requisition was made for that number by the Governor, but only two thousand stand were furnished, and we to-day demand the other eight thousand stand of arms. This is a matter of life and death to us. I am satisfied of the fact that we will need these arms at the South at a very early day. The war cry has gone forth. The rebels say they will rule the country, or exterminate the colored Union men; and, for one, I am disposed to meet them."

Mr. WASHBURNE (of Illinois) had one word to say in reply to the gentleman from Tennessee. "I have no doubt," he said, "of the grievous and perilous state of things which exists in the South, and which the gentleman from Tennessee refers to;

but the question (and it is one of the gravest importance ever thrust upon us) is whether that state of things is to be remedied by sending arms into those States. Sir, I believe that in most of the States, not ten days after those arms are sent there to the negroes, they will be in the hands of rebels."

Mr. STOKES, in reply to that last remark, said in his district they had already drawn two thousand stand of arms, and none of them had gone into the hands of rebels.

Mr. WASHBURNE. I do not allude to that State, but to other States; and I tell the gentlemen to beware before they pass this measure, lest it be an initiation of civil war and insurrection in those States. [Great excitement.] I now yield to the venerable gentleman from North Carolina (Mr. Boyden), who wishes to say a few words, and I ask the attention of the House to what he shall say.

Mr. BOYDEN. Mr. Speaker, I am alarmed at the condition of the country. It is proposed to send arms to North Carolina, that the people may use them against each other. Great God! we can not afford to fight each other. Keep away your arms. Do nothing to irritate our people, but do every thing in your power to assuage and heal the excitement there. We want no arms. I warn the House if arms are sent there we will be ruined. We can not live there. If we need any thing in the way of arms, in God's name send an army of the United States there, but do not arm neighbor against neighbor. There never was a more mischievous measure than this proposition to arm one class of our people against another.

Mr. DEWEES (of North Carolina) addressed the House against adjournment. Some provision, he said, should be made for the new governments of the Southern States, and for the protection of the loyal people, otherwise the rebellion would be re-established. The letter of Mr. Blair would be carried out if Congress adjourned now. Before six months the last traces of republican government in the South would have ceased to exist, and the Ku-Klux Klan, the rebels, the slaveholding, Copperhead, Democratic party would be ruling them, as they ruled in 1865.

Mr. WOODWARD inquired of Mr. Dewees whether the reconstructed governments in the South could be maintained in any other way than by the bayonet.

Mr. DEWEES. We can, if you will give us arms to keep down the rebels, triumph [laughter on the Democratic side], and by no other means.

Mr. WOODWARD. Then I understand the gentleman that the governments which Congress has been at such great pains to reconstruct can only exist by the bayonet?

Mr. DEWEES. The gentleman's party, in 1861, stole the arms that belonged to the Government of the United States to shoot your loyal neighbors' sons, and the guns are still in the hands of the slaveholding Democratic party.

Mr. JONES (of Kentucky) asked whether the militia armed in North Carolina were not under the control of the Governor and Legislature of that State, as now constituted.

Mr. DEWEES. No, sir; we have no militia.

Mr. JONES. It is your own fault.

Mr. DEWEES. Under the rule of the Democratic party, from 1861 to 1865, every musket, shot-gun, and horse-pistol, was taken out of the hands of loyal men, and put into the hands of Southern sympathizers. The support given to this question of adjournment on the side of the House where I occupy a seat, is for the purpose of carrying out the 3d of July letter, stamping out the loyal State governments, and dispersing the United States carpet-baggers. [Laughter.] I say, come on, whenever you feel disposed. Come on. Stretch out, then, your traitorous hands to touch again one fold of the old flag, and the representatives of four millions of men, who, though black in skin, are white and loyal in heart, will throw themselves as a bulwark between you and those loyal governments, and you will only live in sad memories of bad events. Come on! come on! [Unrestrained laughter among Democrats.] If you want to sustain those governments, you have got to give us some assistance.

Mr. ROSS. Is there not some danger of the Republicans losing the election there, unless they get arms?

Mr. KELLEY. Is there not more danger of the Republicans, white and black, losing their lives?

Mr. RANDALL. They would be able to get under a bench, as my colleague did, in Mobile.

[This remark, apparently, did not reach the ear of Mr. Kelley.]

Mr. SCHENCK closed the debate.

This measure, and a kindred one to provide for the government of the States of Mississippi, Virginia, and Texas, in a provisional form, by the bogus conventions thereof, failed for want of time to complete their passage before the hour of adjournment of Congress, on the 27th of July.

PEACE IN SOUTH CAROLINA—HOW TO PRESERVE IT.

The *animus* of the negro government forced by Radicalism on South Carolina is seen in the recommendations of Scott (car pet bag Governor) to the Legislature to confer on him the authority at pleasure to suspend the writ of *habeas corpus*, and also to authorize *the prosecution*, in certain cases, to change the *venue* (whenever desirable to insure a conviction), thus subjecting a defendant to all the embarrassments and expenses of a removal from the vicinage of home, witnesses, and friends, and charging all prosecution costs to the county from which the change is made. The same message claims that, for the first time, a government is inaugurated here "with the consent of the governed," and yet insists on the early organization and equipment of the (negro) militia, and a requisition on the War Department for the State's quota of arms, which will be promptly furnished. When this is done, Scott says, the military forces of the United States "may, with propriety, be dispensed with." Why not before, if the Governor sits in his chair "with the consent of the governed?" Another illustration of Grant's "peace."

Another Revolutionary Measure.
PLANNING A NEW CIVIL WAR.

The Radical Congress has passed the following bill:

Be it enacted, etc., That none of the States whose inhabitants were lately in rebellion shall be entitled to representation in the electoral college for the choice of President or Vice-President of the United States, nor shall electoral votes be received or counted from any such States unless at the time prescribed by law for the choice of electors the people of such States, pursuant to acts of Congress in that behalf, shall have, since the 4th of March, 1867, adopted a constitution of State government, under which a State government shall have been organized and shall be in operation, and unless such election of electors shall have been held under authority of such constitution and government, and such State shall have also become entitled to representation in Congress pursuant to acts of Congress in that behalf; provided, that nothing herein contained shall be construed to apply to any State which was represented in Congress on the 4th of March, 1867.

This bill was vetoed by the President. In his message dated July 20, 1868, he says:

The mode and manner of receiving and counting the electoral votes for President and Vice-President of the United States, are in plain and simple terms prescribed by the Constitution. That instrument imperatively requires that the President of the Senate shall, in the presence of the Senate and House of Representatives, open all the certificates, and the votes shall then be counted. Congress has therefore no power under the Constitution to receive the electoral votes or reject them. The whole power is exhausted when, in presence of the two Houses, the votes are counted and the result declared. In this respect the power and duty of the President of the Senate are, under the Constitution, purely ministerial. When, therefore, the joint resolution declared that no electoral votes should be received or counted from the States that, since the 4th of March, 1867, have not adopted a constitution of State government, under which a State government is organized, a power is assumed which is no where delegated to Congress, unless upon the assumption that the State governments organized prior to March, 1867, were illegal and void. The joint resolution, by implication at least, concedes that these were States by virtue of their organization prior to the 4th of March, 1867, but denies to them the right to vote in the election of President and Vice President of the United States. It follows, either that this assumption of power is wholly unauthorized by the Constitution, or that the States excluded from voting were out of the Union by reason of the rebellion, and have never been legally restored.

Being fully satisfied that they were never out of the Union, and that their relations thereto have been legally and constitutionally restored, I am forced to the conclusion that the faint reason which deprives them of the right to have their votes for President and Vice-President received and counted, is in conflict with the Constitution, and that Congress has no more power to reject their votes than the votes of those of the States which have been uniformly loyal to the Federal Union.

It is worthy of remark, that if the States whose inhabitants were recently in rebellion were legally and constitutionally organized and restored to their rights prior to the 4th of March, 1867, as I am satisfied they were, the only legitimate authority under which the election for President and Vice-President can be held therein, must be derived from the governments instituted before that period. It clearly follows that all the State governments organized in these States, under the acts of Congress for that purpose, and under military control, are illegitimate and of no validity whatever, and in that view, the votes cast in those States for President and Vice-President, in pursuance of the acts passed since the 4th of March, 1867, and in obedience to the so-called Reconstruction acts of Congress, can not be legally received and counted, while the only votes in those States that can be legally cast and counted, will be those cast in pursuance of the laws in the several States prior to the act of Congress on the subject of Reconstruction.

I can not refrain from directing your special attention to the declaration contained in the joint resolution, that "none of the States whose inhabitants were lately in rebellion, shall be entitled to representation in the electoral college, etc." Is it meant that no State is to be allowed to vote for President and Vice-President, all of whose inhabitants were engaged in the late rebellion? It is then apparent that no one of the States will be excluded from voting, since it is well known that in every Southern State there were many inhabitants who did not participate in the rebellion, but who actually took part in its suppression, or refrained from giving it any aid or countenance. I therefore conclude that the true meaning of the resolution is that no State, a portion of whose inhabitants were engaged in the rebellion, shall be permitted to participate in the Presidential election except upon the terms and conditions therein prescribed. Assuming this to be the true construction of the resolution, the inquiry becomes pertinent, may those Northern States, a portion of whose inhabitants were actually in the rebellion, be prevented, at the direction of Congress, from having their electoral vote counted? It is well known that a portion of the inhabitants of New York and Virginia were alike engaged in the rebellion, and it is equally well known that Virginia, as well as New York, was at all times during the war recognized by the Federal Government as a State in the Union, so clearly, that upon the termination of hostilities, it was not even deemed necessary for her restoration that a provisional Government should be appointed; yet, according to this joint resolution, the people of Virginia, unless they comply with the terms it prescribes, are denied the right of voting for President and Vice-President, while the people of New York, a portion of the inhabitants of which State were also in rebellion, are permitted to have their electoral vote counted without undergoing the process of reconstruction prescribed for Virginia. New York is no more a State than Virginia. The one is as much entitled to be represented in the Electoral College as the other. If Congress has the power to deprive Virginia of this right, it can exercise the same authority in respect to New York or any other of the States. Thus the result of the Presidential election may be controlled and determined by Congress, and the people be deprived of their rights under the Constitution to choose a President and Vice-President of the United States. If Congress were to provide by law that the votes of none of the States should be received and counted if cast for a candidate who differed in political sentiment with a majority of the two Houses, such legislation would at once be condemned by the country as unconstitutional and revolutionary, a usurpation of power. It would, however, be exceedingly difficult to find in the Constitution any more authority for the joint resolution under consideration, than for an enactment looking directly for the rejection of all votes not in accordance with the political preference of a majority of Congress. No power exists in the Constitution authorizing the joint resolution, or the proposed law, the only difference being that one would be more palpably unconstitutional and revolutionary than the other, for one would rest upon the radical error that Congress has power to prescribe terms and conditions to the right of the people of the States to cast their votes for President and Vice-President.

For the reason thus indicated I am constrained to return the joint resolution to the Senate for such further action thereon as Congress may deem necessary.

[Signed] ANDREW JOHNSON.
WASHINGTON, D. C., July 20, 1868.

It passed the Senate over the veto of the President on the same day. Yeas 45, all Radicals; nays 8, all Democrats. Passed the House same day. Yeas 134, all Radicals; nays 36, all Democrats; and the Speaker declared it a law.

The States, says the *Chicago Times*, likely to be affected by the enforcement of this revolutionary edict are Virginia, Mississippi and Texas. In all others, the black-and-tan documents called constitutions have been ratified by that small minority of the inhabitants who compose the majority of those allowed to vote—excepting in Alabama, where Congress declared the thing to be, that a majority of more than twenty thousand voted should not be. In Mississippi, the black and-tan production has been rejected. A like result is expected to follow in Virginia and Texas. The same vote that can repudiate the negro infamy under the military Reconstruction acts would give the electoral votes of those States, under the same acts, to the Democratic candidates. This is why the Jacobin revolutionists in Congress, in defiance of the plain letter of the Constitution, declare that their votes in the Presidential election shall not be received and counted.

A contingency is possible in which the declaration of Mr. Trumbull, that the attempt to carry out such an enactment would produce another civil war, might turn out a prophesy Virginia, Mississippi and Texas are entitled to twenty-three electoral votes. If the inclusion of these twenty-three votes would give the majority to Mr. Seymour, and the exclusion of them would give the majority to Mr. Grant, the refusal of a Jacobin Senate to count them would be an extremely hazardous business. Becuase. under the Constitution, such refusal would not make Mr. Grant President. "The President of the Senate *shall*, in the presence of the Senate and House of Representatives, open *all the certificates*, and the votes *shall* then be counted; the person having the greatest number of votes for President *shall be the President*, if such number be a majority of the whole number of electors appointed." Such is the plain language of the Constitution. It is a language that admits of no misconstruction. It is a law that can not be abrogated by an act of Congress.

Trollope on Reconstruction.

THE MOST OUTRAGEOUS TYRANNY EVER IMPOSED UPON A FALLEN PEOPLE—AN INTELLIGENT ENGLISHMAN'S VIEW OF RADICAL POLICY.

[From the Pall Mall Gazette, July 11.]

The following letter is from a well-known English author (Anthony Trollope), now on a visit to the United States:

"WASHINGTON, June —, 1868.

" * * * It has been deemed by Congress that each of these States shall choose a new Constitution *for itself*, but that in choosing it all men, blacks and whites alike, shall have an equal voice, except that white men known to have been leading rebels, and that other white men who will not take a test oath so worded as to be utterly irreconcilable to the feelings of a Southern white man, shall be debarred from voting at all. The upshot is that the framing of the State constitutions is to be given to the men who, four or five years since, were slaves, and who are still negroes. But it must not be supposed that these black men have really been asked to frame their constitutions, or to do anything else than vote. Their constitutions have been sent to them by post, and consist in an undertaking on the part of the State in question that all men shall hereafter vote alike. It will, therefore, go forth to the world that Alabama, Georgia, and the others have themselves declared that white men and black men shall be the same for all political purpose, and that on this basis the States have been 'reconstructed' and restored to the Union. I hold that tyranny never went beyond this. It may be as well at first to point out that in none of the great Western States can a negro vote at all. In Ohio, Indiana, Illinois and Missouri, none but a white man can vote. In Minnesota, Wisconsin, and Michigan, white men and Indians can vote, but never a negro. In the great Eastern States negroes are kept away from the polls, either practically or by actual rule. In Pennsylvania no black man can vote. In New York a negro can vote, but not without a real porperty qualification and three years' residence. In the States of New England, excepting in Connecticut, negroes can vote; but their number is so small as to make their votes of no possible value. Yet it has been ordained by these victorious Northern States that in the conquered Southern States all political power given the whites shall be put into the hands of a race of men who yesterday were their slaves. For myself I am prepared to argue, if it be needed, that a negro is not fitted by his gifts and nature to exercise political power amidst a community of white men. He is so naturally subservient to the white man's greater power of mind that, when passion is over, he will always do as some white man shall instruct him. But putting aside for the present a subject which is very vast in its bearings, and in which men have and will dispute loudly, here has been made a provision for a war of races with the express object of keeping down a people, in order that that people may be debarred from all political power in the empire. It must be remembered that government in the United States is State government for the most part. In Georgia the black men. on these lines of reconstruction, would have the power of making all laws for the restraint of the white They would be enabled to enact that a man should be hung for this or that so-called crime—a white man if you will, for not taking off his hat to a black man. But it has never been for a moment intended really to intrust this power to the negroes. The intention is that, through the negroes, all political power, both State power and Federal power, shall be in the hands of members of Congress from the North—that the North shall have its heels on the South, and that the conquered shall be subject to the conquerors. *Never has there been a more terrible condition imposed upon a fallen people. For an Italian to feel an Austrian over him, for a Pole to feel a Russian over him, has been bad indeed; but it has been left for the political animosity of a Republican from the North—a man who himself rejects all contact with the negro—to subject the late Southern slave-owner to dominion from the African who was yesterday his slave.* The dungeon chains be knocked off the captive in order that he many be harnessed as a beast of burden to the captor's chariot. But it will not be so,

There will in these Southern States be a war of races; hatred from the white man to the poor, timid, incapable, unconscious negro; suffering for both, infinite suffering for poor Sambo, who will gradually begin his appointed task of disappearing; there will be rapid death of negro children, negro want, and all the following of negro vice; but the white man who lives near him will gradually reassume his power. There will be an influx of Northern men into these States, and they will gradually become as the white men of the South. The scheme after a while will fail; but in the mean time all the hatred of a conquering and a conquered people will be maintained. Such, sir, are my ideas of 'reconstruction.'"

WENDELL PHILLIPS ON RECONSTRUCTION.

Seven States have been readmitted and will soon take their places. No one claims that they are ready or fit for places in Congress. But the Grant party needs them. We sink principle and risk the negro in order to elect Mr. Grant. Mark you, he is so popular that there's hardly need to count the votes. Still, we must risk the presence of more Fowlers and Van Winkles, and peril all the results of the war to insure the election of this marvelously popular soldier! And so Mr. Greeley and the *Independent* wheel into line. Every politician must now wear a gag until November. Expect no truth from any man until the vote is declared. How can we so frame our Government that a New York journalist can afford to tell us the truth to-day of General Grant as frankly as he does of Franklin Pierce? Will the abolition of the Presidency abolish the quadrennial gags, this intermittent hypocrisy? If so, we advocate it. Better have a slower and clumsier Government, if that will allow editors to keep a conscience, and Senators to be honest men.

Horatio Seymour.

[From the New York World.]

Horatio Seymour, the Democratic candidate for President of the United States, was born in Pompey, Onondaga county, New York, in the year 1811, and is consequently about fifty-seven years of age. The family to which Mr. Seymour belongs is descended from Richard Seymour, who was one of the original settlers of Hartford, Connecticut. Major Moses Seymour, the fourth lineal descendant, served in the Revolutionary War, and subsequently represented Litchfield in the Legislature of Connecticut for seventeen years. Of his five sons, Henry Seymour, father of Horatio, was born in 1780. He removed to Utica, in this State, served in the State Legislature with signal ability. and was for many years Canal Commissioner, occupying a prominent position in the politics and legislation of the State. One of his brothers was a distinguished member of the United States Senate from Vermont for twelve years. Hon. Origen S. Seymour, for some time Representative in Congress from the Litchfield District of Connecticut, was the son of another brother named Ozias. The maternal grandfather of Mr. Seymour, Colonel Forman, served through the Revolutionary War in the New Jersey line.

Mr. Seymour received a liberal and thorough education in the best institutions of the State. His instincts and preferences naturally led him to the study of the law, which he pursued with great vigor and industry. He was admitted to the bar when only a little more than twenty years of age, and at once commenced the practice of his profession in the city of Utica. The death of his father, however, soon afterward devolved upon him so great responsibilities in connection with the settlement of the family estate, as to require the most of his time and attention, obliging him, much against his wish, to relinquish the practice of his profession. The death of his wife's father, the late John R. Bleecker, occurring about the same time, added to his numerous cares in the adjustment of important property interests. Some of the best years of Mr. Seymour's life were absorbed in this work, but no doubt his mind was being schooled, as it could not otherwise have been, for the graver responsibilities and duties that were to come in after life. Up to this time Mr. Seymour had acted no prominent part in political life, although from his youth, as were his ancestors before him, he had always been strongly attached, through sympathy and taste, to the Democratic party. In the fall of 1841, when not thirty years of age, Mr. Seymour consented to the use of his name as a Democratic candidate for member of Assembly. Although the Whigs were at that time largely in the ascendency in Utica Mr. Seymour was triumphantly elected by a large majority. In the Legislature Mr Seymour at once took a commanding position upon the great questions involving the interests of the State, engaging in the leading debates with great fervency, and assisting largely in shaping the legislation of the session. Among his legislative associates were John A. Dix, Michael Hoffman, David R. Floyd Jones, George R. Davis, Lemuel Stetson, and Calvin T. Hulburd. The Democrats at that time were in the ascendency in both branches of the Legislature, and the great measure of the session was Michael Hoffman's celebrated bill in relation to finances, which was supported and passed by the Democrats. In the success of this measure, which was destined to restore the depreciated financial credit of the State, Mr. Seymour took an active and sympathetic interest, displaying for the first time the forensic ability and oratorical power that have since distinguished him.

In the spring of 1842 Mr. Seymour was elected Mayor of the city of Utica, despite the continued hostility and opposition of the Whigs. In the fall of 1843, he was again elected a member of the lower House of the Legislature, and was re-elected to, and served in the same position during the sessions of 1844 and 1845. The session of 1844 was an important and exciting one, the Assembly being agitated with acrimonious contests, chiefly springing from contemplated opposition to the administration of Governor Bouck. The leaders in the debates of the session were Mr. Seymour and Mr. Hoffman, the recognized leader of the Legislature in 1842, and a formidable antagonist in debate, but Mr. Seymour appears to have coped with him successfully, and to have won not only the plaudits of his political associates, but the praise of his constituents likewise. The session of 1845 opened with a changed spirit, based upon the victorious election of Mr. Polk to the Presidency. At the outset of this session, Mr. Seymour was induced by his friends to enter the contest for Speakership, to which position he was triumphantly elected, despite a violent factional fight, which seriously threatened his prospects. One of the prominent and important events of this session was the election of Daniel S. Dickinson to the United States Senate, in which Mr. Seymour took a leading and active part. He also engaged with fervent spirit in the discussion relative to the call for a convention to amend the Constitution, but voted against the bill providing for the measure. With this session Mr. Seymour's legislative career was brought to a close.

For the succeeding five years Mr. Seymour was not prominent in public life, having resumed the practice of law in the city of Utica. By the action of the Legislature of 1850, providing for the enlargement and improvement of the Erie Canal, and appropriating the revenue of the State in contravention to the provisions of the constitution, Mr. Seymour again assumed a leading position in State politics, and most earnestly resisted this effort to override the provisions of a constitution so recently adopted. On account of his strenuous opposition to that measure, he was that year (1850), for the first time, placed in nomination for Governor of this State in opposition to Washington Hunt. The result of the election was, for Seymour, 214,352 votes; for Hunt, 214,614. Mr. Seymour having been defeated by 262 votes.

In 1852, Mr. Seymour was again placed in nomination by the Democratic party, in opposition to Washington Hunt (Whig), and Minthorne Tompkins (Free Soil), with the following result:

Seymour..................................264,121
Hunt.......................................239,736
Tompkins................................19,299

Mr. Seymour was triumphantly elected over two competitors as the chief executive officer of the State. His administration of State affairs, as generally conceded, was rendered by ability, tact, and good judgment. While occupying the gubernatorial chair in 1852, he vetoed the notorious Maine law, and the correctness of his views as to the power of the Legislature to pass sumptuary laws was subsequently fully established by a formal decision of the Court of Appeals.

In 1854 Mr. Seymour was nominated by the Democracy for re-election, with Myron H. Clark (Republican), Daniel Ullman (American), and Greene C. Bronson (Hard-shell Democrat) as opponents. The following was the result of the election:

Seymour..................................156,495
Clark.....................................156,804
Ullman...................................122,282
Bronson..................................33,850

Although this election resulted in Mr. Seymour's defeat, it demonstrated very satisfactorily his unwaning popularity with the people, and his certainty of success with the party united and working for one candidate. At the conclusion of this contest, Mr. Seymour again resumed the work of his profession at Utica. In everything appertaining to the success of the Democracy he took an active and sympathetic interest. He attended National and State Conventions with great regularity, and was always accorded a leading position in the councils of the same. At the National Democratic Convention at Charleston, in 1860, he was proposed by the Southern delegates as a compromise candidate between Douglas and Breckinridge, but owing to the opposition of the New York delegation his name was withdrawn.

In 1862 Mr. Seymour was for the fourth time placed in nomination for Governor of this State by the Democrats, against General Wadsworth, the Republican nominee. The result of the election was as follows:

Seymour..................................306,649
Wadsworth..............................295,897

Mr. Seymour was thus for a second time elected Governor of this State by the handsome majority of 10,752. After an able administration of two years, he was, in 1864, nominated for re-election, this time against Reuben E. Fenton, by whom he was defeated.

At the National Democratic Convention held in Chicago in 1864, Mr. Seymour was with great unanimity chosen its President, and how ably and efficiently he discharged the duties and responsibilities of that important position, the records and history of the Convention will indisputably show. Since that time Mr. Seymour has delivered many powerful Democratic speeches in various parts of the country, entering each successive campaign in this State with his accustomed vigor, fearlessness and efficiency.

At his home in Utica, as well as throughout the State, he is esteemed and respected with that fervor that springs only from true friendship. He has been from early boyhood a faithful and energetic member of the Protestant Episcopal Church, the interest of which he has labored earnestly to promote, both as an individual member and a leader in her legislative councils. He takes especial interest in educational establishments and in the Sunday schools, whose usefulness and influence he labors zealously to promote and advance.

Such is the Democratic nominee for the Presidency. Well does Thurlow Weed's paper say that Governor Seymour is "not to be beaten by being called a Copperhead. The man who, under the intense pressure of disloyalty brought against him, could poll over three hundred thousand votes in New York, *is more to be feared now than he was in 1864!* Eternal vigilance is necessary to elect Grant."

THE INVASION OF PENNSYLVANIA IN 1863.
[From the Detroit Union.]

While the "idiot" organ of this city is discussing the record of Governor Seymour, in connection with the rebel invasion of Pennsylvania, in 1863, and denouncing him as disloyal, it will serve its readers and add much to the truth of its comments by giving publicity to the following dispatches which passed between the Governor of New York and the Washington officials, and also between New York officials and the Governor of Pennsylvania, not forgetting to add also, that although Governor Curtin was of the "loyal" school of Governors, the first troops in Harrisburg for the defense of that city came from New York, sent by order of Horatio Seymour.

[By Telegram from Washington, June 15, 1863.]

To His Excellency, Governor Seymour:

The movements of the rebel forces in Virginia are now sufficiently developed to show that General Lee, with his whole army, is moving forward to invade the States of Maryland, Pennsylvania, and other States.

The President, to repel this invasion promptly, has called upon Ohio, Pennsylvania, Maryland and West Virginia, for one hundred thousand (100,000) militia, for six (6) months, unless sooner discharged. It is important to have the largest possible force in the least time, and if other States would furnish militia for a short term, to be ordered on the draft, it would greatly advance the object. Will you please inform me immediately, if, in answer to a special call of the President, you can raise and forward twenty thousand militia, as volunteers without bounty, to be credited on the draft of your State, or what number you can probably raise?   E. M. STANTON,
Secretary of War.

ALBANY, June 15, 1863.

Hon. E. M. Stanton, Secretary of War, Washington, D. C.:

I will spare no effort to send you troops at once. I have sent orders to the militia officers of the State.
HORATIO SEYMOUR.

Does this sound like disloyalty?

ALBANY, June 15, 1863.

Hon. E. M. Stanton, Secretary of War, Washington, D. C.:

I will order the New York and Brooklyn troops to Philadelphia at once. Where can they get arms if they are needed?
HORATIO SEYMOUR.

ALBANY, June 15, 1863.

Hon. E. M. Stanton, Secretary of War, Washington, D. C.:

We have about two thousand enlisted volunteers in the State. I will have them consolidated into companies and regiments, and sent on at once. You must provide them with arms.
HORATIO SEYMOUR.

ALBANY, June 16, 1863.

Governor Curtin, Harrisburg:

I am pushing forward troops as fast as possible; regiments will leave New York to night. All will be ordered to report to General Couch.
HORATIO SEYMOUR.

[By Telegraph from Washington, June 16, 1863.]

To Governor Seymour:

The President directs me to return his thanks, with those of the Department, for your prompt responses. A strong movement of your city regiments to Philadelphia would be a very encouraging movement, and do great good in giving strength in the State. The call had to be for six months,

unless sooner discharged, in order to comply with the law. It is not likely that more than thirty days' service—perhaps not so long—would be required. Can you forward your city regiments speedily? Please reply early. EDWIN M. STANTON,
                Secretary of War.

                        ALBANY, June 16, 1863,
Hon. E. M. Stanton, Secretary of War, Washington, D. C.:

Four returned volunteer regiments can be put in the field at once, for three months' service. Can arms and accoutrements be supplied in New York? Old arms not fit for the field. J. T. SPRAGUE,
                Adjutant-General.

[By Telegraph from Washington, June 16, 1863.]
To Adjutant-General Sprague:

Upon your requisition, any troops you may send to Pennsylvania will be armed and equipped in New York with new arms.

Orders have been given to the Bureau of Ordnance. EDWIN M. STANTON.

SEYMOUR PUSHING ON TROOPS.
                        ALBANY, June 16, 1863.
Hon. E. M. Stanton, Secretary of War, Washington, D. C.:

Officers of old organizations here will take the field with their men, and can march to morrow, if they can be paid irrespective of ordnance accounts. The Government would still have a hold upon them to refund for losses. JOHN T. SPRAGUE,
                Adjutant-General.

                        ALBANY, June 15, 1863.
Hon. E. M. Stanton, Secretary of War, Washington, D. C.:

By request of Governor Seymour, who has called me here, I write to say that the New York city regiments can go with full ranks for any time not over three months; say from eight to ten thousand men. The shorter the period the larger will be the force. For what time will they be required? Please answer immediately.

C. W. SANFORD, Major-General.

[By Telegraph from Washington, June 16, 1863.]
To Major-General Sanford:

The Government will be glad to have your city regiments hasten to Pennsylvania for any term of service; it is not possible to say how long they might be useful, but it is not expected that they would be detained more than three (3) months, possibly not longer than twenty (20) or thirty (30) days.

They would be accepted for three months, and discharged as soon as the present exigency is over. If aided at the present by your troops, the people of that State might soon be able to raise sufficient force to relieve your city regiments.

EDWIN M. STANTON,
                Secretary of War.

                        ALBANY, June 18, 1863.
To Hon. E. M. Stanton, Secretary of War, Washington, D. C.:

About twelve thousand (12,000) men are now on the move for Harrisburg in good spirits and well equipped.

The Governor says: "Shall troops continue to be forwarded?" Please answer.

Nothing from Washington since first telegrams.

JOHN T. SPRAGUE, Adj't.-Gen."

[By telegraph from Washington, June 19, 1863.]
To Adjutant-General Sprague:

The President directs me to return his thanks to His Excellency, Gov. Seymour, and his staff, for their energetic and prompt action. Whether any further force is likely to be required, will be communicated to you to-morrow, by which time it is expected the movement of the enemy will be more fully developed.

E. M. STANTON, Sec'y of War.

                        ALBANY, June 20, 1863.
To Hon. E. M. Stanton, Secretary of War, Washington, D. C.:

The Governor desires to be informed if he shall continue sending on the militia regiments from this State. If so, to what extent and to what point.

J. B. STONEHOUSE,
                Act. Ass't. Adj't.-Gen'l.

[By telegraph from Washington, June 21, 1863.]
To Acting Assistant Adjutant-General Stonehouse:

The President desires Governor Seymour to forward to Baltimore all the militia regiments he can raise.

E. M. STANTON, Sec'y of War.

Thus it will be seen that in three days after Stanton wanted to know whether *any* troops could be raised in New York, Governor Seymour had twelve thousand on the way to Pennsylvania.

                        ALBANY, June 18, 1863
To Governor Curtin, Harrisburg, Pennsylvania:

About twelve thousand men are now moving and under orders for Harrisburg, in good spirits and well equipped.

Governor Seymour desires to know if he shall continue to send men. He is ignorant of your real condition.

JOHN T. SPRAGUE,
                Adjutant-General.

[By telegraph from Harrisburg, July 2, 1863.]
To His Excellency, Governor Seymour:

Send forward more troops as rapidly as possible. Every hour increases the necessity for large forces to protect Pennsylvania. The battles of yesterday were not decisive, and if Meade should be defeated, unless we have a large army, this State will be overrun by rebels.
A. G. CURTIN,
Governor of Pennsylvania.

NEW YORK, July 3, 1863.
To Governor Curtin, Harrisburg, Pennsylvania:

Your telegram is received. Troops will continue to be sent. One regiment leaves to-day, another to-morrow, all in good pluck.
JOHN T. SPRAGUE,
Adjutant-General.

In the face of all these facts, when the riots occurred in New York, the Radicals turned upon the Governor and accused him of sending off all the troops and leaving New York unprotected, with an especial view to leaving the city at the mercy of the mob! No other party would have been guilty of so much meanness, or given countenance to such base ingratitude. To day these facts are all of public record and it must require the extreme of impudence and hardihood to attempt to assail Governor Seymour in connection with the history of that period.

STANTON ON SEYMOUR.

The following letter explains itself:

WAR DEPARTMENT, }
WASHINGTON, June 27, 1863.

DEAR SIR: I cannot forbear expressing to you the deep obligation I feel for the prompt and candid support you have given to the Government in the present emergency. The energy, activity, and patriotism you have exhibited, I may be permitted personally and officially to acknowledge, without arrogating any personal claims on my part in such service, or to any service whatever.

I shall be happy to be always esteemed your friend.
EDWIN M. STANTON.

His Excellency Horatio Seymour.

LINCOLN ON SEYMOUR.

Does the *Tribune*, says the New York *World*, believe with Senators Pomeroy that the cant about "Honest Old Abe," which was at first ridiculous, has "now become criminal?" If not, let it have the honesty itself to publish what Lincoln said in 1863 of the candidate whom the Democracy propose in 1868 to put in Lincoln's place.

Just before the battle of Gettysburg, in July, 1863, the officer of Governor Seymour's staff, who had been charged by him with superintending the movements of the New York troops whom Governor Seymour threw forward with such unexampled rapidity and energy to resist the invasion of Pennsylvania by Lee, called to say farewell to President Lincoln. Taking the officer (the *Tribune* knows perfectly well who that officer was) by both hands, President Lincoln said to him: " I wish you to understand that you can not possibly use words too warm to convey to Governor Seymour my thankfulness for his prompt and efficient help given to the Government in this crisis." This language the President thrice repeated, accompanying it with a fervent pressure of the hands, and uttering it each time with increased earnestness and feeling.

President Lincoln is now in his grave. The men who fawned upon him in his lifetime for place and power, but who have never been at the pains to raise even the poorest monument to his memory, now join with the *Tribune* in propagating lies about the Executive of the Empire State who thus stood by him and by the country, when Greeley was hiding under Windust's table, and the Loyal Leaguers of Pennsylvania were hurrying their plate and their cash on special trains at Camden, to escape from the rebel cavalry at Carlisle!

THE TRIBUNE'S RELUCTANT VINDICATION OF GOVERNOR SEYMOUR.

In response to the preceding article of the New York *World*, the *Tribune* is compelled to sweep away all its own slanderous twaddle about Governor Seymour and the battle of Gettysburg, and to confess the mendacious recklessness of the charges it had itself so freely fulminated. Greeley does not come up to this act of justice in a generous and chivalric spirit; but he nevertheless confesses the facts, which are all that is material. We quote his language in the *Tribune* of July 20, 1868:

In June, 1863, General Lee, evading by a flank march, the Army of the Potomac, which confronted and stood ready to fight him on the Rappahannock, invaded Maryland and Pennsylvania. The movement—as Lee's official report virtually confesses—was not defensible on military, nor on other than political grounds. The rebels hoped to win a victory on Northern soil, and thereby to stimulate their Northern friends to declare openly in their favor, and thus, by paralyzing the Union Government end the contest in triumph. The President, justly alarmed and apprehensive, called urgently on the Governors of the Northern States for militia. *Governor Seymour promptly respond* ed, *by sending all the uniformed and disciplined militia of our city, with at least one regiment organized for the occasion. The President and his War Secretary thanked him for so doing.* And, if the forces thus sent were so managed that they did not get within gunshot of an enemy, and nowise contributed to the glorious result of the Gettysburg struggle, the fault was not Governor Seymour's nor their own.

GOVERNOR CURTIN'S (OF PENN.) TESTIMONY.
[From the Philadelphia Age, July 10.]

The *Press* is prompt in the work of defamation, but lacks the "long memory" with which, according to the proverb, it ought to be provided. Here is a specimen of its efforts yesterday:

"Patriots will remember that when Judge Woodward was running for the Governorship of our State, it was openly asserted by the Democracy that, should he be elected, no Union troops should pass to the front through New York or Pennsylvania; that Seymour and Woodward would throttle the Government and end the war."

Not the Democracy but the knaves who libeled them spoke thus; and in doing so, gave the best help they could to the rebellion, in flattering it with false hopes of Northern sympathy. It was by deeds, not words, that the Democracy repelled that lie. When the *Press* uttered it, in 1863, the streets of our city were glistening with the bayonets of regiments sent to the front to defend Pennsylvania, sent from New Jersey and New York, by Horatio Seymour, and by Joel Parker, the Democratic Governors of those States. Governor Curtin was in a condition of hopeless inefficiency. It was his party in this city who were slow to hear his call for troops. George W. Woodward seconded it manfully, when many a blatant Radical was dumb with terror. The candidate of the Democracy, with all his sons in the field, Judge Woodward, issued this stirring appeal, in a letter addressed to the Chairman of the Democratic State Central Committee, and published throughout the State: "There ought to be such an instant uprising of young men in response to this call (Governor Curtin's, of July 26), as shall be sufficient to insure the public safety, and to teach the world that no hostile foot can with impunity tread the soil of Pennsylvania (June 29, 1863)." Few can have forgotten the condition of things in this city, from which the opportune victory of Gettysburg relieved it. It can not be better portrayed than by citing the public speech, made at that crisis by Governor Curtin, from the Continental Hotel, on the first day of July, 1863.

"If General Meade's army is defeated, which God forbid, I need not say to intelligent Pennsylvanians what is next to occur. Military men have concurred in the opinion, and properly, that the defense of Pennsylvania from invasion—certainly of the city—will be found upon the banks of the Susquehanna; and certainly it is pleasant for me to announce that the call made upon the people of Pennsylvania has been responded to all through the State in a manner much beyond all official anticipation, and now from her mountains and valleys, from the homes and public works, our loyal and devoted Pennsylvanians are on their way to the place of rendezvous, and will soon be in arms to protect you on the banks of her great river. I ask for seven thousand eight hundred men from this city. How soon can I get them? Do not measure them by days, let it be hours. * * * *We asked for help from New York—it has come.* We asked for help from New Jersey—it has come. New England will respond; but first let us show that we are true to our honor and protect ourselves."—*Ledger, July 2, 1863.*

Here is a part of the record of Horatio Seymour, in the facts of history, from the lips of the Republican Governor: "*We asked for help from New York and it has come.*" We thank the *Press* for uttering a calumny which we can nail to the counter with the strong, sure blows of truth. The exuberant expressions of gratitude which Mr. Lincoln sent to Governor Seymour for his energy and patriotism, we reserve for another time. We have given the Radicals to day some of the facts of history—let them try to rail them off the record.

New York Riots—Responsibility Therefor
GOVERNOR SEYMOUR'S ACTION APPLAUDED BY THE RADICALS.

In 1863 a draft was ordered in the State of New York, by the Federal Government, to fall principally on the nine Democratic Congressional Districts of New York, and not based upon any just apportionment of the numbers throughout the State. It was a partisan arrangement to conscript Democrats, and to exempt Radicals. Governor Seymour, in a dignified but cordial spirit, called the attention of Mr. Lincoln to the injustice of the arrangement. Mr. Lincoln would do nothing to remedy the outrage. Governor Seymour addressed him a letter which so fully develops the injustice of the scheme of draft that we publish it here as an intelligent account of the whole matter. Though it is of date subsequent to the riots, it forms an appropriate introduction to an account of them, giving as it does a true history of their provoking cause:

ALBANY, August 8, 1863.
To the President of the United States:

I received your communication of the 7th instant to-day. While I recognize the concessions you make, I regret your refusal to comply with my request to have the draft in this State suspended until it can be ascertained if the enrollments are made in accordance with the law of Congress or with the principles of justice. I know that our army needs recruits; and for this and other reasons I regret a decision which stands in the way of a prompt and cheerful movement to fill up the thinned ranks of our regiments. New York has never paused in its efforts to send volunteers to the assistance of our gallant soldiers in the field. It has not only met every call heretofore made, while every other Atlantic and the New England States, except Rhode Island, were delinquent, but it continued liberal bounties to volunteers when all efforts were suspended in many other quarters. Active exertions are now made to organize the new and fill up the old regiments. These exertions would be more successful if the draft were suspended, and much better men than reluctant conscripts would join our armies.

On the 7th instant I advised you by letter that I would furnish the strongest proof of the injustice, if not fraud, in the enrollment in certain districts. I now send you a full report made to me by Judge Advocate Waterbury. I am confident, when you have read it, that you will agree with me that the honor of the nation and of your administration demands that the abuse it points out should be corrected and punished.

You say that we are contending with an enemy who, as you understand, "drives every able bodied man he can reach into the ranks, very much as a butcher drives bullocks into a slaughter pen." You will agree with me that even this, if impartially done to all classes, is more tolerable than any scheme which shall fraudulently force a portion of the community into military service by a dishonest perversion of the law.

You will see by the report of Mr. Waterbury that here is no theory which can explain or justify the enrollment in this State. I wish to call your attention to the tables on pages 5, 6, 7, and 8, which show that in nine Congressional districts, in Manhattan, Long and Staten Islands, the number of conscripts called for is thirty-three thousand seven hundred and twenty nine, while in nineteen other districts the number of conscripts called for is only thirty-nine thousand and six hundred and twenty-six. The draft is to be made from the first-class, those between the ages of twenty and thirty-five. It appears by the census of 1860 that in the first nine Congressional districts there were 164,797 males between twenty and thirty-five; they are called upon for 33,729 conscripts. In the other nineteen districts, with a population of males between twenty and thirty-five, of 270,786, only 39,626 are demanded. Again, to show the partisan character of the enrollment, you will find on the twenty first page of the military report that in the first nine Congressional districts the total vote of 1860 was 151,243; the number of conscripts now demanded is 33,729. In the nineteen other districts the total vote was 457,257; yet these districts are called upon to furnish only 39,626 drafted men. Each of the nine districts gave majorities in favor of one political party, and each of the nineteen districts gave majorities in favor of the other party.

You can not and will not fail to right these gross wrongs. Yours, truly,

HORATIO SEYMOUR.

The riots were excited by this partisan draft, which Governor Seymour so thoroughly sifts in his preceding letter to Mr. Lincoln, written at the close of the correspondence which the excitement and difficulty had made necessary. "When," says the New York *World*, of the 21st of July, referring to Governor Seymour's course in connection with the battle of Gettysburg, "New York had generously stripped herself of all her means of preserving local order, prudence and gratitude alike dictated that the Federal authorities should do nothing during the absence of our militia calculated to kindle the inflammable passions of a vast city. It was well known to the Administration that the conscription was odious, and no attempt should have been made to enforce it until after the return of our local troops. A few weeks' delay would have made no real difference to the Government; and the fact that our militia regiments were then serving at the seat of war might in equity have been accepted as a temporary substitute for drafted men. But no! It was in that critical conjuncture, it was when the city was thus stripped and defenseless, that the Secretary of War thought fit to fling in firebrands, by enforcing, just in that dangerous crisis, the odious conscription by which poor men were to be dragged away from their weeping families, while the rich were to be excused, and let off on the payment of $300. It was reckless tyranny, it was fiendish madness, to select such a moment for enforcing the draft. Justice, prudence, fairness, gratitude, common sense, all forbade this rash experiment on the inflammable temper of the multitude, when their passions were so combustible and the means of repression had been generously given away at the urgent call of the Government. The riots were thus the direct consequence of thankless insolence and blundering tyranny at Washington."

It was on the 13th of July that the riot broke out in New York. On the 14th of July Governor Seymour reached the city from Albany, issued a proclamation that the city and county were in a state of insurrection, the form of law necessary to such an exercise of power having been complied with. On the same day he issued an address to the people of the city, in which he informed them that riotous proceedings must and should be put down. The official documents speak for themselves:

To the people of the City of New York:

A riotous demonstration in your city, originating in opposition to the conscription of soldiers for the military service of the United States, has swelled into vast proportions, directing its fury against the property and lives of peaceful citizens. I know that many of those who have participated in these proceedings would not have allowed themselves to be carried to such extremes of violence and wrong, except under an apprehension of injustice; but such persons are reminded that *the only opposition to the conscription which can be allowed is an appeal to the courts.*

The right of every citizen to make such an appeal will be maintained, and the decisions of courts must be respected and obeyed by rulers and people alike. No other course is consistent with the maintenance of the laws, the peace and order of the city, and the safety of its inhabitants.

Riotous proceedings must, and shall be put down. The laws of the State of New York must be enforced, its peace and order maintained, and the lives and property of all its citizens protected at any and every hazard. The rights of every citizen will be properly guarded and defended by the Chief Magistrate of the State.

I do therefore call upon all persons engaged in these riotous proceedings to retire to their homes and employments, declaring to them that unless they do at once, I shall use all the power necessary to restore the peace and order of the city I also call upon all well-disposed persons not enrolled for the preservation of order to pursue their ordinary avocations.

Let all citizens stand firmly by the constituted authorities, sustaining law and order in the city, and ready to answer any such demand as circumstances may render necessary for me to make upon their services; *and they may rely upon a rigid enforcement of the laws of this State against all who violate them.*

HORATIO SEYMOUR.

NEW YORK, July 14, 1863. Governor.

The other document, issued on the day of his arrival, was the following proclamation, declaring the city and county in a state of insurrection:

Whereas, It is manifest that combinations for forcible resistance to the laws of the State of New York, and to the execution of civil and criminal process, exist in the City and County of New York, whereby the peace and safety of the city, and the lives and property of its inhabitants are endangered; and

Whereas, The power of the said city and county has been exerted, and is not sufficient to enable the officers of the said city and county to maintain the laws of the State, and execute the legal process of its officers; and

Whereas, Application has been made to me by the Sheriff of the City and County of New York, to declare the said city and county to be in a state of insurrection;

Now, therefore, I, Horatio Seymour, Governor of the State of New York, and Commander-in-chief of the forces of the same, do in its name, and by its authority, issue this proclamation, in accordance with the statute in such cases made and provided, and *do hereby declare the City and County of New York to be in a state of insurrection, and give notice to all persons that the means provided by the laws of this State for the maintenance of law and order will be employed to whatever degree may be necessary, and that all persons who shall, after the publication of this proclamation, assist, or aid and assist in resisting any force ordered out by the Governor, to quell or suppress such insurrection, will render themselves liable to the penalties prescribed by law.* HORATIO SEYMOUR.

NEW YORK, July 14, 1863.

At about 12 o'clock on the 14th, says the *World*, a large crowd was listening about the *Tribune* office to a man who was haranguing them, inciting an attack on the *Tribune* building. At that moment, Governor Seymour appearing on the steps of the City Hall, they ran over, joined those in the Park, and to the loud cries of "Seymour, Seymour," the Governor responded. He said, "My friends;" what should he have said? There were no rioters before him; there was a mass of excited laboring men, believing that the draft was illegal, or if not illegal, inequitable and unjust. What was the exact way to talk to such men? First, to tell them that he had sent his Adjutant to Washington to see that their rights should be protected. Second, to tell them to act as good citizens and secure safety to property and person.

Now, why did the mob temporarily get the upper-hand? Mayor Opdyke, whom Republicans can believe, proclaimed, July 15, that the riot "would not have interrupted the peace for a day but for the temporary absence of all our organized local militia." Now let us see how the riot affected military operations. On the night of the 13th, Lee crossed the Potomac and Meade did not pursue. Now let us turn to a venerable memory. Archbishop Hughes, on the 17th, addressed an assemblage. He began—"They call you rioters." He proceeded to tell them that he was their father. What kind of language was that? Was it wise or foolish? The Archbishop had lived long enough to know that, in addressing an excited body of men maddened with a real or fancied grievance, you soothe if you wish quiet, you denounce if you wish fight.

THANKS OF THE NEW YORK LEGISLATURE TO SEYMOUR.

The Legislature, April 16, 1864, passed unanimously the following resolutions:

Resolved, That the thanks of this House be, and are hereby, tendered to his Excellency, Governor Seymour, for calling the attention of the General Government at Washington to the errors in the apportionment of the quota of this State, under the enrollment act of March 3, 1863, and for his prompt and efficient efforts in procuring a correction of the same.

Resolved, That the Clerk of this House transmit to the Governor a copy of this report and resolutions.

Governor Seymour did all he could to suppress this riot. We have Radical testimony to this effect which can not be disputed. We allude to George Opdyke, then the Republican Mayor of New York, and now a leading supporter of Hiram Grant. Mr. Opdyke said of Governor Seymour, in his official letter of July 13, 1863:

"* * * As Governor of the State and Commander in-chief of its military forces, he superseded me in authority over the State militia, commanded by General Sanford; but General Wool, commanding the United States military forces, continued to regard himself as under my immediate directions, subject, of course, to the approval of his own military judgment and to the commands of his superiors at Washington. *It affords me pleasure to add, however, that among all those in authority no diversity of sentiment manifested itself.* ALL CO-OPERATED IN EARNEST EFFORTS *to restore the wonted peace and quiet of the city by the earliest possible suppression of the outbreak.*"

Shortly after 12 M., I sent the following telegram to the Secretary of War:

"MAYOR'S OFFICE, NEW YORK, July 14, 1863.
"Hon. EDWIN M. STANTON, Secretary of War:

"*Sir:* Your dispatch received. Demonstrations very threatening. Governor Seymour is with us, and all the authorities, United States, State and city, are co-operating in efforts to suppress them. But our military force at command is altogether inadequate. If you can render any assistance, by sending a military force, please do so. I will keep you advised.

"GEORGE OPDYKE, Mayor."

From a later letter, at the close of the riot, we quote the following:

"*Party interests and prejudices were ignored by them; their action was united and harmonious; the riot was speedily suppressed;* and, considering the magnitude of the danger and the slenderness of our means of resistance, with extraordinary exemption from loss of life and property. In all my efforts I was ably and steadfastly seconded by those heads of the city departments who may be regarded as the representatives of the Democratic party, Street Commissioner Cornell, Controller Brennan, City Inspector Boole, Supervisors Tweed, Blunt and Purdy, and William H. Armstrong, Esq., of the Mayor's office, were faithful and courageous advisers."

That disposes of the draft lie.

Prominent among the Radical journals engaged in giving vitality to this slander, is the Albany *Evening Journal*, the central organ of the Radical party of New York. What the *Evening Journal* now charges against Governor Seymour, it distinctly denied four years ago, when the events were fresh in the public mind, and when the *Journal* had no object or interest but to tell the truth. See what the *Journal* says now, and what it said then:

[From the *Albany Evening Journal*, July 13, 1868.]
Then came the riots. Seymour went down there. Had it been Andrew Jackson, instead, there would have been no palaver with the bloody criminals. He would have dispersed them by some other method, than by promising them all they asked. * * * Look at the scene. Rebel armies mustering; rebel conscripts hastening to the field; rebel energies gathering. On the other hand: a bleeding Union, a palsied army, brave and daring, but reduced. A nation calls for help. It decrees assistance. A yelping crew, filled with the spirit of rebellion, thirsty for blood, fired with rage, resist their country's pleas and demands, and assail the officers of the nation and the innocent poor of their city. What does Horatio Seymour do? Does he point them to the obligations of the citizen, the dangers of the nation, and the imperiled brethren of the army? Not at all.

[From the *Albany Evening Journal*, in July, 1863.]
Governor Seymour, in so PROMPTLY "DECLARING THE CITY IN A STATE OF INSURRECTION," contributed largely to the suppression of the mob. It gave immediate legal efficiency to the military arm, and enabled the civil authorities to use that power with terrible effect. IT SHOWED, ALSO, THAT IT WAS GOVERNOR SEYMOUR'S PURPOSE TO GIVE "NO QUARTER" TO THE RUFFIANS who seized upon the occasion of a popular excitement, to rob and murder. The exercise of the power thus called into service was effective. The "insurrection" has been quelled. THE MOB HAS BEEN OVERPOWERED. LAW and order have TRIUMPHED, and the RIOTOUSLY DISPOSED every-where have RECEIVED A LESSON WHICH THEY WILL NOT SOON FORGET.

The following communication, in regard to the conduct of Governor Seymour during the New York riots of 1863, is from a gentleman who was in the employ of the Telegraph Company at the time, and who speaks from personal knowledge when he refutes the foul calumnies started by Radical journals on this subject:

CINCINNATI, July 21, 1868.

To the Editors of the Enquirer:

The Radical papers of this and other cities seem to find in the July (1863) riots of New York a sweet morsel for rolling under their tongues, when all other subjects for vituperation of Governor Seymour fail.

* * * * *

The position which I held at the time, in New York State, gives me the opportunity of making a statement in contradiction of these charges, which, if necessary, can be verified by several gentlemen, Republicans and Democrats, who were associated with me at the time.

It is well known that among the first acts of the rioters was the destruction of all, or nearly all, the telegraph lines leading from the city to the Capital at Albany, thus hoping to cut off means of communication between the Governor and the municipal authorities from the Adjutant-General's office in Albany, from whence orders for the movement of troops would be issued. Every wire was cut, the polls thrown down for a great distance through the streets, with the single exception of one wire connecting Jersey City with New York, through a cable unknown to the mob. This wire was owned by the Erie Railroad, and intended for their business alone.

Governor Seymour took possession of this line, and, in the language of telegraphers, kept it red-hot for three days and nights, transmitting orders for his Adjutant-General by the circuitous route from Jersey City *via* Binghampton to Utica, New York, and from thence back to Albany, for the organization and immediate marching orders of a sufficient force of State militia to quell the disturbance. In a very short time companies and regiments were formed and sent forward without delay, many of them composed, in part or wholly, of the "brutal Irishmen" that haunt our Radical friends' slumbers. Every thing that was possible was done with the limited and uncertain means of communication in the hands of the Governor.

While the Republican Mayor, Opdyke, was trembling in his shoes behind the City Hall doors, Governor Seymour, alone and unprotected, stood manfully forth, and by the use of calm words recalled the insane rioters to a sense of their duty as citizens, promising them that their claims should be heard, and their wrongs, if any existed, should be righted. His cool manner and earnest assurances of his intention to investigate any grounds they had for complaint, had the effect of quieting the passions of a populace in a manner that could not have been done by three times their number of armed men.

Yet these Radical papers, from behind their breastworks of print-paper with coffee-mill rifles for defense, set up a howl of rage because this one man did not stand there and denounce the rioters as thieves, cutthroats, murderers, incendiaries and such like invectives.

The effect of such language upon a mass of people excited to feelings worse than insanity itself, by real or imaginary wrongs, would have been like adding fuel to the fire. Numerous were the verbal and written expressions of gratitude received from the citizens of New York for his efforts in quelling the riot, prominent among them the names of gentlemen who, though they differed from him in political views, yet had the manliness to express their thanks and appreciation of efforts which were and are continually being denied by those who knew nothing of the facts, or perverted what they did know.

The citizens of Central New York, regardless of politics, know and respect Horatio Seymour as a Christian gentleman, against whom charges of complicity in, and encouragement of, riotism and mob-law, rebound to the injury of the authors of such falsehoods.

After the fall of Vicksburg, when the Eastern troops were being sent home *via* the New York Central Railroad, dying by the score on the route for want of proper food, rest and medical attendance, Governor Seymour and his brother, the Hon. John F. Seymour, while returning from a Missionary Sunday-school, near Utica, one Sabbath evening, suggested to the writer of this article, and some other friends, that the soldiers be fed and cared for on their passage through the city. The idea was acted upon at once. In two hours a regiment was expected. Mr. Seymour made a detail to solicit contributions of food, coffee, tea, wines, cordials, etc., for the soldiers, and by the time the regiment arrived, more than sufficient was collected to feed and refresh the worn-out and haggard-looking men. Several were taken from the train and cared for in the city until they recovered, at Mr. Seymour's expense. This impromptu suggestion led to the formation of a society, with Mr. Seymour at its head, that provided refreshments and medical care for twenty-five or thirty regiments from Maine, New Hampshire, Connecticut, Rhode Island, and other States.

Mr. John F. Seymour, a gentleman of the same political opinions as his brother, was State Agent for New York in the Army of the Potomac during the war, and by his care and attention to the soldiers in that army, gained for himself and the State authorities manifold blessings from the thousands whose lives were saved and health regained by his personal devotion to their wants. Hundreds of mothers and children bless him from their hearts for restoring to their lives and homes the only ones whom they had to care for and protect them; and yet, he, like his brother, was called a Copperhead, traitor, and rebel sympathizer, by the Radicals, because he dared to differ from the powers that were, in political views. Out upon such Pharisees! Their only counterparts were the rabble of Pontius Pilate, who, not knowing, or knowing, did not trust in their Redeemer, but cried, "Crucify him!" "Crucify him!"

Yours, J. J. F.

Governor Seymour's Record as a Union Man.

DIALOGUE BETWEEN AN EX-CONFEDERATE AND A RADICAL.

A violent ex-Confederate surprised his hearers the other day in New York by exclaiming: If this supporting of Horatio Seymour don't show me to be more reconstructed than ever I expected to be, then I will be d—d.

A Radical standing by asked: How is that?

Why, says the Confederate, I was an original secessionist. My heart was in the cause. I was early to go into the war and late to go out of it. I was wounded twice in the struggle, and yet here I am in New York, for the sake of peace and quiet, supporting a man for the Presidency who denounced the movement of the South as a most wicked rebellion.

Radical. I guess not. He was on your side all the time, and I am not surprised that you are for him. He was a Copperhead—an anti-War Democrat.

Ex-Confederate. Well, if he was anti-War, I should like to know what being for the war is.

Radical. You can not point out where he ever aided it by act or word. He was an open enemy of the 'loyal' cause.

Ex-Confederate. Just listen to this, and then answer me if I have not become very loyal to hurrah for such a man. Here is what he said at the meeting of the State Military Association in January, 1862:

We denounce the rebellion as most wicked because it wages war against the best Government the world has ever seen. There is guilt in negligence as well as in disobedience, and there is danger, too. We complain that the arms of the General Government were heretofore unequally distributed. This was owing in part to the treasonable purposes of officials, but it is due in part to our own neglect of our constitutional duties. Our enrolled militia should count more than five hundred thousand, but they do not exceed one-half of that number. Hence our quota of arms was diminished, and that of the Southern States increased. The want of these arms and a proper military organi-

zation has added immensely to the cost of this war, and to the burdens of taxation. More than this, if we had respected our constitutional obligation we might at the outset *have placed in the field a force that would have put out this rebellion when it was first kindled.*

Radical. This is the first time I ever heard that speech.

Ex-Confederate. Why, did he not say, in his message of June 9, 1863, "Under no circumstances can the division of the Union be conceded."

Radical. No, did he?

Ex-Confederate. Why, yes, and at Utica, in 1861, he said in an address to his townsmen :

We owe our duties to our Government. We must strengthen our armies and furnish it with means to conduct this war to a successful issue. The day has gone by for efforts to avert it. When the American people refuse to live together in the spirit of the Constitution, when they reject all adjustment of controversies, they make the sword the only arbiter. Consistency demands that we who strove to avert the war, should now strive to make it productive of those ends which we sought to reach by peaceful measures. All theories of Government, that of centralization, or that of State rights, requires that we should *stand by the standard of our Government and the standards of our State in the battle-field.*

Radical. Why, Greeley has been lying on Seymour. That is good war talk.

Ex-Confederate. Well, then, just listen to his speech in 1862, in which he said :

To-day we are putting forth our utmost efforts to reinforce our armies in the field. Without conditions or threats we are exerting our energies to strengthen the hands of the Government and to replace it in the commanding position in which it can either propose peace or conduct successful war. And this support is freely and generously accorded. We wish to see our Union saved, our laws vindicated, and peace once more restored to our land.

Radical. Somebody must have been imposing on you.

Ex Confederate. No, he spoke every word I have read. In addition to that, he aided personally in raising a company for the war. Hear to what he said in a speech in New York, October 13, 1862 :

I was gratified that while I was in a remote part of the great West it was in my power to promote the formation of a company of as bold and as sturdy men as ever rallied in defense of our country's flag. I recall with pride their array when drawn up before my lodgings; they expressed, through their commander, their good will toward myself, and their obligations for such assistance as I had been able to give them.

Radical. Well, I must confess that this looks like he was a good Union man.

Ex-Confederate. I should say it did ; and do you not think that our desire to harmonize and reconstruct is sincere, when a man with my antecedents supports Seymour, with such a war record. But what I have read is not all, here is some more of the same sort. Just listen to what he said in a speech in New York, in 1862.

Now, when the men of the South make the bayonet and the sword the arbiter (they elected and not we), when they determined to settle it with blood, and not we—the sword, so far as the present is concerned, must be the arbiter; and in our strong arms it shall make vigorous and strong blows for the life of our country, for its institutions, and for the flag. Now, let me say this to the higher law men of the North, and to the higher law men of the South, and to the whole world that looks on, witnesses to the mighty events transpiring in this country, that this Union shall never be severed—no, never. Whatever other men may say, as for the conservative people of this country, and as for myself as an individual—let other men say and think what they please—as for the division of this Union and the breaking up of that great natural alliance which is made by nature and by nature's God, I never will consent to it—no, never, as long as I have a voice to raise or a hand to fight for this, our native land.

Radical. Well, if I have not had my eyes opened wonderfully. What else is that you have got?

Ex-Confederate. Some more of the same sort, listen : on the the 8th of October, 1862, Hon. Hiram Ketchum addressed the following letter to Governor Seymour :

HON. HORATIO SEYMOUR:

Sir—I take the liberty of sending you the inclosed article, signed by my name, and which expresses my views, without consulting with any political organization whatever, upon the duty, and sole duty of the Government of the United States at this time, which is TO SUPPRESS THE REBELLION

BY THE MILITARY FORCE OF THE COUNTRY BY THE MOST VIGOROUS MEASURES POSSIBLE. I should be pleased to know from yourself wherein these views meet your approval, and wherein you dissent from them. I have the honor to be, very respectfully, your obedient servant and fellow citizen,

HIRAM KETCHUM.

To which Governor Seymour replied:

NEW YORK, October 14, 1862.

DEAR SIR—I have read with great pleasure your letter published in the *Journal of Commerce*. Although the questions you put to Congressional candidates are not addressed to me, I wish to express my satisfaction with your able and clear statement of the great questions upon which the people are to decide at this election. I have already spoken at length upon the topics of your communication. The limits of a letter will not allow me to state my views as I have already done in my published speeches. I SHALL, THEREFORE, ONLY SAY THAT I CORDIALLY CONCUR IN YOUR VIEWS.

Yours truly,
HORATIO SEYMOUR.

In a speech in 1862, Governor Seymour said:

Let us confront the truths of our national position. We must accept the facts as they stand. Overlooking all the past, we find the armed strength of the Government and of the rebellion engaged in deadly conflict. The sword is now the arbiter. Not only are the ranks of the armies arrayed for the defense of our flag filled by our friends and relatives, but *we know that upon the results of battles hang the destinies of our country. Its greatness, its prosperity, its glory, are poised upon the turn of the conflict.*

In his Message of 1864, Governor Seymour said:

We must seek to restore the Union and to uphold the Constitution. To this end—while we put forth every exertion of material power to beat down armed rebellion—we must use every influence of wise statesmanship to bring back the States which now reject their constitutional obligations.

Here is an extract from a message appointing a day of fasting, August 4, 1864:

Let us repent of our manifold sins and offenses, and humbly pray that Almighty God will put down all rebellious resistance to rightful authority, all sectional hatred, all bigotry and malice, all hurtful ambition or partisan purposes which tend to discord and strife. That He will restore the Union of our States, and fraternal affection between the inhabitants thereof, and give peace to our land. Acknowledging the justice of His punishments upon us for our national and personal sins, let us entreat Him to have mercy upon us, to turn away His wrath, to stop the shedding of blood, to return our soldiers to their homes, to relieve the sick, wounded and suffering, to comfort those in mourning, to reward the industry of our people to relieve them from heavy burdens, to make them safe in their persons and homes from all violence and oppression, and to give the protection of law to all conditions of men. To these ends let us pray that God will give wisdom to our rulers, purity to our legislators, uprightness and boldness to our judges, meekness and charity to our clergy, and virtue, intelligence, and godliness to our people.

Radical.—You need not read any more. I am satisfied that Governor Seymour was as good a war man as there was. I can not conceive how it is that I have been the dupe of a different impression all this time, unless it is that the New York *Tribune* is the only paper that I read.

Francis Preston Blair, Jr.

[From the New York Herald.]

The gallant soldier and statesman who has been nominated for the office of Vice-President of the United States by the National Democratic Convention, and who will certainly fill that office, was born in the quaint old town of Lexington, Kentucky, February 19, 1821, and is now in his forty-eighth year. In his twentieth year he graduated at Princeton College, and removed to St. Louis, Missouri, and there began the study of law, in which profession he made rapid progress. In 1845, being then in his twenty-fifth year, he made a journey to the Rocky Mountains with a party of trappers for the improvement of his health, which had failed somewhat, owing to close pursuit of his studies; and on the breaking out of the Mexican war Blair joined the force under Kearney and the gallant Doniphan in New Mexico, and served as a private soldier until 1847, when he returned to St. Louis and resumed the practice of his profession. In 1848, like his father, Francis P. Blair, sr., he gave his support to the Free Soil party, and in a speech delivered at the Court-house in St. Louis, contended against the extension of slavery into the Territories of the nation. In 1852 he was elected from St. Louis county, Missouri, to the Legislature as an avowed Free Soiler, and he was re-elected in 1854, though Thomas H. Benton, the Congressional candidate of the Free Soilers, was beaten. In 1856 Mr. Blair was returned to Congress, from the St. Louis district, over Mr. Kennett, who had defeated Colonel Benton two years before. In 1857 he delivered an elaborate speech in the House of Representatives in favor of colonizing the black population of the United States in Central America. Mr. Blair was also an editor and writer on the Missouri *Democrat* at one time. The father of General Blair was a firm and fast friend of Andrew Jackson; the General, when a child, was wont to play on the knees of Andrew Jackson in the White House. His father was at that time editor of the *Globe*, in Washington. In 1860 Mr. Blair contested the seat in Congress of Mr. Barrett, from the St. Louis district, but did not get it, and soon after was returned to the House, after which he resigned his seat. In 1860 General Blair made a speech in Brooklyn in favor of Mr. Lincoln for the Presidency, and also delivered a speech at the Metropolitan Hotel, in this city, in June, 1861, in favor of strong war measures, hinting that General Scott was rather a slow campaigner. Mr. Blair was very assiduous in raising volunteers in St. Louis, and was the first volunteer of the State of Missouri. He raised the First Regiment of Missouri Volunteers, and acted as its Colonel, albeit he did not hold a commission as Colonel of the regiment. A difficulty arose between Colonel Blair and General Fremont, and Colonel Blair was unjustly placed under arrest by that officer, who was commander of that department. This arbitrary measure of General Fremont's aroused great excitement in St. Louis, where General Blair was universally known and respected, the journals of that city taking part in the quarrel at the time. President Lincoln ordered Colonel Blair to be released from arrest in September, 1861, thereby causing a great feeling of relief to the numerous friends of Colonel Blair in St. Louis. He was again arrested by General Fremont, but finally released after considerable trouble, and newspaper discussion by both parties. Colonel Blair rapidly rose as a soldier and became one of the most skillful Generals in the Western armies. On the 22d of May, 1862, General Blair commanded a division in Sherman's attack on Vicksburg. The brigades of Ewing, Smith, and Kilby Smith, composed his division. Frank Blair had the honor of leading the attack in person, five batteries concentrating their guns on the rebel position. The attack was terrific, and was repulsed. As the head of the column passed over the parapet a dense fire of musketry swept away all its leading files. The rear of the column attempted to rush on, but were driven back. Here, by the bad management of Grant, Blair was not supported, as the supporting division were too far away to give him assistance. At the capture of Vicksburg, Blair's division participated, and did the heaviest fighting in Sherman's command. It was at this time that Grant pronounced Frank Blair to be the best volunteer General in the United States Army, an opinion that was fully sustained by his conduct in action and his judgment as a campaigner. In the great march of Sherman to the sea, General Frank P. Blair commanded the Seventeenth Army Corps, the finest corps in the whole army. He crossed the Ogeechee near Barton, and captured the first prisoners. His division laid pontoons across the river, and the two wings were thus united before Savannah. His division was the first to march into Savannah. From Savannah the Fourteenth Corps was taken by water to Pocotaligo, whence it threatened Charleston, while Slocum, with the Twentieth Corps and Kilpatrick's cavalry marched up the Augusta to Sister Ferry, threatening an advance on Savannah at Tallahatchie. Blair waded through a swamp three miles wide with water four feet deep, the weather being bitter cold. Here the Seventeenth had another fight and lost a number of killed and wounded, but drove the Confederates behind the Edisto, at Branchville. The army then directed its march on Orangeburg. Here the Seventeenth carried the bridge over the South Edisto by a gallant dash, Blair leading his men, as usual, up to the battery's mouth, which was covered by a parapet of cotton and earth extending as far as could be seen. Blair threw Smith's division in front, while his other division crossed below and carried the bridge after a hard fight. A half a dozen men of Blair's corps were the first to enter Columbia. The Seventeenth Corps, however, were not guilty of the burning of this city, as has been charged. At the battle of Bentonville, N. C., on the march up to Richmond, the Seventeenth were engaged heavily.

It is not necessary to go further into detail of the glorious services of General Blair. The *Missouri Democrat* (Radical) of July 6, 1861, referring to his absence from St. Louis at that time, said:

The lack of Colonel Blair's energetic spirit has been apparent in every attempt at progress made since he left for Washington. In the absence of Col. Blair the General (Lyon) lacks a strong right hand. The adroitness and facility with which he grasped the State then reeling under secession influence, and pinned the star with increasing firmness to the constellation of the Union, will in due time cause grateful recollections to spring up in the breast of every honest, loyal citizen. Turn which way we will we can find no one who contributed more successfully to this great object than Colonel Blair.

As soon, says the New York *Herald* (a Grant paper) of July 10, 1868, as the war was over and General Blair perceived that the people of the South were honestly disposed to abide the result of the conflict in good faith, he urged a liberal and generous treatment of the ex-rebels. At first he continued his connection with the Republican party, and endeavored to change its course in his State to a policy of conservatism. The Legislature of Missouri had passed a law disfranchising all who participated in or gave aid and comfort to the rebellion, and another law requiring all the citizens of the State to take a test oath. Both of these measures were opposed by General Blair as proscriptive and unconstitutional. He urged that, the war being over, there was no need of any further rigor toward the men who had engaged in rebellion, and regarded it as dangerous to the peace and prosperity of the State to deprive them of the right to vote. With regard to the test oath he absolutely refused to subscribe to it, and upon presenting himself at the polls in St. Louis his vote was refused for that reason. For this act he brought a suit before the courts for the purpose of testing the constitutionality of the law. The case is now before the Supreme Court of the United States, and is not yet decided. Gradually General Blair severed his connection with the Republican party, after having been a member of that organization from its incipiency. When the present Reconstruction laws of Congress were passed he denounced them as despotic, revolutionary and unconstitutional, and declared that the people of the South would not be in the wrong if they resisted their execution. He opposed, with great earnestness, the policy of universal negro suffrage as a disgrace and an outrage upon the people, and in a recent letter declared that the first duty of a Democratic President, if elected, would be to overthrow the present Radical governments in the South and restore the States to the rule of the whites. This declaration of his has been severely commented upon by the Radical organs.

General Blair's military reputation has gained him considerable popularity in the West, and particularly among the late Union soldiers in that section of the country.

General Blair's war on the Test Oath, referred to in the preceding article, is eminently characteristic of his earnest character as a man and his integrity as a statesman. He pursued it and the party which was the parent of the proscription, though he had theretofore acted with it, with all the restless energy of his nature, and the uncompromising firmness of his antagonism. He fought it at the polls in the presence of elements of violence which might easily be turned upon him. In courts of lower degree, as in the higher tribunals of the State, he engaged it despite the opposition of partisan judges and the fierce defense which it invoked from Radical advocates. In the Supreme Court of the United States, where it now reposes for a final determination, it was the recipient of his sturdiest and most effective blows.

The persecution of the Catholic priesthood, in Missouri, with this test oath, enlisted an opposition from General Blair no less zealous than that which his own individual case had aroused into exercise. In the case of the State v. Father Cummings, he rendered great assistance to the defense of this pious, persecuted priest, which finally resulted in a decision by the Supreme Court of the United States in favor of Father Cummings, which may be found in another part of this book. Thus this high tribunal, though it has not yet decided General Blair's individual case, has determined the application of the test oath to the Roman Catholic clergy of Missouri to have been an outrage, and has vindicated in one of its most material aspects the noble stand taken by General Blair on this question. A beautiful commentary upon the existence of Radical power anywhere, is furnished by the proscription of General Blair in Missouri from the exercise of the elective franchise. It presents the figure of a gallant soldier who, for four years, periled his all upon the dangerous hazard of battle in a war waged, it was said, for the Union, and who is now the candidate of the majority party in the country for the second office in their gift, driven from the polls as a voter by the proscriptive tests of Radicalism, against subscribing which his proud spirit revolts, and which his chivalric manhood determines him to spurn.

General Blair has in him all the pa

triotic elements calculated to enlist Radical antagonism in its most violent forms in the present canvass. He will be, as he has already been, the target of the fiercest assaults, and the undismayed object of its most refined and slanderous detraction. His pen has more terrors for them than an army with bayonets, unless that army has General Blair at its head, a fear which their cowardly apprehensions have already excited, and in which they pretend to be justified by what they call the revolutionary and bloody character of the following letter:

WASHINGTON, June 30.

Colonel James O. Broadhead:

DEAR COLONEL—In reply to your inquiries, I beg leave to say that I leave you to determine, on consultation with my friends from Missouri, whether my name shall be presented to the Democratic Convention, and to submit the following as what I consider the real and only issue in this contest: The Reconstruction policy of the Radicals will be complete before the next election; the States so long excluded will have been admitted; negro suffrage established, and the carpet-baggers installed in their seats in both branches of Congress. There is no possibility of changing the political character of the Senate, even if the Democrats should elect their President and a majority of the popular branch of Congress. We can not, therefore, undo the Radical plan of Reconstruction by Congressional action; the Senate will continue a bar to its repeal. Must we submit to it? How can it be overthrown? It can only be overthrown by the authority of the Executive, who is sworn to maintain the Constitution, and who will fail to do his duty if he allows the Constitution to perish under a series of Congressional enactments which are in palpable violation of its fundamental principles.

If the President elected by the Democracy enforces or permits others to enforce these Reconstruction acts, the Radicals, by the accession of twenty spurious Senators and fifty Representatives, will control both branches of Congress, and his administration will be as powerless as the present one of Mr. Johnson.

There is but one way to restore the Government and the Constitution, and that is for *the President-elect to declare these acts null and void, compel the army to undo its usurpations at the South, disperse the carpet-bag State governments, allow the white people to reorganize their own governments, and elect Senators and Representatives.* The House of Representatives will contain a majority of Democrats from the North, and they will admit the Representatives elected by the white people of the South, and with the co-operation of the President, it will not be difficult to compel the Senate to submit once more to the obligations of the Constitution. It will not be able to withstand the public judgment, if distinctly invoked and clearly expressed, on this fundamental issue, and it is the sure way to avoid all future strife to put this issue plainly to the country.

I repeat that this is the real and only question which we should allow to control us: Shall we submit to the usurpations by which the Government has been overthrown, or shall we exert ourselves for its full and complete restoration? It is idle to talk of bonds, greenbacks, gold, the public faith, and the public credit. What can a Democratic President do in regard to any of these, with a Congress in both branches controlled by the carpet-baggers and their allies? He will be powerless to stop the supplies by which idle negroes are organized into political clubs—by which an army is maintained to protect these vagabonds in their outrages upon the ballot. These, and things like these, eat up the revenues and resources of the Government and destroy its credit, make the difference between gold and greenbacks. We must restore the Constitution before we can restore the finances, and to do this we must have a President who will execute the will of the people by trampling into dust the usurpations of Congress, known as the Reconstruction acts. I wish to stand before the Convention upon this issue, but it is one which embraces everything else that is of value in its large and comprehensive results. It is the one thing that includes all that is worth a contest, and without it there is nothing that gives dignity, honor, or value to the struggle.

Your friend,

FRANK P. BLAIR.

This letter fell like a bomb into the camp of the Radicals. They felt that there was in it a Jacksonian ring which betokened the true metal of the author. The revolutionists in Congress were first seized with the panic which its manly tone excited, and it seemed as if their vision had been opened for the first time to the form of an antagonist who was earnest in his purpose, and their compact front wavered and fluttered like that of an army panicked by the impetuous onset of a foe determined in his purpose. Whatever may be said of this letter of General Blair, it struck the popular heart North and South, and though it may be injurious to the questionable nerve of Radicalism which has indulged so much of bully and bluster, and may be too strong for the weak-kneed and whispering advocates of an unmanly expediency, the great Democratic masses admire its spirit and recognize in it the printed exposition of their own feelings, and embrace it as the oracle of their own manly convictions.

The Washington correspondent of the New York *World* telegraphs what occurred in the House at the time:

Soon afterward, General Blair's letter having been read, Mr. Boutwell asked Mr. Brooks, who had been speaking, what he thought of it; whereupon, Mr Brooks, who made a Yankee bargain with Mr. Boutwell that the latter should not interrupt him until he got through telling what he thought of it, went on to explain that General Blair probably meant this, to-wit: it was perfectly well known in Congress that the Supreme Court had been about to decide, when its decision was interrupted by the action of Congress, to the effect that the Reconstruction acts passed by Congress, were null and void; that it was generally expected that the Supreme Court, when it again assembled, would render such a decision, and that it would become the duty of the President, in such an event, to declare according to that verdict; and, as General Blair's letter suggested, that all acts done and accomplished under such a system of reconstruction were without warrant from the Constitution or the laws, therefore they would have to be done away with. A great silence succeeded in the House, and Mr. Brooks' exposition of the Blair letter was acknowledged to be a perfectly consistent one, which met the Radical misinterpretation of it squarely at the beginning of the campaign.

We regret that our space precludes a more detailed account of the eventful career of the second man on the National Democratic ticket. His life and services will be the theme of many biographies, more extensive than the space this book is able to afford, and will furnish the lovers of personal history the interesting and instructive treat which the subject is ample to gratify, and the reader will be repaid to peruse.

GENERAL BLAIR'S LETTER OF ACCEPTANCE.

General GEO. W. MORGAN, Chairman of the Committee of the National Democratic Convention:

GENERAL: I take the earliest opportunity of replying to your letter notifying me of my nomination for Vice-President of the United States by the National Democratic Convention recently held in the city of New York.

I accept without hesitation the nomination tendered in a manner so gratifying, and give you and the committee my thanks for the very kind and complimentary language in which you have conveyed to me the decision of the Convention.

I have carefully read the resolutions adopted by the Convention, and most cordially concur in every principle and sentiment they announce.

My opinion upon all the questions which discriminate the great contending parties have been freely expressed on all suitable occasions, and I do not deem it necessary at this time to reiterate them.

The issues upon which the contest turns are clear, and can not be obscured or distorted by the sophistries of our adversaries. They all resolve themselves into the old and ever-recurring struggle of a few men to absorb the political power of the nation. This effort under every conceivable name and disguise has always characterized the opponents of the Democratic party, but at no time has the attempt assumed a phase so open and daring as in this contest. The adversaries of free and constitutional government, in defiance of the express language of the Constitution, have erected a military despotism in ten of the States of the Union, have taken from the President the power vested in him by the supreme law, and have deprived the Supreme Court of its jurisdiction. The right of trial by jury, and the great writ of right, the *habeas corpus*—shields of safety for every citizen, which have descended to us from the earliest traditions of our ancestors, and which our Revolutionary fathers sought to secure to their posterity forever in the fundamental charter of our liberties—have been ruthlessly trampled under foot by the fragment of a Congress; whole States and communities of people of our race have been attainted, convicted, condemned, and deprived of their rights as citizens, without presentment or trial or witnesses, but by Congressional enactment of *ex post facto* laws, and in defiance of the constitutional prohibition, denying even to a full and loyal Congress the authority to pass any bill of attainder or *ex post facto* law. The same usurping authority has substituted as electors in place of the men of our own race, thus illegally attainted and disfranchised, a host of ignorant negroes who are supported in idleness with the public money, and are combined together to strip the white race of their birthright through the management of the Freedmen's Bureau and emissaries of conspirators in other States. And to complete the oppression, the military power of the nation has been placed at their disposal in order to make this barbarism supreme. The military leader, under whose prestige this usurping Congress has taken refuge—since the condemnation of their schemes by the free people of the North, in the elections of the last year—and whom they have selected as their candidate, to shield themselves from the result of their own wickedness and crime, has announced his acceptance of the nomination, and his willingness to maintain their usurpations, over eight millions of white people at the South, fixed to the earth with his bayonets. He exclaims, "Let us have peace?" "Peace reigns in Warsaw," was the announcement which heralded the doom of the liberties of a nation. "The empire is peace," exclaimed Bonaparte when freedom and its defenders expired under the sharp edge of his sword. The peace to which Grant invites us is the peace of despotism and death. Those who seek to restore the Constitution by executing the will of the people condemning the Reconstruction acts, already pronounced in the elections of last year (and which will, I am convinced, be still more emphatically expressed by the election of the Democratic candidate as President of the United States), are denounced as revolutionists by the partisans of this vindictive Congress Negro suffrage (which the popular vote of New York, New Jersey, Pennsylvania, Ohio, Michigan, Connecticut, and other States has condemned as expressly against the letter of the Constitution) must stand, because their Senators and Representatives have willed it. If the people shall again condemn these atrocious measures by the election of the Democratic candidate for President, they must not be disturbed! Although decided to be unconstitutional by the Supreme Court, and although the President is sworn to maintain and support the Constitution, the will of a fraction of a Congress, reinforced with its partisan emissaries sent to the South, and supported there by the soldiery, must stand against the will of the people and the decisions of the Supreme Court, and the solemn oath of the President to maintain and support the Constitution! It is revolutionary to execute the will of the people! It is revolutionary to execute the judgment of the Supreme Court! It is revolutionary in the President to keep inviolate his oath to sustain the Constitution! This false construction of the vital principle of our Government is the last resort of those who would have their arbitrary reconstruction sway, and supersede our time-honored institutions. The nation will say that the Constitution must be restored and the will of the people again prevail. The appeal to the peaceful ballot to attain this end is not war—is not revolution. They make war and revolution who attempt to arrest this quiet mode of putting aside military despotism and the usurpations of a fragment of a Congress asserting absolute power over that benign system of regulated liberty left to us by our fathers. This must be allowed to take its course. THIS IS THE ONLY ROAD TO PEACE. IT WILL COME WITH THE ELECTION OF THE DEMOCRATIC CANDIDATE, AND NOT WITH THE ELECTION OF THAT MAILED WARRIOR WHOSE BAYONETS ARE NOW AT THE THROATS OF EIGHT MILLIONS OF PEOPLE IN THE SOUTH, TO COMPEL THEM TO SUPPORT HIM AS A CANDIDATE FOR THE PRESIDENCY, AND TO SUBMIT TO THE DOMINATION OF AN ALIEN RACE OF SEMI-BARBAROUS MEN. NO PERVERSION OF TRUTH OR AUDACITY OF MISREPRESENTATION CAN EXCEED THAT WHICH HAILS THIS CANDIDATE IN ARMS AS AN ANGEL OF PEACE.

I am, very respectfully, your most obedient servant, FRANK P. BLAIR.

GENERAL HANCOCK'S LETTER.
NEWPORT, RHODE ISLAND, July 17, 1868.

S. T. GLOVER, ESQ., ST. LOUIS—*My Dear Sir:* I am greatly obliged for your favor of the 13th instant. Those who suppose that I do not acquiesce in the work of the National Democratic Convention, or that I do not sincerely desire the election of its nominees, know very little of my character.

Believing as I really do, that the preservation of the Constitutional Government eminently depends on the success of the Democratic party in the coming election, were I to hesitate in its candid support I feel I should not only falsify my own record, but commit a crime against my country.

I never aspired to the Presidency on account of myself. I never sought its doubtful honors, and certain labors and responsibilities, merely for the position. My own wish was to promote, if I could, the good of the country, and to rebuke the spirit of revolution, which had invaded every sacred precinct of liberty.

When, therefore, you pronounced the statements in question false, you did exactly right. *"Principles and not men,"* is the motto for the *rugged crisis* in which we are now struggling.

Had I been made the Presidential nominee, I should have considered it a tribute, not to me, but to the principles which I had proclaimed and practiced. But shall I cease to revere those principles because by mutual political friends another has been appointed to put them into execution? *Never! never! never!*

These, sir, are my sentiments, whatever interested parties may say to the contrary; and I desire that all may know and understand them.

I shall ever hold in grateful remembrance the faithful friends, who, hailing from every section of the Union, preferred me, by their votes, and other expressions of confidence, both in and out of the Convention, and shall do them all the justice to believe that they were governed by patriotic motives; that they did not propose simply to aggrandize my personal fortunes, but to save their country through me, and that they will not now suffer anything like personal preferences or jealousies to stand between them and their manifest duty.

I have the honor to be, dear sir,
Very respectfully, yours,
WINFIELD S. HANCOCK.

THE FIRST BLOODY FRUITS OF UNIVERSAL SUFFRAGE—MURDER AND RAPINE IN WASHING.

[From the New York Herald.]

THE NEGRO DISTURBANCES AT WASHINGTON.—The riotous and murderous conduct of the blacks at Washington, after the charter election had resulted in a Radical victory, may well alarm the country. It matters but little whether the first blow, which was the proximate, accidental cause of the riot, was struck by a white or by a black hand. All accounts seem to agree, however, that an inoffensive white man, a soldier, was the first victim of negro violence. Cut across the ribs with a razor, he died in a short time. Another white man was killed by a negro, who cut him across the wrist with a razor, severing an artery. The house of a conservative judge of election was entered and gutted by a negro mob, which was prevented only by the strategy of a policeman from demolishing the office of the *National Intelligencer*. Restaurants were stoned, forcibly entered and robbed. The windows of other buildings were broken, and the wife of a police officer was struck on the shoulder by one of the missiles. Throughout the city a large number of negroes were arrested, most of whom were found to be armed with muskets, clubs and pistols, but, as if indicating the savage ferocity of the infurated blacks, their favorite weapon was found to be the razor.

What strikes us, however, as a still more horrible detail, is the incendiary speech addressed to the negro mob by Mr. Forney. Our correspondent, in his letter which we published yesterday, states that the ex-Secretary of the Senate told this mob that there were two regiments of Lee's troops in the city, with hostile intent against the colored people.

No language can be too strong in reprobation of such a direct appeal to the worst passions of an ignorant and excitable race. Its tendency to provoke dangerous, if not fatal, collisions between whites and blacks is inevitable. Yet this is the tendency of the entire policy of the Jacobin leaders of the dominant Radical party. What Charles Lamb would have classed among the imperfect sympathies between the two races, these blind leaders of the blind are trying their utmost to convert into cruel antipathies. An infinity of painful consequences must ensue, culminating, if not providentially checked, in a repetition on a grander scale of the horrors of the St. Domingo massacre.

We firmly believe that both the former slaveholders of the South and their emancipated slaves would gradually have adapted themselves to their new relation to each other, reaping mutual advantages from it, if fanatical intermeddlers had not wickedly sown the seeds of a dreadful conflict of races. The first fruits of this conflict are visible in the recent deplorable scenes at Washington. A full harvest of destruction will be the final and terrible result.

[From the Washington Evening Express.]

* * That numbers of them have been misled by the teachings of the demagogues who are seeking their own preferment, is perfectly apparent to any one who witnessed the conduct of the procession on Tuesday night. Then, and afterward, threats were abundant against this office, against the residence of the publisher of this paper, against the *Intelligencer* office, and against the residences of certain citizens; and every one at all familiar with mobs knows full well that it needed but a bold, reckless leader or two to excite that crowd to the utmost violence and outrage. Notices to leave town have been served on certain individuals, of which one we have seen says: "It is deemed advisable by the committee that you should leave town within two weeks, or suffer the vengeance of an outraged people."

Since writing the above the following has been handed us:

"WASHINGTON, June 2, 1868.

"F. G. CALVERT—*Sir:* You are hereby notified to leave the city in twenty-four hours. We are on the track of one more. "A DETERMINED RADICAL"

Mr. Calvert was a conservative judge on election day in the First Ward.

"WASHINGTON, D. C., June 3, 1868.

"MR. HOH.—You have been violent in your denunciations of us as a race since the just laws of Congress enfranchised us, and it is deemed advisable by the committee that you should be made to leave the city within two weeks, or suffer the vengeance of an outraged people. Unless you publicly denounce the odious doctrines of modern Democracy within that time, beware.

"Yours, in the cause of progress and liberty.   LOUIS JOHNSON,
"*Of the Committee.*"

Forney's Speech Inciting the Blacks.

[From the Washington Chronicle (Forney's Paper), June 4.]

FELLOW-CITIZENS—This is a different reception from that which honored me in the noon of last night [Laughter.] Then the *Chronicle* office was an object of the polite attention of the other side of the house [laughter], and as I sat in my editorial room I was regaled with exulting rebel shouts and delighted with the strains of "Dixie." [Cheers and laughter.] The shouts came from men who had rallied under the stars and bars, and fought to the melody of that air of treason, and they came here for the purpose of rejoicing over what they conceived to be another victory of the rebellion. [Cheers and cries of "That's so."] But, gentlemen, there are some things that do not lie; and, in saying this, I do not desire to be understood as including the virtuous gentleman at the one end of the avenue and his seven imitators at the other end. [Laughter.] The things that do not lie are the figures casting up the ballots of our independent yeomanry. [Cries of "good" and tremendous cheering.] You are here to rejoice over a well-won and reluctantly conceded victory. [Cheers.] What were the adverse influences against which you had to contend? In the first place you had, in my opinion at least, two regiments of the army of Robert E. Lee quartered in your midst, who voted in your ballot boxes. ["Yes, that is true."] In the next place you had a trained band of officials, driven to the polls to save their bread and butter. [Laughter.] Then you had the whisky ring, located here in all its power, and reinforced by large contributions from other quarters. This victory to-night, my fellow-citizens, means more than the election of your worthy and high-minded candidate for Mayor, Sayles J. Bowen. [Three cheers for Bowen.] It means that you who have been deprived of your rights by the slave tyrants—and now I am speaking for the freedmen before me—have at last attained the privilege of exercising these rights, and have exercised them with prudence, intelligence and moderation.

CLERICAL POLITICIANS.

During the trial of the President the following telegram flashed through the country with the preamble and resolution of the General Conference of the Methodist Episcopal Church, in session at Chicago:

WHEREAS, There is now pending in the Senate of the United States the most important question which has ever engaged its attention; and whereas, the evidence and pleadings in this case have been fully spread before the people, so that all may form an enlightened opinion; and whereas, we are deeply impressed that upon its rightful decision will largely depend the safety and prosperity of our nation, as well as the religous privileges of our ministers and members in many parts of the South; and whereas, painful rumors are in circulation, that, partly by unworthy jealousies, and partly by corrupt influences, pecuniary and otherwise, most actively employed efforts are being made to influence Senators improperly, and to prevent them from performing their high duty; therefore,

Resolved, That we hereby appoint an hour of prayer, from nine to ten o'clock, A. M., to-morrow, to invoke humbly and earnestly the mercy of God upon our nation, and beseech him to save our Senators from error, and to so influence them that their decision shall be in truth and righteousness, and shall increase the security and prosperity of our beloved Union.

In the same body the Rev. Dr. Waldro, a prominent member of the Conference, after much skirmishing by others, boldly took the ground "that all government is based upon the religious ideas of those who carry it on, and that the Northern Methodists have acquired, by conquest, the right to control the religion of the South."

The Rev. Waldro further contended that the Southern Methodists had no more right to meet and worship in their way than Lee and Johnson would have, at this time, "to call together again and drill their armies." He predicted that these heretical Southern Methodists "would soon be prohibited" from worshiping God except in the manner dictated by Northern Methodists. He then went on to say, "The religion of the North is bound to rule this Continent, and *it proposes* to make a proper application of our Bible to the Southern States and people. *A subjugated people have no more right to apply their own peculiar moral ideas, than to use their physical implements of war."*

How it Works.

In November, 1865, Maj.-Gen. H. W. Slocum, the brave commander of the Twelfth Army corps, ran against Gen. Barlow, another brave officer, for Secretary of State for the then Republican State of New York, and was beaten 27,857 votes. General Slocum was subsequently named, by President Johnson, for the post of Naval Officer of the Port of New York, and rejected by the Radical Senate for his Conservatism. The verdict of the Conservatives of the State last November was a change of 75,000 votes in favor of Slocum.

In 1866, Gen. Curtis, of St. Lawrence county, New York, the fighting hero of Fort Fisher, where he lost an eye, was nominated, by the President, Collector of the Port of Ogdensburg. The Senate rejected him for Conservatism, although the Radicals claim to be *par excellence* the friends of the soldier.

In 1866, the Republicans carried St. Lawrence county by 7,500 majority. Last November the Radicals obtained only about 6,000 majority, being a change of 1,500 in favor of Gen. Curtis. Query: At this rate of progress, how many more brave soldiers can the Senate afford to reject?

Shellabarger's Bill.

Mr. Shellabarger, a member of Congress from Ohio, attempted a great blow at States Rights generally, and his own State particularly, at the last session of Congress. He endeavored to shove a bill through regulating suffrage in Ohio, and compelling the concession of it by his State to certain classes of persons having negro blood in them.

The preamble denounces what is called the "Visible admixture act" of the Legislature of Ohio, of 1868, and asserts the right of Congress to determine the qualification of electors for Congressmen in Ohio. In other words, the right of Congress to override the 40,000 majority in Ohio against negro suffrage last year.

The first section proposes to set aside the "Visible admixture act" aforesaid.

The second section instructs the judges of elections to receive, in elections for Congressmen, the votes of certain persons possessed of African blood, in violation of the act aforesaid, and, in the event that the judges refuse to receive their votes, the persons so refused are authorized to hold a visible admixture election separate and apart from the poll at which they are refused the vote, which poll is to be counted in determining the election of members of Congress.

Section three prescribes a heavy penalty, as follows:

And be it further enacted, That any judge or other officer of election, who shall enforce or attempt to enforce any of the provisions of the act hereby declared void, so as to prevent any such elector from voting at the same poll with the other electors of said State for Representative alone, or so as to hinder, delay, or control his casting such ballot for Representative alone, at either the regular or said separate poll, shall be deemed guilty of a high crime, and upon conviction thereof, in any court of the United States having jurisdiction, shall be fined in any sum not exceeding ten thousand dollars, or imprisonment not exceeding one year, or both, at the discretion of the court.

Carpet-bags and Commerce.

[From the New York World.]

We invite all the merchants and traders of the Union to ponder the following eloquent figures:

In the year ending June 30, 1867, the total sales of merchandise by wholesale and retail dealers, auctioneers, and brokers, or, in other words, the business done by the people of the United States, amounted to $11,870,337,207
Of this sum, the three States of New York, Pennsylvania and Ohio, contributed 5,854,948,560
Or just about one-half of the whole.
While the three States of Florida, North Carolina, and South Carolina, contributed 115,719,060
Or just about one-tenth of the whole.

But, under the Congressional reconstruction represented by General Grant, more than *seven hundred thousand ignorant negroes in North and South Carolina, and Florida, not one of whom would be allowed a vote in New York, Ohio, or Pennsylvania, secured the presence in the Senate of six Senators, counterbalancing the Senatorial vote of New York, Pennsylvania, and Ohio.*

And these six negro-chosen Senators are committed to a policy whose mouthpiece in the House, one Dewees, openly *demands arms for the purpose of controlling* the polls in November next, and thus beginning a war which will impose new and unimaginable burdens on the commerce and the industry of this people.

A HIGH-MINDED KING.

Radicalism has much to learn. It has even to stoop down at the foot of a German throne, and learn true magnanimity. On his way to Worms, where the present King of Prussia intended to inaugurate the Luther monument, he for the first time since the late aggrandizement of his dominions visited the city of Hanover, the capital of a formerly independent kingdom. He was officially addressed by the Mayor of the city, and here is in substance his response:

"We meet for the first time since great events resulted in changes which brought you and me into close connection. Like myself, you must be moved by very contradictory sentiments. Do not believe that I disapprove of sentiments which personally you must entertain in favor of former relations. On the contrary, your attachment to myself would be worthless, if the sudden change of our reciprocal condition had been accepted by you with indifference!"

Another notable act of imperial clemency is reported from Vienna. The Emperor Francis Joseph, in an autograph letter addressed to Gen. Kuhn, the Minister of War, has directed that the retired officers of the imperial army, who in consequence of the events of 1848-9 lost their right to pension, shall now be placed on the pension list under the same regulations as all other officers. This measure applies chiefly to the Hungarian officers who took part in the revolution of 1848, and may be thus regarded as effacing the last trace of the old division between Hungary and Austria.

THE FENIANS FOR OUR TICKET.

The following dispatch was sent to the ratification meeting at Tammany Hall the night after the nomination of our ticket:

"Philadelphia sends greeting to New York. She promises the city by at least 7,000 majority, and perhaps 10,000, and the State by from 15,000 to 20,000. Pennsylvanians appreciate the fact, that, while they were preparing for an attack, the troops of New York, thrown forward by Governor Seymour, were here and on the battle-ground, and not only saved the State, but the Republic. We also believe that in the nomination of Francis P. Blair the eighth article of the Democratic platform—'Protection to Americans abroad or fight'—will be sustained. JOHN HASSON,

"Representative of the Fenians of Philadelphia."

In this grave matter the Fenians of Philadelphia no doubt represent the Fenians of the whole country. The Fenians everywhere warm to our ticket. And so do all other true friends of civil liberty. Well they may.

PROPOSAL TO EXCLUDE KENTUCKY AND MARYLAND.

It was even hinted, at a meeting of the Jacobins, that, under the Fourteenth Amendment, and the act regulating the electoral votes of the Southern States, they will exclude Kentucky and Maryland from the Electoral College. The bill excludes from the Electoral College all States not represented in Congress, while the Fourteenth Amendment denies representatives on a colored basis unless the colored population is allowed to vote. The present apportionment of Kentucky and Maryland is based partly on the colored population. The Radicals claim that these States are not entitled to be represented after the reapportionment; hence they can not be counted in the Electoral College. — *Washington Correspondence of the Cincinnati Enquirer.*

RADICAL PROPOSAL TO SELL OUT THE DEAF AND DUMB.

On the 15th of July a bill appropriating money for the District of Columbia Deaf and Dumb Institution being before the House, Mr. Elihu B. Washburne, of Illinois, popularly accredited with the ownership of U. S. Grant, moved to amend by farming out that charity, even as in the good old days—perhaps now—the paupers of New England are let to the lowest bidder. Being remonstrated with, the said Washburne, owner as aforesaid, did then justify his measure by saying, "it will save $40,000," and forthwith clapping the previous question thereto, did thereon take a vote—yeas, 63; nays, 71; the deaf mutes, whom an inscrutable Providence has committed to the care of madmen, thus escaping sale by eight votes. A narrow escape from being put on the block.—*N. Y. World.*

WENDELL PHILLIPS ON THE CHURCH AND STATE, RELIGION AND POLITICS.

[Speech of Wendell Phillips at a Convention of Free-Thinkers, held in Boston, May 31.]

* * * * * * * *

In all reverence be it said, that if Jesus was preaching what he did preach when on earth, in our streets to-day, he would be in jail in less than a week, and there is not a church which would be able to recognize him. [Sensation.] We will have the ballot for the negro by agitation, soon.

(A voice)—How do you propose to do it?

Mr. Phillips—I propose to do it just as Christianity occupied the throne of the Cæsars. [Loud cheers.] I propose to do it by telling man just what God tells me. I will do it by doing what the temperance societies, which are as hide-bound as the churches, dare not—examine a Republican candidate for the Presidency—the most popular man in America, who can not stand up before a glass of liquor without falling down. [Great silence, succeeded by applause.] I will do it by opposing the Republican party when it bids me "be silent about negro suffrage North, it will hurt our party. Be silent about General Grant's drinking, it will hurt his chances." I reply, God bids me speak what you bid me forbear. I will speak, and let the dead bury their dead, whether they bury him in the White House or not.

Another Outrage by Congress.

On the 22d of July the House of Representatives rushed through that body, under the operation of the previous question, the Senate bill to incorporate and establish a great National Life Insurance Company, with a home office in the District of Columbia, and the right to establish branches in the States and Territories. This franchise is granted to Defrees, Government Printer, and Associates. Jay Cooke is the chief capitalist, and it is understood that E. A Rollins is to be the President of the concern, when he ceases to be the head of the Internal Revenue Bureau.

This kind of legislation is unprecedented in the history of Congress, and should be frowned down by the people, so that it may not become, by silent acquiescence, an admitted power of Congress to establish national corporations. If Congress can incorporate insurance companies to operate in the States without the consent, and in defiance of the wishes of the States, it can establish other corporations with like powers of superiority to State authority. This is a bold step in the direction of central consolidation, and toward the overthrow of the legitimate rights of the States; and we hope the President will mark his disapprobation of this assumption of power on the part of Congress by vetoing this iniquitous bill.

A gentleman perfectly responsible (Mr. Fernando Wood) said, while the bill was being put through the House, that he would give one million of dollars for the franchise it conferred upon the corporators. They are authorized to buy and sell real estate as well as insure lives. Indeed, it is difficult to say what they may not do under the authority vested in them by this bill. Such is republican legislation!

Schuyler Colfax as an Advocate of Mob Law and Murder.

On page 188 of this book, the decision of the Supreme Court of the United States, in the case of Lamden P. Milligan, will be found. In it the facts of his conviction by a Military Commission, and the sentence that he be hung, are fully set forth. The Supreme Court interposed its high authority and saved his life. Colfax brutally desired President Lincoln to order him to be hung before the high court could act. Here are the facts from the Indianapolis *Sentinel*, May 21, 1868:

After the Circuit Court of the United States for the District of Indiana, on a petition of Milligan for a writ of *habeas corpus*, had heard the argument, and a divided opinion had been given in order that the case could be carried up to the Supreme Court, Governor Morton and a number of prominent citizens made application to the President to suspend the sentence until the Supreme Court could pass upon the appeal, and in response he finally ordered a commutation of the sentence to imprisonment for life. In this connection, we will add, and we give the authority of Governor Morton for the statement, that President Lincoln did not intend to allow the sentence of the Court to be carried out, but it was his purpose to release Milligan after the war was over. And so anxious was Governor Morton to obtain a postponement or commutation of the sentence that he sent a special messenger to effect the object. While this effort was being made, and the parties to it had a full knowledge of the facts that we have related, the following cruel, infamous, malignant and blood thirsty protest was forwarded to the President:

WASHINGTON, February 3, 1855.

His Excellency, the President of the United States:

SIR—The undersigned, members of Congress from the State of Indiana, in behalf of the loyal people of the State, respectfully but earnestly protest against any commutation of the sentence of the Military Commission against the Indiana conspirators recently tried by it, and against any interference in any manner or form with that sentence.

[Signed]
H. S. LANE,
SCHUYLER COLFAX,
Speaker H. R. U. S.,
GODLOVE S. ORTH,
GEORGE W. JULIAN.

We are informed that Henry S. Lane reconsidered the murderous intent of the protest, for such it was, and withdrew his recommendation. Having led a comparatively blameless and honorable life, and reached an age when, in the due course of human events, he might reasonably expect that his own dissolution was near, he perhaps remembered in that sober second thought the terrible reality of meeting his Creator with the blood of innocent men on his hands, and shrunk from the responsibility. His younger and more unscrupulous companions in this assassination scheme were not moved by even those considerations, but were ready to have the crime of murder upon their souls, for such it would have been under the decision of the Court, to gratify their partisan malignancy and hate.

A Proclamation of Amnesty.
By the President of the United States.
* * * * * *

Now, therefore, be it known that I, Andrew Johnson, President of the United States, do, by virtue of the Constitution, and in the name of the people of the United States, hereby proclaim and declare, unconditionally, and without reservation, to all and to every person who directly or indirectly participated in the late insurrection or rebellion, excepting such person or persons as may be under presentment or indictment in any Court of the United States having competent jurisdiction upon a charge of treason or other felony, a full pardon and amnesty for the offense of treason against the United States or of adhering to their enemies during the late civil war, with restoration of all rights of property except as to slaves, and except also as to any property of which any person may have been legally divested under the laws of the United States.

In testimony whereof I have signed these presents with my hand and have caused the seal of the United States to be hereunto affixed.

Done at the City of Washington, the fourth day of July, in the year of our Lord, 1868, and of the Independence of the United States of America the ninety-third.

ANDREW JOHNSON.
By the President.
WILLIAM H. SEWARD,
Secretary of State.

THE RADICALS AND THE WORKINGMEN.

The significance of the following correspondence is found in the fact that Defrees is Schuyler Colfax's next friend. He was the law preceptor of Schuyler, and to his tactics the Indiana sophomore is indebted for his nomination for the Vice-Presidency. A few days ago Mr. Whaley issued the following circular to the leaders of the Workingmen's movement throughout the country:

WASHINGTON, June 22, 1868.

SIR—You are respectfully invited and requested to meet me in council at French's Hotel, New York city, at ten o'clock, A.M., on the 2d day of July next, to take counsel as to what course shall be pursued by the Workingmen, and what action taken, if any, in this crisis in our National affairs, upon the settlement of which depends so much of paramount importance to the workingmen, and of deep and lasting influence upon the present prosperity and future welfare of the industrial classes.

Other prominent workingmen and advocates of reform have had like invitations extended them, and it is hoped that you may find it convenient to give us the benefit of your presence and judgment.

Please let me hear from you immediately.
Respectfully, J. C. C. WHALEY,
President National Labor Union.

Mr. Defrees, happening to hear of this, and to receive a copy, wrote as follows to Mr. Whaley:

OFFICE OF CONGRESSIONAL PRINTER,
WASHINGTON, June 25, 1868.

Mr. J. C. C. Whaley:

DEAR SIR—I am informed that you, as President of the National Labor Union, have called a meeting to take place in New York on the 2d of July next, to endeavor to induce the Democratic Convention to incorporate the eight-hour movement into their platform *for the purpose of aiding that party to obtain control of the Government they so recently attempted to destroy.*

Of course, I do not object to your advocacy of the eight-hour movement, but I do object that you should, while holding position in this establishment, make any movement whatever, or take any part calculated to aid that party in its effort to again control the affairs of this country.

Have I been rightly informed?

Yours, &c.,
[Signed.] JOHN D. DEFREES.

Mr. Whaley thereupon replied to Mr. Defrees, resigning his position without waiting for the formal discharge in store for him:

WASHINGTON, June 25, 1868.

John D. Defrees, Esq., Congressional Printer:

DEAR SIR—In reply to your letter, dated to day, I would respectfully state that you have been incorrectly informed in the statement that I, "as President of the National

Labor Union have called a meeting in New York on the 2d of July next, to endeavor to induce the Democratic Convention to incorporate the eight-hour movement into their platform, for the purpose of aiding that party to obtain control of the Government they so recently attempted to destroy."

* * * * * *

That call has been sent irrespective of party, for the purpose stated, and *not for the purpose* of aiding the Democratic party. I owe no allegiance to any party, and am governed by no other wish than to faithfully serve those who have chosen me as their President, who believe in "measures, not men; principles, not party."

I do not wish to violate, in any manner, the regulations of your establishment, nor, at the same time, do I intend to surrender the right of independence of action. Therefore, I feel constrained to most respectfully resign my position as proof reader in the Executive Department of the Government Printing-office.

Before closing, allow me to return my sincere thanks for the uniform kindness and courtesy with which you have always treated me, and to say that I will ever bear in kind recollection my official relations with you, running through six eventful years of our country's history.

Respectfully, J. C. C. WHALEY.

THE WAY THE PUBLIC LANDS FLY.

A summary from Mr. Julian's report shows the following result of the dispensation of the public lands:

The Government, since its organization, has sold lands amounting to over 154,000,000 acres.

Of the lands sold, there remain in private hands, not reduced to occupancy as farms, over 30,000,000 acres.

The Government grants of lands to Western and Southern States, to aid in constructing railroads, amount to over 57,000,000 acres.

The grants to aid in the construction of canals amount to over 17,000,000 acres.

The grants to different lines of Pacific Railroad Companies, 124,000,000 acres.

The amount of land granted and to be granted to the States under the act of Congress of July 2, 1862, to aid in the establishment of agricultural colleges, reaches 9,600,000 acres.

The lands granted to the States under different acts of Congress as "swamp and overflowed lands," amount to 43,000,000 acres, making a total of 248,000,000 acres of land; this is exclusive of the Indian lands previously enumerated, and also of the sections given to the Western States for the benefits of their school systems.

The lands granted to the Pacific Railroads alone amount to 193,759 square miles—a territory within 11,075 square miles as large as France, with its population of 36,000,000. If we take the grants to secondary roads (as, for instance, the 9,000,000 acres and more of public lands given to Kansas, on admission, for railroad purposes), we shall probably have a domain equal to Great Britain, Ireland, Prussia, and Switzerland combined.

A correspondent of the Worcester *Spy* predicts the future political influence of these gigantic corporations created by land grants, in the following style:

"Now for the moral—a political one worth heeding, to my mind. At the present time there can be but little doubt that the interests of these great roads control the States of Iowa, Nevada, Missouri and California in great part, and of Nebraska and Kansas altogether. Just now these interests do not run counter to, but with the national interests. But let anything happen here to change, and we shall see the Senators and Representatives from those States—the first especially—acting as a unit for the corporations. Six States are already under their control—virtually so, at least. How long will it be before all the country lying between the Missouri and the Pacific, or at least the Coast Sierras of the North American Cordilleras, will be, as States, controlled politically and legislatively in the interests of these great corporations?"

Radicals v. Catholics.

REV. DR. R. J. BRECKINRIDGE IN ALBANY—KEY-NOTE OF THE RADICAL CANVASS—RELIGIOUS PROSCRIPTION.

[From the Albany (N. Y.) Argus, June 2.]

OPENING OF THE CAMPAIGN OF HATE—AN INCENDIARY THREAT.—The opening of the Radical campaign in this city, in behalf of Grant and Colfax, was an ominous one.

Everything seemed auspicious to a great meeting. The Radical Senate was in session, engaged in the trial of the Dorn impeachment. The Presbyterian Convention attracted many visitors. The getters up of the meeting turned to this latter body to get their orator, instead of to the Senate. The Rev. Dr. Breckinridge was solicited to open the campaign. He had presided over the Baltimore Convention which nominated Lincoln and Johnson, and his name was relied upon to give character to the new demonstration.

Dr. Breckinridge not only made a partisan speech at the behest of a political committee—invoking the name of God repeatedly to give it a pious air—but in his zeal he overdid his work. Pointing out how, in the future, New England and the South would have little to do in directing the politics of the country, which would be in the hands of the great Middle States reaching to the West, and particularly New York, he said that "New York must be redeemed from the disgrace she had brought upon herself last fall." He alluded to the city of New York as containing 50,000 Roman Catholic voters, whom he denounced as the cause of the Radical defeat; and he said the State must be redeemed, even if to do so, New York had to be burned to the ground!

"At the close of his remarks," according to the *Evening Journal*, "the audience rose to their feet and gave him a hearty round of cheers, followed by another for the ticket;" but the *Journal* suppresses all mention of the infamous sentiment, and all reference to the deprecatory remarks of Mr. Townsend, of Troy, who followed, and who evidently regarded this incendiary declaration as one in every way utterly unfit to be made!

We have waited to hear if the sentiment should be disclaimed by the author, or repudiated by his party! He seems to have no explanation to make, and they no disclaimer; so we may regard these words as the key-note of the campaign.

A war of sects is to follow a war of sections; and the spirit of hate which has swept over the country, blasting its fields and blighting human lives, is to be invoked to a new career. Not State against State, but family against family, and brother against brother, are to be armed for the encounter, which these bloodhounds of Zion are baying on.

RADICAL OPINION OF CATHOLICS.

The following extract is from the *Sedalia Times* of the 30th ult., a leading Radical paper in Missouri. It is, says the Missouri *Republican*, an echo of the sentiment of such men as George P. Strong, who declared his desire that the Catholic clergy of this State should be set to digging canals for a living, and of Charles D. Drake, who hoped by the imposition of his "oath of loyalty," to compel these clergy to leave the State, and make their living elsewhere as best they could. In commenting on the statement of the New York *World*, of the action of the Catholic Church among the freedmen in the South, the *Times* says:

"Now, if this report is true—and we presume it is—if the Catholic Church is working with vigor to make converts among the colored people of the South—it means that that church is not only interested in the spiritual welfare of the *World's* children, but is seeking temporal power also. The Catholic Church and the Democratic party have always understood each other wonderfully well. Religious intolerance and bigotry have harmonized so well with the spirit of *caste* and the barbarism of slavery in this country that, while all Democrats have not been Catholics, all Catholics, or, at least nineteen-twentieths of them, have been Democrats. When Romanists get possession of the Southern blacks, we shall hear no more howls about a 'White Man's Government;' for, in that event, every colored Catholic will vote the straight Democratic ticket. Hence it is that such a loud-mouthed advocate of Democracy as the New York *World* is so solicitous and anxious for the success of the 'truly missionary work' of Catholicism in 'the new Africa in America.'"

THE FRANKFORT IRISH MOB.
[From the New Castle (Ky.) Constitutionalist.]

Some months since, an Irish girl was found above the tunnel at Frankfort in a state of insensibility, and bearing on her person several severe injuries. It was supposed that she had accidentally fell over the bluff, which at that point forms almost a precipice. She was taken home to her father's, and medical and surgical aid employed. She remained insensible or unconscious for some considerable length of time, and no hope was entertained of her recovery. But, finally, she revived and recovered her reason. She now stated that she had not fallen over the precipice by accident, but that a negro man, whom she knew well, had met her, forcibly outraged her person, and then threw her over the precipice. This was the simple statement of the girl.

It was thought that, perhaps, her mind was still wandering—that she was but dreaming, as it were, and that the dreadful deed, so unnatural to many families of the brutes, and so utterly and inexpressibly disgusting to every feeling and sentiment of humanity, had not been committed.

But the friends of the injured girl were not long left in suspense. Several negro men were brought before the dishonored and suffering girl, to test the accuracy of her reason. She, of course, said of each he was not the person. At last the man, whom she had charged, was brought in and she at once recognized him, and accused him to his face of the crime. There was no doubt of her perfect sanity—there could be none. She knew the negro well, and her statements were natural and simple. They forced conviction on every mind. Not a particle of doubt was left on the minds of sober, reflecting people in Frankfort of his guilt, and we are assured that no doubt exists among such now. We believe that this is strictly true.

The sequel is soon told. A large number of Irishmen forcibly took the accused negro from the jail, and hung him near the spot where he had committed the deed so inexpressibly worse than murder in its most shocking form. Thus the countrymen of the dishonored girl avenged her injuries and her shame.

But the Radicals were determined to make political capital out of the negro's crime and out of the injuries of the poor girl. Men were arrested and examined in Frankfort. Finally the case was carried before Judge Ballard. Some four or five persons have been confined for months in the Jefferson county jail, accused of being parties to the hanging of the execrable negro at Frankfort. These are the simple facts.

Now, we are no advocates of mobs, but on the contrary we are utterly opposed to them. We know that they endanger all civil interests and the lives of innocent men.

There are some crimes that so shock and move the highest indignation of the human mind, that they have ever been visited by summary popular violence. Rape is one of them. All ages and civilized people have felt alike about it.

PERSECUTION OF A CATHOLIC PRIEST BY A RADICAL JUDGE—HIS IMPRISONMENT BY ORDER OF THE JUDGE.

In connection with this case, so feelingly referred to in the preceding article, the Rev. Lambert Young was requested by the officers of the law to visit the mob, and endeavor by the influence of his holy place to prevent them from hanging the negro. This he did, and an endeavor was made by this Radical, Judge Ballard, to coerce him into a witness against the parties involved. Before the Grand Jury, he declined to answer the questions propounded to him, for the following reasons:

THE PRIEST'S OBJECTIONS.

To the Hon. Bland Ballard, U. S. Judge for the District of Kentucky.

* * * * * * * *

On the evening when it is said a man of color named Jim Macklin was hanged in or near Frankfort during the past winter by a mob, or riotous assemblage of persons, I was sent for and appealed to by Jno. L. Scott, Esq., Commonwealth's Attorney for that district, to use my influence to disperse the mob, which he then informed me was gathering, and would perhaps violate the law. I am a Catholic priest, and was then and yet temporarily stationed at Frankfort. I had been at Frankfort only since the month of May preceding the events herein spoken of, and had consequently a limited acquaintance in that community. I am a native of Holland, and had been in this country only about eight years, and neither speak the English language fluently nor understand it perfectly. I have not been naturalized, yet I came to the United States as the Government of my adoption, and expect to make it my home for life. With a sincere desire to render any and all aid in my power to prevent a violation of law, and especially to use whatever of influence I had or might be supposed to have in favor of the peace and good order of society, and to prevent violence, I went as requested, and exerted all my humble, and as the sequel proved, too inefficient, powers in trying to prevent the breaking of the County jail, or the summary or unlawful execution of the negro. I understood the appeal to be made to me on the ground that I was a Catholic priest, and because it was supposed the mob was in great part composed of Irish Catholics. It was on this ground and for this reason that I hoped I might exert an influence. It was as a priest I went. I am fully persuaded that it was on account of my priestly office, and on that account only, that I was permitted to go into that excited crowd, a large portion of whom were to me personally unknown, and of a different nationality from myself, while others better known, and of more personal influence than myself dared not go among them. When I had, as I verily believe, saved the life of the jailer, and was leaving in despair of wielding further influence, the Mayor of Frankfort appealed to me to return into the jail and request the crowd to hear him speak to them. This I did, being permitted again to pass in as I verily believe only on account of my office of priest.

Now I am asked to inform the grand jury of the names of the persons whom I saw in that maddened and infuriated assemblage, to whom I went solely because of my priestly office, and among whom I was permitted to go and to remonstrate because of my office, and without which I could not have gone in among them. It was because of my office that I was requested to go by the civil authorities. It was in my character of priest that I went in. It was on account of my clerical position that I was enabled to go in and come out unmolested. Now the civil authorities ask me to state whom I there saw, as evidence against them for their punishment. It seems to me on my conscience that for me to depose on the subject would be a prostitution of my office and a disgrace to my character as a priest. That I would stand in the attitude of having taken advantage of my priestly office at the instance of the civil authorities to act the part of a public informer That it would be a breach of implied faith and confidence. And that the probable good from a statement of all the facts within my knowledge would be more than counterbalanced by the evils to be wrought by the apparent betrayal of those who trusted in me as a priest and not otherwise.

I do not claim to put this case strictly or technically on the ground of a sacramental confession. But the reasons, though not so strong, nor so conclusive as that case, differ from it only in degree. The principle is the same. The trust, if it were trust—the forbearance, if it were forbearance—was to my sacred office, not to my humble and comparatively unknown self. Can I afford to testify? If I am compelled to do so, could another of my office dare to thrust himself into such a position? Would he be permitted under like circumstances to raise his voice? Is it right, is it fair for the civil authorities thus to use and abuse my office? With all respect, bowing with all due reverence to the laws of my adopted country, I am bound, in my conscience as a man and as an office-bearer, as I believe and hope in the Church of Christ, to answer all of these questions in the negative.

I do not refuse to answer in any spirit of contempt. As God is my judge, I desire to respect and obey the temporal laws of the country I have voluntarily chosen for my home on earth. I act not hastily, but upon profound and prayerful search of my own heart. I believe in all truth that I ought to be excused from testifying to facts thus obtained. I do not know that my testimony would produce the conviction of any man, accused or not accused. I did not see the execution of the colored man, nor did I see him at the jail, nor at any time in the possession of the mob, nor do I know, except from heresay, that he was executed. But it is not the importance or effect of any testimony that concerns me. It is the principle of deposing as evidence, facts which I came to know in my office as priest, and which I would not otherwise, as I verily believe, have been requested or permitted to have seen or heard. It is not to screen any offender, or supposed offender, against the law, nor from any sympathy with mob violence in this case, or any other, but to protect, as far as in me lies, spotless and unblemished my sacerdotal robes. For these reasons, and these only, I humbly and earnestly pray the court to hold the facts known to me as privileged from exposure on the witness stand. Respectfully,

LAMBERT YOUNG.

The court ordered Mr. Young to answer the questions propounded to him by the grand jury.

Mr. Young, however, persisted in refusing, whereupon he was adjudged to be in contempt, and was ordered to be committed to jail until he answered the questions.

In obedience to this order the Marshal committed him to jail.

He remained in jail until the 6th of July, when he was called before the United States Court, fined $50 for contempt, and put under $2,000 bonds to appear at the October term. He paid the fine, gave the required bond, and was discharged.

The wholesale persecution of the Catholic priests, in Missouri, by the Radical oligarchy who control that State, shows the bitter hate with which this revolutionary party regard the Catholic church. The opinion of the Supreme Court, contained in this volume, delivered in the case of Father Cummins, who was imprisoned in that State for refusing to take the test oath, puts the seal of unconstitutionality upon the Missouri Radical proscription of Roman Catholic priests.

RADICAL KNOW-NOTHINGISM IN CONNECTICUT.

The Radical Legislature of Connecticut has passed two bills for the express purpose of preventing the naturalization of foreigners, and to throw as many obstacles as possible in the way of laboring men to keep them from the ballot-boxes. The plain object of both bills is to embarrass the franchise as much as possible. The party which prates of "equal rights," and which makes every adult male black at the South a voter, does its best to disfranchise white citizens at the North, especially if those citizens are of foreign birth. The Know-Nothing politics of Colfax are revived in Connecticut, by William T. Minor, the last Know-Nothing Governor in that State, who pressed to its passage a bill which will prevent many foreigners from naturalization in time to vote in the coming election. We do not believe that even these foul means will enable the Radical party to carry Connecticut, and the very movement shows the desperation of that party. It is well enough, however, for our citizens of foreign birth to understand that the forces of the old Know-Nothing party, in which Colfax was a leading member, are to be brought to bear in the coming election.

The party which is willing that negroes shall vote in the South will prevent, as far as possible, foreign-born white citizens from voting at the North.

THE GERMANS OF NEW YORK AND THE DEMOCRATIC NOMINEES.

A very largely attended meeting of the General Committee of the German Democratic Union party of New York City was held last week. Oswald Ottendorfer, Esq., editor of the *Staats Zeitung*, presided, and A. Gottman, Esq., acted as Secretary. After brief speeches the following resolutions were adopted:

Resolved, That we heartily indorse the nominations of the Democratic National Convention, and that we shall do all in our power to secure the election of Horatio Seymour, the foremost man in the ranks of the Democracy of the Empire State, and of Francis Preston Blair, the brave and gifted warrior of the Union.

Resolved, That we consider a perfect understanding to exist between the platform of the Democracy, adopted at the last Convention, and the principles of the nominees, and we are satisfied that their election will rid the people of the burden and woes which have befallen them since a corrupt Radical party has taken charge exclusively of the National affairs.

Resolved, That in our sincere belief a continuation of the prevalence of the Radical party must unavoidably lead to the ruin of the credit and welfare of the country, and its happiness and progress, and that we consider it an imperative duty to put an end to Radical Republicanism for all time to come.

SCHUYLER COLFAX AND CATHOLICISM.

We have shown in a previous part of this work the oath taken by the Radical candidate for Vice-President. Let us see how he was instructed before taking that oath. We extract this from the recognized ritual of that intolerant order. President of the order addressing Colfax:

It has, no doubt, been long apparent to you, brothers, that foreign influence and Roman Catholicism have been making steady and alarming progress in our country. You can not have failed to observe the significant transition of the foreigner and Romanist from a character quiet, retiring, and even abject, to one bold, threatening, turbulent, and despotic in its appearance and assumptions. You must have become alarmed at the systematic and rapidly augmenting power of these dangerous and unnatural elements of our national condition. So it is, brothers, with others beside yourselves in every State of the Union. A sense of danger has struck the great heart of the nation. In every city, town, and hamlet, the danger has been seen and the alarm sounded. And hence true men have devised this order as a means of disseminating patriotic principles, of keeping alive the fire of national virtue, of fostering the national intelligence, and of advancing America and the American interest on the one side, and on the other of checking the strides of the foreigner or alien, or thwarting the machinations and subverting the deadly plans of the papist and Jesuit.

Is it at all wonderful that when their leaders are loaded with allegiance to such intolerance that we hear of such speeches as that of the Rev. Dr. Breckinridge, and of the cases of persecution of priests of which we have cited.

RADICAL PAPERS ON THE CONGRESS.

The New York Evening *Post*, edited by William Cullen Bryant, says of the new amendment to the Reconstruction bill which proposes to set aside the Supreme Court:

* * * * "Congress got into a quarrel with the President; it took counsel of its resentments, not its wisdom; more onerous conditions were imposed; until this legislative folly culminated in the MILITARY DESPOTISM *which has produced no solitary good effect*, which has widened the chasm between the races at the South, and which has at length run to such an extravagance that unless arrested it will provoke a general and most disastrous reaction. *It is an extremity into which we shall not follow any leaders; but on the other hand, we shall continue to protest against it until the voice of reason shall once more make itself heard amid the noisy clamors of Washington.*"

The Cincinnati *Gazette* says:

"If the wholesale striking off of taxes, without the capacity to adjust the means of revenue to the expenditures and the demands of the public faith; if the cutting down of appropriations, without curtailing expenses; if the impeachment failure, and more enormous land grants to railroads, are the principal items that this session can show, it is really not a vital matter to the public that the members shall be re-elected. And we have a notion that if this Congress has not the courage to cut down the army and navy to a peace footing, and to rigidly cut down all the military paraphernalia that has grown upon a great war, and to stop the land plunder, and to bring the Freedmen's Bureau to an end with the gathering of the present crop, and to adjust the expenditures and revenue, it will have to give place to another."

"Let Us Have Peace.".

In a letter to the Anti-Slavery Society, Wendell Phillips, who is the engineer of the Radical engine, said :

Our duty is to put there (in Congress) men who will at every hazard save the nation, remembering that they stand where the Long Parliament stood in 1649; and *though the* BLOCK AND AX *in front of the palace may be no fitting measure* NOW, *they are bound to* FIND *and to* USE *some measures fit and efficient to secure their purpose—the* DEPOSITION OF THE PERJURED AND USURPING TRAITOR.

In his speech as President of the Republican State Convention at Syracuse, of 1866, Lyman Tremain, assuming the pretext for a renewal of the civil war, said :

At the first tap of the drum, an army composed of veteran troops capable of overcoming all opposition, would come to the rescue, and, adopting the President's opinion that traitors must be punished, soldiers would proceed to punish them. And I assume further that this time it would be effectually done—*done without the intervention of President or Congress, court, jury or military commission.**

Governor Yates, of Illinois, in his speech at the Radical Convention in Philadelphia, in 1866, said :

He would apply to President Johnson the language of an amiable Illinois Judge to a man who had been convicted before him of murder: "Mr. Smith, it is my duty to pronounce sentence upon you. It is a painful duty, but the law requires me to fix some time when you shall be hanged. Now, Mr. Smith, I want to know when it will suit you to be hanged?" ILLINOIS HE SAID, HAD RAISED TWO HUNDRED AND FIFTY THOUSAND TROOPS TO BATTLE IN THE CAUSE OF THE COUNTRY, AND WAS NOW PREPARED TO RAISE FIVE HUNDRED THOUSAND MORE TO FINISH THE SAME GOOD WORK.

Senator Chandler, of Michigan, said in a speech at the same Philadelphia Convention :

The obstacle that is now in the way the people will remove in a very short time. Who is Andrew Johnson, and what is Andrew Johnson's policy? Andrew Johnson has no more right to a policy than my horse has * * * * * William H. Seward is to-day a traitor at heart to the Government of the United States. Andrew Johnson once said that treason was a crime, and that traitors should be punished and treason made odious. If Andrew Johnson does not stop about now, he will ascertain that treason is a crime, and that traitors shall be punished and treason be made odious.

Senator Wilson, at Philadelphia, played upon the passions of the crowd after this fashion:

Now, according to the acts of Andrew Johnson, these things, were all true, and what ought they to do with him? [A voice—"Hang him with Jeff. Davis."] What are you going to do with him? [A voice—"Hang him."]

The following is an extract from the prayer made by the clergyman who opened the Philadelphia Radical Convention :

Oh, grant that we may do right at this time though the heavens fall. [Shouts of "Amen! amen!"] Hear us we beseech Thee for our nation at large. *Deliver us from the rule of bad men, especially from him who, through Satanic agency, has been raised to authority over us, and who, abusing that authority, is not only endangering the life of our Republic, but our personal liberty.* Great God, interpose, and in making bare Thine

---

*This same Lyman Tremain, said at the beginning of the war: But gentlemen, while I do not justify secession in the abstract, we must not forget that the South has had the most terrible provocation to which civilized man has ever been subjected. * * * *
When they found the Government turned into an engine of war and oppression—make the case your own—and then when you make all proper allowances for the fact that *our Southern friends* are more impulsive than we, that they live under a warmer sun and act more from impulse than the cooler, calculating Yankee sons of the North, I ask whether they are doing very differently from what human nature would do anywhere under such circumstances?

arm FOR VENGEANCE, save us from his infamous and ruinous policy, and from the bad counsels of bad men that surround him. [Shouts of "Amen! amen!"] And we beseech Thee to discover to the American people the base hypocrisy of that party that seeks to sustain him. O, send a spirit from Thy throne *to arouse the American people to* ACTION *in this tremendous hour.* [Renewed cries of 'Amen! amen!"]

General B. F. Butler in his speech at Gloucester, Massachusetts, just before going on to the Philadelphia Radical Convention, said:

He contended that by their rebellion they had forfeited their property, their rights, and their lives, if rebels were hanged, which, unfortunately, he said, they were not. If this state of things can not be altered, the General continued, *we will march once more, and woe to him who opposes us!*

Again General Butler, said:

If I am asked how long I would keep these men out of the Union, *I say keep them out until the heavens melt with fervent heat; and if it should not come in this generation, we will swear our sons to keep them out.*

Parson Brownlow, before leaving home for the Philadelphia Radical Convention said, speaking of the prospects of another civil war:

The loyal masses, who constitute an overwhelming majority of the people of this great nation, intend it shall be no child's play. They will, as they ought to do, make the entire Southern Confederacy as God found the earth when he commenced the work of creation, "without form and void." *They will not and ought not to leave a rebel fence-rail, out-house or dwelling in the eleven seceded States. And as for the rebel population, let them be exterminated.* And when this war is wound up, which should be done rapidly and with swift destruction, let the land be resurveyed and sold out to pay the expenses of the war, and settled only by people who will respect the stars and stripes.

Again, at the Philadelphia Convention, he reiterated this sentiment in returning to the subject, as follows:

I want to have something to say about the division of your forces the next time. *I would divide your army into three grand divisions. Let the first go armed and equipped as the laws of the army require, with small arms and artillery. Let them be the largest division and do the killing.* LET THE SECOND DIVISION BE ARMED WITH PINE TORCHES AND SPIRITS OF TURPENTINE, AND LET THEM DO THE BURNING. *Let the third and last division be armed with surveyors' compasses and chains, and we will survey out the land and settle it. We will first sell it out to pay the expenses of the war with the proceeds,* and then settle it with men who will honor this glorious banner. [Great applause.] These are my sentiments.

Again, having left Philadelphia, Brownlow was received by the Radicals of Trenton, New Jersey, and made a speech, saying:

I can tell you that *you are to have another war.* The devil is in the people of the South, and in the man at the White House in particular. [Cries of "Put him out."] If you are to have another war I want to have a finger in that pie. I want your army to come in three divisions—*the first to kill, the second to burn, the third to survey the land out in small parcels and give it to those who are loyal in the North.*

Governor Hamilton, of Texas, said in his address before the Loyal League at Philadelphia:

Prepare your heart, and your arms, too, perhaps, for another conflict. [Cries of "We are ready."]

Again, on being received at Trenton, with Parson Brownlow, he said:

The great question upon which he (President Johnson) claims your support is that he wants to restore the Union. I can not respond to the sentiment so often expressed. "The Union as it was and the Constitution as it is." I want the Union as it wasn't and the Constitution as it is not.

In his speech in the House of Representatives, in 1867, on Confiscation, Thaddeus Stevens sneers at mercy, and at the fine parable by which it is taught in the *New Testament*:

"Shall he who brought this misery upon the State be permitted to control its destinies? If this be so, then all the precious blood of our brave soldiers and officers, so freely poured out, will have been wantonly spilled. All the glorious victories won by our noble armies will go for naught, and all the battlefields which have been sown with dead heroes during the rebellion will have been made memorable in vain. Why all this carnage and devastation? It was that treason might be put down and traitors punished. I say the traitor has ceased to be a citizen, and in joining the rebellion has become a public enemy. Treason must be made odious, and traitors must be punished and impoverished; their great plantations must be seized and divided into small portions, and sold to honest, industrious men. The day for protecting the land and negroes of these authors of rebellion is past. It is high time it was. I have been most deeply pained at some things which have come under my observation. We get men in command, who, under the influence of flattery, fawning and carressing, grant protection to the traitor, while the poor Union man stands out in the cold." All this is the eloquent language of Andrew Johnson, "as he was." This was the text which I took up and elaborated in a speech to my constituents at Lancaster, in September, 1865, and which has been much criticised by humane sympathizers with rebels. Andrew Johnson was the apostle whose preachings I followed. His doctrine pervades and animates this whole bill. Whatever of justice is in it is due to him. I call upon his friends to stand by him in this, his favorite policy. If you now desert him, who can you expect to defend the "much enduring man" at the other end of the avenue? Having thus rendered unto Cæsar the things that are Cæsar's, I will proceed to defend the course recommended by him, who, above all others, knows what is due to traitors. This bill, it seems to me, can be condemned only by the criminals and their immediate friends, and by that unmanly kind of men whose intellectual and moral vigor has melted into a fluid weakness which they mistake for mercy, and which is untempered with a single grain of justice, and to those religionists who mistake meanness for Christianity, and who forget that the essence of religion is to "do unto others what others have a right to expect from you." It is offensive to certain pretentious doctors of divinity, who are mawkishly prating about the "fatted calf, the prodigal son and forgiving father."

Animus of the Carpet-Bag Patriots.

Richard Busteed, now a judge of the Alabama territory, but formerly a New York Democrat, lately made a speech to the Grant Club in New York city, well filled with the outgushings of his "loil" heart, from which the following is extracted:

I would keep them (the rebels) out in the cold till their teeth chattered to the music of the Union. [Applause.] Keep them out in the cold till they had learned that treason was the greatest crime of the century—and I would keep them there till the last trumpet sounded. Better, I say, a boundless waste of territory, filled with owls and bats, than that the Southern States should be occupied with men bearing antipathies to this Union. [Cheers.] I tell you that although there may be forgiveness before God for the crime of the South in compassing rebellion against our Government, there can be no forgiveness for it before man. [Applause.]

Stanton Covering up his Tracks.
[From the N. Y. World.]

Before surrendering the War Office, Stanton destroyed many, very many, papers on file there relating to secret interior party matters, particularly of detective matters and confidential reports, upon which his high-handed action was in many instances based. It will never be known how much the independence of his subordinates has been suppressed. In all the branches of his office—the Freedmen's Bureau, the detective and the army—he has had hosts of satellites in secret correspondence with him, the matter of which has no doubt been destroyed. In the army the purest and best have had to be extremely cautious of speech among even intimate associates. The army has been degraded by his minions. A better time dawns.

An Unconstitutional Law.

The Radical Congress is as apt at playing the sneak as the bully. Here is what they slipped into a general appropriation bill in order to work an indignity to the President, and make him subject to the complete observation of Grant:

War Department, Adjutant-General's Office, }
Washington, March 12, 1867. }
General Orders No. 15.]

The following extract from an act of Congress is published for the information and government of all concerned: "An act making an appropriation for the support of the army, for the year ending June 30, 1868, and for other purposes.

"Sec. 2. *And be it further enacted,* That the headquarters of the General of the Army of the United States shall be at the City of Washington, and all orders and instructions relating to military operations, issued by the President or Secretary of War shall be issued through the General of the Army, and in case of his absence, through the next in rank. The General of the Army shall not be retired, suspended, or removed from command, or assigned to duty elsewhere than at headquarters, except at his own request, with the previous approval of the Senate, and any orders or instructions relating to military operations issued contrary to the requirements of this section shall be null and void, and any officer issuing orders or instructions contrary to the provisions of this section shall be deemed guilty of a misdemeanor in office, and any officer of the army who shall transmit or obey any order or instruction so issued, contrary to the provisions of this section, knowing that such orders were so issued, shall be liable to imprisonment for not less than two years and not more than twenty years, on conviction thereof in any court of competent jurisdiction. Approved, March 2, 1867."

By order of the Secretary of War.
E. D. TOWNSEND,
Assistant Adjutant-General.

NORTHERN EMIGRANTS TO THE SOUTH.

The following resolutions, passed by the Conservative State Convention of Alabama, are a sufficient answer to all the Radical lies that have been industriously circulated in the premises. We commend them to the reader:

WHEREAS, Radical emissaries at the South have basely circulated reports throughout the country that the hatred of the Southern whites toward Northern men is so intense as to endanger the lives of the latter who settle in their midst; and,

WHEREAS, These reports are greatly to the prejudice of our people, and calculated to seriously retard the restoration of the Union under the Constitution; therefore,

Resolved, by the white men of Alabama, in Convention assembled, That good men from the Northern States and from foreign countries are invited to settle in Alabama, with the assurance that they will be received with true Southern hospitalities.

SUMNER ANXIOUS TO HAVE A NEGRO PEER IN THE SENATE.

The following letter was written by Senator Sumner to a citizen of Norfolk:

"SENATE CHAMBER, June 22.

DEAR SIR: I have your letter of the 18th, in reference to the eligibility of a colored man in Congress. I know of no ground on which he could be excluded from his seat if duly elected, and I should welcome the election of a competent representative of the colored race to either House of Congress as a final triumph of the cause of equal rights. Until this step is taken, our success is incomplete. Yours truly,
CHAS. SUMNER.

Senator Sumner again expresses his anxiety to see a negro in the United States Senate, and has written the following letter:

"SENATE CHAMBER July 3, 1868.

DEAR SIR: I have never given any opinion in regard to the Senatorial question in your State, except to express a regret that the golden opportunity should be lost of making a colored citizen Senator from South Carolina. Such a Senator, if competent, would be a powerful support to the cause of equal rights. His presence alone would be a constant testimony and argument. Nothing could do so much to settle the question of equal rights forever in the United States. The howl against the negro which is sometimes heard in the Senate would cease. A colored Senator would be as good as a constitutional amendment, making all backward steps impossible. I write now frankly in reply to your inquiry, and without any purpose of interfering in your election. You will pardon my anxiety for the cause I have so much at heart.

Accept my best wishes, and believe me, dear sir, faithfully yours,
CHAS. SUMNER.

To Thaddeus K. Sasportas, Esq., Columbia, S. C.

THE OBJECT OF RECONSTRUCTION CONFESSED.

The New York *Tribune* makes the confession that the whole "reconstruction" policy of Congress—which the Radicals have been proclaiming as the only hope for a complete restoration of the Union —was conceived simply for the purpose of keeping that party in power, despite of its utter condemnation by the people. Here is the confession, in the language of the *Tribune* itself:

The Republicans, therefore, were absolutely compelled to enfranchise the Southern blacks or *submit to be expelled from power by the Southern whites.* Had they attempted to bid against the Democrats for the favor and support of the late Rebels, they would inevitably have been outdone. "Blood is thicker than water," and the Democrats and Rebels united *would have outnumbered and ousted the Republicans* as surely as that five are more than four.

As a further illustration of this policy of "reconstruction," advocated and defended by the *Tribune*, we append the following paragraph:

In Tennessee an hundred thousand white men are disfranchised, and the State is governed by a minority composed of sixty thousand blacks and twenty thousand whites. In Louisiana about thirty thousand whites were disfranchised by General Sheridan, and the State was carried, at the recent

The Boys in Blue v. Grant—A Military Monarch Indignant.

MONTGOMERY, ALA., June 12.

On the 5th of June, the Montgomery *Advertiser* contained the following paragraph:

We are requested by the soldiers on duty at this place to state that at the nigger, carpet-bag and scalawag meeting, held at the capitol on Saturday night, the soldiers gave three groans for Grant, and three cheers for McClellan, and three cheers for Andrew Johnson. They were given by soldiers with a hearty good will, and rolled from the capitol to the artesian basin. We are also requested by these soldiers to state that any assertion contrary to this is a base falsehood. The soldiers say they are white men, and have no love for carpet-baggers and scalawags.

In consequence of the above the following order has been issued by General Shepherd, commanding the Sub-District of Alabama:

MONTGOMERY, June 6, 1868.

General Orders No. 22.]

The issue of the Montgomery *Advertiser* of yesterday contains a statement which, if in the slightest degree true, deserves the reprobation of every right-minded soldier in this Sub-District. The statement alluded to applauds, excites and stimulates soldiers to insubordination and disgrace by the publication that some have uttered groans against the General of our army, to whom the country has awarded such a commission for his services in suppressing a rebellion aimed at the destruction of our republic and our freedom as a people. The soldiers in the Sub-District are, therefore, assured that it is their plain duty to rebuke in a becoming manner every effort made by the publishers of newspapers, or by other individuals, tending to incite disgraceful acts and insubordination, and also to abstain from any expression of political opinion as to persons or parties. Thus may soldiers make manifest that they are meritorious, and incapable of being led astray by evil-minded persons, and least of all by those who have caused the pall of death to cover a million soldiers. By order of

O. L. SHEPHERD,
Col. and Brevet Brig.-Gen.

W. T. HARTZ, Brevet Major, U. S. A., A. A. G.

Shepherd is the valiant officer who fought a Firemans' procession in attendance on a funeral in Mobile, because the deceased had been a Confederate soldier, and would not let it pass his headquarters.

A Relic of the Past—Stanton the Eulogist of President Johnson.

WAR DEPARTMENT,
WASHINGTON CITY, March 3, 1865.

His Excellency, Andrew Johnson, Vice-President, elect:

SIR—This Department has accepted your resignation as Brigadier-General and Military Governor of Tennessee. Permit me on this occasion to tender to you the sincere thanks of this Department for your patriotic and able services during the eventful period through which you have exercised the highest trust committed to your charge.

In one of the darkest hours of the great struggle for national existence against rebellious foes, the Government called you from your comparatively safe and easy duties of civil life, to a place in front of the enemy, and in a position of personal toil and danger perhaps more hazardous than was encountered by any other citizen or military officer of the United States. With patriotic promptness you assumed the post, and maintained it under circumstances of unparalleled trials, until recent events have brought safety and deliverance to your State and to the integrity of the Constitutional Union, for which you so long and so gallantly periled all that is dear to man on earth. That you may be spared to enjoy the new honors, and perform the high duties to which you have been called by the people of the United States, is the sincere wish of one who, in every official and personal relation, has found you worthy of the confidence of the Government and the honor and esteem of your fellow-citizens.

Your obedient servant,
EDWIN M. STANTON.

Affairs at the National Capitol.

DISGRACEFUL SCRAMBLE FOR CLERK OF THE SENATE.

[Correspondence of the Cincinnati Commercial.]

WASHINGTON, June 5, 1868.

The story of the man who called upon General Jackson for the English mission, but finding that post already occupied, compromised after some disputation, on a suit of old clothes, is not so much of an exaggeration after all, when read or told, in the light of the actual events of to-day. Only yesterday two or three ex Senators were scrambling for the position of clerk of the body of which a year or two ago they were honorable members. One of them, Mr. Foster, of

Connecticut, was President *pro tem.* of the Senate, and, *ex officio,* Vice-President of the United States, until the 4th of March a year ago, when his term of office expired. Another, Mr. Cresswell, of Maryland, was the nominee of his State delegation at Chicago, for Vice-President under Grant. Both were candidates for Mr. Forney's successorship, but neither got it. The lucky person was a gentleman who, a year ago, ran as the Republican candidate for Governor of California, but was defeated. One's idea of greatness and statesmanship are not easily reconciled with that india-rubber adaptability to circumstances which will either aspire to be a Governor or condescend to be a clerk, as the prospect of success in the one or the other tempts to the contest.

Burbridge's Reign of Terror in Kentucky.

HEADQUARTERS DISTRICT KENTUCKY,
FIFTH DIVISION, THIRD ARMY CORPS.
LEXINGTON, KY., July 16, 1864.

Rebel sympathizers living within five miles of any scene of outrage committed by armed men not recognized as public enemies by the rules and usages of war, will be arrested and sent beyond the limits of the United States. In accordance with instructions from the Major-General commanding the Military District of the Mississippi, so much of the property of rebel sympathizers as may be necessary to indemnify the Government or loyal citizens for losses incurred by the acts of such lawless men, will be seized and appropriated for this purpose. Whenever an unarmed Union citizen is murdered, four guerrillas will be selected from the prisoners in the hands of the military authorities, and publicly shot to death in the most convenient place near the scene of outrage.

By command of Brev. Major-General S. G. Burbridge.

J. B. DICKSON,
Captain and A. A. General.

[From the Maysville Eagle.]

We have been requested to publish the following, which shows how affairs were conducted at General Burbridge's head quarters:

MAYSVILLE, KY., April 11, 1868.

My name is B. D. Nixon. When the war broke out I was living near Owensville, in Bath county. I entered into the Confederate service in 1862, and served for some time on the bodyguard of Gen. H. Marshall. I afterward joined Thos. Johnson's battalion. I was regularly enlisted, never belonged to any band of guerrillas or partisans, and, in what I did in furtherance of the Confederate cause, acted under the orders of my superiors. Late in the spring or early in the summer of 1864, I entered the State of Kentucky with John Morgan's command when he made his last raid into this State. I was at the battle of Cynthiana, and was there cut off and separated from my command. The vigilance of the Federal soldiers prevented me from immediately rejoining my command or leaving the State, and I spent several weeks in Scott and Owen counties while watching an opportunity of leaving the State. During this time I participated in no acts of hostility against the Government, nor did I molest any private citizen, nor did I have any connection with any predatory band. In July an opportunity was afforded me for leaving the State, and in going out I stopped to see my family whom I had not seen for eleven months. I had been only two days at home when I was captured by Lieutenant Denton, and was taken to Mt. Sterling and made to work on the fortifications for two weeks. I was then sent to Lexington and placed in military prison No. 3. Afterward I was taken to prison No. 2. I had been in Lexington several days when a soldier of a Michigan regiment entered the prison, measured my hight, weighed me, and took down a general description of my appearance. On the same evening an old gentleman from Franklin county was placed in prison, who informed me that he had been before the Provost-marshal, and heard the names of myself and fifteen others as read under sentence of death. On the same evening I was ironed. The next morning I was taken before the Provost-marshal, Major Vance. He cursed me and abused me as a thief and a robber, said I ought to be hung, and that he would have me shot in thirty six hours. It was evidently the intention that I should be executed. I defended my character, and seeing Major Downey in the room, I discovered myself to him as a Freemason, and he immediately clasped me by the hand and interceded in my behalf. Through his intervention my life was saved. I was then transferred to prison No 4 and handcuffed for five weeks. At this prison I met the fifteen men who were condemned. These men were kept ironed and taken from the prison in irons. They never returned to the prison. The guard told me they had been shot. I have never heard of any of them since, and my belief is that they were all executed. None of these men were guerrillas, but all belonged to the regular Confederate army. Some of them had been taken through some form of trial, and may have been sentenced as guerrillas, but none of them were. I remember the names of some of them. Two Linkenpelters, Berry, and Lieutenant Hamilton, all of whom I knew. I was released on the 15th day of October, and sent north of the Ohio, where I remained until I had obtained permission from General Burbridge to return to Kentucky.

B. D. NIXON.

The above was dictated by B. D. Nixon, in my presence; it was then read to him and he understood it perfectly. He then signed it in my presence as his own statement and as the truth.

W. P. BALDWIN.

We might add to this damnable record that of a General named Paine, in Tennessee and Kentucky, and that of the atrocious butcher, McNeil, in Missouri, but the story of their bloody outrages is too horrible for republication.

The New Orleans Riots.

STANTON RESPONSIBLE FOR BLOODSHED.

In a document addressed to the Senate, December 12, 1867, giving his reasons for removing Mr. Stanton, the President said:

The sanguinary riot which occurred in the City of New Orleans, on the 30th of August, 1866, partly aroused public indignation, and public inquiry, not only as to those who were engaged in it, but as to those who, more or less remotely, might be held to responsibility for it occurrence. I need not remind the Senate of the effort made to fix that responsibility on the President. The charge was openly made, and again, and again reiterated all through the land, that the President was warned in time, but refused to interfere.

By telegrams from the Lieutenant-Governor, and Attorney-General of Louisiana, dated the 27th and 28th of August, I was advised that a body of delegates claiming to be a Constitutional Convention, were about to assemble in New Orleans; that the matter was before the Grand Jury; but that it would be impossible to execute civil process without a riot; and this question was asked: "Is the military to interfere to prevent process of court?" This question was asked at a time when the civil courts were in full exercise of their authority, and the answer sent by telegraph on the same 28th of August, was this: "The millitary will be expected to sustain and not interfere with the proceedings of the Court."

On the same 28th of August, the following telegram was sent to Mr. Stanton, by Major-General Baird, then, owing to the absence of General Sheridan, in command of the military at New Orleans.

"*Hon. E. M. Stanton, Secretary of War*:

"A Convention has been called with the sanction of Governor Wells, to meet here on Monday. The Lieutenant-Governor and City authorities think it unlawful, and propose to break it up by arresting the delegates. I have given no orders on the subject, but have warned the parties, that I would not countenance or permit such action without instructions to that effect from the President. Please instruct me at once by telegraph."

The 28th of August was on Saturday. The next morning, the 29th, this dispatch was received by Mr. Stanton, at his residence, in this city. He took no action upon it, and neither sent instructions to General Baird himself, nor presented it to me for such instruction. On the next day (Monday) the riot occurred.

* * * * *

The dispatch of General Baird, of the 28th, asked for immediate instructions; and his letter of the 30th, after detailing the terrible riot which had just happened, ends with the expression of regret that the instructions which he asked for were not sent.

* * * * *

No one regrets more than myself that General Baird's request was not brought to my notice. It is clear from his dispatch and letter, that if the Secretary of War had given him proper instructions, the riot which arose on the assembling of the Convention, would have been averted.

* * * * *

The following is the testimony given by Mr. Stanton before the Impeachment Investigating Committee, as to this dispatch:

"Q. Referring to the dispatch of the 28th of July, by General Baird, I ask you whether that dispatch, on its receipt, was communicated?

"A. I received that dispatch on Sunday forenoon; I examined it carefully and considered the questions presented. I did not see that I could give any instructions different from the line of action which General Baird proposed, and made no answer to the dispatch.

"Q. I see it stated this was received at 10:20 P. M. Was that the hour at which it was received by you?

"A. That is the date of its reception in the telegraph office Saturday night; I received it on Sunday forenoon, at my residence. A copy of the dispatch was furnished to the President several days afterward. * * * I suppose it may have been ten or fifteen days afterward.

"Q. The President himself, being in correspondence with those parties on the same subject, would it not have been proper to have advised him of the reception of that dispatch?

"A. I know nothing about his correspondence, and know nothing about any correspondence, except this one dispatch."

Affectation of Generosity.

The Commissioners of the Antietam Cemetery have decided that the remains of the Confederate soldiers be buried in a part of the ground separately from that of the Union army. The question was one which elicited much discussion among the Board, and, while it was pending, Governor Fenton wrote a letter to the special Commissioner from the State of New York, in which he said:

Conquerors as we were in that great struggle, our stern disapproval of the cause in which they fought need not forbid our admiration of the bravery with which they died. They were Americans, misguided indeed, and misled, but still our countrymen, and we can not remember them now either with enmity or unkindness. The hostility of the generous and heroic ends with death, and, brief as our history is, it has furnished an early and striking example. The British and Americans who fell at Plattsburgh sleep side by side; and a common monument on the plains of Abraham attests the heroism of Wolfe and Montcalm.

To-day, nothing, perhaps, could sooner awaken a national spirit in the heart of the South than the thought that representatives of the Northern States were gathering the remains of its fallen sons for interment in our national cemetery; and in future days, when our country is one, not alone in its boundaries, but in spirit and affection, and the recent struggle is remembered as a war less of sections than of systems, the cemetery at Antietam, with its colossal statue of a Union soldier keeping guard over the ashes of all who fell in the opposing ranks of McClellan and Lee, will have a common interest for the descendants of those who died on either side in that sad and memorable civil war.

Why does not Governor Fenton in his political course illustrate the ennobling spirit of that letter? Why is he the bitter, unrelenting, cruel, and proscriptive Radical? Are such lofty and generous thoughts, so well expressed, real and heartfelt, or are they the mere imitation of what he would have us believe he feels; but which he really expels from repose in his breast? A genuine Radical and honest author of the above extract can not consist. We are reluctantly compelled to regard him as counterfeit.

Significant and Suggestive Facts for Northern Capitalists and Creditors.

The editor of the *Metropolitan Record*, Mr. Mullaly, writes from Charlotte, North Carolina, under date of January 26, in regard to the pestilential influence of Messrs. Kelley, Wilson, and other Radical emissaries, who went down to give the negroes advice last fall:

All at that time were doing well. The land had been tilled, the seed planted, the various products were duly ripening for the harvest, when, worse than the army worm, worse than the blight, worse than inclement and unfavorable seasons, came the Radical missionaries with their blasting, withering influence. Now, mark the results. When the crops reached their maturity, when the harvest was ripe and ready to be gathered, the freedmen refused to work. They had been told that they were to have a share in the distribution of the lands, that their Radical friends in the North would put them on a level with their former masters, and that, as their labor had mainly built up the wealth, they were now entitled to a portion of that wealth. The negro, in his simplicity, believed all this. By such vile trickery, by such knavery and deception, these emissaries succeeded in utterly breaking down the obligations of the contract system throughout an immense portion of the South. We have been told, by authority in which we place the most implicit confidence, that in consequence of the speeches of these Radical incendiaries, no less than one million bales of cotton were lost to the country.

Let the capitalists of the North weigh well the vital importance of this huge, overwhelming fact. One million bales of cotton which were ready to be gathered, lost to the capital and industrial wealth of the country—lost to commerce, lost to manufactures, and lost to trade. There is hardly a dealer in the North who has not a special interest in this matter—hardly one. There is hardly a shopkeeper who is at present suffering from a want of trade who has not been affected to the same degree by this loss. By these infamous appeals to the negroes, Kelley and Wilson succeeded in destroying a proportion of the cotton crop, worth at the time over *sixty millions of dollars!*

Bear that in mind, all ye Northern creditors who have been trying in vain to make collections throughout the South. The reason you could not obtain payment of your bills was because the people have no money, and the reason the people have no money is because Radical incendiaries and disseminators of agrarianism succeeded in demoralizing the freedmen and disorganizing the whole labor system of the South.

Sale of the Sea Island Lands—Only Negroes Permitted to be Purchasers.

The House of Representatives, under the operation of the previous question, has passed, by a vote of 75 to 34, a bill for the sale of the Sea Island lands and lots off the South Carolina coast. The bill provides for the sale of a portion of the lands and lots at a dollar and a half per acre, and the rest at a dollar per acre—all the sales to be made to negroes. The bill involves three great outrages; *first*, the confiscation of the property of the former owners of the land; *secondly*, the sales of the lands at such ridiculously small rates; *thirdly*, the restriction of the sales to negroes.

The Sea Island lands, says the Louisville *Journal*, it is well known, are incomparably the most valuable lands in the United States. They produce cotton in exceeding abundance, and the Sea Island cotton is famed throughout the world. The cotton has been regularly sold at a dollar per pound. And yet the land is ceded to the negroes at a dollar per acre. Every pound of cotton that the negroes raise is to pay for a whole acre of land. Could legislation by any possibility be more infamous? We don't see how.

But, after all, we don't believe that the Sea Island negroes, with all the advantages of productive lands and cotton at a dollar a pound, will maintain themselves. If a negro can live upon ten dollars a year, and can't steal the money or its equivalent, he may so far overcome his nature as to raise ten pounds of cotton—not an ounce more. Relief will have to be extended to the Sea Island savages through the Freedmen's Bureau.

Reconstruction in the Massachusetts Legislature.

[Special Correspondence of the World.]
Boston, June 3, 1868.

The House, to-day, by special assignment, had under consideration a series of resolutions upon National Affairs, among which was one drawn in the strongest manner possible indorsing the so called "Reconstruction policy" of the present Congress. Those resolves were acted upon separately, the vote upon most of them being very close; so close that no one considers the indorsement as of any weight, or as in the least backing up the Grant-Colfax platform. The second resolve was the one relating to reconstruction, and when the vote was taken there seemed to be much anxiety depicted in the faces of the Grant and Colfax adherents.

While the roll was being called many members had their pencils at work recording the result. The vote ran very even, neither party, as the turfmen express it, being able to hold the "inside track" for any length of time. At last the voting was concluded, when the Speaker announced that fifty-three members had voted in the affirmative and fifty-three in the negative, and the resolve was passed. Mr. Jewell, the Speaker (brother of the Connecticut Jewell, who was recently defeated for Governor in that State), casting his vote in the affirmative, in order to save the resolve.

As the vote was declared, Mr. Jackman, of Newburyport, reminded the Speaker that the count, as announced by the Clerk, did not agree with the record kept by several members, Mr Jackman's count making 54 nays to 53 yeas. But just at this time the Speaker was hard of hearing, or something of that sort, and due attention was not paid to the suggestion of Mr. Jackman. So the resolve was declared "indorsed," when there are reasons for believing that it was squarely defeated.

No Congress.

The New York *Express* presents a strong argument to prove that "the body of usurpers at present occupying the Capitol of the United States *is not a Congress at all*." There is, as the *Express* intimates, nothing absolutely new in the argument, but it presents it tersely and forcibly.

After considering the question in connection with the preamble to the Federal Constitution, the *Express* continues as follows:

One might stop at the preamble, and rest the case, as against the usurpers, there; but, in order to convict them beyond appeal, it is only necessary to glance at the body of the Constitution itself—

Article 1, sec. 2, says:

The House of Representatives SHALL be composed of members chosen every second year, by the people of the several States.

If this is a constitutional Congress, then, why are there no representatives from no fewer than ten of the States? Why are there between sixty and seventy vacant chairs in the so-called House of Representatives?

Again—

Sec. 3. The Senate SHALL be composed of two Senators from each State, etc.

If this is a constitutional Senate, why are there some twenty names missing—ten chairs vacant—ten States without a Senator? Again—

Representatives and direct taxes shall be apportioned among the several States which may be included within its Union.

The cotton, the income, the internal revenue taxes, are all there, in these Southern States—but (if this is a constitutional Congress), where are the Representatives?

Again—

Sections 1 and 2. The President shall be Commander-in-chief of the Army and Navy of the United States.

If this is a constitutional Congress, how comes it that one branch of it has just "be it enacted" that General Grant, and *not* the President, shall be Commander-in-chief in and over ten States of this Union?

Again—

Article 3, sec. 1. The judicial power of the United States shall be vested in one Supreme Court, etc.

If this is a constitutional Congress, why has it just "be it enacted" that the majority power of that tribunal shall be taken away from it, in order to deprive it of an anticipated decision against a certain act of their own (the Military Reconstruction bill)—in regard to the unconstitutionality of which there is no doubt?

Again—

Article 4, sec. 3. The United States shall guarantee to every State in the Union a republican form of government.

If this is a constitutional Congress, where is that guarantee? How is it that at this moment ten States of this Union have no governments whatsoever, save the grossest forms of military despotism?

Senator Doolittle upon the Reliance of a Citizen upon his State.

In a letter to a recent meeting in New York, Senator Doolittle, after opening with the statement that there were two measures now pending, which, if passed, would tend to revolutionize the Government, proceeds to analyze them briefly, and then said:

In the defense of the great mass of my rights and liberties as a citizen of Wisconsin, I must rely upon the government of the State. First of all, the State defends my life; Congress has nothing to do with that. The State defends my person from assault; Congress has nothing to do with that. The State defends my reputation; Congress has nothing to do with that. The State defends my wife and children; Congress has nothing to do with that. The State defends my home from trespass, from arson, from burglary, and all my property from theft and from robbery; Congress has nothing to do with that. In all my dearest rights, relations, interests, family, character, person, liberty and life, I am defended by the laws of Wisconsin, not by the laws of Congress at all.

Nothing is more clear, therefore, than the necessity of guarding with a jealous care against all encroachments by the Federal Government upon the just rights of the State governments; for it is only under their authority that my most precious interests are secured. The Supreme Court is organized by the Constitution for the purpose of holding, not a false balance, but a just and even balance between these rights which the State government secures, and certain other rights, just as sacred, if not so near and dear, secured to me by the Federal Government against encroachment by the State, against insurrections in the State, against invasions from abroad, and in controversies which may arise between me and the citizens of another State, all of which it is the duty of Congress to defend or secure. * * * *

There is another measure proposed in the House. It may pass that body. It has been reported by a majority of the Judiciary Committee. It is proposed by law to compel the Supreme Court to dismiss the appeal of McArdle, and to make all similar appeals to the Supreme Court impossible. I can hardly believe such a law can pass the Senate. It is an open confession that Radical Reconstruction is unconstitutional, and that they dare not come to a decision in the Supreme Court. Pass that bill, in addition to the rest, and the last vestige of civil law or civil jurisdiction is swept away, from the Potomac to the Rio Grande.

From where I stood this morning, upon the steps of the Capitol, with the flag of the Union over me, I can look across a river and look upon a land of absolute, unqualified despotism. If I visit Mount Vernon, and sit down by the tomb of Washington, I sit under the shadow of military dictatorship, more unlimited than can be found in any civilized country upon the globe. Constitutional liberty is already bound, scourged, and crowned with thorns here—here, in her own sacred temple.

Shall the General of the Army, urged on by radical chief-priests, crucify her on the sacred Capitol Hill? in her own home? under her own banner, amid the scoffs and jeers of all the despots of the world? Let the people answer.

A Terribly Significant Fact—2,500 Coffins in One Year.

[From the Hartford Times.]

Bishop Atkinson, of North Carolina, in an address delivered in Christ Church, in Hartford, referring to the rapid extinction of the negroes in the South, and in illustration of the state of things even in North Carolina, he spoke of a negro town opposite or near Newbern, consisting of 10,000 inhabitants. In that town, said the Bishop, one coffin-dealer alone filled orders for 2,500 coffins in a single year!

What We may Expect.

The New York *Herald*, which now espouses the cause of Grant, showed some time ago what the country had to expect in the event of his election. The *Herald* said:

Military despotism, supported by immense taxation and ruling at the will of an oligarchy of arrogant politicians in Congress, is what the Republicans have labored for in the past. Within this simple and comprehensive programme lie all their principles, all their political ideas; and for this programme they will labor more energetically and with more resolute persistency in the future. They will extend the sphere of its operations also. Grant accepts their programme fully, unreservedly, slavishly, and deliberately promises beforehand, that he will not oppose any obstruction to it, that no "policy" of his shall stand in the way of the prearranged policy of the men who pull the wires of his political existence. If such a party succeeds in electing such a President, the country can judge what must be the result. What is the conduct of the impeachment managers in their present investigation but a foretaste of what would follow with such men in power? Here we have all the personal rights of the citizen invaded at once. Without any process of law whatever, a man is deprived of his liberty and thrust into a cell at the mere bidding of a political bully. The secrecy of the telegraph and postoffice is violated as no man would dare to violate it in despotic France. Men who do such things merely because they have the power, will know no limit but that of their power in enforcing their will.

Mr. Lincoln on Carpet-baggers.

When it was proposed to reconstruct Louisiana during the war, and fill the offices of that State and its representation in Congress with foreign adventurers, "Old Abe" wrote the following letter, which is applicable to these times. Under date of November 21, 1863, Mr. Lincoln wrote as follows:

"DEAR SIR—Dr. Kenedy, bearer of this, has some apprehension that Federal officers, not citizens of Louisiana, may be set up as candidates for Congress in that State. In my view there could be no possible object in such an election. We do not particularly need members of Congress from those States to enable us to get along with legislation here. What we do want is conclusive evidence that respectable citizens of Louisiana are willing to be members of Congress, and to swear support to the Constitution; and that other respectable citizens there are willing to vote for them. To send a parcel of Northern men here as representatives, elected, as would be understood (and perhaps really so), at the point of the bayonet, would be disgraceful and outrageous; and were I a member of Congress there, I would vote against admitting any such man to a seat."

Senator Harlan on Grant.

SPEECH OF SENATOR HARLAN AFFIRMATORY OF GRANT'S MILITARY INCOMPETENCY.

In the Senate of the United States, on the 9th of May, 1862, the following speech, taken from the *Congressional Globe*, was delivered. (Second Session Thirty-seventh Congress, Part 3, pages 2,036–37.) Mr. Harlan said:

Mr. President—So far as the remarks of the Senator from Ohio may have been intended to defend the troops of that State from any unjust aspersions, I have not a word to say. They were well-timed, and it was probably a proper subject for the consideration of the Senate, as their courage had been called in question, as it seems, by a Senator from another State. But at part of his speech which may have been intended to bolster up the reputation of General Grant, I think, may have an injurious effect in the future, and hence I rise to repudiate every word he has said that may have that tendency. *From all I can learn on the subject, I do not think General Grant is fit to command a great army in the field. Iowa had eleven regiments in the field at the battle of Pittsburg Landing. He can never make one of those men believe that General Grant is fit to command.* I have seen many of them, have conversed with the officers and privates, and they believe that our army was surprised. I will read one or two short extracts from a letter written by a gentleman of my State, who is now the presiding Judge of one of the district courts, and who spent several days on the battlefield immediately after the conclusion of the battle. He says:

"During the whole time I was with the army I availed myself of every means to gain correct information as to the battle and all the details connected with it. No one can get the truth by a reading of the newspaper correspondence so well as by conversation with the officers and soldiers who were in the fight. There is no use trying to disguise or cover up the fact that our army was badly surprised on Sunday morning. *Up to the time that General Grant assumed command at Pittsburg Landing, General Sherman was in command, and kept his pickets of infantry and cavalry out in front of his lines for three or four miles, but after Grant arrived this was entirely neglected, and, notwithstanding scouts, deserters from the enemy, and citizens reported to General Grant, through the proper officers, that the main body of the enemy were approaching our lines, he indignantly scorned the idea of an attack, saying that Generals Johnson and Beauregard were not d—d fools enough to attack us here.* * * * * *

On Saturday night before the battle the rebel army was moved up so close to our front lines that, as a rebel prisoner informed me, they could hear the soldiers talking in their camps. At daylight the enemy commenced the attack with not less than seventy five thousand men. They rushed into some of our camps before our soldiers had time to fall into line of battle, and while many of our officers were asleep."

In the concluding part of the letter, he says:

"Although our victory on Monday was complete, and the rebels utterly routed, yet it was too dearly purchased. *The criminal carelessness, or something worse, on the part of General Grant, whereby so many brave soldiers were slaughtered, admits of no palliation or excuse. Newspaper correspondents may write as they please, but the united voice of every soldier in Grant's army condemns him, and it is now time that the Government should do likewise.*"

From all I can learn from the troops from Iowa who participated in this battle, with whom I have conversed, both officers and men, this is but an expression of a conviction made on the minds of all of them. *The Iowa troops have been in battle repeatedly under command of General Grant; they have no confidence in his capacity and fitness for the high position he now holds. They regard him as the author of the useless slaughter of many hundreds of their brave comrades in arms. It is not necessary, nor is it right, to compel them to serve under him.* The speech of the Senator from Ohio might, if unnoticed, induce those in authority to continue him in the field. I understand he has been virtually suspended; that he now really has no command; that each division and army corps of the Western Department is under the command of another General, and the whole under the command of General Halleck; that General Grant is *second* in command of the whole, which is, of course, merely nominal. *In my opinion he ought not to have multiplied thousands of men placed in his hands after the record which he has made.* And the only practical tendency of that part of the speech of the Senator from Ohio would be to induce the President to assign him an active command. This I can not consent to have done in the presence of my countrymen, maimed and slaughtered, as I believe, through his carelessness or incompetency I say this not on account of any public or private grievance of a personal nature. I do not know General Grant, have never met him at any time, and could, therefore, have no personal grief to redress.

I think it much better to present our personal convictions in relation to the character of our Generals to the Secretary of War and to the President. For myself, I uniformly pursue this course, and regret that it has, in my judgment, become necessary to depart from it in this case. *But, sir, it is often as dangerous and as wicked to praise the unworthy and incompetent as to detract from the meritorious. If my convictions are correct, it would be a crime for me to remain silent, and suffer influences to originate in the Senate Chamber which may result in restoring a General to an active command whom I and the people I in part represent deem unworthy of such a trust.* Iowa has sent to the field about twenty thousand troops. They have behaved, I think, well on every battle-field where they have appeared. As far as I know, no Iowa regiment has ever faltered in the discharge of duty, however perilous. Their numbers have been reduced by the casualties of the field and camp nearly one-fourth. They gave their lives with firmness to aid in restoring the supremacy of the laws. But, sir, they believe, and I believe, that a large per cent. of this loss was useless, and is justly attributable to the carelessness or inability of General Grant. And he shall not, with my consent, be continued in command. There is nothing in his antecedents to justify a further trial of his military skill. *At Belmont he committed an egregious and unpardonable military blunder, which resulted in almost annihilating an Iowa regiment. At Fort Donelson, the right wing of our army, which was under his immediate command, was defeated and driven back several miles from the enemy's works. The battle was restored by Gen. Smith, the enemy's works were stormed, and thus a victory was finally won.* And so on the battle-field of Shiloh, his army was completely surprised, as I believe from all the facts I can procure, on Sunday, and nothing but the stubborn bravery of the men fighting by regiments and brigades, saved the army from utter destruction. The battle was afterward restored and conducted by General Buell and other Generals, who came on the field during the evening and night; and our forces ultimately succeeded in completely routing the enemy. Now, sir, with such a record, *those who continue General Grant in an active command will, in my opinion, carry on their skirts the blood of thousands of their slaughtered countrymen.* With my convictions, I can neither do it myself nor silently permit it to be done by others.

SPOONS FOR BUTLER—PONIES FOR GRANT.

[From the Port Gibson (Miss.) Standard, July 23.]

We read in a Mobile paper that a little son of General Grant rides about in the City of Washington on a pony, followed by a soldier in the uniform of the United States army. We think the occupation of the soldier might be more aptly filled by an eunuch of the Eastern hemisphere. But to the pony there hangs a tale: If it is a Shetland pony, it belongs to James W. Watson, of this county. After the surrender of Vicksburg, Grant's little boy rode a pony about the streets of that city attended by a negro. The little boy used to say that *Pa captured* him from the rebs. But the rebs thought his Pa had *stolen* him from the owner; and that stealing ponies for his children was not leading them in the way they should go. People in this region talk freely about the thefts of Butler and Washburne; but in our ethics there is little or no difference between stealing spoons and stealing ponies—since neither should be taken for public military use, or accounted for in the quartermaster's department. If there is truth in history, General Scott would have had all three of the foregoing Generals arrested, tried, and punished by court-martial.

The Radicals of the Georgia House of Representatives endeavored to elect a negro door-keeper the other day, but ingloriously failed

---

Hon. Mr. Ela, of New Hampshire, now canvassing for the Republican party in the Valley of Virginia, was asked the question: "Whether he would consent for his daughter to marry a negro?" He replied, "I decline to answer that question."

The negro who attempted to assassinate Judge Ogden, in New Orleans, because the Judge "had abused carpet-baggers," has been sentenced to only two year's imprisonment, in that he used a club instead of a knife or pistol in his attempt to murder.

Numerous anonymous letters have been received through the Columbus (Ga.) post-office within the past few days addressed to various citizens, and containing fiendish threats of burning the town. Great excitement prevails, and should such a calamity occur, the people are firmly resolved to try the virtues of hemp, steel and lead, as antidotes to negro incendiarism.

Rev. Crammond Kennedy, of New York, now in the service of the Freedmen's Union Commission, enjoyed, on a recent Sunday, the hospitality of Biddeford, Maine. He was recommended to the Mayor by the ministers of the various churches, in order to obtain the City Hall free, and was promised its use for half price. After enduring many petty vexations that night, and gaining the munificent sum of $7 77 to support a lady from that city now teaching in Columbia, S. C., he was the next morning charged by the Mayor full price, $25, for the hall, insulted when he remonstrated, and arrested and put under charge of a Constable till he could find security for $30.

Mr. Trumbull says: "When we say that all men are created equal we do not mean that every man in organized society has the same rights. We do not tolerate that in Illinois. I know that there is a distinction between the two races, because the Almighty himself has marked it upon their very faces, and, in my judgment, man can not, by legislation or otherwise, produce a perfect equality between those races so that they will live happily together. * * * There is a distinction between the white and black races made by Omnipotence himself. I do not believe these two races can live happily and pleasantly together and enjoy equal rights without one domineering over the other; and, therefore, I advocate the policy of separating these races by a system which shall rid the country of the black race as it becomes free."

Mr. Woolley has been informed by three responsible gentlemen here that they heard Manager Logan say he had arranged with the negro waiters at Willard's Hotel to allow him (Logan) to inspect all of Woolley's dispatches before delivering them into the telegraph office, and had by this means possessed himself of every dispatch which Woolley had sent off. It will test public credulity to believe this statement, but the gentlemen, one of them a member of Congress, are all here to make good what they say.—*Washington Correspondence.*

It is now ascertained that the recent Democratic victory in South Carolina, is mainly attributable to the fact that the ballot-boxes were not tampered with after the polling was concluded, as they were after the preceding election.

Two negroes, named respectively Josh Middleton and John Dixon, who claim to be brothers, had a quarrel in Savannah, Ga., which resulted in the latter being severely stabbed in the arm by the former.

About three weeks ago, L. S. Owen, Esq., of Tupelo, Miss., was arrested by a Federal Lieutenant named Morrison, for exercising his authority as United States Commissioner, in arresting a scalawag who was publicly endeavoring to incite the blacks against the whites in his county. Mr. Owen has been in close confinement until the 22d instant, when he was released upon a writ of *habeas corpus* issued by Judge Hill.

Meade returns 16,089 African voters in Florida. The State census of 1867 shows only 15,104 negro males of twenty-one and over. Queer, isn't it?

Colfax and his family will leave Chicago, August 3, on their proposed Rocky Mountain excursion, and the Springfield *Republican* in announcing the fact says brass bands are strictly forbidden on the route. The party will furnish all the brass necessary.

Among the fighting Generals whom the Senate has recently rejected is General Francis L. Price, of New Jersey, who was named as Consul to Havana. General Price went in as Adjutant and came out commanding the famous Second New Jersey Brigade. He will give the Radicals more trouble in New Jersey than the Senate could have given him pleasure by a confirmation.

One of Brownlow's pets, recently pardoned out of the penitentiary by that tender-hearted saint, has recently been arrested in Nashville, on the charge of administering chloroform to a whole family in East Tennessee, from the effects of which an old lady died, and robbing the house of one thousand dollars in money.

John A. Bingham undertook to address a Grant meeting at Bangor the other day, when the ghost of Mrs. Surratt appeared to him on the stage, and he hastened back to Washington.

A large and enthusiastic meeting of Israelites was held in Memphis, Tenn., on the evening of July 15. Stirring speeches by the Rabbi and others were made, and a series of strong resolutions adopted, denouncing Grant and his infamous order. The proceedings indicate that the Jews of Memphis, at least, are a unit against the Radical standard bearer.

Senator Wilson introduced a joint resolution requiring all civil officers of Virginia and Texas to take the iron clad oath, or be removed. This he calls Reconstruction. General Grant would call it Peace.

Radical ex-Congressman Whaley, of West Virginia, has come to grief. It is reported that he is connected with a ring engaged in smuggling, and will shortly be removed from office.

Hundreds of colored voters were in the Seymour and Blair procession in Macon, Ga., a few nights since, and thousands more cheered it on with right good will.

In 1864, Grant wrote, in relation to his proposed nomination for the Presidency: "I would regard such a consummation as being highly unfortunate to myself, if not to my country." In 1868, the country agrees with him, in both respects, and will take him at his word.

At a West Point, Mississippi, Democratic jubilee, recently, says a Mississippi paper, 195 freedmen, who voted the Radical ticket at the late election, acknowledged their error, "professed strong faith in Democracy, and were admitted into full membership into our Democratic Club, took badges, and received certificates of their membership."

The *Courrier des Etats Unis*, the organ of the French population in this country, says: "The Radicals have had their day and done their work. It is upon the Democratic party that the work devolves of rebuilding where they have cast down, and of reconstituting upon a solid basis the elements of social reorganization which they have sacrificed to a narrow spirit of personal authority."

A North Carolina Congressman carpetbagger has just escaped the chance to do the Radicals great service. For weeks he was missing, not having been seen since he started from Tarboro' to Washington. He was trooly loil, and his friends grew alarmed. They were anxiously looking to find his hair in one county and his boots in another, and were desirous to make a first class martyr out of him for campaign consumption.

Two days ago, however, he (Lash is his name) turned up, and declared he had been suffering a "severe indisposition." The quotation is understood.

Will some of Grant's dozen biographers tell a curious world why that hero drops out of his captaincy in 1854 and goes to chopping wood at $40 a month?

Only one member of Lincoln's original Cabinet is now acting with the Radicals, and that one is the notorious corruptionist, Simon Cameron.

The Radical papers insist that Governor Seymour is liable to become insane; "thank God, he is not liable to delirium tremens," says the New Hampshire *Patriot*.

The statement of the public debt for July will show an increase of at least five or six millions of dollars during the month. Forty-five millions in coin have been taken from the vaults of the Treasury to pay the principal and interest due on bonds.

What Governor Wise said was, "Secession is not yet dead. The people are going to secede from Radicalism." Yet the Radicals (including the always harmless and generally decent *ad interim* New York *Times*) leave off the last sentence and make the first a test.

"Rebel"—The watchword of Treasury thieves.

"The Rebels"—Two-thirds of the white people of the country.

"Loyalty"—The Radical apology for public robbery.

"Traitor"—A Radical argument which costs the country $500,000,000 a year in time of peace.

The Cleveland *Leader* admits that a "change of one vote in every ward and township would give Ohio to the Democracy." Well, the Democracy will go them one better in "every ward and township."

Orville Grant, a brother of the General, lives in Chicago, and has just given $100 to a Seymour and Blair club. And a man's foes shall be those of his own household.

Another Southern "citizen" appears in the reconstruction of Willard Warner as an United States Senator from Alabama. Warner is not only a citizen of Ohio, but he was actually a member of the last Legislature of that State.

The Israelites of Nashville, Tenn., have held a large and enthusiastic meeting to consider their action in the coming Presidential election. Grant's famous Order No. 11, in which he banished all Jews from his army lines was read and received with groans and hisses. Strong resolutions were adopted, denunciatory of the order and its author.

In 1859 Charles D. Drake, now Radical United States Senator, tried to get a bill through the Missouri Legislature, of which he was then a member, the object of which was to drive Francis P. Blair, jr., from the State of Missouri because of his opposition to the extension of slavery. Soon Vice-President Blair will have the pleasure of calling this fellow Drake to order.

General Scott predicted that, when the war should be over, it would be "impossible to restrain the fury of non-combatants!"

General McClellan resigned on the 8th, the day of the election, and before the result of the election was known. Will General Grant do as much?

When Donnelly said Washburne carried Grant in his breeches pocket, General Butler remarked, "It was the proper place for small change."

A few months ago Greeley said: "Probably Gen. Grant can afford to be a deaf and dumb candidate, but this country can not afford to elect a deaf and dumb President."

Mrs. Stowe is reported to be starting a school for mulatto children at Aiken, S. C. If this be true, it shows what Sumner calls "the accursed spirit of Caste" in great violence, since white and black are both excluded.

The Charleston *News* asserts that Gen. Canby appointed a negro alderman because the people did not pay him social respect, this motive being to punish and humiliate them for their ostracism.

A disgusted Virginia Conventionist, named John Hodgskin, recently published the following card: "I this day sever my connection with all political organizations, and shall hereafter endeavor to pay more attention to my future salvation."

The North Carolina (Mongrel) Convention has decreed that the word negro must no longer be used in speaking of those persons whom the custom of ages has thus denominated, and who constitute the majority of that assembly.

Mr. Sherman, in the debate in the Senate applauding Stanton's course, said: He (Mr. Sherman) was of opinion Mr. Stanton would stand higher in history in the minds of the people, had he voluntarily resigned the office to the President, who, in Mr. Sherman's opinion, had power to remove him.

The "voice of New York," hot for impeachment, is proclaimed to us through Hon. John Cochrane and C. S. Spencer. We are reminded by this couple of the three tailors that once held a mass meeting in a room on a back street in the city of London, and styled themselves, "We, the people of England!"

There is no knowing what "Reconstruction" costs. The $87,000 deficiency voted for Alabama and Georgia, is only one of numerous like deficiencies to come. Millions upon millions are the taxes Northern white laborers pay to govern the whites of the South by the use of the negroes.

Thurlow Weed remarks: "We do not say that Mr. Greeley was paid like a common lobby man, but we do know that Dean Richmond—"peace to his ashes"—has often said in our presence that "Greeley was a d—d expensive cuss."

If the war was fought, says the Cairo *Democrat*, to free and enfranchise the negro; to create a bondholding aristocracy, and to weigh the laboring classes to the earth with taxes to support that aristocracy, were not a million soldiers grossly deceived as to its object?

The Radical campaign in the country begins with the expulsion, at the National Capitol, of one hundred and fifty soldiers' votes from the ballot-box—soldiers residing there with their families. It is thus that they claim the control of the city government, and by such acts only can they hope for success. This disfranchisement of the soldiers is the first victory of Radicalism.

Thurlow Weed says the pending measures of Congress to wipe out all vestige of civil authority in the South will accomplish two objects, viz: "Inaugurate negro supremacy at the South, and overthrow Radical supremacy in the North. If this be the only way of relieving the country from a political scourge, let us submit to it patiently. Indeed, the Scriptures teach that evil is permitted that good may come."

Forney, in a letter from Chicago to the Philadelphia *Press*, says that the Radical party, five hundred thousand strong, composed of the black Union Leagues of the South and the white Loyalists of the North, are armed *cap-a-pie*, and are ready with the ballot or bayonet to carry the election this fall.

In New York, William Roche was recently indicted and placed on trial for divulging the contents of a telegram without the consent of the company. "Pshaw," said Mr. Oakley Hall, the District Attorney, "I move, your Honor, that he be discharged. I don't believe the time of the court should be wasted in trying this man for what Congress has been doing recently by wholesale." Mr. Roche was accordingly discharged.

Mr. Sherman, on the 21st of June, 1868, in advocating a bill to give twenty millions additional currency to the National Bank circulation, said the attempt to postpone it was a dodge on the part of the men who held stock in the country banks, or words to that effect, whereupon, Mr. Cameron jumped up and said it might be shown that Mr. Sherman held as much stock as others and at any rate the word "dodge" was not a proper one to use. The customary disclaimer was entered immediately and debate went on smoothly.

As General Sherman's name has been brought into the controversy between the President and General Grant, it may not be amiss to state that the President is in receipt of a letter from General Sherman, which is understood to have this paragraph in it: "If Stanton won't resign, and there is no other way of getting rid of him, ulterior measures should be resorted to." This letter, together with one other of a very important character, may reach the public eye if the unfortunate controversy is pressed any further.

There is a lesson for the people of Missouri (says the Missouri *Republican*), in the position of Senator Henderson, and every fresh aspersion on his name gives it additional cogency. It illustrates the bitter vindictiveness of that political organization which seeks to permanently rule this State. It shows that this Radical party requires of those it elects to office a practical abnegation of honor and integrity where they interfere with party interests and schemes; and that even where the officer has talent and influence, if through pure motives he act contrary to the wishes of Radicalism, he is to be thrown overboard without ceremony.

Seymour's Letter of Acceptance.

The following is Horatio Seymour's acceptance of the Democratic nomination for the Presidency. It does not appear in its appropriate place because the book had gone to press before the letter was made public:

GENTLEMEN—When in the city of New York, on the 11th ult., in the presence of a vast multitude, on behalf of the National Democratic Convention, you tendered to me its unanimous nomination as their candidate for the office of President of the United States, I stated that "I had no words adequate to express my gratitude for the good will and kindness which that body had shown to me." Its nomination was unsought and unexpected. It was my ambition to take an active part, from which I am now excluded, in the great struggle going on for the restoration of good government, of peace and prosperity to our country; but I have been caught up by the whelming tide which is bearing us on to a great political change, and I find myself unable to resist its pressure. You have, also, given me a copy of the resolutions put forth by the Convention, showing its position upon all the great questions which now agitate the country. As the presiding officer of that Convention, I am familiar with their scope and import. As one of its members, I am a party to their terms. They are in accord with my views, and I stand upon them in the contest upon which we are now entering, and I shall strive to carry them out in the future, wherever I may be placed, in political or private life. I then stated that I would send you these words of acceptance in a letter, as is the customary form.

I see no reason, upon reflection, to change or qualify the terms of my approval of the resolutions of the Convention. I have delayed the mere formal action of communicating to you in writing what I thus publicly said, for the purpose of seeing what light the action of Congress would throw upon the interests of the country. Its acts, since the adjournment of the Convention, show an alarm lest a change of political power will give to the people what they ought to have—a clear statement of what has been done with the money drawn from them during the past eight years. Thoughtful men feel that there have been wrongs in the financial management, which have been kept from the public knowledge.

The Congressional party has not only allied to itself the military power, which is to be brought to bear directly upon the elections in many States, but holds itself in perpetual session, with the avowed purpose of making such laws as it shall see fit, in view of the elections which will take place within a few weeks. It did, therefore, not adjourn, but took a recess, to meet again if its partisan interests shall demand its reassembling. Never before, in the history of our country, has Congress thus taken a menacing attitude toward its electors. Under its influence, some of the States organized by its agents, are proposing to deprive the people of the right to vote for Presidential electors, and the first bold steps are taken to destroy the rights of suffrage. It is not strange, therefore, that thoughtful men see in such action the proof that there is, with those who shape the policy of the Republican party, a motive stronger and deeper than the mere wish to hold political power; that there is a dread of some exposure, which drives them on to acts so desperate and so impolitic. Many of the ablest leaders and journals of the Republican party have openly deplored the violence of Congressional action and its tendency to keep up discord in our country. The great interests of our Union demand peace, order, and a return to those international pursuits, without which we can not maintain the faith or honor of our Government. The minds of business men are perplexed by uncertainties. The hours of toil of our laborers are lengthened by the costs of living, made by the direct and indirect exactions of Government. Our people are harassed by the frequent demands of the tax-gatherer. Without distinction of party, there is a strong feeling in favor of that line of action which shall restore order and confidence, and shall lift off the burdens which now hinder and vex the industry of the country. Yet, at this moment, those in power have thrown into the Senate chambers and Congressional halls a new element of discord and violence. Men have been admitted as Representatives of some of the Southern States with the declaration upon their lips that they can not live in the States they claim to represent without military protection. These men are to make laws for the North as well as the South. These men, who, a few days since, were seeking, as suppliants, that Congress would give them power within their respective States, are to-day the controllers of the actions of these bodies. Entering them with minds filled with questions, and demands from Congress that it should look upon the States from which they come as in a condition of civil war, and that a majority of their populations, embracing their intelligence, shall be treated as public enemies; that an army shall be kept up at the cost of the people of the North, and that there shall be no peace and order at the South save what is made by arbitrary power.

Every intelligent man knows that they not only owe their present positions to disorder, but that every motive springing from the love of power, of gain, of a desire for vengeance, prompts them to keep the South in anarchy. While that exists, they are independent of the wills or wishes of their fellow-citizens While confusion reigns, they are the defenders of the profits and the honors which grow out of a government of mere force. These men are now placed in positions where they can not only urge their views of politics, but where they can enforce them.

When there shall be admitted in this manner men from the remaining Southern States, although they will have in truth no constituents, they will have more influence in the Senate than a majority of the people of this Union, living in the line of the great States. In vain, members of the Republican party protested against the policy that led to this result. While the chiefs of the late rebellion have submitted to the result of the war, and are now quietly engaged in useful pursuits for the support of themselves and their families, and are trying, by the force of their example, to lead back the people of the South to the order and industry not only essential to their well-being, but to the greatness and prosperity of our community, all see that those who, without ability or influence, have been thrown by the agitations of civil convulsion into positions of honor and of profit, are striving to keep alive the passions to which they owe their elevation, and they clamorously insist that they are the only friends of our Union. Proof of that can only have sure foundation in fraternal regard, and a common desire to promote the peace, the order, and the happiness of all portions of our land.

Events in Congress, since the adjournment of the Convention, have vastly increased the importance of a political victory by those who are seeking to bring back economy, simplicity and justice, into the administration of our national affairs. Many Republicans have heretofore clung to their party, who have regretted the extremes of violence to which it has run. They have cherished a faith that while the action of their political friends has been mistaken, their motives have been good. They must now see that the Republican party is in that condition that it can not carry out a peaceful policy, whatever its motives may be. It is a misfortune, not only to the country, but to the governing party itself, that its action is unchecked by any form of opposition. It has been the misfortune of the Republican party that the events of the past few years have given it so much power that it has been able to shackle the Executive, to trammel the judiciary, and carry out the views of the most unwise and violent of its members. When this state of things exists in any party, it has ever been found that the judgment of its ablest leaders does not control it. There is hardly an able man who has helped to build up the Republican organization who has not, within the past three years, warned it against its excesses, and who has not been borne down and forced to give up his convictions of what the interests of the country call for; or, if too patriotic to do this, who has not been driven from its ranks. If this has been the case heretofore, what will be its action with this new infusion of men who, without a decent respect for the views of those who had just given them their positions, begin their legislative career with calls for arms, and demands that the States shall be regarded as in a condition of civil war, and a declaration that they are ready and anxious to degrade the President of the United States whenever they can persuade or force Congress to bring forward new articles of impeachment. The Republican party, as well as we, are interested in putting some check upon this violence.

It must be clear to every thinking man, that a distribution of political power tends to check the violence of party action, and assures the peace and good order of the country. The election of a Democratic Executive and a majority of Democratic members of the House of Representatives would not give to that party organization power to make sudden or violent changes, but would serve to check those extreme measures which have been deplored by the best men of both organizations. The result would most certainly lead to that peaceful restoration of the Union and re-establishment of fraternal relationship which the country desires. I am sure the best men of the Republican party deplore as deeply as I do the spirit of violence shown by those recently admitted to seats in Congress. The condition of civil war, which they contemplate, must be abhorrent to every right-thinking man.

I have no mere personal wishes which mislead my judgment in regard to the pending election. No man who has weighed and measured the duties of the office of President of the United States can fail to be impressed with the cares and toils of him who is to meet its demands. It is not merely to float with popular currents, without a policy or a purpose. On the contrary, while our Constitution gives a just weight to the public will, its distinguishing feature is that it seeks to protect the rights of minorities; its greatest glory is, that it puts restraints upon power; it gives force and form to those maxims and principles of civil liberty for which the martyrs of freedom have struggled through ages; it declares the right of the people to be secure in their persons, houses and papers, against unreasonable searches and seizures; that Congress shall make no law respecting the establishment of religion or the free exercise thereof, or abridging the freedom of speech or of the press; or the right of the people to petition for redress of grievances. It secures the right of a speedy and public trial by an impartial jury. No man can rightfully enter upon the duties of the Presidential office, unless he is not only willing to carry out the wishes of the people, expressed in a constitutional way, but is also prepared to stand up for the rights of minorities. He must be ready to uphold the free exercise of religion; he must denounce measures which would wrong personal or home rights, or the religious conscience of the humblest citizen in the land; he must maintain, without distinction of creed or nationality, all the privileges of an American citizenship. The experience of every public man who has been faithful to his trust, teaches him that no one can do the duties of the office of President unless he is ready not only to undergo the falsehoods of the bad, but to suffer from the censure of the good, who are misled by prejudices and misrepresentations. There are no appreciations in such positions which deceive my judgment, when I say that a great change is going on in the public mind. The mass of the Republican party are more thoughtful and tempered and just than they were during the excitement which attended the progress and close of the civil war.

As the energy of the Democratic party springs from their devotion to their cause and to their candidates, I may, with propriety, speak of the fact that never, in the political history of our country, has the action of any like body been hailed with such universal and real enthusiasm as that which has been shown in relation to the position of the National Democratic Convention. With this the candidates had nothing to do. Had any others of those named been selected, this spirit would have been, perhaps, more marked. The zeal and energy of the conservative masses spring from a desire to make a change of policy, and from a thought that they can carry out their purposes. In this faith they are strengthened by the co-operation of the great body of those who served in the Union army, and many during the war. Having given nearly 16,000 commissions to the officers of that army, I know their views and wishes. They demand the Union for which they fought. The largest meeting of these gallant soldiers ever assembled was in New York, and indorsed the action of the National Convention in words distinct with meaning. They called on the Government to stop in its policy of hate, discord and disunion, and, in terms of fervid eloquence, demanded restoration of the rights of the American people.

When there is such accord between those who proved themselves brave and self-sacrificing in war, and those who are thoughtful and patriotic in council, I can not doubt we shall gain a political triumph which will restore our Union, bring back peace to our land, and give us once more the blessings of a wise, economical and honest government.

I am, gentlemen, truly yours, etc.,
HORATIO SEYMOUR.

To Gen. G. W. MORGAN and others, Committee, etc.

INDEX.

Alabama, vote of, on Constitution of 1868, 139. Readmission of, to representation, 138.

Aldrich, Judge, of S. C. Removal of, by General Canby, 133.

Ames, Oakes, of Mass. A disinterested Legislator, 62.

Amnesty. President Johnson's Proclamation of, 363.

Andrews, ex-Governor, of Mass. Indisposition to avert Disunion, 77.

Argus, Albany. On violation by Radicals of Declaration of Independence, 18.

Arkansas. Mr. Lincoln's movement to reorganize State, 14. Startling provisions in Constitution of, 130. Readmitted to Representation, 134. Veto of act readmitting, 135. Vote of, on holding Convention, 135. Protest against admitting Representatives from, 136. Act to make stallion-keepers and other business and professional men take the Test-oath, 334. Bill to prescribe Confederate uniform for penitentiary convicts, 334.

Army, U. S. Possession of polls at Nashville by, 208.

Arnell, Samuel M., of Tenn. Opposition in House to admission of, 200.

Ashburn, G. W. Military arrest and trial of citizens of Columbus, Georgia, for alleged murder of, 157, 333.

Ashley, Jas. M., of Ohio. Impeachment resolutions of, 98.

Atkinson, Bishop, of N. C. On mortality among negroes, 379.

Baldwin, A. C., of Michigan. Refused a rightful seat in Congress, 92.

Ballard, Judge, of Ky. Imprisonment of a Catholic priest by, 366.

Banks, N. P., jr., of Mass. Disunion sentiments of, 72.

Bastile, at National Capitol. Character of, 90.

Bayard, James A., of Delaware. On the capacity of Mr. Wade as a trier of the President, 108.

Beck, James B., of Ky., and James Brooks, of New York. Protest of, 122.

Beecher, Henry Ward. Letter of, to Soldiers' and Sailors' Convention at Cleveland, 50. Disunion sentiment of, 72.

Beef. Taxes paid by a, 296.

Bingham, Jno. A., of Ohio. On the reduction of the Supreme Court, 48. On admission of Kansas, 143.

Blair, Gen. C. W., of Kansas. Casts vote of Kansas for F. P. Blair., jr., 235.

Blair, General Francis P., of Mo. Nominated as Democratic Candidate for Vice President, 235. Speech of acceptance of, 239. Letter of acceptance of, 396. Biography of, 352. His war on the Test-oath, 354. His letter to J. O. Broadhead, 355.

Blasphemy of Radical leaders. Specimens of, 212.

Bonds, U. S. Vote on taxing, 278, 279, 280, 286. Herald on the proposition, 287. Character of, 299. Gold-bearing, outstanding, 300.

Boston Post. On imprisonment of C. W. Woolley, 90.

Bowen, C. C., of South Carolina. Antecedents of, 330.

Boyden, Nathaniel, of North Carolina. On bill to arm the militia, 336.

Boyer, Benjamin M., of Penn. On the action of Congress in the McArdle case, 263.

Bradley. A negro Senator in Georgia Legislature, speech of, 330.

Brooks, James, of New York. Turned out of his seat in Congress, 92. Protest of J. B. Beck, of Kentucky, 122. On redeeming 5-20s in greenbacks, 302.

Breckinridge, Rev. R. J., of Kentucky. Incendiary denunciation of Catholics by, 364.

Brown, ex-Governor Joe, of Georgia. A delegate to Radical Convention, 180. War record of, 180.

Brown, John Young, of Kentucky. Refused a seat in Congress, 93.

Brown, Simeon, of Mass. Disunion sentiments of, 72.

Brown, T. W., of Tenn. Reads address of people to Democratic National Convention, 228.

Brown, W. Matt., Mayor of Nashville. Correspondence with Major-General G. H. Thomas, 205.

Browning, O. H. On the question of veracity between the President and Gen. Grant, 172.

Brownlow, W. G., Gov. of Tennessee. Exercise of pardoning power by, 204. His plan of disposing of the negroes, 204. Usurpations of, sustained by the United States army, 204. Speech at Philadelphia Convention, 370. On redeeming 5-20s in greenbacks, 300.

Buchanan, ex-President. Disrespect to memory of, by Radical House of Representatives, 214.

Burbridge. Reign of terror of, in Kentucky, 374.

(389)

Buckner, Gen. S. B., of Ky. Speech of, at Soldiers' and Sailors' Convention, 254.

Burlingame, Anson, of Mass. Disunion sentiment of, 72.

Burnside, A. E., Governor of Rhode Island. Dispatch on impeachment, 104.

Busteed, Judge Richard, of Alabama. Fierce rhetoric of, 371.

Butler, B. F., of Massachusetts. Tilt of, with C. Wendell, 59. Short count of Mr. Wooley's money, 59. His system of espionage, 212. His corruptions in New Orleans, 60. His remarks on impeachment, 102. His bets on impeachment, 108. His exposure of the National Bank system, 308. His speech at Philadelphia, 370.

Butler, R. R., of Tennessee. Debate in House on admission of, 197. Record of, in Tennessee Legislature, 197. Candidates' oath taken by, 202.

Cabinet, Letters of five members of, verifying the President's position in the Grant controversy, 171.

Callicott, ex-Speaker of the New York Assembly, sent to the penitentiary, 66. Retained in office by the Senate while a convict, 216.

Campbell, Jas. B., speech of, on casting vote of South Carolina for Mr. Seymour, 231.

Campbell, Lewis D., of Ohio. Indorsement of Democratic Platform by, 254.

Carpet-baggers, harvest for, 145. Intelligence of, 153. Mr. Lincoln's opinion of, 379.

Carpet-bags and Commerce, 360.

Cary, General S. F., of Ohio, approves the Democratic platform, 256.

Catholics, War of the Radicals on, 364. Radical opinions, 365.

Chandler, Zachary, of Michigan, cowhided by General Grant, 34. Blood-letting letter of, 77.

Chicago Times on the new Electoral College Bill, 338.

Chipley, Wm. S., father of one of the Columbus prisoners, petition of, 160.

Church, Sanford E., of New York. Presentation of name in National Convention, 227.

Civil Rights Bill, 269.

Clerical Politicians. Resolutions of, at Chicago, on impeachment, 359.

Cody, Mr., of Georgia. Imprisonment and treatment of, by military, 161.

Coffroth, A. H., of Pennsylvania, turned out of his seat by the Radicals, 92.

Colfax, Schuyler. Letter of acceptance of, 22. Know-Nothingism of, 44. His record, 181. His resolutions on Mr. Alexander Long, 182. Turnkey at Capitol, 90. His hurry to have Mr. Milligan hung, 362. His views of Catholicism, 368.

Columbus, Georgia. Arrest and treatment of citizens of, by military, 160.

Conjury. Practice of, under military in the South, 158.

Congress. Responsibility of, for expenditures, 63. Reconstruction Acts of, 116. Usurping act of, placing Grant and the army beyond the direct orders of the President, 371. Act snatching from the Supreme Court jurisdiction in the McArdle case, 263. Nonentity of, 377. Corruption of, 57.

Curtin, A. G., Governor, of Pennsylvania. His acknowledgment of aid from Governor Seymour, 345.

Congress, Democratic members of. Protest Against the Indemnity Act, 85. Protest against admission of Arkansas members, 136.

Conservative Convention, at Philadelphia, in 1866. Platform, officers and committees of, 176.

Constitution of the United States, 5. Violation of, by Radicals, 5, 6, 7, 8 and 9. Abnegation of, by Chicago Convention, 20. Abnegation of, by Grant and Colfax, 20–22. Fourteenth Amendment to, 117, 209. Thirteenth Amendment to, 209. Mr. Seward as to ratification of Fourteenth Amendment, 274. Power to amend treated by the New Orleans Picayune, 210. Bogus ratification of the Fourteenth Amendment, 274. Chas. O'Conner on, 276.

Constitutions of rotten boroughs admitted to representation in lieu of Southern States, 126. The builders of, 124. Social equality of, 127. Qualification of voters and officeholders under, 127. Public school provisions of, 127. Monstrosities of, 139. Cost of, 134.

Constitutional Eagle, Camden, Arkansas, office of, destroyed by military, 163.

Corruption of the Radical party, 57.

Cox, S. S., of Ohio. Resolutions of, against military imprisonment of citizens, 82.

Covode, John, of Pennsylvania, on the purchase of high officials, 57.

Crittenden, John J., resolutions by, declaring the object of the war, 68. Peace resolutions of, in Senate, March 2, 1861, 74.

Cromwell, negro delegate in Louisiana Convention. Speech of, 125.

Cross, Col. David C., of Arkansas. Military imprisonment of, 157.

Cummings, Rev. John A., of Missouri. Decision of Supreme Court in Test-oath case of, 191.

Cunningham, L. B., State Treasurer of Arkansas. Removal of, by Gen. Ord, 132.

Davis, Judge David, of Supreme Court. Decision in the Milligan case, 188.

Deaf and dumb of the District of Columbia. Proposal to sell out the, by E. B. Washburne, 361.

Declaration of Independence, 16. Radical violations of, 18–19. Indorsement of, by, 18.

Defrees, J. D., Superintendent of Public Printing, on National Labor Convention, 363.

Delano, C., of Ohio, takes Gen. Geo. W. Morgan's seat in Congress, 95.

Delegates to Democratic National Convention. List of, 240.

Democratic members of Congress. Protests of, against Indemnity act, 85. Against admission of Arkansas members, 136.

Democratic Party. Proceedings of National Convention of, in 1868, 217.

Democratic Platforms. Of 1864, 51. Of 1868, 224.

Dewees, Carpet-bagger, of North Carolina, on bill to arm the militia, 336.

Dodge, Augustus C., of Iowa. Presentation of, for Vice-President, 233.

Donnelly and Washburne. Congressional courtesies of, 60.

Doolittle, Jas. R., Senator from Wisconsin. Presentation of name of, for the Presidency, 227. Letter in favor of Blair and Seymour, 255. Extract from a letter of, to New York

meeting, 378. Speech of, on Reconstruction, 144.
Douglas, Stephen A., of Illinois, on the Republican opposition to adjustment, 75–76.
Dunn, O. J., (negro), Lieut.-Governor, of Louisiana, 149.
Dunbar, Edward E. Expose of condition of the U. S. Treasury by, 289.
Duvall, W. O. Disunion sentiment of, 72.
Eldridge, Chas. A., of Wisconsin, reports against impeachment, 98. On resolution of sympathy for Ireland, 273.
Electoral Colleges. Act with reference to counting vote of, 337. No of, in each State, 259.
English, James E., of Connecticut, presented for President in Democratic National Convention, 227.
Etheridge, Emerson. Arrest of, 258.
Evidence. Of pretended election frauds, 153. How obtained by Radicals in Georgia, 153.
Ewing, Gen. Thomas, jr. Speech of, in Soldiers' and Sailors' Convention, 243. Financial proposition of, 253. Speech of, in National Democratic Convention, 223. Named for Vice-President, 233.
Executive, Judicial and Legislative departments. Views of Washington on the necessary independence of each, 57. Views of Madison, 57. Of John Adams, 57. Of Judge Woodward, of Pennsylvania, 57.
Exemption. Amount of, covered in bogus constitution of Arkansas, 131.
Expenditures of England and United States contrasted, 284.
Fenians, of Philadelphia, for the Democratic ticket, 361.
Fenton, Reuben E., of New York. Antietam letter of, 376.
Fessenden, W. P., Senator from Maine, on the impeachment pressure, 106. On the Tenure-of-Office bill, 106.
Fields, Judge S. T., of the Supreme Court. Decision of, in Father Cummings' case, 191. In A. H. Garland's case, 194. In R. H. Marrs' case, 196. Named for President in Democratic National Convention, 228.
Finances. National, 277.
Financial view of Reconstruction, 133.
Florida. Olustee expedition to, 115. Vote on admitting her to representation, 139. Election frauds in, 152.
Forney, John W. Address of, to Washington negroes, 359.
Forrest, Gen. N, B., casts vote of Tennessee for Gen. F. P. Blair, jr., 234. Fort Pillow libel on, 213.
Foss, Rev. A. T., of New Hampshire. Disunion sentiment of, 72.
Frankfort, Ky. Mob at, 365.
Franklin, Gen. W. B., of Connecticut. Speech as President of Soldiers' and Sailors' Convention, 250. Letter of, to Democratic National Convention, 222.
Freedmen's Bureau. Outrages of, 183. Law creating the, 184. President's veto of, 184. Expenses of, 186. Salaries of officers of, 186. Amalgamation doctrines of, 186. Further continuance of, 188.
Funding bill, 329.
Garland, A. H., of Arkansas. Decision of Supreme Court in case of, 194
Garrison, W. Lloyd. Disunion sentiment of, 72.
Gazette, Cincinnati. Its opinion of Congress, 367.
Generals, Federal. Radical proscription of, 360.

Georgia and Mississippi. Injunction cases, 260–262.
Germans, of New York. On Democratic nominations, 368.
Giddings, J. R., of Ohio. Noted sentiment of, 72.
Gilbert, Colonel C. C., U. S. A. His views of the Freedom of the Press, 163.
Gold-bearing Bonds. Amount of, outstanding, 300.
Gorham, G. C., Secretary of the Senate. Antecedents of, 63.
Grant, U. S. Letter of acceptance of, 21. Record of, 23. Order relative to slaves, 23. How he voted for Douglas, 23. On Iowa soldiers voting, 23. His views on slavery, 23. Terms of General Lee's surrender, 23. Indorses General Lee's petition for pardon, 23. Protests against his indictment and trial, 24. Recommends that Senator Hunter be let alone, 24. Recommends clemency to General Pickett, 24. His views on negro suffrage, 24. Against arbitrary arrests, 24. Report on the condition of the Southern States in 1865, 25. His order looking to the suppression of newspapers, 25. His speech at Cincinnati, in 1866, 25. His father's letter on his candidacy, 26. Against sending troops to Baltimore, in 1866, 26. Against martial law, 26. His testimony before the impeachment committee, 26. He plays mum with his father on negro suffrage, 28. He indorses Congress, 28. His order expelling Hebrew citizens from his lines, 28. Resolution of Mr. Pendleton, of Ohio, thereon, 29. Resolution and speech of Senator Powell, of Kentucky, on same, 29. General Grant and the bondholders, 31. Wendell Phillips on Grant, 32-37. Grant's proper name, 33. He was not for an anti-slavery war of abolition, 33. He cowhides Senator Chandler, 34. The law conferring the rank of General, 34. The Israelites of St. Louis, on Grant, 34. Radical denunciation of Jews, 35. Senator Harlan on Grant as a General, 35. His tail, Colfax, 35. His suppression of newspapers, 36. His indorsement of the swingin'-round the-circle speeches of President Johnson, 36. He could not be induced to be President, 38. His murderous tactics, 38. His cruelty to prisoners, 39. His instructions to his military commanders to carry out the views of the Radicals, 40. His indorsement of his commanders of the several Districts of the South, 40. His career as Sam. Grant, 41. His opinion of himself as a statesman, 42. The cotton speculation of Grant, the father, aided by the son, 42. Grant's punishment of private soldiers, 43. What he thinks of the soldiers, 44. Question of veracity between Grant and President Johnson, 164. Certificate of Cabinet officers as to understanding between Grant and the President, 171. Correspondence between Grant and the President, 165. Telegrams to General Thomas, with reference to Nashville election, 206-207. Appropriation of Mr. Watson's pony by, 381. Groans for, by United States soldiers at Montgomery, 373. Recommends increase of force in Southern States, 131. Telegraph to General Buchanan, on administering oath to Louisiana Legislature, 150. Responsible for military arrests and outrages in the South, 162.

INDEX.

Great Britain and United States. Contrast of debt and expenses of, 284.
Greeley, Horace. Plan of adjustment proposed to Mr. Lincoln by, 175. Reads Mr. Thaddeus Stevens out, 304.
Greenbacks, legal-tender, 277. Payment of bonds in, 288. Views of Mr. Brooks on payment of 5-20s in, 302. Of Thaddeus Stevens on, 303. Of Senator Morton, of Indiana, on, 304. Of Brownlow on, 300. Of Horace Maynard on, 300.
Grier, Associate Justice of the Supreme Court. Protest of, in McArdle case, 269.
Griswold, John A. Radical candidate for Governor of New York. Legislative proprieties of, 213.
Habeas Corpus. Vote on suspension of, 85. Resolution with reference to, 82, 83.
Hale, J. P. Disunion sentiment of, 71.
Hamilton, A. J., of Texas. Speech of, at Philadelphia, 370.
Hampton, General Wade, casts the vote of South Carolina for General F. P. Blair, jr., 234.
Hancock, General W. S. Presentation of name of, for the Presidency, 227. Celebrated order of, 272. Letter of, to Mr. Glover, 357.
Harlan, James, of Iowa. Mysterious wealth of, 60. Speech of, on Grant, 379.
Harrington, Henry W., of Indiana. Habeas Corpus resolutions of, 83.
Helper, Hinton Rowan. Extracts from Book of, 70.
Henderson, J. B. Dispatch of E. W. Fox to, 103. Letter of Missouri Congressmen to, 103. Reply thereto, 103.
Hendricks, Thomas A., of Indiana. Presentation of name for the Presidency, 228. On bill to arm the militia, 335.
Herald, New York, on effect of Radical success, 379. On negro riots in Washington, 358.
Humphrey, Governor, of Mississippi, ejection of, by military force, 148. Himself and family ejected from Governor's mansion, 332.
Impeachment. History of case of President Johnson, 97. Vote on, in House, 98-100.
Indemnity Act, 84. Protest of Democratic members against, 85.
Independent, New York, on dishonesty of Radical Congress, 214.
Intelligencer, National, on the Military reign of terror in the South, 162.
Ireland. Sympathy for, action of House on, 272.
Iron-clad Oath, 117.
Isabel, R. H., (negro,) temporary Chairman of Louisiana House of Representatives, 149.
Jacobs, Lieutenant-Governor, of Kentucky, arrest and banishment of, 258.
Jefferson, Thomas, refusal, as President, to execute an unconstitutional law, 110.
Jenkins, C. T., Governor of Georgia. Removal of, by military, 132.
Johnson, Andrew, President. On disunionism of Sumner, 77. History of impeachment of, 97. Appointment of General Thomas Secretary of War ad interim, 101. Last Amnesty proclamation of, 363. His correspondence with General Grant, 165. Question of veracity between him and General Grant, 164. Veto of Freedmen's Bureau bill, 184. Veto of Arkansas bill, 135. Veto of Omnibus bill, 141. Veto of act amending Judiciary act of 1789, 265. Veto of Electoral College bill, 337.
Johnson and Sherman armistice, 85.

Jones, George W., of Iowa. Arrest of, 258.
Jones, John, Treasurer of Georgia. Removal of by military, 133.
Judiciary, Military. Order substituting, for civil, in Virginia, 133.
Kemper, General J. M., of Virginia, casts the vote of Virginia for General F. P. Blair, 235.
Kent, Chancellor, on the power of removal, 112.
Kiernan, Francis, of New York. Response to the nomination of Mr. Seymour by Ohio, 230.
Kentucky. Treatment of her Representatives to Fortieth Congress, 94. Neutrality of, 94.
Kentucky and Maryland. Proposal to exclude votes of, 361.
Know-Nothing Radicalism, 367.
Legal-tender, Acts making greenbacks a, 277.
Legislative usurpations. Views of the framers of the Constitution on the dangers of, 45.
Legislators, Negro. Specimens of, 152.
Lincoln, Abraham. Letter to Horace Greeley, 52. Letter to Fernando Wood, promising to protect Southern Senators and Representatives, 70. On the right of secession, 78. On the imprisonment of General Stone, 84. On carpet-baggers, 379. On forming a State government in Louisiana, 113. Proclamation of, on Reconstruction, 114. To General Steele on proposed State government in Arkansas, 114. Proclamation of, in 1862, 260. His messages of thanks to Governor Seymour, 343-344.
Logan, John A., of Illinois. Resolution on the Kentucky Representatives, 93.
Long, Alexander, of Ohio. Colfax's resolution to expel, 182.
Louisiana. Mr. Lincoln's movement to organize a State, 113. Bogus Legislature of, 149. Negro Lieutenant-Governor of, 149. Grant snubbed by negro officers of, 149. Military called out, 150. Antecedents of bogus Senators from, 330.
Louisville Journal. Position of, in 1861, 94.
Lusk, Mr., of Mississippi, sentenced to death by a military court, 157.
Marr, R. H., of Louisiana. Decision of Supreme Court in case of, 196.
Marshall, S. S., of Illinois, on official stealing, 57. On corruption, 66. On finances and expenditures, 315. Reports against impeachment, 98.
Massachusetts. Legislature of, on Reconstruction, 377.
Maynard, Horace, against redeeming bonds in greenbacks, 300.
McArdle, W. H., of Mississippi. Military imprisonment of, 157-163. Arrest of action in case of, by Radical Congress, 263. Postponement of, by Supreme Court, 269. Protest of Judge Grier, 269.
McClellan, George B. Resolutions of respect to, by Soldiers' and Sailors' Convention, 254.
McClernand, John A., of Illinois. Speech declining the nomination for Vice-President, 233.
McCook, George W., of Ohio. Speech nominating Horatio Seymour, 229.
McCulloch, Hugh, Secretary of the Treasury. On the retention of corrupt officials, 64. On the question of veracity between the President and General Grant, 172.
McDonald, Alex., Senator from Arkansas. Antecedents of, 147.
McKee, Samuel, of Kentucky, given John D. Young's seat in Congress, 95.

INDEX. 393

McQuade, General, of New York. Remarks in Soldiers' and Sailors' Convention, 253.
Meade, General G. G. Removal of Governor Jenkins by, 132. Of Treasurer Jones, of Georgia, 133. Administration of, 153, 331. His use of detectives to convict the Columbus prisoners, 333.
Methodists. Conference of at Chicago. Resolutions of, 359.
Military interference in elections. Vote in Congress on, 211. Order of Stanton on, 211.
Military Judiciary in Virginia. General Scofield's orders to create, 133.
Military terror. Reign of, in the South, 156.
Militia, Loyal, in Tennessee. Rampage of, 202. Jurisdiction of, 203.
Militia, Loyal, in South. Bill to arm the same, 334. Debate in Congress on, 335.
Milligan, L. P. Decision of the Supreme Court in the case of, 188. Colfax's effort to hang, 362.
Milliken, Wm., of Tennessee. Arrest of, and imprisonment, by General Thomas, 162.
Morgan, George W., of Ohio, turned out of his seat in Congress, 95. Speech notifying Mr. Seymour of his nomination, 238. Speech on the public debt, 317.
Morton, O. P., Senator from Indiana, on negro suffrage, 54. On redeeming Five-twenties in greenbacks, 304.
Mullaly, John. Suggestions of his Southern trip to capitalists, 376.
Mullins, James, of Tennessee. Debate in the House on the admission of, 199. Letter of Lieut. A. M. Trolager on, 201.
Mumford, Mr., of New Orleans. The wrong man hung by Butler, 60.
Nashville. Military interference at the charter election of, 204.
"National" struck from prefix to name of Republican party, at Chicago, in 1860, 71.
National Banks. Creation of, 278. Status of, 289. Vote in the House of Representatives to withdraw currency of, 310. How they work, 308.
National Democratic Convention in 1868. Proceedings of, 217. Platform adopted by, 224. Ballots in, 236-237. List of delegates to, 240.
National Democratic Executive Committee for 1868, 227.
National Intelligencer on bastile at Capitol, 88.
National Life Insurance Company. Charter of, by Congress, 362.
Negroes. Vote in Senate on giving privileges in cars to, 52. Mortality of, 379. Riot of, in Washington, 358. Forney's Address to, 359. Notification of, to white citizens to leave town, 358. Outlawry of, in the South, 154, 331.
Negro officials, 149-151. Letter of the Tennessee Congressional delegation in favor of, 203.
Negro rule in the South, 151.
Negro suffrage. Views of Stephen A. Douglas on, 53. Of Abraham Lincoln on, 53. Of Daniel Webster on, 53. Of Henry Clay on, 53. Of Thomas Jefferson on, 53. Of Senator Morton, of Indiana, on, 54. Of R. P. Spalding, of Ohio, on, 54. Of James Hughes, of Indiana, on, 54. Constitution of Pennsylvania on, 54. Votes in Congress on, 79, 80, 81 and 82. Popular votes of States on, 269. Exercise of, in the Southern States, 151.

Negro testimony. Votes in Congress on, 273.
New Orleans riot. Stanton responsible for, 375.
New York riots. Governor Seymour's course with reference to, 345.
Niagara Falls. Account of proposed negotiation at, 175.
Oath. Test, or Iron-clad, 119.
O'Bierne, Col., of District of Columbia, reads address of Soldiers' and Sailors' Convention, 222.
O'Connor, Charles, on the power of States to withdraw ratification of 14th amendment, 276.
Office. Indecent hunt for, by ex-U. S. Senators, 373.
Officials. Radical, in Tennessee. Taxes paid by, 204.
Olds, Edson B. Arrest of, 258.
Omnibus bill, 138. Vote on, 141. Veto of, 141.
Opdyke, George, Mayor, of New York. His testimony to Gov. Seymour's course during the riots, 348.
Ord, Gen. E. O. C., favors increase of force in Southern States, 131. Removes Legislature of Arkansas, 132. Removes State treasurer of Arkansas, 132.
Packer, Asa, of Pennsylvania, presented for the Presidency, 227.
Palmer, H. L., of Wisconsin, temporary President of National Democratic Convention, 217.
Peace Conference. Propositions of, 73.
Pendleton, George H., of Ohio, presented for the Presidency, 227. His letter of withdrawal to Washington McLean, Esq., 228. His private letter to same, favoring Seymour, 214. His speech at Grafton, Va., 310.
Personal liberty. Vote on, in Congress, 82.
Phillips, Wendell. Disunion sentiments of, 72-73. Letter of, on the church and politics, 361. On the rotten boroughs, 340. On Mr. Chase, 105. On the President, 369.
Pickering, T.T. Removal of, by Jno. Adams,110.
Pomeroy, S. C., Senator from Kansas. Antecedents of, 58.
Pope, Gen. John. Confidential letter of, to Gen. Swayne, 132.
Post, N. Y. Evening, on sale of Senator Pomeroy's vote, 59. On Radical ostracism of Supreme Court, 368.
Prayer. Radical, at Philadelphia Convention, 369.
Presidential elections. Popular vote in, since 1788, 259.
Press. Radical assaults on the liberty of the, 179. Freedom of, in the South, 163.
Preston, Gen. William, of Kentucky, presents the name of Gen. F. P. Blair, jr., for Vice-President, 233.
Prussia. Magnanimity of the King of, 361.
Public debt, 282. That of England and United States contrasted, 284.
Public lands. The way they have been disposed of, 364.
Pugh, George E., of Ohio, on the Crittenden resolutions, 75. On the proposed 14th amendment to the Constitution, 275.
Picayune, New Orleans, on the power to amend the Constitution, 210.
Radicals. Disunionism of leaders of, before the war, 70. Platform of, in 1868, 20. Antagonism to Catholicism, 365. Mob of, in United States Senate, 48. Know-Nothingism of, in Connecticut, 367.

Radical Congress. Conscription of, 57. New York Independent on dishonesty of, 214. New York Evening Post on the, 368. Cincinnati Gazette on the, 368.
Radical financiers. Ignorance of, 301.
Radical rule. Cost of, since the war, 298.
Railroads. Land grants to, 364.
Randall, A. W., on the question of veracity between the President and Gen. Grant, 172.
Ream, Miss Vinnie. Radical persecution of, 86.
Receipts and expenditures of the United States for 1867, 280.
Reconstruction. Military acts of Congress authorizing, 116. Confession by New York Tribune of purpose, 372. History of, 113. Effect of, 154. Northern perils from, 163. Prejudice to workingmen of, 164. Registration returns of, 151. Expense of, 134, 329.
Representation. Blows struck at, by Radical power in Congress, 91.
Revolution. Attempts at, by Radicals in Congress, 121.
Rice, B. F., Senator from Arkansas. Letter of, 148.
Richardson, W. A., of Illinois, against military imprisonment, 83.
Riot of negroes in Washington after municipal election, 358.
Ross, E. G., Senator from Kansas. Telegrams to, pending impeachment, 105.
Salaries. Sizes of, in bogus States, 133.
Saulsbury, W., Senator from Delaware, on Radical violation of Constitution and Declaration of Independence, 19.
Schenck, R. C., of Ohio. Dispatch of, on impeachment, 104. On official corruption, 63. Statement of Government receipts and expenditures by, 280.
Scott, Gov., of South Carolina. His mode of having peace, 336.
Sea Island lands. Outrageous disposition of, 377.
Sedalia Times. A Radical paper, in Missouri, on the Catholics, 365.
Seizure of private papers, in violation of Constitution, indorsed by Radicals, 216.
Senate of the United States responsible for corrupt officials, 63, 64. Election of Mr. Stockton, 91. Its action on Senator Thomas, 93. Its use of the contingent fund, 296. Its retention of the convict Callicott, 216.
Senators of the United States. Proposed sale of five, 58.
Sergeant-at-arms of the House of Representatives. Enormous fees of, 286.
Seward, W. H. His letter declining French mediation, 69. On the ratification of the Fourteenth amendment, 211. On the question of veracity between General Grant and the President, 173. His proclamation certifying hypothetical ratification of Fourteenth amendment, 274.
Seymour, Horatio. President of Democratic National Convention of 1868, 219. Speech of, on taking the chair, 219. Declines the Presidency, 227. Again declines, 229. Is nominated, 232. Speech of acceptance, 238. Letter of acceptance of nomination, 385. Speech at Cooper Institute on the Finances, 320. Biography of, 340. War record of, 342, 350. His course during the New York riots, 345. Thanks of the New York Legislature to, 348. Albany Evening Journal on, 349. Letter to President Lincoln on the draft, 346.
Shellabarger, Samuel, of Ohio. Bill in Congress to regulate suffrage in Ohio, 360.
Shepherd, Colonel O. L., U. S. A. Order condemning Democratic soldiers, 373.
Sherman, John. Cincinnati Gazette on funding talent of, 294. Greenback letter of, 295. On Tenure-of-office bill, 107.
Sherman and Johnston armistice, 85. Report of General Sherman on, 86.
Slocum, General, of New York. Resolutions reported by, in Soldiers' and Sailors' Convention, 252.
Smith, General Ashbel, of Texas, casts her vote for F. P. Blair, jr., 234.
Soldiers' and Sailors' Convention of 1868, 243. Adoption of the Democratic platform by, 254. Officers of, 250. National committee appointed by, 250. Address of, to Democratic National Convention, 251.
South Carolina. Debt of and cost of reconstruction in, 329.
Southern States. Provisional governments in by President Johnson, 115. Rotten boroughs in some of, 134, 141.
Speed, James, Attorney-General, against the execution by the President of an unconstitutional law, 111.
Stanton, E. M. Suspension of, 110. Abdication of, 113. Removal of, indorsed by Soldiers' and Sailors', 254. Covering up of tracks by, 371. Letter of, praising President Johnson, 373. Letters of thanks to Governor Seymour by, 343, 344.
States, reservations of. Instructions to delegates in Continental Congress, 55.
States Rights. Debate on, in the Convention which framed the Constitution, 55. Views of Mr. Calhoun on, 56.
Steedman, James B., of Louisiana. On the nomination of General Blair, 233.
Stevens, Thaddeus. His opinion of Senatorial perjury, 58. Blasphemy of, 212. His letter on Mr. Buchanan's death, 214. His views on redeeming the 5-20s in coin, 303. Horace Greely on, 304. Sneers of, at mercy, 370.
Stockton, John P., Senator of New Jersey. Ejection of, from his seat, 91.
Stokes, W. B., of Tennessee. Objection in House to admission of, 200. Letter of, to Duncan, 200. Remarks on bill to arm the militia, 335.
Stone, Brigadier-General C. P. President Lincoln on imprisonment of, 84.
Stuart, Charles E., of Michigan. Speech of, on Governor Seymour's nomination, 231.
Stubblefield, George J., of Tennessee. On Brownlow's exercise of the pardoning power, 204.
Suffrage, Negro. Votes on in Congress, 78. Negro Suffrage, 78.
Sumner, Charles. On election of negroes to Congress, 372
Supreme Court of the United States. Decision of, in the Milligan case, 188. In Father Cumming's Test-oath case, 191. In A. H. Garland's case, 194. In R. H. Marr's case, 196. In Mississippi and Georgia cases, 260-262. In W. H. McArdle's case 269. Judge Grier's protest, 269. Act of Congress forbidding action of, on Reconstruction cases, 263.

INDEX.   395

Taxing bonds. Votes on, 278.
Tennessee. Reconstruction of, 115. Condition of, 196. Debate in House on admitting Representatives of, 196. Letter of Congressional delegation of, in favor of negroes holding office, 203.
Tenure-of-Office bill, 96.
Testimony. Coercion of negroes to manufacture, by military in Georgia, 159.
Thomas, General George H. His arrest and imprisonment of Wm. Milliken, 162. Telegrams between, and General Grant, with reference to Nashville election, 205, 206, 207. His correspondence with W. Matt. Brown, 205.
Thomas, Phillip Frank, of Maryland. Refused his seat in Senate, 93.
Thurman, A. G., of Ohio. Startling financial facts by, 288.
Tilden, S. J., of New York. Speech casting vote for Governor Seymour, 232. Speech at meeting notifying candidates, 238.
Times, London. On Democratic platform, 257.
Tortugas. Military confinement of citizens of Alabama at, 157.
Treasury. Condition of the United States, exposed by W. E. Dunbar, 289.
Tremaine, Lyman. Extracts from speeches of, 369.
Tribune, New York. On right of the South to secede, 78. Vindication of Governor Seymour by, 344.
Trimble, John, of Tennessee. Objection in House to admission of, 200.
Trollope, Anthony. On reconstruction, 339.
Troluger, A. M., United States Army. On loyalty of James Mullins, 201.
Trumbull, Lyman. On the corrupt pressure to secure conviction of the President, 59. On the admission of Alabama, 142.
Two-thirds rule adopted by Democratic National Convention, 226.
Vallandigham, C. L., of Ohio. Remarks withdrawing Mr. Pendleton, 228. Remarks pressing Mr. Seymour, 229. His resolution relative to workingmen, 235. His trial and banishment, 257.
Van Trump, P., of Ohio. His resolution on Capitol bastile, 90.
Van Wyck, C. H., of New York. Course with reference to memory of Mr. Buchanan, 215.
Veracity. Question of, between the President and General Grant, 164.
Virginia Convention of 1868. Character of, 124.
Voorhees, D. W., of Indiana. Ejected from his rightful seat in Congress, 92.
Vote. Latest popular, 259. For President in 1864, 258. For President since 1788, 259. Electoral, 259.

Wade, B. F., of Ohio. Disunion sentiments of, 73, 77. Blasphemy of, 212. Rebuke of Senator Bayard to, 108.
Waldo, Rev. Dr. Remarks in Methodist Conference at Chicago, 359.
War. Object of, the restoration of the Union, 68.
War and Navy Departments. Cost of, 300.
Washburne, E. B., of Illinois. On bill to arm the militia, 335.
Washington. Negro riot in, after the municipal election, 358.
Washington, George. Efforts to impeach, 109.
Webb, James Watson. Disunion sentiment of, in 1856, 73.
Webster, E. H., of Michigan. Proposition against negro suffrage, 79.
Weed, Thurlow. On the proposed sale of Senator Pomeroy's vote, 59. On the Abolition disunionists, 77.
Welles, Gideon. On the question of veracity between the President and Gen. Grant, 171.
Whaley, J. C. C., President of the National Labor Union. Correspondence with J. D. Defrees, 363.
Whisky Ring. Grief of, at Richmond, 64. Grief of, at New York, 66. New York Times on, 65.
Williams, G. H., Senator from Oregon. On Tenure-of-office bill, 106.
Wilson, James F., of Iowa. Report of, against impeachment, 99.
Wilson, Henry. On the President, 369.
Wood, Fernando, of New York. Resolution of sympathy with Ireland, 272.
Woodbridge, F. E., of Vermont. Report of, against impeachment, 99.
Woodward, George W., of Pennsylvania. On resolutions of impeachment, 111. On the death of Mr. Buchanan, 215. On the action of Congress in interfering with the Supreme Court, 266.
Woolley, C. W. Imprisonment of, by the House of Representatives, 88.
Woolford, Colonel Frank. Arrest of, 258.
Working-men of the United States. Resolution of sympathy with, of the Democratic National Convention, 235. Proscription of, by Radical Superintendent of Public Printing, 363.
World (New York). On the conditions prescribed by Omnibus Bill, 142. (Valuable articles from this able Democratic organ are abundant in this book.)
Yates, Richard, of Illinois. On the President, 369.
Young, John D., of Kentucky. Refused his rightful seat in Congress, 94.
Young, Rev. Lambert. Imprisonment of, by Judge Ballard, 366.

www.ingramcontent.com/pod-product-compliance
Lightning Source LLC
Chambersburg PA
CBHW030429300426
44112CB00009B/912